Eastern Orthodox Encounters of Identity and Otherness

Eastern Orthodox Encounters of Identity and Otherness

Values, Self-Reflection, Dialogue

Edited by

Andrii Krawchuk and

Thomas Bremer

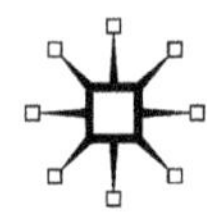

EASTERN ORTHODOX ENCOUNTERS OF IDENTITY AND OTHERNESS

Softcover reprint of the hardcover 1st edition 2014 978-1-137-38284-9

First published in 2014 by
PALGRAVE MACMILLAN®
in the United States—a division of St. Martin's Press LLC,
175 Fifth Avenue, New York, NY 10010.

Where this book is distributed in the UK, Europe and the rest of the world, this is by Palgrave Macmillan, a division of Macmillan Publishers Limited, registered in England, company number 785998, of Houndmills, Basingstoke, Hampshire RG21 6XS.

Palgrave Macmillan is the global academic imprint of the above companies and has companies and representatives throughout the world.

ISBN 978-1-349-48018-0 ISBN 978-1-137-37738-8 (eBook)
DOI 10.1057/9781137377388

Library of Congress Cataloging-in-Publication Data

Eastern Orthodox encounters of identity and otherness : values, self-reflection, dialogue / Andrii Krawchuk and Thomas Bremer, eds.
p. cm.
Includes bibliographical references.

1. Orthodox Eastern Church—Doctrines. 2. Identification (Religion) 3. Other (Philosophy) 4.Ethnicity. I. Krawchuk, Andrii. II. Bremer, Thomas, 1957–

BX250.E377 2013
230'.19—dc23 2013027150

A catalogue record of the book is available from the British Library.

Design by Newgen Knowledge Works (P) Ltd., Chennai, India.

First edition: January 2014

10 9 8 7 6 5 4 3 2 1

Contents

Figure, Tables, and Maps

Figure

Tables

Maps

General Editor's Preface

The core of this volume consists of papers presented at the eighth World Congress of the International Council for Central and East European Studies (ICCEES), and it is the third time that I have the privilege of seeing congress volumes published by Palgrave Macmillan. That this is happening is an indication not only that ICCEES appreciates its fruitful relationship with Palgrave Macmillan, but also of the enduring importance, excellence and relevance of Central and East European Studies as an area of study in the evolving global environment.

In the prefaces to the volumes from the Warsaw (1995) and Berlin (2005) congresses, general editors Professor Ronald Hill of Trinity College Dublin and Roger E. Kanet of the University of Miami outlined the historical conditions that brought about the creation of ICCEES and emphasized the importance of publishing the research that is presented at the congresses. After the founding of ICCEES (in Banff, Canada, in 1974), its world congresses studied Central and Eastern Europe through the lens of various disciplines. They mirrored the changes that were taking place in the region since Western scholars came together to organize the research they were engaged in, but lacked an organizational structure that could collate their results and offer an opportunity for debate and discussion on the other side of the Iron Curtain. This is why the International Committee for Soviet and East European Studies (ICSEES) was created; today it is known as the International Council for Central and East European Studies (ICCEES).

The change in name reflected transformations in the region and in the field of study. Since 1989, as a result of major political, economic, and social changes in Central and Eastern Europe, Western scholarship shifted its focus from "Communist studies" to an area that was undergoing redefinition as a geopolitical region in a broader quest for understanding and cooperation.

The themes of the more recent ICCEES world congresses have also echoed the transformations in the region. The 1990 ICCEES World Congress in Harrogate, England, celebrated the end of the Cold War; the 1995 Warsaw Congress focused on the democratic development of the former "Communist states"; the 2000 Congress in Tampere, Finland, stressed the divergences, convergences, and uncertainties in Central and Eastern Europe; the 2005 Berlin congress focused on the European Union; and the 2010 Stockholm Congress examined the prospects for wider cooperation in Eurasia. The contributions to this volume include papers from the Stockholm meeting and reflect its theme.

An impressive list of publications issuing from the ICCEES world congresses is available on the council's webpage (www.iccees.org). Putting together a volume that has thematic unity from the plethora of papers presented at a world congress is a major challenge. There was a time when it was sufficient to bring together high-quality papers and publish them as congress proceedings. This is no longer the case, and the list of ICCEES publications testifies to the vitality of research in the area. The present volume brings together innovative research findings and scholarly insights into the new dynamics of religion in Central and Eastern Europe. It marks a major contribution to the field and will significantly enhance our understanding of the ongoing transition in the region, besides promoting scholarly cooperation and exchange across cultural and political borders.

Stanislav J. Kirschbaum
York University, Glendon College
Toronto, Canada

Introduction

Andrii Krawchuk

The dissolution of the Soviet Union in December 1991 heralded a period of political transformation and social euphoria, the beginning of a tectonic shift with global repercussions. While some of us were privileged to experience those first weeks and months firsthand, it was not long before these signs of the changing times were felt in the West as well—and expressed through unexpected, pithy observations. At St. Vladimir's Seminary in Crestwood, New York, Professor John Erickson was taken aback when a student from the former Czechoslovakia took issue with his enthusiasm for ecumenism and pronounced: "When the communists were in control, we had to be ecumenical. Now we can be Orthodox."[1] No less than many other cross-cultural insights voiced even as the changes were still occurring, this one may well have encapsulated more than what the student had ever imagined. The paradigm shift was not only political, but extended to the social and religious spheres as well. Religious believers, Orthodox Christians, Catholics and Protestants, Jews, Muslims, and Buddhists, suddenly received the opportunity to practice their faith without fear of persecution. The new sociopolitical climate also opened the way to reflection about the future: how would it be shaped and determined by citizens and communities, who now possessed religious freedom? To what extent would they imagine their future in relation to their past? What kinds of new partnerships and relationships would be forged now that they were possible? As this dramatic and still unfinished chapter of our shared global history approaches the quarter-century mark, scholarly studies are contributing significantly to our understanding of what has already occurred and what is yet in the process of becoming.[2]

Post-Soviet law reforms restructured the social dynamics of religion, as official state atheism and the brutal suppression of religion gave way to a secular state committed to religious tolerance. The 1993 Russian Constitution guaranteed freedom of worship, conscience, and religion, and the equality of all religions. Yet before long, some familiar patterns reemerged: inconsistencies between the lofty declarations and the reality on the ground. New legislation on religion conferred a privileged status on "traditional" religious communities and placed restrictions on "nontraditional" groups. As a result, the Orthodox churches have enjoyed a special relationship with governments while, at the other extreme, some religious communities have been targeted as threats to the social order. Religious life in the region has indeed undergone a fundamental change, but states remain vigilant and reserve the right to intervene at their own discretion. Increasingly, they view religion as integral to state security, formulating laws and implementing policies that enhance its capacity for social consolidation and prevent its inclinations to conflict.

In the wake of fundamental legislative reform, questions of Orthodox identity have preoccupied church leaders, adherents, and scholarly analysts. To what extent should religious identity be connected to ethnic culture and to national discourses of historical memory? The old model of a predominant majority culture may provide a sense of continuity, clarity, and stability, but its hegemonic thrust is undermined by the newly embraced principles of equality and respect for minority cultures and values. Similarly, the once convenient fusion of national and religious identities now flies in the face of a global quest for encounter, dialogue, and peace, and must confront the growing Christian consensus that phyletism or any other form of religious exclusion is not a constructive option. In Central and Eastern Europe, the commitment of churches and their communities to universal human and Christian values frequently remains declarative, but requires confirmation in practice. As in the Soviet period, the world continues to watch for real progress on human rights and freedoms. It is in the international setting, too, that the relational dimension of identity is put to the test—how do religious (and national) communities relate to others, especially those who do not share their history, culture, and values? The reflexive response might be to regress to past ideologies and stereotypes that disqualified or demonized the meddling "other," and "revert" to a climate of isolation, exclusion, and fear. But the times have truly changed and Cold War constructions of the other no longer reflect reality. Religious identities may continue to be defined in terms of borders between the self and the other, yet the new environment of encounter and cross-cultural understanding calls for more openness, a restoration of relationships with "the West" and the global community, and a lively engagement with ideas that can unite the international community. Both of these competing orientations, the inward reflex, looking to the past, and the outward movement, opening up to encounter and new relations with the other, are essential to understanding the dynamics of current religious debates in the former Soviet sphere.

Orthodox churches, as communities and institutions, have made serious efforts to respond to the unprecedented transformation. The Jubilee Bishops' Council of the Russian Orthodox Church (ROC) in 2000 and its major document *Bases of the Social Concept of the Russian Orthodox Church* addressed the complex issues of Orthodox relations with states, society, and the world. That initiative inspired Orthodox communities in other countries to undertake similar reflections, returning to the sources of the faith and developing responses to the social and political challenges of the present day. Nor is it at all surprising that explorations of identity and the other, and of tradition and change, are central to these debates as well. Much of this thinking is informed by deep-rooted models and values, such as the Byzantine *symphonia* and *philanthropia*, yet there is also an appreciation that many issues are without precedent and will require creative reason as well as new, critical readings of the past.

In addition to these top-down initiatives, the post-Soviet transition has ushered in a significant wave of grassroots religious exploration. New ideas on the very nature of religion and its place in a more democratic society are being expressed and debated at all levels of society—from the lower clergy and monastic communities to lay theologians, from secular intellectuals to writers, artists, and the youth. A diverse range of unofficial proposals are being explored in the increasingly globalized and pluralistic marketplace of ideas. These forces of spontaneity and free expression are occasionally prone to criticizing the status quo, and in turn both church anase in point was the arrest and imprisonment in 2012 of members of the feminist punk rock group Pussy Riot. While the group's radical iconoclasm may not have won them widespread support on the home front, their critique of the ROC's views on women and its close ties with Vladimir Putin did resonate with broader public debates on those very issues. Lesser-known developments, such as rock bands comprised of Orthodox monks and religiously inspired literary works by Orthodox women, are blurring the religious-secular distinction and demonstrating that powerful forms of creative religious expression can occur outside the boundaries of what is officially sanctioned.

In the West over the past several decades, ecumenical and interreligious encounters have taken decisive steps away from the era of proselytizing missions and exclusivist claims on absolute truth and salvation. There is an emerging global consensus that religious dialogue is not about producing relativism or facile unions, but about bringing together the forces of diverse traditions in a common quest for global peace, human equality, social justice, and environmental responsibility. Significantly, leading Orthodox figures have been part of these processes. These priorities, collectively addressed across religious boundaries, can become an enduring source of authenticity and social relevance for religion in present-day Central and Eastern Europe. In the face of recent setbacks in ecumenism, such new forms of solidarity may also generate constructive ideas and perspectives for fruitful encounters. As millions of religious believers continue to vote with their feet by adopting alternative, nontraditional modes of religious living and being, churches and religious organizations are faced with a fundamental option: either the well-worn path of isolation, condemnation, and a retreat to the past, or a new path of attentiveness to the signs of the times, encounter with the world, and a self-critical pursuit of truth wherever it may be found. Arguably, it is not polemics against a constructed religious or geographical "other" that will ensure the ongoing social relevance of traditional religious institutions, but the hard, unpredictable and humbling rediscovery of self through encounter with the other.

The present volume is an effort to contribute to an understanding of Christian Orthodoxy in its various encounters, especially since the late 1980s. It comprises a core of chapters relating to the general theme "Orthodoxy in Encounter," which were originally papers presented at the VIII World Congress of the International Council for Central and East European Studies (Stockholm, 2010). Subsequently revised and expanded, they are accompanied here by additional contributions, with a view to rounding out the picture. The result is a collective inquiry into diverse contexts of contemporary Orthodoxy and represents numerous scholarly approaches and methods, including those of political science, law, sociology, history, philosophy, theology, and cultural studies.

The contributions from political science and legal perspectives provide a basis for grasping the frameworks of church-state relations, the pivotal debates over the implementation of human rights provisions in new laws and constitutions, and the local, contextual receptions of their European and Western counterparts. Samuel Huntington's "clash of civilizations" theory, excoriated in the West, nevertheless has some resonance in Orthodox countries. In Central and Eastern Europe, the idea that the collapse of communism replaced the Cold War clash of East-West ideologies with a revival of deep-rooted, civilizational cleavages between the "West" and the Eastern "Orthodox" civilization is supported by scholars who see interpretive links with their own readings of the changing situation. Sociological perspectives inform inquiries into the social dimensions of change and such questions as the renegotiation of church-society relations, particularly as reflected in recent official documents on the social role and responsibility of Orthodox churches and in the discourses of ethnoreligious fusion. Here, Western sociological perceptions of variations on the theme of secularization as "believing without belonging" are occasionally stood on their head by the post-Soviet phenomenon of "belonging without believing." The theological and philosophical approaches of numerous contributions shed light on the foundational underpinnings of Orthodox encounters at all levels: from church-state-society relations to ecumenical dialogues, and from Christian social ethics to critiques of Western movements and ideas (chiefly: proselytism, pluralism, and materialism) and to questions relating to the nature of human dignity. Ecumenism is also a recurring major theme here, especially in connection with recent developments, which have been cited as indications of an Orthodox "retreat from ecumenism."[3] Cultural perspectives provide unprecedented insights into recent unofficial, creative reflection on foundational questions of Orthodox identity, focusing, in particular, on recent literary works that explore the role of women and of the laity in the church. And the historical approaches situate the current debates with reference to interpretations of the past, normative understandings of tradition, and the impact of past experiences of encounter on current practice. In the true spirit of interdisciplinarity, many of these perspectives and analyses intersect and intertwine in their methods and issue focuses alike.

What exactly have the "Orthodox encounters" been, and what do they aspire to be in the future? This collection explores a wide range of encounters: questions of self-identity and its reassessment; encounters with Europe and the West; encounters with the states and societies of one's immediate environment; ecumenical and interfaith encounters; and emerging encounters in new regions. In working out its place and role in the present world, Orthodoxy is engaging in a rediscovery and a rearticulation of its origins, nature, concerns, and aspirations—particularly through its contacts and relationships with "others." The overriding aim of the contributions to this volume is to analyze and assess diverse experiences, challenges, and responses of Orthodox churches in the period since the late 1980s. Beyond the immediate sphere of transformations in former Soviet countries, Orthodox churches in satellite states (notably, postcommunist Bulgaria, 1989–; post-Ceaușescu Romania, 1989–; and post-Milošević Serbia, 2000–) have entered into their own periods of transition. Ultimately, Orthodox churches worldwide have been deeply affected by these transformations in Eastern and Central Europe. Orthodoxy in Western Europe and the Americas has direct, historical links through its emigré communities, while elsewhere as in Greece it has identified closely with many of the discussions that these changes have inspired.

Whereas in the Soviet period the principal challenge for traditional Eastern Christian churches was survival in the face of antireligious policies and persecution, since the collapse of the Soviet Union the introduction of religious freedom has created new challenges for religious life. As formerly isolated churches entered into contact with the global environment, they found themselves in a bewildering marketplace of ideas, religious and secular alike. Religious freedom, initially understood as liberation from the communist yoke, was found to contain further connotations in the understanding of the international community, relating to the equality of religions before the law. As Orthodox and other religious communities move past their Soviet experience and resume activities in their respective social and political environments, they are facing new realities and are discovering that there can be no return to an idealized, pre-Soviet status quo. The arrival of new religious movements and organizations has brought to the fore a new, pluralist reality and has elicited debates about who is indigenous to a country, who has a historical track record and linkage to the story of the people, and who does not. Proselytism may not have been an issue for evangelical missionaries or the representatives of new religious movements, whose very purpose was to convert. But it has been a key concern for the faith communities of Central and Eastern Europe, whose religious identities have traditionally been expressed through a connectedness to land and history, a fusion of ethnic and religious culture, and the aspirations of national self-determination. Traditional values are therefore being challenged and reassessed, and this too is a major theme of the present collection.

This volume is presented in six sections:

Part I, "The Ecclesial Self: Traditional Identities and the Challenges of Pluralism," considers some of the ways in which the post-Soviet transition is radically altering how traditional churches express their identities. Within the global environment of religious diversity, the principles of religious freedom and equality are core values of democratic nations. They inform the underlying assumptions and the explicit provisions of national constitutions, of legislative systems, and of international human rights agreements. As Orthodox churches in post-Soviet countries began to work out new modes of relationship with their states and societies, this international consensus has served as a point of reference, for both imitation and critique. The churches are responding to new questions about their identity and role in society through official pronouncements and by adapting their policies to the new circumstances. The restoration of legal status was only the first hurdle—the second involves taking steps to recover their authoritative voice in the ongoing restructuring of the social and political order. For this, there are no short-cuts since, along with political transformations, social paradigms are shifting and along with them new questions are arising that cannot be answered only by appeals to historical memory. Effective, future-oriented ideas and action by the churches require reliable readings of the signs of the present time. Four chapters explore this rethinking of ecclesial identity in the context of the post-Soviet transitions.

Jennifer Wasmuth (Humboldt University, Berlin) studies the ROC's self-understanding in post-Soviet Russia through some of the key principles that have informed its relations with the state and the nation. The idea of a "new symphony" maintains the traditional recognition of the importance of cooperation with the state, but balances it with a sharper distinction between the divine and worldly domains, and with the principles of noninterference and of the right to resist. In the church's relations with the Russian nation, the principle of a multinational church represents an attempt to respond to the challenge of phyletism and the reality of ethnic diversity within the church, while the principle of "canonical territory" has been expanded from its original, ancient reference to the territorial jurisdiction of bishops to the scope of activity of the ROC as a whole, within Russia's borders and beyond. Highly controversial in contemporary Orthodoxy, this latter principle is sometimes connected to the preservation of national identity, which appears to create a tension with the notion of a multinational church.

Alfons Brüning (St. Radboud University, Nijmegen) analyzes the categories of morality and patriotism in the ROC's current discourse on church and society, and compares their understanding in the Soviet and post-Soviet periods. While the West has been criticized on moral grounds in both periods, the Soviet régime, a former ally, is now portrayed within the enemy camp. The Russian Orthodox notion of patriotism had two distinct meanings in the Soviet period: through its ecumenical and peace initiatives, the ROC observed a political patriotism by defending Soviet religious and foreign policy, while its official references to Christian teaching or to the Russian homeland suggested a cultural understanding of the term. Within the restrictions of the system, the ROC thus tried to maintain a separation between its allegiance to the state and its Christian identity. In the post-Soviet period, the church has stepped up its engagement with society, and has reaffirmed the notion of patriotism as integral to its self-identity.

Daniela Kalkandjieva (Sofia University) approaches the question of ecclesial identity from legal and historical perspectives. She sheds light on two social orientations within the postcommunist Bulgarian Orthodox church (BOC): (1) continuity with the traditional, ethnoreligious idea of the church as a guardian of the nation; and (2) efforts to respond to the demands of religious freedom and equality. Citing the uniqueness of the Bulgarian case where, due to five centuries of Ottoman rule, nationalism emerged in the absence of a national or state Orthodox church, the author points to external factors that produced the ethnoreligious fusion, in particular: Tsarist Russia's diplomatic efforts to promote the unity of Orthodox subjects in the Ottoman Empire, the sultan's decree establishing the Bulgarian Exarchate (1870), and the Bulgarian communist regime, which despite its antireligious policies acknowledged the church's historical role as protector of national identity. In its relations with other religious communities, the BOC is tolerant toward Jews and Muslims, but at best wary of Protestants, Catholics, and new religious movements.

Anna Briskina-Müller (Halle-Wittenberg University) examines recent debates in Russian Orthodoxy, which suggest the emergence of a new religious self-consciousness, both in the official church and in Russian society at large. The author explores Russian Orthodox encounters with Western Orthodox ideas, and instances of innovative rethinking in theological and literary works. She looks at recent advances in critical reflection on the question of women in the church (purity rules and the ordination of women), literary explorations of clerical vices and uncertainties, and a new self-critical capacity in Russian Orthodox reinterpretations of history. Such explorations are indicative of a wide range of issues that have come to the surface in recent years and which have generated heated debates within the church. While the outcome of these processes of rethinking is far from certain, there can be no doubt that Russian Orthodoxy is astir with new ideas and debates about religious identity.

Part II, "Perceptions of the Religious Other: Difference and Convergence," focuses on perceptions of religious difference that have arisen from processes of dialogue and from historical discourses of identity and alterity. Whether in the historical context of efforts to restore unity since the East-West schism, or in the international framework of Orthodox-Protestant encounters and dialogues under the aegis of the World Council of Churches or in Orthodox-Catholic conversations in Romania and Ukraine, studies of the perceptions and expressions of the religious other provide substantive material for reflection on foundational issues and constructive insights into more effective methods of religious dialogue. Sustained encounters with the other and truthful, respectful appreciation of the other's perspectives, motivations, concerns, sensitivities, and distinctiveness are all vitally important to religious dialogue, interdenominational understanding, and personal growth. Even the most extreme expressions of otherness—embedded within deep-rooted, exclusivist interpretations of the other as "wholly other," as disqualified, or even as "the enemy"—can inform new, self-critical proposals for the restoration of relationships inspired by faith. The chapters in this section focus on the perceptions of the religious Other in various discourses and contexts, and provide seminal reflections on ways forward that can work.

Thomas Bremer (University of Münster) explores the historical and contemporary dimensions of Catholic-Orthodox encounters, focusing on Catholic perceptions and initiatives since the East-West Schism of 1054. For over a millennium the encounters were rare, though not insignificant. While they did not achieve reconciliation, they inspired a broadening of perspectives through scholarly inquiry into the historical evolution of liturgy and prompted reappraisals of the supposed supremacy of the Latin rite. Vatican Council II (1962–1965) was a key turning point that marked the beginning of Catholic ecumenism, paved the way for the current dialogue, and hammered out seminal ideas ("sister Churches" and "two lungs") about the nature and shape of that relationship within a new framework of mutuality. While the road to Catholic-Orthodox understanding has not always been smooth and numerous challenges still remain, the author argues that further ecumenical progress stands to gain from a new understanding of each church as diverse and multifaceted in its own right.

Dagmar Heller (Ecumenical Institute at Bossey) surveys Protestant-Orthodox dialogues and multilateral encounters since the 1950s. Her analysis of the most contentious issues reveals Orthodox sensitivities and the connection of ecclesiological and ethical concerns to apostolic tradition: hence, their exclusion of interconfessional worship and women's ordination, their condemnation of the ordination of homosexuals, their critique of the use of human rights to promote opinions viewed as anti-Christian and their objections to the proselytizing of Orthodox believers. While Orthodox leaders have attributed such impediments to dialogue to a confrontation of their own traditional worldview and the secular neoliberalism of the West, the author proposes that the real line of demarcation cuts across confessional affiliations and indicates diverse Christian responses to modernity.

Ciprian Ghişa (Babes-Bolyai University, Cluj-Napoca) studies the identity discourse of the interwar Romanian Orthodox press and presents it as a set of oppositions, with Roman Catholicism in the position of the "other." Through an essentially dualistic narrative, Romanian Orthodox identity was articulated as a kind of mirror image of everything that the Roman Catholic Church stood for, or was accused of being. Despite this predominantly aggressive, polemical discourse of alterity, there was room for positive assessments of Catholicism. Since the 1989 Revolution, the traditional identity discourse has persisted, along with more conciliatory and ecumenically minded elements.

Natalia Kochan (Ivan Kuras Institute, Kyiv) views religious otherness through the prism of fault lines between Orthodox and Catholic churches in Ukraine. She assesses their relation to civilizational differences (between the Catholic West and the Orthodox East) and to differences of regional culture and history. National narratives, which typically conflate religious and ethnic identities, create obstacles to interdenominational understanding by virtue of their exclusivist orientations, while the Uniate model of ecclesiastical unification is not accepted by the Orthodox as a viable alternative—as illustrated by the negative responses to proposals of church unification by the head of the Ukrainian Greek Catholic Church in 2006 and 2008.

Part III, "Orthodox Critiques of the West," focuses on another level of the Orthodox understanding of the "Other." Beyond the experience of encounter and references to specific ecclesial communities, Eastern Orthodox discussions of the religious "Other" typically include a broader dimension—a critical attitude toward the West. While some writers take pains to delineate the specific meaning of the "West" historically and geographically, most commonly the primary points of reference are Western Christianity and post-Enlightenment modernity, along with the attendant values associated with such developments as political liberalism, empirical science, economic materialism and commercialism, and humanist or "anthropocentric" theologies. As a constructed category, the West has proven to be of immense utility to Orthodox discourses, whether for explanatory illustrations of identity and difference, for reasoned critiques, or for outright polemical denunciations. In the process, for better or worse, this concept has become deeply embedded within Orthodox self-consciousness and modes of self-expression. Even in the present context of globalization and postmodernity, the East-West opposition retains its power and status as a reliable touchstone for fundamentally different understandings of Christianity. The perception of the West as "Other" is seen by many as the root cause of numerous difficulties for ecumenical encounters and the search for understanding across religious borders. The three chapters in this section focus on critical Orthodox appraisals of the West and contribute to a better understanding of this ongoing challenge to religious encounter.

Vasilios N. Makrides (University of Erfurt) studies Christos Yannaras' critique of the West, and in particular the notion of the "Barbarian West," which sets up a civilizational divide with Eastern Orthodoxy. In the author's analysis, despite Yannaras's own denial of anti-Westernism, his approach is ultimately one that polarizes and thus obstructs encounter and dialogue: its views of the Greek Orthodox past as ideal and normative, of Eastern Orthodoxy as superior, and of the West as moribund and in need of solutions from the East. Such a posture offers little for fruitful exchange with the West, which in fact reads the past critically and historically, which embraces pluralism in the pursuit of cross-cultural understanding, and which has replaced the triumphalism of the past with self-critique.

Julia Anna Lis (University of Münster) analyzes Orthodox anti-Western and anti-Europe discourses in Greece and Serbia, and finds that such critiques are often informed by a pattern of linking religion with culture and nation. She traces the development of such critiques in the ideas of Christos Yannaras, Nikolai Velimirović, and Justin Popović, whose thinking shows significant convergence: in their idealization of historical memory, in their assessment of Western culture as anthropocentric, rationalist, and secular; and in their related critiques of Europe as technologically driven, soulless, and destructive of the human person and of the natural environment. The author concludes that such conceptual dichotomies only perpetuate stereotypes, impede religious dialogue, and complicate European integration.

Regina Elsner (University of Münster) examines the ROC's critique of modern Western values, focusing on two key ideas expressed in official church statements and central to the Russian critique of the West. In speaking of the human person, Russian Orthodoxy accentuates the relational dimension and communion with other persons and with divinity—and contrasts this with the Western, post-Enlightenment emphasis on the individual. The idea of tradition is identified in the ROC with a conservative principle of static truth, codified once and for all. The contrast is with a dynamic "principle of growth and regeneration," associated with the West, but affirmed by Georges Florovsky. The author finds that these ideas are fused with political and ideological considerations, which require sorting out in the interest of more fruitful East-West encounter.

Part IV, "Encounters with European Values," continues some elements from the previous section, inasmuch as Orthodox discourses also refer to European values as part of the constructed, and polemically "Other," image of the "West." However, here the principal focus is not on metaphorical representations, but on the legal framework of the European Union (EU), and the way in which its foundational principles and provisions are understood and received in Orthodox countries. The entry into the post-Soviet period was marked very quickly in most countries by the enactment of new laws that guaranteed religious freedom and equality. But it was not long before Orthodox churches developed strong reservations about the new religious pluralism and began to press for legislative amendments that would recognize and restore their place of privilege as "traditional Churches," possessing historic roots in their respective countries and organic connections to their traditional cultures. Such patterns can potentially undermine, or invalidate, the commitment to full religious freedom and equality for all, including minorities and irrespective of traditional rootedness. The crucial notions of human dignity and human rights are also at stake, and Orthodox receptions and interpretations of those principles have occasionally appeared to depart from their generally accepted understanding in Europe and the West. Such cognitive dissonances are matters of serious concern to the EU, and can lead to legal or constitutional challenges at home, or before the European Court of Human Rights. Thus, in different countries, Orthodox encounters with European values still involve ongoing struggles over the terminology and the sociopolitical values of democratic societies.

Tina Olteanu (University of Vienna) and Dorothée de Nève (FernUniversität, Hagen) consider the tenuous relationship between Orthodoxy and the EU. The critical attitude of Orthodox churches toward the EU arises from their sensitivity to external interference in the church-state relations of particular nations, and from their traditional preference for a close connection between the political and religious spheres. Further difficulties arise with religious pluralism, which Orthodox churches see as a threat to their claims on privileged access to the political sphere and to their self-understanding as bearers of national identity. Divergence also exists over social pluralism, where the EU's civil liberties and antidiscrimination standards conflict with Orthodox norms and teachings, such as the vehement condemnations of homosexuality and the more restrained objections to abortion.

Mikhail Zherebyatyev (Voronezh State University) analyzes the post-Soviet evolution of the ROC's ideas about European law and sheds light on an important shift. While maintaining its commitments on the home front to church-state harmony and collaboration on matters of Russian identity, as well as its status as the church of the majority, by virtue of its engagement with the international community the ROC has taken stands that represent a significant departure from its traditional position on human rights. In responding to the problem of anti-Christian persecution and discrimination in other countries, the ROC set aside its well-established emphasis on collective rights and affirmed the principle of religious freedom as an individual right, and has also acknowledged that the principle should apply to religious minorities.

Olga Kazmina (Moscow State University) identifies three phases in the ROC's responses to challenges in post-Soviet Russia. The 1990 Law on Freedom of Beliefs lifted restrictions on religion, recognized all denominations as equal, and permitted entry to foreign missionaries. Such changes elicited a defensive, nationalist reaction, opposition to religious diversity, and calls for a restoration of traditional links between religion and historical culture. When a new law (1997) conferred a special status to traditional religions, the ROC promulgated a major social document, established an Inter-Religious Council, restated its commitment to Christian unity, and bolstered its efforts to counter Roman Catholic proselytism. From the mid-2000s, a more self-assured ROC expanded its missionary activity, toned down its antiproselytism rhetoric, and affirmed human dignity as attained, not given, and human rights as subordinate to the interests of the motherland, community, and family.

Part V, "Prospects for Religious Encounter, Consensus, and Cooperation," focuses on ideas and initiatives that have opened up new possibilities for progress in religious encounter and cooperation in Orthodox environments. The chapters in this section study the advances and achievements of religious encounter that contain lessons or suggest constructive paths for future work. Here we move from the hard considerations of difference and obstacles to a somewhat more optimistic, or hopeful, affirmation that meaningful progress in ecumenical and interreligious encounter is indeed attainable. From the ecumenical ideas, commitment, and experience of Georges Florovsky to the sustained meetings of German and Russian theologians at Arnoldshain, Bad Urach, and Zagorsk, and to the consensus statements of Jewish, Christian, and Muslim leaders in Ukraine, what emerges is a source for further visionary, programmatic reflection and action. It is the goal of religious encounters today to break through the barriers of religious isolation and exclusivism, to embrace the other and thereby rediscover new depths of one's own identity—and, through productive ecumenical and interreligious understanding and cooperation, to respond collectively to ethical challenges on a global scale.

Matthew Baker (Fordham University, New York) makes a case for the ecumenical character of Georges Florovsky's program of neopatristic synthesis, a proposal to bridge patristic theology with Western learning. Profoundly concerned with ecumenism, which he saw as centered primarily on the problem of schism, and convinced that "both East and West are incomplete," Florovsky laid out his constructive proposals and moral rationale for genuine Orthodox engagement with Western theology and culture, with a view toward reintegrating the two traditions. Inspiring further work by Vladimir Lossky and John Zizioulas, Florovsky's ecumenical thought provides constructive challenges to Orthodox and Western reflections on the tasks, methods, and goals of ecumenical encounters.

Christoph Mühl (University of Münster) examines the dialogue between German Protestant and Russian Orthodox theologians that focused on the respective notions related to salvation: justification by faith alone and *theosis*. Although the differences in Eastern and Western thinking about salvation are often viewed as opposites, the theological conversations revealed unexpected levels of convergence between Lutheran and Orthodox positions on justification and the relation between faith and good works. A closer study of the resulting consensus statements suggests that further clarifications will be required to overcome differences in confessional terminologies, develop a common theological language, and address remaining issues of soteriology and anthropology. The consensus already achieved can inspire this further work.

Andrii Krawchuk (University of Sudbury) studies the interreligious work of the Ukrainian Council of Churches and Religious Organizations. In identifying religious common ground and responding to social and political issues, the leaders of the major religious communities in Ukraine have issued joint statements for nearly two decades. While their encounters are not ecumenical in that they deliberately avoid direct dialogue on matters of doctrine, the very existence of the council and the broad-based consensus that it has produced on social ethics does constitute a robust track record. The council's evolution, from a common voice of religious solidarity addressing the state on law reform and religious freedom to a herald of social morality, may set the stage for a further expansion of its mandate and goals into the sphere of interreligious dialogue and understanding. At the same time, serious concerns have begun to appear on the international front, notably on the status and rights of religious and sexual minorities, and on abortion.

Part VI, "Emerging Encounters and New Challenges in Post-Soviet Central Asia," represents a significant new area of interest and research on religion in Central and East European Studies, and one of the largest Muslim regions of the former USSR. In this cluster of newly independent countries, the post-Soviet transition has been especially difficult, marked by an extreme deterioration of the economy. Orthodox Christianity occupies a minority status in the region, with less than 10 percent of the population in Uzbekistan and Turkmenistan, but is more significantly represented in Kyrgyzstan (20 percent) and Kazakhstan (44 percent). The ROC has two main jurisdictions in the region: the Metropolitan District of Kazakhstan, comprising one eparchy established in the Soviet period (Astana and Alma Ata, 1945) and eight others since Kazakhstan's independence in 1991—Karaganda (2010), Kokshetau (2011), Kostanay (2010), Pavlodar (2010), Petropavlovsk and Bulayevo (2011), Uralsk and Guryev (1991), Ust-Kamenogorsk (2011), and Shymkent (1991); and the Central Asian Metropolitan District (established in July 2011), which comprises the eparchies of Bishkek (Kyrgyzstan, 2011), Dushanbe (Tajikistan, 2011), and Tashkent (Uzbekistan, 1871). The ROC is also present in Turkmenistan, with ten parishes and one monastery in 2012, under the jurisdiction of the Eparchy of Tashkent. These structures, most of which were established recently, give a sense of both historic roots and the current pattern of concerted activity by the mother church. While the subject of Orthodox encounters in Central Asia remains a matter for further scholarly exploration, the predominantly Muslim environment is a factor with potential impact on the Christian minorities.[4] In recent years, the rise of radical Islam has turned Central Asia's Ferghana Valley into a hot spot of Islamic radicalization and extremism. The contributions to this section introduce Muslim-Orthodox relations and study processes in Central Asia in the wake of the post-Soviet sociopolitical transformations.

Andrii Krawchuk (University of Sudbury) examines Muslim-Orthodox relations in the Russian Federation, where Russian Orthodoxy and Islam are pursuing similar goals of institutional consolidation and stabilization in response to internal and external issues. Orthodox responses to *A Common Word between Us and You* (2007) have provided a theological reflection that shifts the focus of dialogue from the sphere of social and political concerns to that of foundational scriptural texts and core values. They have also opened up new opportunities for the two communities to pursue a relationship that is informed by their religious identities, rather than one merely subsumed under the pragmatic agenda of the state. Despite conceptual and doctrinal differences that remain to be resolved, this exchange has identified significant areas of shared concern, not the least of which is the global quest for the rights of religious minorities.

Galina Yemelianova (University of Birmingham) studies the parties, ideology, and factors of radicalization and observes that in Central Asia the post-Soviet transition produced a climate that has fueled polarization. The termination of subsidies from Moscow created a socioeconomic crisis, while the end of state atheism and the relaxation of border controls permitted new contacts with other Islamic countries. Radicalizing *Salafi* Muslims appeared on the scene, some of them possibly recruited to replace the leaders of traditional Islam in the region. Despite some counterbalances to radicalization, like the enduring Soviet legacy of secularism and the strength of a more moderate, "folk" Islam, the factors behind the emergence of the process—the socioeconomic crisis, as well as the ineffectiveness, corruption, and repressions of authorities—appear to be shaping the course of events.

Michael Fredholm (Stockholm University) analyzes the activities of Uzbek Islamic extremists and finds that, although their Islamic rhetoric has little theological content and is outweighed by their belief in the righteousness of their cause and that salvation can be assured by armed violence in the name of the religious duty of holy war (jihad), they have indirectly contributed to the rise of authoritarianism in the new states of Central Asia. In responding to terrorism, governments in the region bolstered their security services and enacted harsher legislation. The persistence and expansion of these extremist groups over the past two decades, their significant roles in civil conflicts, and their destabilization of fragile states appear to set the course for the foreseeable future in the region, in which coincidentally the ROC has also become much more active in the same period.

The present collection is a significant contribution to the understanding of Orthodox Christianity in its local and global contexts. The essays provide groundbreaking studies of major religious trends and processes that are central to the rethinking of community identities and of encounter with the "other" in Central and Eastern Europe today. They explore the richness and diversity, as well as the challenges and difficulties, of religious responses to an unprecedented social, cultural, and political transformation. In the post-Soviet sphere, after decades of struggling for survival, Orthodox Christianity is beginning to rediscover itself and to redefine its relationship with the world community. Its dramatic journey and its vision for the future may still remain works-in-progress, but the emerging practical reflection and action already contain the seeds of a new self-identity as Orthodoxy responds to urgent global issues and debates.

A brief note on transliteration: given the diversity of authors, native languages, and ways of transliterating Slavic languages, a certain degree of variability is only to be expected in a collection like the present one. While serious attention was given to standardize and harmonize our texts as much as possible, scholars of Eastern and Central Europe will be quite familiar with numerous possible transliterations, particularly in the rendering of names. Indeed, even official sources can sometimes vary in their transliterations. Also, if an author followed the German transliteration of her cited published sources, harmonizing the text with other standards would have created inconsistency in the chapter. Our goal was to ensure consistency within the chapters first of all and, as far as possible, throughout the book. In this volume, both transliterated and the original Cyrillic versions of texts coexist. As for names, the index at the end attempts to facilitate searches by capturing some of the variations (e.g., Kyrill/Kirill, Florovsky/Florovskii, etc.).

The editors are grateful to Allison Tremblay of Desmarais Library, Laurentian University (Sudbury, Canada), who prepared the Central Asian maps for the final section of this book. As the scholarly study of religion in Central and Eastern Europe expands its scope of inquiry and encounter eastward into Asia, these visual aids will be a useful point of reference for readers who may be unfamiliar with specific locations in the region.

Notes

1. John H. Erickson, "A Retreat from Ecumenism in Post-Communist Russia and Eastern Europe?" *Ecumenical Trends* 30:9 (October 2001), 129–138. See also: Harriman Institute, Columbia University April 7, 2000: www.orthodoxresearchinstitute.org/articles/ecumenical/erickson_ecumenism_russia.pdf (accessed December 28, 2012).
2. See Lucian Leustean, ed., *Eastern Christianity and Politics in the Twenty-First Century* (New York and London: Routledge, forthcoming in 2014); George E. Demacopoulos and Aristotle Papanikolaou, eds., *Orthodox Constructions of the West* (New York: Fordham University Press, 2013); Alfons Brüning and Evert van der Zweerde, eds., *Orthodox Christianity and Human Rights* (Leuven: Peeters, 2012); Jarret Zigon, ed., *Multiple Moralities and Religions in Post-Soviet Russia* (New York: Berghahn Books, 2011); Chris Hann and Hermann Goltz, eds., *Eastern Christian Churches in Anthropological Perspective* (Berkeley—Los Angeles—London: University of California Press, 2010); Ines Angeli Murzaku, ed., *Quo Vadis Eastern Europe? Religion, State, and Society after Communism*, Series on Balkan and East-European Studies 30 (Ravenna: Longo Editore, 2009); Thomas Bremer, ed., *Religion and the Conceptual Boundary in Central and Eastern Europe: Encounters of Faiths*, Studies in Central and Eastern Europe (Basingstoke: Palgrave-Macmillan, 2008); Mark D. Steinberg and Catherine Wanner, eds., *Religion, Morality and Community in Post-Soviet Societies* (Washington: Woodrow Wilson Center Press, 2008); Victor Roudometof, Alexander Agadjanian, and Jerry Pankhurst, eds., *Eastern Orthodoxy in a Global Age: Tradition Faces the Twenty-First Century* (Walnut Creek, CA: AltaMira Press, 2005); Jonathan Sutton and Wil van den Bercken, eds., *Orthodox Christianity and Contemporary Europe* (Leuven: Peeters, 2003); and William H. Swatos, Jr., ed., *Politics and Religion in Central and Eastern Europe: Traditions and Transitions* (Westport, CT: Praeger, 1994).
3. The withdrawal of the Orthodox churches of Georgia and Bulgaria from membership in the World Council of Churches (in 1997 and 1998, respectively) and the substantially reduced Orthodox participation in the WCC's eighth Assembly (Harare, 1998) may well have been symptomatic of a larger pattern within Orthodoxy in the post-Soviet period—a "retreat from ecumenism." In Catholic-Orthodox relations, the Joint International Commission for Theological Dialogue between the Catholic Church and the Orthodox Church, which was established in 1979 by Pope John Paul II and Ecumenical Patriarch Dimitrios, and which held 12 plenary meetings between 1980 and 2010, appears to be in a hiatus since 2010.
4. In addition to the monographic studies of our contributors, a number of recent works reflect the emerging scholarly focus on the religious factor in Central Asia: Russell Zanca,

"Fearing Islam in Uzbekistan: Islamic Tendencies, Extremist Violence, and Authoritarian Secularism," in *Religion, Morality and Community in Post-Soviet Societies*, Mark D. Steinberg and Catherine Wanner, eds. (Bloomington, IN: Indiana University Press–Woodrow Wilson Center Press, 2008), pp. 247–280; J. Rashid, *Jihad. The Rise of Militant Islam in Central Asia* (New Haven: Yale University Press, 2002); V. Naumkin, *Radical Islam in Central Asia* (Lanham: Rowman & Littlefield Publishers, 2005); Bartholomew I, Ecumenical Patriarch; Rabbi Arthur Schneier, President Appeal of Conscience Foundation Sheikhul-Islam; Allahshukur Pashazadeh, Chairman of the Muslim Board of Caucasus, Declaration Conference on "Peace and Tolerance II: Dialogue and Cooperation in Southeast Europe, the Caucasus and Central Asia," *Greek Orthodox Theological Review* 50:1–4 (Spring–Winter 2005), 451–455; R. Foltz, "Islamic Communities in Central Asia," in *The Oxford Handbook of Global Religions*, Mark Juergensmeyer, ed. (New York: Oxford University Press, 2006); and Sébastien Peyrouse, "The Partnership between Islam and Orthodox Christianity in Central Asia," *Religion, State & Society* 36:4 (December 2008), 393–405. See also the historical studies: J. Dyck, "Revival as Church Restoration: Patterns of a Revival among Ethnic Germans in Central Asia after World War II," in *Mission in the former Soviet Union*, Walter Sawatsky and Peter Penner, eds. (Schwarzenfeld, Germany: Neufeld Verlag, 2005); and David M. Johnstone, "Czarist Missionary Contact with Central Asia: Models of Contextualization?" *International Bulletin of Missionary Research* 31:2 (April 2007), 66–70, 72.

Part I

The Ecclesial Self: Traditional Identities and the Challenges of Pluralism

1

Russian Orthodoxy between State and Nation

Jennifer Wasmuth

Introduction

Since the collapse of the Soviet Union in 1991 there has been an astonishing development of religion in Eastern Europe. In contrast to the predominant atheist doctrine in Soviet times, a massive religious renaissance has taken root since the early 1990s. The increasing influence of religion is especially true in the case of the Russian Orthodox Church (ROC). Polls conducted by diverse organizations indicate a high level of acceptance of the ROC. More than 70 percent of Russians (more than 80 percent, according to some sources) consider themselves Orthodox.[1] Also, 40 percent of the population declare that they completely trust the church[2] and 53 percent (including Muslims) praise the public efforts of Patriarch Kirill.[3]

The aim of this study is to demonstrate how the ROC defines its role in the present situation. Of particular interest here is the question of the extent to which it is able to fulfill political and social expectations. In focusing on the self-assessment of the ROC, our analysis is based on official church documents and on statements of leading representatives of the ROC. Such an approach seeks to avoid the risk of imposing Western theoretical frameworks and concepts, which may not apply to developments in Russia.[4]

The ROC and Service to the World

In 2000, the Bishops' Council of the ROC adopted the *Bases of the Social Concept of the Russian Orthodox Church* (hereafter, *Social Concept*; for text references, *SC*). For the first time, the ROC issued a comprehensive statement dealing with the most relevant political and social issues or, as the *Social Concept* put it, setting forth "the basic provisions of her teaching on church-state relations and a number of socially significant problems."[5]

Although it may be a stereotype to think of Orthodoxy primarily in categories of liturgy and piety and of Orthodox belief as an attitude totally directed to "another world," there is certainly a strong ascetic tradition within Orthodoxy that is oriented toward a withdrawal from the world. A case in point was the movement of the "Non-Possessors" (Нестяжатели), which opposed ecclesiastical land ownership at the turn of the fifteenth–sixteenth centuries. Very telling in this regard was the way in which Patriarch Nikon (1605–1682) defended

> the ideal of contemplative monasticism, arguing that the goal of monastic life was personal salvation through continual prayer and purification of one's heart. Though critics might call this egoistical, Nikon declared that it was "holy egotism" and that monasteries served the world precisely by providing a refuge from the turmoil of the world—and not for the monks only, but for the faithful as well.[6]

The Orthodox tradition thus contains a well-established conviction of its own "otherworldliness," a "holy egotism" that can potentially impede social concern and social assistance.

In light of this tendency and the legal prohibition on social service by the ROC during Soviet times, it seems all the more remarkable that the Bishops' Council of the ROC adopted the *Social Concept*. In doing so, the ROC affirmed that the "Church is called to act in the world in the image of Christ, to bear witness to Him and His Kingdom" and likewise "the members of the Church are called to share in Christ's mission, in His service of the world" (*SC* I.2). Scott M. Kenworthy describes the *Social Concept* as a "deliberate attempt of emancipation from the mystical-ascetical stream of Orthodox tradition, an attempt to articulate the Church's relevance to modern society in a language that is still conservative and imbued with tradition."[7]

It is important to understand that the *Social Concept* "deals primarily with fundamental theological and ecclesio-social issues" (*SC* Introduction), and that it does not work out a detailed social-ethical program. Consequently, many questions are left open. However, the document does outline the ROC's basic ideas of engagement in the service to the world "at the end of the 20th century and in the near future" (*SC* Introduction).

In this study we will focus on the chapters in *Social Concept* relating, first, to church-state and, then, church-nation relations.

Church-State Relations

The chapter on church-state relations sets forth the differences between the church, a "divine-human organism," and the state, "which exists for the purpose of ordering worldly life" (*SC* III.1), and acknowledges a need for the state: "God blesses the state as an essential element of life in the world distorted by sin" (*SC* III.2). Despite their fundamentally different functions, the church and the state must work together. The ROC defines its relationship toward the secular state, "not bound by any religious commitments," as follows: While cooperation with such a state should be "limited to several areas and based on mutual non-interference into each other's affairs,"[8] this does not imply "that religion should be radically forced out of all spheres of social life." In sum, the principle of a secular state "presupposes only a certain division of domains between church and state and their non-interference in each other's affairs" (*SC* III.3). This "new symphony"[9] distinguishes the domains far more than the classical Byzantine model ever did and formulates a right to resistance: "If the civil authorities force Orthodox believers to apostatize from Christ and His Church and to commit sinful and spiritually harmful actions, the Church should refuse to obey the state. Following the will of his conscience, a Christian may refuse to fulfill commands of the state that could force him into a grave sin" (*SC* III.5). From the perspective of the ROC, the view that it is becoming more of a state church has no basis in fact. As Archpriest Vsevolod Chaplin, head of the Synodal Department for Church and Society Relations, explained, the

> fact that the Church is growing and becoming more active by no means implies a change in its position on relations between the state and religion...the Church is not trying to substitute some state or form some politicized ideology...We do not want [the Church] to become part of the state apparatus, state machinery, or to assume secular functions.[10]

Church-Nation Relations

In the chapter on the relationship between church and nation, the ROC formulates a complex position, which is not without tensions and contradictions. Two principles, which were the subject of fierce controversies, are set forth here. These principles were previously voiced in the *Statute of the Russian Orthodox Church*, which declared: "1. The Russian Orthodox Church is a *multinational* Local Autocephalous Church in doctrinal unity and in prayerful and canonical communion with other Local Orthodox Churches. [...] 3. The jurisdiction of the Russian Orthodox Church shall include persons of Orthodox confession living on the *canonical territory* of the Russian Orthodox Church."[11] The principles of a multinational church and a canonical territory are of central importance to the ROC, and we examine them more closely in the following sections.

The ROC as a "Multinational Church"

In its official statements, the ROC describes itself as "the great and multinational Russian Orthodox Church."[12] Though the term "multinational church" is not used in the *Social Concept*, its biblical foundation is found in the chapter "Church and Nation": "By His Blood Christ 'hath redeemed us to God out of every kindred, and tongue, and people, and nation' (Rev. 5:9)." Upon this soteriological base the *Social Concept* points to the universal, supranational nature of the church:

> In the Church "there is no difference between the Jew and the Greek" (Rom. 10:12). Just as God is not the God of the Jews alone but also of the Gentiles (Rom. 3:29), so the Church does not divide people on either national or class grounds: in her "there is neither Greek, nor Jew, circumcised nor uncircumcised, Barbarian, Scythian, bond nor free: but Christ is all, and in all" (Col. 3:11). (*SC* II.1)

The *Social Concept* draws upon the biblical notion of a new community, united in faith:

> The community of the children of God, "a chosen generation, a royal priesthood, an holy nation, a peculiar people...which in time past were not a people, but are now the people of God" (1 Pet. 2:9–10)...The unity of this new people is secured not by

> its ethnic, cultural or linguistic community, but by their common faith in Christ and Baptism. (*SC* II.1)

The reference to biblical texts situates the ROC's reflection in a framework that is shared by all Christians. The emphasis on the universal nature of the church is especially relevant in relation to the risk of "phyletism," or national tribalism within the church, a phenomenon to which Orthodox churches are particularly sensitive. The classic historical reference point for this has been the 1872 Council in Constantinople, which condemned the establishment of a Bulgarian Exarchate as a case of phyletism and a negation of the catholicity of the church.[13]

Further, the ROC necessarily stresses its universal and supranational nature because it truly is a multinational church. Its members include Karelians, Komi, Mordovians, Ukrainians, Belorussians, Chuvash, Yakuts, Armenians, Tatars, and Buryats. The ROC thus must cope with ethnic diversity and also the tensions that arise when some minorities define their own identities in contradistinction to the ROC.[14]

This challenge is by no means new. The ROC is traditionally a multinational church. Ever since Muscovy became an imperial power in the sixteenth century and had to integrate non-Russian people, the ROC has had to develop a strategy to deal with ethnic and religious differences. In spite of the widespread opinion that in those times the ROC left nothing undone to strengthen its position in proclaiming the idea of Moscow as the "Third Rome," recent research has shown that the ROC acted very pragmatically and focused its "modest efforts not on the conversion of pagans or Muslims, but on bringing a more perfect faith to the Russians who were already Orthodox."[15] In practical terms, the idea of Russia as the "New Israel" has been far more important than the idea of Moscow as "Third Rome."

Today the ROC responds to ethnic and religious tensions arising from diversity within the church and in society by proclaiming universal Orthodox values. Thus Metropolitan Hilarion has called on Christians of all confessions to forge a "strategic alliance" grounded in shared, traditional Christian values like the family—even allowing the possibility that the Roman Catholic Church could become an important ally in that alliance. For his part, Patriarch Kirill had repeatedly stressed that "interethnic, interreligious problems in Russia can be resolved only by improving public morals." In a July 2011 address to Prime Minister Vladimir Putin and prominent members of religious and other nongovernmental organizations, he stated: "It is impossible to neutralize differences by ignoring the values of human life. If we want to build a society isolated from these values, an absolutely secular one and tolerate multiple forms of behavior, we will abandon something that people of any religion have in common and that unites them, we will destroy the moral foundation of our life."[16]

The emphasis on traditional Christian values goes along with a strong criticism of Western social concepts. In the aforementioned address, Patriarch Kirill related to the Western model of multiculturalism: "[This] model smoothes out differences between religions and cultures and neutralizes traditional values. [...] Values go away from a multicultural society, but differences remain in place and these differences prompt people to throw bombs and Molotov cocktails at each other and turn over cars. The melting pot idea doesn't work."[17] Such criticism applies to current developments in Russia—in particular, the widespread acceptance of what the political establishment calls a "guided" or "managed democracy" (управляемая демократия). In fact, 93 percent of the population believes that Russian society needs law and order first and foremost, as compared with only 49 percent who want a democratic system.[18]

From a Western perspective, the ROC's emphasis on traditional Christian values may seem problematic because it does not support democratic development. Moreover, the notion of "plurality" is reduced to a multiplicity of nations. There comes to light a longing for unity and harmony, which is deeply rooted in the history of the ROC.[19] But there is no sense of "plurality" that would correspond to any concept of civil society, understood as the social spaces between the individual and the family, the individual and the state, and the space for communities, nonprofit organizations and associations pursuing various types of public utility,[20] which constitute the basis of democratic processes. While accepting a democratic system in principle,[21] the ROC does not acknowledge any need for civil society. It therefore becomes possible to argue that the ROC bears some responsibility for what appears to be the failure of the Russian democratic experiment.[22] And the question remains open as to whether the ROC's return to traditional Christian values will enable it to address effectively the social and political problems of Russia as part of the modern, globalized world.

The "Canonical Territory" of the ROC

The principle of a "canonical territory" is equally important for the understanding of the ROC's relation toward nation. But its meaning is not self-evident, and no detailed explanation of it is given in any official document of the church. Historically, it can be traced back to the principle of "one city—one bishop—one Church," which was elaborated in the first three centuries of Christianity and defined in the *Canons of the Apostles*. As Metropolitan Hilarion has explained, the purpose of this principle in the ancient church was to "point out the inadmissibility of violating the boundaries of ecclesiastical territories by bishops or clergy,"[23] that is, to avoid or to reduce conflicts *within* the church. Thus, in its original intent, this was first of all a principle of church order and not a political strategy, although in "defining the boundaries of ecclesiastical territories, the Fathers of the ancient undivided Church took into account civil territorial divisions established by secular authorities."[24]

Even Metropolitan Hilarion has to admit that for historical and political reasons it is impossible today to implement fully the ancient principle of "one city—one bishop—one Church."[25] So what does "canonical territory" mean today? What exactly does the ROC have in mind when talking about its "canonical territory"—the territory of Kievan Rus', the Moscow Empire, the Soviet Union, the Russian Federation? The *Statutes of the ROC* give a fairly precise definition: "The jurisdiction of the Russian Orthodox Church shall include persons of Orthodox confession living on the *canonical territory* of the Russian Orthodox Church in Russia, Ukraine, Byelorussia, Moldavia, Azerbaijan, Kazakhstan, Kirghizia, Latvia, Lithuania, Tajikistan, Turkmenia, Uzbekistan and Estonia and also Orthodox Christians living in other countries and voluntarily joining this jurisdiction" (Section 1, Paragraph 3). In this definition, "canonical territory" encompasses not only the present-day Russian Federation, but also the whole area of the post-Soviet states, including Ukraine and Belarus. Only Georgia and Armenia are not mentioned because of their own Orthodox churches.

The principle of "canonical territory" has thus become one of the most controversial topics in the contemporary Orthodox world, prompting Daniel P. Payne to suggest that the "ROC and the Patriarchate of Constantinople are in a war for souls concerning the issue of canonical territory."[26] Conflicts around the issue also exist within the Roman Catholic Church. From the perspective of the ROC, the Roman Catholic Church is working hard to expand its influence, primarily through the Greek Catholic Church in Ukraine, which was restored to legal status in 1988, and through the establishment of "parallel hierarchies" in Russia.

Nor are jurisdictional questions the only source of controversy. The tendency to connect "canonical territory" with national aspirations has drawn criticism. Payne points to the Diocese of Sourozh under the leadership of Metropolitan Anthony Blum, which did not want to "understand itself as 'a vehicle for preserving Russian national identity.'"[27] And Cardinal Walter Kasper, former president of the Pontifical Council for Christian Unity, openly accused the ROC of "ecclesiological heresy by defining the canonical territory of the Moscow Patriarchate according to the principle of cultural and ethnic identities."[28]

Indeed, the ROC generally does have a strong national attitude even if we allow for Irina Papkova's threefold distinction within the church: "a fundamentalist wing (a small but activist group imbued with virulent nationalism and xenophobia), a currently dominant conservative wing, and a quietly liberal democratic, reformist wing."[29] In this connection, the *Social Concept* declares that in spite of its universal nature the church bears responsibility for national welfare: "Orthodox Christians, aware of being citizens of the heavenly homeland, should not forget about their earthly homeland" (*SC* II.2). The document lists a number of saints (Prince Michael of Tver, 1271–1318; Sergius of Radonezh, *ca.* 1314–1392; Prince Dimitry Donskoy, 1350–1389; Patriarch Hermogen of Moscow and All Russia, *ca.* 1530–1612; Metropolitan Filaret of Moscow, 1782–1867) who "became famous for the love of their earthly homeland and fidelity to it" (*SC* II.2). It further explains that "love of the fatherland" includes a specific territory as well as the "brothers by blood, who live everywhere in the world" and demands that the "patriotism of the Orthodox Christian should be active [...] preserve and develop national culture and people's self-awareness" (*SC* II.3). Clearly, the ROC sees itself in a special relationship with the Russian people over and above any other people, and with Russian culture as opposed to any other culture.

Even if the *Social Concept* condemns "aggressive nationalism, xenophobia, national exclusiveness and inter-ethnic enmity" (*SC* II.4), the emphasis on the Russian nation and the related identification of Orthodoxy and Russianness seem to contradict the principle of a multinational church. "Canonical territory" in fact becomes a principle of *missionary* territory, since it proposes that Russians both inside and outside of Russia should be tied closer to the ROC and, through it, to the Russian state.[30] The ROC, therefore, is eager to stress publicly its national importance[31] and to strengthen its social role as an integral feature of national identity, for example, through the introduction of Orthodox chaplains into the army[32] or of Russian Orthodox teachings into the educational system.[33]

According to one perspective, this is a promising strategy insofar as patriotic feelings may be said to characterize Russian society today. Angelika Nußberger, director of the Institute of Law in the East, has identified a new trend in Russian juridical literature, "die 'vaterländische Tradition' in der Rechtswissenschaft zu betonen und den Blick nach Westen als 'Verrat' zu brandmarken."[34] For many Russians, the core of their patriotic feelings seems to be "Orthodoxy." Hence, the ROC stands not only for national identity, as with the veneration of Tsar Nicholas II and his family in

Ekaterinburg, which "attracts all kinds of 'patriots.'"[35] More broadly, the ROC offers (through pilgrimages) the "authentically Russian" life that many people seek.[36] Thus, "traditional religions," especially Orthodoxy, are highly respected and enjoy a privileged legal status.[37] Zoe Knox's case study analysis of religious freedom during the Putin presidency "suggest[s] that religious freedom in post-communist Russia is understood as freedom *from* the influence of certain religions and confessions... The threat posed by artists critical of the Russian Orthodox Church was the intrusion of secularism into Russian tradition and culture. The process of Westernization is regarded as a corruption of Russian national traditions."[38]

From another perspective, the ROC's emphasis on patriotic sentiment needs to be called into question. This strategy has stirred up conflicts with national, religious, and nonreligious minorities.[39] There is also a risk of the instrumentalization of Orthodoxy by nationalistic groups and organizations and its degeneration into a political ideology. We also have to ask if the ROC can really live up to the expectations of caring for *all* Russians that are placed upon a "national" church. As Melissa Caldwell has shown, because of its market-style behavior and its involvement in financial transactions, the ROC is reputed to be a "corrupt and immoral institution."[40] Moreover, the ROC undermines its public image when it distributes charitable aid only to specific groups of Russians, who regularly attend the Divine Liturgy. The ROC is well aware of the phenomenon of "belonging without believing" and it therefore encourages people to deepen their knowledge of Orthodox belief and strengthen their spiritual life. Patriarch Kirill has stressed that "the hardest task facing the church today is to transform the Orthodox faith from the level of folklore, where our contemporaries often place it, to the level of a worldview."[41] Of course, such efforts run counter to the proclaiming of a sort of "national birthright" on Orthodoxy for every Russian. Melissa Caldwell captures the essence of the problem: "The Orthodox Church finds itself caught in an untenable position in which its efforts to regain its status as the national church are at the same time undermining its popularity. By emphasizing its legitimate claim to Russia's historical and national legacy, the Orthodox Church has itself disentangled the spiritual and theological from the practical."[42] The emphasis on patriotic sentiment, although embracing Russia as a whole, seems to underestimate the importance of recent tendencies toward individualization in Russian society. It has been argued that "individualization must be recognized as one of the key features of... the new popular Orthodoxy."[43] As opposed to "belonging without believing," there is also an inverse phenomenon of "believing without belonging," in which people with particular religious needs may be attracted to the ROC, but only temporarily and with no intent to become a regular, active member of that church.[44]

Concluding Remarks

Our inquiry into Russian Orthodoxy "between the state and the nation" shows that the church-state relationship is—at least from the ROC's point of view—fairly clear. However, the church's relationship with the nation raises some important questions. In this area, the ROC espouses its two key principles of multinationalism and canonical territory, which may be illustrated as shown in table 1.1.

Considering the high level of social acceptance of the ROC, various surveys have suggested that both principles—the "multinational Church" and the "canonical

Table 1.1 The Russian Orthodox Church's self-understanding: Two Principles

Principle	**"Multinational church"**	**"Canonical territory"**
Foundation	Mainly New Testament	Mainly Canon Law ("Canons of the Apostles")
Idea	Universal Promise of Salvation	"One City—One Bishop—One Church" One Nation—One Belief (Reduction of Conflicts)
Function	ROC as integrating factor (emphasis on universal Christian values)	• Strengthening the social and political position of the ROC • Preventing "Westernization"

territory"—serve to strengthen the position of the ROC, even though they contradict each other. The ROC claims to be multinational in the sense that anyone, regardless of national identity, can be a true Orthodox. At the same time, the ROC also claims that every *Russian* should at some point become an Orthodox believer since Russia is the "canonical territory" of the ROC.[45] Both principles respond to a widespread desire for unity, order, historical continuity in the post-Soviet context, and national identity in the age of globalization. However, the principles are problematic in this respect too: multinationalism does not really support the democratization processes of Russia, since it retains the categories of "nation" and "blood of brothers," and because it understands "plurality" as simply a multiplicity of nations. As for the principle of canonical territory, it runs the risk of transforming Orthodoxy into a political ideology and undermining the proper theological understanding that the ROC is striving to proclaim.

Notes

1. Veniamin Simonov, "Religion und Religiosität in Rußland," *Osteuropa* 59:6 (2009), 189–216.
2. Lew Gudkow, "Die politische Kultur des postsowjetischen Russland im Spiegel der öffentlichen Meinung," in *Länderbericht Russland*, Bundeszentrale für politische Bildung—Schriftreihe 1066, Heiko Pleines and Hans-Henning Schröder, eds. (Bonn, 2010), 424.
3. Interfax Religion—www.interfax-religion.com (August 5, 2011). The high level of acceptance of the ROC does not necessarily mean that all of the 70 or 80 percent are active, practicing Orthodox. For example, young, well-educated people are known to have very critical attitudes. There is thus a "discrepancy between the official, 'monolithic' image and anthropological reality." On this, see Alexander Agadjanian and Kathy Rousselet, "Individual and Collective Identities in Russian Orthodoxy," in *Eastern Christians in Anthropological Perspective*, Chris Hann and Hermann Goltz, eds. (Berkeley, Los Angeles, London: University of California Press, 2010), 312.
4. Chris Hann rightly emphasizes that the prevailing concepts of "modernity" and "secularization" are helpful for understanding why the situation in the West cannot be simply transferred to post-Soviet states. See his "Broken Chains and Moral Lazarets: The Politicization, Juridification and Commodification of Religion after Socialism," in *Religion, Identity, Postsocialism*. The Halle Focus Group 2003–2010, Chris Hann, ed. (Halle/Saale, 2010), 3–21.

5. The document is published. See www.mospat.ru (Russian) and www.mospat.en (English).
6. Scott M. Kenworthy, "To Save the World or to Renounce It: Modes of Moral Action in Russian Orthodoxy," in *Religion, Morality, and Community in Post-Soviet Societies*, Mark D. Steinberg and Catherine Wanner, eds. (Washington: Woodrow Wilson Center Press, 2008), 22.
7. Ibid., 46, with reference to Alexander Agadjanian, "The Social Vision of Russian Orthodoxy," in *Orthodox Christianity and Contemporary Europe*, Jonathan Sutton and Wil van den Bercken, eds. (Leuven-Paris-Dudley, MA: Peeters, 2003), 163–182.
8. The *Social Concept* lists the relevant areas in detail in III.8.
9. Pauliina Arola and Risto Saarinen, "In Search of *Sobornost* and 'New Symphony.' The Social Doctrine of the Russian Orthodox Church," *The Ecumenical Review* 54:1 (2002), 130–141.
10. Interfax Religion—www.interfax-religion.com (July 15, 2011).
11. See the English version at https://mospat.ru/en/documents/ustav/i/; and the Russian version: https://mospat.ru/documents/ustav/i/ (author's emphasis).
12. See, e.g., the address of Metropolitan Hilarion of Volokolamsk to the Primate of the Russian Church Abroad in February 2011: www.russianorthodoxchurch.ws/synod/eng2011/20110207_print_enmethilarionvisit.html (The official website of the Synod of Bishops of the Russian Orthodox Church Outside of Russia).
13. Anastasios Kallis, "Phyletism," *Lexikon für Theologie und Kirche* 11 (2001), 220f.
14. Sergei Filatov and Roman Lunkin, "My Father's House Has Many Mansions: Ethnic Minorities in the Russian Orthodox Church," *Religion, State and Society* 38:4 (2010), 361–378.
15. Paul Bushkovitch, "Orthodoxy and Islam in Russia 988–1725," in *Religion und Integration im Moskauer Russland. Konzepte und Praktiken, Potentiale und Grenzen. 14.-17. Jahrhundert*, Ludwig Steindorff, ed., *Forschungen zur Osteuropäischen Geschichte* 76 (Wiesbaden: Harrassowitz Verlag, 2010), 117–143.
16. Interfax Religion—www.interfax-religion.com (July 20, 2011).
17. Ibid.
18. Gudkow, "Die politische Kultur des postsowjetischen Russland im Spiegel der öffentlichen Meinung," 416.
19. On the romantic-inspired idea of "sobornost," which is fundamental for the *Social Concept*, see: Jennifer Wasmuth, "Sozialethik in der russisch-orthodoxen Kirche der Gegenwart. 'Die Grundlagen der Sozialkonzeption' in kritischer Betrachtung," *Evangelische Theologie* 64:1 (2004), 37–51.
20. Jens Siegert, "Zivilgesellschaft in Russland," in *Länderbericht Russland*, Bundeszentrale für politische Bildung—Schriftreihe 1066, Heiko Pleines and Hans-Henning Schröder, eds. (Bonn, 2010), 172. Siegert mentions the following criteria to identify the actors in a civil society: volunteerism (*Freiwilligkeit*), independence from state control (*Staatsunabhängigkeit*), and commitment to the public good (*Verpflichtung zum Gemeinwohl*).
21. *Social Concept*, V.
22. Irina Papkova, "The Freezing of Historical Memory? The Post-Soviet Russian Orthodox Church and the Council of 1917," in *Religion, Morality, and Community in Post-Soviet Societies*, Mark D. Steinberg and Catherine Wanner, eds. (Washington: Woodrow Wilson Center Press, 2008), 55f.
23. Orthodoxy Today.org—www.orthodoxytoday.org/articles6/HilarionOneBishop.php.
24. Ibid..
25. Orthodoxy Today.org—www.orthodoxytoday.org/articles6/HilarionOneBishop2.php.
26. Daniel P. Payne, "Spiritual Security, the Russian Orthodox Church, and the Russian Foreign Ministry: Collaboration or Cooptation?" *Journal of Church and State* 9 (2010), 10.

27. Ibid., 11. Payne argues that the ROC is a willing instrument in the hands of the Russian minister of foreign affairs, promoting its concept of "spiritual security" (1) "for the purpose of expanding and consolidating the Russian world" (15).
28. J. Buciora, "Canonical Territory of the Moscow Patriarchate. An Analysis of contemporary Russian Orthodox Thought," in: www.orthodox-christian-comment.co.uk/canonical_territory_of_the_moscow_patriarchate. See also Zoe Knox, "Religious Freedom in Russia: The Putin Years," in *Religion, Morality, and Community in Post-Soviet Societies*, Mark D. Steinberg and Catherine Wanner, eds. (Washington, 2008), 293–298.
29. Mark D. Steinberg and Catherine Wanner, "Afterword: Policy Implications of the Research and Analysis," in *Religion, Morality, and Community in Post-Soviet Societies*, Mark D. Steinberg and Catherine Wanner, eds. (Washington: Woodrow Wilson Center Press, 2008), 317. See also Papkova, "The Freezing of Historical Memory?" 71ff.
30. Alexander Agadjanian and Kathy Rousselet, "Globalization and Identity Discourse in Russian Orthodoxy," in *Eastern Orthodoxy in a Global Age: Tradition Faces the Twenty-First Century*, Victor Roudometof, Alexander Agadjanian, and Jerry Pankhurst, eds. (Walnut Creek, CA: Alta Mira Press, 2005), 40f.
31. William Yoder, "Vorsprung oder Krise?—Die russische Sehnsucht nach dem christlichen Staat," in *Pressedienst der Russischen Evangelischen Allianz*, Moskau/Rußland; Quelle: CBS KULTUR INFO: www.kirchen-in-osteuropa.de/index.php?action=archiv&jahr=2011&monat=&noek&nummer=16/11&mail=B#2 (April 19, 2011). Yoder quotes Archpriest Vsevolod Chaplin as saying: "Es ist heute offensichtlich, daß Volk und Kirche eins sind. Das russische Volk wird wieder zu einem christlichen Volk, zur Heiligen (Kiewer) Rus werden, völlig unabhängig davon, ob das anderen gefällt oder nicht."
32. Joachim Willems, "Kirche und Armee. Religion und Politik in Rußland," *Osteuropa* 59:6 (2009), 235–248.
33. Joachim Willems, "Religions- und Ethikunterricht in Russland. Was wollen Staat und Kirche? Zur Einführung des neuen Schulfaches 'Grundlagen der religiösen Kulturen und der weltlichen Ethik,'" *Erfurter Vorträge zur Kulturgeschichte des Orthodoxen Christentums* 9 (Erfurt, 2010).
34. Angelika Nußberger, "Rechtswesen und Rechtskultur," in *Länderbericht Russland*, Bundeszentrale für politische Bildung—Schriftreihe 1066, Heiko Pleines and Hans-Henning Schröder, eds. (Bonn, 2010), 149.
35. Agadjanian and Rousselet, "Individual and Collective Identities in Russian Orthodoxy," 318.
36. Jeanne Kormina, "Avtobusniki. Russian Orthodox Pilgrims' Longing for Authenticity," in *Eastern Christians in Anthropological Perspective*, 267–286.
37. See the preamble of the *Law on Freedom of Consciences and Religious Associations* (1997): on the one hand, Nußberger affirms that Russia is a secular state, on the other, she acknowledges: "Christianity, Islam, Buddhism, Judaism, and other religions, constituting an integral part of the historical heritage of the peoples of Russia" and in particular underlines "the special contribution of Orthodoxy to the history of Russia and to the establishment and development of its spirituality and culture." Zoe Knox has criticized the law for establishing a hierarchy of religions, with the ROC at the top. See her article, "Religious Freedom in Russia: The Putin Years," 284–287. Chris Hann suggests that the law is not that unusual, as numerous "EU member states continue to offer their citizens legal protection against 'sects' of various kinds." Chris Hann, "Broken Chains and Moral Lazarets: The Politicization, Juridification and Commodification of Religion after Socialism," in *Religion, Identity, Postsocialism*, 16.
38. Zoe Knox, "Religious Freedom in Russia: The Putin Years," 304f.
39. Students protested against the building of more churches on the University of Moscow campus and increased the public presence of the ROC as compared with other religions: *Newsletter von Radio Vatikan*—www.radiovaticana.de (April 13, 2011).
40. Melissa M. Caldwell, "The Russian Orthodox Church, the Provision of Social Welfare, and Changing Ethics of Benevolence," in *Eastern Christians in Anthropological Perspective*,

Chris Hann and Hermann Goltz, eds. (Berkeley, Los Angeles, London, 2010), 344; Hann, "Broken chains and Moral Lazarets," 17.

41. Interfax Religion—www.interfax-religion.com (July 18, 2011). Similarly, Archpriest Vsevolod Chaplin urges "the flock to be more courageous in manifesting faith. 'We should cross ourselves without hesitation any place wherever we want to and place a crucifix wherever we work or live,' he wrote in an article published by the Orthodox newspaper *Rus Derzhavnaya* in April." *Interfax Religion*—www.interfax-religion.com (May 19, 2011).
42. Caldwell, "The Russian Orthodox Church," 346.
43. Jeanne Kormina, "Avtobusniki. Russian Orthodox pilgrims' longing for authenticity," in *Eastern Christians in Anthropological Perspective*, Chris Hann and Herman Goltz, eds. (Berkeley, Los Angeles, London, 2010), 280–282.
44. However, Alexander Agadjanian and Kathy Rousselet, "Individual and Collective Identities in Russian Orthodoxy," 324, argue that "within contemporary Russian Orthodoxy, as a thick religious tradition, individuality, while always present, does not exceed the limits set by the tradition itself." It should be mentioned that the principle of "canonical territory" also affects church-state relations in Russia, since it appears that the ROC is not always guided by the political decisions of the Russian state. For example, the ROC and the Georgian Orthodox Church maintain good relations even though diplomatic contacts between Russia and Georgia were severed by the Five-Day-War between the two states in 2008. Patriarch Kirill repeatedly emphasizes, as he did at a meeting with the Catholicos-Patriarch Ilia II of All Georgia in July, that "Abkhazia and South Ossetia remain canonical territories of the Georgian Orthodox Church" (Interfax Religion—www.interfax-religion.com [July 27, 2011]). However, with Ukraine and Estonia we find the opposite: the Russian government recognizes the independence of Ukraine and Estonia, while the ROC refuses to accept the autocephaly of the local Orthodox churches of these countries.
45. Thomas Bremer, "Die orthodoxe Kirche als gesellschaftlicher Faktor in Russland," in *Länderbericht Russland*, Bundeszentrale für politische Bildung—Schriftreihe 1066, Heiko Pleines and Hans-Henning Schröder, eds. (Bonn, 2010), 454.

2

Morality and Patriotism: Continuity and Change in Russian Orthodox Occidentalism since the Soviet Era

Alfons Brüning

"The West" continues to be a subject of suspicion for many Orthodox church leaders from Russia—a somewhat surprising carryover from Soviet times to this day. In numerous statements and documents on the mission of the Russian Orthodox Church (ROC), its leading hierarchs—Patriarch Kirill, Archbishop Hilarion, Archpriest Vsevolod Chaplin, and others—identify their main opponent as "aggressive Western liberalism and secularism." They claim that this opponent's principal aim is to expel religion, in general, and the Orthodox Church, in particular, from society and to diminish the influence of religion on people's behavior and life. An antithetical opposition is framed between "liberalism and secularism" on the one hand, and "morality and traditional values" on the other. The "enemy" is associated with an overriding antireligious tendency in Western societies that dates back to the French revolution and whose influence has continued to be felt in Russian society.

Another image of the "enemy" is rooted in the conceptual framework of the Communist period. In that time, the West was characterized as capitalistic and involving an immoral struggle for the survival of the fittest. The situation of man under Western capitalism was imagined in terms of Friedrich Engels's early writings or Charles Dickens's novels: since morality was a casualty of capitalism, the system was inherently immoral. From the 1960s to the 1980s, the Soviet press consistently presented this image of the West as thoroughly shaped by capitalism, not only in matters of economics, but as a unified culture of exploitation, alienation, and constant conflicts. In turn, this made it possible to affirm the moral superiority and political exclusiveness of Soviet Russia.[1]

These images of the West, as antireligious and capitalist, are often framed within a discourse on morality. Morality is seen as being under a double threat in the present era—in the first place, because of the secularization of laws and customs in the West,[2] and second because of the growing power of transnational economic corporations and the perceived negative consequences of global financial speculation.[3]

Russian Orthodox hierarchs frequently draw a line of continuity from the antireligious beginnings, or "aberrations," of the French revolution to the antireligious campaigns of the Soviet regime, which many hierarchs had experienced personally. For them, a direct line connects Rousseau and the Jacobins with Marx, Lenin, the Soviet regime, and present-day secular voices in Russian society, such as the members of the Russian Academy of Sciences, who addressed a letter to President Putin in 2007 warning of the threat of the clericalization of Russian society.[4] This kind of secularization is regarded in its core as foreign to Orthodoxy and yet another "import" from the West. In the words of Patriarch Kirill: "The Christian East did not denounce the idolization of the individual, which developed since the Enlightenment and which placed itself under the banner of the anti-religious struggle in the Soviet Union."[5]

However, any attempt to fuse these two images of an adversary or enemy inevitably leads to an apparent contradiction. On the one hand, there seems to be a clear continuity between Soviet and Russian Orthodox images of Western societies as "immoral." On the other hand, there is a discontinuity when the ROC refers to the Soviet regime as one of the latest elements in a long line of "aggressive, liberal and secular," antireligious forces bent on eliminating the influence of religion in society. In its time, the Soviet régime may have been an ally in the common struggle against "capitalist immorality," but since its demise, the old régime is also being characterized as part of the enemy camp.

The notion of morality thus occupies a pivotal place in the question of continuity and change in the transition from Soviet to post-Soviet Russian Orthodoxy. The question of continuity and change necessarily requires coming to terms with a delicate balance between imposed accommodation and sincerely held views. In order to be properly understood, Soviet-era statements of leading Orthodox churchmen on the international scene must be checked thoroughly against the prevailing propaganda formulas and the effect of KGB surveillance. Even if their concerns about social injustice, unemployment, poverty, and other negative realities of capitalism were sincere, their collaboration with the Soviets was likely motivated to a significant degree by the principle that "the enemy of my enemy is my friend." The specific nature and the extent of such a strategic alliance between the ROC and the Soviet régime is a source of ongoing interest. Insofar as it accepted the lines of demarcation that defined the Cold War and were popularized by the Soviet media, the ROC could consider the Communist régime as its ally against an "immoral West," and quite obviously it did so. A statement by Metropolitan Nikodim of Leningrad in the 1960s appears to bear this out:

> Can we find a Christian justification of the fact that, in spite of a massive concentration of wealth, in many progressive Western countries millions of people live in slums, in poverty, suffer from systematic unemployment and abide in fear of the next day? Can a Christian coldheartedly pass over with dull and selfish indifference in the face of foreign indigence, of the pain of children deprived of the joy of childhood, of all the physical and moral torments of the oppressed and wretched, and of other evidence of social evils, barely covered by a formal equality of all people before the law? [...] Many reject communism because of its link to the "deadly sin" of atheism. But in doing so, they forget about the atheism within the bones of any given society. An objective examination of atheism reveals the need to distinguish strictly the motives, which lead to an

> atheist worldview. We know that communist atheism represents a system of convictions, including moral principles that do not contradict Christian norms. A different type of atheism—blasphemous and immoral—arises from the wish to live "independently" of the divine law of Truth, which was present in the depths of the old society and which often appeared on the fertile soil of the luxurious and demoralized lifestyle of the possessing classes. Christian teaching indeed considers atheism of the second type a mortal sin, but looks differently on communist atheism.[6]

Here, the opponent is neither communism nor atheism, but the "wish to live independently," as witnessed in "the luxurious and demoralized lifestyle of the possessing classes." As for "atheism" on its own, it can refer to a "moral atheism" that is also found in the West. Current Orthodox perspectives do not depart significantly from this view. Still, such a text must be treated with due caution. Against the backdrop of its political context, a new era of oppressive antireligious policy under party leader Khrushchev,[7] it cannot be taken as a direct expression of the metropolitan's convictions. In that moment, he would have had many reasons to conceal his authentic convictions within formulas convenient to the regime.[8]

The Russian Orthodox clergy is not a homogenous group today, nor was it in Soviet times. An analysis of continuity in the ROC must therefore take account of social change and the relationships among different factions. The present study focuses on a group of leading clergymen, mostly bishops, of the ROC in the Soviet period, which advocated both international contacts and social concerns on the home front. A key figure in this group, Metropolitan Nikodim (Rotov) of Leningrad (1929–1977), is venerated in some circles, in particular by former disciples such as Patriarch Kirill[9]; in other circles, he is disregarded and even disdained. We will focus on two areas of the ROC's activity during the Soviet period, which shaped convictions that in one form or another persist to this day: the ROC's ecumenical and peace initiatives in the World Council of Churches (WCC) and in other venues; and its initiatives in the spheres of social policy and the moral renewal of Russia.

The ROC's Ecumenical and Peace Initiatives

Studies published during the Cold War[10] suggested that, since the early 1960s, the appearance of Russian Orthodox hierarchs at ecumenical organizations such as the WCC and the Christian Peace Conference in Prague had a secondary effect of bolstering the image of the Soviet Union, and that this was why the regime had permitted such activities in the first place. Permission was conditional upon the observance of two main principles of Soviet foreign policy—patriotism and peacekeeping. The church was required to serve the interests and uphold the image of its Soviet homeland, to act as an agency of its peace policy, and to oppose the "capitalistic and imperialistic aggression" of the West.

Regarding the image of the Soviet Union, ROC representatives apparently fulfilled their duties as required. At various ecumenical forums, Russian hierarchs consistently emphasized the vitality of church life in the Soviet Union and were quick to counter any information about restrictions of religious freedom there.[11] In negotiations preceding the ROC's entry into the WCC, and their participation as observers at the Second Vatican Council, the ROC always insisted on assurances that no such forum would be used for anti-Soviet propaganda.[12] During political crises, such as the

Cuban Missile Crisis in 1962, the Soviet invasion of Prague in 1968, the Vietnam War and the invasion of Afghanistan in 1979, Russian hierarchs consistently advocated the Soviet standpoint, even if that standpoint was difficult to defend against the background of Orthodox peace policy.[13] Themes of social justice and peace-building, expressed in the terminology of Soviet foreign policy and often with an unmistakably anticapitalist overtone, prevailed in the sessions of the Christian Peace Conference in Prague after 1958. After its approval of the Soviet invasion in Czechoslovakia in 1968, this forum of Christian denominations from Communist countries was often seen as a propaganda mouthpiece of the Communist countries.[14]

Were propaganda and the Soviet state interest the only guiding concerns of the ROC? Despite these superficial indications, there was always a suspicion that the ROC may also have had its own motives for joining ecumenical organizations. Such motives could have arisen from the ROC's theological reflection applied to patriotism, peace policy, and finally ecumenism.

The ROC's understanding of patriotism was not reducible to a mere accommodation to the regime and a superficial loyalty to the Socialist homeland. Many Russian Orthodox churchmen distinguished between the "political patriotism," or coerced and formal expressions of loyalty to the Soviet regime, and "cultural patriotism," in which Orthodoxy was a constitutive element in Russian national self-consciousness. And, according to contemporary Russian church historians, this distinction was present in Metropolitan Sergii's (Starogorodsky) controversial declaration of loyalty to the Soviet state in 1927, which included the following passage: "We wish to be Orthodox and at the same time to claim the Soviet Union as our civil motherland, the joys and successes of which are our joys and successes, the misfortunes of which are our misfortunes."[15]

Current Russian Orthodox historiography points out that Sergii, as *locum tenens* of the vacant patriarchal see, had used the word *rodina* (motherland, homeland) rather than *otechestvo* (fatherland), which has a more political connotation. Thus, the phrase "successes and joys" referred to the homeland, the country in which the Orthodox lived, and not necessarily to the political regime. Sergii himself had emphasized that his concern was with the good of the people, and not with the advancement of the Communist revolution.[16] This idea survived through the period of World War II, when the ROC was seen as the moving force behind patriotic motivations to stand up and fight the foreign occupants. Thus, in 1960, when Patriarch Aleksii I spoke in defense of his church before the Soviet public at the Kremlin, he referred mainly to cultural patriotism. In a speech that attracted great attention in the Soviet Union and in the West, he presented Orthodoxy as the main source of Russia's culture and moral strength during all the historic invasions, from the time of Napoleon to World War II.[17]

Apart from the theme of patriotism, the patriarch's speech also declared the ROC's support for peace policy, inasmuch as the pursuit of peace is in accordance with Christian teaching and supported by Scripture. This commonplace, which would have the support of most theologians, suggested that in their peacekeeping and ecumenical activities Russian Orthodox churchmen were pursuing their own goals and mission no less than those of Soviet foreign policy. The combination of sincere religious motivations and the performance of a propaganda task was also embedded within depictions of the enemy, identified in ROC statements as the "aggressive capitalistic and imperialistic Western World."[18]

While the context and conditions for the churchmen's external activities are well established, to date few studies have analyzed this particular mixture of religion and politics, and the theological motivations, processes, and achievements that were at play. One exception is a study by Heiko Overmeyer,[19] which examines the bilateral talks between the ROC and the Lutheran Church of Germany (after 1973 comprising the Evangelische Kirchen in Deutschland of Western Germany and the Bund Evangelischer Kirchen in the GDR) in Arnoldshain and Zagorsk between 1959 and 1990. The main issue of these talks, the understanding of peace, was thoroughly treated from both theological traditions. Socialist propaganda was obviously present in all these talks, but the ROC's treatment of the subject often extended beyond the ideological restrictions of Marxist-Leninist ideology. A theological anthropology was employed to discuss the human capacity to realize peace (with or without God's grace), and to explore the nature of sin and the phenomenon of evil as the principal obstacles to peace. The reflection on justice as a precondition for peace repeatedly returned to the matter of social conditions. The view of capitalism as a system that fosters structures of evil was rarely mentioned explicitly, and was only implied on a few occasions. It is therefore difficult to assess to what extent the tacit allusions to the threatening role of liberalism and capitalist economics were a matter of conviction or of propaganda. Overmeyer proposes that the hierarchs followed the thought patterns of a moderate Marxist perspective, but developed it further in a framework of Orthodox theology.

The political considerations behind the ROC's ecumenical initiatives are well known. As the church emerged from isolation, its quest for support on the international scene was complicated by Khrushchev's positive image in the West as a reformer and a liberal. At the same time, the Soviet regime was bent on using the church as a propaganda tool to bolster its image worldwide. The ROC did not at first grasp the full scope of the opportunity that was offered to it, but by the late 1950s a process of intensive theological and political reflection was under way.[20] An early indication of such reflection was given by Metropolitan Nikodim in his inauguration speech to the WCC in 1963,[21] which expressed genuine theological considerations and ecumenical interest, though not without a considerable degree of skepticism. The ROC's opposition to ecumenism had deep roots, ever since its pronouncements on the founding of the WCC in 1948. In that year, responding to invitations to the first assembly of the WCC, a special issue of the *Journal of the Moscow Patriarchate* reflected the ROC's opposition to such an organization.[22]

The ROC's initial reservations were grounded in a fundamental distrust of the term and the very idea of ecumenism. It maintained that there can only be one church and viewed any negotiation on questions of dogma, canon law, and ecclesiology as a threat to the untouchable tradition of the "Holy, Christian, Catholic and Apostolic Faith." Many Russian bishops feared a superficial and effusive "spirit of unity," which neglected essential differences. Thus, in the early years, the ROC categorically rejected any engagement in ecumenism.

A more differentiated approach was found only among Orthodox theologians in the Western diasporas. The eminent patrologist Georges Florovsky attended the preliminary meeting of the Faith and Order Commission in Edinburgh in 1937, and was one of the few Orthodox delegates at the opening conference of the WCC in Amsterdam in 1948. In numerous articles and essays relating to his engagement, he insisted on a clear expression of existing differences and considered it a precondition for real dialogue and unity. "There can only be one church," he repeated time and again. He rejected a simple economic approach, since *oikonomia* (a more flexible interpretation of church law, as opposed to strict adherence) cannot create something that did not exist in the first place. As an Orthodox priest, Florovsky excluded any ecclesiological compromises and believed that the full truth of the faith was found within his own church—as long as this church remained grounded in the faith of the ancient and undivided church. Yet the church's canonical boundaries were not contiguous with her sacramental boundaries. According to Florovsky, sacramental grace exists beyond the canonical limits of the Orthodox Church. Consequently, talks with the adherents of other confessions were useful, necessary and even an obligation of Christian love. The ultimate aim of such talks was the full establishment of faith in its Eastern Orthodox form—even allowing for some changes in form, but not substance.[23]

The similarity between this position and the ROC's guidelines for ecumenism after 1963 is quite evident. Nikodim's aforementioned speech, the ROC's first official representation to the WCC at its New Delhi Assembly in 1963, balanced caution with a rationale for participating in such talks:

> What was it then which incited the Russian Orthodox Church to join the World Council of Churches? My answer is this: firstly, the love of brethren who are distressed by the divisions among Christians, and who declare their desire to eliminate the obstacles to fulfilling the will of our Lord Jesus Christ "that they may all be one" (John 17.21). Secondly, an awareness of the importance of coordinating the efforts of all Christians, in their witness and service to men in the complex conditions of the secularized world of today—subject to rapid changes, divided, but aspiring to unity. The fact that the Russian Orthodox Church has joined the World Council of Churches cannot be regarded as an ecclesial act in the ecclesiological sense.[24]

The last point—that joining the WCC "was never considered as having an ecclesiologically obligatory meaning for the Orthodox conscience"[25]—is repeated throughout the entire speech. The WCC was to constitute a forum for a dialogue between branches of a divided Christianity, but in no way could be regarded as the body of any kind of "ecumenical" church. Moreover, later documents from other churchmen reveal a similar caution with respect to the WCC's "real" significance (considered very limited in terms of ecclesiology), and to potential optimism arising from a superficial "ecumenical spirit."[26]

Apart from some minor differences, this perspective is remarkably similar to Florovsky's approach, so much so that it is difficult to presume that the similarities are only incidental. Is it possible that, in the short period after 1948, Orthodox clerics studied the alternative ideas of the Russians in exile? We know little about the content of theological education and access to new literature in the years after the ROC's first restoration in 1945. In those years, teachers and students relied primarily on prerevolutionary resources. But according to Vitalii Borovoi, a key figure of ROC ecumenism since its beginnings, Florovsky's works were among the inspiring sources behind the change of perspective that took place in the 1950s.[27]

Inspired by sources that were far removed from Marxist-Leninist ideology, this approach provided an element of continuity, one that is still in place today. If we compare this vision of ecumenism from the 1960s with the guidelines for interconfessional relations published by the Moscow patriarchate after 2000,[28] we see much the same essential principles and concerns—that the division of Christianity is a sin that must not be ignored, and that a true restoration of unity can only be achieved by returning to the faith of the Church Fathers. Although the official ROC "principles of the attitude towards the non-Orthodox" developed after the fall of the Soviet Union use a less conciliatory language than did Soviet-era ecumenical statements,[29] they seem to be based on very similar theological considerations.

The "Basic Principles of Attitude to the Non-Orthodox" differs from earlier texts primarily in its stronger focus on pure theology, rather than in its theological affirmations. It maintains a pejorative image of "the other," combining a suspicion of heresy and sin with the potential access to divine grace, while ecclesiastical divisions are described as a falling away from the fullness of the truth, which is preserved within the Orthodox Church:

> Delusions and heresies result from a person's desire to assert himself and set himself apart. Every division or schism implies a certain measure of falling away from the plenitude of the Church. A division, even if it happens for non-doctrinal reasons, is a violation of orthodox teaching on the nature of the Church and leads ultimately to distortions in the faith.[30]

This pertains to any other Christian denomination, including Western denominations. The document also presents disunion among Christians as purely a matter of faith, and unity as "first of all a unity and communion in the Sacraments."[31] What is missing is the second theme raised by Metropolitan Nikodim in 1963: the necessity of a coordinated witness and service of all Christians "to men in the complex conditions of the secularized world." Removed from the ecumenical agenda, this moral issue has found its way into other discussions.

What emerges from the three points we have explored—patriotism, peace policy, and ecumenical engagement—is the image of a church opening up cautiously to the world, but holding on to a strong sense of its own treasures and mission. Along with this, there is an ambiguous image of the West and Western churches as "the Other": one the one hand, potential allies and brethren in faith, and on the other, suspected of either collaboration with "immoral capitalistic forces," or of heresy—or of both. In short: whereas in the past the desire "to live independently" was viewed as the root cause of an immoral system, in the current discourse it is "the desire to assert oneself and to set oneself apart" that is understood as heresy and the cause of disunity. May this, in turn, be a source of the current Orthodox condemnation of the "idolization of the individual"?

After the end of Soviet communism, the theme of "the secularized world" is no longer a central concern within the ROC's ecumenical program. Instead, that moral issue was addressed separately in the first Orthodox social statement of its kind, the ROC's *Basis of a Social Concept* (2000).[32]

Social Policy and the Moral Improvement of Social Life

In analyzing the aforementioned passage from Metropolitan Nikodim's 1963 speech, the first question is to what extent this text is authentic and not distorted by censorship or written by someone else. There have even been doubts as to whether Nikodim was the author of the entire speech.[33]

What then might allow us to presume that the passage is not simply a concession to the propaganda tasks connected with his position? Nikodim is not known to have ever expressed any sympathies toward the Marxist analysis of society. While some Eastern and Western theologians may have had such sympathies in the decades after World War II, they seldom led to open support for the Soviet system. Such was the case, for example, with references to Marxism in the social teaching of the Roman Catholic Church[34] and in the writings of the prominent Lutheran Paul Tillich and his ideas on "religious socialism."[35]

Nikodim and other Russian Orthodox churchmen were in a different situation. Reliable statements on their actual relationship toward Marxism could perhaps have been made privately, beyond the reach of Soviet agents or Western observers, but any public statement would have been subjected to political interpretation. We know of no such statements by Nikodim, and his available bibliography is limited almost exclusively to official texts.[36] The *Journal of the Moscow Patriarchate* frequently published articles by Orthodox theologians on possible areas of compatibility between Soviet ideology and Christian teaching, but censored as this journal was, they hardly reflect a real dialogue in essence.

However, it is known that Nikodim refused to be identified with any suggestion of far-reaching synergies between Christian teaching and Soviet communism. Confronted with some Christian-Marxist theses, including one about Christ's second incarnation during the October revolution (a "theology of revolution"), which had appeared in articles bearing his name, Nikodim emphatically denied being their author: "I am not such a fool as to write this."[37] Not only did he refuse to be identified with "Christian-Marxist ideological mixtures," he also firmly rejected any possibility of a theoretical dialogue with Soviet Marxists.[38] Thus, he was clearer in his opposition toward Marxism than many of his Western contemporaries.

In the earlier passage on morality from the 1963 speech, the inclinations toward Marxist morality went beyond the usual propaganda formulations—so much so that they cannot be discounted as merely one of the "necessary evils" with which ROC bishops had to cope under Soviet rule.

Nikodim may have been referring implicitly to what was known as the moral code of communism. His allusions to "a communist atheism" that "represents a certain system of convictions, including moral principles which do not contradict Christian norms" can be related to the *Moral Code of a Builder of Communism*, which was included in the *Program of the Communist Party* in 1961. This code called on its adherents to embrace such principles as "collectivism, humanity, sincerity and rightfulness, simplicity and modesty." Further, "the guiding principle of the Moral Code is devotion to the cause of Communism, and love for the Socialist homeland."[39] Some of these ideals, such as the notion of patriotism, were not intrinsically antithetical to Orthodox believers, and contemporary churchmen were quick to notice the parallels. Many leading clerics of the ROC, including the patriarch himself, saw possibilities for "a fruitful social work of the Church in the bosom of the socialist society."[40]

On the other hand, the Communist moral code also required "intolerance towards the remains of the old world and towards the enemies of communism, of the cause of peace and the freedom of the people," and it was explicitly stated that "religious prejudices" were seen as the central element in those "remains of the old, bourgeois ideology."[41] So the real opportunities for convergence between what Nikodim saw as morality and the actual approach of the Communist code were limited.

Nikodim delivered his speech shortly after a Khrushchev-era wave of anti-Church persecution that involved the arrests of priests and massive closings of church buildings. He had previously witnessed similar repressions in his Leningrad diocese and in other areas of Russia. Although his personal relations with representatives of the regime were not always inimical (in fact, he was known for having good personal contacts[42]), in those particular circumstances he would hardly have been inclined to praise Communist morality. In light of this, it is possible to argue that the text attributed to Nikodim may have had a different author. It may be that here the Communists received more credit in Nikodim's speech, delivered publicly to a Western audience, than in any other of his statements (leaving aside the question of whether he was in fact the author of the passages). Still, quite a number of convergent points between the "Moral Code" and Christian teaching cannot be ignored.

Two points in Nikodim's argumentation deserve special attention. First, a crucial distinction that he makes is not between different ideologies or "moralities," but between people who adhere to moral principles and those who only seek to "live independently." A generic fidelity to moral principles—whatever their source—is thus contrasted with an outright rejection of any morality. This contrary position corresponds very closely to the traditional, theological understanding of the term "heresy" (from the Greek *hairesis*, or "own choice"). The "desire to assert himself and set himself apart," according to contemporary documents of the ROC, is also responsible for "delusions and heresies" and for any "division, even if it happens for non-canonical reasons."[43]

Second, the "free and independent lifestyle" that Nikodim criticized was seen as a source of social injustice and the suffering of the poor. Freedom, according to the bishop, is hardly imaginable without favorable conditions of social justice and welfare. If these conditions are absent, it is due more to a moral deficit than to flaws of abstract societal structures. On the other hand, if many unbaptized people are truly engaged in the improvement of society, where are the followers of Christ? Without a doubt, as Nikodim pointed out in a 1970 lecture to the EKD in West Germany, they too were "on the side of progress, justice, freedom and peace." He explained: "Faith in Christ calls us to cooperation with non-Christians, when they fight for the same ideals." The improvement of social life was one such area of shared ideals, according to Nikodim, and the church's mission focused largely on "the preaching of the Gospel and the implementation of its moral norms in society."[44]

Nikodim's 1970 lecture employed the vocabulary of the "Communist Moral Code" in identifying "the supporters of the preservation of outdated and unjust relationships in society,"[45] but the argument ultimately goes beyond a merely superficial reliance on this ideological code. This is not at all to say that Nikodim went so far as to promote communism—it is not even mentioned in this speech. Nikodim's key point was that non-Christians—by implication, even Communists—*can* potentially be allies of the church, insofar as they can be receptive toward its moral values. Christians and non-Christians share a common aim, a sense of moral obligation, to overcome the poverty and suffering that result from unjust social relations and structures. Non-Christians were more than welcome to share in this work.

Metropolitan Nikodim's speech gave an early indication of the ROC hierarchs' growing interest in exerting an influence on society. Nikodim promoted a theology oriented toward life in this world, and one that enabled the church to work toward improving human relations.[46] His 1963 speech in Holland singled out an isolationist spirituality and a retreat from the world as key temptations of the church.[47] Nor was this a new issue in Russian Orthodox theology. Discussion of the ROC's social mission and of how it could be harmonized with its spiritual heritage was echoed in the Russian journals of the reform era after 1855.[48] These journals were readily available in the church institutions of higher learning, which were reopened after World War II.

Even under Soviet rule, the church had understood its task as working for the divine Kingdom in the present world. The religious law, still in force since 1929,[49] strictly forbade any church activity beyond ritual services. Education and catechesis were prohibited, as were charitable activities. By the mid-1960s, however, there was a new reality. With the end of the Khrushchev-era persecutions, ever-greater numbers of people turned to the church for moral orientation, and bishops like Nikodim, along with parish priests, had to respond to this growing audience from all sectors of society.[50] In responding to these emerging needs, they combined Christian teaching with diverse references to Russian culture and its Christian origins. Patriotic sentiment was present as the church began to exercise new functions that were still officially prohibited.[51] It was not a matter of propagating a narrow-minded nationalism, but even a priest like Aleksandr Men' saw a long-standing schism between the church and society, and sought ways to overcome this problem. In his view, reconciliation required reacquainting Russians with the foundations of Christian culture in Russia.[52]

By the middle of the Brezhnev era in the early 1970s, there was a renewed societal interest in religion. In a "closed city" like the Ukrainian Dniepropetrovsk, records of the rock opera "Jesus Christ Superstar" were widely distributed, despite official countermeasures, and generated unprecedented levels of interest in religious themes and texts. For many, this first encounter with Christianity was the starting point on a spiritual path that took them to the priesthood or a monastery by the early 1980s.[53] The opportunity for the church to become more socially active grew significantly in the later Brezhnev years, and even more under perestroika. In St. Petersburg and Moscow, interest in religious issues grew significantly and found expression in the emergence of reading circles and intellectual communities devoted to the discussion of religious issues.[54]

With the liberalization of Soviet religious policy under perestroika, the church's social efforts attracted the interest of the regime, which sought to make use of them for its own ends. The explicit goal of strengthening moral values in society led the state to view the potential of religious believers in a new light. As Konstantin Kharchev, chairman of the Department for Religious Affairs under Gorbachev, stated on occasion, the project of renewing socialist society needed people who believed in something—such people were more useful and more advantageous to society than those without any beliefs or moral convictions at all.[55]

In 1988, another significant step was taken in the rebirth of the ROC within the Communist state. The operative notions of social engagement and patriotism became central to a new definition of the church's role in society. On the occasion of the thousand-year anniversary of the baptism of Rus' in 1988, the local ROC synod declared:

> On its thousand-year historical path, the Russian Orthodox Church was always closely linked with its people. It always strove to bring up its children as valuable citizens of their earthly fatherland. And now, guided by the responsibility for the prosperity of its homeland, it blesses them in their effort to contribute to the process of a spiritual, social and economic renewal of the Soviet Community.[56]

The proceedings of this same synod include a resolution (Article 19) to undertake social and charitable activities, and to further support that work by establishing appropriate institutions. It is noteworthy that the restrictive Stalinist religious law remained in force until 1990, when a new law on religion was passed.

Conclusion

The search for modes of coexistence during Soviet period, especially after World War II, led the ROC to define a number of key notions that would prove crucial for its work within the Soviet system and for its relations with the outside world and the West. In that effort, political considerations and the need for compromises were as crucial as theological reflections. This combination of factors often resulted in a peculiar mixture of religious convictions, theological adaptations, and political concessions, all of which can be seen in the official texts and declarations of the ROC in the 1960s and 1970s. Two pivotal notions relating to the church's social and ecumenical activities were those of patriotism and morality.

Patriotism was understood by Orthodox believers and clerics as the close connectedness of Orthodoxy with historic achievements of Russian culture, independent of ruling political regimes. Such patriotic allegiances made it possible for senior clerics to join ecumenical institutions after the early 1960s, because they saw this as a way to protect the church and serve their homeland. However, while engaging in such activities, they still maintained a critical distance toward other Christian denominations, in the theological conviction that the fullness of truth was to be found only within Orthodoxy. Even more virulent was a notion of patriotism associated with the ROC's increasing engagement in society. Service to one's community and society was propagated as a central goal of Orthodox believers and, in order to be up to this task, they had to be thoroughly familiar with the values and the cultural heritage of Russia. Just as the Orthodox could cooperate with members of other Christian denominations in ecumenical settings, Christians in the Soviet Union were called to seek allies among nonbelievers. After all, non-Orthodox and Communists alike could potentially share some portions of truth and of morality with the Russian Orthodox—the former by virtue of being Christians (of another denomination), and the latter by virtue of sharing the ethnic identity of the Russian Orthodox. Morality was thus understood as fidelity to community values, as distinct from any independent-minded, selfish, and egoistic lifestyle. Radical individualism, devoid of any sense of responsibility to God, divine law, one's neighbor, and the community, was considered the principal adversary of morality and the root of all evil—from the deplorable divisions in the Christian Church to the inhuman conditions of life of most people within a capitalist economy.

When the Soviet Union collapsed, all of these concepts were firmly in place, and they constituted a rich ideological treasury for addressing the new circumstances. These ideas did not generate any particularly anti-Western posture, nor were their attendant views of peace, welfare, and social justice based on any Western models. In this Russian Orthodox perspective, Western standards were viewed with suspicion. This aloofness would be further consolidated after the first experiments with Western concepts such as liberalism, market economy, and democracy in Russia during the 1990s. When those experiments brought ruptures, chaos, turmoil, and poverty, there was a decisive retreat to ideological categories and to an increased isolation from the West.[57] In 1992, Deacon Andrei Kuraev, former personal secretary to Patriarch Aleksii II, published an article that criticized Western liberalism and the Western concept of human rights, and proposed that Russia needed to articulate collective moral standards as an alternative to the legalism and individualism of the Western approach.[58]

In the current ROC, it is relatively easy to identify echoes of the social concepts of patriotism and morality, which were elaborated in the previous period. One of the first tasks envisaged by the church after the radical changes in the 1990s was precisely to pave the way for the *Bases of the Social Concept*. Just as Nikodim had done, the document that was released in 2000 and drafted under the guidance of Metropolitan Kirill of Smolensk (now patriarch), in its opening chapters, set aside any idea of renunciation of the world by the church. Instead, Christians were called to actively serve the good of the world and of the society in which they lived.[59] The document continued with a comprehensive passage on "Church and Nation," in which we read:

> Christian patriotism may be expressed at the same time with regard to a nation as an ethnic community and as a community of citizens. [...] The patriotism of the Orthodox Christian should be active. It is manifested when he defends his fatherland against an enemy, works for the good of the motherland, cares for the good order of people's life through, among other things, participation in the affairs of government. The Christian is called to preserve and develop national culture and people's self-awareness.[60]

There may be a question as to whether a sharp distinction was intended between "fatherland" and "homeland" (*otchizna*). The entire second chapter, on patriotism, leaves little doubt that the "nation" (the original alternates between the terms *narod* and *natsiia*) is understood as a cultural rather than a political entity. The nation is the cultural framework, within which faith and tradition (liturgy, language, saints, etc.) find their natural expression. Patriotism involves working for its good and well-being, not necessarily to increase its power in the world, and every people is chosen, just as the Israelites were.[61]

Morality is closely connected to this notion of patriotism. It is understood in terms of community affiliation, as opposed to liberal and individualistic perspectives, and this community is embedded within one's cultural homeland. After the fall of the Soviet Union, patriotic sentiment and a growing sense of Russian distinctiveness inspired a new academic discipline, "culturology," which was established in 1992 by the Ministry of Education to study Russia's cultural and moral heritage and to make it relevant for the future. Western observers were critical of this new discipline, due perhaps in part to its anti-Western overtones, but also because of the similarities between it and Marxist philosophy—both in its content and in its academic staff, whose personnel were often former instructors of Marxist-Leninism. While its root notion of "culture" is not defined, the discipline comprises values that are essential to the life of any community or society, and the study of these values is aimed at formulating moral orientations on supposedly scientific grounds. Orthodox churchmen refer to frameworks of culturology, especially in referring to the application of human rights in Russia, or in their efforts to keep textbooks in line with the provisions of the *Bases of Orthodox Culture*. So too with the concept of a Russian civilization, which in its opposition to all things Western and with its built-in aspirations to cultural hegemony derives its key categories from a discipline that appears to be rooted in Soviet ideas.[62]

It is quite evident that there are elements of both continuity and change in the ROC after the fall of the Soviet Union. Much research remains to be done on the ideological framework within which the ROC operated in the Soviet period, and to determine which of its ideas retain their relevance today. Historians in both the East and the West are only beginning to gain a better insight into these questions. It is equally clear that the radical political transformation did not produce a complete break with the past in Russian Orthodox thinking.

With these considerations in mind and based on our preliminary findings, we can propose a tentative conclusion. Any thorough study of current Russian Orthodox thinking must take serious account of the persistence of ideas or, more precisely, of theological adaptations carried over from the Communist period, rather than discounting them as nothing more than propaganda concessions. Furthermore, this legacy has clearly shaped present-day Russian Orthodox ideas and has reinforced, among other things, a certain distance toward the West. In the period of transformation, numerous potential sources of East-West misunderstanding have also come to the fore—notions like "patriotism" or "morality" (*nravstvennost'*) must be approached and can only be grasped with this transformative context in mind. As for the ROC in the preceding Soviet era, any accommodation that occurred must be set against the background of suffering, pressure, and the search for productive solutions: conditions that were far removed from any Western experience and which still remain very challenging for any historical reconstruction.

Notes

1. To date, there has been little scholarly study of the image of the West among average Soviet citizens in the 1960s and 1970s. For an analysis of the press, see William Peter van den Bercken, *Het beeld van het Westen in de Sovjet pers* (Groningen: Wolters-Noordhoff, 1980). The Khrushchev era brought a certain opening, and a break with the old stereotypes of socialism and capitalism. However, the basic contours of that conceptual framework remained in place. A recent analysis of movies of the time is Anne E. Gorsuch, "From Iron Curtain to Silver Screen. Imagining the West in the Khrushchev Era," in György Péteri (ed.), *Imagining the West in Eastern Europe and the Soviet Union* (Pittsburg: University of Pittsburg Press, 2010), pp. 153–171. Gorsuch's study also suggests that there was even a certain regression in the following period, when differences with the "decadent" West were emphasized more than before.
2. In this sense, morality ("нравственность" in Russian) was often contrasted with human rights, the latter being seen as a Western concept based on external legalism and even libertinism. For a more thorough analysis, see Alfons Brüning, "'Freedom' vs. 'Morality'—On Orthodox Anti-Westernism and Human Rights," in Evert van der Zweerde (eds.), *Orthodox Christianity and Human Rights* (Leuven: Peeters, 2011), pp. 122–148.

3. Chapter XVI.3 of the *Bases of the Social Concept of the Russian Orthodox Church* (2000) reads: "Globalization has not only political and legal, but also economic and cultural-informational dimensions. In relation to the economy, it is manifested in the emergence of transnational corporations which have accumulated considerable material and financial resources and have employed an enormous number of people in various countries. Those standing at the head of international economic and financial structures have concentrated in their hands a great power beyond the control of nations and even governments and beyond any limit, be it a national border, an ethnic and cultural identity or the need for ecological and demographical sustainability. Sometimes they refuse to reckon with the customs and religious traditions of the nations involved in the implementation of their plans. The Church cannot but be concerned also for the practice of financial speculations that obliterates the relationship between income and labor. Among various forms of this speculation are «financial pyramids» the collapse of which causes large-scale upheaval." Cf. also chapter VI of the same document ("Labour and Its Fruits"), all accessible on http://www.mospat.ru/en/documents/social-concepts/.
4. The letter was first published in the supplement *Kentavr* no. 3, 2007, to *Novaia gazeta*, July 23, 2007.
5. Patriarch Kyrill, "Néoliberalisme occidental et traditionalisme orthodoxe," *Istina* 45 (2000), 292–295, quotation 292 (in French). See also Bishop Ilarion of Vienna and Austria, "Der militante Säkularismus und das Christentum. Die religiösen und die 'allgemein-menschlichen' Werte," *Orthodoxie aktuell* no. 5–6 (2005), 12–17.
6. Архиепископ Никодим, "Мир и свобода." Доклад на региональной конференции в Голландии (Archbishop Nikodim, "Peace and Freedom." Lecture at the Regional Conference [of the Christian Peace Conference] in Holland), *Журнал Московской Патриархии* (*Journal of the Moscow Patriarchate*, hereafter: *ZhMP*), no. 1 (1963), 42 (English mine).
7. For further details, see Dimitry V. Pospielovsky, *The Russian Church under the Soviet Regime 1917–1982* (New York: St. Vladimir's Seminary Press, 1984), vol. II, pp. 327–364.
8. According to Pospielovsky (ibid., p. 318), there was a common bias in the texts issued by bishops of these times, dependent on when and where they were published. "Almost every bishop (and to a lesser extent every priest) has acted as a two-faced Janus." Moreover, required propaganda speeches were commonly accepted by the believers, "seeing them as a necessary evil to which they are all immune and for which they pity rather than condemn their pastors" (ibid.).
9. The current Patriarch Kirill, before starting his dazzling career as rector of the Leningrad Theological Academy and bishop, was Nikodim's personal secretary from 1970 onward. See Jane Ellis, *The Russian Orthodox Church. A Contemporary History* (Keston College: Croom Helm, 1986), p. 204. Generally on the so-called Nikodimovcy ("the Nikodimians") in the present ROC hierarchy, see Николай Митрохин, *Русская Православная Церков. Современное состояние и актуальные проблемы* (Nikolai Mitrokhin, *The Russian Orthodox Church. Present State and Current Problems*) (Moscow: Biblioteka Zhurnala Neprikosnovennyi Zapas, 2004), pp. 177–181. One should mention (as Mitrokhin does), first, that these former disciples of Nikodim are not a completely homogenous group, but often divided among themselves, and, second, the term "nikodimovcy" is often used pejoratively by their ecclesiastical adversaries. Nevertheless, what unites these circles at least superficially is a certain openness toward the ecumenical movement (and to Roman Catholicism in particular), a strong concern with developments in society and culture outside the church, and their veneration of Nikodim. For the latter, see the contributions of a number of higher clerics collected in Митрополит Крутицкий и Коломенский Ювеналий, *Человек церкви. К 20-летию со дня кончины и 70-летию со дня рождения Высокопреосвященнейшего митрополита Ленинградского и Новгородского Никодима, Патриаршего Экзарха Западной Европы (1929—1978)* (Москва: изд.

Раритет, 1999) (Metropolitan Yuvenaliy of Krutitsy and Kolomna, *A Man of the Church. On the 20th Anniversary of the Death and the 70th Birthday of His Holiness Metropolitan Nikodim of Leningrad and Novgorod, Patriarchal Exarch of Western Europe* [Moscow: Raritet, 1999]).

10. William C. Fletcher, *Religion and Soviet Foreign Policy* (Oxford: Oxford University Press, 1973).
11. See the interview given by Metropolitan Nikodim to an Italian journalist, in *ZhMP* no. 3 (1970), 2–4. The metropolitan's statements were quite in line with those of other hierarchs of the time, as collected by Ellis, *The Russian Orthodox Church*, pp. 208–211. Ellis comments: "The Russian Orthodox episcopate is [...] a most diverse body of men, and it is therefore surprising to find that their very different backgrounds have not shaped their views on church-state relations to any significant extent and that the views which they express are so similar—indeed, stereotyped" (p. 211).
12. See Архиеп. Брюссельский и Бельгийский Василий (Кривошеин). *Митрополит Никодим (Ротов)* (Archbishop Vasilii [Krivoshein] of Brussels and Belgium, *Metropolitan Nikodim (Rotov)*), on http://www.portal-credo.ru/site/?act=lib&id=2216 (last accessed on May 10, 2011), p. 8 (printed version). For a detailed account of the negotiations preceding the Moscow Patriarchate's delegation to Vatican II, see A. Roccucci, "Russian Observers at Vatican II. The 'Council for Russian Orthodox Church Foreign Affairs' and the Moscow Patriarchate between Anti-religious Policy and International Strategies," in A. Melloni (ed.), *Vatican II in Moscow. Acts of the Colloquium on the History of Vatican II, Moscow, March 30—April 2, 1995* (Leuven: Bibliotheek van de Faculteit Godgeleerdheid, 1997), pp. 45–69.
13. Examples from Fletcher, *Religion and Soviet Foreign Policy*, pp. 130f., 136–139. See also the statement of the Moscow Patriarchate on the Afghanistan invasion in *ZhMP* no. 5 (1980), 4f., also published in P. Hauptmann and G. Stricker (eds.), *Die russische orthodoxe Kirche. Dokumente ihrer Geschichte* (Göttingen: Vandenhoeck & Ruprecht, 1988), no. 371, p. 919f.
14. There is no systematic study so far of the CPC activities between 1958 and its dissolution shortly after 1990. Founded by West German theologians and the Czech theologian Jozef L. Hromadka in 1958, the organization soon came under Soviet influence through financial support, and by a majority of delegates from the Warsaw Pact countries. Nevertheless, the forum enjoyed credibility during the first decade of its existence, due to its effective inner structure and the personal reputation of Hromadka. Only after the events of 1968 in Prague, when Hromadka reluctantly stepped down, followed by Metropolitan Nikodim, the Christian Peace Conference was met with increasing distrust. See Wolfgang Lienemann, *Frieden: Vom 'gerechten Krieg' zum 'gerechten Frieden,'* Bensheimer Hefte no. 92 (Göttingen: Vandenhoeck & Ruprecht, 2000), pp. 143–146; see also Fletcher, *Religion and Soviet Foreign Policy*, pp. 39–56.
15. William C. Fletcher, *A Study in Survival. The Church in Russia 1927–1943* (London: SPCK, 1965), p. 29f.
16. With this, Sergii tried to link his declaration with the considerably less loyal documents that had been issued by his predecessors. See Protoierei Vladyslav Tsypin, *Istoriia Russkoj Cerkvi, 1917–1997 gg.* (Archpriest Vladyslav Tsypin, *History of the Russian Church, 1917–1997*) (Moscow: Izdatel'stvo Spaso-Preobrazhenskogo Monastyria, 1997), p. 161.
17. Cf. *ZhMP* no. 3 (1960), 33–35; also Hauptmann and Stricker, *Dokumente* (as n. 13), no. 323, pp. 812f. The speech drew severe criticism, and eventually led to the removal of Metropolitan Nikolai (Jarushevich), by then head of the Church Department for External Relations and the author of the text, from his duties. Cf. Arkhimandrit Avgustin (Nikitin), *Tserkov plennaia. Mitropolit Nikodim i ego vremia* (The church in captivity. Metropolitan Nikodim and his time) (Moscow: Izdatel'stvo S. Peterburgskogo Universiteta, 2008), pp. 51–54. On patriotic motives in the ROC since World War II, see also the overview by

Kathy Rousselet, "Die Russische Kirche in der Sowjetunion und ihren Nachfolgestaaten," in *Die Geschichte des Christentums*, vol. 13 (Freiburg: Herder, 2002), pp. 393–395.

18. See "Message to Christians all over the World," *ZhMP* 1948 (special issue), 31f.; also in Hauptmann and Stricker, *Dokumente*, no. 308, p. 789.
19. Heiko Overmeyer, *Frieden im Spannungsfeld zwischen Theologie und Politik. Die Friedensthematik in den bilateralen theologischen Gesprächen von Arnoldshain und Sagorsk* (Frankfurt am Main: Otto Lembeck, 2005).
20. Current works by ROC authors focus less on political considerations than on the controversial issue of ecumenism, although they do appear in an account from Archpriest Vitalii Borovoi, who then was himself one of the leading personalities. Cf. Protopresbyter Vitalii Borovoi, "И он был верен до смерти," in *Человек церкви* (see note 9 above), pp. 91–120, esp. 102–107.
21. Metropolitan Nikodim, "The Russian Orthodox Church and the Ecumenical Movement"—The English version is published in Constantin G. Patelos (ed.), *The Orthodox Churches in the Ecumenical Movement: Documents and Statements 1902–1975* (Geneva: WCC 1978), pp. 266–279.
22. Cf. Г. Разумовский, *Экуменическое движение и Русская Православная Церковь* (Москва: Изд. Московской Патриархии 1948 = special issue of *ZhMP*) (see also note 18).
23. See Georges Florovsky, "The Doctrine of the Church and the Ecumenical Problem," *The Ecumenical Review* 2:2 (1950), 151–161. On Florovsky, see Andrew Blane (ed.), *Georges Florovsky. Russian Intellectual—Orthodox Churchman* (Crestwood, NY: St. Vladimir's Seminary Press, 1993).
24. Metropolitan Nikodim, "The Russian Orthodox Church and the Ecumenical Movement," p. 267f.
25. Ibid., p. 269.
26. See the ROC's general statement about the fifth assembly of the WCC in Nairobi in 1976, as quoted in *ZhMP* 4 (1976), 7–13, and in Hauptmann and Stricker, *Dokumente*, no. 367, pp. 895–899.
27. Protopresbyter Vitalii Borovoi, "И он был верен до смерти," in Человек церкви (see note 20), p. 98f.
28. *Basic Principles of the Attitude to the Non-Orthodox*, http://www.mospat.ru/en/documents/attitude-to-the-non-orthodox/ (accessed April 30, 2011).
29. Various opinions about the secondary nature of divisions among Christians are harshly condemned in ibid., Chapter 2, and the term "ecumenism," still controversial in contemporary Russian discussion, is avoided.
30. Ibid., pt. 1.14.
31. Ibid., pt. 2.12.
32. See note 3.
33. Reported and discussed, e.g., by Archbishop Vassili Krivoshein of Brussels and Belgium in his memoir, Архиеп. Брюссельский и Бельгийский Василий (Кривошеин). *Митрополит Никодим (Ротов)*, p. 24f.
34. See R. Uertz, "Die Auseinandersetzung der katholischen Sozialethik mit dem Marxismus und Kommunismus als moderner Ideologie," in I. Gabriel and C. Bystricky (eds.), *Kommunismus im Rückblick. Ökumenischen Perspektiven aus Ost und West (1989–2009)* (Ostfildern: Matthias Grünewald, 2010), pp. 117–136.
35. Cf. Paul Tillich, *Christentum und soziale Gestaltung. Frühe Schriften zum religiösen Sozialismus* (Stuttgart: Evangelisches Verlagswerk, 1962 = Gesammelte Werke, vol. 2). Particularly interesting in this context is another quotation from Tillich, where he praises "the prophetical spirit of self-criticism" that led Pope John XXIII to the reforms of the II Vatican Council: "Ausserdem hat Johannes XXIII. gezeigt, dass die Kirche nicht nur die Brüder erreichen kann, die sich von ihr losgesagt haben, sondern auch diejenigen, die niemals der Kirche angehört haben, die Feinde der Kirche und des Christentums. Auf

Grund meiner Erfahrungen im Religiösen Sozialismus fühle ich mich ihm verwandt. Uns ist die prophetische Selbstkritik gemeinsam, die der Wahrheit offen ist, die die Kirche verloren hat und für die heute säkulare und antireligiöse Bewegungen in einen Kampf eintreten, der gegen die Kirche gerichtet ist." Paul Tillich, *Vorlesungen über die Geschichte des christlichen Denkens, Teil II: Aspekte des Protestantismus im 19. und 20. Jahrhundert*, Ergänzungs- und Nachlassbände zu den Gesammelten Werken von Paul Tillich, vol. 2 (Stuttgart: Evangelisches Verlagswerk, 1967), p. 196.

36. See Igumen Avgustin (Nikitin), "Bibliografiia trudov mitropolita Nikodima," in Митрополит Ювеналий, *Человек церкви*, pp. 133–148. A slightly expanded version is included in *Tserkov plennaia*, pp. 611–623.
37. See note 33. Nikodim expressed a similar refusal of such visions in his interview, *ZhMP* 3 (1970), 2–4.
38. See *ZhMP* 6 (1968), 57; *Kirche im Osten* 12 (1969), p. 106.
39. "Moral'nyi Kodeks stroitelia kommunizma," in *Bol'shaia Sovetskaia entsiklopediia*, vol. 16, 3rd ed. (Moscow: Izdatel'stvo "Sovetskaia Entsiklopediia," 1974), col. 1673f.
40. See *Kirche im Osten* 12 (1969), p. 105f. for additional references.
41. See the excerpt of the program quoted in Hauptmann and Stricker, *Dokumente*, no. 335, p. 829.
42. Because of this widespread reputation, Alexander Men' turned to Nikodim in the 1960s in order to help his fellow priests Gleb Yakunin and Lev Regelson, who had encountered serious trouble due to their critical open letter to the patriarch. Father Aleksandr Men', "The 1960s Remembered," *Religion State & Society* 23:2 (1995), 149. See also the episodes given in the memoir of Archbishop Vasilii (n. 33), p. 24.
43. See note 30.
44. Mitropolit Nikodim, "Sotrudnichestvo kreshchennykh i nekhristian v sovmestnom sluzhenii blagu chelovechestva" [Metropolitan Nikodim, Cooperation of the Baptized with Non-Christians in a Common Service to the Good of Mankind], *ZhMP* 3 (1970), 74–79, quotations 75, 76.
45. Ibid., 75.
46. Many examples from his writings are quoted in Protoierei Vasilii Stoikov, "O bogoslovskikh trudakh Mitropolita Nikodima" (On the theological works of Metropolitan Nikodim), in *Chelovek Tserkvi*, pp. 57–61.
47. Архиепископ Никодим, "Мир и свобода" (see note 6), p. 40f.
48. See the explorations of Julia Oswalt, *Kirchliche Gemeinde und Bauernbefreiung. Soziales Reformdenken in der orthodoxen Gemeindegeistlichkeit Russlands in der Ära Alexanders II.* (Göttingen: Vandenhoeck & Ruprecht, 1975).
49. This law strictly forbade the church any activity except for the pure performance of rites. Education and catechesis were thus prohibited, as were charitable activities of any kind. For the text of this decree, see Hauptmann and Stricker, *Dokumente*, no. 267, pp. 735–738.
50. Nikodim is reported to have adapted the language of his sermons to the average listener, most of whom were non-Christians, but still interested in "knowing about the truth." See Stoikov, "O bogoslovskikh trudakh Mitropolita Nikodima" (n. 46), esp. p. 61. See also Nikodim's lecture "On the Tasks of Contemporary Theology" at the Leningrad seminary and academy in 1968, in *ZhMP* 12 (1968), 63–69. For a similar report of a parish priest at this time, and the difficulties in coping with the overflow of listeners and those interested in religious conversations, see Aleksandr Men', "The 1960s Remembered," p. 150f.
51. On Nikodim's "patriotic" convictions, see Stoikov, "O bogoslovskikh trudakh," p. 60.
52. See Wallace L. Daniel, "Father Aleksandr Men' and the Struggle to Recover Russia's Heritage," *Demokratizatsiya* 17:1 (2009), 73–92. Also on http://www.demokratizatsiya.org/issues/winter%202009/daniel.html.
53. See Sergei Zhuk, "Religion, 'Westernization' and Youth in the 'Closed City' of Soviet Ukraine, 1964–84," *The Russian Review* 67:4 (2008), 661–679.
54. On religious life in late Soviet Russia, see Rousselet, *Die Russische Kirche*, pp. 400–407.

55. Ibid., p. 403. For an analysis of religious policy of the perestroika era, see Jane Ellis, "Some Reflections about Religious Policy under Kharchev," in Sabrina Petra Ramet (ed.), *Religious Policy in the Soviet Union* (Cambridge: Cambridge University Press, 1993), pp. 84–104.
56. See *ZhMP* 8 (1988), 12–13; in German, in *Kirche im Osten* 32 (1989), 169f.
57. A good overview of the crisis of the 1990s in Russia is given by Martin McCauley, "From Perestroika towards a New Order, 1985-1995," in Gregory Freeze (ed.), *Russia—A History* (Oxford: Oxford University Press, 1997), pp. 383–421.
58. Andrei Kuraev, "Prava cheloveka i pravoslavie," *Nezavisimaia Gazeta* (March 5, 1992), quoted after Rousselet, *Die Russische Orthodoxe Kirche*, p. 417. For a detailed description of the inner development of the ROC during this period, see Christopher Selbach, "The Orthodox Church in Post-Communist Russia and her Perception of the West: A Search for a Self in the Face of the Other," *Zeitschrift für Religionswissenschaft* 10 (2002), 131–173.
59. *Bases of the Social Concept*, no. I.1-I.4. This is only one of many places where the will to interact with the secular world is expressed in recent documents. For a thorough analysis, see Alexander Agadjanian, "Breakthrough to Modernity, Apologia for Traditionalism: The Russian Orthodox View of Society and Culture in Comparative Perspective," *Religion, State & Society* 31:4 (2003), 327–346.
60. *Bases of the Social Concept*, no. II.3.
61. Ibid., chapter II.
62. See Jutta Scherrer, *Kulturologie. Russland auf der Suche nach einer zivilisatorischen Identität* (Essener Kulturwissenschaftliche Vorträge, vol. 13) (Göttingen: Wallstein Verlag, 2003); Marlène Laruelle, "La discipline de la culturologie: un nouveau "prêt-à-penser" pour la Russie?" *Diogène* 204:4 (2003), 25–45. See also Brüning, "'Freedom' vs. 'Morality,'" p. 139ff.

3

The Bulgarian Orthodox Church at the Crossroads: Between Nationalism and Pluralism

Daniela Kalkandjieva

On November 10, 1989, a plenum of the Central Committee of the Bulgarian Communist Party removed Todor Zhivkov from his positions as the party's secretary general and chairman of the State Council.[1] This gave a green light to the democratization of Bulgaria. Several months later, the ruling political force changed its name to the "Socialist Party." It also agreed to discuss the country's future with the newly formed democratic opposition at a National Roundtable, which was held in Sofia from January 3 to May 15, 1990. At the end of that forum, the participants signed a joint agreement to disregard Article 1 of the Constitution, which recognized a leading role for the Communist Party. The final break with the totalitarian regime came in June 1991, when the Great National Assembly adopted a new Constitution of Bulgaria.

This change in the country's fundamental law ended the monopoly of official atheism in the public sphere. Without the threat of persecution, people began to demonstrate their religious affiliations openly.[2] All religious denominations registered an increased attendance to their services and a stricter observance of their faith and practices. This religious revival was also accompanied by a growing interest among the faithful in the theological aspects of their beliefs. In the case of the Bulgarian Orthodox Church (BOC), this process is combined with an emphasis on its role in preserving the Bulgarian national identity through the centuries. The fact that 82.6 percent of Bulgarian citizens affiliated themselves with Orthodoxy has turned this religious institution into a key factor shaping social attitudes.[3] The BOC's influence was further enhanced by the widespread notion of Orthodoxy as an inherited characteristic of Bulgarian identity. Therefore, the attitude of this church and its hierarchy toward the increasing pluralism in post-Communist Bulgaria has acquired special significance for the stable development of society.

The Bulgarian Orthodox Church and the Issue of Nationalism

Eastern Orthodox Christianity (Orthodoxy) is often perceived as a religious tradition that is inherently linked with nationalism. Analyzing its modern development, P. S. Ramet states that "Orthodox churches have frequently assumed importance as nationalist institutions."[4] V. Perica explains this state of affairs as a result of the peculiar development of the Orthodox world, where "the Church, ethnic community and state grow together."[5] In fact not all Orthodox churches have experienced such a simultaneous growth along with ethnic communities and states. The history of the ancient patriarchates of Alexandria, Antioch, Jerusalem, and Constantinople reveals significant deviations from this pattern. Even in the cases of Bulgaria, Serbia, and Russia there are discrepancies between state and church developments, since the establishment of their medieval states preceded that of their churches. The experience of Orthodox churches in the Ottoman, Russian, and Habsburgs Empires, that is, the Patriarchate of Constantinople, the Russian Orthodox Church, and the Metropolinate of Karlovci, whose jurisdictions were extended over multi-ethnic communities of believers, also puts into question the link between Orthodox churches and specific ethnic identities. Therefore, it seems that the concurrent development of church, state, and ethnic community is a process typical mostly for the age of nationalism and limited to those Eastern European countries where the majority of the population was Orthodox. Despite some modifications made in such multinational states as the Soviet Union and Tito's Yugoslavia, this pattern survived under Communist regimes and reemerged after their collapse.

At the same time, the post-1991 changes in the political map of Eastern Europe have shaken the model of Orthodox churches as national or state bodies. After the collapse of communism, Orthodox churches did not adjust their territorial jurisdictions according to the new political map of Eastern Europe. For example, the so-called canonical territories of the Russian, Serbian, and Czechoslovakian Orthodox churches retained the contours of states that no longer exist. At the same time, the governments of such states as Ukraine or Macedonia began to contest the jurisdictions of the Moscow Patriarchate and of the Serbian Patriarchate, respectively, over their citizens. The Romanian Patriarchate, an Orthodox church situated in a country whose borders did not change with the fall of communism, extended its jurisdiction beyond the territory of Romania. It took under its protection the newly established Metropolitan Church of Bessarabia that opposed the canonical authority of the Patriarchate of Moscow over the Orthodox population in post-Soviet Moldova. On the one hand, such processes raise questions about the meaning of the term "national churches" in contemporary Orthodox Europe. On the other hand, despite the claims of canonical or supranational rights of such Orthodox churches, the activities of their hierarchy are often driven by purely nationalist motives.[6]

The BOC shares many common features with other Eastern European churches. At the same time, its specific features must be considered in the analysis of its interaction with nationalism. Although the establishment of the Bulgarian Church in 870 brought about a unity of the state, the church, and society, this symbiosis ceased to exist from 1018 to 1185, when Bulgaria was conquered by Byzantium and its church was subordinated to the Patriarchate of Constantinople. The restoration of the Bulgarian Kingdom at the end of the twelfth century revived the unity of the state, church, and people, which only lasted until the beginning of Ottoman rule in 1396. The loss of state sovereignty was followed by the abolition of the Patriarchate of Tarnovo, whose flock was subjected to the patriarch of Constantinople within the framework of the *Millet* system. It organized the sultan's subjects into different social groups according to their confessions, irrespective of their ethnicity. Thus, Orthodox Bulgarians found themselves within the *Rum Millet* together with Greeks, Serbs, and other Orthodox nationalities, while the other non-Muslim communities, such as Jews or Catholics, were organized in separate *millet*s administrated by their own religious leaders. In the case of the *Rum Millet*, the sultan granted this privilege to the patriarch of Constantinople. The patriarch thus became not only the religious leader of the entire Orthodox community in the new empire, but also its lay administrator, responsible for the loyalty of the Orthodox population to the Ottoman authorities, for the regular payment of their taxes to the Sublime Porte, and for a series of civil activities as never before.[7] Bulgarians were able to leave the *Rum Millet* only in 1870, when the sultan issued a special decree for the establishment of their own national church—the Bulgarian Exarchate. Eight years later, the Russian-Turkish War (1877–1878) ended with the establishment of the Principality of Bulgaria and a partial liberation of the Bulgarian nation. We will return to this moment later in the discussion.

Although the Bulgarian neighbors also became dependent on the Ottoman Empire they preserved some degree of church autonomy. The Patriarchate of Ipek followed the destiny of the Patriarchate of Tarnovo but its adherents were subordinated to the archbishop of Ohrid. Moreover, in 1557, the Grand Vesir Mehmed Sokolović, a Serb converted to Islam, restored the Patriarchate of Ipek and appointed his brother Makarii as its supreme hierarch.[8] In 1766 the Orthodox Serbs had lost their church freedom for the second time and were subjected to the patriarch of Constantinople. This situation continued until 1830 when they obtained political autonomy followed by church autonomy granted by Constantinople.[9] The Greeks were in a better situation, benefitting from the survival of the Patriarchate of Constantinople. Still, as soon as the Kingdom of Greece got international recognition, it proclaimed its local church structures as a new autocephalous church in 1833.[10] Among the Orthodox nations ruled by the Ottomans, only the Wallachians and Moldovians preserved some unity of state, church, and ethnic identity thanks to the vassal status of their principalities and the autonomous status of the corresponding metropolitanates.

This state of affairs points to the most peculiar feature of the Bulgarian case, in which the advent of nationalism was not promoted by a national or state Orthodox church, as it did occur in the neighboring Greek, Serbian, and Romanian lands. Until 1870, Bulgarians had no religious or other institution keeping them together as a distinct nation within the Ottoman Empire. Moreover, until the Crimean War (1853–1856), Bulgarians also lacked their own native church hierarchy.[11] Despite these considerations, the idea that the BOC had preserved the Bulgarian national identity during the centuries of Ottoman rule achieved great popularity in post-Communist Bulgarian society. How did this happen?

The Church as Guardian of the Nation

The image of the BOC as guardian of the nation is not simply an ideological construction created by clerical or lay nationalists. It has also been nurtured by the way the Bulgarian Exarchate was set up and functioned in the Ottoman Empire.

The sultan's decree for its founding, issued on February 28, 1870, was in tune with the desire of his Bulgarian subjects for independence from the Patriarchate of Constantinople. They were now free to elect their own bishops, to have a Slavonic liturgy, to control the collection of the church taxes, and to use the collected money for the development of national education, that is, to save their nation from the Hellenizing efforts of the patriarchate.

The sultan's decree also met the demands for a church whose territory would include all Orthodox dioceses where the majority population was Bulgarian. In fact, the decree listed most of those dioceses by name, but left open the question of several eparchies located in present-day Macedonia.[12] Article 10 provided for their integration into the Bulgarian Exarchate on condition that two-thirds of the population would vote for such a change. In 1873, the Sublime Porte permitted such referenda to take place in the Orthodox dioceses of Skopje and Ohrid and they joined the exarchate. In 1878, the same happened with the dioceses of Debar, Bitolja, and Strumitsa (presently situated in FYROM) as well as that of Nevrokop (the present city of Gotse Delchev in Bulgaria).[13] In this way, the territorial jurisdiction of the exarchate delineated the borders of the Bulgarian nation, giving grounds to the notion of the BOC as an embodiment of its nation.

However, the sultan's decree and his subsequent approval of the appointment of Bulgarian hierarchs did not guarantee the smooth functioning of the exarchate. It only gave secular legitimacy to the new church, but did not assure its religious legitimacy. It took Bulgarians 75 years to obtain canonical recognition from the Patriarchate of Constantinople.[14] The very fact that the exarchate was established by a non-Christian authority put into question its existence as a proper Orthodox church. The Patriarchate of Constantinople passed over this issue, since its own existence was impossible without the benevolence of the Ottoman rulers. Still, it was not ready to accept the establishment of the exarchate. Such an acknowledgment would have entailed not only a withdrawal of the patriarchate's claims over the Bulgarian population and its territories, but also a severe reduction of financial resources. Moreover, any such recognition was seen as potentially harmful to the prestige of Constantinople as the primary patriarchate in the Orthodox world. Unable openly to reject the 1870 sultan's decree, the patriarchate found another way to undermine the Bulgarian victory. In September 1872, it declared a schism with the exarchate. This act was justified by canon law, which forbids the establishment of more than one ecclesiastical see in the same city, and preserved Constantinople for its patriarch. Bulgarians, however, ignored those rules and set up the headquarters of their exarchate in Istanbul next to those of the patriarchate.[15] They did so deliberately—situating the exarch's office in Istanbul ensured an effective defense of Bulgarian interests before the Sublime Porte and the ambassadors of the Great Powers.

The schism had a complex effect on the Bulgarian national and church development. On the one hand, it damaged the ecclesiological development of the Bulgarian Exarchate. Until 1945, when it was abolished, the clergy of the other Orthodox churches refused to concelebrate liturgies with Bulgarians. The exarchate also encountered difficulties in performing sacraments due to the shortage of holy oil or myrrh. Until the Bolshevik Revolution, it managed to perform the sacraments by the goodwill of the Russian Church, which provided myrrh through unofficial channels. This practice was continued in the interwar period thanks to good relations between Bulgarian hierarchs and their Serbian and Romanian colleagues in various ecumenical settings.[16] On the other hand, the schism prevented any interference by the Patriarchate of Constantinople in the affairs of the BOC and stimulated a church-centered process of national consolidation: it united membership in the exarchate with membership in the Bulgarian nation.

The role of the exarchate as a guardian of the nation was additionally enhanced by the gradual restoration of Bulgaria's political sovereignty—a process that started with the Russian-Turkish War (1877–1878) and culminated in 1908 with a declaration of the Bulgarian Kingdom's full independence. According to the preliminary treaty signed between the Russian and the Ottoman Empires in San Stefano on March 3, 1878, future Bulgaria had to cover a territory that almost overlapped with that of the exarchate (see map 3.1). Bulgarians welcomed this act and were bitterly disappointed by its revision, as negotiated by the Great Powers at the Berlin Congress in July 1878. That revision divided San Stefano Bulgaria into three parts: the Principality of Bulgaria, comprising the lands between the Danube River and the Balkan Range as well as the region of Sofia; the exarchate's dioceses of Plovdiv and Sliven, united into an autonomous province of the Ottoman Empire called Southern Rumelia; and the dioceses in Macedonia and Edirne Thrace, which were returned under the direct authority of the Sublime Porte. Under these circumstances, the exarchate became the only institution able to preserve the unity of the Bulgarian nation despite its partition.

In 1879, the Constituent Assembly convoked in Veliko Tarnovo—the capital of the Second Bulgarian Kingdom (1187–1393)—and adopted the first Constitution of the new Principality. Its text included a special paragraph confirming de facto the role of the exarchate as a guardian of the national unity of Bulgarians. According to Article 39 of the Constitution, "In ecclesiastical terms, the Principality of Bulgaria constitutes

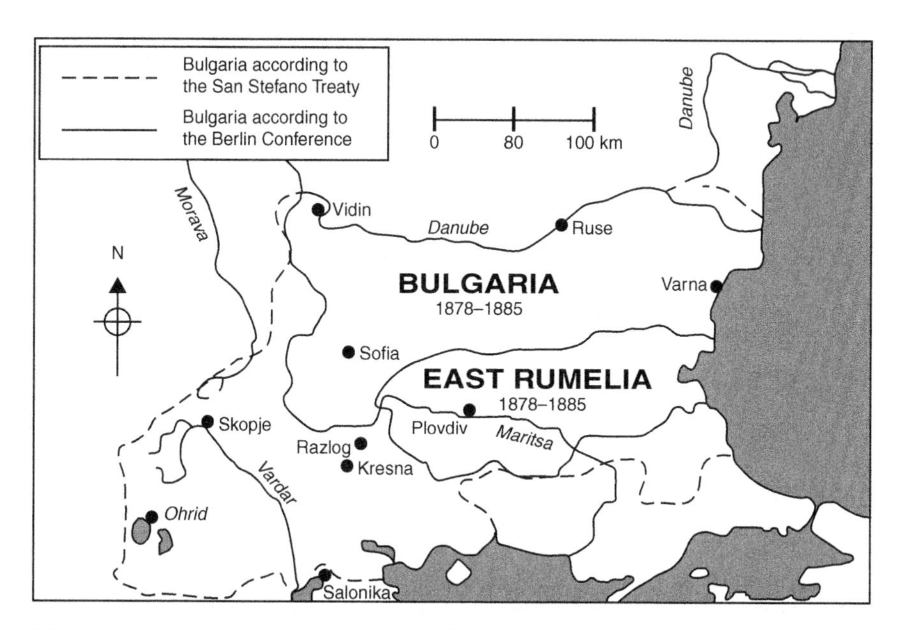

Map 3.1 Bulgaria (1878), Treaty of San Stefano, and Congress of Berlin.
Source: http://www.macedoniainfo.com/docs/macedonian_question.htm.

an inseparable part of the territory of the Bulgarian Exarchate and submits to the Holy Synod—the supreme spiritual authority of the Bulgarian Church wherever this authority is situated."[17] This wording was sensitive to the distinction drawn by the Bulgarian national leaders between their post–San Stefano state territory and that of their church. The fact that the former was much smaller than that of the Bulgarian Exarchate provoked an ecclesiastical irredentism, where the church borders, perceived as national ones, had to become state borders as well. This set a precedent in Orthodox history. Although the situation of the Moscow Patriarchate after the dissolution of the Soviet Union or that of the Serbian Patriarchate after the disintegration of Tito's Yugoslavia are similar to that of the Bulgarian Exarchate, there is an important difference. Bulgarians from the three parts of San Stefano Bulgaria considered the exarchate's territory as their national possession and looked upon this church institution as a guardian and spokesman for the entire nation, regardless of the political borders that divided them.

The hidden agenda of Article 39 met its authors' expectations in the first decades after the adoption of the Tarnovo Constitution. In 1885, the Principality of Bulgaria united with Southern Rumelia. As a result, the dioceses of Plovdiv and Sliven were transferred from the Ottoman Empire to the Bulgarian Principality. Although they remained under the jurisdiction of the exarchate, in administrative terms, these dioceses now moved from the control of the exarch to that of the Holy Synod in Sofia. This change corresponded to the logic of the Constitution's Article 39. Since the exarch, that is, the head of the BOC, remained a subject of the sultan and his appointment depended on the Sublime Porte, the Bulgarian government searched for ways to prevent Ottoman interference in its domestic affairs through the exarch. Therefore in 1883, the Principality adopted a new version of the exarchate's Statutes, the so-called Adapted Statutes, applied only within its territory. Therefore, although the Bulgarian Exarchate continued to exist it now had two administrations: one, under the leadership of the Sofia Synod and the other, under Exarch Josif in Constantinople. This approach aimed to preserve the image of the exarchate as the guardian of national unity, while allowing the two church administrations to function independently from each other and according to the specific needs of their believers. The administration responsible for the dioceses in the Principality of Bulgaria was focused on purely religious activities, while that in Ottoman territories continued to combine its religious responsibilities with civil duties (developing Bulgarian schools, organizing the training and appointment of Bulgarian teachers, collecting state and church taxes from its flock, organizing Bulgarian municipalities in Macedonia and Edirne Thrace, defending the interests of the Orthodox Bulgarians before the Sublime Porte and the ambassadors of the Great Powers in Istanbul, etc.). Thus, the image of the exarchate as guardian of Bulgarian national unity acquired a real meaning in Macedonian dioceses, especially in the period 1885–1912, before the partition of this region by Greece, Serbia, and Bulgaria in the course of the Balkan and the European wars (1912–1918).

Meanwhile the consolidation of Bulgarian state increased the self-confidence of its political elite who declared it as sovereign kingdom in September 1908. This change in status provoked a change in the attitude of statesmen to San Stefano Bulgaria, who began to entertain the idea of a war for the liberation of Macedonia and Edirne Thrace. Their enthusiasm, however, was not shared by the national Orthodox hierarchy. Exarch Josif and the Sofia Synod considered that San Stefano Bulgaria could be restored in a peaceful way. They also insisted that this goal be pursued with Russia's consent, that is, by following the "path of Slavdom and Orthodoxy." As a result, the Bulgarian government abandoned its union with the exarchate and entered in alliance with the other Orthodox Balkan states aligned against Turkey. This new militant Bulgarian nationalism, however, failed to achieve the San Stefano dream during the two Balkan wars (1912–1913). On the contrary, the exarchate lost part of its dioceses in Macedonia. In the hope of restoring or improving the situation, the Bulgarian government joined the Central Powers in World War I. This step had an even more disastrous effect on Bulgarian society, its church, and its state.

The Treaty of Neuilly (1919) increased the losses of territories and people by Bulgaria. The exarchate also lost its dioceses in Macedonia, which were ceded to Serbia and Greece.[18] A considerable part of its flock fled to the Bulgarian Kingdom together with their bishops and priests, while those who remained were put under the jurisdiction of the corresponding Orthodox churches. Moreover, the Bulgarian state lost Southern Dobrudzha, which had belonged to it since its liberation in 1878. After World War I, this region was transferred to and remained part of Romania until 1940. Orthodox Bulgarians in the region were cut off from the exarchate and integrated into the Romanian Patriarchate. This act was facilitated by the fact that they were considered schismatics, that is, their integration in the Romanian Church restored their communion with the canonical Orthodox world. At the same time, they had to face denationalization. As a result, by 1938 only 14 Bulgarian parishes in Southern Dobrudzha still celebrated the liturgy in Church-Slavonic, while in another 46 it was only partly preserved. Meanwhile the regions of Dobrich and Silistra were almost entirely Romanized.[19]

All these losses led to a rapprochement between the Bulgarian government and the Holy Synod, who joined their efforts to overcome the trauma of the national catastrophe of 1919. Their interwar alliance was additionally facilitated by the Bolshevik Revolution that removed another source of conflict between the two. On the one hand, the Russophilism of the Bulgarian hierarchy was no more politically harmful for the pro-Western orientation of the country, while on the other, the fear of the leftist movements reduced the secular overtones in the domestic politics of the Bulgarian governments. Their new partnership with the Orthodox church reflected on the development of the Bulgarian nationalism. In the interwar period, it pursued the restoration of the territorial jurisdiction of the exarchate as one of its major aims. Therefore, despite the loss of all dioceses abroad, neither the Bulgarian government nor the Holy Synod agreed to move the headquarters of the exarchate from Istanbul to Sofia. For its part, the BOC was inclined to make some concessions to its state: during World War II its hierarchy did not oppose the military plan for restoring San Stefano Bulgaria as it had during the previous wars, and it cooperated in the occupation of Macedonia and Edirne Thrace in 1941–1944.

Ethnoreligious Dimensions of Bulgarian Nationalism

The contemporary link between the Bulgarian ethnic and religious identity cannot be directly deduced from the medieval status of Orthodoxy as a state religion. Such a linkage neglects the impact of the five-century Ottoman rule over the Bulgarian people as well as such important nineteenth-century developments as the advent of modern nationalism and the struggles of the Great Powers over the so-called Eastern Question. The ethnoreligious dimensions of Bulgarian nationalism were influenced, in particular, by the Russian policy of maintaining the unity of the different Orthodox nations in the Ottoman Empire as a condition for its control over the Straits. On the eve of the Crimean War, St. Petersburg sent its emissaries to the Bulgarian lands to warn the local people against westerners,[20] who were accused of an evil intent—coaxing Bulgarians into betraying their faith. According to the emissaries, Orthodoxy was the only religion suitable for Slavs. Therefore, those Bulgarians who left Orthodoxy for another religion, and particularly Catholicism, had to know that along with their faith they would lose their Bulgarian identity.[21]

The unity of the Orthodox nationalities in the Ottoman Empire became even more important for Russia after her defeat in the Crimean War, when with the support of the Western Great Powers, Catholic and Protestant churches established their missions in the Orthodox provinces of the Ottoman Empire. St. Petersburg responded by setting up a network of consulates in the main Bulgarian cities. One of their tasks was to monitor the application of the so-called Hatti-Humayun, an act issued by the Sublime Porte in 1856, which allowed local communities to register their own, self-governing bodies along national lines. When ethnic Bulgarians who belonged to Catholicism or Islam tried to register their local councils as Bulgarian, the Russian diplomats intervened with the Ottoman authorities and prevented their recognition as such. Consequently, only Orthodox Bulgarians were able to register their municipal councils as "Bulgarian."[22]

At the same time, the Russian plans to keep the sultan's Orthodox subjects united under the jurisdiction of the Patriarchate of Constantinople was gradually undermined by the advent of nationalism in the Balkans. They were particularly threatened by the Bulgarian church movement. It started in 1820 with requests for native bishops, Slavonic liturgy, and Bulgarian education, but since the Patriarchate of Constantinople refused to satisfy them, Bulgarians changed their mind and put forward the question of the restoration of their medieval church independence. Until the Crimean War, however, they had no success as St. Petersburg supported the jurisdiction of the Patriarchate of Constantinople over the Orthodox population in the Ottoman Empire. Russia's defeat in 1856, however, undermined the position of the patriarchate as protector of Balkan Orthodox unity. Although it had the canonical power to refuse the establishment of an independent BOC, its hierarchy was unable to prevent Bulgarians from looking for alternative solutions, especially when the latter were backed by Western Great Powers.

In March 1861, Bulgarians sent a delegation to the pope, which signed a union with the Catholic Church. This act allowed them to organize their own church administration independently from the Patriarchate of Constantinople. The number of its followers grew so quickly that Russia took extraordinary measures to restore its influence over Bulgarians. In the summer, the Russian Embassy in Istanbul kidnapped Josif Sokolski—the exarch of the United Bulgarians (Greek-rite Catholics) and had him imprisoned at the Great Lavra in Kiev.[23] At the same time, the Russian diplomacy took a more favorable position to the Bulgarian church question and made a series of attempts to negotiate a compromise between them and the Patriarchate of Constantinople. It also provided stipends to Bulgarian boys to study in Russian ecclesiastical academies and seminaries. This training turned them into zealous supporters of Russia. The fact that almost all hierarchs of the Bulgarian Exarchate, established in 1870, were Russian graduates shaped their Russophile positions in the next period. Facilitated by a common language, blood relations, historical memory, and shared folk traditions, the Russian policy toward Orthodox Bulgarians also imparted an anti-Catholic orientation to the nationalism of the first generation of Bulgarian hierarchs (1870–1918).

The sultan's decree establishing the Bulgarian Exarchate (1870) also reinforced the ethnoreligious nature of modern Bulgarian nationalism. The act instituted the "Bulgarian *millet*," a new entity that combined the modern notion of "nation" with the Ottoman principle of *millet*, according to which adherence to a non-Muslim religious community determined the membership of the sultan's subjects in one or another *millet*, that is, Orthodox, Jewish, Catholic, and so on. The Bulgarian exarch became not only a religious leader of his flock, but also a lay administrator of his compatriots, thus replacing the patriarch of Constantinople in the dioceses under the jurisdiction of the Bulgarian Church. The new *millet* enjoyed internal ecclesiastical, cultural, and administrative autonomy, but in excluding the Catholics, Protestants, and Muslims of Bulgarian origin it did not embrace the whole Bulgarian ethnos. In this way, the notion of the modern Bulgarian nation was reduced to an ethnoreligious entity whose members were both Bulgarian and Orthodox. The *millet* concept thus played an important role in the transformation of the exarchate into an institution promoting ethnoreligious nationalism.

This ethnoreligious model of the Bulgarian nation established in the third quarter of the nineteenth century was further developed during the Third Bulgarian Kingdom (1878–1946), when the state and the Orthodox church collaborated in suppressing the religious rights of non-Orthodox ethnic Bulgarians, such as the forceful conversion of Pomaks (Bulgarian Muslims) during the Balkan Wars (1912–1913)[24] or the anti-Catholic repressions in the 1920s.[25] However, the BOC never used force to convert other non-Bulgarian ethnic minorities, such as the Roma, Turks,[26] and Jews, to Orthodoxy. In the process of the forceful conversion of Pomaks in 1912, the church refrained from converting the Roma, who lived in the same region, because its aim was to return the Pomaks to the religion of their Bulgarian forefathers, while the Roma were not regarded as part of the Bulgarian nation.

In the case of the Turkish and Jewish ethnic minorities, the BOC never organized mass campaigns for their conversion to Orthodoxy, but baptized only those of their members who requested it. In this respect, the BOC's stand off on the Jewish question during World War II is very significant. In fact it was the only Christian church whose supreme authority, the Holy Synod, took a decision to rescue Jews in its dioceses and openly protested against the attempts of the government to expel them from Bulgaria.[27] Still while rejecting those measures in the Law for the Nation's Defense that were directed against "Jews as a national minority," the same Holy Synod called the government not only to fight against antireligious and antichurch forces in the country but also to restrict "foreign religious propaganda, which tears up the spiritual unity of the Bulgarian people and by doing so make it vulnerable to falling prey to foreign goals and aspirations."[28] This approach allowed some internal autonomy of the non-Bulgarian ethnic groups, including the freedom to belong to different religious traditions, but obliged all ethnic Bulgarians to confess Orthodoxy as an ultimate religious and national value. Meanwhile, the BOC had zero tolerance for atheism and resisted any form of Catholic or Protestant influence among its flock. The situation changed radically after the Communist takeover, when Orthodoxy lost its status as the dominant religion and the BOC was separated from the state.

Communist Historiography on the National Role of the BOC

Communist historiography also left its mark on the link between Bulgarian Orthodox and national identity. The Communist regime's antireligious stance did not prevent it from using religion for its own ends. The Russian Empire was not alone in employing the unity of Slavic and Orthodox sentiments of Bulgarians to bolster its influence over them. Stalin himself referred to the traditional love of Bulgarians for Orthodox Russia as means of winning their loyalty to the Soviet Union and their support for the Red Army during World War II. In keeping with this same policy, the Bulgarian Communist Party also postponed its attacks against the Orthodox Church after coming to power on September 9, 1944. Although it did not hide its negative attitude toward religion, it showed respect for the historic role of the BOC. On the millennium of the most venerated Bulgarian saint, Ivan of Rila, Georgi Dimitrov, the leader of the Bulgarian Communist Party, delivered a speech with the following statement: "Our Bulgarian Orthodox Church, as opposed to other churches, is an institution with a historical role in preserving Bulgarian national identity and self-consciousness. During our people's struggle for liberation from its foreign yoke, the Bulgarian Church served as a patron and guardian of Bulgarians through centuries of the most severe trials."[29]

Delivered at a time when the Allied Powers had not yet signed peace with Bulgaria and before the Bulgarian Communist Party had consolidated its political power in the country, Dimitrov's speech pursued specific goals: to transform traditional Bulgarian sympathy for Russia into a loyalty toward the Soviet system; to undermine the unity of the Orthodox clergy, whose priests were seen as more progressive than the bishops; and to legitimate references to the BOC in national historiography.[30] After 1948, when the Communist Party consolidated its power, the idea of the national role of the Orthodox church was abandoned. The proponents of scientific atheism promoted the idea that Bulgarians were not only an antireligious nation but also had a deeply rooted anticlericalism.[31]

As for other religious traditions, as soon as Bulgaria's international status was settled and the domestic political opposition was crushed in the autumn of 1947, the Bulgarian Communist Party launched an open attack against their theological teachings, clergy, and institutions. Rather than launching repressions against Jews, the Communist Party facilitated their exodus to the newly established Israeli state. As a result, 45,000 of the 50,000 Bulgarian Jews left the country in 1948.[32] At the same time, the severest antireligious attacks were directed against the non-Orthodox Christian communities, who comprised some 100,000 believers. The leadership of the main Protestant churches was destroyed in a show trial of 15 Protestant pastors in February 1949. Between 1951 and 1953, the Roman Catholic and Greek Catholic Churches were decapitated. Their priests, nuns, and many laymen were tortured and prosecuted in a series of trials. The entire Catholic episcopate was physically liquidated.[33]

The Bulgarian Communist Party's campaign against Islam, the second largest religious community in the country, took into consideration the ethnic differences between the three Muslim communities in the country and thus treated Turks, Pomaks, and Roma separately. Until 1948, the Communist regime tolerated the religious life and traditions of the 700,000 Turks living in the country in the hope of negotiating their extradition to Turkey. When this plan failed, the regime launched repressions against them. Initially, however, their goal was not to eradicate the religiosity of the Bulgarian Turks, but rather to cut their ties with the Turkish state, situated outside of the Iron Curtain and where these people still had relatives. In the case of the Roma Muslims, who numbered 180,000, the Communist regime treated them as an ethnic group along with non-Muslim Roma. The main target of the anti-Muslim measures was the Pomak population, embracing 120,000 believers, with their own Mufti Organization separate from that of the Muslim Turks.[34]

In the late 1960s, the atheist régime began to soften its attitude toward religion and the BOC. A new paradigm emerged in the early 1970s, according to which religion could play a positive role in society.[35] Scientific atheists began to view early Christianity as an ideology of the oppressed classes in their struggle for liberation and favorably assessed the social achievements of churches in the course of history. They began to emphasize the BOC's role as a protector of Bulgarian national identity under the Ottoman rule. However, the absence of a Bulgarian church institution until 1870 put their claims on shaky grounds. To solve the problem, Communist historiography redefined the term "Bulgarian Orthodox Church," linking it to those Orthodox monasteries whose monks had preserved the Slavonic liturgy, who had written many works in Bulgarian, and who ran schools that enabled Bulgarian children to study in their native language.[36]

Pursuing their ultimate goal, Communist scholars focused their attention on particular aspects of this noninstitutional church, namely, its role in sustaining Bulgarian ties with Russia, in resisting Catholic missionaries in the Ottoman Empire, and in struggling for liberation from Ottoman rule. At the same time, the Holy Synod of the BOC canonized two key figures of this liberation struggle: Father Paisii of Hilandar in 1962 and his disciple, Bishop Sofronii of Vratsa, in 1964. These were the only saints proclaimed by the BOC under Communist rule. While the religious virtues of these two clerics have been the subject of some criticism from an Orthodox theological perspective, their contribution to the Bulgarian national cause is beyond doubt.[37] Today it is difficult to say whether their canonization pursued purely domestic goals, that is, to stabilize the BOC's position in an atheist country, or to demonstrate to Christians outside the Iron Curtain that the Bulgarian Patriarchate, a member of the World Council of Churches since 1961, enjoyed freedom of religion.

In the early 1970s, the BOC's role in the struggle for Bulgarian political liberation was framed in a context of interethnic and interreligious conflicts (i.e., the historical fights of Bulgarians against Turks and of Christianity against Islam). Moreover, the introduction of this topic into school textbooks coincided with a mass campaign of the Bulgarian Communist Party to change the names of Pomaks (1970–1974), ethnic Bulgarians who had adopted Islam during the Ottoman rule. This act was presented by the regime as a restoration of historical justice, insofar as the predecessors of the contemporary Pomaks had been forcibly converted to Islam as part of an Ottoman policy to erase their national consciousness.[38] Any resistance against the campaign for the change of the Pomaks' names was regarded as evidence of the damaging effect of those forcible conversions on the national consciousness of this part of the Bulgarian people.

The thirteen hundredth anniversary of the Bulgarian State in 1981 inspired new interpretations of the idea of the BOC as guardian of national identity. The establishment of the Bulgarian Exarchate in 1870 was treated as "a great success of the Bulgarian national revolution" that had led to the recognition of Bulgarians as a distinct nation in the Ottoman Empire.[39] This was a return to the theses of interwar Bulgarian historians Todor Burov and Petar Nikov, and of Bulgarian Orthodox theologians and churchmen Ivan Snegarov and Patriarch Kiril. The idea of the BOC as guardian of national identity made its way into the official historiography of Communist Bulgaria in the mid-1980s during the so-called Revival process, when Bulgarian citizens of Turkish origin were forced to change their names in order to erase their ethnic identity.[40] Thus, by the end of Todor Zhivkov's regime, religious minorities in the country and Western observers considered the BOC as nationalist, rather than merely a national religious institution. On the other hand, most Orthodox Bulgarians considered their church as an institution that had preserved them as a nation through the centuries. Since the collapse of communism, the revival of Orthodoxy in Bulgaria has been accompanied by some manifestations of ethnoreligious nationalism.

The BOC and the Challenge of Pluralism

In their respective contexts, most East European Orthodox churches and their communities entered into contact and lived together with non-Orthodox and non-Christian peoples, but today they still find it difficult to deal with the modern understanding of freedom of religion and legal norms regulating religious pluralism.[41] In this, the BOC is no exception. The baptism of Bulgaria established Byzantine Christian forms of religious and social life, which continued in the period 1018–1185, when there was no Bulgarian state and when the BOC had been abolished by the Patriarchate of Constantinople.

The Ottoman conquest at the end of the fourteenth century changed the religious situation in Bulgarian lands. Since then, Orthodox Bulgarians coexisted with Muslims and practiced their Orthodox faith, although after the abolition of the Patriarchate of Tarnovo at the beginning of the fifteenth century they were subjected to the Patriarchate of Constantinople. Although the Ottoman *millet* system allowed a broader religious diversity, it was still far from the contemporary understanding and practice of pluralism and freedom of religion. It maintained a higher status for Islam, and granted a degree of autonomy for the conquered Orthodox population. Those Orthodox who converted to Islam could not later return to their ancestral religion or join another faith tradition, for example, Catholicism.

The establishment of Bulgarian statehood in 1878 put into place a new model of religious tolerance. The Tarnovo Constitution of 1879 declared Orthodoxy as the dominant religion (Article 37), while recognizing the internal autonomy of religious minorities (Article 40). It also guaranteed the special status of the Holy Synod as the institutional entity responsible for religious affairs in Bulgaria (Article 39). In the twentieth century, the Communists promised freedom of religion, but in the end they simply replaced Orthodox dominance with their own militant atheism. These developments made it difficult for the post-1989 leaders of the BOC and Bulgarian society at large to embrace European principles and values in the sphere of religious rights. Their accommodation to those principles is further complicated by enduring Communist images of religion from the period 1944–1989.

The first democratic Constitution of Bulgaria (1991) broke with militant atheism by making special reference to religion. It preserved the separation between church and state (Article 13.2) as a necessary condition for the democratic development of the country, but developed further the notion of freedom of religion. Whereas the preceding Communist constitutions (1948 and 1971) had limited the freedom of religion to the freedom of worship (Articles 78.1–1947 and 53.1–1971), the 1991 Constitution broadened its meaning: "The freedom of conscience, the freedom of thought and the choice of religion and of religious or atheistic views shall be inviolable. The State shall assist the maintenance of tolerance and respect among the believers from different denominations, and among believers and non-believers" (Article 37.1–1991).

The 1991 Constitution further referred directly to Eastern Orthodox Christianity "as the traditional religion" in Bulgaria. This text, however, did not limit the rights of non-Orthodox believers and agnostics in the country. Their rights were guaranteed by the Constitutional Court's Judgment No. 2 of February 18, 1998, which declared "the traditional character of Eastern Orthodox Christianity expresses its cultural and historical role and meaning for the Bulgarian State and its current meaning for civil life, primarily in the system of civic holidays (Sundays, New Year, Passover and Christmas)." The debate on the traditional role of Orthodoxy was revisited in 2002 when the first post-Communist Denominations Act was promulgated. It too referred to the traditional character of Orthodoxy but linked specifically with the BOC, rather than as a generic faith tradition. According to Article 10.1–2002,

> The traditional religious denomination in the Republic of Bulgaria is Eastern Orthodoxy. It has a historical significance for the Bulgarian state and is important for civil life. Its voice and representative is the autocephalous Bulgarian Orthodox Church which, as a "Patriarchate," is the legitimate successor [*pravopriemnik* in Bulgarian] of the Bulgarian Exarchate and is a member of the United Holy Ecumenical and Apostolic Church. It is governed by a Holy Synod and is represented by the Bulgarian Patriarch, who is also the Metropolitan of Sofia.

The next paragraph (Article 10.2–2002) granted the BOC the status of a juridical entity on the basis of the constitutional affirmation of the traditional character of Orthodoxy (1991 Constitution, Art. 13.3) and of the Constitutional Court's Judgment of 1998 about the church's significance for the state and public life. Its further affirmation of the rights of the Bulgarian Patriarchate over the legacy of the exarchate (1870–1953) fueled apprehension that the definition of the BOC as "the legitimate successor of the Bulgarian Exarchate" restored its claims over the eparchies outside the present state territory of Bulgaria, that is, over eparchies situated in FYROM.[42] By linking the traditional character of Orthodoxy with the patriarchate, the new Denominations Act granted unique privileges to the BOC that no other religious community has.[43]

The new legal status of the BOC also deepened its historic symbiosis with ethnonationalism. On December 16, 2002, just few days before the final vote for the Denominations Act, Patriarch Maxim delivered a speech, declaring that during its 12-century existence the Bulgarian state[44] was legitimated by the BOC. He further stated that any vote against the new Denominations Act, in particular its provision on the special status of the BOC, would reveal who "is on the side of the forces that have been working against our native Church for years" and who does not respect the unity of the Bulgarian state.[45] This position was supported not only by the church hierarchy, but also by many leading politicians and public figures. In their view, any criticism of the act's provisions on the Orthodox church would be detrimental to national and historical consciousness.

The subsequent implementation of the Denominations Act revealed that Article 10 was intended not only to respect traditions and historical memory, but also to address a crisis in the BOC caused by documented revelations that Maxim owed his election as Bulgarian patriarch in 1970 to a Politburo decision.[46] The crisis split the church's leadership into two synods, each of which claimed to be the true canonical representative of Orthodox Bulgarians. In the ensuing years, the conflict between the two groups of hierarchs was heightened by the process of restitution of church properties that had been confiscated by the Communist regime.[47] The Alternative Synod rejected Patriarch Maxim's legitimacy and laid claim to all the church property—subject to restitution. Meanwhile, the Synod of Patriarch Maxim insisted that it was the only canonical BOC leadership recognized by the rest of the Orthodox world. The conflict was also determined by the support that each faction received from the major political forces: the Union of Democratic Forces sided with the Alternative Synod, while the Bulgarian Socialist Party backed Patriarch Maxim. The patriarch's situation was further improved after the return of King Simeon II to Bulgaria and the victory of his National Movement in the parliamentary elections of 2001. In the following year, the new government promulgated a law on religions that recognized the Synod of Patriarch Maxim as the canonical leadership of the BOC and as the only legal entity having full rights over the restored church property. Although the new Denominations Act did not outlaw the Alternative Synod, it enabled state authorities to confiscate properties and to transfer them to the Synod of Patriarch Maxim. The synod thus strengthened its authority over the Orthodox community in Bulgaria, while its adversary appeared doomed to extinction, despite a legal victory against Bulgaria in the European Court of Human Rights.[48] For Patriarch Maxim, it was no less significant to be recognized as the canonical head of the BOC by the leaders of all autocephalous Orthodox churches in the world, as was demonstrated by their visits to Sofia.

The BOC and Other Religious Denominations

Although the BOC has benefited from expanded religious freedoms after the fall of communism, it has maintained a generally negative attitude toward religious pluralism. While it is tolerant toward Jewish and Muslim communities, the Synod of Patriarch Maxim is very wary of non-Orthodox Christian denominations and of new religious movements that appeared and grew rapidly after 1989. Its negative attitude to Western Christianity was evident in its withdrawal from the World Council of Churches (WCC) in 1998 and in its subsequent withdrawal from the Conference of European Churches (CEC). The ostensible reasons were the WCC's disregard of Orthodox opinions in the decision-making process, the failure of ecumenism to develop an authentic theological dialogue among the different Christian churches, and the growing number of new Protestant factions that were seen as a threat to Orthodoxy.[49] Although other Orthodox churches supported this position, the Georgian Orthodox church also withdrew from the WCC (in 1997), no other Orthodox church did so. According to some Bulgarian clerics, both ecumenism and communism threatened the survival of Orthodoxy and, by leaving the WCC and the CEC, the BOC had defended true Christianity.[50]

Similar attitudes were also demonstrated to Catholicism during the visit of Pope John Paul II to Bulgaria (May 23–26, 2002). Until the last moment, there was no clarity whether Patriarch Maxim would attend the official ceremony. Finally, he was persuaded by some members of the Holy Synod to meet the pope but under the condition that he would not refer to him as the head of the Catholic Church.[51] Therefore, the Bulgarian patriarch welcomed John Paul II only with the words "Christ is risen!" Rather than addressing his eminent guest with the title "Your Holiness," Maxim employed the polite form of "you," that is, "Your visit" or "Your delegation."[52] For his part, the pope was highly respectful toward his Orthodox hosts and referred to them with the words: "Your Holiness, Honorable Metropolitans and Bishops, Dear Brothers in Christ!"[53] In spite of that, some observers still considered that the pope diminished the significance of his visit to the Bulgarian patriarch by meeting with the leaders of the local Muslim and Jewish communities. In the view of such critics, the only positive outcome of the pope's visit was his neglect of the Alternative Synod, whose attacks against Patriarch Maxim were considered to have been weakened.[54]

The papal visit revealed the depth of the gap between Orthodoxy and Catholicism in Bulgaria. Metropolitan Nikolay of Plovdiv, at that time vicar bishop of Sofia Diocese, locked the altar's gates of the "St. Alexander Nevski" patriarchal cathedral during the official ceremony in order to prevent its desecration by "heretics," that is, the pope and his clerics.[55] Thus, it seems that the Euro-integration of Bulgaria is the major factor that restrains such instances of Orthodox outrage at Western Christianity. Consequently, Bulgarian Orthodox opposition focuses more on new religious movements (NRMs) and some American evangelical churches that are not welcome in other member-states of the European Union, that is, Mormons, Jehovah's Witnesses, the Unification Church of Moon, or Scientologists.[56] In such cases, the Holy Synod rarely makes open statements, but some Orthodox priests and individual metropolitans take an active part in the public protests against building prayer houses and the door-to-door agitation of NRMs.[57] During such demonstrations, Orthodox icons and gonfalons are typically seen alongside the flags of nationalist political formations, such as the VMRO (Internal Revolutionary Macedonian Organization) and "Ataka" (Attack). The BOC's attitude toward NRMs is also evident in various forms of condemnation and in the establishment of centers dedicated to countering "destructive sects."[58] Still other countermeasures against NRMs include the introduction of mandatory classes of religious instruction (in an Orthodox vein), an idea adopted by the Holy Synod in 2008. This proposal singled out various religious denominations, such as the Mormons, the Unification Church of Moon, the Seventh Day Adventists, the Jehovah's Witnesses, and Scientology as "very dangerous for children."[59]

At the same time, the Synod of Patriarch Maxim maintains good relations with the leaderships of other traditional religious communities, notably Jews and Muslims. The Jewish community is quite small, comprising only 706 members in 2011, while the Muslim community is Bulgaria's second largest religious denomination, with almost 577,139 believers or 7.84 percent of the total population.[60] It is significant that while the public discourse on Islam in Bulgaria can reveal negative attitudes, especially on the issue of Ottoman rule, the post-1989 relations between the Synod of Patriarch Maxim and the Chief Mufti Office in Sofia are quite good. Over the last decade, the leaders of both religious communities joined their efforts to introduce mandatory religious instruction in Bulgarian public schools. While the efforts of the Chief Mufti's Office are focused only on areas with compact Muslim populations, the Synod of Patriarch Maxim seeks to include all non-Muslim children in such classes. So far, there has been no public support for this campaign, and only 1–2 percent of all students from the first to the twelfth grades take such lessons in Bulgaria's public school system.[61]

Conclusion

Our analysis of the BOC's attitude to nationalism and pluralism would not be complete without considering the post–Cold War development of Bulgaria. Although the collapse of communism brought an end to militant atheism and rehabilitated the role of religion in the public sphere, it also challenged the boundaries between the religious and the secular in society. In Bulgaria, as in other former totalitarian states in Eastern Europe, the transnational process has been complicated by the difficulty in distinguishing between the atheist and the secular. On the one hand, Bulgarian society is no exception and it has witnessed an expansion of religion into the public sphere. On the other hand, Bulgarian society views this process through the prism of its recent past. As a result, the defense of secular values can easily be interpreted as a return to Communist or totalitarian values, while the defense of religious values tends to be treated as a defense of democracy. Such a situation has enabled the BOC to justify its attacks against non-Orthodox religious organizations on the grounds that they limit individual freedoms and threaten the dignity of man as God's creation. However, the same situation also has led the majority of Bulgarians to oppose the introduction of mandatory religious instruction in public schools, insofar as it is reminiscent of Communist forms of indoctrination.

Although post-totalitarian developments have provoked disparate and contradictory reactions to Orthodoxy as a religious phenomenon, its institutional representative, the BOC, is widely regarded as the guardian of the Bulgarian nation throughout the centuries. This may be attributed to the weakened role of the state as a source of common identity. That role was diminished by the collapse of communism and the uneasy adaptation of Bulgarian society to a market economy, as well as by the processes of Euro-integration and globalization. Thus, the state underwent a "passage from a national-political nationalism to a cultural nationalism,"[62] which in turn allowed the BOC to be seen as an embodiment of national values. This perception became especially vivid in the attempts of some Orthodox zealots to revive the statement of Metropolitan Kliment (Vassil Drumev) of Tarnovo that there will be no Bulgarian people without Orthodoxy.[63] They interpret these words outside of their historical context and present them as the testament of the eminent hierarch. In fact, Metropolitan Kliment made this statement on the Sunday of Orthodoxy, in February 1893, as a protest against the state's plan to change Article 38 of the Bulgarian Constitution, whose original text had required the heir to the throne to be baptized an Orthodox. Under pressure of Bulgaria's King Ferdinand, the Parliament amended Article 38 and allowed his son Boris to remain Catholic. This created tensions between the Bulgarian Orthodox hierarchy and the ruling dynasty until 1911, when the original constitutional text was restored and Prince Boris was converted to Orthodoxy.[64] The misuse of religion for nationalist ends, such as this anachronistic reading of a century-old text, impedes the current BOC's ability to embrace the EU's principles of pluralism and freedom of religion.

The fusion of religious and national identity is further nurtured by the fact that many Bulgarian statesmen and the public at large cannot distinguish between theology and history in the absence of a critical reading of the Bulgarian church past. While the BOC certainly played a significant role in shaping the history of its people, that does not make it the sole and only factor responsible for their progress and survival. Indeed, there were periods when this church did not exist as institution. The same may be said about Byzantine Christianity, whose enduring influence from the baptism of Bulgaria (864) to today, along with other factors (historical memory, traditions, language, territory, institutions) shaped the national consciousness of modern Bulgarians. Nevertheless, Orthodoxy was not the only religious tradition that contributed to the emergence of the contemporary Bulgarian nation. In its present composition, Bulgaria's future and prosperity will depend on its ability to respect the religious diversity within its own society and to adhere to European principles of religious pluralism.

Notes

1. Evgenia Kalinova and Iskra Baeva, *Balgarskite prekhodi, 1939–2002* (The Bulgarian transitions, 1939–2002) (Sofia: Paradigma, 2002), pp. 252–253.
2. According to Zhivko Oshavkov, by 1968 over 70 percent of Bulgarian citizens were atheists. This research, however, was done by indirect surveys—interviewees were asked about the religious habits of their neighbors and this information was used to arrive at estimates. Although Oshavkov's methodology is criticized today by sociologists, his work remains the main sociological research on religion conducted in socialist Bulgaria. See Oshavkov, *Protsesat na preodolyavaneto na religiyata v Balgariya (Sotsiologicheski izsledvaniya)* (The process of overcoming religion in Bulgaria [Sociological surveys]) (Sofia: BAN, 1968).
3. See the statistical data from the 2001 Census retractable from: http://www.nsi.bg/Census/Census.htm. The latest census of 2011 (http://censusresults.nsi.bg/Reports/2/2/R10.aspx) reveals a drop in the number of Orthodox Bulgarians from 6,552,751 in 2001 to 4,374,135 in 2011. To a great degree, the difference is a result of the changed data collecting methodology, which allows people to choose whether they want to declare their religious affiliation or not. In this way, only 59.4 percent of the Bulgarian population freely registered as Orthodox, whereas in previous years they had been obliged to give information on their family's religious affiliation, rather than their personal affiliation.
4. Pedro Ramet, "Autocephaly and National Identity in Church-State Relations in Eastern Christianity: An Introduction," in *Eastern Christianity and Politics in the Twentieth Century*, P. Ramet (ed.), Christianity under Stress, Vol. 1 (Durham, London: Duke University Press, 1988), p. 6.
5. Vjekoslav Perica, *Balkan Idols: Religion and Nationalism in Yugoslav States* (Oxford: Oxford University Press, 2002), 7.
6. The nationalistic behavior of Eastern European Orthodox churches is discussed by Sabrina P. Ramet, *Nihil Obstat: Religion, Politics and Social Change in East Central Europe*

and Russia (Durham and London: Duke University Press, 1998), pp. 171–175 and 241–243; Perica, *Balkan Idols*; Zoe Knox, "Church, State and Society in Eastern Europe," in *Religion zwischen Kirche, Staat und Gesellschaft—Religion between Church, State and Society*, Irimie Marga, Gerald G. Sander, and Dan Sandu (eds.), (Hamburg: Verlag Dr. Kovač, 2007), pp. 94–95.

7. Steven Runciman, *The Great Church in Captivity* (Cambridge, UK: Cambridge University Press, 2006), p. 175.
8. Konstantin E. Skurat, *Istoriya Pomestnykh Pravoslavnykh Tserkvey* (History of local Orthodox churches), vol. 1 (Moscow: Russkie ogni, 1994), 106.
9. It took the Serbs several decades to obtain full church independence. They were granted autocephaly in 1879, while their patriarchate was restored in 1922.
10. This autocephaly was unilaterally proclaimed by the Greek state in 1833 and was recognized as canonical by the Patriarchate of Constantinople in 1850.
11. Rumyana Radkova, *Bulgarskata inteligentsiya prez Vuzrazhdaneto* (The Bulgarian intelligentsia during the Revival) (Sofia: Nauka i izkustvo, 1986); Olga Todorova, *Pravoslavnata tsarkva i balgarite, XV-XVIII vek* (The Orthodox Church and the Bulgarians, XV–XVIII centuries) (Sofia: Akademichno izdatelstvo "Prof. Marin Drinov," 1997).
12. According to Article 10 of the Sultan's Decree, the Bulgarian Exarchate included the dioceses of Ruse, Dorostol (the present-day city of Silistra), Preslav, Tarnovo, Sofia, Vratsa, Lovech, Vidin, Nish (present-day Serbian city of Niš), Pirot (in present Serbia), Kyustendil, Samokov, Veles (in the present Macedonia), Plovdiv, and Sliven. The Black Sea coast with the regions of Varna and Sozopol and some areas around Plovdiv remained under the jurisdiction of Constantinople because of the compact Greek population living there in the nineteenth century. The same article also allowed new dioceses to join the Bulgarian Exarchate, if two-thirds of their Orthodox population voted for such a change. *Tsarkovno-narodniyat sabor, 1871 g.* (The Church-People's Council, 1871) (Sofia: Universitetsko izdatelstvo "Sv. Kliment Ohridski," 2001), pp. 39–40.
13. Petar Nikov, *Vazrazhdane na balgarskiya narod: Tsarkovno-nacionalni borbi i postizheniya* (The revival of Bulgarian people: Church and national struggles and achievements) (Sofia: Akademichno izddatelstvo "Prof. Marin Drinov," 2008), pp. 364–368.
14. The Bulgarian Exarchate was recognized as a canonical church on February 22, 1945. See D. Kalkandjieva, "The Bulgarian Orthodox Church and the Cold War," in *Eastern Christianity and the Cold War*, Lucian N. Leustean (ed.) (London, New York: Routledge, 2010), p. 81.
15. Although many authors point to *phyletism*, or discriminatory ecclesiastical nationalism, as the main argument of the Patriarchate of Constantinople against the canonical recognition of the Bulgarian Exarchate, the only indisputable argument for the schism declared with Bulgarians in September 1872 was the location of the see of their exarch. See *Protokoli na dukhovnata komisiya za preglezhdane na Ekzarkhiiskiya ustav i na vsichki deystvuvashti vav vedomstvoto na Balgarskata pravoslavna tsarkva tsarkovni naredbi* (Proceedings of the Ecclesiastical Commission, appointed to review the exarchate's statutes and all decrees of the BOC that are currently in force) (Sofia: Sinodalno izdatelstvo, 1920).
16. Stefan Tsankov, "Mezhdutsarkovnoto polozhenie na Balgarskata pravoslavna tsarkva sled Osvobozhdenieto na Balgariya" (The Interchurch status of the BOC in the Orthodox world after the Liberation of Bulgaria), *Godishnik na Sofiyski Universitet—Bogoslovski fakultet* (Annual book of Sofia University—Theological faculty), vol. X (1933), 1–122.
17. The literal translation of "the territory of the Bulgarian Exarchate" is "the Bulgarian church area" or *balgarska tsarkovna oblast* in Bulgarian. This phrase is a direct reference to Article 10 of the 1870 sultan's decree that starts with the words "The church area of this Bulgarian Exarchate consists of the dioceses of Russe, Drostol." See *Tsarkovno-narodniya sabor, 1871 g.* (The church-people's council, 1870), ed. Khristo Temelski (Sofia: Glavno

upravlenie na arkhivite pri Ministerski Savet, Universitetsko izdatelstvo "Sv. Kliment Ohridski," 2001), p. 39.

18. Ivan Snegarov, "Otnosheniyata na Balgarskata pravoslavna tsarkva i drugite pravoslavni tsarkvi sled provazglasyavaneto na skhizmata" (The relations of the BOC with other Orthodox churches after the declaration of the schism), *Tsarkoven arkhiv* (Church Archives), vol. 35 (Sofia, 1929), pp. 72–73; Tsankov, "Mezhdutsarkovnoto polozhenie."
19. Blagovest Nyagulov, "Pravoslavieto i katolitszmat sred balgarite v Romania" (Orthodoxy and Catholicism among the Bulgarians in Romania), in *Balgarskata pravoslavna tsarkva" Traditsii i nastoyashte* (The BOC: Traditions and present developments) (Sofia: IK "Gutenberg," 2009), pp. 247–255.
20. NBKM-BIA (Bulgarian National Library "St. Cyril and St. Methodius—Archives of Bulgarian Revival), f. (fund) 113, a.e. (archival unit) 67, pp. 30–31.
21. D. Kalkandjieva, "Katolitsizmat v balgarskite zemi i zalezat na Osmanskata imperiya (vtorata polovina na XIX vek" (Catholicism in the Balkan lands and the decline of the Ottoman Empire: the second half of the nineteenth century), *Rodina* (historical journal "Motherland"), Sofia, vol. 1–2 (1997), 166–186.
22. Ibid., 161.
23. Ibid., 184.
24. Svetolazar Eldarov, *Pravoslavieto na voyna: Balgarskata pravoslavna tsarkva i voynite na Balgariya, 1877–1945* (Orthodoxy in wartime: The BOC and Bulgaria's wars, 1877–1945) (Sofia: Voenno izdatelstvo, 2004), pp. 98–120; Velichko Georiev and Stayko Trifonov, *Pokrastvaneto na balgarite mohamedani, 1912–1913. Dokumenti* (The Conversion of the Bulgarian Muslims, 1912–1913. Documents) (Sofia: AI "Prof. Marin Drinov," 1995).
25. Svetolazar Eldarov, *Katolitsite v Balgaria, 1878–1944* (Catholics in Bulgaria, 1878–1944) (Sofia: IMIR, 2002), pp. 354–370 and 455–470.
26. It seems that the tolerant attitude of the BOC to the ethnic Turks and their religion is also influenced by the fact that the existence of the exarchate's headquarters in Istanbul was possible thanks to the goodwill of the Sublime Porte and the Turkish governments, who tolerated this situation until 1945 when on January 21 the Bulgarian Synod decided to move the see of the Bulgarian Exarch to Sofia.
27. *The Power of Civil Society in a Time of Genocide: The Proceedings of the Holy Synod of the Bulgarian Orthodox Church on the Rescue of the Jews in Bulgaria, 1940–1944*, eds. Albena Taneva and Ivanka Gezenko, trans. Alex Tanev (Sofia: Sofia University Press "St. Kliment Ohridski," 2005), pp. 66–69, 142–147.
28. Ibid., p. 69.
29. TsPA (Bulgarian State Archives—Bulgarian Communist Party's Files), f. 146, op. 2, a.e. 709, p. 8.
30. See also D. Kalkandjieva, "The Millennium of the Death of Saint Ivan of Rila (May 26, 1946)," *Bulgarian Historical Review*, Sofia, vol. 3–4 (2002), 188–206.
31. The image of antireligious Bulgarians was developed by the advocates of militant atheism in Bulgaria in the 1960s, e.g., Nikolai Mizov, *Antireligioznite vazgledi i traditsii na balarskiya narod* (The antireligious views and traditions of the Bulgarian people) (Sofia: Profizdat, 1960). The antichurchliness thesis is developed by Zhivko Oshavkov in *Protsesat na preodolyavaneto na religiyata v Balgariya: Sotsiologicheski izsledvaniya* (The process of overcoming of religion in Bulgaria: Sociological studies) (Sofia: BAN, 1968).
32. D. Kalkandjieva, "Politikata na Balgarskata komunisticheska partiya kam nepravoslavnite religiozni obshtnosti (1944–1953 g.)" (The politics of the Bulgarian Communist Party towards the non-Orthodox religious communities [1944–1953]), *Trudove na katedrite po istoria i bogoslovie—Shumenski Universitet "Episkop Konstantin Preslavski* (Publications of the departments of history and theology at the University of Shumen "Bishop Konstantin of Preslav") Shumen, vol. 8 (2005), 254.

33. The anti-Protestant and anti-Catholic trials are discussed by Daniela Kalkandjieva in her study "The Catholic Church in Bulgaria and the Cold War," in *L'Europe et la Méditerranée: Stratégies politiques et culturelles (XIXe et XXe siècles), Actes du colloque de Nancy-Malzeville (4, 5, 6 septembre 1997)* sous la direction de G. Meynier et M. Russo (Nancy: Presses universitaires de Nancy, France, L'Hartmattan, 1999), pp. 229–241. See also Svetolozar Eldarov, *Katolitsite v Balgaria, 1878–1989* (Catholics in Bulgaria, 1878–1989) (Sofia: IMIR, 2002), pp. 666–672.
34. Kalkandjieva, "Politikata na Balgarskata komunisticheska partiya kam nepravoslavnite religiozni obshtnosti (1944–1953 g.)," pp. 254–257.
35. Todor Stoychev, "Some Gnoseological and Social Aspects of Religion," in *Pravoslavieto v Balgariya* (Orthodoxy in Bulgaria), Dimitar Angelov, Nikolay Mizov, and Todor Stoychev (eds.) (Sofia: BAN, 1974), p. 22.
36. Georgi Neshev, "The Orthodox Institutions in XV–XVIII cen.," in *Pravoslavieto v Balgariya*, p. 151.
37. Yanko Dimov, *Kiril—Patriarch Balgarski* (Cyril—Patriarch of Bulgaria) (Sofia: Universitetsko izdatelstvo "Sv. Kliment Ohridski," 2005), pp. 210–216.
38. The campaign of replacing Muslim Pomak names with Bulgarian ones is discussed by Mikhail Gruev and Aleksey Kalyonski in their book *Vazroditelniyat protses: Myusyulmanskite obshtnosti i komunisticheskiya rezhim* (The "Revival Process." Muslim communities and the Communist regime: Policies, reactions and consequences) (Sofia: CIELA, 2008), pp. 64–86.
39. Zina Markova, "The Struggle for an Independent Church as a School for the National and Social Progress of the Bulgarian People," in *Balgariya, 681–1981* (Bulgaria) (Sofia: Izdatelstvo na Otechstveniya front, 1981), p. 221.
40. About the "Revival process" among the Bulgarian Turks, see Gruev and Kalyonski, *Vazroditelniyat protses*, pp. 131–175.
41. This part summarizes the author's research accomplished within the REVACERN project on Orthodox Christianity and pluralism (www.revacern.eu) and particularly Kalkandjieva's publication "The New Denominations Act and the Bulgarian Orthodox Church (2002–2005)," in *Religion zwischen Kirche, Staat und Gesellschaft—Religion between Church, State and Society*, Irimie Marga, Gerald G. Sander, and Dan Sandu (eds.) (Hamburg: Verlag Dr. Kovač, 2007), pp. 103–117.
42. Dilyan Nikolchev, "Zakonat za veroizpovedaniyata i Ustavat na Balgarskata pravoslavna tsarkva (normativni problem)" (The Denominations Act and the Statutes of the Bulgarian Orthodox Church [Normative issues]), in *Veroizpovedaniya i zakon: Monitoring na religioznite svobodi v Republika Balgariya* (Denominations and law: Monitoring of the religious freedoms in the Republic of Bulgaria) (Sofia: Institute of Rule of Law, 2004), pp. 210–211.
43. The effect of this text can be discovered in the decision of the minister of finances to exempt the BOC, presented by Patriarch Maxim, from VAT, while the other religious denominations were not exempted. Kalkandjieva, "The New Denominations Act and the Bulgarian Orthodox Church (2002–2005)," p. 114. See footnote 30.
44. The period of 12 centuries is estimated from 865—when the baptism of Bulgarians took place.
45. Kalkandjieva, "The New Denominations Act and the Bulgarian Orthodox Church (2002–2005)," pp. 112–113.
46. According to a document signed by Todor Zhivkov: "The nomination of Metropolitan Maxim of Lovech as leader of the Bulgarian Orthodox Church shall be proposed and supported. Comrade Mikhail Kyuchukov, Chairman of the Committee of Church Affairs at the Ministry of Foreign Relations, is assigned to prepare everything necessary for ensuring the election of Metropolitan Maxim as the patriarch of the Bulgarian Orthodox Church." TsPA, f. 1, op. 35, a.e. 2040, p. 1.

47. The impact of the restitution of church property on the fight between the Synod of Patriarch Maxim and the Alternative Synod is discussed in D. Kalkandjieva, "The New Denominations Act and the Bulgarian Orthodox Church (2002–2005)," pp. 108–110.
48. See the ECHR's judgments on the Case of the Holy Synod of the BOC (Metropolitan Inokentiy) and Others v. Bulgaria (Applications nos. 412/03 and 35677/04)—preliminary issued on January 22, 2009, and the final one issued on September 16, 2010.
49. "Izlozhenie na Sv. Sinod na BPTs vav vrazka s uchastieto na BPTs v ikumenich-estkoto dvizhenie" (Statement of the Holy Synod concerning the participation the BOC in the ecumenical movement), *Tsarkoven vestnik* (Church newspaper), No. 11, May 27, 1998. Available in Bulgarian at: http://www.pravoslavieto.com/docs/CV/ecumenism_1998-2002.htm.
50. Angel Velichkov (priest), "Prizrakat na ikumenizma" (The ghost of ecumenism), *Tsarkoven vestnik*, No. 13, 2002. http://www.pravoslavieto.com/docs/CV/ecumenism_1998-2002.htm.
51. According to media publications, Metropolitan Dometian of Vidin played a decisive role in persuading the Bulgarian patriarch to meet the pope. "The pope blessed the Bulgarians," *Standart*, May 24, 2002.
52. "Negovo Sveteyshestvo Patriarch Maksim: Slovo kam Papa Yoan Pavel II pri posesht-enieto mu v Balgariya na 24 may 2002 godina" (His Holiness Patriarch Maxim: Address to Pope John Paul II during his visit to Bulgaria on May 24, 2002), *Tsarkoven vestnik*, No. 10, 2002. Available in Bulgarian at: http://www.pravoslavieto.com/inoverie/catholicism/slovo_pMaksim.htm.
53. "Privetstveno slovo na Papa Yoan Pavel II kam Patriarkh Maksim (Sofia, 24 May 2002 g.)" (Greeting Address of Pope John Paul II to Patriarch Maxim [Sofia, May 24, 2002]), available in Bulgarian at: http://www.mediapool.bg/site/bulgaria/2002/05/24/0013.shtml.
54. "Debat na denya: Idvaneto na Papata (Sofia, 14 yuni 2002 g.)" (The Debate of the Day: The Pope's Visit [Sofia, June 14, 2002]), *Kultura* (newspaper "Culture") No. 26. June 28, 2002.
55. The anti-Catholic sentiments of Bishop Nikolay were widely discussed by the Bulgarian media after his election as metropolitan of Plovdiv in February 2007. See Diana Petrova, "Vlastta iska mir mezhdu vladikata Nikolay i katolitsite v Plovdiv" (The government calls for peace between Metropolitan Nikolay and Catholics in Plovdiv), (newspaper) *Sega*, February 12, 2007, p. 6; "Tova e pravoslaven fundamentalizam, kaza prof. Matanov" (This is Orthodox fundamentalism, said Prof. Matanov), (newspaper) *24 chasa*, February 14, 2007, p. 4; "Vladika obyavi papata za eretik" (Metropolitan declared that the Pope is a heretic), (newspaper) *Trud*, February 14, 2007, pp. 8–9.
56. Mormons and Jehovah's Witnesses (1998) were registered as legal entities in Bulgaria already in the second half of the 1990s, but the fact that they are not recognized in some European countries is used by their opponents as an argument to ban them in Bulgaria.
57. In recent years, Metropolitan Grigorii of Veliko Tarnovo pronounced many sermons against the activities of Jehovah's Witnesses in his diocese. In February 2009, the Jehovah's Witnesses filed legal complaints against the metropolitan as representative of the Bulgarian Orthodox Church, and against the political parties of VMRO and Ataka, which had objected to the building of their prayer house in the city of Gabrovo. See Tsvetomir Rusinov, "'Jehovah's Witnesses' complain before the prosecutor's office against the Bulgarian Orthodox Church, VMRO and 'Ataka,'" *Darik News*, February 26, 2009, available at: http://dariknews.bg/view_article.php?article_id=333820.
58. One of the most active bodies of the church for the fight against the NRMs is the "Sts. Cyril and Methodius" Center for Religious Studies and Consultations in Sofia (http://www.symvol.org/mm/centarreligiozni). Another is the Center for Research of New Religious Movements that organized a series of conferences aimed at revealing their totalitarian nature. See *Veroizpovedaniya i novi religiozni dvizheniya v Balgariya—problemi i perspectivi na praga na Evropeyskiya sayuz* (Religious denominations and New

religious movements in Bulgaria—problems and perspectives on the eve of its European membership), vol. 1 (Sofia: Center for Research of New Religious Movements, 2007). These conferences were attended by Friedrich Griess and other representatives of the FECRIS (European Federation of Centers of Research and Information on Sects).
59. The text of the concept for the introduction of "confessional instruction classes" is available at: http://mitropolia-varna.org/index.php?option=com_content&task=view&id=547&Itemid=27.
60. National census of 2011, available at: http://censusresults.nsi.bg/Reports/2/2/R10.aspx.
61. About the introduction of religious classes in post-Communist Bulgarian public schools, see D. Kalkandjieva, "Religious Education in Bulgaria Today," in *Religiöse Dimensionen in Schulkultur und Schulentwicklung*, Martin Jäggle, Thomas Krobath, and Robert Shelander (eds.) (Vienna: Lit, 2009), pp. 481–488.
62. Silvio Ferrari, "Nationalism, Patriotism and Religious Belief in Europe," *University of Detroit Mercy Law Review*, vol. 83 (2006), 627–628.
63. Rusi Rusev, "Zashto tryabva da se zashtitava pravoslavieto?" (Why should Orthodoxy be defended?) *Orthodoxy Bulletin*, No. 5 available at: http://www.sarakt.org/viara-bul5.html.
64. *Balgarski konsitutsii i konstitutsionni proekti* (Bulgarian Constitutions and drafts of constitutions), eds. Veselin Metodiev and Lachezar Stoyanov (Sofia: DI "D-r Petar Beron," 1990), p. 24.

4

The Search for a New Church Consciousness in Current Russian Orthodox Discourse

Anna Briskina-Müller

Background

In the course of the twentieth century, contacts between the Russian Orthodox Church (ROC) and Western Christianity, its concepts and values, took place on two levels. The first was occasioned by the emigration of Russian theologians to the West in the first decades of the century, and the second by the "invasion" of Western theological ideas into the "canonical territory" of the ROC through ecumenical contacts and the translation of theological works into Russian since the 1990s. In this context, Orthodox theologians found themselves in a twofold dialogue with the West: an encounter with "heterodoxy" (whether as part of ecumenical dialogue or in polemical opposition to it), and another with the Russian Orthodox diaspora, including such figures as Alexander Schmemann, John Meyendorff, and Metropolitan Anthony (Bloom), whose books appealed to a broad readership in Russia in the 1990s.

From the moment when Orthodox theologians ceased to ignore certain issues that were perceived as "Western" or "modernist" and began to include them in discussions and subsequently accepted the possibility of tension within their own tradition, we may speak of an emerging influence on Russian Orthodoxy of Western ideas or sentiments. These include: the Jewish-Christian dialogue and the concomitant examination of Christian anti-Semitism, or, more specifically, Orthodox liturgical anti-Judaism such as that found in the services for Holy Week; interreligious dialogue, which to date the ROC has conducted in polemical terms at best; religious and cultural pluralism and the resulting changes in missionary theology; the relationship between culture and religion, and culture and the church; the concept of suffering (one's own suffering, the suffering of the Third World, the suffering of Christian martyrs in the twentieth century); human rights (which the ROC interprets in a peculiar way); the women's question; and an emerging dialogue with the natural sciences. These and other issues have only recently become matters of theological debate in Russia.

In the West, the Orthodox Church has readily faced many of these issues. Noteworthy contributions have been made by authors such as Elisabeth Behr-Siegel[1] and her work on the ordination of women, Metropolitan Anthony (Bloom), who argued that women's ordination should be taken up not as a debate among outsiders but as *our* very own issue,[2] and Bishop Kallistos (Ware), who is becoming more and more open-minded on this issue.[3] Thomas Hopko with his book on homosexuality,[4] John and Lyn Breck with their Orthodox perspective on bioethics,[5] and Alexander Schmemann with his reflections on the relationship between Orthodoxy and the (Western) world[6] have also lent their authoritative voices to the Orthodox theological discussion in the West and young scholars have followed in their footsteps, pushing the debates forward.

There are many signs that the ROC is undergoing a theological reawakening. It has now begun to confront some questions that were ignored as "Western" until now. Clergy and laity alike are engaged in the discussions. And although this process of rethinking is far from involving the entire church community, every new wave of discussion leaves its traces: in literature, in theological and historical research, and in church communications.

In the present chapter, we will outline a few of the Orthodox debates in Russia, beginning with the most prominent one.

Rethinking the Women's Question

The women's question, which the Eastern churches are confronting today as a result of their continuing dialogue with Western Protestant churches, is at the core of many issues. It was raised by the Protestants in all of the Orthodox-Protestant dialogues. But in fact, the issue was not new to the Orthodox churches. It had been raised by Orthodox women in Greece, the United States, and France already in the 1970s, and had been given serious consideration by several Orthodox hierarchs.[7] Since that time, numerous Orthodox conferences on this issue—some attended exclusively by women—have taken place (Romania in 1976, Rhodos, Greece, in 1988, Constantinople in 1997, and Bratislava in 2007) and several publications on the issue have appeared in the Orthodox world.

The Orthodox discussion of women's issues has focused on two matters—purity regulations and the ordination of women—that have had the unintended effect of limiting women's participation in church life. In both Eastern and Western Orthodoxy, purity rules have been discussed for some time, but the issue of women's ordination has not generated the same level of interest. But the debate has now definitely arrived in Russia.

Purity Rules

To this day, church canons and Orthodox theology continue to define women as impure during menstruation and after childbirth and to exclude them from the Eucharist. In extreme cases, not rare in Russia, women are even prohibited from entering the church, although that prohibition usually applies only to touching religious objects, such as icons. While women are rarely asked directly about their state of purity, the degree of self-censorship is such that this prohibition is upheld. The *Social Doctrine of the ROC* (2000) emphasizes the natural differences between the sexes but stresses that these do not stand in the way on the path to Christ or to salvation. The issue of participation or nonparticipation of a menstruating woman in the Eucharist is not yet raised here.

It is only in the past few years that this matter has been discussed. A number of opinion pieces were published by the independent Orthodox Internet portal *Pravoslavie i mir.*[8] For example, in December 2009, the document "The place of the woman in the Orthodox church and the question of woman's ordination. Results of the inter-Orthodox Consultation"[9] was published in this website, as was the priest Andrey Posternak's "The Issue of the Priesthood of Women,"[10] and an interview by the portal's editor-in-chief, Anna Danilova, with the well-known missionary protodeacon Andrey Kurayev.[11]

A second wave in the debate was initiated in September 2010 by Sr. Vassa (Larin), an American Orthodox nun of Russian origin and staff member of the Catholic Theological Faculty at the University of Vienna, in her article "On Ritual (Im)purity. What Is It and What Is It For?"[12] Although Sr. Vassa is not a member of the ROC, her comments contributed significantly to the development of the discussion in the Russian Church, and we will briefly examine her core argument.

Sr. Vassa does not examine the women's question on the basis of sociopolitical criteria because these are not valid in the church context. Terms such as "humiliating" or "unjust" function differently in the Orthodox Church since every such form of restriction is seen as a possibility for exercising personal humility and thus has the potential for spiritual growth. The women's question thus needs to be regarded from the point of view of its anthropological content. What is the point of barring women from the Eucharist during menstruation? What does this position say about the Orthodox perspective on childbirth? Sr. Vassa begins with an examination of the concept of "impurity" on the basis of the Old and New Testaments and the works of the Church Fathers. She points out an inconsistency in the Orthodox application of purity rules, since according to Leviticus 15:19–33, it is not only a menstruating woman who is impure but anyone who touches her (Lev. 15:24). In the New Testament, Jesus does not reprimand the menstruating woman who touched him, but praises her faith and heals her (Matt. 9:20–22). St. Paul only accepts the Old Testament purity rules in the interest of Christian charity (Rom. 14). Some of the earlier Church Fathers (Methodius of Olympus, Justin Martyr, Origen) understand the ideas of "purity/impurity" as symbols of virtue and sin, and argue that baptism and the Eucharist are sufficient for the "purification" of Christians. The Didaskalia even goes so far as to forbid Christians from observing Old Testament rules including the purity rules for women, with reference to Matthew 9:20–22. The first church canon to forbid women from going to church during menstruation is Canon 2 of Dionysius of Alexandria (d. 265) from the year 262. Dionysius also argued on the basis of Matthew 9:20–22, but came to the opposite conclusion: menstruating women were to be excluded from the Eucharist because the woman did not touch Jesus himself, but only dared to touch the hem of his clothing. Dionysius interpreted this as a metaphor for exclusion from the Eucharist. St. Gregory the Great, pope of Rome (590–604), reprimands those who considered forbidding menstruating women from receiving the Eucharist. He also argues with Matthew 9:20–22. ROC practices have always been extremely severe in their observation of purity rules. Even today, the reading of the prayer on the first day after a child's birth is prescribed: one prays for the forgiveness of *all relatives*. The prayer that is read on the fortieth day (at the end of postnatal bleeding) reads: "Wash her from bodily defilement (skverna) and spiritual defilement in the completion of forty days, making her worthy of the communion of your precious body and blood." A woman is clearly considered to be *unworthy* of Communion after giving birth.

Sr. Vassa also cites other Orthodox churches that have removed such texts from their liturgical service books, for example, a decision of the Holy Synod of Antioch (1997) or the theological conference in Crete (2000), which called the church to invite women to receive the Eucharist, regardless of the time of the month.

Sr. Vassa further examines the canonical arguments and finds that while some canons are theoretically still valid, many of them have in fact fallen into obscurity. In her view, the purity rules are a fundamentally non-Christian phenomenon in the guise of Orthodox piety. Ultimately, the exclusion of women during menstruation and during postnatal bleeding reveals an inconsistency in the belief in the incarnation and redemption of Christ.

This essay elicited several responses. Fr. Sergei Sveshnikov[13] commented positively on a passage from Pope Gregory (540–604) that was quoted by Sr. Vassa, but considers the other sources to be less tolerant. He cites Romans 14:14 and Acts 15:28–29, where the Apostles warn against the consumption of blood, and then corrects himself and admits that, in this case, the reference to blood is in connection with food. But, despite that self-correction, he still argues that these biblical passages should be applied to menstrual blood as well. Such a line of reasoning becomes even less appropriate when one considers that Christians today no longer observe the Old Testament slaughtering rules and that animal blood is commonly used in food and pharmaceutical industries. Sveshnikov reviews the canons relating to women (Canon 2, Dionysius of Alexandria; Canons 6–7, Timothy of Alexandria; and Canon 18, Hippolytus) and surmises that the restrictions on receiving the Eucharist during menstruation may be explained in connection with the absence of appropriate hygiene products. He mentions Augustine's appeal to married couples to abstain from sexual relations during menstruation and his belief that abstention could sanctify a non-Christian partner and their children.[14] Taking up the idea of sanctification, Sveshnikov argues that this motif not only permeates the purity rules, but that it is a thread running through the entire fabric of Orthodox piety. If one pulls on this thread, one risks destroying the entire fabric. In fact, Augustine was referring to marital abstinence and not to abstention from Communion. Sveshnikov ends his response with a broadside against Sr. Vassa's argument that Orthodox Christians are fully cleansed in the waters of baptism and therefore no further regulations on cleanliness are necessary. Such an argument, he says, could be applied to all pious practices. Sveshnikov is concerned that any discussion of the women's question can potentially undermine Orthodox practice in its entirety.

Hegumen Iosif (Kryukov) of the ROC in the United States (patriarchal parishes of the ROC in the United States) has discussed the role of "prayers of cleansing" after the birth of a child.[15] He admits that the practice of praying for the cleansing of a woman after childbirth is a cause of unease not only for the laity, but often for the clergy too. Most commentaries on such prayers on the first and fortieth days begin with a reference to Old Testament law (Lev. 12). According to Leviticus 12, a sacrifice should be made to conclude a period of cleansing. What remains unclear for Hegumen Iosif is the nature of the sin on account of which the sacrifice is to be made. He notes that Clement of Alexandria, the Apostolic Canons, and Dionysius the Areopagite never refer to any rite of purification after the birth of a child. However, he still concludes, surprisingly, that to change something that is "in good order" is folly because it could lead to schism. In addition, the words of the Seventh Ecumenical Council remain in effect: "May those who alter church traditions—written or unwritten—be anathema."

Such argumentation is impervious to the fact that the cited traditions are themselves modifications of even more ancient church traditions. Both authors demonstrate clearly how unnecessary, inconsistent, and incomprehensible the purity rules are, and yet they still see no need to change the status quo. Their statements show that even the clergy are unsure of how to deal with the women's question in the church.

However, one Orthodox priest's reflection on Sr. Vassa's article represents a clear rejection of the purity rules. Fr. Feodor Lyudogovsky examines the fundamental underlying reasons for the canonical exclusion of menstruating women from Communion.[16] For Lyudogovsky, the prohibition is obviously a form of penance. He argues that there are three reasons why an Orthodox Christian may be prohibited from participating in Communion: moral (e.g., open hostilities with someone), disciplinary (e.g., having breakfast before the liturgy), and technical (e.g., the pathological inability to swallow or the inability to leave one's house). The attempt to include menstruation in this list raises difficulties because it does not fit anywhere. If the prohibition is to be understood in moral terms, then the processes that take place in the woman's body would have to be defined as being a priori sinful. But that would contradict the entire New Testament, in which impurity is understood as a purely ethical category (Matt. 15:17). Menstruation is sometimes interpreted as a result of the fall of man, in that it is an unrealized, or "unused," pregnancy. Following this reasoning, in order to avoid this "sin," a woman would have to become pregnant every year. Additionally, we may suppose that women who had recently given birth could not be excluded from Communion. But such is not the case. As for the second rationale for exclusion on pedagogical or disciplinary grounds, Lyudogovsky argues that it necessarily presupposes free choice: if individuals are required to "improve" their behavior, they must have the capacity to choose the good. But with menstruation, women have no choice. Sometimes the argument is made that as a result of this prohibition to take part in Communion, women are in a position to better recognize the sinfulness of human nature. But according to Lyudogovsky, this sinfulness of human nature is manifested in many ways, few of which are obstacles to Communion. And in contrast to menstruation, they always depend on a person's free will. Nor is it at all clear why only women need to be reminded of the inherent sinfulness of our nature—for half of their lifetime. The third, technical, reason for exclusion from communion has been rendered irrelevant by modern feminine hygiene products, which allow women to move freely during menstruation. For Lyudogovsky, the continued exclusion of menstruating women from Communion is unfounded.

The Ordination of Women

The issue of women's ordination has arisen in the ROC only recently. An early official response to this challenge can be found in the *Social Doctrine of the ROC* (2000). The document declares that the natural differences between the sexes have not been resolved and that the vocations of women and men cannot be considered identical. Women must first and foremost be "protected, in their role as mother." Gender-based differences do not obstruct the path to Christ or to salvation, according to the "social doctrine," but women should not imitate men's roles or try to compete with them.

Andrei Kurayev readily admits that, until about one hundred years ago, along with culture and politics, literature was dominated by men.[17] While he is referring to "literature," and not "theology," he is in fact referring to the Church Fathers. Kurayev speaks in support of women until he is asked about the ordination of women. At that point, his language changes radically: The essence of humankind, he argues, is not the struggle for rights but the exercise of duties and the church does not want to burden the (weak) shoulders of women with the (heavy) cross of ministry. The usual palette of arguments follow: the priest is the icon of Christ (a thesis that many Orthodox theologians perceive as "imposed by the West"); the Eucharist reenacts the Last Supper, at which no women were in attendance; and the priest gives the consecrated Host as a gift, and giving is an exclusively male quality (while women have the capacity to receive). His final argument is that women cannot be admitted to the priesthood for simple psychological reasons, since women have a tendency toward religious radicalism—literally: "Orthodoxy + a woman = a parish witch." It does not occur to Kurayev that this argument might just as easily disqualify many men from the priesthood.

Two related theses merge here: (a) women are lower beings than men, "helpers," created from Adam's rib, relegated to a silent role in the church, impure and mentally unstable; and (b) a little more politely but the same in its intention: women are weak and should therefore be spared.

Most often it is argued that the women's question is of Western provenance and therefore not of interest in an Orthodox context. Yet the establishment of seven sacraments is also of Western provenance. The Western origin of a custom, a rule, or tradition does not mean that it will never find resonance in the East.

Nor is the systematic exclusion of women limited to the question of priestly ordination. Even when the focus is shifted to the ordination of deaconesses, which was practiced in the early church and was never forbidden, all arguments in favor of such a practice are summarily blocked. The exclusionary practice also extends to the consecration of readers, female choir singers, and other lower church offices that do not require access to the sanctuary. Women practicing these offices receive no episcopal benediction, but only a nonliturgical blessing of the parish priest, which is understood as tacit permission.

The closing documents of the international Orthodox women's conferences all end with the recommendation that local churches rethink a number of well-established traditions, attitudes, and practices. Thus, the message has reached the ROC.[18] Whereas in the past this subject was either totally ignored or denied, after a period of highly charged polemics there are now the first signs of readiness to speak about these issues—indeed, a few Russian Orthodox theologians are even positively disposed toward them. For the ROC, the emergence of such an openness signals a very significant shift in Russian Orthodox consciousness in recent years.

Rethinking the Everyday Life of the ROC

While Feodor Dostoyevsky focused on the troubled "little man," in today's ROC there is an emerging literary reflection on the concerns of the troubled "little priest" (or "little nun" or "little church-goer" as the case may be). This reflection contains several innovations: an interest in the day-to-day lives of church people, fearless writing, and the fact that the writers are women.

Maya Kutcherskaya reflects on Orthodox life in her book *The Modern Patericon. Readings for the Desperate* (Sovremennyy paterik. Kniga dlia vpavshih v unynie,

2004). An anonymous "nun N."—possibly an abbess—author of the book *The Cry of the Third Bird* (Plach tretyey pticy, 2008) dares to describe a number of shortcomings or vices in everyday Russian Orthodox monastic life, criticizing them from a perspective of love for her church and at the same time bitterly lamenting the state of affairs. In 2007, N. had also published *Have Courage, Daughter* (Derzay, dsher'!), which cautiously but unambiguously broached the women's question in the church.

These books have been very popular among Orthodox readers and have generated considerable excitement, although not all reactions were positive. *The Modern Patericon* has been recommended reading in some monasteries, but many worldly and otherwise liberally minded priests have flatly rejected the work, arguing that as a woman Kutcherskaya does not have the right to pass judgment on the inner life of the clergy and should instead devote her attention to childbearing.

Other recent novels have focused on life inside the Orthodox Church: *The Rain God* (Bog dozhdya, 2007) by Maya Kutcherskaya, *The Cross of Flowers* (Tsvetochnii Krest, 2010) by Elena Kolyadina, and *Serafim* (2011) by Elena Kryukova. Kolyadina's 2010 Russian Booker winning novel, describing seventeenth-century Russian Orthodox life as a mixture of piety, levity, and superstition, was received by the Orthodox laity as in part a caricature of today's ROC and its priests. It is, in fact, a collective portrait of some readily recognizable Russian "young elders," a veritable plague in the ROC in the last two decades.[19] Loggin, a 21-year-old priest, falls in love with a young girl, dreams of tutoring her to sainthood, and in the end sends her to be burned as a witch. The author describes the inner turmoil of the immature priest and of his spiritual daughter, Feodosya. Classic Russian literary themes are revisited here: the inner faith of some and the spiritual blindness and arrogance of others, the religious and educational potential of women, and the ignorance of the common people. The book has generated significant interest in a public discourse that otherwise offers few alternatives to the usual fare of artificial Orthodox works on the one hand and aggressively anticlerical sound bites on the other. In the same year the author was also awarded the *Абзац* literary antiprize.[20] By ignoring, metaphorically speaking, Feodosya's cries from the flames, zealots of Orthodox purity have demanded that Kolyadina be tried for defamation of the church. But according to one literary critic, the deeper meaning cannot be ignored: Feodosya's cries are a metaphor for "our earth itself crying out as a lonely and violated woman."[21] Indeed, the metaphor may be further paraphrased: it is our church itself that is crying out. But the outcome is uncertain. Feodosya survives the fire, and the child that she had mourned reappears alive and well. Her faith is intact and her repentance and humility are pleasing to God. Loggin moves to Moscow, where he assumes a higher position.

The figures of Father Antoniy in Kutcherskaya's book and Father Serafim in Kryukova's doubt their own sermons and admit to having unorthodox thoughts. At first glance, the subjects of the two novels are similar: the unfulfilled, forbidden love of a priest and a woman from his parish. But a closer look at the figures in Kutcherskaya's novel reveals that they are driven not by love but by a nonromantic, mutual dependency. Father Antoniy and Anna are in search of worthy intellectual partners. They are lonely. The book is about the loneliness of a monastic priest working in an urban parish on the one hand, and the isolation in which the Orthodox "intelligentsia" finds itself in the process of its "in-churching" (*votserkovleniie*) on the other. The details of everyday Orthodox life are well-observed and richly narrated, as are the successive stages of in-churching. Ultimately, the chains of dependence are broken not by the priests, but by the women.

These authors demonstrate, to varying degrees, a good knowledge of clerical psychology and of the everyday life of the Orthodox faithful with all their confessions, temptations, bows, hand-kissing, fasting, exercises in humility, pilgrimages—as well as their arrogance and isolation. They force the reader to ask what the priests would be left with were they to lose all the women in their parish. These two categories of church people serve one another. The one seeks to admire and the other to be admired. Here, the women's question overlaps with the new "priest's question" and with the increasingly pressing question of the relationship between the church and the intelligentsia. Both Feodosya and Anna are portrayed as *thinking* characters.

The message of these books nevertheless remains a definite affirmation of Orthodoxy, even in its sickly state. The authors employ unadulterated irony toward Orthodox life, the clergy, and the faithful, yet they remain constant in their love for their church. This combination of irony and love not only represents a new motif in Russian literature and a new issue for Russian theology, it also marks the emergence of an entirely new attitude toward the church and of a *fundamentally new church consciousness.*

Rethinking the Twentieth-Century Martyrdom of the ROC

Within the ROC a self-critical view is gradually developing and growing regarding its form, its history, its fate, and the substance and *actual* meaning of its martyrdom in the twentieth century. Ever more voices within the church are comparing the current state of Russian Orthodoxy with the situation just before the October Revolution of 1917.

Among ecclesiastical historiographers, perhaps the most prominent is Archpriest Georgiy Mitrofanov. In 2009, he published a collection of his studies in the book *The Tragedy of Russia. "Forbidden" topics of the history of the 20th Century in Religious Preaching and Journalism* (*Tragediya Rossii. 'Zapretnye temy' istorii XX veka v tserkovnoy propovedi i publitsistike*).[22] A second collection, *The Russian Orthodox Church at the Historic Crossroads of the 20th Century* (*Russkaya pravoslavnaya Tserkov' na istoritcheskom pereputye 20 veka*) appeared in 2011.[23] Mitrofanov's core question is about the responsibility not only of those who persecuted and nearly destroyed the ROC in the twentieth century, but first of all of the shepherds and the flock—responsibility for the fact that the largest national Orthodox church with its 900-year history was almost completely destroyed in the first 20 years after the revolution, despite its membership in excess of one hundred million.

Mitrofanov's answer to the question is that the martyrdom of the ROC on such a scale was only possible because apostasy had reached such a high level. In Mitrofanov's view, the martyrdom of a church is inevitably also its fiasco.

The key question for Mitrofanov is not about the role of the ROC in the history of Russia, but about the impact of Russia's tragic twentieth-century history on the life of the ROC—both during and since the Communist era. He considers the canonization of those new martyrs and confessors, who had criticized Metropolitan and later Patriarch Sergiy (Stragorodsky's) accommodation with the Soviet regime and who broke Eucharistic communion with him. Today's ROC is the result of his conviction that the church could only be saved if it collaborated closely with the state.

While Mitrofanov does not say so directly, he implies that the new martyrs recently canonized by the ROC would break Communion today with us, just as they did in the past with Patriarch Sergiy. In order to truly venerate the new martyrs, the church should break with its "Sergianist" subservience to the very state that degraded it.

Mitrofanov also takes issue with the glorification of the suffering of these martyrs. While the immense numbers of these martyrs are a source of Russian Orthodox pride, in fact the Russian Church emerged from the sufferings of the Soviet period as a cripple. Pride in the numerical quantity of suffering is a "sign of the intensive dechristianisation of modern church consciousness." The ROC is wounded and still very deeply Soviet—its famous "sobornost" is little more than Soviet collectivism and its celebrated "humility" is Soviet subservience.

Authors like Mitrofanov, Kutcherskaya, the nun N., and publications on the women's question thus provide insights into the potential for conflict *within* the ROC. Even if the significance of these ongoing discussions should not be overstated, their increasing intensity within the church can certainly no longer be ignored. Nor are these the only questions being raised: other, equally urgent matters include a range of ethical issues (human rights, bioethics, political ethics) and internal church matters (liturgical language, the church calendar, relations with the other Orthodox churches, relations with the "heterodox," the issue of church interference in secular affairs, and the new style of the ROC under the new patriarch). The will to clarify these issues is growing, along with dissatisfaction both from within and without. Where will these sentiments lead to this time: to a new revolution, such as that of October 1917, or perhaps to a new reformation, similar to that of October 1517?

Translated by Andreas Hemming and Silvana Lindner

Notes

1. Michael Evdokimov calls her "one of the most attractive personalities in the Orthodox Church in France, and beyond that in Europe." See the preface to the posthumous English translation of some of her most important articles, *Discerning the Signs of the Times. The Vision of Elisabeth Behr-Sigel*, Michael Plekon and Sarah E. Hinlicky, eds. (Crestwood, NY: St. Vladimir's Seminary Press, 2001), p. ix.
2. "Préface du Métropolite Antoine de Souroge," *Le ministère de la femme dans l'Église* (Paris: Les Éditions du Cerf, 1987). The Russian translation appeared in 2002.
3. Kallistos Ware and É. Behr-Sigel, *L'ordination des femmes dans l'Église orthodoxe* (Paris: Les Éditions du Cerf, 1998).
4. Thomas Hopko, *Christian Faith and Same-Sex-Attraction. Eastern Orthodox Reflections* (Chesterton, IN: Conciliar Press 2006).
5. John Breck and Lyn Breck, *Stages on Life's Way. Orthodox Thinking on Bioethics* (Crestwood, NY: St. Vladimir's Seminary Press, 2005).
6. Alexander Schmemann, *Church, World, Mission. Reflections on Orthodoxy in the West* (Crestwood, NY: St. Vladimir's Seminary Press, 1979).
7. Notably by Kallistos (Ware), Bishop of Diokleia (Patriarchate of Constantinople), and by Anthony (Bloom), Metropolitan of Sourozh (Patriarchate of Moscow).
8. Orthodoxy and the World, www.pravmir.ru.
9. http://www.pravmir.ru/mesto-zhenshhiny-v-pravoslavnoj-cerkvi-i-vopros-o-xirotonii-zhenshhin/.
10. *Vopros o zhenskom sviashchenstve*, in: http://www.pravmir.ru/vopros-o-zhenskom-svyashhenstve/ (December 13, 2009).

11. "Tserkov v mire liudei. Zhenshchina v Tserkvi," published December 13, 2009, on: http://www.pravmir.ru/cerkov-v-mire-lyudej-zhenshhina-v-cerkvi/.
12. "O ritual'noi nechistote. Chto eto i zachem?" in: http://www.pravmir.ru/o-ritualnoj-nechistote-chto-eto-i-zachem/.
13. Fr. Sergei Sveshnikov (USA), "More to the Point: Should Nuns Light Their Icon Lamps?" http://www.pravmir.com/more-to-the-point-should-nuns-light-their-icon-lamps/ (May 27, 2011).
14. Sveshnikov is referring to "On Merit and the Forgiveness of Sins, and the Baptism of Infants" 3:21.
15. Igumen Iosif (Kryukov), "K ponimaniju znacheniia poslerodovykh molitv" ("Understanding the importance of postnatal prayers"), September 10, 2010, http://www.pravmir.ru/k-ponimaniyu-znacheniya-poslerodovyx-molitv/.
16. Fr. Feodor Lyudogovsky, "Pedagogika nelyubvi, ili snova o ritual'noi nechistote v khristanstve" ("The pedagogy of unlove or ritual impurity in Christianity") in: http://www.pravmir.ru/pedagogika-nelyubvi-ili-snova-o-ritualnoj-nechistote-v-xristianstve/; (May 2011).
17. See the interview with Anna Danilova, the editor-in-chief of the Internet portal *Pravoslavie i mir*, "Tserkov v mire liudei. Zhenshchina v Tserkvi," posted December 13, 2009; http://www.pravmir.ru/cerkov-v-mire-lyudej-zhenshhina-v-cerkvi/.
18. The first scholarly monograph on this issue in Russia is the collective work of three female Orthodox church historians: Elena Belyakova, Nadezhda Belyakova, and Elena Emchenko, *Zhenshchina v pravoslavii: tserkovnoe pravo i rossiyskaya praktika* (Woman in Orthodoxy: Canon law and Russian practice) (Moskva: Institut Rossiiskoy istorii Rossiiskoy Akademii Nauk, 2011).
19. With the restoration of its religious freedom after 1990, the ROC was flooded with a massive influx of new believers. Faced with an urgent need of new priests, the bishops hastily ordained devout parishioners, who were often new believers themselves. Despite their lack of formal theological training, these new priests were often imbued with monastic ideals of obedience, and their pastoral approach was quite authoritarian. In the first two post-Soviet decades many people experienced a new form of enslavement to such "spiritual fathers," and this issue is central in Kolyadina's novel.
20. The *Abzats* antiprize is awarded by the newspaper *Knizhnoe obozrenie* (Review of books) together with the General Direction of the International Book Fair to authors, translators, and editors of printed material that does not meet the standards of modern literature.
21. Tatyana Moskvina, "Dushevny krik zemli—odinokoy i opozorennoy baby," *Argumenty nedeli* (December 8, 2010).
22. For reactions, see: Igumen Petr (Meshcherinov), "Svoboda i traditsionalism. Presentatsiya knigi ottsa Georgiya Mitrofanova *Tragediya Rossii*," *Zvezda* 11 (2009), on the web portal *Zurnalny zal*: http://magazines.russ.ru/zvezda/2009/11/ro12.html. Igumen Petr (Mesherinov): krugly stol zhurnala *Kontinent* "V chem sila i slabost khristianstva?" *Kontinent* 142 (2009), http://magazines.russ.ru/continent/2009/142/hr25.html.
23. See the report on the site *Credo.ru* (this site does not belong to the ROC but to the so-called Russian Orthodox Autonomous Church) from September 22, 2011: www.portal-credo.ru/site/?act=news&id=86481.

Part II

Perceptions of the Religious Other: Difference and Convergence

5

Between Admiration and Refusal: Roman Catholic Perceptions of Orthodoxy

Thomas Bremer

The year 1054 became somehow the "official" year of the schism between the Western and the Eastern churches. However, the actual events that occurred in that year do not necessarily indicate such consequences: The Roman delegate to Constantinople, Cardinal Umberto (Humbert) a Silva Candida, excommunicated the patriarch, and subsequently he and his entourage were excommunicated by the patriarch. Umberto probably exceeded his competence. The mutual anathemas did not relate to the churches, but rather to individuals. We have evidence of communion between the Western church and single Eastern churches even after 1054.[1] In addition, this dispute affected only one autocephalous church in the East, namely, the Patriarchate of Constantinople, and did not relate to the other Eastern patriarchates (Alexandria, Antioch, Jerusalem) or to Orthodoxy in the Russian lands. Nevertheless, the relations between the Christian East and West seem to have been already heavily damaged, so that this year could become the symbolic date of the interruption of community between both traditions. Some historians consider 1204, the year of the Fourth Crusade's capture of Constantinople, as the decisive moment; others see it much earlier and perceive the coronation of Charlemagne as Western emperor in 800 by the pope as the definitive rupture between East and West.[2] In any case, in the second millennium there were very few contacts and encounters between the two sides—instead, a process was put in motion and it has certain parallels to what after the Reformation was called "confessionalization." Both traditions developed independently from each other, two distinctive "churches" evolved, the "Catholic" and the "Orthodox," each of which regarded itself as the only true church, from which the other had seceded. The Catholic side in particular developed an exclusive idea of salvation, which denied the possibility that outside its boundaries—that is, in the Orthodox Church—one could gain salvation. According to this theory, one had to become Catholic in order to be saved. Within the logic of this consideration, church unity was not to be sought through the reunification of the two churches, but in the submission of the Orthodox to the Roman Church.

This attitude and the long period of separation led to a high degree of alienation between the two churches. When contacts were reestablished in the twentieth century, there was almost no knowledge about the respective other, and prejudices prevailed. This situation changed and continues to change slowly, depending on different circumstances—whether the faithful of one of the two churches live as homogenous groups or alongside the others, whether identities are connected to national or ethnic principles, and other considerations. In each church, there is a broad range of positions, from an open-minded and full-hearted acceptance of the other to a vehement rejection of it. While there is no single, unified Orthodox (or Catholic) perception of the other church, a certain mainstream attitude may be perceived. In this chapter, we will first explore the historical development of Catholic views of Orthodoxy, and then present the current Catholic position toward the other church, which is informed by that historical development.

Historical Background

For centuries after the schism, there was almost no contact between the two sides. Greek and Southeast European Orthodoxy were gradually subsumed under the Ottoman Empire, and East Slavic Orthodoxy found itself mostly within the Muscovite Empire—both empires had only poor relations to Western countries. Communication was quite difficult between the two parts of the Mediterranean world. Travel was complicated and dangerous, letters took a long time, and the confrontation of two political systems did not favor contacts. The same was true for Central and Eastern Europe. The Muscovite, later Russian, Empire was isolated from the rest of the continent. The reports of Western envoys reveal a complete ignorance of this part of the world, and from Russia very few envoys were ever sent to the West.

If we set aside the attempts of the second Council of Lyon (1274) to come to a union with Orthodoxy, which was exclusively motivated by political reasons, we are left with only the Council of Ferrara-Florence (1438–1439) as perhaps the only significant encounter of the two churches before the twentieth century. Although that concluded union was also highly influenced by the political and military factors, the real, divisive issues between the churches were nevertheless intensively discussed. In the final agreement, the Orthodox side acknowledged the supremacy of the Roman pontiff, while the Catholic side accepted the customs and traditions of the Greeks. However, this union never came into effect, since only a few years later the Ottomans conquered Constantinople and as the grand-prince of Muscovy did not accept the union. But even without those obstacles to a new interecclesial relationship, there would still have remained many misunderstandings and divergent interpretations, as had been clear in the Florentine negotiations.

One of the consequences of this union was the perception of the "West" by the Christian East as traitors and cowards: although the Byzantine emperor had expected (and was promised) military help from the West against the Ottomans, it never arrived. Thus, Constantinople was seized in 1453, some years after the conclusion of the union. This brought the union definitively to an end, and it created an image of the West as people who would betray their Christian brothers rather than enter into a military confrontation with an enemy.

However, the Florence agreement did serve as a blueprint for further unions. The first and most important of these was the one concluded in Brest and Rome in 1595–1596. This union is still alive, and some four million Eastern-rite Catholics in Western Ukraine and in other countries trace their origins to that event. The history of the circumstances under which this union was contracted shows clearly how much it was influenced by a Roman idea of "return": since Eastern Christians had allegedly torn away from the Catholic Church, their return is the only way to restore church unity.[3] In other words, the unity of the church already exists, namely, in the Catholic Church. All other Christian communities are not churches, as there is only one church. Orthodox theology later developed similar convictions concerning its own side. There were cases in which Catholics who converted to Orthodoxy were eventually rebaptized. Although this practice must be traced back to specifics of Orthodox theology, it nevertheless shows how much the two churches changed their attitude to each other in the second millennium.

This developing idea of a "return" was supported by the events connected with the Reformation. The Catholic Church stressed more and more that there can be no salvation inside a Protestant Church; the Protestants had to come "back to Rome." This same stance was transferred to Orthodoxy, although here apostolic succession—the Catholic basis for regarding Protestant sacraments as invalid—was in place. But the unity with the Roman pontiff became the key criterion for salvation, and unity did not mean any more the concordance and mutual acknowledgment as it used to be in the first centuries of Christianity, but rather a formal subordination. Rome now demanded from Eastern and any other churches that they accept the pope's role within the Western church as valid also for the universal church. It is understandable that Eastern churches, which had never before recognized such a Roman role, were reluctant to do so now and regarded it as an illegitimate innovation.

Rome's concentration on itself had other consequences, chief among them being the idea of *praestantia ritus Latini*, the supremacy of the Latin rite. It meant that the dogmatic ideas of the Catholic Church, especially those formulated in the Council of Trent (1545–1563), which were directed against Lutheran ideas, found their best liturgical form and expression in the Latin mass. As there were Eastern churches in union with Rome, one could not say that their rites were invalid, but they were regarded as less adequate than the Latin rite. This led to a gradual Latinization of the Eastern rites in churches that were in union with Rome. Elements that came to be regarded as contrary to Catholic doctrine were deleted (above all the Creed without the Filioque), and piety in connection with the Eucharist (Eucharistic adoration, Feast of Corpus Christi, etc.) was strengthened. Thus, frequently, the respective Eastern rite became a kind of hybrid, with an Eastern form, but many Western elements included. This Latinization was also pursued in church administration, canon law, and other areas of church life. Thus, the Eastern churches were perceived as something of minor value, lacking the fullness of the Catholic (i.e., the Latin) Church, and thus needs to be perfected.

However, one also finds developments that indicate a different approach to the Eastern tradition. An important impetus came from the liturgical perspective as well: Catholic liturgical historians began to study the Eastern forms of worship and discovered their seniority and theological richness. In 1577, the Greek College of St. Athanasius was founded in Rome. It was a papal academy aimed at training priests from and for "the East," which meant at that time concretely from Greek islands under Western (Venetian, Genoese) control. Although the college was not primarily an institution for research on the Eastern tradition, it nevertheless contributed to a consciousness of the existence of an alternative tradition. The French Dominican Jacques Goar (1601–1652), a scholar of Greek who lived for a number of years on the Greek island of Chios and became interested in Eastern liturgy, returned to the West with Eastern liturgical manuscripts. In 1447, after stays in Rome and in Paris, he published his *Euchologion sive Rituale Graecorum*, an edition of the Greek text of the liturgy with a Latin translation, and with his comments.[4] He used an older printed edition of the euchologion (a priest's book of sacraments, services, and blessings) and completed it with the help of the manuscripts that he had obtained. Some years later, Eusèbe Renaudot (1646–1720), a French theologian and orientalist, used Eastern liturgies in order to show their congruence with the Latin rite and so to refute Protestant doctrines. For this purpose, he translated many texts into Latin and published them as *Liturgiarum Orientalium Collectio* in 1715–1716.[5] This collection concentrated on the Eucharistic liturgies; in the nineteenth century, Heinrich Denzinger published Latin translations of the Eastern sacramental services.

Joseph Simon Assemani (or Guiseppe Simone A., 1687–1768), a Lebanese Maronite priest who adopted the Latin rite, worked in the Vatican library and later headed it for 30 years. After two trips to the East, he brought hundreds of manuscripts to Rome and edited many of them. His nephew, Joseph Aloys Assemani (Giuseppe Luigi A., 1710–1782), also lived in Rome for most of his life and assisted his uncle in his work. From 1749 onward, he edited the *Codex liturgicus ecclesiae universae*, which was intended to collect in 15 volumes all the Western and Eastern liturgies. However, in his lifetime, only five volumes (with texts on baptism, confirmation, Eucharist, and ordination in several churches) were published.[6] Still, this work laid the foundation for later research on the Eastern liturgies in the West. Assemani, teaching liturgy in the Pontifical Academy of Theology, opened the way for a broader understanding of the variety of liturgies and of the value of the Eastern rites.

These endeavors by Latin specialists proceeded from a growing interest in the Eastern church. As mentioned, some parts of the Eastern Mediterranean with Orthodox population were under control of the Latins, and among some circles in Rome the hope arose that these areas could become Catholic (or "again Catholic"). But by studying the Eastern Christian texts, these researchers discovered in them elements of the ancient Christian heritage, which had been forgotten in the West. This, in turn, produced a hermeneutical insight: the authors came to appreciate the temporality of all kinds of texts, and therefore also of the Latin liturgy. From a scholarly interest in the liturgy there thus arose an awareness of the variety and broadness of the (old) Christian liturgy.

However, it took much more time for the Catholic Church to acknowledge the full equality of Eastern rites with the Latin rite. The *praestantia* was formulated by Pope Benedict XIV, after all these studies in Eastern liturgy, in his apostolic constitution *Etsi pastoralis* (1742). The pope stated that the Roman Church had always had the right to forbid or to change whatever was not appropriate in Eastern liturgies, since Rome was the head and the mother of all churches. The decree therefore had a strong accent on discipline and on the supremacy of the Roman Church.

It was only in the late nineteenth century that the Roman interest in the East became more open-minded. Pope Leo XIII recognized in *Orientalium dignitas* (1894) the value of the Eastern liturgical traditions and stressed the apostolic origins of the Eastern churches. Benedict XV constituted in 1917 the Congregation for the Eastern Church (since 1967, the Congregation for the Eastern Churches), which up to then had been a department in the *Propaganda Fide*, the Papal Congregation for Missions. This new congregation was in charge of matters relating to Eastern-rite Catholic Churches. In the same year, the Pontifical Oriental Institute was founded in Rome, which became a center for scientific research on Eastern Christianity. In 1929, a *dies orientalis*, that is, a day with lectures about the Eastern tradition and with an Eastern rite liturgy, was recommended for all Catholic seminaries.

This attitude changed completely with the ecumenical movement. Representatives of Orthodox churches participated in ecumenical gatherings from a very early stage, in the first years of the twentieth century. The Catholic Church officially opened itself up to ecumenical contacts with other churches in the Vatican Council II (1962–1965). With Vatican II, a new era started. Already before the council, Pope John XXIII and Ecumenical Patriarch Athenagoras exchanged courteous feast-day messages. From then on, Catholic and Orthodox representatives had frequent and regular contact. Pope Paul VI and Athenagoras met several times, as did all their successors (with the exception of Pope John Paul I who reigned for only four weeks). This process of encounters and contacts was referred to as a "dialogue of love," and when an official joint theological commission was formed in order to discuss the questions in which both churches had dissent, it was known as a "dialogue of truth." Many signs of better relations could be seen, like mutual visits, exchange of students, cooperation at the parish level, and so on. However, in some areas—after decades of silence—the situation remained problematic, and progress was very slow. But in general, more than ever in the almost one thousand years of separation contacts were established and maintained.

This real paradigm shift that Vatican II introduced is evident in two documents: *Orientalium Ecclesiarum*, on the Catholic Eastern churches, and the decree on Ecumenism *Unitatis redintegratio*, which developed an extensive discussion of the Orthodox churches.[7] For the first time, Orthodox churches were recognized as churches, and not as mere groups of (erring) individuals, as had been the case in the past. The dignity of their heritage was underlined, and the council stated that the Catholic Church was not Catholic in the full sense without the liturgical and theological traditions of the East.

The development of the Catholic attitude toward Eastern Christianity shows how much it was dependent on church politics and on the idea of achieving church unity through unions. As long as this idea prevailed, the Christian East was not seen on the same level, but rather as an area of future subordination to Rome. It was above all the consciousness of historical development, an outcome of liturgical research, which led to an acknowledgment of the Eastern traditions. But only in the twentieth century, with Vatican II, this had concrete consequences: it was in the general framework of the opening up of the Catholic Church, when the East came to be seen, at least theoretically, on equal terms.

Another point that becomes evident is that the study of history, as in the case of Eastern liturgical scholarship, leads to an appreciation of diversity. The scholarly study of liturgical history produced an understanding that the traditions were many and various, and that they were historically determined. This necessarily led to a relativization of the Roman tradition. This development hints at the phenomenon that closed ideational systems are always endangered in their identity when a historical perspective is adopted.

The Present Situation

On an official level, the current relationship between the Roman Catholic Church and Orthodoxy is described as one between "Sister Churches,"[8] and the official contacts between them have an explicitly ecumenical character, that is, they aim at a reconciliation and eventual reunification, but without subordination. The notion of a priority of one tradition over another has been set aside. They understand each other as quite close, especially since they both refer to the old tradition of the undivided church, and they claim to have many key elements in common, but which they do not share with other Western churches—such as a sacramental understanding of church ministry, the exclusive transfer of ministry by a bishop, and the exclusion of women from the priesthood. On this, the proximity of Catholic and Orthodox positions is clear. Another area of agreement is frequently cited—namely, the attitude to the modern world, to secularity, and to the pluralism that accompanies modernity. It is primarily the representatives of the Russian Orthodox Church (ROC) who claim this common position of the two churches. In many cases, this refers to questions of ethics, such as the attitude toward homosexuality. The ROC argues that in a world that is hostile to traditional values and to Christianity, the Catholic and Orthodox Churches are the only ones that resist the growing secularism and that form a stable rock in a churning sea of liberalism, subjectivism, and relativism. Even the Protestant Churches are thought to have given in to these challenges and adapted to the modern world, which ROC representatives see not only as non-Christian, but as hostile to Christianity.[9]

There were and still are tendencies within the Roman Catholic Church to accept such a view, for historical reasons: in light of a deteriorated relationship over the last two decades, such an approach was seen by Catholic representatives as an opportunity to reestablish contacts with Orthodoxy. On the eve of his election as Pope Benedict XVI, in his sermon at the opening mass of the 2005 conclave, Cardinal Joseph Ratzinger made a statement that reflects this vision of the world.[10] In the ROC, it is Patriarch Kirill himself and Metropolitan Ilarion, the chairman of the Department for Foreign Church Relations, who advance such opinions.

One could argue that, in the background of these deliberations, there is an ambiguous stance toward modernity. Is the modern world an environment that is hostile toward Christianity and against which Christianity must arm itself, or should the modern world be viewed as the context of the existence of Christianity today? The Catholic Church expressed its position regarding this question in Vatican II, when it accepted the correlation with the world, that is, with everything that is not the church. The famous Council document *Gaudium et Spes* begins with the words: "The joys and the hopes, the griefs and the anxieties of the men of this age, especially those who are poor or in any way afflicted, these are the joys and hopes, the griefs and anxieties of the followers of Christ."[11] This is a clear indication that the

Catholic Church does not regard the world, "the men of this age," as something alien, but rather that it sees a strong connection between the fate of the world and the church. This does not mean that the church accepts all aspects of modernity, but it does recognize the relevance of the contemporary world for the church—by the way, this is something that has always been the case in the course of history. All church decisions and formulations have been influenced by the respective context, and there is no absolute expression of the faith, which would be valid independently from historical circumstances. But now, the Catholic Church expressly acknowledged this dependence of many church decisions and positions upon historical circumstances and—in a certain sense—their relativity.

Nevertheless, the position of the ROC described earlier finds agreement among Catholic leaders. Some used this as an opportunity to renew contacts with Orthodoxy, while others are deeply convinced that Christianity, and especially the Catholic Church, are under threat by the secular world, and they share the opinion of the ROC representatives. Thus, there is no Catholic unanimity on this question: there are Catholic supporters of both orientations and they preclude a single official line. In order to understand the Catholic Church's attitude toward Orthodoxy, it is necessary to distinguish among several approaches.

It is interesting to note that the position depends to a certain degree on the convictions in church politics that a particular person holds. Theologians and church leaders, who are more open-minded and who accept the statement of the Vatican Council quoted earlier as decisive for the Catholic Church today, will tend to be more open with regard to Orthodoxy. They would accept the Orthodox Church as a "sister Church" in similar circumstances, yet they would not favor an isolation of the churches from society. Instead, they would seek ways to express Christian views and values to the modern world. Representatives of such positions are frequently also critical toward attempts within the Catholic Church to address the challenges of modernity with retrospective answers. They advocate the development of the church in dynamic interaction with its social context.

On the other hand, conservative Catholics tend to accept Orthodoxy on the basis of its critique world, rather than on the basis of theological agreement. For them, the Orthodox Church has not given in to negative developments in modern society but resists them. They feel that the Catholic Church should adopt a similarly critical stance toward the modern world. Often they are also critical of phenomena within the Catholic Church that they regard as detrimental, above all in the realm of liturgy. Some of them, in extreme groups, even contest the significance of Vatican II.[12]

That means that the perception of Orthodoxy by the Catholic Church is much more dependent from the position of a person within the broad spectrum of the Catholic Church than from other convictions or arguments. This can be seen in several fields that will be presented in this chapter. The attitude toward modernity seems to play the decisive role. This has many implications, and it sheds new light on the question of church unity and division: in fact, there is not only a split between churches, but also, perhaps even deeper, between the different wings of a church. Christians from different churches who agree on certain questions may feel a greater affinity among themselves than with fellow Orthodox or Catholics, whose opinions they do not share. This complicates the discourse about the relationships between churches.

There are other issues on which the Eastern and Western traditional perspectives differ, and they serve as an occasion for Catholics to address internal problems and issues. One of these is clerical celibacy. While the Catholic Church ordains only unmarried men to the priesthood, who after ordination cannot enter into a marriage, most priests in the Orthodox Church are married. It becomes more and more problematic to find candidates who are prepared to remain unmarried in order to become priests. Sometimes, in internal Catholic discussions of the issue, the Orthodox Church is cited as an example. But here too, there is some diversity of opinion. Catholics who regard clerical celibacy as an advantage or even as a prescription, from which the church cannot or must not deviate, do not view the Orthodox model favorably; but those who argue that compulsory celibacy for Catholic priests hinders the church in its development, and that it should be abolished, see Orthodoxy as an example of fidelity to the ancient Christian practice, which included a married priesthood. This internal debate has shaped the Catholic stance toward the Eastern church and its traditions.

Another internal Catholic discussion concerns the celebration of the mass. In the wake of Vatican II, the Roman rite was reformed, and an important element of that reform has been the introduction of the vernacular language in place of Latin. In Orthodoxy, the texts and prayers said during the liturgy have not been changed for many centuries, and there is no possibility for variation (i.e., the priest cannot formulate prayers by himself). Liturgy is usually celebrated in an ancient form of the local language; especially in Russia, it is not the vernacular that is used, but Old Slavonic, which can hardly be understood by many believers. Such practices are favored by critics of the reformed mass in the Western church. For them, sacred functions require a language other than the secular form of everyday communication and, out of respect for that sanctity, ritual texts cannot be subject to change. Similar arguments are made concerning the direction of celebration, that is, whether the priest usually stands facing the congregation, or toward the East, with his back to the congregation, which was the Catholic practice prior to the reforms, and which remains in Orthodox practice today.

Beyond the areas of discipline and liturgy, there are also theological elements (in a more narrow sense) that make Orthodoxy attractive for some Catholics. One of the most prominent of these is the Orthodox model of the church, which appears to be an alternative to Roman centralism. For many Catholic theologians, the question of papal supremacy, and above all the problem of how the latter is concretely realized in modern Catholic church life, presents a great challenge. These theologians see the Orthodox model as a way of preserving traditional ecclesiastic structures, but at the same time providing more autonomy to local churches. Therefore, they appraise Orthodox ecclesiology as a means by which the Catholic Church could potentially overcome its centralized structure, which became especially significant since the eighteenth century, and which has been reinforced in recent decades. Interestingly, this positive attitude has little to do with the real life of the Orthodox Church. The reality is far from homogenous; and, in some local Orthodox churches, the patriarch plays a central role and all important decisions are ultimately his. Other local churches try to include the faithful as much as possible in decision-making, whether through synods or other structures. In the end, the Orthodox Church is quite focused on its (higher) clergy, and it is doubtful whether this reality would be accepted by Catholics as a viable alternative if it were understood more accurately. But in any case, the theological theory serves as a positive paradigm for a Catholic alternative.

This interest in Orthodoxy concentrates more on theology and theory and less on practice. To a certain degree, it may be seen as a parallel to the interest in earlier epochs in the Eastern liturgy: it serves for a better understanding and eventual changing of one's own practice. The perception of Orthodoxy, therefore, is pragmatic, in that it is oriented toward one's own tradition and aimed at its improvement.

The same holds true for other areas of Roman Catholic interest in Eastern Christianity. A vast field is what may be referred to as spirituality. The Eastern Christian spiritual approach is highly esteemed in the Christian West. This can be seen in areas like the piety toward icons, prayer practices (especially the so-called prayer of the heart, or Jesus prayer), and the experiential dimension of the liturgy. The perception of Russian piety predominates, much more than Greek or Oriental piety. In the Greek tradition, it is Mount Athos, the famous "monastic republic" on a Greek peninsula, that occupies the center of attention. The monastic tradition introduced the significance of the "Elder" (Greek: *geron*, Russian: *starets*), a monk (or a nun) with spiritual expertise and experience who advises younger monks (or nuns) in matters of their inner development. In Russia, these "elders" were frequently asked for advice and counseling by laypeople who came to talk with them or who corresponded with them. The famous nineteenth-century Russian work titled *The Way of a Pilgrim*, which describes the Prayer of the Heart and the author's relationship with his spiritual elder, is an indication of the significant influence of the Eastern Christian tradition on Western Christians. Translated into all the major Western languages, its prominent mention in J. D. Salinger's short story *Franny* (in his 1961 collection, *Franny and Zooey*) also introduced it to people who had no previous interest in Eastern spirituality.

This tradition of spiritual fathers (and also, though quite rarely, mothers) was diminished, but did not cease in Russia during the Soviet period. Nowadays, it is disputed in Russian Orthodoxy, since several monks and priests abused their position and exercised very strong control over people who had approached them for advice. But there are still many Orthodox who would not undertake a major endeavor without the "blessing," or permission, of their spiritual father. Interestingly, this aspect of the phenomenon does not have a very strong echo in the Western world. Westerners may understand the significance of such a method of counseling, but would not accept it as helpful for themselves.[13] Above all, there seems to be a fundamental difference in the understanding of the autonomy of the individual. Most people in Western societies would not accept that their decisions should require someone else's approval. Obviously, the influence of modernity with all its consequences, such as individualism and autonomy, has had its effect. If this is true, it may be an inevitable process, which will also take place in Russia and, in the long term, move Orthodox believers toward more autonomous relationships with their spiritual leaders.

The significance of this kind of interest can be seen in the high volume and popularity of books published and sold on spiritual topics in the West, and in related activities, such as seminars, courses, and so on. Obviously, Western Christians feel a kind of longing for circumstances in which the spiritual aspect of life plays a much more important role and which they expect to find in Eastern Christianity. But this also suggests that there is generally little knowledge of Orthodoxy within the Catholic Church. Most Catholics worldwide have little or no contact with the Orthodox, and their knowledge of Orthodox church life is often limited to vague ideas. On the other hand, while the Catholic Church presents itself as a Western, Latin Church, it in fact neglects the existence of the Eastern Catholic Churches, within its own East-West framework. In the general perception of Catholics and non-Catholics, Catholicism is a Western phenomenon; the Eastern Catholic Churches do not play a significant role, whether inside the Catholic Church or in external perceptions.

It is interesting to note that such activities and perceptions take place on an informal level—they have no parallel at the level of church leaders or in the official theological dialogue. In the West, a few private initiatives began to concentrate on spiritual exchange. At the monastery in Bose, Italy,[14] the community started with the study of ancient Christian traditions and came to an appreciation of Orthodoxy. For several years, the monastery has organized annual conferences on Orthodox spirituality, which attract hundreds of participants, among them bishops, monks, and theologians from Orthodox Churches. Even high-ranking hierarchs attend this event, which therefore also becomes a forum for informal interchurch contacts. In addition, there are several Catholic monasteries in Western countries that observe the Eastern tradition in liturgy and discipline.[15]

On an official level, the Catholic Church has reacted in several ways to the rapprochement toward Orthodoxy. As mentioned earlier, Vatican II was a turning point in many respects, including ecumenism. In its document on ecumenism, *Unitatis Redintegratio*, the council stated that there is a complementarity between Eastern and Western church structures and theological mind systems.[16] This opened the way to a recognition of the value of the Eastern tradition. Pope John Paul II coined the phrase "the two lungs," with which the church should breathe, meaning that it is insufficient to rely only on Western tradition.[17] This expression is quoted frequently and can relate not only to the variety of (Eastern and Western) traditions within the Catholic Church, but also to the need of ecumenical cooperation between the Catholic and Eastern Churches. But there is no clarity about whether this metaphor is more supportive of ecumenical contacts with Orthodoxy or of a strengthening of the Eastern tradition within the Catholic Church.

On the Russian Orthodox side, there is a visible interest to come into closer contact with the Catholic Church. This has to be seen in the context of the perception of the "rotten West," which is predominant in the ROC. Its leading representatives speak about a "strategic alliance" between the Roman Catholic and the Orthodox Church. The background of this proposal is the conviction that an agreed, joint Catholic-Orthodox position on theological issues is unrealistic; ecumenical negotiations and talks will not overcome the theological differences between the two sides. Instead, the churches should struggle together in order to resist the spiritual and societal development in Europe, which the Russian Church regards as detrimental. In the eyes of Russian Orthodoxy, the Roman Catholic Church seems to be the only Christian church that supports such views. This can clearly be seen in the statement of Metropolitan Ilarion, the head of ROC's influential Department for External Church Relations, to the Synod of (Catholic) Bishops in Rome in October 2012:

> I would like to use this opportunity to call my brothers in the Catholic Church to create a common front in order to defend Christian faith in all those countries where it is being marginalized and persecuted. In Europe and America we are witnessing growing pressure from those representatives of militant secularism and atheism, who are attempting to expel Christianity from the public sphere, to ban Christian symbols, to destroy traditional Christian understanding of the family and marriage as a union between a man and a woman, of the value of human life from inception till natural death.[18]

This quotation shows a very biased attitude toward the contemporary situation in the world, and it also shows the solution that Metropolitan Ilarion proposes to the Catholic Church, namely, "to create a common front." The use of military terms such as "alliance," "front," and "struggle" is very telling about how the ROC sees the situation.

How did the Catholic Church respond to this offer? On the one hand, with great openness, partly because it came at a time when the relations between Russian Orthodoxy and Rome were very poor. In February 2002, the Vatican announced that it would found a Catholic "church province" Russia, with four dioceses into which the former "Apostolic Administrations" were transformed. This elicited angry reactions from the Orthodox and led to a significant deterioration of relations.[19] So, when the Orthodox Church came with an offer for cooperation, many Catholic representatives welcomed it as an opportunity to restore contacts with Moscow.

At the same time, other Catholic voices were more reserved. They felt that the ROC's position excluded the Protestant Churches, and implied a negation of all previous ecumenical efforts and accomplishments. It appeared that, for the Orthodox, many ecumenical achievements were invalidated by more recent developments in Protestantism, especially the ordination of women to ministry and the acceptance of homosexuality—whether in the form of blessing same-sex partnerships, or in the consecration of gay ministers. In contrast, the Catholic Church was able to treat differences in ethical positions as separate from ecumenical relations with the Protestants. In the Catholic view, ethical differences should not overshadow an overriding common ground on central principles of Christianity, and they certainly do not terminate ecumenical relations. Catholics would not want to set aside important theological agreements reached in the past, such as the joint Catholic-Lutheran statement on justification, which put to rest the issue that had sparked the Reformation. Thus, for some Catholic representatives, neglecting those achievements seemed too high a price to pay for rapprochement with Russian Orthodoxy.

In the end, Catholic-Orthodox relations were reestablished. The churches now undertake official contacts on different levels. Yet there is a continuing misperception, on which neither side has reflected sufficiently. Although on the surface friendly relations do exist, the attitudes toward modernity have not yet been adequately clarified. The ROC is quite clear on this question, but within the Catholic Church there are different tendencies. This difference does not hinder the dialogue, but its closer examination must be seen as an underlying precondition of any fruitful contacts between the churches—if it were to remain unaddressed, it could give rise to some serious difficulties in the future.

Conclusion

What can we conclude about Roman Catholic perceptions of Orthodoxy? We propose the following observations:

- "The" Catholic Church is not a monolithic or unanimous entity. It consists of a broad variety of different traditions, standpoints, and views. Any attempt to define "the official position" of the Catholic Church toward Orthodoxy must inevitably face internal tensions and contradictions: even as the Catholic Church pursues official theological dialogue with the Orthodox, it continues to affirm that it is the only "true" church. Some Catholic statements on the significance of the notion of "sister churches" seem to contradict others. Moreover, the idea that there is a unified, central institution in Rome that coordinates all actions and statements of the whole Catholic Church is far from reality.
- The Eastern tradition is highly esteemed by the Roman Church—at least according to what is said. But it is not at all clear whether this high regard applies to Orthodoxy, or to the Eastern-rite Catholic Churches (the Greek Catholic or "uniate" Churches). There is no unequivocal Catholic position on this. The Eastern Catholic Churches belong to the Catholic Church and therefore enjoy the solidarity and support of Rome, but they are also frequently regarded as obstacles in ecumenical relations toward Orthodoxy. On this question, two principles of the Catholic Church seem to contradict each other. The background of this contradiction is a completely different understanding of church unity between Rome and basically all other churches.
- The Orthodox Church is mainly perceived as something that is strange, but attractive, and about which little is known. The strongly mystical attitude, which Western Christians attribute to Orthodoxy, appears to indicate that they miss this dimension in their own church. In that way, they may be idealizing something that may not exist at all in Orthodoxy, but which is merely a projection.
- There is also an interest in theology and even in church politics in the background. For Catholics who have a more critical approach toward their own church, Orthodoxy seems to present an attractive alternative that avoids some of the shortcomings that they perceive in their own church, but which preserves the traditional understanding of what church is. In a certain way, there is a parallel to Catholic individuals interested in Eastern spirituality: they tend to see something in Orthodoxy that they miss in their own Catholic Church, but which they feel could enrich the Catholic Church. Sometimes they may have a "romantic" idea of what they are seeking in Orthodoxy. Nevertheless, this phenomenon indicates a perceived lack in the Catholic tradition.
- Finally, if we challenge the idea of "the" Catholic or "the" Orthodox Church, then we must also question the perception that there are clear borderlines between the churches. In many cases, we have overlapping and unclear

identities. We should consider that our ideas of boundaries between churches are mostly a construction, which does not necessarily correspond to reality. Every contact of one church with another changes both of them. Imagining church boundaries in traditional terms is not helpful for analyzing inter-church contacts in modernity.

Notes

1. An example: The "Translation of the Relics of Saint Nicholas from Myra to Bari" is an Orthodox feast that is especially celebrated in Slavic Orthodoxy. This translation took place in 1087—it was originally a feast in the West, and was introduced in Russia after 1054.
2. See John Meyendorff, *The Orthodox Church. Its Past and Its Role in the World Today* (Crestwood: St. Vladimir's Seminary Press, 1996), p. 37.
3. There is an abundant literature on this union. Some years ago, an attempt was made to shed light on the union by Catholic, Orthodox, and Greek Catholic scholars from several countries. The results of this research project are published in: *Internationales Forschungsgespräch der Stiftung Pro Oriente zur Brester Union. Erstes Treffen: 18.-24. Juli 2002*, ed. by Johann Marte (= Das Östliche Christentum. N.F. 54) (Würzburg: Augustinus, 2004); *Internationales Forschungsgespräch der Stiftung Pro Oriente zur Brester Union. Zweites Treffen: 2.-8. Juli 2004*, ed. by Johann Marte (= Das Östliche Christentum. N.F. 56) (Würzburg: Augustinus, 2005); *Die Brester Union. Forschungsresultate einer interkonfessionellen und internationalen Arbeitsgemeinschaft der Wiener Stiftung PRO ORIENTE*, ed. by Johann Marte (= Das Östliche Christentum. N.F. 58) (Würzburg: Echter, 2010).
4. It was reprinted after the Venice 1720 edition in Graz, 1960.
5. Several reprints, available online at http://www.hathitrust.org/.
6. Ibid.
7. All of these documents are readily available at the Holy See's website: http://www.vatican.va/archive/hist_councils/ii_vatican_council/.
8. Thomas Bremer, "Schwesterkirchen—im Dialog? Erfolge und Rückschritte in den orthodox-katholischen Beziehungen seit 1965," in *Die Wiederentdeckung der communio*, Johannes Oeldemann (ed.) (Würzburg: Der Christliche Osten, 2006), pp. 55–80.
9. Numerous statements outlining these positions, mostly by Metropolitan Ilarion and Archpriest Vsevolod Chaplin, may be found on the various websites of the ROC, including http://www.patriarchia.ru/ and http://www.mospat.ru/.
10. http://www.vatican.va/gpII/documents/homily-pro-eligendo-pontifice_20050418_en.html: "How many winds of doctrine have we known in recent decades, how many ideological currents, how many ways of thinking. The small boat of the thought of many Christians has often been tossed about by these waves—flung from one extreme to another: from Marxism to liberalism, even to libertinism; from collectivism to radical individualism; from atheism to a vague religious mysticism; from agnosticism to syncretism and so forth."
11. http://www.vatican.va/archive/hist_councils/ii_vatican_council/documents/vat-ii_const_19651207_gaudium-et-spes_en.html (October 15, 2012).
12. One example is the "Society of St. Pius X," which refutes many decisions of Vatican II, maintaining that they contradict Catholic tradition.
13. I used to tell my students the story of a young Orthodox theologian whom I met; when I asked him whether after finishing his studies he would be a priest, a monk, or a layman, he said "I do not know yet, my bishop will decide." Western students react with astonishment and incomprehension when they hear this story.
14. See http://www.monasterodibose.it/index.php?lang=en.

15. They include the monasteries of Chevetogne (Belgium), Niederaltaich (Germany), and several others in North America.
16. See *Unitatis Redintegratio*, 17: "What has just been said about the lawful variety that can exist in the Church must also be taken to apply to the differences in theological expression of doctrine. In the study of revelation East and West have followed different methods, and have developed differently their understanding and confession of God's truth. It is hardly surprising, then, if from time to time one tradition has come nearer to a full appreciation of some aspects of a mystery of revelation than the other, or has expressed it to better advantage. In such cases, these various theological expressions are to be considered often as mutually complementary rather than conflicting." (http://www.vatican.va/archive/hist_councils/ii_vatican_council/documents/vat-ii_decree_19641121_unitatis-redintegratio_en.html)
17. The famous scholar of Syriac studies Sebastian Brock has challenged this metaphor, as it neglects the third tradition, the Syriac one: Sebastian Brock, "The Syriac Orient: A Third 'Lung' for the Church?" *Orientalia Christiana Periodica* 71 (2005), 5–20.
18. See http://mospat.ru/en/2012/10/17/news73157/.
19. For a more detailed discussion, see Thomas Bremer, "Rome and Moscow, A Step Further," *Religion in Eastern Europe* 23:2 (2003), 1–11.

6

Apostolic Continuity in Contradiction to Liberalism? Fields of Tension between Churches in the East and the West

Dagmar Heller

"We ask you, do not trouble us any more and any longer to write or send anything about these issues…Go now your way! Don't write us any more about dogmas, but only for the sake of friendship, if you so desire."[1] With these words, the Ecumenical patriarch ended his correspondence with Protestant theologians at the University of Tübingen in the sixteenth century. Doctrinal differences between Eastern Orthodox and Western churches thus are nothing new. But it was only in the twentieth century that official and sustainable dialogues were taken up in the framework of the ecumenical movement. These dialogues are taking place in multilateral as well as in bilateral settings, either on an international, regional, or local level.

On the international, multilateral level the encounter between Eastern and Western churches takes place mainly in the framework of the World Council of Churches (WCC). In the history of the WCC, a number of specific difficulties between the two have become evident. In 1902, when Ecumenical Patriarch Joachim invited the views of other Orthodox churches on the pursuit of closer relations with Catholics and Protestants, he already knew about the difficulties in such relationships. He referred to the

> unbroken persistence of these Churches in doctrines on which, having taken their stand as on a base hardened by the passage of time, they seem quite disinclined to embark on a path to union, as is demonstrated by evangelical and historical truth; nor do they evince any readiness to do so, except on terms and bases on which the desired dogmatic unity and fellowship is unacceptable to us.[2]

This statement indicates the incompatibility of distinct understandings of unity and the methods of achieving it, an issue that remains unresolved to this day. The core of the problem was expressed in later Orthodox statements, such as the Statement of the Orthodox delegation at the first World Conference on Faith and Order in 1927 in Lausanne, Switzerland: "We Orthodox cannot conceive of a united Church in which some of its members would hold that there is only one source of divine revelation, namely Holy Scripture alone; but others would affirm that apostolic tradition is the necessary completion of Holy Scripture."[3] The statement went on to emphasize that unity is necessarily related to the "totality of faith."[4] And in 1952, an encyclical of the Ecumenical Patriarchate affirmed that common worship services with heterodox "are contrary to the sacred canons."[5]

While difficulties and tensions have existed since the beginning of the modern ecumenical movement, the difficulties in the relationship between the Orthodox and Western members of the WCC in 1998 reached a point where the fellowship was in danger of being broken. Two Orthodox member churches had left the WCC prior to the eighth Assembly in Harare, Zimbabwe, in 1998. The remaining Orthodox churches then called for a special commission to work on reform proposals for the WCC, in order to prevent any further withdrawals of Orthodox churches. One reason for such a proposal was the perception that the Orthodox position had become more of a minority position within the WCC, and that the Orthodox felt attitudes and teachings contrary to their own, particularly on the ordination of women and on homosexuality, were being imposed on them. In addition, some influential Orthodox circles—referring to canons of the early church[6]—began to voice the opinion that the Orthodox could not pray together with non-Orthodox.[7] This created considerable pressure for ecumenically active Orthodox Church leaders. A Special Commission on Orthodox Participation in the WCC was subsequently established, and its work revealed ecclesiological issues at the root of the difficulties.

On the different bilateral levels, the true picture becomes even more complex: an important element between East and West has always been the relationship of the Orthodox Church with the Roman Catholic Church. This relationship became increasingly difficult after the end of the Cold War. One of the issues was the conflict over Greek Catholic Church properties in Ukraine and in other Eastern European countries. This church had lost its properties in the Soviet period to the Russian Orthodox Church (ROC) and had suffered the persecution of its clergy. While the problem of union with Rome from their beginning in the sixteenth century was interpreted as proselytism by the Orthodox, the revival of Uniate churches after 1990 also revived this conflict.[8] At the same time, the Roman Catholic Church established new dioceses in Russia, which the Moscow Patriarchate also interpreted as proselytism. While other Orthodox churches did not express themselves as critically as the Moscow Patriarchate, they generally shared the same concerns about proselytism. This created a deep crisis in the official international dialogue between the Roman Catholic Church and the Orthodox Church and led to an interruption of the meeting in Baltimore in 2000.[9] Resumed in 2006, this dialogue is currently discussing the primacy of Rome.[10]

Numerous bilateral dialogues between Orthodox and Protestant churches exist on international and national levels: with Old Catholics and the Orthodox since 1871[11]; with the Anglicans since 1973[12]; with the Lutheran World Federation since 1981[13]; and with the World Alliance of Reformed Churches since 1988.[14]

At the same time, several bilateral Orthodox-Protestant dialogues were taken up on national and regional levels. The Protestant Church in Germany (EKD) has engaged in dialogue with the ROC since 1959; with the Patriarchate of Constantinople since 1969; and with the Romanian Orthodox Church since 1979. The Church of Finland has been in dialogue with the ROC since 1989.[15] The Community of Protestant Churches in Europe (CPCE) has held a series of dialogue sessions in recent years with representatives of Orthodox member churches of the Conference of European Churches.[16]

These dialogues and their particular meetings are not the only mode of encounter and cooperation. Most of the dialogues are accompanied by other activities and events, such as partnerships between congregations of dioceses and mutual visits at various occasions.

The dialogues between the Orthodox and Western churches were successful to the extent that both sides got to know each other better and established permanent relations. In particular, the dialogue with the Old Catholics dealt systematically with all dogmatic questions and is the only dialogue that was officially completed. However, the respective churches have not yet implemented its recommendations, mainly because some Old Catholics introduced the ordination of women, which is unacceptable to the Orthodox. The same issue became a stumbling block in Orthodox-Anglican relations. Although that dialogue has continued, it is clear that this issue is a major point of divergence. The dialogues with Lutherans from the outset looked at the differences on matters such as scripture and tradition, soteriology (justification and sanctification), and ecclesiology. In the dialogue between EKD and the ROC over the last years, the issue of human rights came to the forefront. Further evidence that this is a crucial issue for Protestant-Orthodox relations was the Moscow Patriarchate's 2008 statement on human rights,[17] which sparked controversy and drew responses from the CPCE and from theologians from diverse denominations.

In the following section, I propose to expand on this rough sketch of the relations between Eastern and Western churches by analyzing more closely the main fields of tensions that exist and the arguments for the different positions. The central themes may be divided into four groups: (1) ecclesiological issues (common prayer, ordination of women) and (2) moral-ethical issues (human rights, homosexuality). These first two themes lead to the next (3) how the churches relate to the developments in the contemporary world and to secularization. And finally, (4) the recurring and particularly challenging issue of proselytism is presented separately.

Ecclesiological Issues

Common Prayer

Common prayer, which had been mentioned in previous Orthodox documents,[18] became a source of internal tensions within the WCC in 1998. During the work of the Special Commission on Orthodox Participation in the WCC, it became clear that behind the question of prayer there was a deeper, ecclesiological issue: for the Orthodox, worship can only be conducted by the church. If the WCC organizes worship services, it pretends to be a church, even a superchurch. The fear that the WCC could become a superchurch has been expressed by Orthodox churches ever since the foundation of the WCC. Therefore, the Central Committee of the WCC at its meeting in Toronto in 1951 made clear that the WCC was not and never should become a superchurch.[19] The Special Commission wanted to find a way to demonstrate this in the worship services at the WCC's assemblies and related events. With that purpose in mind, new language was introduced that referred to "inter-confessional prayer" and "confessional prayer,"[20] thus avoiding the term "worship."

Behind the question of common worship, the ecclesiological issue arises from the fact that in the fellowship of the WCC the Orthodox are members together with other churches, which they do not recognize as churches. The Special Commission stated that there are two basic types of

> ecclesiological self-understandings, namely of those churches (such as the Orthodox) which identify themselves with the One, Holy, Catholic and Apostolic Church, and those which see themselves as parts of the One, Holy, Catholic and Apostolic Church. These two ecclesiological positions affect whether or not churches recognize each other's baptism as well as their ability or inability to recognize one another as churches. They also affect the way churches understand the goal of the ecumenical movement, its instruments—including the WCC and its foundational documents.[21]

For the first type of church, it is difficult to recognize others as churches. The fact that the mutual recognition of churches was not a condition for membership in the WCC had made it possible for the Orthodox to become members. It was the first time in history that the idea of "bringing others back into my church" was set aside as an acceptable model of unity. But such a situation could not remain without problems in the long run: for how indeed would it be possible to work toward the unity of churches, if some do not recognize others as churches? The matter of recognition will likely remain a source of tension as long as the Orthodox do not clarify among themselves which ecclesiological status they attribute to Protestant churches.

Women's Ordination

The issue of women's ordination led to a deterioration, especially in Anglican-Orthodox relations: in 1977

> a thunderstorm broke out presaging the onset of a "winter." For the Orthodox members realised with regret that the ordination of women was "no longer simply a question for discussion but an actual event in the life of some Anglican churches" and asked themselves "how it will be possible to continue the dialogue, and what meaning the dialogue will have in these circumstances."[22]

The main differences in this matter were expressed in the report of the 1978 Conference at Mont Pendeli, Athens, where the Orthodox side said:

> We see the ordination of women not as part of the creative continuity of tradition, but as a violation of the apostolic faith and order of the Church...This will have a decisively negative effect on the issue of the recognition of Anglican orders...By ordaining women Anglicans would sever themselves from continuity in apostolic faith and spiritual life.[23]

From the Orthodox side, it is emphasized that "men and women are equal but different" and that this diversity needs to be acknowledged. Recognizing the duty of the church to give women more opportunities to use their specific gifts, they list a number of ministries, which can be exercised by women, such as diaconal and philanthropic tasks, prayer and intercession, spiritual help, and administration. The ordination of women to the priesthood is rejected with the argument that "from the time of Christ and the Apostles onwards, the Church has ordained only men to the priesthood."[24] This is considered a binding precedent for Christians to the present day. The Orthodox further cite biblical grounds for this position by referring to Galatians 1:8f: "But if we, or an angle from heaven, preaches to you anything else than what we have preached to you, let him be anathema."

The Anglican position comprises different points of view on this question—opposition, advocacy, and moderation, according to which women's ordination should not be introduced precipitately in light of ecumenical concerns. The arguments against female priesthood relate to the person of Jesus:

> It was in a male that the Word was made flesh and humanity in all its fullness was united to the Godhead... a male priest must be the symbol and image of Christ as Bridegroom, whereas women symbolize the response of humanity in creative obedience—the God-given nature of the ministerial priesthood includes the fact that it is male.

Those who favor the ordination of women do so because they believe that the Church's tradition must grow and develop. They believe that this is a true development, under the guidance of the Holy Spirit, of the patterns of ministry to which God has been calling some churches in response to major changes in the ordering of society. The vocations of women who offer themselves for the priestly ministry therefore need to be tested, and none of the arguments, either from Scripture or tradition, advanced against such vocations seem to those who hold this position to be in principle convincing. For, in the exercise of the priestly ministry, it is not maleness that qualifies the candidate but humanity, since priesthood concerns the relationship between humanity and God.[25]

Although the Orthodox-Anglican dialogue has continued, expectations are lower than they were at the beginning. In 2006 the issue was discussed in a session of this bilateral dialogue in Cyprus, where they compared the different positions. The Orthodox explained that "they see no convincing theological reason for the decision of the Anglican and other Western Churches to deviate from this age-long tradition by ordaining women to the eucharistic priesthood." They argue that the Eucharistic president acts *in persona Christi* and although the Christ in whose person the Eucharistic president acts is the eschatological Christ, that maleness is part of his identity. Theological and ecclesiological considerations are more decisive than the sociological argument that the church should listen to society and its expectations. The Orthodox think "that the theological dimension of this matter remains open."[26]

While this dialogue text leaves the issue more or less open, the ROC has expressed its concern over the ordination of women in recent years. During a visit to the United Kingdom in 2010, Metropolitan Hilarion of Volokolamsk made it clear that the ordination of women is an obstacle to closer relations with the Anglicans: while many Protestant churches were ordaining women by the 1990s, he noted that the relationship with the Anglicans was unique because:

> the Anglican Community had long sought rapprochement with the Orthodox Church. Many Orthodox Christians recognized the existence of apostolic continuity

> in Anglicanism. From the 19th century, Anglican members of the Association of Eastern Churches sought "mutual recognition" with the Orthodox Church and its members believed that "both Churches preserved the apostolic continuity and true faith in the Saviour and should accept each other in the full communion of prayers and sacraments."

And Metropolitan Hilarion referred to a statement issued by the Department for External Relations, saying that the positive decision of the Church of England's General Synod on the female episcopate "has considerably complicated dialogue with the Anglicans for Orthodox Christians" and "has taken Anglicanism farther away from the Orthodox Church and contributed to further division in Christendom as a whole." For him, "the introduction of the female episcopate excludes even a theoretical possibility for the Orthodox to recognize the apostolic continuity of the Anglican hierarchy."[27]

According to the Orthodox, the ordination of women as pastors and especially as bishops indicates the loss of apostolic tradition. It needs to be mentioned that the question of female ordination has been an issue especially in the relationship between Orthodox and Anglicans as well as Orthodox and Old Catholics, because there had been expectations on the Orthodox side that intercommunion could be established.[28] The Orthodox-Lutheran dialogue began at a time when some Lutheran churches had already introduced women's ordination. Thus, from the very beginning, these conversations were aimed toward a mutual recognition of apostolicity. Only recently the fact that EKD had elected a female bishop as president of its Council in 2009 and the protocol implications for ecumenical meetings became a pretext for Metropolitan Hilarion of Volokolamsk to decline from participation in the fiftieth jubilee celebration of the EKD-ROC dialogue.[29]

Moral and Ethical Issues

Homosexuality

In 2003 the ROC suspended contact with the Episcopal Church in the United States after an openly practicing homosexual bishop had been consecrated. In a statement in reaction to this event the Moscow Patriarchate said: "The Church has always regarded homosexual contacts as a grave sin."[30] They saw clear biblical testimonies for this position and "the negation of the direct meaning of the words of St. Paul contradicts the centuries-long Christian tradition of the comprehension of these texts and is contrary to common sense."[31] The ROC highlighted the good relationship of the two churches till then through the establishment of a Joint Coordinating Committee for Cooperation in the 1990s. But they did not see a possibility of continuing the dialogue because

> the "consecration" of a gay priest has made any communications with him and with those who consecrated him impossible. We shall not be able to cooperate with these people, not only in the theological dialogue, but also in the humanitarian and religious and public spheres. We have no right to allow even a particle of agreement with their position, which we consider to be profoundly anti-Christian and blasphemous. Because of this situation the Russian Orthodox Church is forced to suspend the work of the Joint

Coordinating Committee and to freeze her contacts with the Episcopalian Church in the USA.[32]

This issue was also mentioned by Metropolitan Hilarion in 2010 in his aforementioned speech: "Some Protestant and Anglican churches have repudiated basic Christian moral values by giving a public blessing to same-sex unions and ordaining homosexuals as priests and bishops. Many Protestant and Anglican communities refuse to preach Christian moral values in secular society and prefer to adjust to worldly standards." The same reasons led to an interruption of relations with the Church of Sweden in 2005.[33]

Human Rights

Closely related to the attitude toward homosexuality is the issue of human rights. In 2008, the Moscow Patriarchate published a document on *The Russian Orthodox Church's Basic Teaching on Human Dignity, Freedom and Rights.*[34] In the discussion that was initiated by this document the difference between Orthodox and Protestant approaches to human rights became clear: while Protestant churches view human rights in a positive light, in that they guarantee the freedom of faith for churches living in a minority situation,[35] the Russian statement begins with the observation that human rights promote and protect attitudes and opinions that are not compatible with Christian faith and teaching.[36]

One of the major differences in this debate is to be found in the understanding of human dignity: Orthodox as well as Protestants base their understanding of human dignity on Genesis 1:26: "Then God said, 'Let us make humankind in our image, according to our likeness." For the reformers like Martin Luther this image (imago Dei) has been destroyed completely by the fall of humanity.[37] The human being has his/her dignity, which is based on the "imago Dei," only in Jesus Christ, the one who restored the "imago Dei" according to Romans 8:29.[38]

In an Orthodox perspective, human dignity was not lost through the fall of mankind, "for the image of God in it remained indelible, which means that an opportunity remained for restoring human life to the fullness of its original perfection."[39] Through sin this dignity is overshadowed or darkened, because "dignified life is related to the notion of God's likeness achieved through God's grace by efforts to overcome sin and to seek moral purity and virtue."[40]

In the view of the Reformation churches, the human person can do nothing to restore this dignity. It is only through Jesus Christ that he or she receives dignity and not through good works or actions. In the Orthodox understanding "the notion of 'dignity' has first of all a moral meaning, while the ideas of what is dignified and what is not are bound up with the moral or amoral actions of a person and with the inner state of his soul."[41] The Russian Orthodox view human rights as problematical, because they defend the right of freedom of choice without giving due consideration to the moral dimension of life: "Every individual is endowed by God with dignity and freedom. The use of this freedom for evil purposes however will inevitably lead to the derogation of one's own dignity and to the humiliation of the dignity of others."[42]

On the Protestant side, as was expressed in the response of the CPCE, this matter is viewed differently: "Human dignity is not governed by a person's own achievements but solely by God's grace."[43] Thus, human dignity cannot be diminished by human sinfulness. This different approach to the understanding of human dignity has consequences, for example, in the respective positions regarding the death penalty: the CPCE accuses the ROC of not condemning the death penalty with sufficient clarity.[44]

A second difference related to the two approaches is the issue of the relation of the human person to community. The Orthodox emphasize community responsibility, while—in their view—a human rights focus is too individualistic.[45] The primary concern with community responsibility figures prominently in the ROC text: "One's human rights cannot be set against the values and interests of one's homeland, community and family."[46] In other Orthodox statements, this critique of human rights is stated even more strongly. Christos Giannaras, who considers the "individuum-centered (human) right" of modernity as a "tragic regression,"[47] refers instead to the Greek understanding of "person," which is different from being an individual. Persons are understood only in light of their relationships with others.[48] But even in the intra-Orthodox discussion, others have stressed that "the correctness of the Orthodox critique of the anti-communitarian spirit does not justify and sanction the rejection of the individual rights in the name of the community."[49]

In this discussion, the differences center on two anthropological issues: the understanding of human dignity and the understanding of a person or individual. While on the human person there can be some convergence with Protestant positions, the matter of human dignity inevitably leads to a difference of opinion on the relation between human rights and soteriology. Protestants emphasize the "secular character of human rights"[50]—for them, human rights have nothing to do with soteriology. But in the Orthodox paper, human rights are understood as "norms that obliterate or altogether cancel both the Gospel and natural morality."[51] Behind this position is the fear that immoral attitudes that the Orthodox consider to be sinful, such as sexual perversions or profit-oriented thinking and violence, could gain support and become norms of conduct.

Modernity, Secularism, and Enlightenment

The ROC's positions on human rights, homosexuality, and women's ordination are linked to its views on the relation of faith and life in modern society. This is made clear in the introduction to the church's document on human rights.[52] The entire document maintains a critical posture toward human rights. This attitude is further confirmed by Patriarch Kirill, who has stated on different occasions that for him the greatest challenge today is the confrontation between a conservative, traditionally oriented view of the world and a liberal worldview, which he sees as based on the "forcible and potentially violent implementation of neo-liberal values."[53] He was referring to the further development of the liberalism that spread through Europe during the Enlightenment, accusing it of having put the individual in the center without considering his brokenness because of sin.[54] He voiced his concern about an "ethical secularization" of public life[55] and lumped together the promoters of the Renaissance, of the Reformation, the Enlightenment, and of the later Revolutions as the ones "who created the idea of freedom in secularized form and gave it an anti-ecclesial and anti-Christian character."[56]

Protestants would readily point out that "the secularization of modern thinking...did not begin in Protestant countries, but in Italy, which was governed by the papacy."[57] Also, Protestant churches at first had found it difficult to recognize human rights,[58] and only saw things differently after World War II, when they discovered that human rights are based on basic Christian values. The churches had learned that human rights have their boundaries, but within these boundaries they have an important meaning for human coexistence. Some Orthodox writers, mainly Greeks, realized this by saying: "The discourse of Orthodoxy with the Enlightenment should not take a defensive course, as if it were a threat to our identity. The identification of the Enlightenment with its anti-ecclesial or atheist dimension must finally be overcome... Orthodoxy must definitively accept the modern and secular character of human rights."[59]

Proselytism

While the ecclesiological and moral issues for the most part concern the Orthodox-Protestant relationship, the issue of proselytism also touches on the relations with the Roman Catholic Church.[60] For example, in 2006, Patriarch Alexii told the RIA-Novosti news service that the "extremely unfriendly policy" of the Catholic Church was straining relations between the Moscow Patriarchate and the Holy See. Until the Catholic Church changed policies, the prospects for ecumenical progress would remain bleak.[61] He also criticized Roman Catholic missionaries for taking away Orthodox believers from their parishes. Various Orthodox churches within the WCC have voiced similar concerns regarding Protestant groups and sects in Eastern Europe and the Middle East.

> After the disintegration of the Soviet Union and of the communist system we have encountered still another danger for the ecumenical movement, namely, the growth of proselytism and competition in missionary service. These activities are not only carried out by sects, but unfortunately also by some WCC member churches...They send missionaries to us who are telling us that we are unable to carry out missionary activities...And they do it by bringing not only a word, but dollars.[62]

Consequently, in 1995 the Joint Working Group of the WCC and the Roman Catholic Church published a document on *The Challenge of Proselytism and the Calling to Common Witness*.[63] And in 1997 the WCC issued the statement *Towards Common Witness. A call to adopt Responsible Relationships in Mission and to Renounce Proselytism*.[64]

In Orthodox-Protestant relations, the issue is rooted in the specific understanding of mission in some evangelical churches. Petros Vasiliadis has proposed that, historically, "an undue emphasis was put on the individualistic and anthropocentric understanding of '*making disciples*'" (emphasis in the original). As a result, this led to an expansionist attitude and even destroyed the spiritual character of the church's mission. In his view, the divisions between the churches created a denominational antagonism supporting proselytizing attitudes.[65] In an Orthodox understanding "the subject of mission is not the individual believer, the missionary or even the church as an impersonal corporate entity, but the Triune God ... Mission does not aim primarily at the propagation or transmission of intellectual convictions, doctrines, moral commands, etc., but at the transmission of the life of communion, that exists in God."[66]

The problem is related to the fact that Orthodox ecclesiology follows the ancient Christian principle of one church/one bishop in one territory. The Orthodox feel that Rome violated this principle of the early church when it established a Latin Patriarchate in Jerusalem during the Crusades. Although the ROC under Patriarch Kirill has modified its attitude toward the Roman Catholic Church, the root problem will remain as long as both churches hold to their current positions. For their part, even those Protestant churches that do not evangelize aggressively would see individual religious freedom as contravened by a system in which citizenship is connected to membership in a particular church. The principle of one bishop in one territory seems archaic and incompatible with the realities of the modern, pluralistic world.

Concluding Remarks

While many of these religious debates have become more heated during the last 20 years, few of them are new. They are therefore likely to remain sources of tensions and conflict into the future. Within the framework of the WCC, the introduction of a consensus model for decision-making and the introduction of guidelines for common worship have softened the tensions to some degree, but they certainly did not solve the problems.

At the same time, it must be recognized that the tensions around these issues are not limited only to the dialogues between Orthodox and Western churches, but that they are sources of conflict inside confessional families as well: the ordination of women within the Lutheran World Federation, homosexuality within the Anglican Communion, proselytism among Protestant churches. Even within the Orthodox discussions, these issues are treated differently by diverse individuals. Patriarch Kirill may well be right to distinguish between two worldviews, one conservative and the other progressive, but the line of demarcation does not necessarily coincide with confessional lines. The real border on these issues is not between traditional churches and new(er) churches. Rather, it cuts through the churches themselves. And since this whole issue is closely related to the question of how to relate to the modern world, it has to be seen not only in the framework of interchurch relations, but also within the broader context of churches in relation to increasingly diverse societies.

Notes

1. "Letter No. XIV of Patriarch Jeremias II to the professors in Tübingen on 6 June 1581," in *Wort und Mysterium. Der Briefwechsel über Glauben und Kirche 1573 bis 1581 zwischen den Tübinger Theologen und dem Patriarchen von Konstantinopel*, Außenamt der Evangelischen Kirche in Deutschland (ed.) (Witten: Luther-Verlag, 1958), p. 213. (My translation from the German.)
2. "Patriarchal and Synodical Encyclical of 1902," in *Orthodox Visions of Ecumenism. Statements, Messages and Reports on the Ecumenical Movement 1902–1992*, Gennadios Limouris (ed.) (Geneva: WCC Publications, 1994), p. 3.
3. Statement at the First World Conference on Faith and Order, in *Orthodox Visions of Ecumenism*, p.13.

4. Ibid.
5. "Encyclical of the Ecumenical Patriarchate, 1952," in *Orthodox Visions of Ecumenism*, p. 21.
6. See Apostolic Canon 45.
7. Konstantin Scouteris, "Hat der Ökumenische Rat der Kirchen eine Zukunft? Der Ursprung des ÖRK und die 'Sonderkommission zur orthodoxen Mitarbeit im ÖRK,'" *Ökumenische Rundschau* 50:2 (2001), 147–154; Mary Tanner, "Die Sonderkommission zur orthodoxen Mitarbeit im ÖRK: Rückblick auf die Halbzeit aus nicht-orthodoxer Sicht," *ÖR* 2 (2001), 155–166; Dagmar Heller and Barbara Rudolph (Hg.), *Die Orthodoxen im Ökumenischen Rat der Kirchen. Dokumente, Hintergründe, Kommentare und Visionen*, "Beihefte zur Ökumenischen Rundschau, 74" (Frankfurt a.M.: Verlag Otto Lembeck, 2004).
8. Jutta Koslowski, "Der Streit um die Einheit: das Problem des Uniatismus und der orthodox-katholische Dialog," *Una Sancta* 66:1 (2011), 50–60.
9. Johannes Oeldemann, "Der orthodox-katholische Dialog steht vor einer Bewährungsprobe," *G2W* 9 (2010), 12–14.
10. Johannes Oeldemann, "Zeugnis für die Wahrheit geben—im Spannungsfeld von Theologie und Ethik. Die Orthodoxe Kirche im ökumenischen Dialog," *Una Sancta* 66:1 (2011), 63.
11. After some interruptions due to the two world wars, this dialogue was resumed in 1973. *Growth in Agreement I. Reports and Agreed Statements of Ecumenical Conversations on a World Level. 1972–1982*, Harding Meyer and Lukas Vischer (eds.) (New York: Paulist Press and Geneva: WCC, 1984), p. 390.
12. Ibid., p. 40.
13. *Growth in Agreement II. Reports and Agreed Statements of Ecumenical Conversations on a World level, 1982–1998*, Jeffrey Gros, Harding Meyer, and William G. Rusch (eds.) (Geneva: WCC and Grand Rapids: William B. Eerdmans, 2000), p. 219.
14. Ibid., p. 275f.
15. See Risto Saarinen, *Faith and Holiness. Lutheran-Orthodox Dialogue 1959–1994* (Göttingen: Vandenhoeck & Ruprecht, 1997), for more detailed information about the Lutheran-Orthodox dialogues mentioned earlier.
16. The results are published in *Consultations between the Conference of European Churches (CEC) and the Community of Protestant Churches in Europe (CPCE)*, Leuenberg Documents 11, Michael Beintker, Martin Friedrich, and Viorel Ionita (eds.) (Frankfurt am Main: Verlag Otto Lembeck, 2007); and *Baptism in the Life of the Churches. Documentation of an Orthodox-Protestant dialogue in Europe*, Leuenberg Documents 12, Michael Beintker, Viorel Ionita and Jochen Kramm (eds.) (Frankfurt am Main: Verlag Otto Lembeck, 2011).
17. See note 34.
18. See note 5.
19. *A Documentary History of the Faith and Order Movement 1927–1963*, Lukas Vischer (ed.) (St. Louis, Missouri: The Bethany Press, 1963), pp. 167–176.
20. *Final Report of the Special Commission on Orthodox Participation in the WCC*, Section B, chapter V, par 42f. http://www2.wcc-coe.org/ccdocuments.nsf/index/gen-5-en.html#Anchor—SECTI-1786 (accessed October 10, 2011).
21. Ibid., Section B, chapter III.
22. *The Dublin Agreed Statement 1984*, Introduction, http://www.anglicancommunion.org/ministry/ecumenical/dialogues/orthodox/docs/pdf/the_dublin_statement.pdf (accessed October 17, 2011).
23. Ibid.
24. Ibid., Appendix 2.
25. Ibid.
26. "The Church of the Triune God"—The Cyprus Statement 2006 International Commission for Anglican-Orthodox Theological Dialogue.

http://www.anglicancommunion.org/ministry/ecumenical/dialogues/orthodox/docs/pdf/The%20Church%20of%20the%20Triune%20God.pdf (accessed October 10, 2011).
27. Address by Metropolitan Hilarion of Volokolamsk, Chairman of the Moscow Patriarchate's Department for External Church Relations to the Annual Nicean Club Dinner (Lambeth Palace, September 9, 2010), http://www.mospat.ru/en/2010/09/10/news25819/ (accessed November 18, 2011). See also: http://www.orthodoxytoday.org/blog/2010/09/russian-metropolitan-blasts-anglican-communions-sexual-innovations/ (accessed November 18, 2011).
28. "Historical Introduction to the Old Catholic—Orthodox Conversations," *Growth in Agreement I*, p. 390f.
29. "Ökumenisches Forum für Glauben, Religion und Gesellschaft in Ost und West," G2W 1 (2010), p. 7f. (referring to www.kommersant.ru, November 11, 2009; and www.religio.ru, November 2, 12, 13, 2009).
30. "The Church cannot approve of the perversion of human nature created by the creator himself." *The Statement of the Department for External Church Relations of the Moscow Patriarchate* http://www.mospat.ru/archive/en/ne311176.htm (accessed October 10, 2011).
31. Ibid.
32. "Address by Metropolitan Hilarion of Volokolamsk, Chairman of the Moscow Patriarchate's Department for External Church Relations, to the Annual Nicean Club Dinner" (Lambeth Palace, September 9, 2010), http://www.mospat.ru/en/2010/09/10/news25819/ (accessed November 18, 2011).
33. Ibid.
34. The English version can be found at http://www.mospat.ru/en/documents/dignity-freedom-rights/ (accessed October 10, 2011).
35. *Human Rights and Morality. A Response of the Community of Protestant Churches in Europe (CPCE)—Leuenberg Church Fellowship—to the Principles of the Russian Orthodox Church on "Human Dignity, Freedom and Rights,"* Chapter 2, p. 3, http://www.leuenberg.net/daten/File/Upload/doc-9806-2.pdf (accessed October 12, 2011).
36. Preamble of the cited document.
37. Wolfhart Pannenberg, *Anthropologie in theologischer Perspektive* (Göttingen: Vandenhoeck & Ruprecht, 1983), p. 46.
38. Martin Luther, *Disputatio de homine*, par. 24. http://dtserv2.compsy.uni-jena.de/__C1257B4400443401.nsf/0/539DD564D4E85B42C1257B49005B9434/$FILE/Luther_Disputatio_De_Homine.pdf (accessed October 26, 2013).
39. Par. I.1 in *The Russian Orthodox Church's Basic Teaching on Human Dignity, Freedom and Rights.*
40. Ibid., Par. I.2.
41. Ibid.
42. III.1, Ibid.
43. *Human Rights and Morality*, Chapter 1, p. 2. http://www.leuenberg.eu/sites/default/files/Human_rights_and_morality%20(final).pdf (accessed October 26, 2013).
44. *Human Rights and Morality*, Chapter 5, p. 6. http://www.leuenberg.eu/sites/default/files/Human_rights_and_morality%20(final).pdf, referring to the Russian paper IV.2.
45. III.4.
46. III.5.
47. *Die Inhumanität des Rechts* (Athen, 1998), p. 47 (gr.), quoted by Konstantinos Delikostantis, "Die Menschenrechte im Kontext der Orthodoxen Theologie," *Ökumenische Rundschau* 1 (2007), 25.
48. Ioannis Zizioulas, "Wahrheit und Gemeinschaft in der Sicht der griechischen Kirchenväter," *Kerygma und Dogma* 26:1 (1980), 34.

49. Konstantinos Delikostantis, "Die Menschenrechte im Kontext der Orthodoxen Theologie," *Ökumenische Rundschau* 1 (2007), 30. (Translation mine).
50. *Human Rights and Morality*, Chapter 2, p. 4. http://www.leuenberg.eu/sites/default/files/Human_rights_and_morality%20(final).pdf (accessed October 26, 2013).
51. *The Russian Orthodox Church's Basic Teaching on Human Dignity, Freedom and Rights*, Par. III.3.
52. "In the world today there is a widespread conviction that the human rights institution in itself can promote in the best possible way the development of human personality and social organization. At the same time, human rights protection is often used as a plea to realize ideas, which in essence radically disagree with Christian teaching. Christians have found themselves in a situation where public and social structures can force and often have already forced them to think and act contrary to God's commandments" ("Introduction," *The Russian Orthodox Church's Basic Teaching on Human Dignity, Freedom and Rights*).
53. Kyrill, Patriarch von Moskau und der ganzen Rus', "Die Zeichen der neuen Zeit" (first published in *Nesavisimaia Gazeta*, Mai 1999), in *Kyrill, Freiheit und Verantwortung im Einklang. Zeugnisse für den Aufbruch zu einer neuen Weltgemeinschaft*, Barbara Hallensleben et al. (eds.) Fribourg: Institut für ökumenische Studien der Universität Freiburg (Schweiz, 2009), p. 25 (translation mine).
54. Ibid., p. 26. And: "So wurde im Zentrum eines anthropozentrischen Universums der Mensch zum Maß aller Dinge. Doch nicht einfach der Mensch, sondern namentlich der gefallene Mensch im Stand der Sünde" (p. 27). This opinion is repeated in variants in other places: "Die Glaubensnorm als Lebensnorm," in *Kyrill, Freiheit und Verantwortung*, pp. 33–49; and "Das liberale Wertesystem als Bedrohung der Freiheit," in ibid., pp. 64–69.
55. "Einheit der Kirche und Erneuerung der Menschheit. Eine gemeinsame Suche (Vortrag auf einem internationalen Seminar in Budapest, Dezember 1987)," in *Kyrill, Freiheit und Verantwortung*, p. 57.
56. *Kyrill, Freiheit und Verantwortung*, p. 76 (translation mine). See also: "Was die westliche Welt betrifft, so hat sich in ihr eine besondere zivilisatorische Norm behauptet, die als Ergebnis einer philosophischen und gesellschaftlich-politischen Entwicklung entstanden ist, welche in der Epoche der Renaissance und der Reformation begonnen hat und auch das Zeitalter der Aufklärung und der europäischen Revolutionen einschließt. Grundlage dieser Norm ist das sogenannte liberale Prinzip, das die individuellen Freiheiten als höchstes Gut bezeichnet" (p. 101).
57. Gerhard Ritter, *Die Weltwirkung der Reformation* (Leipzig 1941), p. 221f.. See also Wolfgang Huber, *Gerechtigkeit und Recht. Grundlagen christlicher Rechtsethik* (Darmstadt: Wissenschaftliche Buchgesellschaft, 2006), p. 273: "Auf diese Weise bereitete der italienische Renaissance-Humanismus, in Aufnahme stoischer Gedanken, jene anthropologische Wende vor, welche die Würde des Menschen in seiner Vernunftnatur verankerte."
58. Huber, *Gerechtigkeit und Recht*, p. 515.
59. Ibid., p. 24.
60. Roman Catholics have entered the discussion about human rights with the Orthodox in a controversial way: Some defend the position of the ROC (Barbara Hallensleben in Fribourg, Switzerland), while others distance themselves (Ingeborg Gabriel in Vienna).
61. http://directionstoorthodoxy.org/mod/news/view.php?article_id=198 (accessed October 10, 2011).
62. Metropolitan Kyrill of Smolensk, "Orthodox relations with the World Council of Churches," in *The Ecumenical Movement, the Churches and the World Council of Churches. An Orthodox Contribution to the reflection process on "The Common Understanding and Vision of the WCC,"* George Lemopoulos (ed.) (Geneva/Syndesmos, Bialystok: World Council of Churches, 1995), p. 52.

63. http://www.oikoumene.org/en/resources/documents/wcc-commissions/joint-working-group-between-the-roman-catholic-church-and-the-wcc/challenge-of-proselytism.html (accessed October 10, 2011).
64. http://www.oikoumene.org/resources/documents/wcc-commissions/mission-and-evangelism/towards-common-witness.html?print (accessed October 10, 2011).
65. Petros Vassiliadis, "Mission and Proseytism. An Orthodox Understanding," *International Review of Mission* 85 (1998), 262.
66. Ibid.

7

The Image of the Roman Catholic Church in the Orthodox Press of Romania, 1918–1940

Ciprian Ghişa

Preliminary Considerations

Confessional identity is a construct in the *longue durée*, formed and sustained by the ecclesiastical hierarchy and by the clergy[1] through a well-defined discourse of identity. The identity discourse of an institutional church has an official character, insofar as it is formulated and transmitted by clerical elites. The sequence usually involves clergy first attaining a certain level of spiritual and intellectual training, then the formulation of a message of identity, and finally the transmission of that message to the faithful. The message is "controlled, selected, organized and redistributed"[2] by its authors, in order to serve specific aims and needs, which can change as it is addressed to each successive generation. The methods of transmission include preaching, catechism, canonical visitations and pastoral activity, religious literature, sacred images, pamphlets, booklets, calendars, and, since the mid-nineteenth century, the religious press. In the process of constructing the identity message, the constitutive elements of church identity (denomination, rite, tradition, institutional structure, historical past, the relation between church and nation, and otherness) are assimilated in progressive stages and degrees.

One theory that has gained acceptance by historians asserts that the process of identity construction is accelerated by the notion of alterity.[3] The need to define one's self-identity becomes imperative as soon as one interacts with *the other*. Otherness often attests to the existence of a conflict or a rivalry. It leads to controversy and triggers defense mechanisms of positive self-evaluation. In turn, an identity discourse is formulated in terms of opposite values, such as good-evil, truth-lie, fidelity-treason, salvation-damnation, and so on.[4] These dual categories set up a polarization that is heightened when sensitive questions such as that of salvation are raised. Church identity typically comprises two levels of alterity: ecclesiastical, which focuses on the differences between one's own and the other's faith traditions, and national, which considers the respective ethnic identities within each of the two faith traditions.

This chapter focuses on the interwar alterity relationship between the Romanian Orthodox Church (RomOC) and the Roman Catholic Church (RCC), and the ways in which this relationship was reflected in the identity discourse of the RomOC and transmitted to the clergy and the faithful by the religious press.

Origins of the Romanian Orthodox Identity Discourse

The identity discourse of the RomOC was elaborated during the seventeenth and the eighteenth centuries, at a time when Eastern Orthodox churches were responding to Catholic and Calvinist proselytism by formulating precise and exclusive categories of identity. Western proselytism was perceived as a threat, and the Romanian polemical reaction to it was developed within the medieval, East-West paradigm of alterity. In Eastern Europe, as in the post-Tridentine Catholic environment, numerous Confessions of faith appeared, such as: the Confession of Patriarch Cyril Lukaris (Geneva, 1629), the *Orthodoxa Confessio Fidei Catholicae et Apostolicae Ecclesiae Orientalis* of Metropolitan Peter Moghila (approved in Constantinople in 1643),[5] and the Confession of Patriarch Dositheos II of Jerusalem (1672).

Many anti-Calvinist and anti-Catholic books in Greek were published in Wallachia and Moldavia with state support.[6] They included the former Jerusalem patriarch Nectarius's work *Against the pope's primacy* (Jassy, 1682); two fifteenth-century writings, *Against the Heresies*, by Archbishop Simeon of Thessaloniki, and *Explanation of the Canons of the Church*, by Metropolitan Mark Eugenikos of Efes (1683); *Against the Schism of the Papists*, by Maxim from Peloponnese (Bucharest, 1690); a book by Meletios Sirigos against Catholic doctrine and the positions of Patriarch Cyril Lukaris; the *Tome of Reconciliation* (Jassy, 1692–1694); the *Word for Combating the outlaw and false Decision composed in Florence at the Synod held by the Latins* by John Eugenikos (Jassy, 1694); the *Tome of Love against the Latins* (1698); and the *Tome of joy* (Jassy, 1705). Some of this literature was translated into Romanian, for example, *On the Schism of the Papists*,[7] which became a cornerstone of anti-Uniate polemical literature and was distributed widely in Transylvania.

In nineteenth-century Romania, the RomOC focused more on the threat of Roman and Greek Catholicism, and the theme of a Protestant threat disappeared for a while from the discourse. Toward the end of the century, new Protestant denominations (Baptist, Anabaptist, Nazarene, or Adventist) arrived on the scene, in modest numbers at first but growing steadily by the turn of the twentieth century. This elicited a strong reaction from traditional Orthodox and Greek Catholic Romanian Churches, which intensified in the interwar period.[8] The Orthodox perspective on identity was further shaped by three significant historical achievements and transformations. First, the political, economic, and cultural rapprochement of Romania with the West was deepened after the promulgation of the 1866 Constitution, the coronation of Charles I of Hohenzollern as prince of Romania, the international recognition of Romanian independence in 1878, and its political unification in 1918.[9] Second, the elevated status of the church was ensured by the 1923 Constitution, which declared the RomOC as the official church in the land and by the establishment of the Romanian Patriarchate in 1925.[10] And third, through its involvement in the ecumenical movement, the RomOC came into contact with numerous religious communities (Old Catholics, the Anglican Church, the Evangelical Churches in Germany and Sweden) and organizations.[11] These developments inspired a new self-awareness and a corresponding Orthodox identity discourse that dispensed with the medieval geographic designation of the enemy or threat as "the West" or the Western church.

The Romanian Orthodox Press

The Orthodox press in Romania, which emerged in the nineteenth century (after 1850 in Transylvania),[12] aimed to reflect church life and to become "a channel of information and cultural support for the people, an instrument of education for the clergy, and a defender of Romanian national and cultural interests."[13] The press developed significantly in the interwar period with the support of various levels of the institutional church.[14] It had a diversity of formats and content depending on their patrons and target audiences.

Official publications of the RomOC included *Biserica Ortodoxă Română* (Romanian Orthodox Church), the Bucharest journal of the Patriarchal Synod; *Apostolul* (The Apostle), the journal of the archbishop of Bucharest; *Telegraful Român* (The Romanian Telegraph) in Sibiu, the journal of the Transylvanian metropolitan. Eparchial journals included *Renașterea* (Renaissance) in Cluj; *Legea Românească* (Romanian Law) in Oradea; *Calea Mântuirii* (The Way of Salvation) in Arad. Other journals were published by priests: *Ortodoxia* (Orthodoxy) in Bucharest; *Misionarul* (The Missionary) in Chișinău; *Clujul Ortodox* (Orthodox Cluj) in Cluj; *Fântâna Darurilor* (The Fountain of Grace); and *Calea Adevărului* (The Way of Truth). *Studii Teologice* (Theological Studies) was the Yearbook of the Faculty of Theology in Bucharest. The Romanian Orthodox Brotherhood published *F.O.R.* in Craiova; and *Viața Ilustrată* (Illustrated Life) in Sibiu. *Glasul Monahilor* (The Voice of the Monks) in Bucharest was edited by hieromonk Dionisie Lungu. Their content was diverse, covering theological, dogmatic, historical, and moral issues, and discussing such matters as interconfessional relations, political and national problems, and the evolution of the church-state relations. While the journal *Biserica Ortodoxă Română* maintained a more moderate and official tone, others like *Legea Românească* and *Glasul Monahilor* adopted more radical positions on the controversies and issues of the day, and engaged in polemics with the Catholic and the secular press.

As the main source for the present research, these journals contain official statements of the church and articles by religious leaders and thinkers. Among those key figures were: Archmandrite Iuliu Scriban,[15] perhaps the most active Orthodox publicist of the time, former principal of the theological seminary in Bucharest, and important Orthodox theologian; Irineu Mihălcescu, the future metropolitan of Moldavia[16]; Nicodim Munteanu, the former bishop of Huși, superior of Neamț Monastery, and future patriarch (1939–1948)[17]; Nicolae Colan, Metropolitan of Sibiu[18]; Ioan Vască, dean of the Theological Academy in Cluj[19]; Ștefan Munteanu, rector of the Theological Academy in Oradea[20]; and the theologian Teodor M. Popescu, future dean of the Faculty of Orthodox Theology in Bucharest.[21]

The Negative Image of Catholicism

In the interwar period, Catholicism was perceived as the RomOC's most formidable adversary largely because of the position of the RCC in Romania after 1918: the considerable number of Catholics—1,234,151 Roman Catholics and 1,427,391 Greek Catholics (1930)—compared to 13,108,227 Orthodox believers at a total of 18,025,829 inhabitants; a sizeable Greek Catholic Church in Transylvania; the Catholic model of proselytism, an extension of the Union with the Church of Rome; the Concordat between the Romania and Vatican (1929)[22]; and the national problem, in particular the status of the majority Hungarian Roman Catholics of Transylvania and their loyalty to Hungary.[23] The negative image of the RCC in the Orthodox press consisted of traditional theses, whose origins can be traced to eighteenth-century Orthodox discourses of alterity.[24] To these, new theses were added in the twentieth century. Together, they constituted the RomOC's critical view of Catholicism during the interwar period.

1. *The Catholic Church as papist*[25]—The image of the pope was superimposed over the image of the RCC and qualified by negative attributes: "the pope with all his antichrist tyranny, with all his frightening heresies"[26]; "this false representative of Christ," who puts on "the airs of a god descended among unfortunate mortals"[27]; "the papacy is a political foundation with religious appearance, that tends more towards idolatry than piety."[28] On the same theme of idolatry, the author of an article in 1924 wrote: "On Catholic medals and postcards one sees the portrait of the pope right alongside the image of Our Lord's Mother...and such words about the pope as though he were an object of worship...these, without question, are acts of idolatry, because the pope is not the proper person to be worshiped."[29] Also cited as idolatrous were the practices of priests and bishops kneeling before Pope Leo XIII and of cardinals kissing the feet of a newly elected pope. The author wondered: "Is this not a path towards pope-worship?"[30] This was only one step away from a direct accusation of paganism. In fact, Nicodim Munteanu wrote in 1932: "In the case of the popes, during the Middle Ages there was outright paganism. The Popes had the title of Christ's *locum tenens*, but in fact, they were nothing less than pagans. Perhaps not openly, but unconsciously and implicitly, that old paganism manifests itself today in the spirit of those who call themselves the successors of Christ."[31]

2. *Centralized Catholic authority*—An article in 1934 argued that centralized Catholic authority prevented the development of any national spirit inside the church. "The centralized system of the pope" (the derogatory term "papism" was used) led to a

> distortion of the genuine constitution of the Church of Christ and to an abdication of traditional principles that guaranteed people the right to express their national and religious character within a framework of ecclesiastical autocephaly...in the West, a new church system was created, replacing the spiritual unity and fruitful ecumenicity of the old church with the juridical patterns of a coercive uniformity and centralization.

In this view, the people of Western Europe had been "handcuffed by the pope's imperialism," and this led to the Reformation "as an escape from the restraints of papal centralism."[32] The vocabulary of interwar Orthodox authors created the image of a system akin to those of imperialist states. The use of terms such as "imperialism," "centralism," and "papism" underlined the political nature of the papacy and its character as autocratic, aggressive, and devoid of spiritual values. The system created a suffocating environment in Western Europe, pushing people to embrace a radical solution: the tearing apart of church unity. The accusation that Catholicism and the pope were responsible for the division of Christianity was repeated often in the Romanian Orthodox press.[33]

3. *Aggressive Catholic proselytism*—The RCC was portrayed as applying its political influence in the pursuit of its political objectives. Discussing the expansion of Christianity throughout the world, an article in the Cluj journal *Renaşterea* pointed out that "in seeking to build an earthly empire and absorb the entire non-Catholic world, the RCC created the Institute for the Propagation of the Faith [Propaganda Fide]."[34] Formulations like "in a time of serious hardship and troubles, when our Romanian Orthodox Church is thoroughly battered by the Roman-Catholic offensive"[35] put forward the image of an Orthodox Church under siege. Catholic proselytism was seen as a grave threat to the RomOC: "Catholics are the most dangerous of all. Compared to them, the [new-Protestants] are mere playthings that can always be restrained by state mechanisms," which was not possible with the Catholics.[36] In an article titled "Politics and the Vatican," the author, I. Mihălcescu, said that "one of these enemies and the most dangerous of all is, of course, Catholicism."[37]

4. *The RCC as deceptive*—In response to a text in the Roman Catholic journal *Albina*[38] (The Bee) from Bucharest, one author wrote: "[The Catholics] praise our weaknesses because of delight and not out of sincere feelings. This Jesuit-Catholic system casts the scale of values into darkness, introduces confusion, makes people unable to recognize the real aspects of life and forces them to think only according to their misleading Catholic patterns."[39] On another occasion, responding to an article published in *Cultura Creştină* (Christian Culture), the Greek Catholic magazine in Blaj, the author voiced the following observations regarding Catholic adaptability to virtually any political circumstances: "Rome is the servant of the ages and she guides the boat of her interests among the Hungarians, the Hottentots, the men on the moon, just to stay alive. She does not care about the Hungarians or about us, she just wants to use everybody, as long as they have some power."[40]

5. *The RCC as heretical*—Numerous articles contested Catholic doctrines and practices (the Immaculate Conception, papal infallibility, the doctrine on Hell, the Catholic perspective on the divorce, the indulgences) and declared them erroneous.[41] Some of these were described as "novelties," a term that was taken over from eighteenth-century polemics.[42] Catholics were therefore "far removed from the dogmatic truth as established the holy ecumenical councils."[43] Moreover, the Catholic Church was described as vulnerable to heresy and schism. The author of an article in *Biserica Ortodoxă Română* in 1924 claimed that Protestantism could not spread inside the Orthodox world. "[Protestantism] haunted only Catholic countries and only there it was successful. It had to stop the moment it tried to pass over into Orthodoxy. Thus, [the best Orthodox] defense against Protestantism is to remain Orthodox... Protestantism flourishes in the Catholic body that has turned away from the Gospels, but it is powerless before us."[44] In contrast, the Orthodox Church was presented as the sole preserver of redemptive truth, of the authentic apostolic tradition, and of doctrine as defined by the fathers of the church and the ecumenical councils. The Orthodox discourse typically included positive self-assessments: "The Christian Orthodox Church strictly preserved its attributes [of unity, holiness, catholicity, and apostolicity]. That is why it remained and still is the only Church based on the foundational truth that was revealed to the world."[45]

6. *Pagan theatrics and spiritual death*—An article in 1930 revealed that in organizing anniversary celebrations commemorating St. Augustine and the Council in Ephesus, Rome had spent over two million francs, which were secured by the pope through political negotiation with the French government.[46] A new notion was added

to this line of argument: Rome was depicted as a place of spiritual death[47]—an ancient theater, with religious ceremonies full of theatrical, extravagant materialism but without spiritual content. In his 1928 article "In Rome," G. D. Mugur presented the following impressions from his visit to St. Peter's Basilica:

> Here comes the Pope. Smoke, frankincense, lights, bells and organ. A steward, guards with spears, crusaders with capes and swords, then the pope's palanquin. On his throne, Leo XIII wearing the pontifical tiara, heavy silk robes, with a *pallium*, the diamond cross and the traditional ecclesiastical ring, called the Holy Ring of the Fisherman. Behind the palanquin and the papal cross, the Swiss guard entered in party-colored uniforms, reminiscent of the soldiers of Henry IV of France. Spears, halberds, flags with the pope's coat of arms, censers, an opera cortège walking in the thundering organ music. Over the heads of the crowd, the *Sedia gestatoria* with the *Servus Servorum Dei* rose as in the ancient processions of triumph. We can always see the diamonds of the tiara, the papal cross and the gesture of the pontiff blessing the crowd and the Catholic universe. I don't know how the emperors from the golden age of the Antonins made their entrance in Rome, but I cannot imagine a more theatrical parade than the cortège of the Catholic sovereign on the feast days in St. Peter's Cathedral. And the organ was playing... in the very place where St. Peter was buried, who was barefoot while fishing. Confused and amazed, I thought of being in an ancient theater under the spirals of sacrificial smoke, watching the spectacle of a pagan procession. I was confused by the spears, the bells, the weapons and the organ. [This was] an hour during which I did not feel in communion with the tragedy on Golgotha... Along with the first successors of the first Apostles, we had covered the truth and the beauty of Christianity with fiction. We created a drama, parodying God in a theater décor... As I re-entered the city the stars were weeping over Rome.[48]

This type of Orthodox description of a Catholic event was not unique. A theology student who attended a mass celebrated in St. Joseph's Roman Catholic Cathedral at Bucharest remarked: "The moment I entered, I had the impression of being in a large pagan temple two thousand years ago, the pagan appearance coming from the statues aligned along the walls"; "almost theatrical gestures of the celebrants"; then Bishop Cisar preached, exalting the pope and uttering his name dozens of times, whereas the name of Our Lord was spoken only three or four times.[49]

7. *Intolerance, exclusivism, and antiecumenism*—The press reminded its readers of the Inquisition, its tortures, and crimes.[50] Similarly, critical and ironic reference was made to the Crusades, the Borgia family, and the questionable morality of popes such as Julius II and Innocent VIII.[51] Introducing a new element into its interwar critique, the RomOC accused the RCC of avoiding ecumenical dialogue. An article on the RomOC's ecumenical activities in 1924 commented, "Only the voice of the Church of Rome is missing. Of course, the reason is well-known: the Church of Rome occupies an extremely exclusive position that could be overcome only on the condition of a total abdication by the other side, which is a totally unacceptable condition."[52] Another author asked,

> Hasn't the Church of Rome been invited to congresses where cooperation is debated? Why doesn't she want to come? Because there, one has to join others as brothers, and the Church of Rome wants to participate only as a master among servants. But we know only God as our master. Whoever wants to have the Roman Caesar as master, so be it![53]

The accusation of Roman Catholic exclusivity was further supported by the frequent use of the expression "*Roma locuta, causa finita*."[54]

The RomOC had a very different experience with the Anglican Church in its pursuit of ecumenical dialogue and the cause of church unity. It took part in ecumenical conferences that sought to improve mutual understanding.[55] Its dialogue with the Anglican Church was amply reflected in the Orthodox press[56] in a very positive light: "The Anglican Church stands ahead of all churches that are working to restore the body of Christ to its original beauty"[57]; "we cherish those people [Anglicans] who love the East, seek new links, revere the Orthodox Church, desire to help and ask nothing in return. They do not share the interests of the Pope. They want Christian cooperation; a unified Christian action against paganism in the world and to build worldwide fraternity through church action. If through all these efforts unity could be reestablished, all for the best. We [the Orthodox] have compromised nothing in our doctrine because of them"[58]; the Anglican Church "is not Protestant, but something between Catholicism and Orthodoxy. With only a few minor dogmatic changes, she could easily rejoin Catholicism or Orthodoxy"[59]; the Anglican hierarchy decisively helped the patriarch of Constantinople in his conflict with the Turkish state in 1921–1923, whereas the papacy tried to exploit the situation and plotted against him[60]; the Anglican priesthood is similar to the Catholic and Orthodox one[61]; "the Anglican Church [is] a traditional Church that seeks unity with us."[62] The Orthodox press also discussed the activity of the Faith and Order Movement, and suggested that its conference debates and exchanges were informed by a "spirit of Christian love," since the goal of church unity had considerable support among Protestants.[63] This increasingly positive image of the Anglican Church and the benevolent attitude toward other Protestants changed the RomOC's attitude toward the West. As long as some of its members were so inoffensive, respectful, and anxious for mutual understanding, it appeared that the entire West could no longer be called an enemy. Consequently, the traditional opposition to "the West" and its direct association with the RCC was set aside in the interwar period, along with the RomOC's defensive posture toward it. Orthodox voices occasionally expressed reservations about this rapprochement with Protestants. An article in *Apostolul*[64] (1928) on the encyclical *Mortalium animos*[65] reaffirmed the charge of Catholic exclusivism,[66] but then proceeded to comment favorably and to express tacit agreement with the general principles of the papal text. The author argued that some limitation of the RomOC's dialogue with Protestants would have been advisable.

Catholicism remained the only real opponent. In 1923, Rev. Ştefan Munteanu argued that even "cooperation with papal Rome would carry the germs of danger that would threaten permanently our national liberty and the objective, divine origin of our religion."[67] The "West" was perceived as dangerous too, but for a different reason: the social modernization spawned by revolutions, rationalism, secularization, intellectualism, and materialism. Since each of these factors was believed to lead potentially to atheism, the Orthodox press attacked the spiritually decadent and "anarchical" lifestyles after World War I; and the nationalization of church properties, civil marriages, freemason doctrines, pornography and adultery, Malthusianism, prostitution, and anticlerical literature.[68] While some of those factors had originated in the West, the blame for them did not necessarily rest with Western churches.

8. *Unscrupulous opportunism*—Sometimes the victim of such activity was the Orthodox Church: "Whenever misfortune strikes the Orthodox Church, instead of

unselfish, Christian help, Catholic leaders see only another opportunity to go fishing in the waters of Orthodoxy."[69] The image was again bolstered by comparisons with loathsome behaviors: "like crows that smell misfortune and come to feed on flesh, so too the leaders of the Catholic Church" hoping to exploit every opportunity. These ideas took form within a specific context: the disastrous position of the Orthodox Church in Russia after the communist takeover, where Catholics were seen as no better than the new Protestants[70]; the difficult situation of the Greek Church of Jerusalem—one article alleged that Patriarch Damianos had been offered bribes to embrace Catholicism, which he refused[71]; and the Constantinople patriarch's disputes with the Turkish state.[72] The resulting image was one of a Catholic Church always in contact with the governments of states in regions of interest, dominating them and profiting from their weaknesses.

9. *The RCC as persecutor*—This image was promoted particularly in relation to the situation of recently established Orthodox Churches in Czechoslovakia and Poland. An article in 1930 related that in eastern Czechoslovakia and southwestern Poland the populations converted massively to Orthodoxy and many new parishes were founded, only to be faced with grave material problems, since they did not have their own churches, properties, or parochial houses. The only such ownership was reserved for Uniates and Roman Catholics.[73] C. Tomescu showed that Orthodoxy was born in the country in 1874, when the first parish was established in Prague, by bishop Gorazd, "the founder of the Czechs' redemption." Seizing upon the "danger," the papists launched an offensive, mocking press campaign, which was duly answered.[74] In Poland, the situation was similar. The fledgling Orthodox Church also faced calumnies and struggled with serious material problems, since all ecclesiastical properties in the country were owned by Catholics according to the Concordat.[75]

10. *The RCC as antinational*—This accusation was invariably linked with two sensitive issues for Romanians: the RCC's relations with Hungary, with which Romania had a long history of political and national disputes; and the contestation of the Concordat,[76] negotiated since 1920 and signed in 1929—"the most dangerous enemy of Orthodoxy."[77] In contrast, the RomOC was consistently depicted as the national church. In the classic fashion of identity and alterity discourse, the fusion of religious and national sentiments was presented as an essential trait of the Romanian experience. History had proven the existence of a strong bond between this particular religion and the Romanian people, who had survived numerous hardships thanks to their faith and their Orthodox Church: "Our society is bound more strongly to its Orthodoxy than any other"[78]; "only inside Orthodoxy one can find the true synthesis between Christianity and the national spirit of peoples, the true symbiosis between Church and Nation. In other Christian communities, the natural rapport between the Church and national factors has been altered"[79]; "Orthodoxy entered our blood at the same time as our mothers' blood."[80] Thus, Orthodoxy was called "the faith of the forefathers," and within this church "Romanian law" was preserved without change.[81]

Positive Images of the RCC

Despite the overall negative image of the RCC, the interwar Romanian Orthodox press was not without some positive assessments of the RCC. The RCC's support for missionary activities was viewed favorably, indeed with admiration, as an example that could be followed by the RomOC: "The Church of Rome supports great institutes for the training of specialized missionaries who sustain Catholic propaganda in Catholic countries and among other people still beyond the light of Christianity...The Western Church [i.e., the RCC] is supported by thousands of philanthropic societies and associations."[82] The Catholic youth ministry was also viewed as remarkably well organized. The journal *Apostolul* mentioned the "strongest organization for the religious education of the youth, the Catholic association *Neudeutschland*"[83] in Germany. Archimandrite Iuliu Scriban wrote: "One of the ways by which Catholicism is strengthened and maintains its positions is that it doesn't let its youth get out of control. This is certainly a very important skill and consists of a very serious method of work. [...] Indeed, the Catholic Church always uses all available means to stimulate the religious consciousness of its faithful"; the RCC knows the psychology of its believers and very actively fulfills their expectations with a broad range of activities, such as processions, congresses, and other kinds of events.[84]

Orthodox authors also spoke favorably of individuals and phenomena that transcended denominational borders. On Augustine, N. Cazacu wrote:

> I will not insist on his teaching, which is not fully approved by the Orthodox Church, the blessed Augustine being unable to keep completely within the true doctrine of the Church of Christ as did the Eastern Fathers, St. Athanasius, St. Basil the Great, St. John Chrysostom and others. Still, because of his writings, so very helpful for the entire Church, and his fruitful life, so tenderly described in his *Confessions*, this great bishop enjoys the respect of all Christianity. The occasion of his 15th centenary is a proper moment for us Orthodox to meditate on the life and work of the most important representative of Western Christian theology.[85]

Of course, this text could also have been read as a critique: the most important Western theologian could not escape error. But, based on the article as a whole and considering other references to Augustine in the RomOC press, it appears that the intention of authors was to reflect positively on the subject. Similarly, the miraculous occurrences in Lourdes were mentioned favorably, but only as proofs of the protective power of Mary, and not that of Catholicism.[86]

Conclusions

The alterity-based identity discourse of the RomOC was evident in the entire Orthodox press throughout the entire interwar period, continuing and developing ideas born in the seventeenth and eighteenth centuries. The discourse was accusatory, aggressive, unequivocal, and aimed at an opponent rather than a dialogue partner. It centered on a set of oppositions and contrasts: the Catholic Church was all that the Orthodox Church was not and vice versa. In using such mirror images and contrasting ideas and concepts, interwar writers drew upon a long polemical tradition that had been constructed over centuries. The harshness of the discourse reflected in part the hotly debated political and religious issues of the day, such as the Concordat. But its intensity also increased in step with the growth of nationalism, which had a considerable influence in the 1930s. The discourse evolved from a general focus on the "West" into a virtually exclusive focus on the RCC. In criticizing the moral issues and decadence that were brought on by secularization, modernization, and rationalism, the blame was not put on Catholicism or Protestantism, or on churches alone, but on the general evolution of civilization. But for Orthodox traditionalists, Western civilization remained the root cause of evil. On this point they were closer to the Western religious press than they might have realized.

In postwar Romania under communism and after the 1989 Revolution, the RomOC's identity discourse in the religious press remained fairly constant. Alterity with Catholics continued to be the most significant constitutive element. As noted in the interwar period, subsequent identity discourse has continued to be determined largely by the historical context. RomOC attitudes were also affected by changes in the RCC. The Second Vatican Council (1962–1965) and the visit of Patriarch Athenagoras of Constantinople to Pope Paul VI (1967) created a new climate for dialogue between the Catholic and Orthodox Churches. Bilateral discussions were started with the creation in 1980 of the Joint International Commission for Theological Dialogue between the Catholic Church and the Orthodox Church, which had three meetings before 1989.

After the 1989 Revolution, Greek Catholic ("Uniate") Churches renewed their existence in Eastern Europe, which created profound tensions between Orthodoxy and Catholicism, both locally and internationally. The Orthodox used this as a pretext to block further ecumenical dialogue with the Catholic Church. In Romania, as Greek Catholics demanded *restitutio in integrum* of its churches and properties confiscated after its abolition in 1948, tensions and conflicts arose with the RomOC that required legal resolution in the courts. In 1993, the Joint International Commission for the Theological Dialogue between the Roman Catholic Church and the Orthodox Church issued a document at Balamand, Lebanon, stating that Uniatism was not a solution for the realization of church unity, a principle that satisfied the Orthodox but drew sharp criticism from Greek Catholics.[87] In 1998, the Commission for Dialogue between the RomOC and the Greek Catholic Church was constituted, focusing on a principle of dialogue with a view toward overcoming differences. And in May 1999, Pope John Paul II visited Romania—this first visit of a Roman pontiff to an Orthodox country was seen as a very significant step for ecumenism.

In light of these diverse factors, the image of the RCC in the Romanian Orthodox press after 1990 was marked by its own diversity of tones and clichés, combining traditional expressions with new ones inspired by the changing political and religious context. Themes that regularly appear in the Orthodox alterity discourse include: proselytism,[88] which occasionally is also associated with the activity of new Protestant denominations; the political influence of the Vatican and its involvement in international relations; the idea of resorting to any means to achieve its goals and interests; the reluctance to engage in ecumenical dialogue[89]; historical errors[90]—the Inquisition, the struggle for supremacy against states, religious wars, the Concordats[91]; the promotion of rationalism from a Catholic standpoint, which led to religious indifference and atheism[92]; the RCC as responsible for the schism of 1054 and for the secessions of the Reformation.[93] These themes attest to the continuity of what we have called a traditional Orthodox identity discourse, and to its resilience in the face of historical changes. On the other hand, in light of various Orthodox-Catholic encounters, there have also been more favorable references to the RCC as a "Sister Church" or "that post–Vatican II Rome, open to Orthodoxy."[94] The implicit message appears to be that such fraternal contacts highlight the involvement of the RomOC in ecumenism and its commitment to church unity.[95]

Notes

The present study is the result of research as part of the project "Alte Grenzen und Neue Fronten—die Orthodoxie und die Europäische Integration," financed by the Volkswagen Foundation. Project leader, Prof. Dr. Thomas Bremer (Faculty of Catholic Theology—University of Muenster, Germany).

1. For this idea, see: E. Van der Zweerde, "Beyond Occidentism and Philosophic Geography: Reflections on Europe's Eastern Border," in *The New Europe. Uncertain Identity and Borders*, M. Kowalska, ed. (Bialystok, 2007), pp. 48–49. Also see the study of W. Reinhard, who used the concept of *Konfessionsbildung*. W. Reinhard, "Disciplinamento sociale, confessionalizzazione, modernizzazione. Un discorso storiografico," in *Disciplina dell' anima, disciplina del corpo e disciplina della società tra medioevo ed età moderna*, P. Prodi, ed. (Bologna, Società editrice il Mulino, 1994), pp. 101–123.
2. M. Foucault, *Ordinea discursului. Un discurs despre discurs* (Bucureşti, 1998), p. 15.
3. In support of this idea, see: S. Nicoară and T. Nicoară, *Mentalităţi colective şi imaginar social. Istoria şi noile paradigme ale cunoaşterii* (Cluj-Napoca: Ed. Presa Universitară Clujeană, 1996), pp. 198–200; or S. Mitu, "De la *Imaginea Celuilalt* la geografiile simbolice: trasee metodologice," in *Identitate şi alteritate. Studii de istorie politică şi culturală*, Vol. 3, N. Bocşan, S. Mitu, and T. Nicoară eds., (Cluj-Napoca, 2002), pp. 9–14.
4. Nicoară and Nicoară, *Mentalităţi colective şi imaginar social*, pp. 198–200.
5. J. Meyendorff, *Biserica Ortodoxa ieri si azi* (Bucuresti: Ed. Anastasia, 1996), pp. 81–82.
6. B. Murgescu, "Confessional Polemics and Political Imperatives in the Romanian Principalities (Late 17th—early 18th Centuries)," in *Church & Society in Central and Eastern Europe*, M. Crăciun and O. Ghitta eds., (Cluj-Napoca: European Studies Foundation Publishing House, 1998), pp. 174–175.
7. M. Păcurariu, *Legăturile Bisericii Ortodoxe din Transilvania cu Ţara Românească şi Moldova în secolele XVII-XVIII*, Sibiu, 1968, p. 42; I. Mateiu, "O carte din 1699 contra desbinării religioase," *Revista Teologică* 28:7–8 (1938), 299–302.
8. In the Austro-Hungarian Empire, the Baptist denomination was legalized in 1905. In Oradea region, e.g., the first signs of the presence of these denominations were noticed immediately after 1900. A first pastoral letter issued by an official of the Romanian Orthodox Church from this area dated in 1901. See Marius Eppel, *Un mitropolit şi epoca sa. Vasile Mangra (1850–1918)* (Cluj-Napoca: Presa Universitară Clujeană, 2006), pp. 316–318.
9. The issue of national development provoked a long and complex debate in Romanian society, which began in the mid-nineteenth century and continued in various forms into the interwar period. The historian Keith Hitchins presented these two main directions as follows: "The first, inspired from the model and the experience of the West would have led to industrialization and urbanization, causing major change at all the layers of the society; the second perspective started from the agrarian past of Romania and focused on the preservation of the traditional social structures and of cultural values." In the nineteenth century, this situation was reflected in the debate between the members of the group Junimea, led by Titu Maiorescu (the theory of the forms without the ground) and then the cultural and political trends of Poporanism and Sămănătorism, on one hand, and the liberals on the other; in the interwar period, this was the debate between the Europeanists (Eugen Lovinescu, Ştefan Zeletin) on one hand, and the Traditionalists (the group around the magazine *Gândirea*—represented by Nichifor Crainic, its editor between 1926 and 1944 and the main theoretician of "Orthodoxism"; the philosopher Lucian Blaga; the philosopher Nae Ionescu, who published his views in the magazine *Cuvântul*, the theoretician of "trăirism," a Romanian version of existentialism). See: K. Hitchins, *România 1866–1947*, ed. II (Bucureşti: Ed. Humanitas, 1998), pp. 67–99, 292–332; E. Pintea, "A Leading Publication: Gândirea," *Transylvanian Review* 7:3 (1998), 124–131; N. Sălcudeanu, "Present Day Reverberations of the Traditionalism—Nationalism—Orthodoxism Synthesis Professed by Gândirea

Magazine," in *Ethnicity and Religion in Central and Eastern Europe*, M. Crăciun and O. Ghitta, eds., (Cluj-Napoca: Cluj University Press, 1995), pp. 338–344.

10. On the evolution of the RomOC after 1918, see: Al Moraru, *Biserica Ortodoxă Română între anii 1885-2000. Biserică. Națiune. Cultură*, vol. III, tome I (București, 2006), pp. 90–148; S. Trîncă, "Constituția din 1923 și Biserica Ortodoxă," in *Anuarul Facultății de Teologie Ortodoxă* din cadrul Universității Babeș-Bolyai Cluj-Napoca, tome VII, 2002–2004, pp. 144–151.
11. I.-V. Leb, *Ortodoxie și Vechi-Catolicism* (Cluj-Napoca: Ed. Presa Universitară Clujeană, 1996), pp. 67–150; M. Păcurariu, *Istoria Bisericii Ortodoxe Române*, vol. 3 (sec. XIX–XX) (București: Ed. Institutului Biblic și de Misiune al Bisericii Ortodoxe Române, 1994), pp. 476–478; Al Moraru, *Biserica Ortodoxă Română între anii 1885-2000*, vol. III, tome II, pp. 235–298; A.-A. Podaru, "Mișcarea ecumenică. De la Edinburgh (1910) la Amsterdam (1948)," in *Ortodoxie și ecumenism*, I. V. Leb, ed., (Cluj-Napoca: Ed. Renașterea, 2008), pp. 19–27.
12. Out of some 80 Romanian newspapers and magazines that were issued after 1850 until the end of the nineteenth century, 12 can be described as church journals. Of those, 5 came from the Orthodox environment: *Biserica și școala* (Arad, 1877); *Foaia diecezană* (Caransebeș, 1886); *Lumina* (Arad, 1872); *Speranța* (Arad, 1869); *Telegraful Român* (Sibiu, 1853). M. Bedecean, *Presa și bisericile românești din Transilvania (1865–1873)* (Cluj-Napoca: Ed. Presa Universitară Clujeană, 2010), p. 18. The *Amvonul* magazine, issued in Oradea from 1868 under the supervision of Iustin Popfiu, had a strictly theological and religious character and was addressed to Orthodox and Greek Catholics alike, which made it an exception in the religious Romanian press. See Bedecean, *Presa și bisericile românești din Transilvania (1865–1873)*, pp. 26–27.
13. See Bedecean, *Presa și bisericile românești din Transilvania (1865–1873)*, p. 22.
14. For a general presentation of the Orthodox press in the interwar period, see M. Păcurariu, *Istoria Bisericii Ortodoxe Române*, vol. 3, pp. 466–467; I. V. Leb, "Presa bisericească transilvăneană," in *Biserică și implicare: studii privind istoria Bisericii Ortodoxe Române* (Cluj-Napoca: Ed. Limes, 2000), pp. 97–115.
15. For information on the life and activity of Archmandrite Iuliu Scriban, see M. Păcurariu, *Dicționarul Teologilor Români* (București: Ed. Enciclopedică, 2002), pp. 432–434.
16. See ibid., pp. 293–294.
17. Ibid., pp. 321–323.
18. Ibid., pp. 112–113.
19. Ibid., pp. 510–511.
20. Ibid., p. 323.
21. Ibid., pp. 382–384.
22. The Romanian Orthodox press participated actively in the debate on the Concordat, expressing its virulent, active, and constant protest. The press argued that the Concordat was a threat to both the Romanian stata and the Orthodox Church, which was severely disadvantaged by it. It further condemned the political influence of the Vatican. For the way these issues were reflected in the Cluj journal *Renașterea*, see C. Ghișa, "Întărind vechi alterități, ridicând noi frontiere: Concordatul dintre România și Vatican—1929," *Studia Universitatis Babeș-Bolyai, Theologia Catholica* LV: 4 (2010), 43–56.
23. For a general presentation of the situation of the Catholic Church of both rites in interwar Romania, see I. M. Bucur, *Din istoria Bisericii Greco-Catolice Române (1918–1953)* (Cluj-Napoca: Ed. Accent, 2003), pp. 29–77.
24. See C. Ghisa, *Biserica Greco-Catolica din Transilvania 1700–1850. Elaborarea discursului identitar* (Cluj-Napoca: Ed. Presa Universitara Clujeana, 2006), pp. 255–260.
25. *Glasul Monahilor* I:13 (București,1924), pp. 3–4.
26. *Misionarul* II:2 (1930), p. 132.
27. *Glasul Monahilor* V:114 (București, 1928), p. 3. The idea of the pope's deification also appeared in *Biserica Ortodoxă Română* 42:6 (1924), p. 380.

28. *Biserica Ortodoxă Română* 42:3 (1924), p. 141.
29. *Biserica Ortodoxă Română* 42:9 (1924), p. 538.
30. Ibid., pp. 539–540.
31. Nicodim Munteanu, "Lustru fals" (fake façade), in *Calendarul Arhiepiscopiei Iaşilor* (1932), p. 66.
32. *Viaţa Ilustrată* 1:1 (Sibiu, 1934), p. 3, see also p. 6
33. *Misionarul* 2:1 (Chişinău, 1930), p. 38; *Calea Mântuirii* 1:17 (Arad, 1935), p. 3, also see 3:42 (1943), p. 2; *Calendarul bunului creştin* (Sibiu, 1936), p. 136; *Glasul Monahilor* 7:211 (Bucureşti, 1930), p. 1.
34. *Renaşterea* 5:16 (Cluj, 1927), p. 5.
35. *Viaţa Ilustrată* 1:1 (Sibiu, 1934), p. 16—in no. 10, p. 23, referred to the "systematic attacks of Catholicism of both rites against Orthodoxy." The article "Biserica noastră să vegheze" claimed that "Catholicism is moving its attacking forces, seen or occult"—*Clujul Ortodox* 1:12 (1931), 1. See also the article "Religia adevărată şi religiile false. Atacul neputincios al catolicismului" (True religion and false religions. The powerless attack of Catholicism), *Glasul Monahilor* 5:114 (Bucureşti, 1928), p. 3. See also the article from *Misionarul*, presenting RCC tactics to attract new believers in Bulgaria, through the "bribing of souls than are to be sold": *Misionarul* 2:9 (Chişinău, 1930), p. 807.
36. *Glasul Monahilor* 7:237 (Bucureşti, 1930), p. 1.
37. *Biserica Ortodoxă Română*, series II, year 41 (1922), pp. 71–73.
38. *Albina* is called "the journal of Catholic contempt in Romania"—in *Biserica Ortodoxă Română* 9 (1924), p. 534.
39. *Biserica Ortodoxă Română* 13 (1923), p. 1010.
40. *Biserica Ortodoxă Română* 6 (1924), p. 379.
41. *Apostolul* 3:11–14 (Bucureşti, 1926), pp. 102–103; *Viaţa Ilustrată* 1:10 (Sibiu, 1934), p. 3; *Glasul Monahilor* 7:218 (Bucureşti, 1930), p. 3; *Glasul Monahilor* 8:257 (Bucureşti, 1931), p. 4.
42. *Biserica Ortodoxă Română* 3 (1924), p. 138.
43. *Glasul Monahilor* 6:162 (Bucureşti, 1929), p. 3.
44. *Biserica Ortodoxă Română* 6 (1924), p. 380.
45. *Calea adevărului* 1:6 (Bucureşti, parish St. Voivodes, 1932), pp. 33–35—author pr. Haralambie Popescu; for the same idea, see *Credinţa* 1:9 (Bucureşti, 1927), p. 1; *Renaşterea* 7:3 (Cluj, 1929), p. 4.
46. *Apostolul* 7:9 (Bucureşti, 1930), pp. 167–168. Another article referred to "fairy-tale fortunes"—see *Glasul Monahilor* 1:13 (1924), p. 4; and in 1932 the same journal commented ironically and negatively about the new pope's automobile, the most luxurious in the world—"What a huge difference between the donkey used by our Lord and the pope's automobile!"—*Glasul Monahilor* 8:313 (Bucureşti, 1932), p. 6.
47. *Apostolul* 3:11–14 (Bucureşti, 1926), p. 103.
48. *Fântâna Darurilor* 1:1 (Bucureşti, 1928), pp. 9–11.
49. *Glasul Monahilor* 8:257 (Bucureşti, 1931), p. 4.
50. *Misionarul* 2:2 (Chişinău, 1930), p. 114; *Glasul Monahilor* 5:114 (Bucureşti, 1928), p. 4; *Renaşterea* 8:12 (Cluj, 1930), p. 5.
51. *Glasul Monahilor* 7:218 (Bucureşti, 1930), p. 3; *Biserica Ortodoxă Română* (1922), pp. 144–145; *Biserica Ortodoxă Română* 9 (1924), pp. 535–536; Teodor M. Popescu, "Cucerirea Constantinopolului de către latini ca mijloc de unire a bisericilor," *Studii Teologice* series II, 1:1–2 (1929), pp. 63–99.
52. *Apostolul* 2:1–2 (Bucureşti, 1925), pp. 5–6. The RomOC's ecumenical activities included contacts with other Orthodox Churches, with representatives of the Anglican Church, with French Protestants, and a conference at Sinaia, Romania, organized by the national council of the International Alliance for Peace through Church. See also: *Calea Mântuirii* 1:17 (Arad, 1935), p. 3—"Only the Catholics do not want to talk!" I. Vască's article "Church and Union," presented the relation between states and churches. He wrote: "The RCC did

not want to have relations with any other church, living in isolation and raising more and more the walls that separated it from all other churches... On so many occasions it stressed its superiority over all the other Christian communities and presumed the exclusive right to speak in the name of Jesus Christ. Therefore, it became an isolated island." *Renaşterea* 7:2 (Cluj, 1929), pp. 4–5.

53. *Biserica Ortodoxă Română* (1922), p. 71.
54. *Apostolul*, Bucureşti 3:11–14 (1926), p. 102; *Biserica Ortodoxă Română* (1922), p. 145.
55. See: *Misionarul* 2:1 (Chişinău, 1930), p. 7; *Biserica Ortodoxă Română* 43 (1923), pp. 532–533; *Renaşterea* 7:4 (1929), p. 2. Ioan Vască argued that the Orthodox Church was the true Church of Christ, thus having the vocation of achieving church unity.
56. The visit of bishop John Greig of Gibraltar in Bucharest, in 1922, the visit of bishop Charles Gore, "a great theologian" in 1923: *Biserica Ortodoxă Română* 43:9 (1923), pp. 647–648. The visit in Bucharest of another Anglican delegation in 1935: *Viaţa Ilustrată* 2:7 (Sibiu, 1935), p. 1; *Calea Mântuirii* 1:17 (Arad, 1935), p. 3; *Calendarul bunului creştin* (Sibiu, 1936), pp. 132–133.
57. *Viaţa Ilustrată* 2:7 (Sibiu, 1935), p. 1.
58. *Biserica Ortodoxă Română* series II, 41:1 (1922), p. 71.
59. *Legea Românească*, Oradea 3:4 (1923), p. 1.
60. *Biserica Ortodoxă Română* (1922), pp. 144–145, also see 41:8 (1922), p. 469.
61. *Biserica Ortodoxă Română* 43:9 (1923), p. 648.
62. *Biserica Ortodoxă Română* 44:6 (1924), p. 342.
63. *Biserica Ortodoxă Română* 43:7 (1923), pp. 532–533.
64. *Apostolul* 5:4 (Bucureşti, 1928), pp. 63–64.
65. Pope Pius XI's encyclical criticized the ecumenical movement for its direction, arguing that the result would be a pan-Christianity based on mutual love, but this would have meant the relativization of the faith. But real unity meant primarily unity in faith. See Podaru, "Mişcarea ecumenică," p. 30.
66. It was said: "One cannot conceive of union outside the formula: the return and obedience of the Churches that had separated from the Catholic, Apostolic and Roman Church, the only one deposit and exclusive protector of the revealed treasury of the Truth." *Apostolul* 5:4 (Bucureşti, 1928), p. 63.
67. *Legea Românească* 3:35 (Oradea, 1923), p. 1.
68. *Renaşterea* 8:8 (1930), p. 5; *Renaşterea* 10:12 (1932), pp. 5–6; *Renaşterea* 13:22 (1935), p. 2; *Apostolul* 3:11–14 (Bucureşti, 1926), p. 103; *Ortodoxia* 4:49 (Bucureşti, 1937), p. 7; *Misionarul* 2:1 (Chişinău, 1930), p. 36; *Misionarul* 2:11 (Chişinău, 1930), p. 1079; *Viaţa Ilustrată* 1:1 (Sibiu, 1934), p. 7.
69. Archm. I. Scriban, "The Vatican's Negotiations with the Bolsheviks," in *Biserica Ortodoxă Română* (1922), p. 68.
70. *Apostolul* 5:3 (Bucureşti, 1928), p. 46. On the issue of the diplomatic relations of the pope with the Bolsheviks, see the article "Amestecul Papei în treburile Rusiei" (The Pope's interference in Russia's internal politics), in *Clujul Ortodox* 1:12 (1931), p. 4.
71. *Misionarul* 2:4 (Chişinău, 1930), pp. 381–382. The same idea of corruption appears also in *Glasul Monahilor* 7:235 (Bucureşti, 1930), p. 1.
72. *Biserica Ortodoxă Română* (1922), pp. 145–146.
73. See *Misionarul* 2:1 (Chişinău, 1930), p. 5.
74. See *Misionarul* 2:4 (Chişinău, 1930), pp. 338–347.
75. *Misionarul* 2:4 (1930), pp. 371–377.
76. See the articles referring to the Concordat in: *Apostolul* 6:12 (Bucureşti, 1929), pp. 177–178; *Viaţa Ilustrată* 2:11 (Sibiu, 1935), pp. 20–21; *Glasul Monahilor* 1:13 (Bucureşti, 1924), pp. 3–4; 1:16 (1924), p. 3; 6:177 (1929), pp. 1–2; *Biserica Ortodoxă Română* series II, 43:6 (1924), p. 339.
77. *Renaşterea* X:12 (Cluj, 1932), pp. 5–6.

78. *F.O.R.* 3–4 (Craiova, 1934), p. 6. See also *Biserica Ortodoxă Română* 1 (1922), p. 447—the speech of Metropolitan Miron Cristea; *Misionarul* 2:11 (Chişinău, 1930), pp. 1077–1078; *Renaşterea* 1:7 (Cluj, 1923), p. 2; *Legea Românească* 3:10 (Oradea, 1923), p. 6.
79. *Viaţa Ilustrată* 1:1 (Sibiu, 1934), p. 2—article by Nicolae Colan, chief editor. The idea can also be found in N. Stoicescu, "Ortodoxia noastră" (Our Orthodoxy), *Ortodoxia* 1:7 (Bucureşti, 1933), p. 2.
80. *Calea Mântuirii* 1:5 (Arad, 1935), p. 3.
81. *Viaţa Ilustrată* 1:1 (Sibiu, 1934), pp. 1–2; *Ortodoxia* 5:45 (Bucureşti, 1938), p. 1; *Renaşterea* 5:21 (Cluj, 1927), p. 1. The expression "the Romanian law" was given the following recent definition: "*Romanian law* has always been understood as that Orthodoxy which remained Romanians' distinctive religion in spite of all the attempts to attract them to other religions, thus contributing to the ethnic survival of our people." I. Gh. Retegan, "Biserică şi naţiune—simbioză şi identitate," in *Anuarul Facultăţii de Teologie Ortodoxă Cluj-Napoca*, tome V, 1996–1998 (Cluj-Napoca, 2000), p. 136.
82. *Misionarul* 1:1 (Chişinău, 1929), p. 25.
83. *Apostolul* 4:5 (Bucureşti, 1927), p. 38.
84. *Biserica Ortodoxă Română*, series II, 40:1 (1921), p. 68.
85. *Apostolul* 7:19 (Bucureşti, 1930), p. 287. See also *Legea Românească* 3:48 (Oradea, 1923), pp. 1–2.
86. *Credinţa* 1:1 (Bucureşti, 1927), pp. 2–3; 1:13, p. 13.
87. See *Biserica Ortodoxă Română* 111:4–6 (1993), pp. 43–69—articles by Prof. D. Radu and Metropolitan Antonie Plămădeală of Ardeal on the dialogue of the RomOC with Catholics regarding Uniatism and on the Balamand document. See also *Renaşterea* 8:4 (1997), p. 9. For the discussions at the Balamand meeting, see *Catholiques et Orthodoxes: Les Enjeux de l'Uniatisme. Dans le sillage de Balamand* (Paris: Cerf-Bayard, 2004).
88. Dan Ciachir, "Misionarism, prozelitism, toleranţă" (Mission, proselytism, tolerance), *Renaşterea* new series 8:2(86) (1997), p. 4. See also Radu Preda, "Orthodoxy and Catholicism 1996–1997," in *Renaşterea* 8:1 (1998), pp. 4–5.
89. *Biserica Ortodoxă Română* 111:4–6 (1993), pp. 43–45; *Renaşterea* 10:1 (1999), p. 5.
90. Ion Alexandru Mizgan, "De ce Ortodoxia?" [Why Orthodoxy?], *Renaşterea* 8:4 (1997), p. 9.
91. Metropolitan Bartolomeu Anania of Cluj: Valeriu Anania, *Pro Memoria. Acţiunea catolicismului în România interbelică*, ed. II (Cluj-Napoca: Ed. Renaşterea, 2005). The book reasserts all the elements of the interwar discourse against the Concordat between Vatican and the Romanian state, using all the same references to Catholicism that were formulated in the 1920s and 1930s.
92. *Legea Românească* 19:2, new series (2008), p. 39. Article by Dumitru Megheşan on Augustine, Thomas Aquinas, Anselm of Canterbury, or Bonaventura as precursors of this antireligious phenomenon.
93. Article by Metropolitan Antonie Plămădeală in *Biserica Ortodoxă Română* 111:4–6 (1993), p. 43.
94. Radu Preda's article in *Renasterea* 10:1 (1999), p. 3. The formula is relevant, even though it was employed in the discourse on relations with the Greek Catholics of Romania.
95. See the discussions of Pope John Paul II's visit to Romania in *Biserica Ortodoxă Română* 117:1–6 (1999), pp. 31–205. The visit was presented as the pope's pilgrimage to Romanian Orthodoxy, p. 48; *Legea Românească* 10:1 new series (1999), pp. 5–8; Patriarch Teoctist's evaluation of the papal visit to Romania, in the journal of the Romanian Patriarchate, *Ortodoxia* 50:1–2 (1999), pp. 3–5. The text also referred to the Balamand document.

8

"Oh, East Is East, and West Is West…": The Character of Orthodox-Greek Catholic Discourse in Ukraine and Its Regional Dimensions

Natalia Kochan

The notions of East and West can be rather confusing in the Ukrainian context. The stock phrase "between East and West," often used to describe Ukrainian specificity, is too broad in its outlines when applied to a country with a vast territory, comparable to that of France, and profound regional differences. The latter belong to taboo topics in Ukrainian public discourse, since state-building is promoted here within a nation-state paradigm where nation is understood in essentialist, ethnic terms and is believed to constitute an organic entity, "one nation." The age of ideology and nation-state paradigm has not yet ended here.

East and West do exist in Ukraine, shaped by the distinctive, centuries-long history and culture of their respective populations. Cultural patterns in the Ukrainian West—of an agrarian, traditional type, which is closed and exclusive by definition—do not have much in common with what is usually referred to as patterns of Western civilization. And Ukraine's East, which came into being as a result of inland colonization/extension of a rising Russian empire with intensive labor migration to undeveloped virgin lands, can hardly be characterized as "Eastern." The exploration of the Ukrainian historical Wild Steppe region (scantily populated—or rather depopulated—lands on the border with the Islamic world) was accompanied by intensive ethnic migrations of Slavic peoples from Turkish-occupied territories in the southwest, by economically active adventurers and independent spirits from all over Russia, and by intensive labor migration and the further industrialization of the region. This type of colonization—as distinct from Western overseas colonization—is linked to an ethos and epos/mythology that break with traditionalism and transform society into an open, inclusive, and dynamic "melting pot," where the local and regional identifications of its population predominate over ethnic identities and where individual merits and corporate values prevail over rural communalism. Ukraine's East (Donbas), despite the current deep depression of the region, can hardly be described in terms of an Eastern-type society.[1]

The regions of contemporary Ukraine for centuries constituted peripheral parts of stronger neighbor states (Russia, Austro-Hungary, Poland), sharing their history, integrating into and contributing to their culture and traditions, undergoing oppressions and discriminations, as any minority does under a stronger power, especially one that builds a nation-state/empire or whose political regime is of an authoritarian or totalitarian nature.

Ironically, the unification of Ukrainian historical territories into one political unit, the Soviet Socialist Republic, happened as a consequence of Soviet expansionist and aggressive policy before, during, and after World War II. Eastern Halychyna (Galicia), Volyn', Bukovyna, and Sub-Carpathian (or Trans-Carpathian) regions were annexed in the course of the war, and the Crimean peninsula was attached to its territory in 1956 for political reasons. Thus for the first time Ukrainians of different regions found themselves in one quasi-state body. After the collapse of Soviet experiments with the construction of a "new historical entity—one Soviet people" they were confronted by many different images of the Ukrainian "other," hidden behind nonethnic principles of the Soviet nation-building policy, despite the fact that the Soviet interpretation of ethnicity was basically essentialist.

Regional "otherness" in Ukraine was and still is too profound to match with the Procrustean bed of *Volksgeist, Blut und Boden*,[2] as romanticized by Ukrainian nationalists, or with the concepts of "one people—one faith" and "one independent state—one local, independent Church" that were supposed to be the cornerstones of post-Soviet Ukrainian nationhood. At the same time, Ukrainian political classes (rather than "elites") failed to create any civic and democratic integrative prospects for social and political development, being focused exclusively on a state-building process that finally resulted in the creation of a Ukrainian version of Leviathan—an almost failed state without a self-organized and self-sufficient society.[3]

To date, it remains impossible to speak of Ukrainian identity in the singular, or as an accomplished fact. A broad variety of identifications position themselves as Ukrainian—in particular, ethnic ones, referring to themselves as authentic and native, claiming to be the "only true" and exceptional identity, and trying to dominate public discussions on nationhood and state-building. Samuel P. Huntington's theory of the clash of civilizations is not popular in independent Ukraine, since it undermines the nation-state building myths of "one, united (*soborna*) Ukraine," "one people, one nation," "one national Church." Huntington's theory emphasizes objective "fault lines" between civilizational groups, determined by cultural and religious differences, and explicitly separates the Western part of Ukraine from the rest of it, especially, from the southeast. The author classifies Ukraine as a "cleft country," where large groups of people identify with a separate civilization, and argues his hypothesis with the example of a "cleft" between the Orthodox-dominated East and the Greek-Catholic dominated West.[4]

But—as usually happens with national myths based on reductions—the reality is far more complicated. Ukrainian historian Yaroslav Hrytsak has suggested with bitter humor that there are not two but at least twenty-two Ukraines.[5] Dominique Arel argues that the regional divisions in Ukraine are deep-rooted and permanent, rather than transitory, and that they cannot be explained by nation-state building processes alone. He shows that even in the regions defined by Huntington as belonging to the same civilization matrix there are many additional inward divisions. For example, the ethnic structure of southeastern Ukraine is inclusively dual: Ukrainian self-identification coexists with a sense of the Russian language as native, and Ukrainian political loyalties are combined with friendly sentiments toward Russia and memories about common elements of culture and idealized historical past.[6] To Ukrainian essentialists, the statement sounds like a contradiction in terms, in spite of the objective reality behind it and the prevalence of a dual identity among the Ukrainian population in the southeast. The Ukrainian Orthodox Church, under the jurisdiction of the Moscow Patriarchate (UOC-MP), has no competitors in the region.

The national narrative presupposes that a "true" Ukrainian should be strictly Ukrainian-speaking and attend a "Ukrainian national Church." The list of "national" churches currently in Ukraine includes two Orthodox Churches with irregular status (the Ukrainian Orthodox Church of the Kyiv Patriarchate—UOC-KP and the Ukrainian Autocephalous Orthodox Church—UAOC), and the Ukrainian Greek-Catholic Church—UGCC, not without reason characterized by Sophia Senyk as being "a victim to nationalism."[7] On many questions—from positive affirmations of nationhood and patriotism to xenophobic statements and resentful witch-hunting of speculative enemies of the nation—nationalism unites all three "national" churches.[8]

In its dealings with the "national" Orthodox structures, the UGCC has found it difficult to keep to the rules officially established in relations between the Roman Catholic Church (RCC) and the Orthodox Churches, when the RCC committed herself to respect Orthodox canonical regulations and to minimize communication with Orthodox Churches with irregular status. Thus, it was common for the "national" churches to concelebrate non-Eucharistic worship commemorating "national heroes" or events of national history, which were interpreted within an ethnic nationalist paradigm with its high level of resentment. The "national" churches do not miss an opportunity to participate in important events of one another's inner life. For instance, the head of the UOC-KP (excommunicated by the Patriarchate of Moscow) earlier was a guest of honor at the installation ceremony of Bishop Husar as Exarch of Kyiv and Vyshgorod and later at the installation of Major Archbishop Sviatoslav Shevchuk as head of the UGCC, and was the first to congratulate him. The UOC-KP's official media interpreted such contacts as a gradual recognition of the church with irregular status by the Catholic Church[9] (to compensate for their complete isolation in the fullness of Orthodoxy).

The hierarchy of the UOC-KP still preserves an awareness of the impossibility of liturgical concelebration with the UGCC, whereas the latter is less sensitive to the respective canonical requirements. When in the autumn of 2009 the bishop and clergy of the UOC-KP participated in liturgical vestments in a liturgical celebration of the Greek Catholic bishop of Kolomyja-Chernivtsi, the Synod of the UOC-KP publicly exercised disciplinary measures against them and issued a special communiqué with an explicit prohibition of intercommunion with Greek Catholics. Greek Catholic participants interpreted the case as a "unification of Orthodox and Greek-Catholics," but there was no reaction or comment from Greek Catholic authorities.[10]

The grassroots "ecumenism" between the "national" churches exceeds officially established limits. In the aforementioned provincial mountain town of Kolomyja, it also includes the joint construction of a church by the UGCC and the UOC-KP for their shared use. The local Orthodox bishop explained by saying that the UOC-KP has a common aim with Greek Catholics "to build one/united Church in Ukraine."[11] As it usually happens when nationalism comes to the fore, nationalist affiliations overrule religious ones. No matter what forms such cooperation may take in the future, it is already clear that it does not strengthen the position of the Catholic Church in its international dialogue with the Orthodox Churches.

The rivalry and animosity between Orthodox and Greek Catholics that characterized Ukrainian religious life in Halychyna during the 1990s have largely been resolved by the restoration of confiscated church properties to the UGCC and by the construction of new church buildings by the Orthodox. The proportion of Orthodox parishes in Western Ukraine was reduced during 1992–1999 from 51.5 percent to 35.4 percent.[12] As for the UOC-MP, labeled by the "national" churches as a servant of the Communist regime, an oppressor, an invader and so on, it lost almost two-thirds of its parishes in Halychyna, which led the ROC to speak of a *pogrom* of Orthodoxy in Halychyna. Many former Orthodox parishes joined the UGCC, while others opted for newly founded "national" Orthodox Churches. The new Orthodox structures reidentified themselves within nationhood and the nation-state building paradigm, and paid for it by losing their regular status. The members of those new Orthodox institutions in Halychyna were mostly former Greek Catholics who made their choice in favor of an "independent national church in the independent nation-state," free from subordination to any center abroad (whether to the Vatican or to Moscow).

As Western Ukraine is the region with the highest level of ethnic mobilization in the country, it is natural that most of the communities of "national" churches are located there. In 2008, the UOC-KP had 42.9 percent of its communities in the western region, and the UAOC—70.7 percent. In addition, 93–95 percent of the Greek Catholic communities in Ukraine (excluding the Mukachevo eparchy, which has no administrative link with the UGCC) were located in the West in 2002–2008, mostly in the Lviv, Ivano-Frankivs'k, and Ternopil' oblasts.[13]

Exclusive identity prevails in the "national" churches. "Others" are welcomed on condition that they appropriate the Ukrainian culture and traditions as they are cultivated in one or another "national" church. Mobilized ethnicity can see no contradiction in the following statement: "The UGCC should be aware of its Catholicity not only in theology but also in ethnic and cultural aspects,"[14] in which universality is reduced to particularity.

The UOC-MP predominates in all regions except Halychyna.[15] As has been noted, dual identity (Ukrainian-Russian or Russian-Ukrainian depending on the prevalence of certain ethnic and cultural markers) dominates in the UOC-MP, a fact that does not exclude explicit Ukrainian or Russian self-identifications within the church as well, as it also includes Ukrainian Greeks, Romanians, Georgians and so on, who maintain their own linguistic, liturgical, and cultural patterns in worship and liturgical practice.

Thus, Samuel Huntington's "fault line" in Ukraine separates not only the Orthodox from Greek Catholics, but Greek Catholics and Orthodox with a mobilized ethnic identity from Orthodox with either dual Ukrainian Russian identity, or with another non-Ukrainian identity, or with marginalized and irrelevant ethnic self-identifications.

Finally, in order to put cultural and religious divisions in the country into proper perspective, one should take account of the 2002–2008 annual surveys of the Institute of Sociology of the Ukrainian Academy of Sciences, according to which 75 percent of Ukrainians identified themselves with Orthodoxy and 6.8 percent with Greek Catholicism.[16] In 2009, 41.7 percent identified themselves as members of the UOC-MP, while 27 percent were members of the UOC-KP, 16.5 percent of the UGCC, and 2.3 percent of the UAOC.[17]

In situating the fault line between Eastern Catholics and Orthodox in Ukraine, Samuel Huntington associates Eastern-rite Catholicism with Western civilization, as most Westerners do, considering "Catholic" as the key word in the expression "Eastern Catholics." The supposition is logical, and as long as Western theological content shapes the Eastern rite, the gradual Latinization/hybridization of ritual forms is unavoidable. Yet, in the current Ukrainian Greek Catholic milieu, the stress is placed on the word "Eastern" (and Ukrainian) rather than "Catholic." Some theologians point out the fact that Ukrainian Greek Catholic theology "goes beyond not only Catholicism but also Orthodoxy"[18] and try to substantiate the phenomenon of Eastern-Catholic theology.[19] Others go further and question the legitimacy of papal supremacy over the UGCC, stressing that it is Orthodox by nature but in communion with Rome.[20] Still others, on the contrary, argue that the Latinized rite is the most important marker of their identity—"the rite of the UGCC is sacred" and "leads to salvation."[21]

A significant number of Greek Catholics in Ukraine deny any form of Easternization of their church, as it has strong association with Orthodoxy. The older generation's memories of the forcible liquidation of the UGCC, which was supported by the ROC, and of the persecutions that followed are still an open wound. The knowledge of the younger generation is affected by nationalist resentment with a paradoxical combination of victimization and triumphalism. This milieu recalls that "the purification of the rite ('Easternization') always led to tragic and even catastrophic consequences in the history of our Church."[22] The opposition to "Easternization" and the defense of local Latinized tradition has already provoked a split within the UGCC and brought to life parallel structures, each of which claims to represent the "true faith of the fathers."

Samuel Huntington's "fault line" marks in Ukraine the frontier (*limitrophe*) zone between Orthodoxy and Western Christianity rather than separates them—in between there is the compact unit of Greek Catholicism that produces specific tensions and divisions. The line runs between:

1. *Orthodox and Greek Catholics.* This combination contains an intrinsic contradiction. From an Orthodox perspective, all Eastern Catholics are understood as unconditionally Catholic. Greek Catholics identify themselves in terms of an Orthodox-Catholic fusion, and it is precisely this matter that Orthodox can neither understand nor accept.

2. *Greek Catholics and Roman Catholics.* The settlement pattern of Ukrainian Roman Catholics does not correlate with the "fault line" but corresponds to historical settlements of the Polish minority in Ukraine. The line separates

Halychyna and Volyn' in the west, which for a long time has been densely populated by Roman Catholics. But the settlement of Roman Catholics stretches over the line to the east and southeast—to Podillja, Braclavschyna, and Zhytomyrschyna in the central and northern part of the country. It is in those regions that the RCC in Ukraine has almost 40 percent of its parishes.

The historical relations between Greek Catholic Ukrainians and Roman Catholic Poles in Halychyna were burdened with mutual rivalry, where religion was a marker not only of ethnicity but also of social status. The RCC in Ukraine until recently was negatively stereotyped by the UGCC as Polish and practicing proselytism among Ukrainians.[23] In fact, the Polish minority is one of the most assimilated groups in Ukraine. The national census in 2001 indicates that 71 percent of Ukrainian Poles consider Ukrainian as their native language and only 12.9 percent view Polish as their mother tongue.[24] In addition, Orthodox accusations of proselytism in Ukraine are addressed to Greek Catholics and never to Roman Catholics—unlike in Russia.

It took some time to contain the tension between the two Catholic structures in Ukraine and to put an end to nationalist resentment in the media (Greek Catholic in Ukraine and Roman Catholic mostly in Poland). But the current mutual initiatives of the two churches proceed to a large extent from the Vatican rather than from inner needs and dispositions.[25] The recently established annual conferences of the RCC and UGCC hierarchies owe their appearance to a direct order of the pope.[26] The predominant national discourse in the UGCC hampers further closer relations between Catholics of Eastern and of Latin rites.

3. *Greek Catholics and Greek Catholics with two competing identities*: "Ukrainian Eastern Catholic" as it was shaped after World War II in the Ukrainian Catholic Church abroad with reference to Metropolitan Sheptytsky and was exported to Ukraine in the early 1990s; and "Ukrainian Greek Catholic" local, traditional, Latinized piety as it was practiced during the interwar period and in the church underground.

Each of these lines of division contains contradictory, sometimes exclusive, elements that could be attributed to different types of civilization (Western/Catholic or Eastern/Orthodox) and, when these elements are mobilized and instrumentalized, they lead to divergence. This makes theological dialogue between Ukrainian Orthodox and Catholics even more important as a means of overcoming objective obstacles and limitations.

Strictly speaking, the full-fledged Orthodox-Catholic dialogue in Ukraine presupposes Greek Catholics from the Catholic side as the major interlocutor of the local Orthodox Church with regular status—the UOC-MP. The Greek Catholic attitude to canonical rules as they are understood in Orthodoxy is evident from the examples given earlier. But there is another fundamental question—to what extent could the UGCC, without an internal consensus about the essence of its identity—Easternized or Latinized, Catholic or Orthodox, be a credible partner of the Orthodox in a dialogue that the Orthodox see as basically theological?

Cardinal Husar has characterized the level of contemporary Ukrainian Greek Catholic theology as "very weak,"[27] yet stressing repeatedly in numerous interviews to Ukrainian media that Greek Catholics have the same theology as the Orthodox. The metaphorical language of religion allows one to express such ideas while using contradictory statements. "To be a Catholic—says the Cardinal—does not exclude being Orthodox in the theological and traditional understanding." The cardinal states that the center of the church is constituted not only by Jesus Christ but also by the successor of St. Peter—the pope of Rome[28]—as if papal primacy does not constitute one of the major hindrances in Orthodox-Catholic dialogue, and as if the Orthodox do not view the bishop of Rome as the patriarch of the West (a title that was cancelled by Pope Benedict XVI), equal among equals or at most *primus inter pares*.

The newly elected head of the UGCC Major Archbishop Sviatoslav Shevchuk, commenting on the identity of Eastern theology in the context of confessional diversity, argued that in order to understand "the definition 'Eastern,' one should from the very beginning go beyond the limits of one Church, either Catholic or Orthodox,"[29] describing the identity of the UGCC as having existed in the time of an undivided Christianity,[30] thus contributing to the foundation myth of the UGCC.

One may suppose that in this case we are dealing with the phenomenon of local theology, if that phenomenon were not so different from both Catholic and Orthodox ways of theologizing. A certain theological amorphousness could be considered as an inner problem of the UGCC. But it is precisely from such a starting point that the leaders of the church propose to the Orthodox Churches in Ukraine theologically failing models of unification (in which the formula "one people—one church" prevails[31]): whether one patriarchate under Roman supremacy,[32] or a self-proclaimed, autonomous structure with established intercommunion and under the jurisdiction of their respective ecclesiastic administrative centers—Rome, Moscow, and, possibly, in the case of the UAOC, Constantinople. Since the Orthodox Churches see the UGCC as a part of the Catholic Church bound with a somewhat modified church discipline and order, they might suppose that such initiatives have the approval of Rome, but that is not the case.

The character of Orthodox-Greek Catholic discourse at the highest level about the possibility of interconfessional dialogue illustrates a profound misunderstanding by Greek Catholics of what Orthodox and Roman Catholics expect from such encounters and how they see the ways of achieving better mutual understanding.[33]

The former head of the UGCC Cardinal Lubomyr Husar wrote letters to the leaders of the two major Orthodox Churches in Ukraine—to Metropolitan Volodymyr (Sabodan) of the UOC-MP (April 26, 2008) and to self-proclaimed Patriarch Filaret (Denysenko), the head of the UOC-KP (February 14, 2006), explaining his understanding of the possible unification of the "Churches of the Kyivan tradition" (a key concept in the UGCC's national and theological narrative) and of the fruits of such unification. According to Cardinal Husar, a future "united local Ukrainian Church will be resurrected through a communion of the Churches of Kyivan tradition" on condition that (i) the future, united church will recognize the churches of Constantinople, Rome, and Moscow as sister churches; (ii) the latter churches will recognize the Ukrainian Church as their sister church; and, finally (iii) all of them will confess the faith of the first seven Ecumenical Councils and recognize the validity of the sacraments in each of the churches. The "Kyivan Church" should be represented by a patriarch, who would be elected by Ukrainian churches of the various jurisdictions. Such a visionary project may come to fruition, according to Lubomyr Husar, when all "our Churches," the state, and broad masses of Ukrainian society unite their efforts. The fruit of these efforts may become "a powerful factor in the consolidation of society and a foundation for the Ukrainian national idea."[34]

Cardinal Husar's letters evoked predictably negative responses from both of the Orthodox Churches, irrespective of their regular or irregular status. The head of the UOC-KP wrote on behalf of its Synod:

> The Ukrainian Orthodox Church of the Patriarchate of Kyiv belongs to the family of local Orthodox Churches and constitutes an integral part of Universal Orthodoxy. The Ukrainian Greek-Catholic Church constitutes a part of the Roman Catholic Church despite all her distinctiveness as a Church of the Eastern tradition. That is why the only possible path to the unification of our Churches is to return to their former unity in faith, as it was in the time of the Metropolitan See of Kyiv under the jurisdiction of the Patriarchate of Constantinople before the Union of Brest 1596, and even better—to the unity of faith between Christian West and East that was broken in 1054.
>
> History has proven that attempts to unite East and West on the ground of Roman dogmatic tradition led not to understanding but to even deeper division [...]. On the question of the unity of the Christian East and West, our Church will continue to keep to Eastern Orthodox dogmatic and canonical tradition...the model of forcible institutional unification without the achievement of true unity in faith is mistaken and unstable.[35]

In numerous interviews with the Ukrainian media, the head of the UOC-KP has added that the Ukrainian Orthodox and Ukrainian Greek Catholics "are native by blood" and, therefore, have much in common.[36] He states that "the unity and independence of the Church is inseparable from the unity and independence of the state." As the Greek Catholic Church entered into union with Rome "when Ukraine already had lost its statehood," now that Ukraine has gained its independence, the reason for a separation between Orthodox and Greek Catholics no longer exists.[37] But, he further adds:

> I think that Greek-Catholics may unite with the Orthodox Church only when Ukrainian Orthodox Churches unite into one local Church and the latter will be recognized. At that point, the Greek-Catholic Church will return to the Orthodox Church and separate from Rome. Although members of the Greek-Catholic Church will definitely lose their Orthodox rite and become Roman Catholics. [...] It would be necessary either for the Orthodox to become Catholics, or for Catholics to become Orthodox in order to unite the Greek-Catholic and the Orthodox Churches in Ukraine. Only under such conditions is unification possible.[38]

A stern response to Cardinal Husar came from the Synod of the UOC-MP. The letter pointed out that the suggested model of unity does not differ from the "uniate" one, contradicts the general context of Orthodox-Catholic dialogue, which aims to "arrive at a common theological understanding of dogmatic differences between our Churches," and has already been rejected by the Catholic and Orthodox Churches as a method of achieving unity. The UOC-MP hierarchs questioned the UGCC's credentials to put forward such initiatives (i.e., being a part of the Catholic Church, to speak on behalf of the whole ecclesiastic body) and declared them invalid on ecclesiological, canonical, and liturgical grounds.

At the same time, the synodal decision contains suggestions for clearing the way to unity as understood by the Orthodox. Generally, it presupposes a deconstruction of the structures of the UGCC. Some members of the UGCC, "who identify themselves with Eastern Christianity may come back to Orthodoxy, and those for whom their link with the Church of Rome is dear, may join it keeping their Eastern rite." The Orthodox hierarchs refer to such Catholic structures as monasteries in Chevetogne (Belgium) and Bose (Italy), where the Byzantine rite is practiced and they form no separate canonical unit. "This is how one of the important obstacles in the way of restoring the universal unity between the Orthodox and Roman Catholic Churches may disappear. We are aware that it is not easy, but in this case it depends exclusively on us—Orthodox and Greek-Catholics in Ukraine."[39]

Summing up the "ecumenical" Greek Catholic-Orthodox exchange of opinions at the highest level, one may see that on the Greek Catholic side it fails theologically, being too dependent on national and nativist discourses. The Greek Catholic vision of a forthcoming ecclesiastical unity is dominated by a chiliastic expectation of "national/ethnic unity." The UOC-KP fully shares with Greek Catholics their ethnic and nationhood mythology, and at the same time keeps—selectively—its ties to Orthodox theological foundations. Characteristically, the nationalist standpoint of Ukrainian "national" churches was (mis-)used by some members of Parliament, when in October 1995 they founded a group with the aim "to gather an All-Ukrainian Unifying Council of the Orthodox and Greek-Catholic Churches, that eventually would merge into one Ukrainian self-governing Church."[40]

The position of the UOC-MP proceeds from its multiethnic composition and extends beyond the national discourse, although the idea of Eastern Slavic unity—currently reformulated in Russia into a political and religious concept of "Rus' world" that aims to strengthen the ties between the Orthodox Churches in Russia, Ukraine, and Belorus—forms an essential part of its identity. At the same time, the UOC-MP has such a firm theological background that it could hardly ever be fully set in practice. However, there is little doubt that this standpoint will undergo a process of contextualization as soon as Greek Catholics elaborate a more clearly defined confessional identity—either Catholic or Orthodox—and adapt their theology accordingly. The "third way," the Greek Catholic option between Catholicism and Orthodoxy (in the role of a "mediator"),[41] does not elicit any response from Orthodox or Catholic milieus.

While it may be argued that ethnic nationalism cannot be an intrinsic state of mind of the "national" churches, it does have a history of its own and roots in the local cultures of certain regions of Ukraine. Among them, Halychyna—stereotyped in the national narrative as a "Ukrainian Piedmont"—occupies the leading position. Its population demonstrates the highest level of mobilized ethnicity in the country and its representatives (irreligious included) constantly strive to bring a local, ethnic version of nationalism to the national level. The fact that most parishes of the "national" Ukrainian Orthodox Churches and the absolute majority of the Greek Catholic parishes are concentrated in Halychyna illustrates the high level of dependence of religion on local culture and history. Similarly, most Orthodox parishes with predominantly Russian or Russian-Ukrainian identities are located in the southeast of the country.

The dependence is also illustrated by regular monitoring data of the integral index of distance between different ethnic groups (within a Bogardus social distance scale) prepared by the Institute of Sociology, Ukrainian Academy of Sciences, as well as by the data from the International Sociological Survey Program.[42] In 2006, sociologists again pointed out a rather high level of psychological distance between representatives of different ethnic groups and the growth of xenophobic feelings in

Ukraine. The level of tolerance was diminishing from eastern to western Ukraine. Ludmila Rjazanova analyzed the confessional dimension of those tendencies and showed that the highest level of isolationism and xenophobia was demonstrated by Greek Catholic respondents. According to the study, among "nonbelievers" and "Orthodox" the deviations from average levels of isolationism and xenophobia in the country were negligible, while Greek Catholics demonstrated rather radical opinions on some points.[43]

At the same time, Maxim Paraschevin shows that the

> lower level of tolerance among the populations of Western regions would be noticeable even if Greek Catholics were excluded from the overall picture. It may have been assumed that it was the domination in the region of the Greek-Catholics with their lower level of tolerance that determined the level of tolerance in the West. But even looking exclusively at Orthodox believers, lower levels of tolerance in the West remain.[44]

We already know that the overwhelming majority of Orthodox believers in the West are members of the "national" churches.

These sociological observations bring us back to Huntington's civilizational "fault lines." It will no doubt be a challenge for future Ukrainian politicians to build a harmonized Ukrainian political nation and a functional state. In the case of the Ukrainian churches, what is needed is an honest answer to the question: who will transform whom?—will the world transform the church, or will the church transform the world, bearing a convincing witness to its faith and hope? For now in Ukraine, "East is East, and West is West" and it remains to be seen whether "the twain shall meet, till earth and sky stand presently at God's great Judgment Seat." There is also the "mediator" between East and West, whose specific contribution to that meeting of "the twain" still requires specification and an accompanying theological argumentation that will be convincing to both the East and the West.

Notes

1. On regional differences and identities in Ukraine, see: Лариса Нагорна, *Регіональна ідентичність: український контекст* (К.: ІПіЕНД ім. І.Ф. Кураса НАН України, 2008).
2. The newly elected head of the UGCC, Major Archbishop Sviatoslav Shevchuk, in arguing for the unification of all Ukrainians into "one people"—"one great European nation, one of the most populous European nations" characteristically refers to them as "children of the same motherland." *Нова Зоря* (орган Івано-Франківської єпархії УГКЦ)—№ 5—2012—С. 5. The head of the Commission for Catechisation of the UGCC emphasized during the presentation of a new version of the Cathechism of the UGCC its integrative, national function: "common traditions, spirit, Ukrainian blood." "Церква як добра мати старається дати настільну книгу, яка повинна допомогти кожній людині осягнути святість." Інтерв'ю із с. Л. Цюпою, головою Катехитичної комісії УГКЦ — *Патріярхат* (Published by the Ukrainian Patriarchal Society in the United States by a Ukrainian editorial board in Lviv)—№ 5—2011—С. 9.
3. The critical questions of the broken bonds of Ukrainian society and its "normlessness" (*anomie*) were analyzed at the Institute of Sociology of the Ukrainian National Academy of Sciences on the basis of annual sociological surveys in the years 1992–2010 within the framework of "anomie theory." *Українське суспільство 1992–2010. Соціологічний*

моніторинг /За ред. Ворони В., Шульги М—К.: Інститут соціології НАН України, 2010—С. 505.

4. Samuel P. Huntington, *The Clash of Civilizations and the Remaking of World Order* (New York: Simon & Schuster, 1996).
5. See: Я. Грицак, *Страсті за націоналізмом. Стара історія на новий лад* (К.: Критика, 2011).
6. Dominique Arel. "Залучення відокремленого" (The hidden face of the Orange Revolution: Ukraine in denial toward its regional problem)—*Критика*—Ч. 109—2006—С. 10-13.
7. Sophia Senyk, "Victim to Nationalism: The UGCC in its own Words," *Het Christelijk Oosten* 3-4 (Nijmegen, 1999), pp. 167-187; "The UGCC Today: Universal Values Versus Nationalist Doctrines," *Religion, State & Society* 30:4 (2002), 317-332.
8. The UOC-KP is profiling its identity as a national church through resentment toward elements of its former ROC identity. Thus, its major object of resentment is everything connected with Russia. From that perspective, the UOC-MP is characterized by UOC-KP spokesman Dmytro Stepovyk as "deprived of Christian virtues" in its "total hatred towards everything and everybody," as Ukrainian in name but not in essence and spirit, and as an "Orthodox Taliban" (Дмитро Степовик, "Коли в овечі шкури вбираються вовки. В Україні діє православний Талібан."—*Голос Православ'я*—№ 5—2006—С. 8). The official UOC-KP newspaper *Holos Pravoslav'ja* (№ 13—2009—С. 3) referred to Moscow patriarch Kirill as an ethnic Mordvin who pretends to be Russian and claims that Ukrainian land is his land; it also emphasized that the patriarch's visit to Ukraine cannot be compared with the visit of Pope John Paul II to Ukraine because the pope had "some Ukrainian blood" in his veins.

   Greek Catholics have a twofold object of resentment—Poles and Russians. Poles are mostly treated as "occupiers who came to our ethnic lands as invaders" *Арка* (орган Стрийської єпархії УГКЦ)—№ 11—2002—С. 1. The same argument of "land" was addressed to Polish Roman Catholics in Ukraine by Cardinal Husar in his interview in *Tygodnik Powszechny*. № 46—17.11.2002. The UOC-MP and Moscophiles in Halychyna are stereotyped as a "fifth column" (*Жива вода*, Трускавець—№ 1—2003—С. 6, 10), and the ROC is accused of providing "anti-Ukrainian, pro-Russian, anti-state activity, ruining in all possible ways national morality in Ukraine on individual and collective levels, using chauvinistic reactionary forces for the aggressive propaganda in the mass-media against the Catholic world, precisely the UGCC, and against the independence of Ukraine." *Мета* (орган УГКЦ)—№ 4—2003—6. These are but a few examples, and many more can be found in the various church-related media.
9. *Голос Православ'я* (орган УПЦ-КП)—№ 7—2011—С. 2.
10. *Голос Православ'я*—№ 19—2009—С. 5;№ 21—2009—С. 2.
11. *Нова Зоря*—5 серпня 2010 р—С. 2.
12. Unless otherwise specified, all figures cited here are based on the annual statistical reports of the Ukrainian state department on religion (whose official name and administrative status are constantly changing).
13. This figure appears to contradict the statements of Greek Catholic leaders about the nationwide character of the UGCC and its diffusion all over the Ukrainian territory after it shifted its administrative center from Lviv to Kyiv. Such figures as two communities in the Chernihiv region, three each in Cherkassy and Luhans'k, and four each in Sumy, Kirovohrad, and Zaporizhja do not yet establish a significant presence of the UGCC on a national level.
14. *Патріярхат*—№ 3 (418)—2010—С. 13.
15. Наталія Кочан, "Релігійність в Україні: регіональний вимір."—*Збірник наукових праць. Політологічні студії* (Кам'янець-Подільський)—Вип. 1—2010—С. 197-208; Войналович Віктор, Кочан Наталія. "Регіональні особливості інституалізації релігійного простору України."—*Наукові Записки ІПіЕНД ім. І.Ф. Кураса НАН України*—№ 2—2010—С. 76-100.

16. Людмила Рязанова, "Релігійне життя України: сучасні тенденції пристосування."—*Українське суспільство. 1992-2009. Динаміка соціальних змін.* /За ред. Ворони В., Шульги М.-К.: Інститут соціології НАН України, 2009—С. 341.
17. "Результати національного опитування 'Громадська думка в Україні—2009'. Омнібус."—*Українське суспільство. 1992-2009. Динаміка соціальних змін.* /За ред. Ворони В., Шульги М.-К.: Інститут соціології НАН України, 2009—С. 545.
18. о. Мирон Бендик. "Про концепцію богословської освіти в Україні."—*Богословія*—№ 64—2000—С. 33.
19. See the special issue of *Logos: A Journal of Eastern Christian Studies* 39:1 (Ottawa, 1998) on "What is Eastern Catholic Theology" with contributions by Robert F. Taft, SJ, Myroslav Tataryn, and Petro Galadza. The Ukrainian reflections on the phenomenon of Eastern Catholic theology are focused on arguing for the recognition of a patriarchal status to the UGCC. See the Pastoral letter by Cardinal Husar "On the Affirmation of the patriarchal strcture of the UGCC" (Lviv, September 2, 2002) and articles that reduce the papal functions of the bishop of Rome (о. Мирон Бендик, "Еклезіологічні перспективи УГКЦ: до питання про патріархат."—*Патріярхат*—№ 2—2003) or denounce any kind of subordination of the UGCC to the Catholic Church (о. Іван Гаваньо, гол. редактор журналу *Богословія*, "Навколо проголошення патріярхату УГКЦ."—*Патріярхат*—№ 6—2003—С. 16-18).
20. о. Михайло Димид. "Від патерналізму до прямого батьківства."—*Патріярхат*—№ 4—2003—С. 14-15; "Християни покликані запобігати руйнуванню системи цінностей."—*Жива вода*—6 червня 2003—С. 9, 13.—"А що після візиту єпископа Риму в Україну."—*Богословія.*—№ 6—2002.
21. о. Йосиф Смішко. "Наш обов'язок."—*Божий сіяч* (орган Тернопільсько-Зборівської єпархії УГКЦ)—№ 7—2002—С. 6.
22. о. Ігор Пелехатий. "Рускій мір"—руїна України."—*Нова Зоря*—№ 23—2012—С. 1. See also the response, in support of a local, Latinized rite in the UGCC by Sofron Dmyterko, Bishop of Ivano-Frankivs'k (1991-1997), in Софрон Дмитерко "Поцілунок Папи."—*Поступ* (Львів)—1-2 червня 2002.
23. See: Наталія Кочан, "Етноконфесійні стереотипи сучасної УГКЦ: РКЦ як 'польська церква' в Україні."—*Наукові Записки ІПіЕНД ім. І.Ф. Кураса НАН України*—№ 29—2006—С. 300-328.
24. *Національний склад населення та його мовні ознаки за даними Всеукраїнського перепису 2001 року* (К.: Державний комітет статистики України, 2003)—С. 11.
25. On the clash between the leaders of the UGCC and the RCC, see the interview of Cardinal Lubomyr Husar and the response to it by Cardinal Marian Jaworski in *Tygodnik Powszechny* (November 17, 2002, and January 5, 2003, respectively).
26. The Vatican's efforts to normalize relations between the UGCC and the RCC in Ukraine are predictably nonpublic. Yet it is known that the problematic character of those relations was discussed during Pope John Paul II's visit to Ukraine in June 2001 at the meeting of Greek Catholic and Roman Catholic hierarchy with the Pontiff at the building of the Apostolic Nuncio in Kyiv, and the Pope referred to it in his sermons to Catholics of both rites. See: Проповіді Святішого Отця Івана Павла ІІ під час відправлення літургій латинського (26.06.2001) і візантійського (27.06.2001) обрядів у Львові.—*Парафіяльна газета* (орган римо-католицьких парафій в Україні)—1-8 липня 2001—С. 16, 21. In addition, according to the acting head of the UGCC Sviatoslav Shevchuk, it was the order of Pope Benedict XVI to the Conference of Bishops of the Roman Catholic Church in Ukraine and the Synod of Bishops of the UGCC to hold joint meetings twice a year (*Католицький вісник* [орган римо-католицьких парафій в Україні]—№ 4—2012—С. 5).
27. *Патріярхат*—Ч. 6—2011—С. 11.
28. "Помісність УГКЦ як вона є. Інтерв'ю з главою УГКЦ кардиналом Л. Гузарем."—*Патріярхат*—№ 4—2009—С. 11.

29. о. Святослав Шевчук. "Ідентичність східного богослов'я та питання конфесійності."—С. 36.
30. See the interview of Major Archbishop Shevchuk: "Наша ідентичність—це свідчення Церкви часів неподіленого християнства. Патріярх (Святослав) Шевчук про сьогодення та перспективи УГКЦ."—*Патріярхат*.—№. 4.—2011.—С. 3–8.
31. Cf. Bishop S. Mudryj on Greek Catholic relations with the UOC-KP: "We are one people, one Church of Christ and only afterwards one or another confession." *Мета*—№ 3—2002—С. 3.
32. Cardinal L. Husar, Pastoral letter "One people of God on the Kyivan hills" (Один народ Божий на Київських горах"), April 13, 2004 (http://risu.org.ua/ua/index/resourses/church_doc/ugcc_doc/34078). The newspaper of the Ivano-Frankivs'k eparchy *Nova Zorja* suggests that local communities include in their list of monthly intentions prayers for the "conversion of all those who fell away from unity with the Catholic Church" *Нова Зоря*—№ 2—2010—С. 3). The bishop emeritus of the Ivano-Frankivs'k eparchy Sofron Mudryj stated in one of his interviews: "Christ instituted the Church only on Peter the Rock and not on ten apostles. Yet, Constantinople and then Moscow are building [something] of their own. Let them do that, but it is not true. Christ built the Church only on Peter, and not in any other way." See: "Тепер це буде знак побіди Христа над атеїзмом.' Інтерв'ю з ректором Івано-Франківської теологічної академії єпископом Софроном Мудрим."—*Нова Зоря*—№ 23—2011—С. 4. See also the similar statement of S. Mudryj in: Idem., "Християнське мучеництво—свідчення Церкви XX століття."—*Богословія*—№ 63—1999—С. 89.
33. See, for instance, comments on documents approved by the synodal meetings of the bishops of the UGCC of June 16–22, 2000: "The Conception of the Ecumenical Standpoint of the Ukrainian Greek-Catholic Church" and "Practical Measures for Carrying out the Ecumenical Standpoint of the Ukrainian Greek-Catholic Church," in Natalia Kochan, "The Ukrainian Greek-Catholic Church on Ecumenism," *The Journal of Eastern Christian Studies* (formerly *Het Christelijk Oosten*) 3–4 (2002), 269–285.
34. "Лист Блаженнішого Любомира до Блаженнішого Митрополита Володимира, Предстоятеля Української Православної Церкви," http://risu.org.ua/ua/index/resourses/church_doc/ugcc_doc/33942.
35. *Голос Православ'я*—№ 6—2006—С. 4.
36. "Патріарх Філарет: Київський патріархат зростає, незважаючи на спротив."—*Голос Православ'я*—№ 6—2010—С. 3.
37. See the interviews in: *Голос Православ'я*—№ 7—2012—С. 4; № 15—2011—С. 4.
38. "Греко-Католицька Церква не може бути одначасно в єдності з Православними Церквами і з Римом." Інтерв'ю патріарха Філарета (Денисенка) під час прес-конференції в агенстві *Главред* 8 квітня 2010 р—*Голос Православ'я*—№ 8—2010—С. 5.
39. "Заседание Священного Синода от 16.07.2008. Журнал № 50."—*Церковная Православная газета* (орган УПЦ)—№ 14—2008—С. 4–5.
40. *Голос України* (газета Верховної Ради України)—21, 25 листопада 1995.
41. Cardinal Husar formulated the "special task" of the UGCC as that of a "mediator who interprets the East to the West and the West to the East." *Мета* (Львів)—№ 1—2003—С. 3. Cf. E. Lanne, "Églises unies ou Églises-soeurs: un choix inéluctable—-*Irénikon*, 1975—p. 322f.
42. Ukrainian scholars have participated in the European Sociological Survey program (ESS) since 2008. For the full data of the ESS, see: www.europeansocialsurvey.org. On Ukraine in general. Also see: Головаха Євген, Горбачик Андрій. *Тенденції соціальних змін в Україні та Європі за результатами "Європейського соціального дослідження" 2005-2007-2009*. -К.: Інститут соціології НАН України, 2010. On religion in Ukraine in 2008 according to the ESS, see: Максим Паращевін, *Релігія та релігійність в Україні*.—К.: Інститут політики, Інститут соціології НАН України, 2009.
43. Людмила Рязанова, "Влияние религиозной и конфессиональной идентичности на этнонациональную толерантность/интолерантность (украинский контекст)"

//*Национально-гражданские идентичности и толерантность. Опыт России и Украины в период трансформации* /Под общей ред. Дробижевой Л., Головахи Е.—Киев: Институт социологии НАН Украины, Институт социологии Российской академии наук, 2007—С. 248.

44. Максим Паращевін. *Релігія та релігійність в Україні.* —С. 13.

Part III

Orthodox Critiques of the West

9

"The Barbarian West": A Form of Orthodox Christian Anti-Western Critique

Vasilios N. Makrides

Introduction: Orthodox Anti-Westernism

As is known from history, the Orthodox Christian critique of the West has exhibited many facets and variations, premised on different considerations and evaluations and caused by multiple sociohistorical developments. Byzantine Orthodox anti-Westernism is certainly not identical with the modern Orthodox anti-Western critique. But various lines of continuity can be located between the two, as both are part of a long chain of critical attitudes toward the West. Orthodox opposition to the West goes back to the early Middle Ages and the progressive alienation between Eastern Orthodox and Western Latin Christendom and the concomitant worlds, culminating in the schism of 1054. Aside from this, modern Orthodox anti-Westernism is a more varied phenomenon and flourishes in different local contexts, religious and otherwise. The close connection of anti-Westernism with anti-Americanism and antiglobalization nowadays constitutes a case of a modern transformation and adaptation of a specific tradition within the Orthodox world. Literature on such phenomena and developments abounds today.[1] Needless to say, this phenomenon concerns not only the Orthodox world, but also relates to other religions, cultures, states, groups, and individuals worldwide. There is a growing interest in interdisciplinary and comparative studies of anti-Westernism beyond merely religious perspectives.[2] This has to do not only with the historical rise and worldwide significance of the West (or more specifically: of Western Europe), but also with the contemporary situation. In the present global context, "the West" with its Eurocentric connotations may have lost its past predominance,[3] but many critics still use the term pejoratively to denote a civilization that created "numerous troubles" for the rest of the world through its overseas expansion and colonialism.

The particular Orthodox understanding of the West has been scrutinized more in recent years than in the past. Particular attention has been given to the process of the "construction" of the West by various Orthodox institutions and individuals across history.[4] This means that the Orthodox understanding of the West has often been artificially construed and used for various purposes. The category of "the West" thus reflects the particular ideological underpinnings of its promoters[5]—the same of course can be said about the category of "the East" as construed and used by Western actors. The problem is simply that such ideological constructions of the West were often elevated by their promoters as intrinsically connected with the authentic Orthodox Christian identity, which had to be rediscovered and purged of all adulterating Western influences. In other words, Orthodox self-identification and self-definition were related to the line of demarcation between itself and what was perceived as "the West." This is not, of course, to deny the major or minor differences between East and West, which are historically more than obvious. The problem remains the constant attempt at self-definition through the demarcation and negation of the "Other" (in our case: of the West). Such a process can hardly remain immune to ideological uses of sources and history, which is in fact evident by looking at the different and sometimes contradictory criteria used by the Orthodox anti-Western thinkers in critically evaluating the West. The Slavophile anti-Western critique in the nineteenth century did exhibit many variations and was not fully homogeneous[6]; further, it is different from the critique of the West formulated by the Russian theologians of the diaspora in the course of the twentieth century.[7] The same holds true for two contemporary Greek anti-Western thinkers, John Romanides[8] and Christos Yannaras—the latter will concern us more in the present chapter. It suffices to examine how Augustine has been evaluated by such thinkers in an anti-Western context in order to understand how subjective and perhaps arbitrary their differently applied "criteria of Orthodoxy" are.[9]

Christos Yannaras and His Critique of the West

One of the internationally best-known Orthodox thinkers associated with an anti-Western critique is the Greek theologian and philosopher Christos Yannaras (born 1935). A very prolific author, he has published an impressive number of books dealing with a wide variety of topics over the last 50 years. Many of his books have been translated into various European languages, including English, which means that they had a wide readership beyond Greece. For many decades he has also been publishing his comments and views in well-known Greek newspapers, where he touches upon actual and everyday developments, such as Greek politics or the current Greek economic crisis. His work has thus attracted both domestic and international attention,[10] and has been the subject of various dissertations[11] and comparative studies.[12] At the same time, his views have generated numerous debates in Greece[13] and abroad,[14] and thus they remain controversial.

The central axis of Yannaras's thought relates to the deep and decisive differentiation between the Hellenized Orthodox Roman East and the Latin West.[15] His overall work may be described as an attempt to locate and explain the crucial characteristics differentiating the two worlds, as well as their long-term repercussions. To summarize his argument: He is deeply convinced that the Western Latin world has deviated from the Orthodox East for a number of reasons and followed another path. This was not a fortuitous or unimportant deviation, but a catalytic one that later gave rise to the much-admired Western civilization. The latter lies thus at the antipodes of the Orthodox world, one that has developed almost throughout the long period of the Hellenized East Roman (Byzantine) Empire. Sadly enough for Yannaras, the impact of the West became stronger and stronger, and was felt in the East since the late Byzantine period. Consequently the East was gradually Westernized, and this process has continued until today. Given these premises, Yannaras argues that the modern Orthodox world is deeply alienated from its authentic roots, which have been violently distorted in the wake of formative Western influences. The Orthodox therefore need to rediscover their lost past and realize their enormously rich, pre-Westernized heritage, which is essentially different from the Western one.

Yannaras then goes on and meticulously tries to locate the key aspects of this lost heritage. Yet, the Orthodox East and specifically Greece are already fully Westernized. Only a few traits of this lost heritage are still discernible today, but only by those tuned into the genuine and authentic Orthodox criteria. This is simply the outcome of generations of Westernized elites (political, intellectual, economic, etc.), who have turned the coordinates of Orthodox civilization upside down. Hence, Yannaras puts himself in the tradition of those "Orthodox detectives," who are dedicated to locating the problems caused by Westernization, bringing to light the surviving traces of this heritage and offering a new orientation for a better future to his compatriots, whom he clearly regards as uninformed and naive. In attempting this, he also delved into a deep study of Greek antiquity and tried to find the elements intrinsically connecting Hellenism and (Orthodox) Christianity. He concludes that the West's reception of Greek antiquity, commonly regarded as the cradle of Western modernity, constitutes a false appropriation of this rich heritage since it is based on Western premises and underscored by specific Western objectives.

As expected, this schematic summary of Yannaras's main ideas on East and West involves a serious and hard critique of the West and its civilization. The West is held responsible for forgetting the apophatic mode of knowledge and existence, for the genesis of theological rationalism and intellectualism, for the objectification of the Christian truth, for the rise of authoritarianism and totalitarianism, for the ideologization of Christianity and the religionization of the church (i.e., its transformation into an individualistic ideology and authoritative institution), and for many other distortions of the original Christian church and meaning. Interestingly enough, Yannaras does not consider himself to be guided by an anti-Western spirit. He attributes anti-Western sentiments and actions basically to the broad and varied field of Orthodox rigorists or fundamentalists, who try to compensate for various psychological and other deficits by outspokenly attacking and rejecting the West. But he does not put himself in this category. His entire work, he argues, undertakes the painful task of self-critique and self-understanding in order to methodically explain what happened after the schism between East and West.[16] Thus, when he addresses Western readers, who can easily misjudge his positions and critique of the West, he tries to clarify his objectives and avoid misunderstandings. To this purpose, he adds sometimes a short new preface in some translations of his books, specifically destined for Western readers.

Thus, in the preface to the French translation of his book condemning Western Christian legalism and supporting the freedom of the Orthodox ethos, he rejected the label of being anti-Western himself. His aim, he argued, was to begin a dialogue; not in the way that this is usually done in the context of the Ecumenical Movement or church diplomacy, but rather with reference to the existential human questions and the need to find real answers to the dilemmas of life. He considered, on the one hand, ecclesial Orthodoxy, namely, the theology and experience of the undivided church of the first eight centuries, which were intrinsically connected with the experience, popular piety, and practice in Orthodox Greece. On the other hand, he took into consideration the theology of the West with all its social, political, and cultural consequences, which in fact represented, to a great extent, his own way of life within the modern consumerist world too, either in Greece, in Europe, or elsewhere. He thus considered himself to have fallen victim to this pervasive Westernization process. In this respect, he was not addressing some merely theoretical issues, which bore no relevance to real life; neither was it his intention to call Roman Catholics or Protestants into question. His was an agonic search for the false theological paths that have led our individualistic civilization and consumerist way of life to concrete problems and impasses. After all, Westernization is evident in both East and West and encompasses everyone nowadays. In this highly emotional frame, Yannaras looks for "answers of life," namely, those that can offer solutions to the many deadlocks within ecclesial Orthodoxy. In the end, his critique of Western theology is also directed against his own Westernized self. Can something from the historically uncontaminated Orthodoxy, from the truth and the lived experience of the undivided church of the first eight centuries, be saved in such a radically Westernized world? This question underlines Yannaras's main aim and hope for the modern world, which is moribund because of its Western roots and moorings.[17]

The same convictions also appear in Yannaras's survey of the relations between Orthodox Greece and the West. In the preface to the abridged English translation of this book, [18] he wrote:

> What concerns me is to study the consequences of the differences between "Orthodoxy" and the "West" in today's world [...] I attempt to identify the cultural consequences of some of the West's deviations from the Greek embodiment of ecclesial experience, to trace these consequences in the social body of the historical transmitter of Orthodoxy, to study in Westernized modern Hellenism a cultural tragedy which is perhaps of general human interest, and to highlight the real spiritual problems that have been created by the Western "religionizing" of the Church.[19]

In addition, he tried again to explain the motives of his anti-Western critique in order to avoid misunderstanding among his Western readers:

> The critique of Western theology and tradition which I offer in this book does not contrast "Western" with something "right" which as an Orthodox I use to oppose something "wrong" outside myself. I am not attacking an external Western adversary. As a modern Greek, I myself embody both the thirst for what is "right" and the reality of what is "wrong": a contradictory and alienated survival of ecclesiastical Orthodoxy in a society radically and unhappily Westernized. My critical stance towards the West is self-criticism; it refers to my own wholly Western mode of life. I am a Western person searching for answers to the problems tormenting Western people today. The threat to the environment, the assimilation of politics to business models, the yawning gulf between society and the state, the pursuit of ever-greater consumption, the loneliness and the weakness of social relations, the prevailing loveless sexuality—all these seem to go back to the theological differences that once provoked the "Schism" dividing Christendom into two. Today's individualism and absolute utilitarianism appear to have theological origins.[20]

Yannaras believes that such explanations suffice to portray him not as an ideological adversary of the West, but as a person worrying about the "cultural tragedy" of the modern world, caused by the global spread of Western culture. He thus regrets that the statements given in the extract have been ignored by his many critics, who have labeled him as anti-Western. He bemoans that this label still unjustly follows him, since this is not at all his main objective and orientation.[21]

Yet there is probably a misunderstanding here about the significance of the term "anti-Westernism." What exactly constitutes anti-Westernism? Among other things, the formulation of an ambitious theory claiming that the Western world as a whole has chosen a false path and thereby went wrong constitutes a particular form of anti-Westernism. If one further claims that one's own religious culture (here: the Hellenized Orthodox Roman East) is, in its authentic and ideal form, qualitatively superior to the Western one, then this is again a form of anti-Western critique. The same holds true if one talks about the evils of the Westernization process or if one believes that the Western world is full of impasses and needs some regenerating and vital forces from outside (in our case: from the Orthodox world) to be revived and finally saved. The fact that Yannaras calls himself a Westernized person and that he exercises self-critique does not render his arguments any less anti-Western. All this belongs without doubt to a broader civilizational critique that commonly falls under the category of anti-Westernism and can be found in many contexts in past and recent times alike, not only in the Orthodox world. After all, in contrast with other civilizations worldwide, Western civilization is probably the only one that has generated so many negative comments from external perspectives, especially in modern times. In the related discussion anti-Westernism often implies an extreme hatred of the West and the plan to destroy it, even through the use of violence.[22] But there also exist milder forms of anti-Westernism, like the one formulated by Yannaras.

In his most recent book, in which he offered a summary of what he believes to have been his major contributions to philosophy and theology, Yannaras explains again the main points of his critique against the West and the reasons lying behind it. In this context, he uses the expression "the Barbarian West" as a catchword with a particular emphasis. He also cites a book by John Michael Wallace-Hadrill (1916–1985), a scholar of Medieval Western Europe, about "the Barbarian West" (between 400 and 1000 AD) as the classic that established this expression internationally.[23] This is an interesting extension of Yannaras's civilizational anti-Western critique, which requires particular attention. Generally, it has been observed that Yannaras replaced his earlier theological anti-Westernism with a strongly Hellenocentric and civilizational anti-Westernism from the late 1970s onward.[24] Yannaras thus distinguishes the Roman West (up to the fifth century) from "the Barbarian West" (after the fifth century). He refers to the invasion and settlement of numerous tribes (Goths, Huns, Franks, Vandals, Burgundians, Longobards, Angles, Saxons, Normans, etc.), mostly Germanic, but also of Hunnish and Alanic provenance, in the West Roman Empire between the fourth and sixth centuries, which altered not only its ethnic composition, but also its future course in all respects. These "hordes" were mostly nomadic, living under "primitive conditions" and characterized by the "lowest underdevelopment" at that time. They were Christianized, not because they were looking for satisfactory answers to their metaphysical quests, but because to be Christian at that time meant a radical change of social status. In this way, they could "enter civilization and live by qualitatively higher standards." These barbarian tribes replaced their previous pagan traditions with Christianity, which they adapted to their stereotypes. In fact, they had no idea at all about the ontological and existential aims of the "ecclesial event."[25] We should keep in mind here that Yannaras does not consider Christianity a religion, but ideally a church (*ecclesia*), while he criticizes its pernicious religionization, which was brought on by Latin deviations in the West.[26]

In addition, in his view, the Christianized barbarians in the West had no idea about the majestic achievements in the Hellenized Orthodox Roman East, namely, the long-standing apophatic tradition and the key criterion of verifying knowledge not individually, but always in communion. By contrast, in the West there prevailed "the primitivism of the need for individually-centered certainties" and the utilitarian, instrumental understanding of Greek philosophy and Christianity. Ironically, the West today claims and is proud of having continued the ancient Greek heritage (in philosophy, sciences, etc.), but utterly ignores the main coordinates of the ancient Greek world. Its reception of Greek antiquity thus constitutes a distortion of its main parameters, apophaticism and communality, which were embraced, transformed, and perpetuated by the Hellenized Eastern Roman world after Christianization.[27] No doubt, for Yannaras Western civilization is to be admired for its numerous fantastic achievements, yet all of these are subjected to utilitarian ends and have nothing to do with the achievements of the ancient Greek world.

A case in point: When the "enthusiastic barbarian West...in its medieval adolescence"[28] discovered Aristotle, it considered only his rational theory of knowledge and ignored its socially determined, communal verification. For Yannaras, all this attests to the initial intellectual and cultural immaturity of the West and the concomitant distortions of the ancient Greek and Christian heritage. The result was an instrumentalized, utilitarian understanding of Aristotelian logic, a fixation on a false empiricism, and a need to verify faith and knowledge intellectually with rational arguments and unshaken certainties. This orientation remained the dominant one in Western civilization, although there have been several "iconoclastic" critics of it in modern times, such as Pascal, Nietzsche, Heidegger, and Wittgenstein. Yet, even these ingenious and brave thinkers remained unaware of the crucial, socially determined verification of truth as a communal achievement that continuously permeated the Greek world in the East since the time of Heracleitus. Yannaras emphasizes that he is referring here to a particular way of life (civilization), not to a special scientific method.[29] He also mentions that even the Latin West in its prebarbarian period exhibited characteristics that had already set it apart from the Greek Orthodox East; for example, a utilitarian, individualistic, and legalistic theology, apart from the communal church experience, which found its peak in Augustine's voluminous output.[30] Yet, the barbarian conquest of the West intensified these trends, further widened the gap with the East, and rendered it practically unbridgeable.

All this, Yannaras goes on, brought an avalanche of distortions to the ecclesial experience and witness by the "newly baptized barbarians." Under these circumstances it was very difficult to maintain the political and the ecclesiastical unity of the entire Roman Empire. During its post-Roman, barbarian period, Western Europe was politically highly differentiated, since every local political leader could define "Christian Orthodoxy" according to his own will. One of the greatest falsifications of Christian dogma took place through the arbitrary insertion of the *filioque* into the already established Christian Creed, despite early reactions from the popes. This change signified for Yannaras that the West was completely unaware of the ontological content of the ecclesiastical theology about the Trinitarian God. The Trinitarian dogma was not an ideological axiom, but contained an existential experience and gave expression to a related hope.[31] In contrast, the Latin Church under Frankish control was deeply influenced by the developments in the West and adapted its policy accordingly. Christian unity in the West was no longer related to the lived and proven catholicity of ecclesial Orthodoxy, but was subjected to the logic of political rivalry between the various "barbarian kingdoms" for supreme authority and forcible imposition of an ideologized Christian faith. Finally, all this led to the creation of the Papal State in the eighth century (in modern times known as the Vatican State), a monstrous creation, far removed from the standards of the ecclesial body of the East. It was exactly this "post-Roman barbarian West" that would definitely mark subsequent world history; for example, by giving birth to ideology (the transformation of experience and a way of life into an intellectualized system of acceptance and an obsessive psychological conviction) and totalitarianism (the forcible and authoritative imposition of an ideology).[32] Due to the unavoidable separation of the two churches and the two worlds into East and West, the "schismatic and still barbarian West" remained without any significant external control or pressure. Arbitrariness, individual appropriation, and distortion of the previous ecclesiastic experience went hand in hand. The newly arrived barbarian tribes were instrumental in initiating and achieving these dramatic changes. Although they "lived for many dark centuries like animals on their way to development and civilization," they finally gave birth to a new civilization, which was diametrically opposed to the ancient Greek and Christian ecclesial way of being, communicating, and coexisting.[33] Yannaras acknowledges that both the Hellenized Roman East and the post-Roman barbarian West do not lack mistakes, even grave ones, through the course of history. There is also no lack of exceptional Christian personalities in the medieval West. But the crucial, "caesarean difference" between East and West lies precisely in the fact that the East never institutionalized sin and never accepted it to serve various sacred goals, as the West did.[34]

To sum up, Yannaras does not deny that the West was able to create a unique civilization with universal appeal and dynamics. But he explains this achieved universality by means of the highly distorted and problematic nature of this civilization (religionization, instinctive individualism, individual rationality, utilitarianism, etc.). Interestingly enough, he opines that a value-laden assessment and comparison of the two civilizations, East and West, is not possible, since the criteria used are not commonly shared, but are diametrically opposed. It is also precarious, he argues, to talk about "higher" and "lower" or "better" and "worse" civilizations. But it is possible to locate cardinal differences between them; for example, the fact that Western civilization never felt the need to move from a society of utility to one of truth. Through an impressive inventiveness in all possible domains it solely serves human utilitarian needs and the individual. The community-centered civilization of the Hellenized Orthodox Roman East can thus never be compared or compromised with the individualistic civilization of the post-Roman West. The differences between them are profound and diametrically opposed; in fact, the one contradicts the other.[35]

"The Barbarian West": A Critical Discussion

It is not possible within the limited space of this chapter to deal with every aspect of the "Western deviation" according to Yannaras and to examine the validity of his criteria and the heuristic power of his arguments. But his particular emphasis on the barbarian character of the West after the fifth century is very striking in this recent book. But this was not the first time in his overall oeuvre that he underlined the notion of the barbarian character of the West.[36] In the English translation of his aforementioned book about the relations between Orthodox Greece and the West (including Greece's "Western captivity"), he also referred to the barbarian tribes and hordes, which invaded Central, Western, and Southwestern Europe. They were Christianized, but were not in a position to grasp fully the implications of the Christian dogma, as it had been developed in the Orthodox East. This is why they started making arbitrary innovations in the Christian tradition and differentiating themselves from the Eastern Orthodox world, to which they were feeling inferior and which they deeply resented.[37] The original Greek edition of this book included an even more elaborate version of the same topic. There Yannaras cited extensive passages from the works of Western scholars (H. Butterfield, J. B. Bury, M. Rouche, and G. Duby), who underlined the barbarian character of the West during the early medieval period.[38]

In another article on church and civilization, he also talked about the "primitive hordes" of the barbarians that swept the West. These nomadic tribes were Christianized, but they could not enter into a fruitful relationship with the ecclesial Orthodoxy of the East for many reasons. In the end, they made out of the church an instinctive natural religion to satisfy their basically "childish," individualistic, and utilitarian needs. The long-term consequences of this tragedy can be discerned in many instances nowadays; for example, in the films of Ingmar Bergmann and Federico Fellini, which masterfully show how Latin Christianity has tormented Western peoples across history.[39] Thus, Yannaras's main ideas remained the same. But again the particular expression "the Barbarian West" did not appear there as a catchword. Further, in some other previous works, for example, in his concise exposition of the Orthodox faith[40] or in his introduction to philosophy,[41] he hardly emphasized the barbarian nature of the West. There he put more emphasis on the particular development of the Latin Christian church and theology, especially after Augustine, which moved in a different direction from that of Eastern Orthodoxy. This gave rise to new forms of individualistic and rationalistic theological reasoning (e.g., in the context of Scholasticism) and finally led to the formation of the Western intellectual world, which has acquired such a great importance worldwide.

What role does the argument about "the Barbarian West" play in this recent book, and why is it emphasized so prominently? We should briefly mention here that this topos is not altogether absent from the general Orthodox anti-Western critique.[42] The deep antithesis between the Greek-speaking and Latin-speaking Romans in East and West, respectively, and the Frankish invaders in the West forms the backbone of the interpretative scheme of John Romanides as well.[43] Although Yannaras acknowledges Romanides's theological contribution, he thinks that his particular presentation and assessment of the East-West opposition belongs rather to conspiracy theories and scenarios. This makes Romanides's ideas in this area less persuasive, although they do not completely lack historical grounds.[44] But our purpose here is to focus on Yannaras's catchword "the Barbarian West" and its implications.

First: Yannaras's observation about the completely different Eastern and Western civilizations and the alleged impossibility of a comparison between them is hardly convincing. The same holds true for his claim regarding the impossibility of an evaluation and ranking among "higher" or "lower" civilizations. The reader of his book will probably be left with a big question reading these lines. What else does Yannaras accomplish with all his arguments if not precisely such a comparison? Does he not consider the Hellenized Roman civilization of the Orthodox East, both explicitly and implicitly, as superior to the Western one? Consider the following statements: "Behind the Greek and the barbarian (civilizational) products lie two clearly different hierarchizations of human needs and divergent evaluations of human priorities."[45] Or further: "The notion of catholicity had quite other connotations and pragmatic consequences in the Hellenized Roman East and in the barbarian West."[46] As a matter of fact, he locates the crucial differences between East and West, offers a devastating critique of the entire Western civilization, emphasizes its barbarian character, talks negatively about the "Western deviation" and its catastrophic consequences across the globe, constantly compares the West with the Hellenized Orthodox Roman East, which he considers incomparably superior, and laments the infatuation that many in the East have historically shown for Western achievements. All this undoubtedly belongs to a category of value-laden arguments in the context of a comparative examination of two civilizations that are viewed as completely different. Such a conclusion can hardly be avoided by readers of his latest book. Of course, he has every right to formulate his critique against the West and to explain what, in his opinion, went wrong. But to claim a value-free perspective in doing this is highly questionable and totally unconvincing. The only plausible explanation for this could be his desire to present his criticism as more "objective" and to persuade readers of the correctness of his arguments. As mentioned before, he also denied the label of being an anti-Western for similar reasons. Nevertheless, such apologetic tactics are quite weak, given that his entire oeuvre is fundamentally premised on a value-laden critique of the West.

Second: Yannaras talks about "the Barbarian West" (also with particular reference to Western scholars) as if this were a kind of new discovery or a new idea that many people have ignored, neglected so far, or forgotten. But again this is hardly the case. By referring to Western scholars he seeks to show that the expression "the Barbarian West" was not coined by him and that he actually follows their *ipsissima verba* in describing this historical period of Western civilization. This, of course, is true and correct—earlier and current scholarship has dealt amply with the invasions of numerous tribes that led to the end of the Western Roman Empire and its eventual transformation. But this is hardly a new topic and cannot occasion surprise. There was, among other things, a very interesting exhibition in Venice in 2008 entitled *Rome and the Barbarians: The Birth of a New World*. There, an effort was made to avoid past stereotypes about the barbarian hordes that invaded the Western Roman Empire and instead to identify the new developments during this formative period, especially in the domain of art, which demonstrate an impressive cultural encounter, diversity, and mutual enrichment.[47] It is obvious that the Western world as such has no problem at all with this particular phase of its history. Even from the perspective of the Eastern Romans (Byzantines), the Western part of the Roman Empire was considered to have been subjected to barbarian peoples after 476. The distinction between Romans and barbarians, which included not only wild nomads but also Latin Christians and by extension all peoples living outside the East Roman Empire (Byzantium), was quite common in Byzantine sources.[48] We should not, however, forget that the term "barbarian" experienced a development in the West between the fifth and seventh centuries, as the "the old antithesis of Roman and barbarian was becoming less and less accurate as a description of prevailing social and cultural conditions in Europe as the two cultures mingled and their opposition diminished."[49] The distinction was thus gradually blurred, while attention was placed more and more on the emerging new conditions in the West, in which barbarians slowly disappeared, once they accepted Christianity, a civilizing force par excellence. Characteristically enough, forms of barbarism were attributed by Western Christians even to the Byzantines. Thus, Pope Gregory II (715–731) wrote once to the Byzantine emperor Leo III (717–741): "It is regrettable that the savages and barbarians have become cultured whilst you as a cultured individual have degraded yourself to the level of the barbarians."[50] This means that, historically speaking, the label of barbarism was attributed even to the Eastern Orthodox world by the West, not only in Byzantine times but also later on, especially when the Orthodox were under Ottoman domination. Thus, it is understandable that the term "barbarian" and the condition of barbarism have historically acquired many connotations and were not used exclusively for only this one case, but for a variety of different cases. It is therefore highly precarious to try to evaluate entire cultural complexes, like the Western one, by way of a normative reference to such a relative characterization, as Yannaras does.

Third: More important, however, is the issue of the specific evaluation of the particular expression "the Barbarian West." When J. M. Wallace-Hadrill and Yannaras use this expression, they hardly mean the same thing. The implications they also give to this term are hardly identical. It appears impossible that J. M. Wallace-Hadrill and other Western scholars would ever agree with or accept Yannaras's civilizational comparison and analysis regarding the crucial differences between East and West, which in the end amount to a complete negation of Western civilization. By using the expression "the Barbarian West," they are simply pointing to a historical period in Western history, not to a means of downgrading the significance of Western civilization as such. In attempting a genealogy of the modern Western world, they are also unavoidably confronted with this particular period, which is examined along with other periods. Western scholars have no difficulty in acknowledging that the Eastern Roman Empire (Byzantium) was in many respects by far superior to the West for a long period during the early Middle Ages and that this situation resulted in a pronounced inferiority complex in the West vis-à-vis Byzantium. The extreme anti-Byzantine sentiments of Bishop Liutprand of Cremona in the tenth century have also been explained with reference to such an inferiority complex.[51] All of this is readily accepted by Western scholarship, especially in the context of postmodern and postcolonial efforts, to be self-critical toward one's own past. But such critical perspectives are not meant to negate Western civilization as such, which is widely accepted as an exceptional achievement in world history. The same also applies to the discourse on "the Barbarian West." For Yannaras, the Frankish ruler Charlemagne was basically a barbarian, who was envious of Eastern Roman (Byzantine) superiority and intended to alienate East and West, among other things, by claiming the Roman imperial political continuity for his own kingdom. In contrast, Western scholarship on Charlemagne is well aware of his "barbarian roots," but still hails him as a great political leader, as a precursor of European unification and as a great reformer (cf. the so-called Carolingian Renaissance[52]). It is not our aim here to determine which evaluation is correct. The point is that for Western scholars the expression "the Barbarian West" has quite a different meaning, and therefore Yannaras's reference to Western scholarship to support his position is misleading. Generally, this constitutes a major inconsistency in the entire Orthodox anti-Western critique. In order to substantiate their anti-Western arguments, many Orthodox cite Western scholars critical of certain developments in the overall Western project. After all, it is well-known that there is an internal anti-Western critique originating from the very ranks of the Western world. Yet, the Orthodox like to present such arguments from their own particular perspectives and never do justice to the intentions of these Western scholars. When scholars such as Jürgen Habermas or Cornelius Castoriadis, for example, criticize certain trends of the Enlightenment and of the Western modernity, they still situate themselves within the overall Western project and do not reject or call it into question. They simply want to rectify certain things that, in their opinion at least, went wrong and offer various alternative solutions. But when Yannaras discusses all this in the context of his anti-Western discourse,[53] he intends to call into question Western modernity itself, which he considers to belong to the long chain of deviations from the authenticity and the superiority of the Orthodox East, at least in its uncontaminated form during the first eight centuries. Needless to say, such an alternative could never be accepted by the aforementioned Western thinkers.

Fourth: Yannaras's particular emphasis on "the Barbarian West" fulfills various specific goals. It can be understood as an additional modern civilizational criterion in the long line of similar qualitative distinctions, which go back to the well-known demarcation between Greeks and barbarians in antiquity. This distinction, which was taken by the East Romans (Byzantines) as well, resurfaces in Yannaras's anti-Western critique in another form. As commonly understood, a barbarian is an uncivilized person, one that lacks literacy, culture, development, and refinement, or at least one who is found at a very early stage of civilization. It is expected that the term and the label "barbarian" immediately evoke negative connotations. As already mentioned, this is not to deny that the new tribes invading the West were more or less in such a civilizational state. After all, the term "barbarians," as already mentioned, is commonly used for them in scholarly publications. For example, Odoacer is considered to be the first Germanic barbarian ruler, who in 476 took over the throne of the West Roman Empire from its last Roman emperor Romulus Augustulus and ruled in his place. Yet, this particular emphasis on the expression "the Barbarian West" fits well into Yannaras's anti-Western objectives. It reminds his Orthodox readers that the modern West, despite its great and much admired achievements, has in fact barbarian roots and origins, as well as a concomitant background. From this perspective, Western civilization as a whole is thus, at least partly, a "barbarian product." In the present context of Orthodox anti-Westernism such a characterization puts Western civilization automatically on a qualitatively lower level than the Hellenized Roman civilization of the Orthodox East. In addition, it functions as a constant reminder to the numerous Westernized Orthodox, who have been and still are infatuated with Western progress and achievements. In Yannaras's view, this uncritical admiration is tricky and misleading, because it is based on false assumptions, interpretations, and evaluations. The very fact that Western civilization has barbarian origins renders it inferior and unworthy of admiration. The Westernized Orthodox could do much better by discovering their own outstanding, rich, superior, and uncontaminated tradition, whose cultural achievements were incomparably better at the time when the West was coming of age. From this perspective, the emphasis on "the Barbarian West" functions as a new compensation mechanism against the traditional inferiority complex felt by many Orthodox vis-à-vis the West and aims at strengthening their civilizational identity and concomitant real superiority.

Fifth: It is obvious that the whole issue under discussion revolves around a civilizational comparison of East and West, and Yannaras is certainly not the only one who has attempted something like this. In fact, it is about a comparative cultural history of Christianity in Europe, which is done by many including the present author. There is nothing wrong with this discipline as such, for it enables us to understand historical differentiations and transformations that have influenced the course of Europe, and not only in the strict religious domain. The repercussions of religious changes are felt in many other domains, even until today. The problem arises when specific criteria are used to make such civilizational comparisons and to draw normative and value-laden conclusions. The issue here is not about a quest for objectivity, which is illusory and unattainable in such comparisons. Even Max Weber, who initiated and left a strong legacy in such a comparative research frame, was not fully "objective." This is because, according to modern views, his interpretations reflected for most part a "Protestant meta-narrative," which was dominant at that time in Germany; for example, regarding the intrinsic compatibility between Protestantism and modernity.[54] No doubt, there are many crucial differences in the overall development between the Orthodox East and the Latin West, which still need serious and interdisciplinary examination. The problem is, however, how to locate and evaluate them, so that persuasive arguments and credible positions may be formulated. This does not seem to be the case with Yannaras, who, although he correctly identifies many Eastern and Western particularities, evaluates them in the end from a normative, prescriptive, value-laden, confessional Orthodox, right, and proper perspective. His theory about the religionization of Christianity through its Westernization exhibits many flaws and is highly ideological, although he himself castigates ideology as a Western product. More importantly, all of this is situated within a fundamental anti-Western frame, which in fact amounts to a complete negation of Western civilization and a yearning for an elapsed Orthodox one, which unfortunately could not survive Western domination, except in fragments. With his entire work Yannaras thus calls into question the whole Western project, depicting it in extremely negative colors as a thorough distortion of and deviation from the authenticity of the Orthodox East. The history of the West turns out to be a history of constant decadence and decline, despite the fact of its universal appeal and significance. Such an evaluation can hardly be accepted in the contemporary world, although we are certainly not lacking critical voices against the West and its worldwide influence. In addition, the language and the categories (primitivism, animal-like people, dark Middle Ages, etc.) that Yannaras uses to describe the barbaric tribes in the West and their impact is not—to say the least—"politically correct." In the contemporary, postmodern context such expressions are generally avoided. Culture and comparisons are conceptualized and analyzed in other ways.[55] One also tries to use more neutral and dispassionate terms in such scholarly endeavors. By using such expressions Yannaras intends to downgrade even further "the Barbarian West" and to show its, at best, elementary civilizational stage, which is totally unworthy of imitation by others. Certainly, one cannot argue that the barbaric tribes between the fourth and sixth centuries were at the peak of their civilizational development. But they became an inseparable part of the Western world, which gave rise, in the end, to an exceptional civilization. It is therefore strange to the Western audience today if one evaluates the entire "Western miracle" from the narrow perspective of the barbarian invasions in Late Antiquity and as a concomitant deviation from the authenticity of the Orthodox East—yet that is exactly what Yannaras tries to do. Nobody in the West today considers the medieval universities, the scholastic theology and philosophy, the conflict between papacy and Western rulers, the Reformation or the Enlightenment—to mention just a few examples—from such a perspective and a concomitant negative genealogy. What is emphasized more is the outcome of all these sociohistorical transformations, rather than the specific historical phase of the barbarian invasions, which, as already mentioned, is treated from quite another perspective.

Sixth: The main problem with Yannaras's aforementioned ideas is inextricably linked with his axiomatic presuppositions about the "fallen West." He is convinced that the Western world constitutes a major problem, not only for the East, but also for the rest of the world. He also believes that there is a worldwide wish to be liberated from this Western catalytic influence. However, no one today idealizes the West and its wider impact and no one denies its dark sides. There exists a very critical literature toward the West from many different perspectives. Critical voices and self-reflection about Western civilization and its amelioration abound. But there is a cardinal difference here. There is one critique of the West by Western thinkers who seek to correct its mistakes and thereby improve it. But there is another critique of the West, which rejects it as a whole and looks for a completely new alternative. The latter is exactly what Yannaras does with his entire anti-Western critique. To mention a concrete example: when Max Horkheimer and Theodor Adorno talked about the "dialectic of the Enlightenment,"[56] their intention was to reflect upon some antinomies of the Enlightenment legacy, not to deny it altogether. Despite many criticisms (e.g., by postmodernists), the legacy of the Enlightenment is still an inseparable part of the Western civilizational paradigm, and one that enjoys general acceptance today.[57] From Yannaras's perspective, though, the Enlightenment is a later outcome of the fundamental Western deviation. The strong anticlericalism of the Enlightenment confirms, in his view, that Latin Christianity had previously gone wrong. In the end, the Enlightenment teaches Orthodox Churches and Christians what they should preferably avoid doing in the future, not what they should possibly gain from it in terms of various accomplishments. It is thus no wonder that the legacy of the Enlightenment never entered into a fruitful conversation with Orthodox Christianity until today.[58] In addition to this, Yannaras's civilizational comparisons imply a value-laden, axiological ranking of cultures, in which both the ancient Greek and the Hellenized Orthodox Roman East occupy a superior place.[59] In one instance, he even talks about the "aristocracy" of the Greek nation, which can set correctly the various priorities in life in contrast to Western peoples, who are driven by the constant, instinctive, and collective thirst to produce, to accumulate wealth, and to consume.[60] Although he claims that his intentions are not axiological and that instead he refers to these cultures in a supraethnic, non-nationalistic, and nonchauvinistic way, one can hardly avoid this conclusion, which emerges, whether implicitly or explicitly, from his many East-West comparisons.[61] This is again a perspective that does not fit into the pluralistic, relativist, and multicultural orientation of our age. All of this taken together renders Yannaras's work and views highly controversial and problematical from numerous perspectives.[62]

Concluding Remarks

By way of conclusion, let me reiterate that the objective of this chapter was not to judge the whole oeuvre of Yannaras, which is certainly broad in scope, impressive, and worth reading. Nor was it our goal to assess the validity and the rectitude of his theological and philosophical presuppositions, reflections, interpretations, or extrapolations. Rather, our focus has been on his constant anti-Western obsession, which has led him in recent years to add new arguments to his already full anti-Western arsenal, in particular, his emphasis on "the Barbarian West." Not only because of this, but in general Yannaras's perspectives can hardly be accepted in our postmodern world, primarily because of his guiding principles. First, he undertakes romantic regressions to an idealized Greek Orthodox past, which serves as a model for future orientation. He sees this idealized past as normative, supplying solutions to current and future problems. While it may be considered a classical orientation by the Orthodox generally, it has less resonance in the Western world today, which views the past historically rather than normatively. In addition, Yannaras constantly tries to demonstrate the supposed superiority of the Greek Orthodox East over the Latin West. This is in fact a compensation mechanism for the many shortcomings that the Orthodox feel in many domains vis-à-vis the West. Such claims of absolute certainty and superiority are critically viewed in today's tolerant, pluralistic, and relativistic social context and have no real chance to be taken seriously into account. Finally, Yannaras, along with many other Orthodox in the past and in the present, considers himself as fulfilling some kind of a mission toward the allegedly moribund West, which needs to be saved from impending disaster. It is a kind of quasi-messianic, salvation syndrome aimed at helping the West to overcome its numerous deadlocks and impasses. The problem is that the West today neither wants to be saved nor needs such self-declared saviors. It acknowledges its own limitations, mistakes, and weaknesses, expresses a strong self-critique, and is ready to learn from others. Today, we no longer hear only the voice of a triumphalistic West, as in previous periods, but also a self-critical awareness of enduring problems and challenges lying ahead. But in no way does the West accept that it has reached its own limits or that it is at a dead end. For the most part, such attitudes are also shared nowadays by the Western Christian churches, including the Roman Catholic one, which has become much more self-critical and appears to be more compatible with modernity. These churches do not deny their past mistakes or wrongdoings, and all these fermentations are considered vital for the articulation of their future agenda. As such, the Western world today has no need for a savior figure like Yannaras. On the contrary, a Western reader, perhaps an offspring of the old "barbarians" of the Late Antiquity, might suggest that Yannaras could instead try to save his own Orthodox compatriots and country, which has been deeply afflicted in recent years by a profound crisis of values and orientations far beyond the immediate economic sphere. Frankly, the Greek crisis that erupted in 2009 is connected, among other things, to a specific Orthodox-based cultural discourse, which was formulated during the last three decades and was highly popular and influential. Many of Yannaras's ideas and evaluations discussed in this chapter contributed significantly to the articulation of this discourse, which in turn formed the ideological backdrop to the current crisis. But that is a topic for another essay.

Notes

1. See, among others, Selbach 2002; Makrides and Uffelmann 2003; Makrides 2009.
2. Buruma and Margalit 2005.
3. See Goody 1996; Chakrabarty 2007.
4. This was the topic of a conference organized at Fordham University, June 28–30, 2010, aimed at deconstructing such false caricatures of the West. See Demacopoulos and Papanikolaou 2013.
5. See Carrier 1995.
6. See Uffelmann 1999.
7. See Stoeckl 2006.
8. On his work and theological thinking, see Sopko 1998.
9. For more details, see Demacopoulos and Papanikolaou 2008.
10. See, among others, Petrà 2004; Louth 2009; Petrà 2010.

11. See Grigoropoulou 2008; Payne 2011; Lis 2013.
12. Payne 2008.
13. For details, see Kalaitzidis 2008: 209–543; 2009: esp. 479–513.
14. See, among others, Murray 1971; Konstantinides 1972; Nissiotis 1972; Petrà 1984; Dupuy 1991.
15. See, e.g., Yannaras 1972; 1974.
16. Yannaras 2011: 282–284.
17. Yannaras 1982: 9–10 (also reprinted in Yannaras 2011: 285–286).
18. The English translation is not identical to the Greek original (Yannaras 1992). As the translators Peter Chamberas and Norman Russell noted (Yannaras 2006a: xi), all changes in the English version of the book were made in previous consultation with the author. These changes included, among other things, the modification of the "polemical tone" of the original, but not of its passion in criticizing the evils of Western civilization. They also mentioned that the author (xi) was "anxious [...] that his work should not be seen as an attack on the Western religious tradition as such, but as an examination of how Greek Orthodox historically have approached their own ecclesiastical culture."
19. Yannaras 2006a: viii.
20. Ibid., viii–ix.
21. Yannaras 2011: 286.
22. Buruma and Margalit 2005: 1–12, 101–149.
23. Yannaras 2011: 232, 247. The book by Wallace-Hadrill is entitled *The Barbarian West, 400–1000*. Yannaras mentions a 1962 edition of this book. The book was, however, first published in 1952, while subsequent editions were revised and brought up to date. Yannaras also mentions other studies by Western scholars, who refer to "the Barbarian West" or generally to the barbarian invasions and their consequences (see ibid., 232–233, footnote 2).
24. Kalaitzidis 2008: 257–272, 287–319.
25. Yannaras 2011: 232–233.
26. For more details, see Makrides 1994 and 2007.
27. See Yannaras 2009.
28. This particular expression goes back to Duby (1984). Needless to say, Duby could never share Yannaras's interpretations, implications, and conclusions concerning "the Barbarian West."
29. Yannaras 2011: 34–36.
30. Ibid., 242–245.
31. Ibid., 233–234.
32. Ibid., 235–236.
33. Ibid., 247–248.
34. Ibid., 267–268.
35. Ibid., 247–249. In the second edition of the same book, Yannaras has added a new preface, in which he offers an additional, even shorter summary of his entire oeuvre and thought. There he talks again of the "post-Roman, Barbarian West" and the "Dark Middle Ages" in Western Europe, which produced an ill-guided civilization, completely different from and inferior to the one in the Hellenized Orthodox Roman East.
36. See, e.g., Yannaras 1998: 46, 83, 87; 2006b: 144–145, 225–226; 2008: 136–137. See also Kalaitzidis 2008: 443–456.
37. Yannaras 2006a: 11–22.
38. Yannaras 1992: 21–42.
39. Yannaras 2003: 13–14.
40. Yannaras 1991: 154–164.
41. Yannaras 1986: 89–244.
42. Gallaher 2011: 679–683. In the 2008 Russian documentary film *Gibel' imperii: Vizantiiskii urok* (The Fall of an Empire: The Lesson of Byzantium), directed and narrated by the

archimandrite Tikhon Shevkunov, the superior civilization of Byzantium is also contrasted with the barbarian state of development in the Latin West.
43. Romanides 1981.
44. Yannaras 1992: 441–444.
45. Yannaras 2011: 237.
46. Ibid., 251.
47. Aillagon 2008.
48. Lechner 1954: 73–128; Kazhdan and Cutler 1991: 252–253.
49. Jones 1971: 386.
50. Cited in ibid., 390, footnote 79.
51. Rentschler 1981.
52. See Stiegemann and Wemhoff 1999.
53. See, e.g., Yannaras 1984.
54. Carroll 2007.
55. See Lincoln 2000.
56. Horkheimer and Adorno 1947.
57. Todorov 2010.
58. See Makrides 2008.
59. See Kalaitzidis 2008: 273–286.
60. Yannaras 1994: 50–51.
61. Yannaras 2003: 15–17. See Yannaras 2009: 15–22.
62. See Gounelas 1996; Kalaitzidis 2008: 287–353; Gallaher 2009.

References

Aillagon, Jean-Jacques, ed., 2008: *Rome and the Barbarians: The Birth of a New World.* Milano: Skira.

Buruma, Ian, and Avishai Margalit, 2005: *Occidentalism: A Short History of Anti-Westernism.* London: Atlantic Books.

Carrier, James G., ed., 1995: *Occidentalism: Images of the West.* Oxford: Clarendon Press.

Carroll, Anthony J., 2007: *Protestant Modernity: Weber, Secularization and Protestantism.* Scranton and London: University of Scranton Press.

Chakrabarty, Dipesh, 2007: *Provincializing Europe: Postcolonial Thought and Historical Difference.* Princeton, NJ: Princeton University Press.

Demacopoulos, George E., and Aristotle Papanikolaou, eds., 2013: *Orthodox Constructions of the West.* New York: Fordham University Press.

Demacopoulos, George E., and Aristotle Papanikolaou, eds., 2008: *Orthodox Readings of Augustine.* Crestwood, NY: St. Vladimir's Seminary Press.

Duby, Georges, 1984: *Le Moyen Âge. I: Adolescence de la chrétienté occidentale: 980–1140.* Genève: Éditions d'art Skira.

Dupuy, Bernard, 1991: "La 'philosophie néohellénique' de Christos Yannaras." *Istina* 36: 385–388.

Gallaher, Brandon, 2009: "Review of Christos Yannaras, *Orthodoxy and the West: Hellenic Self-Identity in the Modern Age*, Brookline, MA: Holy Cross Orthodox Press, 2006." *Logos. A Review of Eastern Christian Studies* 50: 537–542.

———, 2011: "'Waiting for the Barbarians': Identity and Polemicism in the Neo-Patristic Synthesis of Georges Florovsky." *Modern Theology* 27: 659–691.

Goody, Jack, 1996: *The East in the West.* Cambridge: Cambridge University Press.

Gounelas, Sotiris, 1996: "Kritiki theorisi orismenon theseon tou Christou Yannara" (Critical perspectives on some views of Christos Yannaras). *Synaxi* 58: 67–76.

Grigoropoulou, Evaggelia, 2008: *The Early Development of the Thought of Christos Yannaras*. PhD doctoral thesis, Durham University.
Horkheimer, Max, and Theodor W. Adorno, 1947: *Dialektik der Aufklärung*. Amsterdam: Querido.
Jones, W. R, 1971: "The Image of the Barbarian in Medieval Europe." *Comparative Studies in Society and History* 13: 376–407.
Kalaitzidis, Pantelis, 2008: *Ellinikotita kai Antidytikismos sti "theologia tou '60"* (Hellenicity and anti-Westernism in the "theology of the 1960s"). PhD dissertation, University of Thessalonica.
———, 2009: "I anakalypsi tis Ellinikotitas kai o theologikos Antidytikismos" (The discovery of Hellenicity and the theological anti-Westernism). In Pantelis Kalaitzidis, Thanassis P. Papathanassiou, and Theophilos Ambatzidis (eds.), *Anataraxeis sti metapolemiki theologia. I "theologia tou '60"* (Turbulences in post-war theology: The "theology of the 1960s"). Athens: Indiktos, pp. 429–514.
Kazhdan, Alexander, and Anthony Cutler, 1991: "Barbarians." In *The Oxford Dictionary of Byzantium*, Vol. 1. Oxford: Oxford University Press, pp. 252–253.
Konstantinides, Chrysostom, 1972: "Orthodoxy and the West: A Response." *The Greek Orthodox Theological Review* 17: 143–166.
Lechner, Kilian, 1954: *Hellenen und Barbaren im Weltbild der Byzantiner*. Dissertation, Universität München.
Lis, Julia Anna, 2013: *Antiwestliche Diskurse in der serbischen und griechischen Theologie. Zur Konstruktion des "Westens" in den Schriften von Nikolaj Velimirović, Justin Popović, Christos Yannaras und John S. Romanides*. ThD dissertation, University of Münster (forthcoming in "Erfurter Studien zur Kulturgeschichte des Orthodoxen Christentums," 2014).
Lincoln, Bruce, 2000: "Culture." In Willi Braun and Russell T. McCutcheon (eds.), *Guide to the Study of Religion*. London: Cassell, pp. 409–422.
Louth, Andrew, 2009: "Some Recent Works by Christos Yannaras in English Translation." *Modern Theology* 25: 329–340.
Makrides, Vasilios N., 1994: "Christian Orthodoxy versus Religion: Negative Critiques of Religion in Contemporary Greece." In Ugo Bianchi (ed.), *Selected Proceedings of the XVI Congress of the I.A.H.R. (Roma, 3–8 September 1990): The Notion of "Religion" in Comparative Research*. Rome: "L'Erma" di Bretschneider, pp. 471–479.
———, 2007: "Religion, Kirche und Orthodoxie. Aspekte orthodox-christlicher Religionskritik." *Zeitschrift für Religionswissenschaft* 15: 53–82.
———, 2008: "Orthodoxes Christentum und westeuropäische Aufklärung: Ein unvollendetes Projekt?" *Ökumenische Rundschau* 57: 303–318.
———, 2009: "Orthodox Anti-Westernism Today: A Hindrance to European Integration?" *International Journal for the Study of the Christian Church* 9: 209–224.
Makrides, Vasilios N., and Dirk Uffelmann, 2003: "Studying Eastern Orthodox Anti-Westernism: The Need for a Comparative Research Agenda." In Jonathan Sutton and Wil van den Bercken (eds.), *Orthodox Christianity and Contemporary Europe*. Leuven: Peeters, pp. 87–120.
Murray, Robert, SJ, 1971: "A Brief Comment on Dr. Yannaras's Article." *Eastern Churches Review* 3: 306–307.
Nissiotis, N. A., 1972: "Orthodoxy and the West: A Response." *The Greek Orthodox Theological Review* 17: 132–142.
Payne, Daniel, 2008: "Orthodoxy, Islam and the 'Problem' of the West: A Comparison of the Liberation Theologies of Christos Yannaras and Sayyid Qutb." *Religion, State and Society* 36: 435–450.

———, 2011: *The Revival of Political Hesychasm in Contemporary Orthodox Thought: The Political Hesychasm of John Romanides and Christos Yannaras.* Lanham: Lexington Books.

Petrà, Basilio, 1984: "Christo Yannaras e la verità dell'ethos." *Rivista di Teologia morale* 16: 539–548.

———, 2004: "Christos Yannaras (1935–)." *Credere oggi* 24: 121–130.

———, 2010: "Christos Yannaras. Un'introduzione alla sua vita e al suo pensiero." In Ch. Yannaras, *Ontologia della relazione.* Troina (EN): Città Aperta, pp. 7–27.

Rentschler, Michael, 1981: *Liudprand von Cremona: Eine Studie zum ost-westlichen Kulturgefälle im Mittelalter.* Frankfurt am Main: Klostermann.

Romanides, John S., 1981: *Franks, Romans, Feudalism, and Doctrine: An Interplay between Theology and Society.* Brookline, MA: Holy Cross Orthodox Press.

Selbach, Christopher, 2002: "The Orthodox Church in Post-Communist Russia and her Perception of the West: A Search for a Self in the Face of an Other." *Zeitschrift für Religionswissenschaft* 10: 131–173.

Sopko, Andrew J., 1998: *The Theology of John Romanides: Prophet of Roman Orthodoxy.* Dewdney, BC: Synaxis Press.

Stiegemann, Christoph, and Matthias Wemhoff, eds., 1999: *799. Kunst und Kultur der Karolingerzeit. Karl der Große und Papst Leo III. in Paderborn.* Mainz: Philipp von Zabern.

Stoeckl, Kristina, 2006: "Modernity and its Critique in Twentieth Century Russian Orthodox Thought." *Studies in East European Thought* 58: 243–269.

Todorov, Tzvetan, 2010: *In Defence of the Enlightenment.* London: Atlantic Books.

Uffelmann, Dirk, 1999: *Die russische Kulturosophie. Logik und Axiologie der Argumentation.* Frankfurt am Main: Peter Lang.

Yannaras, Christos, 1972: "Orthodoxy and the West." *The Greek Orthodox Theological Review* 17: 115–131.

———, 1974: "Scholasticism and Technology." *Eastern Churches Review* 6: 162–169.

———, 1984: *Orthos logos kai koinoniki praktiki* (Right reasoning and social practice). Athens: Domos.

———, 1986: *Philosophie sans rupture.* Genève: Labor et Fides.

———, 1991: *Elements of Faith: An Introduction to Orthodox Theology.* Edinburgh: T&T Clark.

———, 1992: *Orthodoxia kai Dysi sti neoteri Ellada* (Orthodoxy and the West in modern Greece). Athens: Domos.

———, 1994: *Aoristi Ellada. Kontserto gia dyo apodimies* (Undefined Greece: A concert about two travels abroad). Athens: Domos.

———, 1998: *I apanthropia tou dikaiomatos* (The inhumanity of the right). Athens: Domos.

———, 2003: "Ekklisia kai Politismos" (Church and civilization). *Synaxi* 88: 11–17.

———, 2006a: *Orthodoxy and the West. Hellenic Self-Identity in the Modern Age.* Brookline, MA: Holy Cross Orthodox Press.

———, 2006b: *Enantia sti thriskeia* (Against religion). Athens: Ikaros.

———, 2008: *To ainigma tou kakou* (The riddle of evil). Athens: Ikaros.

———, 2009: *Wem gehört die griechische Antike?* (Erfurter Vorträge zur Kulturgeschichte des Orthodoxen Christentums, 8). Erfurt: Universität Erfurt.

———, 2011: *Exi philosophikes zografies* (Six philosophical paintings). Athens: Ikaros.

10

Anti-Western Theology in Greece and Serbia Today

Julia Anna Lis

In their attitudes toward the West, Serbia and Greece represent two very different cases. Greece has long been a member of Western structures such as NATO and can therefore be regarded as a member or partner of the West. In contrast, Serbia's relationship with the West is more complicated because of historical circumstances in the twentieth century, in particular the wars in the 1990s in Croatia, in Bosnia-Herzegovina, and in Kosovo, the latter including the NATO bombings of Serbia. Whereas Greece has been a member of the European Union since 1981, Serbia has only recently taken its first steps toward such membership.

However, Greece and Serbia share a common history of centuries under Ottoman rule. With their predominantly Orthodox populations, both countries share a similar understanding of ethnoreligious identity: Orthodox identity is not limited to religious sentiments, but often includes cultural and national ones as well; in some cases, Orthodox identity is understood mainly in cultural and national terms. Conversely, the Orthodox Churches in both countries also have significant constituencies, whose sense of ethnic identity necessarily entails an Orthodox identity.

The aim of this chapter is to consider the implications of this relationship between nation and religion in Greece and Serbia for the images of the West and of European integration, and for the understanding of the social role of Orthodoxy in these countries. I will try to show how important twentieth-century Orthodox thinkers and theologians have constructed the interconnected religious, national, and cultural elements of Orthodox identity and opposition to the West.

Anti-Western Elements in Orthodox Discourse and Their Origins

Groups that stress the links between culture, religion, and nation often accuse the European Union or the West in general of weakening the nation and the church by promoting the processes of globalization and modernization.

In Greece, the Free Monks, a rock band comprised of Orthodox monks, uses its music to protest against civil marriage, atheism, sects, and treaties with Europe. Considering Orthodoxy a tool for maintaining Greek national unity, the Free Monks promote strong bonds between Greek and Orthodox identities.[1] Anti-Western and Euro-skeptical statements have been made by the former Greek archbishop Christodoulos. In his opinion, human rights and globalization serve only the imperialistic needs of the West, which employs these ideas in order to destroy the national and religious identity of Greece.[2] In 1999, he warned against "the EU melting pot and its tragic consequences for Hellenism and Orthodoxy."[3] The theologian Georgios Metallinos presented similar views on Greece and the EU in a pamphlet entitled *Threat or Hope?* According to Metallinos, the problems Greece has with the European Union are not chiefly economic or political, but spiritual and cultural.[4] The dominant culture of the EU is not merely different from Greek culture, but it is also anti-Hellenic.[5] The strongest critique of the West can be found in rigorist groups, which claim to be the only representatives of true and pure Orthodoxy. Their aim is to protect Greek society from what they consider to be the evil influences of the West, such as European integration, the teaching of evolution in schools, and books and films that are critical of Christianity. Their relationship to the official church is complex: on the one hand, there are alliances between official church representatives and rigorist groups during conflicts between state and church, like the identity cards issue,[6] but on the other hand, there are Greek bishops who have condemned Orthodox rigorists as schismatics.[7]

In Serbia, anti-Western statements criticized Western policy during the Yugoslavian war and linked the NATO bombings and the situation in Kosovo with a critique of Western culture. Prominent church leaders such as Bishop Amfilohije Radović portray the West as atheistic and enmeshed in earthly materialism and totalitarianism. According to Radović, the decadence of Europe consists of abolishing traditional values and the pursuit of economic gain.[8] The attitude of the West toward the conflict in Kosovo is described by Bishop Radović as "tyrannically enslaving individuals and entire nations by trampling on human hearts and human conscience."[9] Some Serbian theologians, for example, Radomir Popović, consider Western materialism and secularism as a bigger danger for Orthodoxy than communism was in earlier times.[10] There are also efforts in Serbia, similar to those of the Free Monks in Greece, to mobilize anti-Western opinion using rock music[11]: for example, Hieromonk Jovan Čulibrk released a CD album entitled *Songs above East and West*. The idea was to popularize the thoughts and words of Bishop Nikolaj Velimirović by combining his lyrics with rock music.[12]

Such processes raise the question: What are the theological roots of this anti-Western thinking? In Serbia, the two most important proponents of anti-Western theology were Nikolaj Velimirović (1881–1956) and Justin Popović (1894–1979), who developed their ideas mostly in the first half of the twentieth century. At that time, Greek theology was largely under the influence of the West.[13] It began to take an anti-Western orientation in the 1960s, in connection with the neo-Orthodox movement. Its chief protagonist is the philosopher Christos Yannaras (b. 1935), the most famous and controversial theological thinker in Greece. He criticized the Western and, in particular, scholastic influences in Greek theology,[14] and set out to establish a new line of Orthodox thinking. In the following we will examine and compare the views of Yannaras, Velimirović, and Popović on the West, and their images of their own countries and Europe in order to illustrate the roots of anti-Western positions in Serbian and Greek theology today.

The enduring importance of Velimirović and Popović is readily evident, since the church recently canonized them as saints. The most important Serbian theologians and bishops such as Amfilohije Radović, Atanasije Jevtić, or Irinej Bulović were students of Popović[15] and some of them did academic work on Velimirović. In his biography on Velimirović, former bishop of Kosovo Artemije Radosavljević wrote that Velimirović "pushes various foreign customs and superfluous Westernism away from himself and his people. He is entirely imbued with the warm currents of Orthodoxy; he is excited and captivated by Christ's magnificent and salutary image and Saint Sava's church and social activity."[16] Considering the great number of books about him, Velimirović is surely one of the most popular authors in postsocialist Serbia.[17]

Yannaras, Velimirović, and Popović thus create an image of Orthodox culture that is completely and fundamentally different from Western culture. Popović's views of Europe are much more centered on theological considerations, while Velimirović stresses more the cultural differences between Serbia and the West.

The Idealization of Historical Memory: *Svetosavlje* and Byzantium

In Serbian Orthodox self-understanding, Saint Sava is a key point of reference. Sava was the younger brother of the first Serbian king, Stefan Nemanjić, and became the first Serbian bishop.[18] His cult in oral culture, religious tradition, and national epics was established especially in the nineteenth century.[19] In the interwar period, *Svetosavlje* became a movement of philosophical and theological ideas, which praised Saint Sava's cultural and religious heritage and regarded it as the foundation of the Serbian nation.[20] Nikolaj Velimirović is one of the most prominent representatives of *Svetosavlje*.

For Velimirović, the main characteristic of *Svetosavlje* was the attitude of *Theodule*, or serving God. In his view, Saint Sava's main achievement was the liberation of Serbs from Greek domination[21] and the foundation of the Serbian church in which Orthodoxy and Serbian nationality were unified: in serving God one also serves one's own people.[22] Thus, service to God became the first goal of the Serbian church and the Serbian state in the Middle Ages,[23] the "Golden Age" of Serbia. The structure of a monastery with its harmonic unity between work and prayer, daily and spiritual life became a model for the structure of society.[24]

The Serbian Saint-Sava-identity discourse also established a dichotomy between Serbia and the West. According to Velimirović, Saint Sava opposed papal supremacy and Western theocracy by arguing for a uniquely Serbian form of *Theodule*.[25] Velimirović constructs a dichotomy between Serbian *Theodule*, based on voluntary service, and Western European theocracy meaning the domination of a ruler over his servants.[26] *Theodule* refers to a harmonious unity between church and state, which serve God together, whereas in a theocracy church and state are in a constant struggle because they have no common goal of service but only the pursuit of domination and mastery.[27]

In essence, Velimirović's notion of *Theodule* entails a sacralization of the nation and the state. Despite the idealized image of the Serbian people, it lacks emancipatory potential.[28] The sacral dimension of the state and its rulers does not allow any rebellion against them. The common goal of the entire society, peasants as well as the nobility, is to serve God, and not pursue their separate rights or leadership. The idea of the spiritual unity of all Serbians and the denial of any form of oppression in traditional Serbian society make emancipation unnecessary. The ideal of liberation was understood exclusively in relation to foreign oppression.[29] Saint Sava thus became a symbol of a glorious Serbian past and of resistance to foreign influences and oppression.[30]

The concept of *Theodule* is fundamentally opposed to any separation of church and state.[31] On the contrary, if the goal of the state and his ruler is to serve God, it has a sacral dimension. For Velimirović, any separation of church and state along Western lines is essentially misguided. Also connected with the image of Saint Sava is the idealization of the whole period before the battle of Kosovo Polje in 1389. This historical image serves as a contrast with the West and as an alternative model of a true Christian civilization. Velimirović suggested that the reason why nothing remains of this civilization is the influence of the West.[32]

A similar notion of an ideal historical time is also found in Yannaras's depiction of Byzantium as a society governed by Orthodox principles. For him, the teachings of the Church Fathers are not only a theological doctrine, but a way of life and a way to act in the world,[33] above all, respecting human personhood and the personal nature of the cosmos. All dimensions of life—culture, art, technology, economy, and politics—are subsumed under the overarching goal of a life in truth. [34] The only historical example of a society in which this concept was fully realized in a social structure, according to Yannaras, was Byzantium.[35] The Byzantine way of life was characterized by the priority of liturgy as "an event of personal communion."[36] This communal ethos was the foundation of the church, and it influenced economics, politics, legislation, and art.[37] Yannaras considers this communal ethos as a fundamental difference between the underlying cosmologies of Gothic and Byzantine architecture: Byzantine architecture was distinctive in creating a connection between the natural form and the human being interacting with it, a personal relationship or dialogue between the builder and the material—through the material, the builder enters into a personal relationship with God, who manifests himself in his creation.[38] But apart from this example, Yannaras does not show what this ethos really meant in Byzantium, how it was realized concretely, and how it influenced daily life and political decisions. Nor does he explain how Byzantine inner struggles and problems fit within the idealized image of Byzantine society.

Ultimately, the "historical traditions" that Velimirović and Yannaras present are not actual historical reality, but invented, utopian constructions of societies inspired by Orthodox values and truth. In a romanticized fashion, each author presents his own, invented tradition as historical truth, as a way of drawing upon the past in search of answers to the challenges of modernity. They see the root cause of all the problems of modernity in the erroneous culture that developed in the West.

The Humanist Culture of the West

According to all three authors, the basic reason for the erroneous development of the Western world is a mistaken understanding of the relationship between God and man, which is anthropocentric and rooted in the theology of St. Augustine.

Yannaras argues that Western thinking regards the human being as an individual, autonomous, isolated being, and not as a person, open to relationships with others and with God (as does Orthodoxy). For Popović, the key term that distinguishes Orthodox and Western world is "God-manhood." The goal of every human being should be to become like Christ, the God-man, in order to realize his God-given potential.[39] Velimirović and Popović believe that only those who seek God and God-manhood have personal, human dignity. The Western view is seen as denying God-manhood, because its idea of human self-sufficiency implies that man does not need God. According to Popović, anthropocentrism is focused on individual demands, and that amounts to devil-centeredness.[40]

A key point of focus in the Orthodox critique is Western rationalism, including Scholastic theological rationalism. Humanity should be studied as the image of God, rather than trying to understand God's nature by investigating man, as Western theology does, according to Yannaras.[41] The West reduces the knowledge of God to a purely intellectual process, which leads to a division between immanence and transcendence, the separation of religion from life, and ultimately to the "death of God" in Western thought.[42]

Popović accuses Western culture of ignoring the God-man Jesus Christ and of replacing him with a humanist worldview.[43] In his opinion, this has profound consequences for the theological and philosophical thought of the West. Through his concentration on rationalism, Western man focuses exclusively on himself and is trapped in immanence. Popović constructs a sharp distinction between the predominantly humanist philosophy of the West and the theological philosophy of Orthodoxy. In his view, Western philosophy is a philosophy of radical division, while Orthodox God-manhood represents unity and community between God and man.[44]

In their critiques of the modern Western world, all three authors connect secular Western culture and the erroneous perception of Christianity held by Western churches. Popović argues that the divinization of the pope, expressed in the dogma of infallibility, is the "heresy of heresies"[45] because it manifests the anthropocentrism of Western culture. Since infallibility is a divine prerogative, the dogma of papal infallibility means that one man claims to be divine. It was arrogant of popes to try to replace Jesus Christ instead of remaining humble and striving for holiness through the imitation of the God-man.[46] In this view, secular modern culture is the consequence of a Fall, which for Popović began with the conflicts over the position of the bishop of Rome between the Western and the Eastern churches and for Yannaras with the Augustinian theology on which scholasticism was based.[47] In light of this, the alienation of the Western world from Christianity is not accidental but the result of an erroneous understanding of the relationship between God and humanity—since the very beginnings of the Western church.[48] The West does not preach Christ but an Antichrist, as Yannaras states, quoting Dostoyevsky.[49]

Concepts of Europe

In their views of Western Europe, Yannaras, Velimirović, and Popović are in agreement. Europe's main flaw is that it has departed from Jesus Christ as the center of civilization. The replacement of God by man has consequences for Western culture, science, politics, and fashion. Man has become the measure of all things, and European liberalism and socialism have created a secularized worldview, which denies Christianity.

According to Yannaras, the Western technological understanding of the cosmos is a consequence of a utilitarian approach to reality: Western man does not seek a relationship to the world but only wants to exploit it for his own purposes.[50] The consequences of this development include the destruction of natural environment[51] and the crisis of the family and marriage.[52] Popović also argues that Western anthropocentrism transforms the human person into a soulless robot, the *homo faber* of technological and scientific progress.[53] Therefore, its consequences are nihilism and the death of humanity.[54]

Velimirović advances a differentiated concept of the West. In the first phase, he expresses admiration for the United States[55] and Great Britain,[56] which for him are true democracies. He admires their civil religion, which prevented them from becoming secular states like other countries in Western Europe. In a second phase, he radicalizes his critique of Western Europe. The evil of Europe has gone so far that there is no way out. European man does not trust in God but only in human beings and follows human and not divine laws.[57] Only Serbia can be saved, but only if it returns to its true national and religious identity and stops imitating the West.

Popović's image of Europe is inspired by Dostoyevsky—a strong emphasis on nationalism rooted in religion, the search for a distinctive, non-Western cultural and religious identity, and a return to one's own traditions instead of imitating Europe.[58] Without Christianity, Europe has lost its inner self. According to Popović, the destructive power of the Western world seems to be endless, capable of creating such evil as the Nazi concentration camps.[59]

According to Yannaras, Velimirović, and Popović, nothing good can be expected from the faulty foundations of Western theology and philosophy, and the only solution for Europe is to return to authentic Christianity as practiced by the Orthodox Church. In their view, Orthodoxy can offer an alternative to modern, technological, and consumer culture, with beneficial consequences for art, politics, economy, and technology. In a truly Orthodox society, the unity of morality, politics, and economics, and of transcendence and immanence—which have been eroded by Western influence—could be restored. The salvation of Europe, and an effective response to its social, economic, and political challenges, requires repentance and social transformation toward Eucharistic community and God-manhood. The secular world should be integrated into the community of believers, and the pursuit of social justice should focus on the true spiritual good within a loving, fraternal community of believers, as found in monastic life.

Conclusion

The dichotomy between East and West in the views of Yannaras, Popović, and Velimirović can thus be traced to a distinctive line of theological thinking and a unique approach to politics and culture. The evils of modernity are attributed to Western influence in Orthodox societies, which in turn prevents them from holding on to their own traditions. The strongest Manichean worldview is represented by Popović, who presents the conflict between East and West as a struggle of God and his servants against the demonic powers of the devil.

All three thinkers view the East and the West as monolithic, static blocks and leave no room for dialogue or mutual understanding. All instances of Western influence are interpreted as a sign of the decline of Orthodox culture. The only solution they see is in a return to the invented traditions of one's own idealized past.

Many of the aforementioned observations on individualism, technologization, and rationalism are present in Western conservative critiques of modernity since the Romantic period. But Velimirović, Yannaras, and Popović go further by presenting Orthodoxy as an alternative. By stressing the fundamental difference between Orthodox and Western cultures, they relate the problems of modernity to spiritual decline and moral evil, and propose Orthodoxy as a solution. But, despite their critique of the West in general and Western ideas in particular, these critics themselves employ Western concepts. The concept of nation, so important to Velimirović's thinking, is quite similar to that of Western Romanticism: the construction of a national culture, history, and national heritage, the invention of traditions like *Svetosavlje*, and the imagination of a Golden Age in the past are important elements of this idea.

The anti-Western perspective of Velimirović, Yannaras, and Popović can also have consequences for the attitudes of Serbian or Greek Orthodoxy toward Western Europe and European values such as human rights, pluralism, and the separation of church and state. Human rights as individual rights are difficult to reconcile with a worldview that is fundamentally opposed to individualism. Velimirović and Popović would reject them as examples of Western anthropocentrism. Similarly, the nation as a concept constructed under specific historical circumstances is in stark contrast to Velimirović's image of a nation as a spiritual and ethnic community.

The very concept of Europe can have different meanings for the anti-Western thinkers. Usually Europe means the West and is therefore criticized. For example, Popović speaks about Europeans or European philosophy and contrasts them with their Orthodox counterparts. But there is also a notion of Europe as the homeland of true Christianity. In this case, anti-Western Orthodox thinkers would not deny that they are part of Europe but would regard themselves as the only true Europeans. In Greece, this is expressed in the idea that Europe developed out of the synthesis between Christian faith and Greek culture. Serbians refer to the historical role of Serbia as an *Antemurale Christianitatis*, defending Europe and Christianity. From such a perspective, the Orthodox task is to bring Europe back to its roots and to true Christianity.

As long as the conceptual dichotomies of East versus West or "true, Orthodox" Europe versus "decadent, secular" Europe persist, they will remain obstacles to dialogue and integration. Religious voices will likely continue to play a key part in the complex discourse on the European Union and European integration. Their constructive contribution to that discussion will depend on their ability to avoid stereotyping the West as "the other" and as a source of evil.

Notes

1. Lina Molokotos-Liederman, "Sacred Words, Profane Music? The Free Monks as a Musical Phenomenon in Contemporary Greek Orthodoxy," *Sociology of Religion* 65:4 (2004), 411–412.
2. Alfons Brüning, "Spannungsverhältnis. 'Orthodoxe Werte' und Menschenrechte," *Osteuropa* 59:6 (2009), 66.

3. Elizabeth Prodromou, "The Ambivalent Orthodox," *Journal of Democracy* 15:2 (2004), 70.
4. Effie Fokas, "Greek Orthodoxy and European identity," *Harvard Kennedy School—Kokkalis Programme on Southeastern and Central Eastern Europe*, http://www.hks.harvard.edu/kokkalis/GSW2/Fokas.PDF (accessed December 17, 2010), p. 17.
5. Georgios Metallinos, "Orthodox and European Culture. The Struggle between Hellenism and Frankism," http://www.romanity.org/mir/me04en.htm, 1995 (accessed December 17, 2010).
6. In 2000, the Greek government decided to remove any reference to religious affiliation from identity cards, in order to avoid discrimination against non-Orthodox Greeks. This provoked a conflict with the Greek Orthodox Church, which regarded this measure as an attack on the link between Hellenism and Orthodoxy. More about the identity card conflict in Greece can be found in: Vasilios N. Makrides, "Between Normality and Tension: Assessing Church-State Relations, in Greece in the Light of the Identity (Cards) Crisis," in Vasilios N. Makrides (ed.), *Religion, Staat und Konfliktkonstellationen im orthodoxen Ost- und Südosteuropa. Vergleichende Perspektiven* (Frankfurt am Main: Peter Lang, 2005), pp. 137–178.
7. More about Greek rigorists can be found in Vasilios N. Makrides, "'L'autre' orthodoxie: courants du rigorisme orthodoxe grec," *Social compass* 51:4 (2004), 511–521.
8. Ivan Čolović, "Europa als Gegenstand der zeitgenössischen politischen Mythologie in Serbien," in Harald Heppner and Grigorios Larentzakis (eds.), *Das Europa-Verständnis im orthodoxen Südosteuropa*, Institut für Ökumenische Theologie und Patrologie (Graz, 1996), pp. 194–195.
9. Atanasije Jevtić, "The Cry of Serbs from Kosovo and Metohija," http://www.mitropolija.co.me/duhovnost/vatanasije-cry.htm, 1999 (accessed January 26, 2010).
10. Klaus Buchenau, "Kleines Serbien, große Welt: Serbiens Orthodoxie über Globalisierung und europäische Integration," in *Religion, Staat und Konfliktkonstellationen im orthodoxen Ost- und Südosteuropa. Vergleichende Perspektiven*, p. 99.
11. Anna Di Lellio, "The Missing Democratic Revolution and Serbia's Anti-European Choice: 1989–2008," *International Journal of Politics, Culture, and Society* 22 (2009), 382. The following is an example of the Free Monks' lyrics: "Hold on tight to the faith, hold on to the great ideals / We won't sell the fatherland off / The church will not die / History won't be forgotten / This atheist civilization signs treaties and agreements / You're not a person anymore, just a bar code number." http://www.youtube.com/watch?v=mGTePB-dups (accessed February 24, 2012).
12. Dijana Gaćeša, "Fundamentalist Tendencies of Serbian Orthodox Christianity," *Western Balkans Security Observer* 7–8 (2007–2008), 77–78. See also the *Poem to St. Sava*: "Sweet Lord speaks when he walks the earth / Of spiritual drink and of living water: / Blessed is the one who drinks it in this age, / Living rivers will flow from him. / No one in the Serbian nation could / Drink in living water like you. / Hence the rivers gushed out of you / And watered wonderfully all the Serbian land: / Grace and justice and holy truth, / Hope and brotherhood and upright education, / Strong patriotism, gentle brotherly love / These are your waters, each deeper in turn. / You watered living seedbeds with them / You watered them till now, you'll water them from now on. / Just like Egypt is waterless without the Nile / So is your homeland without you." http://www.mitropolija.co.me/ustrojstvo/radio/vladika/vladika/index_eng.html (accessed February 24, 2012).
13. Vasilios N. Makrides, "Neoorthodoxie—eine religiöse Intellektuellenströmung im heutigen Griechenland," in Peter Antes and Donate Pahnke (eds.), *Die Religion von Oberschichten. Religion—Profession—Intellektualismus* (Marburg: Diagonal, 1989), p. 286.
14. Christos Yannaras, "La Théologie en Grèce aujourd'hui," *Istina* 16 (1971), 131–150.
15. Di Lellio, "The Missing Democratic Revolution and Serbia's Anti-European Choice," p. 381.

16. Artemije Radosavljević, *Život svetog vladike Nikolaja Velimirovića—Novi Zlatoust*, Parish of Lelić and Ćelije Monastery, 1991, cited in Helsinki Committee for Human Rights in Serbia, "The Serbian Orthodox Church and the New Serbian Identity," http://www.helsinki.org.rs/doc/Studija-Kupres-eng.pdf, 2006 (accessed February 4, 2011), pp. 10–11.
17. Jovan Byford, "From Traitor to 'Saint': Bishop Nikolaj Velimirović in Serbian Public Memory," *The Vidal Sassoon International Center for the Study of Antisemitism—Studies in Antisemitism Series*, http://sicsa.huji.ac.il/22byford.pdf (accessed January 28, 2011), p. 13.
18. Klaus Buchenau, "Svetosavlje und Pravoslavlje. Nationales und Universales in der serbischen Orthodoxie," in Martin Schulze Wessel (ed.), *Nationalisierung der Religion und Sakralisierung der Nation im östlichen Europa* (Stuttgart: Franz Steiner, 2006), p. 206.
19. Maria Falina, "Svetosavlje. A Case Study in the Nationalization of Religion," *Schweizerische Zeitschrift für Religions- und Kulturgeschichte* 101 (2007), 520.
20. Ibid., p. 521.
21. Nikolaj Velimirović, *Srpski narod kao Teodul* (Beograd: Evro, 2003), p. 225.
22. Ibid., p. 259.
23. Ibid., p. 226.
24. Ibid., p. 244.
25. Ibid., p. 225.
26. Ibid.
27. Ibid., p. 229
28. Buchenau, "Svetosavlje und Pravoslavlje," p. 219.
29. Ibid.
30. Bojan Aleksov, "Nationalism in Construction: The Memorial Church of St. Sava on Vračar Hill in Belgrade," *Balkanologie* 7:2 (2003), 51.
31. Buchenau, "Svetosavlje und Pravoslavlje," p. 219.
32. Velimirović, *Srpski narod kao Teodul*, p. 260.
33. Christos Yannaras, *Person und Eros. Eine Gegenüberstellung der Ontologie der griechischen Kirchenväter und der Existenzphilosophie des Westens* (Göttingen: Vandenhoeck & Ruprecht, 1982), p. 99.
34. Ibid.
35. Christos Yannaras, *The Freedom of Morality* (Crestwood, New York: St. Vladimir's Seminary Press, 1984), p. 220.
36. Ibid., p. 221.
37. Ibid.
38. Yannaras, *Person und Eros*, p. 105.
39. Justin Popović, *Orthodox Faith and Life in Christ* (Belmont, MA: Institute for Byzantine and Modern Greek Studies, 2005), p. 100.
40. Ibid., p. 101.
41. Yannaras, *Person und Eros*, pp. 236–237.
42. Ibid., p. 71.
43. Popović, *Orthodox Faith and Life in Christ*, p. 56.
44. Justin Popović, *L'homme et le dieu-homme* (Lausanne: L'age d'homme, 1989), p. 45.
45. Popović, *Orthodox Faith and Life in Christ*, p. 112.
46. Ibid., pp. 102–104.
47. Christos Yannaras, "Orthodoxy and the West," *Philotheos* 2 (2002), 79–80.
48. Yannaras, "Orthodoxy and the West," p. 72.
49. Ibid., p. 86.
50. Yannaras, *Person und Eros*, p. 44.
51. Ibid., p. 108.
52. Yannaras, *The Freedom of Morality*, p. 170.
53. Popović, *Orthodox Faith and Life in Christ*, p. 61.

54. Ibid., p. 110.
55. R. Chrysostomus Grill, *Serbischer Messianismus und Europa bei Bischof Velimirović* (St. Ottilien: EOS, 1998), pp. 155–157.
56. Nikolaj Velimirović, *Serbia in Light and Darkness* (London: Longmans, Green and Co., 1916).
57. Nikolaj Velimirović, *Kroz tamnički prozor* (Beograd: Evro, 2007), p. 138.
58. Grill, *Serbischer Messianismus und Europa bei Bischof Velimirović*, pp. 72–74.
59. Popović, *Orthodox Faith and Life in Christ*, p. 63.

11

The Russian Orthodox Church on the Values of Modern Society

Regina Elsner

In the official statements of the Moscow Patriarchate over the last 20 years, primarily those of the Department of External Church Relations, the topic of the modern values of the so-called West has been a central concern. "Modern values" in these documents refers to the phenomena of individuation, social secularization, and pluralization, while "the West" indicates Western Europe and North America.

The Russian Orthodox position on modern values emerged from an extensive discussion of the *Basis of the Social Concept*, which was adopted at the Bishops' Council of the Russian Orthodox Church in August 2000,[1] its further elaboration in the document *Basic Teaching on Human Dignity, Freedom and Rights*, adopted at the Bishops' Council of the Russian Orthodox Church in June 2008,[2] and the official statements of key figures of the Russian Orthodox Church (ROC) on a range of subjects, such as religious freedom, art exhibitions (i.e., "Ostorozhno Religia" and "Dvoeslovie"), and family ethics. These statements focus special attention on liberalism, modernism, and so-called militant secularism, which are treated critically—sometimes aggressively—and it is not easy to discern the theological foundations of the rather polemical discourse.

In an effort to identify theological categories within the Russian Orthodox discussion of modern values, I have studied the recent statements of leading representatives of the ROC. While my observations are by no means exhaustive, their goal is to broaden our perspective for the interpretation of Orthodox statements on modernity. I concentrated mainly on texts of the patriarch of Moscow and All-Russia, formerly metropolitan of Smolensk and Kaliningrad and head of the Department of External Church Relations Kirill (Gundjaev)—and of the current head of the Department of External Church Relations, Metropolitan Hilarion (Alfeev) of Volokolamsk, former ROC representative at the European Union and bishop of Vienna. In his previous capacity as head of the Department of External Church Relations, Patriarch Kirill was directly involved in the development of the *Basis of the Social Concept* and the documents on human rights. His successor in the Department of External Affairs,

Metropolitan Hilarion, is responsible for the implementation of the positions adopted in the basic documents.

In studying the documents two theological topics attracted my attention in particular: the image of the human person and the notion of tradition.

The Human Person

In 1999 Kirill, while still metropolitan of Smolensk and Kaliningrad, expressed the core of the Orthodox position in the modern world at the end of an article entitled "The Circumstances of Modern Life. Liberalism, Traditionalism and Moral Values of a Uniting Europe": "We come from a theocentric spiritual tradition which considers anthropocentric humanism as an alien world-view. We are prepared to treat it with respect, but we shall never accept it as the absolute and unconditional positive value."[3] Such a theocentric perspective resists the contrary worldview, according to which the human subject, rather than God, occupies the central position and the highest value. From an Orthodox perspective, precisely such an anthropocentric view is present within modern liberalism and Western society. Similarly, the statements of Metropolitan Hilarion put the question of the human person and its problematic definition by Western civilization at the center of the discussion. In 2005, he wrote: "At the core of the modern ideology of globalization is the humanistic idea of the absolute dignity of man and of the existence of universal, 'common human' values, which should serve as the foundation of a single world civilization."[4]

The image of the human person thus seems to be a key category in the ROC's engagement with the modern world. It is therefore important to grasp the concept of the human person as it is understood in Orthodox theology. Metropolitan Kirill gave a basic description of the concept at the tenth World Council of Russian People in 2006.[5] At the center of this definition is the person as image of God, which is derived from the biblical understanding of the person as "God's image and after His likeness" (Gen. 1:26). Referring to John of Damascus, Kirill demonstrates how this biblical statement establishes a dynamic, basic principle through the distinction between *value* and *dignity*. According to that principle, the human person possesses an inalienable *value* as an image of God, but still must act justly in order to achieve his full *dignity*. Dignity, in other words, is no fait accompli, but can increase or decrease, depending on how a person uses his freedom in choosing between good and evil. Because of sin, it is impossible for a human being always to choose good, and to attain full dignity through his own effort. Elaborating further on this, the *Basic Teachings on Human Dignity* (2008) pointed out that human dignity is a gift from God and that the individual is responsible for his life according to this gift: "Therefore, the human being as bearing the image of God should not exult in this lofty dignity, for it is not his own achievement but a gift of God. Nor should he use it to justify his weaknesses or vices, but rather he should understand his responsibility for the direction and way of his life. Clearly, the understanding of responsibility is integral to the notion of dignity."[6]

Such reflections reveal the particular Orthodox perspective on the modern image of the human person. First, this dynamic understanding of dignity does not permit any static understanding of human rights—human dignity can never become an unconditional value, regardless of human action. Second, sinful humanity cannot be at the center of a universal scale of values. Metropolitan Hilarion cites the *Basis of the Social Concept of the ROC*: "The Church cannot favour a world order that puts the human person, darkened by sin, at the centre of everything."[7]

It is noteworthy that this official discourse on the human person argues the need for moral norms. In the *Basic Teachings on Human Dignity*, we read: "According to Orthodox tradition, a human being preserves his God-given dignity and grows in it only if he lives in accordance with moral norms, because these norms express the primordial and therefore authentic human nature not darkened by sin. Thus, there is a direct link between human dignity and morality."[8] This need for moral norms originates in the inability of the sinful person to distinguish between good and evil, to act according to this differentiation, which is essential for salvation. Norms help the individual to use his freedom and to attain the dignity corresponding to him, thus attaining salvation and becoming a *person* in the profound sense. These moral norms are available in the Christian tradition—observing them leads to the good life and salvation, while setting them aside entails a loss of dignity and worth in life. From a Russian Orthodox point of view, these Christian norms formed the culture and people in Russia and Europe and are the foundation of their civilization. Western European society since the Enlightenment is challenged by secularization and "Christian values are being more and more marginalized, God is being driven to the outskirts of human existence."[9] Accordingly, from the point of view of the ROC these norms should be protected institutionally, that is, legally, against the individualism that already threatens Western civilization.

In this connection, a crucial theological point is the supraindividual character of what makes the human being a *person* by virtue of being the image of God. Just as God in his trinitarian dimension is not individual, but personal living communion between Father, Son, and Holy Spirit, so the human person as image of God is called to communion and, through communion, to become a person. Relatedness is constitutive of the human being as image of God. *Collective* norms and values therefore are fundamental in both a soteriological and a social sense. On his own, the individual person is unable to achieve personhood as image of God by merely following some private moral norms. Thus, all official ROC statements emphasize collective values like the nation, the family, the religious community, and sacred objects as higher than individual human rights. It is precisely around this notion that many Western critics of the Orthodox position have developed their counterarguments. The notion of collective values has been central to their skepticism toward the Orthodox perspective, their defense of universal human rights, and their argument that Russian Orthodoxy has a predisposition toward (totalitarian) collectivism.

However, the theological roots of this position are much more complex. The linking of individual and community is founded in the constitutive relatedness of the person as an image of the trinitarian God to something or someone above or outside himself, as introduced earlier in this chapter. Although this is elaborated only in a few places in the basic social documents and in official statements of the ROC, this connection has deep roots in the traditional Orthodox interpretation of the person as an image of the trinitarian God. The works of Vladimir Lossky and other theologians of the New York and Paris Russian Orthodox schools, the current Russian philosopher and theologian Sergei Horuzhij, as well as the Greek Orthodox theologians Christos Yannaras[10] and Metropolitan John Zizioulas[11] emphasize the importance of patristic theology and introduce complex anthropological approaches, which are distinct from Western anthropologies. Zizioulas sees the difference as a confrontation of two notions: the "individual" and "personhood."[12] The Orthodox interpretation is thus quite different from the post-Enlightenment, Western accentuation of the human person as a subject, focusing instead on the aspects of relatedness and communion. While this has led to some misunderstanding in the interpretation of modern values by Western observers, it also contains significant parallels to the current Western discourse on postsecularism and postmodernism, and could potentially produce constructive insights for rethinking the nature of the human person.[13]

Preserved and Living Tradition

In addition to theological anthropology, which is a key factor determining the ROC's ambivalent stance toward the modern world, the category of *tradition* is also an important element of Russian Orthodox theological argumentation. Besides the emphatic stress on the moral norms, which are preserved by tradition, it is noteworthy that the basic social documents of the ROC and the statements of the church representatives refer almost exclusively to the Bible and the Church Fathers. This seems to be surprising, if not outright anachronistic, considering earlier Russian-Orthodox theological discussion of the modern world, Enlightenment thinking, and questions of modernization and secularization—for example, eighteenth-century responses to the reforms of Peter the Great, nineteenth- to twentieth-century responses to the reforms of czar Alexander II and to the Slavophile movement, and the twentieth-century responses of the Orthodox schools of Paris and New York to the new political challenges and totalitarianism in Europe and Russia.

Since the nineteenth century and certainly since the beginning of the twentieth century, Russian Orthodox theology reoriented itself toward the Church Fathers. This return to the Patristic heritage, along with a commitment to preserve it without change, appears to be yet another reason for a certain skepticism within Russian Orthodoxy toward the integration of new philosophical, cultural, and social ideas into its theological thinking. In contrast, Western Christian theology from the Reformation up to the Second Vatican Council engaged in intense debates and struggle with the dominant social and philosophical developments. As a result, and in the quest for a common language with the emerging secular worldview, Western theology and churches adopted the terms and concepts of their own time. No such development took place within the ROC, partly because the church was isolated for many decades from the philosophical-theological discussions in Europe, and partly because of the ROC's desire to distance itself from the perceived theological excesses of the Latin Church. According to Metropolitan Hilarion, "Russian theological thought had been bound for nearly three centuries in the tight chains of Latin scholasticism."[14] And, according to Metropolitan Kirill, today the ROC maintains a critical distance toward "some Christian denominations" that seek systematically to remove apostolic religious norms from the social sphere and replace them with a liberal value system.[15]

In 1999, Metropolitan Kirill underlined the ROC's deep commitment to tradition: "The preservation and affirmation of the inviolate norm of faith is the mission of Orthodox Christianity in the world, since the rejection of Tradition actually entails an unwitting embrace of the notion that people can do anything."[16] It is a fundamental conviction of Russian Orthodoxy that all essential moral norms are contained in the Bible and the writings of the Church Fathers. These sources, along with the liturgical tradition, are considered to hold the truth in an essential and salvific sense. In responding to contemporary issues, what is required is a constant return to these texts and reading them anew, rather than recognizing any other sources as authoritative. In turn, this means a different understanding of contextual reading, as Bishop Hilarion explained in 2001[17]: A "contextual reading" of the fathers refers to a search for answers to the questions of our time in the writings of the fathers. Understanding the historical limitations of theological terms and the search for new meanings under contemporary conditions are secondary matters, which cannot change the unfaltering teaching of the church. In the words of Metropolitan Hilarion, the fathers preserve the image of human personhood "far more universally" than any modern approaches, such as psychoanalysis, and therefore the fathers must remain the foundation for rethinking the human person.[18] This again confirms the conviction that tradition, as currently understood by Russian Orthodoxy, is not a dynamic system of practices and doctrines that accrue, but rather the static truth codified once and for all by the fathers without any permissible subsequent modification.

In sum, the recent statements of ROC leaders show a definite tendency to "conserve" the tradition as a way of preventing disorientation amid the ever-changing trends of the modern world. By laying strong emphasis on this Conservatism, another aspect of Orthodox tradition—the "living tradition" (живое предание) with a dynamic character—is in danger of being ignored. According to Florovsky, that sense of tradition is an essential characteristic of Orthodoxy as well: "Tradition is not only a protective, conservative principle; it is, primarily, the principle of growth and regeneration."[19] In such an interpretation, tradition offers a great openness toward particular elements of the surrounding world, without dismissing long-held traditions and convictions. Furthermore, it avoids a negative assessment of the ever-changing world in a direct contrast to the conservative perspective. The recent focus on "preserving" rather than on "changing" could lead to an increasing loss of that understanding of living tradition with all its potential.

At the same time, the traditional ways of thinking about the world and the person beyond "modern" (enlightened, humanistic, and liberal) ideas have to be taken into account insofar as they raise serious questions about universal rights and norms. Both Hilarion and Kirill repeatedly emphasize how in the past the suppression of religious traditions in favor of seemingly more universal ideas led to schism, war, and inhuman behavior.[20] For them, this is a crucial consideration in addressing current issues of globalization and universal human rights claims.

Conclusion

According to this preliminary analysis of official ROC statements, we are confronted with a difficulty, which was probably at the root of the widespread uneasiness that accompanied the process of their reception in the Western world. These texts are not scientific theological works, and their interest in questions of the modern world is not primarily theological, but social and political. Theological elements are fused here almost organically with political and ideological considerations, thus inviting questions about the potential instrumentalization of politics by the church, and also the risk of the reverse. For example, the need to maintain collective moral norms as guidelines for the future becomes an argument for the exclusive religious authority of the ROC in Russian society, and for its legal protection by the state. Further, the protection of the Patristic tradition serves as an argument in support of the particular Russian Orthodox perspective, as opposed to "Western" thinking. Also, the fundamental mistrust of individual rights and freedoms appears to be grounded in a view of the inherent sinfulness of the human condition. The authors of the Orthodox statements do not make clear the complex *theological* bases of their arguments, and as a result leave them open to ideological interpretations. Whether this was intentional or not, it will be the task of future study to sort out to what extent these complementarities of theological and political intents are uniquely a phenomenon of the last 20 years, or whether they are rooted in past confrontations with renewal and reform (such as the liturgical reforms under Peter the Great, or at the council of 1917). However, it is also clear that genuine theological concerns—in particular, theological anthropology and the notion of tradition—inform the ROC's position on modern social values in a very direct way. These concerns can support a fruitful dialogue of Russian Orthodoxy with the modern world, as long as they are not used to further political aims, but rather to enrich the ongoing discussion of modernity, postmodernity, and the role of religion in society.

Notes

1. *The Basis of the Social Concept.* http://www.mospat.ru/en/documents/social-concepts/ (accessed September 10, 2010).
2. *The Russian Orthodox Church's Basic Teaching on Human Dignity, Freedom and Rights.* http://www.mospat.ru/en/documents/dignity-freedom-rights/ (accessed September 10, 2010).
3. Kirill (Gundjaev), "The Circumstances of Modern Life. Liberalism, Traditionalism and Moral Values of a Unifying Europe," *Nezavisimaya Gazeta* (May 26, 1999). http://www.mospat.ru/archive/ne906081.htm (accessed September 10, 2010).
4. Hilarion (Alfeev), "Traditional and Liberal Values in the Debate between Christianity and Secularism," *Europaica Bulletin* 63 (April 2005). http://orthodoxeurope.org/page/14/63.aspx#1 (accessed September 10, 2010).
5. "Vystuplenie mitropolita Smolenskogo i Kaliningradskogo Kirilla na X Vsemirnom Russkom Narodnom Sobore."http://www.vrns.ru/syezd/detail.php?nid=101&binn_rubrik_pl_news=307&binn_rubrik_pl_news=307 (accessed September 10, 2010). Kirill's definition of the human person was repeated almost verbatim in the *Declaration on Human Rights and Dignity* in 2006 and in the document on human rights from 2008, *Vsemirnyi russkij narodnij sobor': Deklaratsia o pravah i dostoinstve cheloveka.* http://www.vrns.ru/syezd/detail.php?nid=780&binn_rubrik_pl_news=306&binn_rubrik_pl_news=306 (accessed September 10, 2010).
6. *The Russian Orthodox Church's Basic Teaching on Human Dignity, Freedom and Rights,* I.2. http://www.mospat.ru/en/documents/dignity-freedom-rights/i/ (accessed September 10, 2010).
7. *The Basis of the Social Concept,* XVI.4. http://www.mospat.ru/en/documents/social-concepts/xvi/ (accessed September 10, 2010).
8. *The Russian Orthodox Church's Basic Teaching on Human Dignity, Freedom and Rights,* I.5. http://www.mospat.ru/en/documents/dignity-freedom-rights/i/ (accessed September 10, 2010).

9. Hilarion (Alfeev), *Major Challenges for Christianity in Europe. Address to the 12th Assembly of the Conference of European Churches*, June 30, 2003, Trondheim, Norway. http://hilarion.ru/en/2010/02/25/1090 (accessed January 8, 2011).
10. See, e.g., Christos Yannaras, *Human Rights and the Orthodox Church*. Address at the international conference of the World Council of Churches "The Orthodox Churches in a Pluralistic World: An Ecumenical Conversation," October 3–5, 2002, Holy Cross Greek Orthodox School of Theology, Brookline. http://jbburnett.com/resources/yannaras/yannaras_rights&orth.pdf (accessed September 10, 2010).
11. See, e.g., John D. Zizioulas, *Communion & Otherness* (London: T & T Clark, 2006); *Being as Communion: Studies in Personhood and the Church* (Crestwood, NY: St. Vladimir's Seminary Press, 1997).
12. John D. Zizioulas, *Communion and Otherness*. http://www.incommunion.org/2004/12/11/communion-and-otherness/ (accessed November 5, 2010), also: Zizioulas, *Communion and Otherness* (2006), pp. 155–176.
13. Kristina Stoeckl, *Community after Totalitarianism. The Russian Orthodox Intellectual Tradition and the Philosophical Discourse of Political Modernity* (Frankfurt: Peter Lang, 2008); Kristina Stoeckl, "Postsekulyarnaya sub'ektivnost' v zapadnoj filosofskoj diskussii i pravoslavnoe bogoslovie," bogoslov.ru *Nauchnyj Bogoslovskij Portal*, June 9, 2010. http://www.bogoslov.ru/text/863182.html (accessed June 15, 2010).
14. Hilarion (Alfeev), "Orthodox Theology on the Threshold of the 21st Century." http://en.hilarion.orthodoxia.org/6_3 (accessed September 10, 2010).
15. Kirill (Gundjaev), "The Circumstances of Modern Life." http://www.mospat.ru/archive/ne906081.htm (accessed September 10, 2010).
16. Ibid.
17. Hilarion (Alfeev), "The Patristic Heritage and Modernity." http://orthodoxeurope.org/page/11/1/2.aspx (accessed September 10, 2010).
18. Ibid.
19. Georgij V. Florovsky, "The Catholicity of the Church," in *Bible, Church, Tradition. An Orthodox View* (Belmont, MA: Nordland Publ., 1972), p. 47.
20. See Hilarion (Alfeev), "Christianity and the Challenge of Militant Secularism." http://hilarion.ru/en/2010/02/25/1044 (accessed November 5, 2010).

Part IV

Encounters with European Values

12

Eastern Orthodoxy and the Processes of European Integration

Tina Olteanu and Dorothée de Nève

Introduction

In the public debate on the European integration process, the religious dimension did not play a significant role until the focus of attention moved to the European constitution and questions about the religious identity of the European Union (EU; Weninger 2007, 178ff.). The present study applies a political science methodology to analyze the ambivalent relation between Orthodoxy and the European integration process in Bulgaria, Cyprus, Greece, Romania, and Serbia.

From a social science perspective, the political sphere and the religious sphere are thought of as subsystems of society as a whole. Their independence and autonomy are the products of social processes of differentiation. Each of the two spheres generates its own patterns of action and rules of behavior, geared to its own horizon of values. Thus, interactions between them are also shaped by the confrontation of their competing systems of norms. The two spheres are independent and self-organized and mark areas of control and influence. Their effect on their own frontiers is one of intermediation, extension, and control. They interact—sometimes in a conflictual and competitive manner—with other spheres and influence the conditions of their operations (de Nève 2011a, 76ff.).

The figure 12.1 illustrates the structural, procedural, and content dimensions of the political and religious spheres, hypothetically assuming that there are interdependent relations among all of the dimensions (de Nève 2011a, 80ff.).

The present study employs this model to analyze systematically the relations between Orthodoxy and the EU. The analysis consists of three sections: (i) an overview of existing Orthodox Churches, of Orthodox populations in European countries and their attitudes toward political institutions; (ii) an examination of the relationship between Orthodoxy and the EU from the perspective of European religious policy and of Orthodox religious actors; and (iii) a description of the tensions between European politics and Orthodox teaching through the prism of three issues: religious pluralism, homosexuality, and abortion. The analysis focuses on the Orthodox Churches as

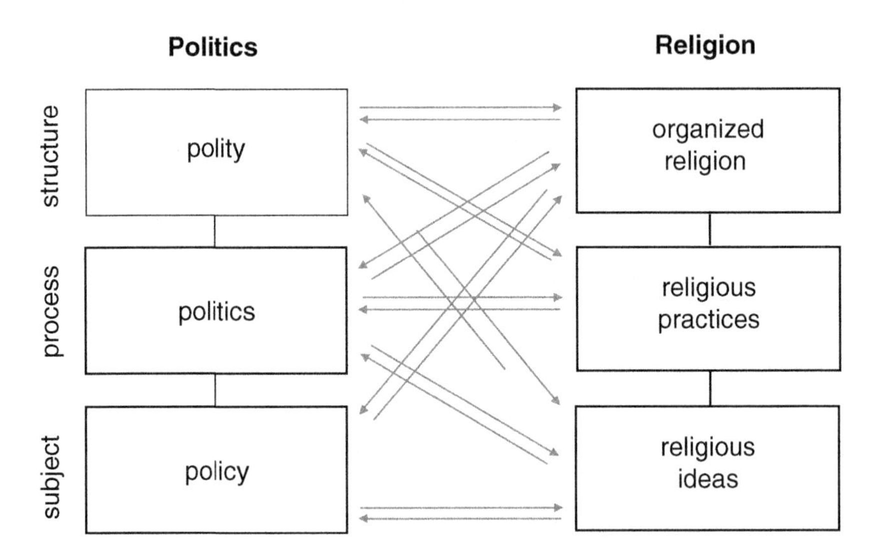

Figure 12.1 Interdependence between Religion and Politics.

institutions of organized religion, on their interdependent relations with the political system of the EU (polity), and on their interpretation of political decisions (policy).

Orthodox Christians in Europe

While there are numerous Orthodox Churches in Europe today, their membership in the five aforementioned countries cannot be determined precisely, since neither European nor national statistics provide complete data on religious affiliation. In four of the countries, which became EU members at different stages of European integration (Greece in 1981, Cyprus in 2004, Romania and Bulgaria in 2007), the majority of the population is Orthodox (table 12.1). While the Orthodox Churches in Romania, Serbia, and Cyprus are autocephalous and canonical, Orthodoxy in Bulgaria is divided. Because of the Holy Synod's close ties with the socialist government, a schism split the Bulgarian Orthodox Church in 1992. The governing party Union of Democratic Forces (UDF) supported and accelerated this split, which had far-reaching consequences for Bulgarian Orthodoxy (Broun 1993, 2000, 2002). Currently, the Bulgarian Orthodox Church under Patriarch Maxim is recognized as canonical, while the alternative Synod under Pimen and after his death in 1999 under Metropolitan Innoketij is not recognized by other Orthodox Churches. Serbia, a potential EU candidate, has a predominantly Orthodox population (84,1 percent).[1] While Montenegro, Serbia, and the Republika Srpska (BiH) are subsumed under the canonical jurisdiction of the Serbian Orthodox Church, the status of the Macedonian church is not yet clear (Zečević Božić 1994). Albania, another potential candidate country, has its own autocephalous church, but only comprises 20 percent of the population. Numerous Orthodox Churches exist in Western Europe, but their communities are minorities.

Within the wider frame of Europe there are a number of Orthodox churches with different prospects of joining the EU. Ukraine has a strong Orthodox tradition but no

Table 12.1 Orthodox Christian Populations in Europe

	Orthodox Christian population	*Orthodox Christians as a percentage (%) of total population*
Greece	11,080,059	99.2
Moldova	3,510,343	98.5
Romania	18,817,975	86.8
Bulgaria	6,894,843	83.7
Serbia	6,371,584	85.0
Belarus	7,577,520	80.0
Cyprus	625,444	78.0
Russia	106,445,473	75.0
Montenegro	464,742	72.2
Macedonia	1,372,575	67.0
Bosnia and Herzegovina	1,353,600	36.0
Albania	639,000	20.0
Croatia	492,291	11.1
Lithuania	133,169	4.0
Austria	177,597	2.2
Poland	763,347	2.0
Switzerland	131,913	1.8
Germany	1,424,500	1.7
Finland	59,028	1.1
Sweden	103,027	1.1
Slovakia	50,363	0.9
Czech Republic	21,002	0.2
Norway	7,835	0.2

References: http://www.3saints.com/orth_population.html; http://www.remid.de/index.php?text=Info_Zahlen; National Consensus for Austria 2001, Bulgaria 2001 (in this census, the data include all Christians and no further details on Orthodox, Catholics, or Protestants are given; but it is estimated that Catholics and Protestants constitute around 1 percent of Christians), Serbia 2002, România 2002, and Switzerland 2005.

real prospects for EU membership at the moment. Here, the ecclesiastical situation is complicated by the coexistence of three Orthodox Churches: the autonomous Ukrainian Orthodox Church (Moscow Patriarchate), the independent Ukrainian Orthodox Church (Kiev Patriarchate, founded in 1992) not recognized by other Orthodox Churches, and the Ukrainian Autocephalous Orthodox Church, which was founded in 1921 and also not recognized as canonical (French 2011, 608; see Bociurkiw 1995, 143).

The Russian Orthodox Church (ROC), by far the largest Orthodox Church, remains outside of the EU debates, since Russia has not sought entry into the EU. It includes the Belarusian Orthodox Church, which essentially comprises Russian Orthodox eparchies on the territory of Belarus.

In Moldova, the Orthodox are divided ethnically between Romanians and Russians. There is also a differentiation in the religious sphere, between the autonomous Moldovan Orthodox Church under ROC jurisdiction and the Metropolitanate of Bessarabia within the Romanian Orthodox Church (RomOC; Kenworthy 2011, 391).

Orthodox Christianity is thus present in both the old member states of the EU and in the new and potential members. In a few countries, Orthodoxy is the church of the majority (Bulgaria, Greece, Cyprus, and Romania). In other countries, Orthodox Christians are a religious minority and their minority status is partly overlaid by ethnic cleavages, as with Russians in the Baltic States, Serbs in the Yugoslavian succession states,, or Greeks in Albania. In Western Europe, the Orthodox Churches are basically comprised of immigrants.

On its own, religious affiliation may not say much about the relevance of religion in a particular society. But the analyses of the European Values Study (2008)[2] suggest that religious bonds do in fact play an important role. Religion was important or very important to significant majorities of interviewees in Cyprus (93.2 percent), Greece (80.9 percent), Romania (82.5 percent), and Serbia (80.5 percent) (table 12.2). Even in Bulgaria, religion was important or very important for 58.6 percent of the respondents.

Table 12.2 Evaluation of the importance of Religion for Orthodox Christians by Country (in % of Orthodox denomination)

	Very important	*Important*
Bulgaria	18.4	40.2
Cyprus	63.9	29.3
Greece	42.1	38.8
Romania	51	31.5
Serbia	21.6	58.9

Note: Values for *N*—Bulgaria, 2,131; Cyprus, 996; Greece, 2,541; Romania, 3,587; Serbia, 1,029.
Source: European Values Study 2008. Own calculations.

Table 12.3 Religious persons by Religious Denomination and Country (in % of denomination)

	Orthodox	*Other*
Bulgaria	70.1	83.8 (Muslim)
Cyprus	92.9	93 (Roman Catholic)
Greece	87.1	81 (Muslim)
Romania	81.9	85.6 (Roman Catholic)
Serbia	95.7	92.1 (Roman Catholic)

Note: Values for *N*—Bulgaria, 2,131; Cyprus, 996; Greece, 2,541; Romania, 3,587; Serbia, 1,029.
Source: European Values Study 2008. Own calculations.

In all of these countries, a large percentage of Orthodox Christians consider themselves religious. In Serbia, 95.7 percent of the interviewees considered themselves religious, with similar results in Cyprus (table 12.3). A comparably high self-characterization as a "religious person" also holds true for Muslims and Roman Catholics in these countries.

However, religious practices do not reflect the same level of commitment as self-identification—the highest rate of weekly church attendance, which is in Cyprus, represents only 32 percent of the Orthodox population (table 12.4). Still, the proportion of Orthodox Christians praying outside of religious services is considerably higher: 85.3 percent of the Orthodox Christians in Romania pray at least once a week. Thus, while religious identity plays an important role for Orthodox Christians in these countries, it does not necessarily entail the same levels of religious practice that can be quantified and measured by the displayed survey results.

The relation of Orthodox Christians and politics is ambivalent: there is little confidence in political institutions, whether that refers to the government, the parliament, or to political parties (table 12.5). Confidence in the EU is much higher, particularly in the new member states Bulgaria, Cyprus, and Romania. But compared with other institutions, the churches enjoy the highest levels of confidence in Cyprus, Greece, Romania, and Serbia (see Roth and de Nève 2002, 183f.).[3] The churches

Table 12.4 Religious Practices of Orthodox Christians by Country (in % of Orthodox denomination)

	Attendance at religious services at least once a week	*Pray to God outside of religious services at least once a week*
Bulgaria	9.0	34.3
Cyprus	32.0	72.9
Greece	18.3	63.8
Romania	22.8	85.3
Serbia	8.5	56.6

Note: Values for *N*—Bulgaria, 2,131; Cyprus, 996; Greece, 2,541; Romania, 3,587; Serbia, 1,029.

Source: European Values Study 2008. Own calculations.

Table 12.5 Degree of Confidence in various Institutions among Orthodox Christians by Country (in % of Orthodox denomination)

	Churches	*EU*	*Government*	*Parliament*	*Political Parties*
Bulgaria	44.7	53.6	9.6	22.1	7.6
Cyprus	69.9	55.8	62	57.5	32
Greece	56.2	39.1	23.8	29.2	16.7
Romania	82.2	49.7	24.1	21	17.6
Serbia	67.1	27.3	14.1	13.8	7.1

Note: Values for *N*—Bulgaria, 2,131; Cyprus, 996; Greece, 2,541; Romania, 3,587; Serbia, 1,029.

Source: European Values Study 2008. Own calculations.

Table 12.6 "Religious leaders should not influence how people vote"—responses from Orthodox Christians by country (in % of Orthodox population)

	Agree strongly	*Agree*	*Neither agree or disagree*	*Disagree*	*Strongly disagree*
Bulgaria	42.4	45	8.1	3.3	1.3
Cyprus	—	—	—	—	—
Greece	33.5	44.9	15	5.3	1.2
Romania	39.7	38.8	10.8	8	2.7
Serbia	—	—	—	—	—

Note: Values for *N*—Bulgaria, 2,131; Cyprus, 996; Greece, 2,541; Romania, 3,587; Serbia, 1,029.
Source: European Values Study 2008. Own calculations.

therefore hold a strong position in the respective societies. However, this does not mean that Orthodox Christians want their religious leaders to be more involved in the political sphere. An overwhelming majority of respondents in Bulgaria, Greece, and Romania feel that religious leaders should not influence how people vote (table 12.6).

Orthodox Christians and their churches are thus a relevant factor in the EU. The believers are highly committed to their churches and express confidence in religious institutions. In the following section, we analyze the EU's religious policy as it relates to Orthodoxy.

Religious Polity and Policy in the EU

Political science research has elaborated numerous typologies aimed at analyzing the institutional relations between the state and the church (*polity* and organized religion, see figure 12.1). However, these typologies always refer to the relatedness of states and various institutions of the organized religions (de Nève 2011a, 83ff.). The analysis of these relations in the multilevel system of the EU certainly exhibits some specific characteristics. In the following, we will first outline the constitutional specifics and then describe the religious policy of the EU in the process of enlargement.

The regulatory claims of the EU vary in different political fields. Whereas, for example, the will to shape policies is far-reaching in the field of agricultural policy, this is not the case with religious policy. The Lisbon Treaty makes no mention of religious and denominational groups or of their relation to the EU. Within the EU, the regulatory relations between the state and churches are found on the national level. Religion is understood as part of national identity or culture (Weninger 2007, 65ff.). In the member states, there are different kinds of relations between the state and churches (Robbers 2005). For its part, the EU has no master plan—the harmonization of the various models of church-state relations is not an aim—rather, it protects the existing diversity within their respective legal frameworks. Thus, the so-called Amsterdam Declaration in the final act of the Amsterdam Treaty states: "The European Union respects and does not prejudice the status under national law of churches and religious associations or communities in the Member States. The European Union equally respects the status of philosophical and non-confessional organizations" (Treaty of Amsterdam 1997, Declaration 11).

This does not mean that the EU does not act with respect to religious policy and does not attach importance to religion at all. For example, the Lisbon Treaty explicitly indicates the significance of "the cultural, religious and humanist inheritance of Europe, from which have developed the universal values of the inviolable and inalienable rights of the human person, freedom, democracy, equality and the rule of law" (Treaty of Lisbon 2009, Preamble). Therefore, on the one hand it is acknowledged that religion has made an important contribution to the development of European values, but on the other it is declared that the EU functions on the basis of universal principles such as democracy and constitutional legality. Beyond that, the EU shapes religious policy by guaranteeing the basic right of religious freedom in the EU and the member states. The individual and collective right as well as the right to have no faith adherence are fixed in Article 10 of the Charter of Fundamental Rights in the Lisbon Treaty:

> (1) Everyone has the right to freedom of thought, conscience and religion. This right includes freedom to change religion or belief and freedom, either alone or in community with others and in public or in private, to manifest religion or belief, in worship, teaching, practice and observance. (2) The right to conscientious objection is recognized, in accordance with the national laws governing the exercise of this right. (Treaty of Lisbon, Charter of Fundamental Rights 2009)

However, the regulation of the actual exercise of these freedoms and the question of how far the states are obligated to perform certain services remain unsettled. Furthermore, the normative guidelines of the EU do not stipulate the equal treatment of different denominations—which is of interest especially with regard to countries with Orthodox majorities. Yet the right to religious freedom as guaranteed in the Lisbon Treaty sets clear limits on state intervention in the realm of organized religion and citizens, and on the behavior of religious institutions toward people of another religion or of no religion at all.[4]

Beyond these judicial basics, there are close contacts between religious communities and the EU institutions on different levels. From the point of view of the EU this represents the legitimate claim of civil society organizations to participate in the shaping of the European legislative processes.[5] The Orthodox Churches in Eastern Europe have associated themselves with the most influential federation, the Conference of European Churches (CEC), which was founded as early as 1959. This organization represents the interests of the numerous Christian churches in Europe, for example, with the help of special commissions (The Church and Society Commission):

> The Church and Society Commission of CEC links member churches and associated organizations of CEC with the EU's institutions, the Council of Europe, the OSCE, NATO and the UN (on European matters). Its task is to help the churches study church and society questions from a theological and social-ethical perspective, especially those with a European dimension, and to represent common positions of the member churches in their relations with political institutions working in Europe. (Conference of European Churches 2009)

On the European level churches also organize as individual actors, as the Russian, Romanian, and Serbian Orthodox Churches did by opening offices in Brussels.

Within the framework of the EU, religious institutions are welcome like any other civil society organization to participate in policy and decision-making processes. This EU principle of the equal treatment of churches and other civil society organizations and lobby groups is not without some controversy: in particular, Orthodox Churches do not usually define themselves as part of civil society and do not want to be classified in this way. The advisor to the state secretary for religious communities and denominations in Romania commented on this question, with reference to the biblical passages in Romans 13:2–7: "This commandment proves that Church and civil society, in which is also included the state [*sic*!], are two different realities, the first one deals with the salvation of its believers while the state is occupied with the daily life of people." (Gombos 2009). It is quite surprising that an adviser to the state secretary has such a distinct understanding of political and religious affairs; it is also quite astonishing that the state is seen as part of civil society. In this view, which is fairly prevalent in Romania, church and political players alike distinguish very clearly between civil society and the church. This runs counter to the understanding of the EU that treats religious denominations as part of organized civil society.

On the whole, the EU evidently has only a limited interest to interfere in the church-state relations of its member countries. One important exception, as mentioned earlier, is in the monitoring of compliance with religious freedom. This political tendency is also reflected in the EU enlargement process (2004 and 2007) as well as in negotiations with candidate countries. In the progress and monitoring reports there are no remarks on church-state relations going beyond the norms of the Charter of Fundamental Rights. It is merely monitored to determine how far the free practice of religion is possible in the particular country.

Within the monitoring reports[6] on Romania, for example, the EU commission examines the fulfillment of EU requirements. It is constantly mentioned that there are no de facto violations against freedom of religion, but that Romania's 1948 law needs revision due to its references to "non-recognized cults and sects" (European Commission 1999, 17). But in 2002 Orthodox clergy, along with the local administration, were cited as driving forces that hamper religious freedoms of other groups on the local level (European Commission 2002, 33). It is also interesting to note that the topic of a new law regulating the freedom of religion disappeared from the 2005 monitoring report, even though the new law on "freedom of religion" was not adopted until 2006 and entered into force in January 2007, shortly after Romania`s accession (Legea No. 489/2006).

The same holds true for criticism of the restitution to the Greco-Catholic Church of properties confiscated during communism (see de Nève 2011b, 179ff.), first mentioned in the 2001 report (European Commission 2001, 27). In the 2003 report, the RomOC is indirectly accused of obstructing restitution (European Commission 2003, 27). The 2004 report suggests that a new regulation might speed up this kind of restitution but needs further monitoring (European Commission 2004a, 27). There was no further mention of this in the 2005 report (European Commission 2005).

As for Serbia, the situation is similar, as freedom of religion is seen to be endangered by a 2006 law and by violent attacks against members of religious groups and denominations. At the same time, the two Orthodox Churches of Serbia and Macedonia are in conflict with each other (European Commission 2009, 15f.). The dispute is about the autocephaly, or at least autonomy, of the Macedonian Orthodox Church, which considers the Serbian Orthodox Church to which it officially belongs as too closely linked to the political sphere (Shea 1997, 174). As a result, the Orthodox Ohrid Archbishopric is autonomous and recognized by the other Orthodox Churches, while the Macedonian Orthodox Church unilaterally declared an independence that remains unrecognized (Kuzmič 2003, 381). The same holds true for the Montenegrin Orthodox Church (Bardos 2011, 569).

The case of the Serbian Orthodox Churches and its unrecognized separatist churches illustrates the overlapping of national and religious identities and the conflicts resulting from the splitting up of Yugoslavia on the one hand and the strong ties between Orthodox Churches and the state on the other. Therefore the need for autocephaly of the Orthodox Churches (in the successor states of Yugoslavia and in Ukraine) might be interpreted as a part of nation-building, as Yelensky (2005, 166) points out: "The autocephalous status for a church of Orthodox people is still in effect an act of general recognition of their nation, an act that demonstrates mature statehood."

From the perspective of the EU, this is not a matter of concern as long as it does not enter the political sphere. In this sense, the European Commission 2009 report simply concludes: "Unresolved issues concerning relations between the Orthodox churches in the two countries had no major political implications" (15f).

In the case of Bulgaria, the EU concluded in its first Progress Report that "Freedom of religion continues to be guaranteed. As regards 'non traditional' religions and their registration, the climate seems to be more relaxed and practical solutions are usually found" (European Commission 1998, 11). Still, in 2004 the European Commission mentioned certain problems:

> As regards freedom of religion, a lack of clear procedural guidelines in the Law on Denominations has resulted in some difficulties related to the implementation of registration requirements at the local level. In July 2004, the executive intervened through police raids in more than 200 Orthodox churches, on the grounds of a conflict over the restitution of properties within the Bulgarian Orthodox Church, which split in 1992. Some clergymen were temporarily detained. The property rights of local churches will need to be clarified. (2004b, 23)

All in all, first there can be identified a comparatively low claim of validity with reference to religious policy on the part of the EU. The legal norms of the EU regulate freedom of religion, but they do not regulate the structural relations between the political sphere and organized religion. The existing church-state relations are a matter of national politics.

Second, following this logic we can observe in the enlargement process that the EU monitors religious freedom only in the broadest terms, and is reluctant to stress or monitor in more detail potential fields of conflict. It is interesting that the question of property rights in Bulgaria and Romania is given more attention than other matters.

Third, in the documents of the EU (Amsterdam Treaty, Lisbon Treaty) religion and the contribution of organized religion to the construction of a European identity and values are appreciated, but at the same time the secular conception of the EU as a political actor is maintained. In the structures of the EU, religious organizations are consequently assigned to the arena of civil society. In this respect, they are put on a level with other civil society actors on the one hand while on the other they are granted a legitimate say in political processes of decision-making.

This setting of religious policy in the EU contains considerable potential for conflict, as will be seen in the following explanations.

Orthodox Perspectives on the EU

The relationship between Orthodox Churches and the EU is ambivalent. One might expect that Orthodox Churches do not differ significantly from other religious denominations in the way they look at the EU, since their (often privileged) national position within one state is not challenged by the EU and the integration process. Nevertheless, there have been lively debates over the EU and potential accession within the Orthodox Churches of Eastern Europe. Here, Makrides (2009: 79) distinguishes three types of Orthodox perspective toward the EU: ambivalent approval, Euroskepticism, and axiomatic disaffirmation. While the first attitude is usually shaped by pragmatic considerations and very often the official position of the Holy Synod, the other two are common among the Orthodox clergy and among believers irrespective of the state in which they are situated. These diverse attitudes toward the EU show that Orthodox Churches have differentiated approaches toward the state and society, and that diversity shapes the specific challenges of unity for the church in each country.

This partly critical attitude of the Orthodox Churches toward the EU is grounded in a practice of very close, harmonious church-state relations at the national level, which is considered the ideal (Halikiopoulou 2011, 80). From a political science perspective, it is significant that the Orthodox Churches challenge the EU's paradigm of secularization through their close ties with the political sphere. They are keenly interested in the fusion or at least in maintaining close connections between the political and the religious spheres, as expressed by the traditional concept of *symphonia*: the idea of harmonious relations between the state and the (Orthodox) church. Brüning (2009, 73) argues that nowadays it is more a matter of legal or customary privileges that Orthodox Churches enjoy in states with Orthodox majorities, as opposed to other religious groups and denominations. In practice, while church-state relations are unique in every Orthodox-majority country, in all of those countries nation and church are very highly interconnected (Perica 2002, 165ff.).

In some of the countries under consideration, the formal framework for church-state relations is provided by the respective constitutions. The Romanian and Serbian constitutions, however, do not mention the Orthodox Churches. The RomOC had tried unsuccessfully to secure a status similar to that of the Greek Orthodox Church in the course of drafting the constitution. The Greek constitution (2008) describes the Orthodox Church as the "prevailing" religion, and translation of the Bible without permission of the Orthodox Church of Greece and Constantinople is forbidden (Constitution of Greece, Article 3). Even though this article does not set forth any particular form of church-state relations, it definitely favors a privileged relationship. The Constitution reflects the traditional view that Greek ethnic identity and Orthodox belief are intertwined and that they are at the root of civil rights (Lorenz 2008, 110). Thus, the Greek Orthodox Church successfully opposed EU intervention in the constitutional process, and preserved its own privileged status (Article 3) and the special rights of the Regime of Aghion Oros (Mount Athos) (Article 105) (Constitution of Greece 2008).

> The traumatic and defensive elements of Greek national identity are deeply embedded in Greek history and are imperative in understanding how Greeks currently perceive their nation. Greek national identity was formed around the concept of threat of national extinction, and this remains a dominant feature of contemporary official state discourse. [...] This enables political and church actors to portray the need to defend the church as synonymous with defending the Greek nation. (Halikiopoulou 2011, 81)

The Bulgarian constitution (1991) guarantees religious freedom and bans both state interference in religious matters and the instrumentalization of religion for political ends; but according to Article 13, (3) "Eastern Orthodox Christianity shall be considered the traditional religion in the Republic of Bulgaria." Even though it has no immediate effect on church-state relations, it does indicate the importance of Orthodoxy for the Bulgarian national identity.

Beyond this look at formal church-state relations, close but informal relations can be found in most countries with an Orthodox majority. The case of Romania may serve as an example. In the early 1990s, there were efforts to establish a state church in Romania and to include the Holy Synod in the senate (Stan and Turcescu 2008, 75). In its efforts, the church hierarchy was willing to include the leaders of other recognized religious denominations. In 1998, they again sought to allow religious leaders to serve in parliament, arguing that the church and the Romanian state had never been separated and that, with such a change, the well-being of the country would become the mission of all citizens, including religious leaders (77; Hitchins 1977, 224ff.). Andreescu (2004) has described in detail how the RomOC tried to influence the electoral process in Romania, when their admission into the senate was refused. For a time, priests and other church dignitaries entered politics by running for office and being elected, or by telling voters how they should vote (53). Thus, the RomOC deliberately pressured the political parties, irrespective of policy fields. In the local elections of 1998, the active suggestions on how to vote resulted in the nomination for election of numerous religious dignitaries (53). In addition, politicians do not hesitate to demonstrate publicly their connection to Orthodoxy, whether by drawing media attention when going to church or by making donations to the church (Stan and Turcescu 2008, 264f.). Thus, the enduring influence of Orthodoxy depends not only on the legislative framework, but also on the influence of religious communities on national policy, which is considered legitimate.[7] Despite the RomOC's failure to obtain constitutionally guaranteed access to political power and representation in parliament, political life cannot be imagined without it.

The relationship between the Orthodox Churches and the EU is therefore problematic, because—regardless whether they are state churches (as in Greece) or the churches of predominant majorities (as in Bulgaria and Romania)—these churches assume the role of defending the nation against external threats. This tendency is further intensified by their close ties to nationalist figures. Considering their participation in nationalist rituals and campaigns, the Orthodox Churches of Bulgaria and Romania may be associated with the political camp of EU skeptics and EU critics—notwithstanding any official, contrary statements on the EU by those same churches.

As has been shown, the EU has no guidelines for church-state relations, nor does it challenge the laws or privileged position of Orthodox Churches on the national level. But the very existence of a superordinate form of government is perceived by the Orthodox as a threat: the EU as a key player in law-making is to a large extent beyond the influence of the Orthodox Churches. And, in actual practice, most laws passed by the national parliaments of EU members do take account of EU regulations and directives—over these, Orthodox Churches can have only a limited influence by lobbying in a competitive environment along with other players of civil society. Thus the Orthodox Churches, having a greater and more direct capacity to act in the national context, are very sensitive to political decisions regarding religious pluralism or other matters that may potentially contravene religious norms or undermine the privileged status of those churches in society.

Religious and Social Pluralism

One of the significant points of conflict in the relations between the Orthodox Churches and the EU is related to religious pluralism. Social pluralism serves a fundamental function in democracies; it concerns the idea that citizens have their own distinctive worldviews and bring their unique needs, ideals, and interests into their community, to the public, and to the body politic. This plurality is not only desired but purposefully supported, and in the interest of fair competition and representation in a democracy. In line with this, the national legislatures of Bulgaria, Greece, and Romania have established rules to preserve and promote social, economic, and political pluralism (e.g., protection of minorities, political party acts, etc.). Similarly, EU policies advance social pluralism through legally formulated basic rights, minority protection, and antidiscrimination provisions.

From the point of view of democracy, pluralism is not a threat but a precondition for its proper functioning. Religious pluralism, too, is considered a source of cultural and political enrichment for democracy—inasmuch as citizens of different denominations also develop different attitudes, ideas, and interests, which they bring into the democratic process. Most denominations—by no means only the Orthodox—have a tenuous relationship with religious pluralism. In many cases, citizens show little or no trust toward members of other denominations (de Nève 2011b, 175). In Romania and Bulgaria, less than half of the citizens trust people of other faith traditions, Jews and Muslims in particular (175; Halikiopoulou 2011, 82).

Religious Pluralism

The Orthodox emphasis on nationhood and references to "one" homogenous religion set the stage for potential conflict. Their fundamental reservations about religious pluralism are derived from the aforementioned principle of *symphonia*, from which they lay claim to an exclusive, privileged access to the political sphere, which is not open to others. Seeing themselves as the bearers of national identity, they consider religious pluralism as a threat to national integrity. Furthermore, Orthodox Churches challenge the legitimacy of proselytism, whether by well-established groups, such as Catholics, or by newcomers to the religious marketplace, such as evangelical Christians (Knox 2005, 160). This idea is deeply rooted in Orthodoxy, and it is invoked even when those churches are acting outside of the national borders. For example, an American priest who converted to Orthodoxy is quoted as saying: "The real danger to the Romanian Orthodox community lies with some of the fellow Christian survivors of the old regime and—incredibly—with otherwise well-intentioned American evangelicals" (quoted in Hill 1992, 173).

Although the Orthodox Churches with majority status normally have a privileged position in the state, their contact with members of other denominations is often problematic. This creates a risk of conflict with European legal norms, which provide clear guidelines for EU member states. Such norm violations are especially apparent in the context of escalations of violence. In various countries, priests and laity have resorted to violence and threats against sacred buildings and religious minorities (Turcescu and Stan 2008, 106; see Forum 18, May 25, 2005). The question of restitution of church properties became the setting for limitations of religious pluralism and the unequal treatment of different religious communities. The restitution of non-Orthodox church properties expropriated during communism continues to complicate interreligious relations, for example, between Greek Catholics and the RomOC in Romania. The RomOC strives to prevent the implementation of restitutions, while the Romanian state has long since abdicated its responsibility in this matter (de Nève 2011b, 179). Numerous legal proceedings have been taken to the European Court of Human Rights by the Greek Catholic Church and have been decided there. These cases—currently there are still more than 2,000 real properties, which the Greek Catholic Church would retrieve (181)—demonstrate a serious problem of deficient constitutional legality. In these conflicts, EU interference is limited in light of two considerations: European institutions, such as the Council of Europe, only become active when a charge is brought before the European Court of Human Rights; when the court's decisions are not implemented, the available punitive instruments are so restricted or so radical that they are not utilized. In Serbia, Jewish and Muslim communities are affected by fragmentary restitution legislation. Here, the limitation on restitution claims was set at 1945, although the expropriations in question took place before that year (US Department of State: International Religious Freedom Report on Serbia 2010).

The European Court of Human Rights is the primary addressee for violations of Article 9 of the European Convention on Human Rights (ECHR) that constrict religious pluralism. The Convention on Human Rights (1950), in this respect, similarly worded as the Charter of Fundamental Rights in the Lisbon Treaty, also permits legal action by nonmembers of the EU.

> *Article 9—Freedom of thought, conscience and religion*
>
> 1. Everyone has the right to freedom of thought, conscience and religion; this right includes freedom to change his religion or belief and freedom, either alone or in community with others and in public or private, and to manifest his religion or belief, in worship, teaching, practice and observance.
>
> 2. Freedom to manifest one's religion or beliefs shall be subject only to such limitations as are prescribed by law and are necessary in a democratic society in the interests of public safety, for the protection of public order, health or morals, or for the protection of the rights and freedoms of others.

Violations of this article are a good indicator of problematic issues of religious freedom and pluralism in the European countries, including nonmember states. It is also a good indirect indicator of the extent to which rule of law is guaranteed. The European Court of Human Rights is responsible for determining whether a violation of Article 9 took place or not. Individuals or institutions may submit legal actions to this court after exhausting all available legal avenues in their national courts.

Table 12.7 Violations of Article 9 of the European Convention on Human Rights, 1959–2010

Country case number	*Case number/short description*	*Individual (I) or collective (C) practising of religion*
Countries with Orthodox majorities of population		
Bulgaria 4	39023/97 Nomination of religious leader by the state (Muslims)	C
	52435/99 Dismissal from an administrative position at a school (Evangelical group)	I
	412/03 and 35677/04 State intervention in a conflict between two Orthodox Churches	C
	30985/96 Nomination of a religious leader by the state (Muslims)	C
Georgia 1	71156/01 Insufficient investigations after attacks on Jehovah's Witnesses by a former Orthodox priest and his followers	C
Greece 9	14307/88 Proselytism, Jehovah's Witnesses	I
	38178/97 Nomination of a religious leader by the state (Muslims)	C
	19516/06 Oath of judges, forced declaration of religious belief (religion unknown)	I
	23372/94, 26377/94, 26378/94 Proselytism in the army (Pentecostal)	I
	50776/99; 52912/99 Nomination of a religious leader by the state (Muslims)	C
	42837/06; 3237/07; 3269/07; 35793/07; 6099/08 forced declaration of religious belief in court	I
	24095/94 Exemption from school for one day because of religious belief (Jehovah's Witnesses)	I
	21787/93 Exemption from school for one day because of religious belief (Jehovah's Witnesses)	I
	34369/97 Refusal of military service in times of general mobilization (Jehovah's Witnesses)	I
Moldova 3	45701/99 State interference in conflicts between two Orthodox Churches	C
	952/03 Denial of registration to an Orthodox Church	C
	6303/05 Collective religious practice of a nonrecognized group (Muslims)	C

Russia 5	2512/04 Reentry was denied to an American because of proselytism (Unification Church)	I
	76836/01 and 32782/03 Denial of registration as "legal entity" (Scientology)	C
	302/02 Denial of registration as "legal entity," delays in legal procedures (Jehovah's Witnesses)	C
	184/02 Police obstruction of collective religious practices (Jehovah's Witnesses)	C
	18147/02 Denial of registration as "legal entity" (Scientology)	C
Ukraine 3	77703/01 Affiliation of Orthodox Churches with patriarchate	C
	39042/97 Denial of access to a priest for a prisoner on death row (religion unknown)	I
	38812/97 Denial of access to a priest for a prisoner on death row (religion unknown)	I
Countries with other religious configuration of the population		
Poland 1	18429/06 Provision with food in line with religious belief in prison (Buddhist)	I
Latvia 3	798/05 Inner Orthodox Churches conflict and state intervention	C
	61638/00 Access to church service during trial (religion unknown)	I
	30273/03 Denial of residence permit due to religious activities (Muslim)	I
San Marino 1	24645/94 Oath of parliamentarians with religious denomination (religion unknown)	I
Switzerland 1	Case could not be identified	
Turkey 3	21924/05 Mentioning of Alevi in the passport was denied as Alevi is understood by the state as a subtype of Muslim	C
	41135/98 Wearing a headscarf in public	I
	One case could not be identified.	

Source: European Court of Human Rights: Violation by Article and by Country, 1959–2010. (Number of cases); identification of case laws via ECHR: Document Collection (HUDOC). Own research (two cases, one in Switzerland and another in Turkey, could not be identified more clearly).

The summary of Article 9 proceedings regarding before the European Court of Human Rights since 1959 (table 12.7) shows that problems with religious pluralism are especially virulent in countries with an Orthodox majority—for the first time in 1988. It was seen that 71.4 percent of all actions before the European Court of Human Rights relate to these countries, whereas 28.6 percent of all proceedings relate to countries without an Orthodox majority population. It is also noteworthy that a great part of the proceedings are related to Greece (nine actions, 25.7 percent) and Russia (five actions, 14.3 percent). Romania and Serbia have not been convicted of violations against Article 9, but two other postsocialist democracies have. The overview demonstrates that the problem is by no means limited to postsocialist states.

In the case of Bulgaria, three of the four convictions were directed at the state's influence in the nomination of religious leaders (one of an Orthodox Church, and two of Muslim communities). The fourth case involved a violation of individual religious freedom when a member of an evangelical church was dismissed from a position at a public school. The Georgian case was based on insufficient state investigations of violent attacks led by a (dismissed) Orthodox priest against Jehovah's Witnesses. The cases against the Greek state are connected to its verdicts against proselytism by Jehovah's Witnesses, constraints on the freedom to adhere to no religion, and the allegedly unauthorized assumption of authority of Muslim leaders. For the Republic of Moldova two cases tackle Orthodoxy (the Metropolitan Church of Bessarabia wanted to change from the Moscow Patriarchate back to the one in Bucharest; recognition of the "True Orthodox Church of Moldova"). One case was on the collective practising of religion (in this case Muslims) that was not officially recognized. The Russian cases deal mainly with the registration of religious groups and denominations as legal entities (Scientology, Jehovah's Witnesses). One case deals with proselytism as grounds for refusal of reentry into Russia for an American member of the Unification Church. One case is also of special interest as the police obstructed a religious gathering of the Jehovah's Witnesses. In Ukraine, one case involved intra-Orthodox conflicts over affiliation, while two other cases dealt with the individual right of access to a priest for prisoners on death row.

Human rights cases in countries with non-Orthodox majorities are rather rare. In Poland, a violation of Article 9 was documented when a Buddhist prisoner did not get vegetarian food according to his religious conviction. The Latvian state intervened in a conflict between two rival Orthodox Churches, while in another case a prisoner was denied access to church service while in prison. The Austrian case was over the denial of registration of Jehovah's Witnesses as a legal person, followed by procedural delays. In San Marino, the conflict was over the oath parliamentarians were required to take and which refers to God. In Turkey, two cases dealt with the mentioning of Alevi on the passport and the sentencing of a woman for wearing a headscarf in public.

In countries with an Orthodox majority, beyond the high incidence of violations of Article 9, conflicts between Orthodox Churches are quite prevalent. As for European integration, it is remarkable that Greece entered the EU in 1981 but did not undergo monitoring of religious freedom; it also violates Article 9 quite often (table 12.7). Here, the Jehovah's Witnesses are especially hampered, proselytism being the prime pretext for conflict. In other countries with Orthodox majorities and which are either in the process of accessing the EU or have recently been admitted, individual violations of religious freedom are infrequent (e.g., Romania, Serbia). Russia is a good example of a country with an Orthodox majority and where religious discrimination has occurred through the denial of registration as legal entities. The EU has only a limited capacity to influence Russian legislation—Russia has no interest in EU membership and therefore does not need to comply with EU norms.

It appears that accession to the EU can induce states to embrace religious pluralism. While some violations of religious freedom result from individual actions (property damage, violence) and the actions of organized religion, others are due to state activities. In countries with an Orthodox majority population, the states tend to uphold the interests of Orthodox Churches in their competition with other denominations; but they also interfere in internal conflicts of the Orthodox Churches (Bulgaria, Ukraine). This leads us back to the close church-state connections in these countries and to the complex intertwining of national and religious identities (as in the case of the Republic of Moldova). In this sense, the Council of Europe and EU's approach to religious pluralism creates a significant potential for conflict, especially in countries with an Orthodox majority, regardless whether or not they are EU members.

Pluralistic Society

Social pluralism, too, as defined by the EU, harbors a significant potential for conflict in the interactions of the EU with the Orthodox Churches and their members. Makrides (2008, 126) describes this contradiction as follows: "Even in pro-European Orthodox statements Western culture is often described with negative denotations such as consumerist, materialistic, individualistic, irreligious, oriented to the here and now, etc., whereas Orthodox culture—in its ideal—depicts the opposite." The civil liberties and antidiscrimination standards fixed in European law come into conflict with the religious norms and teachings of Orthodox Christianity. The EU has a very clear approach to (individual) human rights, which serves as the basis for its antidiscrimination regulations (Ellies 2005).

Orthodox Churches sometimes contravene basic human rights (Brüning 2009),[8] particularly in their negative attitudes toward certain social groups. We will illustrate this with reference to two specific policy areas: the antidiscrimination of sexual minorities and abortion regulations. The EU has handled each of those two controversial policy areas differently. Whereas the EU implemented strong antidiscrimination guidelines and demands compliance with them, it does not enforce any comparable measures that would harmonize diverse abortion regimes. In antidiscrimination, the Orthodox Churches' scope of action is subject to EU regulations, while abortion policy is determined only on the national level.

Antidiscrimination and Sexual Orientation

The European Values Study shows that social intolerance is widespread among members of Orthodox Churches (table 12.8). In particular, there is a strong rejection of homosexual neighbors among the polled Orthodox Christians, with highest proportions in post-Communist countries. The respondents are quite intolerant toward other specific social groups as well such as Gypsies, Jews, or Muslims. In Cyprus and Greece, the rejection of gypsies is highest, followed by prejudices against homosexuals.

This overall negative attitude toward sexual minorities is also very prevalent within the Orthodox Churches on different hierarchical levels. The most obvious form of politicization of the Orthodox Churches concerning homosexuals are gay parades,

Table 12.8 Undesired Neighbors: Responses (%) of Orthodox Christians by Country

	Homosexuals	*Gypsies*	*Jews*	*Muslims*
Bulgaria	55.2	53	17.6	25.7
Cyprus	40.4	46.7	25.6	36.6
Greece	29.6	36.5	15.2	18.9
Romania	67.3	49.9	24.1	30.1
Serbia	57.7	24.1	18.3	29.8

Note: Values for *N*—Bulgaria, 2,131; Cyprus, 996; Greece, 2,541; Romania, 3,587; Serbia, 1,029.

Source: European Values Study 2008. Own calculations.

where Orthodox clergy try to obstruct this form of public expression by rallying against it. The latest Gay Pride in Serbia in September 2011 was prohibited, on grounds that the police could not guarantee the security of the protesters. "The Serbian Patriarch Irenej himself called on the government to ban this 'parade of shame' on Friday. He expressed concern that this event would 'eclipse the sad and tragic situation of Serbs in Kosovo' in favor of 'a group of perverted people who want to force their minority point of view on the vast majority of society'" (Klotz 2011). The same wording was used a year before. The same situation holds true for Romania and Bulgaria, where this event triggers violent protests and harsh comments from Orthodox clergy. Besides the clergy and believers, right-wing nationalist groups also mobilize against gay prides (Mediafax, June 4, 2011). In June 2011, the protest event of the right-wing party Noua Dreaptă in Timişoara, the so-called march for the traditional family, ended in front of the Orthodox cathedral (Noua Dreaptă TV, June 5, 2011). The close connection between national to nationalistic tendencies and Orthodox clergy is evident.

The widespread negative attitudes toward homosexuals also influence the controversial debates over the EU's antidiscrimination regulations, which set a very high standard of tolerance toward specific social minorities (Ellies 2005). While the EU does not actively promote certain collective rights for minority groups such as ethnic minorities, it very much safeguards individual human rights. In the case of sexual minorities, this means first of all that any legislation that punishes or discriminates against homosexuality is not in compliance with EU standards. While the EU does not demand collective rights for homosexuals, such as same-sex-marriage or the right of adoption, its antidiscrimination law was and still is hotly debated in the new member states, potential member states, and those that are part of the neighborhood policy of the EU.

When Romania officially applied for EU membership, paragraph 200 of its Criminal Code (Buletinul Oficial nr. 79–79 bis/21 iun. 1968), stemming from Communist times and punishing same-sex sexual relations with up to five years of imprisonment, came under discussion. This law contravened the EU's approach to minorities and had to be abolished. Stan and Turcescu (2008) describe the debate between the constitutional court, parliament, church organizations, and the public at large. It began in 1994, when the constitutional court was asked to take a stand on the paragraph. The constitutional court invited religious denominations to voice their position on the subject. Not surprisingly, all of the religious denominations that were asked concluded that homosexuality was to be condemned (331f.).[9] Even though the religious groups were quite united on the subject, the constitutional court decided that paragraph 200 is in part unconstitutional, as long as people are not underage and do not have sexual intercourse in public or cause a "public scandal" (333). The Holy Synod tried until the very last moment to retain the original article without change, and then asked President Emil Constantinescu to refuse to sign the abolition of the paragraph in 2000. Finally, the paragraph was annulled due to external pressure. But when it became clear that the prospect of Romania's EU membership was seriously endangered, the Romanian legislator dismissed paragraph 200, mere hours before the deadline set by the Council of Europe. The Romanian churches, and especially aggressively the RomOC, tried to lobby against the abolition of paragraph 200 of the Romanian Criminal Code. "During her fight against homosexuality, the church used state television to criticize the changes of article 200 of the Criminal Code. Through a number of religious programs, Orthodox theologians, priests and monks bravely praised the traditional position with regards to sexual relations and rejected any "occidentalization" of Romanian morals" (339).

Even today, after the abolition of paragraph 200, there are still initiatives that advocate the "healing" of homosexuals and arguing against homosexuality based on the Orthodox faith and the traditional position of the Orthodox Church (Speranţă şi vindecare pentru homosexual n.d.). Profamily organizations engage in targeted lobbying and, in one case, pointed to a politician who was not reelected because he had stood up for the acceptance of homosexuality (Alianţa Familiilor din România n.d.). Though the self-descriptions of these organizations do not explain the extent of their institutional or financial cooperation with the Orthodox Church, it is obvious that they base at least some of their arguments on the official teaching of the church.

Regarding Serbia, Sabrina Ramet (2006, 170) has explained, "The Serbian Church's view of homosexuality does not differ from that of its Romanian and Russian sister Churches. What it adds is an intense nationalism, in which homosexuality comes to be seen not merely as a betrayal of Christ and as a grievous sin against nature, but also as a betrayal of the Serbian nation." In this sense, the discussion concerning the antidiscrimination law also triggered discussions of sexual orientation. Here the Serbian Orthodox Church, together with other religious denominations, objected to the idea that people can express their sexual orientation in public and that they should not be discriminated against. Due to these protests, the new law was once sent back to the parliamentary assembly, but two weeks later (on the March 26, 2009) it was adopted in parliament. The argumentation of the Orthodox Churches shows that there has been a learning process with regard to the EU:

> The Bill that the Government has sent to the Assembly consists of something that has nothing to do with discrimination on the basis of the sexual orientation. That Bill guarantees the right to express sexual orientation. Such a right does not exist in any international agreement on anti-discrimination, nor in any European directive, nor in any relevant European or other nation's legislation. The right to express publicly some inclination, which is neither in the scope of thoughts or ideas nor in the scope of culture, is not a means of fighting against discrimination. The practice of such a right, actually expressing publicly any kind of sexual orientation, offends the right of citizens to privacy and family life, and also offends their religious rights, as well as the sanctity of personal dignity. (Serbian Orthodox Church, March 17, 2009)

Thus, antidiscrimination in itself was not disputed but rather limited to certain fields, while the aspect of expressing one's sexual orientation was simply moved to the private sphere. Still, the statement viewed pressure from the EU and the Council of Europe as illegitimate and continued to denounce the European legal position.

As the conflicts between the Orthodox Churches and the legal norms of the EU demonstrate, social pluralism is restricted or opposed. Homosexuals in postsocialist countries with Orthodox majorities are especially affected by this, as are homosexuals in the postsocialist space in general (e.g., in Poland or the Baltic states). The Orthodox Churches and most of their believers, including political elites, generally share negative attitudes toward this group. On this particular issue, the Orthodox Churches have collaborated with religious denominations against whom they would readily discriminate against under any other circumstances. Political lobbying by the Orthodox Churches was quite successful, since they could present themselves as the preservers of national traditions and managed to postpone liberal legislation on several occasions. In the end, only the pressure of the EU and CoE made legislative changes possible. Still, official demonstrations for the rights of sexual minorities continue to elicit loud opposition when Orthodox believers, clergy, and nationalists unite.

Abortion Rights

Orthodox citizens hold surprisingly liberal views on abortion (table 12.9). Particularly in post-Communist countries, the majority of respondents do not oppose abortion in principle. According to the European Values Study, significant proportions of respondents feel that abortion is acceptable when the couple/mother does not want any more children (Bulgaria—77.3 percent; Serbia—66.7 percent; Romania—43.9 percent). Outside of the post-Communist countries, there is considerable variation, however (Cyprus—55.6 percent; Greece 11.9 percent). In circumstances where the mother's health is at risk, the proportion of Orthodox Christians who approve of abortion is much higher.

The legislative frameworks concerning abortion vary widely among EU member states, while the EU itself has no regulations in this field. In Malta, any kind of abortion is strictly prohibited; in Ireland it is only allowed if the mother's life is endangered. Spain, Portugal, and Poland also have strong restrictions on legal abortion (a mother's physical and mental health, rape, disease of child), while the remainder of Europe has rather liberal abortion laws for the first trimester. This also holds true for countries like Serbia, Ukraine, and Russia. Abortion regulations tend

Table 12.9 Abortion can be approved: Frequency of Answers (%) of Orthodox Christians by Country

	Mother's health at risk	*Physically handicapped*	*Unmarried woman*	*Unwanted children*
Bulgaria	91.4	90.5	64.1	77.3
Cyprus	—	—	52.1	55.6
Greece	—	—	16.3	11.9
Romania	89.1	81	51.7	43.9
Serbia	—	—	57.9	66.7

Note: Values for *N*—Bulgaria, 2,131; Cyprus, 996; Greece, 2,541; Romania, 3,587; Serbia, 1,029.

Source: European Values Study 2008. Own calculations.

to be rather strict in countries with Catholic majorities and liberal in countries with Protestant and Orthodox majorities. This is somewhat surprising, since the official Orthodox and Catholic positions on abortion do not differ significantly.

In Serbia, abortion legislation was very liberal under communism; it became slightly more restrictive in 1994. The Serbian discourse on abortion has also focused on national concerns first and foremost: "But religious discourses against abortion remained focused on the issue of national survival, i.e. pronatalism, and only next to that presented the argument of the sanctity of life" (Drezgić 2009, 21).

In Romania, the debate has been connected to religious considerations. As the RomOC puts it: "The Church has always considered the abortive medicines, the mechanic barriers (Intra Uterine Device and certain pills, such as RU 486) with contraceptive effect, as well as the contraceptive medicines, as a very serious sin, equal to abortion" (Biserica Orthodoxă Română).

The Romanian situation is unique as compared with other Orthodox countries in the region. Under the socialist regime of Nicolae Ceausescu, family planning was not a private matter but state policy, including the prohibition of any kind of contraception and abortion. As a result, illegal abortions became very common, even at the risk of severe health problems or criminal prosecution. It also led to disabilities among children where unsuccessful abortions took place (de Nève 1998, p. 69ff.). This high degree of state interference in reproduction led to a change in legislation very shortly after the power shift in 1989, liberalizing abortion in the first trimester. Since then, there have been several attempts to introduce tougher laws on abortion.

Those efforts have generally been more moderate than the aggressive assaults against sexual minorities. As Daniel Barbu (1999, 254) has observed: "Not even one per cent of the energy that was devoted by the Orthodox hierarchy and different Orthodox associations to the punishment of homosexuality in the 1990s was invested in the prohibition and limitation of abortion." In 1994, on behalf of the RomOC, one parliamentarian condemned a new legislative draft on abortion, calling the Romanian abortion rate "a disaster for our nation that occupies the first place in Europe in killing newborns" (Stan and Turcescu 2008, 349). Shortly after this parliamentary initiative, the RomOC issued an open letter on the same matter. But that intervention was not successful. Another attempt to prohibit abortion took place in 1997–1998 when a Greek Catholic priest and parliamentarian introduced a restrictive law—it was rejected by the Senate's parliamentary commission on human rights, although the Health commission issued a favorable statement (349f.). The RomOC follows a cautious line on this subject in view of the legacy of socialism in Romania, as a result of which many Romanian Orthodox people are in favor of abortion (table 12.9). At the same time, the church has a clear idea who is responsible for this development:

> Unfortunately, abortion and the use of contraceptives are a reality in the modern secularized world. In the name of immediate "happiness" and comfort, generations are killed and a young woman dies, mother or not. The church cannot be indifferent to this alarming and tragic reality that is maintained by institutions that call themselves "charitable," "humanist" and even "medical." (Patriarchia Romania n.d.)

As we have seen, Orthodox believers generally do not oppose abortions for medical reasons. The idea that the broad acceptance of abortion within Romanian society is ultimately caused by secularization and European integration is quite common within the clergy. "During a press conference at Alba Iulia in the spring of 1998, Archbishop Bartolomeu Anania declared, 'Europe advises us to accept homosexuality, electronic devices, drugs, abortion and genetic engineering" (Andreescu 2004, 14f.).

The debate on abortion, illustrated here in the case of Romania, shows that the Orthodox Churches find themselves in a dilemma: while the EU has no overriding jurisdiction on matters of abortion, the Orthodox discourse sees secularization and "Europe" as the root of the evil. In the process, they disregard the positions of their believers and their own inability to advance more restrictive abortion laws. In the countries with a significant Orthodox presence, Europe is thus accused of being the source of moral decay, while the churches themselves are absolved from any responsibility in this regard.

Conclusion

The EU has evolved significantly over the last two decades. Twelve new member states have entered the union, and the level of political integration has deepened. With regard to Orthodoxy, this development has had two effects. The number of countries with a majority of Orthodox believers within the union has risen from one (Greece) to four and will grow further with the accession of other Western Balkan countries and countries with strong ties to the EU in the frame of European Neighborhood Policy (ENP). The expansion of the EU has also brought into focus the relevance of religion in polities and politics, as was seen in the Lisbon Treaty discussions over references to divinity.

While the EU does not interfere in church-state relations, it is secular in the sense that religious denominations are invited to participate in political decision-making just like any other form of organized civil society. At the same time, it reflects positively on the (historical) merits of religions in constituting the universal values that are the basis of the EU. The EU influences the religious landscape in member states and candidate countries through the ENP as well as through antidiscrimination regulations and the safeguarding of religious pluralism. Beyond that, even Russia, which is neither part of the ENP nor in an accession process to the EU, is challenged by the European norms whenever the European Court of Human Rights decides upon alleged violations of Article 9 of the ECHR. As this analysis has shown, countries with Orthodox majorities are convicted of human rights violations more frequently than others, while candidate countries and new member states with Orthodox majorities are convicted less often. Here Greece is something of an exception—its high number of convictions being a function of its long-standing membership in the EU.

The official positions of the Orthodox Churches support the existing or future EU membership of their countries. "Many Orthodox leaders now guardedly support the EU, but their support is predicated on the preservation of it as a Christian European project" (Toft, Philpott, and Shah 2011, 55). What is reflected here is not only a reservation against non-Christian religions such as Islam but also the desire for a greater role for Christianity in Europe.

The tensions between the Orthodox Churches and their members and with the EU's legal principles become evident in concrete policy fields. Irrespective of how far the political claims of the EU actually reach, the EU is depicted as a threat:

1. Historically, Orthodox Churches have strong ties to the political sphere. Though many have lost their de jure privileged position with regard to other

religious denominations, they remain de facto privileged and very influential. In the current environment, the EU's legal provisions are considered to undermine this de facto influential position. The *symphonia* model of church-state relations stands in sharp contrast to the idea of secularization. Secularism as a principle is perceived in Western societies as one of the great achievements of the Enlightenment and is an operating principle of the EU. But in the view of Orthodox clergy, it is a sign of moral and spiritual decay. On the whole, while church-state relations in countries with Orthodox majorities are not in direct conflict with the EU, the question of religious pluralism and the churches' antisecular views do set the stage for anti-EU sentiments.

2. In the past, Orthodox Churches were seldom challenged by religious pluralism, since national and religious identities were closely intertwined. But subsequent to the split-up or newly won independence of states (such as in former Yugoslavia, Moldova, Ukraine) the dominant Orthodox Churches face religious pluralism from "within," when Orthodox entities have formed autocephalous churches. Such changes have led to conflicts over property, state interference in Orthodox structures, and to problems of interstate conflicts. Problems relating to religious pluralism have also been intensified by denominations, which recently entered the religious marketplace. These religious newcomers have encountered state-sanctioned delays with registration or the obstruction of their religious practices. In some cases, states have acted as agents of the majority religions, which inevitably undermined the rule of law.
3. The acceptance of pluralist ways of living is also a major concern for Orthodox Churches. As we have observed, religious and pluralist norms and values often collide. The issue is not whether religious communities can accept certain ways of living (such as sexual orientations or abortion), but how they try to interfere with values that they perceive as "deviant." It is here that the EU is depicted as the source of "deviant" attitudes and behavior. Such anti-Occidentalism is convenient for Orthodox Churches, and it obscures the fact that the EU has only limited influence on local decision-making processes, in which the diversity of electoral opinions are really at play—as on the issue of abortion. On that matter, there is no EU-wide regulation, and the Orthodox lobby for stricter abortion laws was unsuccessful or only partially successful, and it was convenient to blame the EU. In the case of antidiscrimination against sexual minorities, the case is quite clear. Here, the EU's clear regulations require implementation by member countries. Orthodox churches, clergy, and groups have mobilized in opposition to these rules and to public manifestations of sexual minorities. They have also publicly pressured national parliaments to stand up against this instance of "EU interference" with religious (and national) values. On this issue, the churches know that they have the support of the majority of believers.

As this chapter has shown, European integration and Orthodoxy is an ambivalent field. It is not necessarily de jure church-state relations that create difficulties, but rather the idea of religious pluralism the EU advances. The official Orthodox Churches have rather followed a pragmatic approach toward EU accession and toward the dialogue with EU institutions. But beneath the surface, the EU is seen as a challenge or even as a danger to the perceived religious foundations of society and its Orthodox majority. The Orthodox Churches may have been successful in some of their lobby efforts, but the political sphere is also well aware of the highly diversified attitudes among the voting public. The Orthodox Churches' decreased influence in the decision-making process within their states is not necessarily the result of pressure from the EU.

Notes

We thank Nils Arne Brockmann, Fabian Klein, and Nicu Olteanu for their support in research and useful comments in the process of writing this chapter.

1. The EU differentiates between candidate countries and potential candidate countries. Candidate countries are those whose membership requests have been accepted by the EU. Potential candidate countries, such as Albania and Serbia, have only received the prospect of membership. There are no accession negotiations with potential candidate countries. The third category comprises countries within the frame of the European Neighborhood Policy and which have not yet received a prospect of EU membership. An example is Ukraine.
2. The European Values Study (third wave 2008) is a large-scale, cross-national, and longitudinal survey research program on basic human values. It provides insights into the ideas, beliefs, preferences, attitudes, values, and opinions of citizens all over Europe. It is a unique research project on how Europeans think about life, family, work, religion, politics, and society.
3. The question posed by the European Values Study unfortunately does not allow a differentiation between different churches in this context.
4. See the section titled "Religious Pluralism."
5. Religious communities are seen as civil society organizations in the logic of the EU. Therefore, they do not enjoy a special status (see European Glossary).
6. The monitoring reports are accessible under: http://ec.europa.eu/enlargement/press_corner/key-documents/index_archive_en.htm.
7. From table 12.5 it is clear that religious dignitaries can certainly be a relevant factor, since churches generate far more confidence than political institutions.
8. In part this is equally valid for other denominations (see Kunter 2010, 163ff.).
9. The Romanian Orthodox, Greek Catholic, and Old Calendar Romanian Orthodox Churches, the Jewish community, Muslims, Seventh Day Adventists, and Pentecostals.

Bibliography

Andreescu, Gabriel (2004). Biserciaortodoxăromanăcaactorul al integrăriieuropene. http://www.constiinta-critica.ro/upload/documente/doc78.pdf (accessed October 1, 2011).

Alianța Familiilor din România (n.d.). POLITICĂ ȘI LEGISLAȚIE. http://www.alianta-familiilor.ro/politica.html (accessed October 25, 2011).

Barbu, Daniel (1999). *Republica absentă*. București: Nemira.

Bardos, Gordon (2011). "Serbia, Patriarchal Orthodox Church Of." In: *The Encyclopedia of Eastern Orthodox Christianity*, John Anthony McGukin (ed.). Malden: Wiley-Blackwell, pp. 559–570.

Biserica Orthodoxă Română (n.d.). Avortul. http://www.patriarhia.ro/ro/opera_social_filantropica/bioetica_1.html (accessed October 24, 2011).

Bociurkiw, Bohdan (1995). "Politics and Religion in Ukraine. The Orthodox and the Greek Catholics." In: *The Politics of Religion in Russia and the New States of Eurasia*, Michael Bourdeaux and Karen Dawisha (eds.). Armonk: M.E. Sharp, Inc., pp. 131–162.

Broun, Janice (1993). "The Schism in the Bulgarian Orthodox Church." *Religion, State & Society* 21:2, 207–220.

——(2000). "The Schism in the Bulgarian Orthodox Church, Part 2: Under the Socialist Government, 1993–97." *Religion, State & Society* 28:3, 263–289.

——— (2002). "The Schism in the Bulgarian Orthodox Church, Part 3: Under the Second Union of Democratic Forces Government, 1997-2001." *Religion, State & Society* 30:4, 365–394.

Brüning, Alfons (2009). "Spannungsverhältnis. 'Orthodoxe Werte' und Menschenrechte." *Osteuropa* 59:6, 63–78.

Bucur, Ioan-Marius, and Raluca Dima (2010). "The Romanian Orthodox Church in the Process of Romania's EU Accession (1990–2004)." *Transylvanian Review* 19:3, 237–254.

de Nève, Dorothée (1998). "Zwanghafte Gleichberechtigung und kontrollierte Körper: Zu den Lebensbedingungen von Frauen im sozialistischen Rumänien." In: *Frauen in Südosteuropa. Aus der Südosteuropa-Forschung*, Anneli Ute Gabanyi and Hans Georg Majer (eds.), vol 9. Munich: Südosteuropa-Gesellschaft, pp. 59–67.

——— (2011a). "AgentInnen in fremden Sphären—Politikwissenschaftliche Analyse der interdependenten Beziehungen zwischen Politik und Religion." In: *Sphärendynamik I—Zur Analyse postsäkularer Gesellschaften*, Georg Pfleiderer and Alexander Heit (eds.). Zurich: Pano/Nomos, pp. 59–130.

——— (2011b). "Grenzen der Religionsfreiheit" In: *Religionsfreiheit im Kontext der Grundrechte. Religionsrechtliche Studien 2*, Adrian Loretan (ed.). Zurich: Theologischer Verlag, pp. 163–188.

Döpmann, Hans-Dieter, ed. (1997). *Religion und Gesellschaft in Südosteuropa.* Munich: Südosteuropa-Gesellschaft.

Drezgić, Rada (2009). *Religion, Politics and Gender in Serbia. The re-traditionalization of gender roles in the context of nation-state formation. Final Research Report for UNRISD and Heinrich-Böll Foundation.* http://www.fondacija-boell.eu/downloads /Serbia_Final_Research_Report.pdf (accessed October 1, 2011).

Ellies, Evelyne (2005). *EU Anti-Discrimination Law.* London: Oxford University Press.

Enyedi, Zsolt (2003). "The Contested Politics of Positive Neutrality in Hungary." *West European Politics* 26:1, 157–176.

European Court of Human Rights (2010). *Violation by Article and by Country 1959–2010.* http://www.echr.coe.int/NR/rdonlyres/2B783BFF-39C9-455C-B7C7-F821056BF32A/0 /Tableau_de_violations_19592010_ENG.pdf (accessed October 1, 2011).

Forum 18 (2005). "GEORGIA: Georgian Orthodox priests incite mobs against religious minorities." http://www.forum18.org/Archive.php?article_id=569 (accessed October 25, 2011).

Fosztó, László (2006). "Mono-Ethnic Churches, the 'Undertaker Parish,' and Rural Civility in Postsocialist Romania." In: *The Postsocialist Religious Question. Faith and Power in Central Asia and East-Central Europe*, Chris Hann, et al. (eds.). Berlin: LIT Verlag, pp. 269–292.

French, Todd E. (2011). "Ukraine, Orthodoxy in." In: *The Encyclopedia of Eastern Orthodox Christianity*, John Anthony McGukin (ed.). Malden: Wiley-Blackwell, pp. 604–609.

Gombos, Stelian (2009). "Biserica Ortodoxa si societatea romaneasca actuala." http: //www.crestinortodox.ro/drept-bisericesc/biserica-ortodoxa-societatea-romaneasca-actuala-120210.html (accessed October 16, 2011).

Halikiopoulou, Daphne (2011). *Patterns of Secularization—Church, State and Nation in Greece and the Republic of Ireland.* Farnham/Burlington: Ashgate.

Hill, Kent R. (1992). "The Russian Orthodox Church and a Pluralistic Society." In: *Russian Pluralism—Now Irreversible?* Uri Ra'anan, Keith Armes, and Kate Martin (eds.). New York: St. Martin's Press, pp. 165–188.

Hitchins, Keith (1977). *Orthodoxy and Nationality. Andreiu Şaguna and the Romanians of Transylvania, 1846–1873.* Cambridge: Harvard University Press.

Kenworthy, Scott (2011). "Moldova, Orthodoxy in." In: *The Encyclopedia of Eastern Orthodox Christianity*, John Anthony McGukin (ed.). Malden: Wiley-Blackwell, pp. 390–391.

Kissane, Bill (2003). "The Illusion of State Neutrality in a Secularising Ireland." *West European Politics* 26:1, 73–94.

Klotz, Wolfgang (2011). "Verbotene Gay-Pride Parade in Serbien: Der Kampf war wichtiger als der Erfolg." http://www.boell.de/demokratie/geschlechter/feminismus-geschlechterdemokratie-verbotene-gay-pride-parade-in-serbien-der-kampf-war-wichtiger-als-der-erfolg-12987.html (accessed October 23, 2011).

Knox, Zoe (2005). *Russian Society and the Orthodox Church: Religion in Russia after Communism.* London: RoutledgeCurzon.

Kunter, Katharina (2010). "Der lange Weg der Anerkennung: Die Kirchen und die Menschenrechte nach 1945." In: *Religion, Menschenrechte und Menschenrechtspolitik*, Antonius Liedhegener and Ines-Jaqueline Werkner (eds.). Wiesbaden: Verlag für Sozialwissenschaften, pp. 153–174.

Kuzmič, Peter (2003). "Macedonia." In: *The Encyclopedia of Christianity* (vol. 3), Erwin Fahlbusch and William Bromiley (eds.). Grand Rapids: Eerdmans, pp. 379–382.

Lorenz, Astrid (2008). *Verfassungsänderungen in etablierten Demokratien. Motivlagen und Aushandlungsmuster.* Wiesbaden: Verlag für Sozialwissenschaften.

Makrides, Vasilios (2008). "Orthodoxe Kulturen, der Westen und Europa: Die eigentlichen Schwierigkeiten einer Beziehung am Beispiel der serbischen Orthodoxie." In: *Serbien in Europa. Leitbilder der Moderne in der Diskussion (Forschungen zu Südosteuropa. Sprache—Kultur—Literatur, Band 3)*, Gabrielle Schubert (ed.). Wiesbaden: Harrassowitz, pp. 117–137.

——— (2009). "Orthodoxe Kirchen in Europa." *Osteuropa* 59:6, 79–92.

Mediafax (2011). "About 150 People Attend Gay Pride Parade in Bucharest." http://www.mediafax.ro/english/about-150-people-attended-gay-pride-parade-in-bucharest-8313983 (accessed October 24, 2011).

Merkel, Wolfgang, Hans-Jürgen Puhle, Aurel Croissant, Claudia Eicher, and Peter Thiery (2003). *Defekte Demokratie. Band 1: Theorie.* Opladen: Leske + Budrich.

Noua Dreaptă TV (2011). "Marşul pentru familia tradiţională din Timişoara 2011 II." http://www.youtube.com/watch?v=8ERhGWHsQRE&feature=player_embedded (accessed October 24, 2011).

"Patriarchia Romania" (n.d.). Avortul. http://www.patriarhia.ro/ro/opera_social_filantropica/bioetica_1.html (accessed October 1, 2011).

Perica, Vjekoslav (2002). *Balkan Idols. Religion and Nationalism in Yugoslav States.* Oxford: Oxford University Press.

Ramet, Sabrina P. (2006). "The way we were -and should be again? European Orthodox Churches and the 'Idyllic Past.'" In: *Religion in an Expanding Europe*, Timothy Byrnes and Peter J. Katzenstein (eds.). Cambridge: Cambridge University Press, pp. 148–175.

Robbers, Gerhard, ed. (2005). *Staat und Kirche in der Europäischen Union.* Baden-Baden: Nomos.

Roth, Alexander, and Dorothée de Nève (2002). "Rumänien—Zustimmungsmaschinerie oder 'einziger Gesetzgeber des Landes'?" In: *Parlamente und Systemtransformation im postsozialistischen Europa*, Susanne Kraatz and Silvia von Steinsdorff (eds.). Opladen: Leske + Budrich, pp. 183–206.

Schoenauer, Andreas (2010). *Die Kirchenklausel des § 9 AGG im Kontext des kirchlichen Dienst- und Arbeitsrechts.* Frankfurt/Main: Lang.

Serbian Orthodox Church (2009). "Statement: Anti-discrimination on the Basis of Some Personal Inclination Is Not the Same as Freedom of Expression of That Person." http://www.spc.rs/eng/statement_antidiscrimination_basis_some_personal_inclination_not_same_freedom_expression_person (accessed October 24, 2011).

Shea, John (1997). *Macedonia and Greece: The Struggle to Define a New Balkan Nation.* Jefferson: McFarland.

Speranţă şi vindecare pentru homosexual (n.d.). "DECLARAŢIA CREŞTIN-ORTODOXĂ CU PRIVIRE LA HOMOSEXUALITATE." http://www.homosexualitate.ro/declaratie.html (accessed October 25, 2011).

Stan, Lavinia, and Lucian Turcescu, eds. (2008) *Religie şi Politică în România postcomunistă*. Bucureşti: S.C. Curtea Veche.

Stanley, Arthur Penrhyn (2003). *Lectures on the History of the Eastern Church*. New Jersey: Kessinger.

Tamcke, Martin (2007). *Das orthodoxe Christentum*. Munich: Beck.

Toft, Monica Duffy, Daniel Philpott, and Timothy Samuel Shah (2011). *God's Century: Resurgent Religion and Global Politics*. New York: W.W. Norton & Co.

Turcescu, Lucian, and Lavinia Stan (2008). "Romania." In: *Churches in-between: Greek Catholic Churches in Postsocialist Europe*, Stéphanie Mathieu and Vlad Naumescu (eds.). Berlin: LIT Verlag, pp. 99–109.

Walzer, Michael (1998). "Drawing the Line: Religion and Politics." *Soziale Welt* 49:3, 295–307.

Weninger, Michael H. (2007). *Europa ohne Gott? Die Europäische Union und der Dialog mit den Religionen, Kirchen und Weltanschauungsgemeinschaften*. Baden-Baden: Nomos.

Willems, Ulrich (2001). "Bedingungen, Elemente und Effekte des politischen Handelns der Kirchen in der Bundesrepublik Deutschland." In: *Verbände und Demokratie in Deutschland*, Annette Zimmer and Bernhard Wessels (eds.). Opladen: Leske + Budrich, pp. 77–105.

Yelensky, Victor (2005). "Globalization, Nationalism, and Orthodoxy: The Case of Ukrainian Nation Building." In: *Eastern Orthodoxy in a Global Age: Tradition Faces the Twenty-First Century*, Victor Roudometof, Alexander Agadjanian, and Jeffrey Pankhurst (eds.). Oxford: AltaMira Press, pp. 144–178.

Zečević Božić, Jure (1994). *Die Autokephalieerklärung der Makedonischen Orthodoxen Kirche*. Würzburg: Augustinus-Verlag.

Data and Population Census

Austria (2001), http://www.statistik.at/web_de/statistiken/bevoelkerung/volkszaehlungen_registerzaehlungen/index.html (accessed October 25, 2011).

Bulgaria (2001), http://www.nsi.bg/Census_e/Census_e.htm (accessed October 25, 2011).

European Values Study (2008). GESIS Data Archive for the Social Sciences ZA4804. http://www.europeanvaluesstudy.eu/.

Romania (2002), http://www.insse.ro/cms/files/RPL2002INS/vol4/tabele/t7.pdf (accessed October 25, 2011).

Serbia (2003). Book 3. http://webrzs.stat.gov.rs/WebSite/Public/PublicationView.aspx?pKey=41&pubType=9 (accessed October 25, 2011).

Switzerland (2005), http://www.pxweb.bfs.admin.ch/dialog/statfile.asp?lang=1 (accessed October 25, 2011).

Other Official Documents

Buletinul Oficial nr. 79–79 bis (21 iun 1968). *Criminal Code of Romania*, Art. 200.

Conference of European Churches (2009). *European Churches and EU Institutions Discuss Economic Crisis*, Press Release No. 09–19/e. http://www.ceceurope.org/news-and-media/news/?tx_ttnews%5BbackPid%5D=229&tx_ttnews%5BpS%5D=1255885210&tx_ttnews%5Bpointer%5D=13&tx_ttnews%5Btt_news%5D=79&cHash=2c772442ca36836fbe5eaf115ef02362 (accessed October 16, 2011).

Constitution of Bulgaria. http://www.parliament.bg/en/const (accessed October 25, 2011).

Constitution of Greece (2008). http://www.hellenicparliament.gr/UserFiles/f3c70a23-7696-49db-9148-f24dce6a27c8/001-156%20aggliko.pdf (accessed October 20, 2011).
Constitution of Greece. http://www.hri.org/docs/syntagma/ (accessed October 25, 2011).
Constitution of Romania. http://www.cdep.ro/pls/dic/site.page?id=371 (accessed October 25, 2011).
Constitution of Serbia. http://www.srbija.gov.rs/cinjenice_o_srbiji/ustav.php?change_lang=en (accessed October 25, 2011).
European Commission (1998). *1998 Regular Report from the Commission on Bulgaria's Progress towards Accession*. Brussels. http://ec.europa.eu/enlargement/archives/pdf/key_documents/1998/bulgaria_en.pdf (accessed October 25, 2011).
——— (1999). *1999 Regular Report from the Commission on Romania's Progress towards Accession*. Brussels. http://ec.europa.eu/enlargement/archives/pdf/key_documents/1999/bulgaria_en.pdf (accessed October 25, 2011).
——— (2001). *2001 Regular Report from the Commission on Romania's Progress towards Accession*. Brussels http://ec.europa.eu/enlargement/archives/pdf/key_documents/2001/ro_en.pdf (accessed October 25, 2011).
——— (2002). *2002 Regular Report from the Commission on Romania's Progress towards Accession*. Brussels. http://ec.europa.eu/enlargement/archives/pdf/key_documents/2002/ro_en.pdf (accessed October 25, 2011).
——— (2003). *2003 Regular Report from the Commission on Romania's Progress towards Accession*. Brussels. http://ec.europa.eu/enlargement/archives/pdf/key_documents/2003/rr_ro_final_en.pdf (accessed October 25, 2011).
——— (2004a). *2004 Regular Report from the Commission on Romania's Progress towards Accession*. Brussels. http://discutii.mfinante.ro/static/10/Mfp/control_prev/regular_rep_ro_041006.pdf (accessed October 25, 2011).
——— (2004b). *2004 Regular Report from the Commission on Bulgaria's Progress towards Accession*. Brussels. http://europe.bg/upload/docs/Regular_Report_2004_EN.pdf (accessed October 25, 2011).
——— (2005). *Romania. Comprehensive Monitoring Report. Brussels.* http://discutii.mfinante.ro/static/10/Mfp/control_prev/comprehensive_rep_ro_051025.pdf (accessed October 25, 2011).
——— (2009). *Serbia 2009 Progress Report*. http://ec.europa.eu/enlargement/pdf/key_documents/2009/sr_rapport_2009_en.pdf (accessed October 25, 2011).
European Convention of Human Rights 1950. http://www.hri.org/docs/ECHR50.html#C.Art5 (accessed October 21, 2011).
European Court of Human Rights: Document Collection (HUDOC). (Accessible via http://www.echr.coe.int/ECHR/EN/Header/Case-Law/Decisions+and+judgments/HUDOC+database (accessed October 24, 2011).
European Glossary (n.d.). *Civil Society Organizations*. http://europa.eu/legislation_summaries/glossary/civil_society_organisation_en.htm (accessed October 16, 2011).
Legea Nr. 489/2006 Privind libertarea religioasă și regimul general al cultelor. http://www.crestinism-ortodox.ro/TEXTE/LegeaCultelor-Nr489-2006.pdf (accessed October 25, 2011).
Treaty of Amsterdam (1997). Treaty of Amsterdam amending the treaty on European Union, the Treaties establishing the European Communities and related acts, Official Journal C 340, 10 November 1997. http://eur-lex.europa.eu/en/treaties/dat/11997D/htm/11997D.html#0133040028 (accessed October 16, 2011).
Treaty of Lisbon (2009). http://register.consilium.europa.eu/pdf/en/08/st06/st06655-re07.en08.pdf (accessed October 25, 2011).
US Department of State (2010). *International Religious Freedom Report on Serbia*. http://www.state.gov/j/drl/rls/irf/2010/148980.htm (accessed October 25, 2011)

13

The Russian Orthodox Church's Interpretation of European Legal Values (1990–2011)

Mikhail Zherebyatyev

Background

Russian attitudes toward Europe, manifested today in intellectual milieus including the Russian Orthodox Church (ROC), have been shaped by views that originated in Russia almost two centuries ago in the dispute between the Slavophiles and the Westernizers. In those constructions, the notion of Europe generally appeared as a personification of the West and the fundamental difference between Europe and Russia was the apparent juridicism of all aspects of European life.

The roots of this perception of Europe can be traced primarily to the Catholic tradition and, to some extent, the Protestant one too. According to this perspective, the secular component of public life is seen as the direct consequence of the secularization of Catholicism since the Renaissance. The Protestant discussions and ideas of a separation of church and civil institutions were not, however, within the sphere of interests of nineteenth-century Russian social thought.

Despite their differences, the Slavophiles and many Westernizers were in fact united in their view of juridicism as a negative organizing principle. According to Russian legal philosopher Vladimir Pristenskij, the Slavophiles "viewed the law as first and foremost a matter of coercion and, since they considered it impossible to achieve social integration through coercion, they renounced the idea of law."[1] Prerevolutionary Westernizers such as Boris Chicherin, Boris Kistyakovsky, Pavel Novgorodtsev, and Nikolai Berdyaev drew attention to the coercive nature of laws, which, in their view, reduced the significance of rights, as opposed to religious faith or morals. They felt that full and genuine social unity could only be guaranteed by faith and morals. Thus, because of its understanding of the law as an instrument of coercion, Russian social thought lost its sense of emancipatory significance of the law.

The ROC remained aloof from this important public debate. In the nineteenth century, its position on the nature of the law was rooted in the existing state ideology, as formulated in the time of Emperor Nicholas I (1825–1855):

"Orthodoxy—Autocracy—Nationality" (*Православие—Самодержавие—Народность*). A key promoter of this line was Konstantin Pobedonostsev, chief procurator of the Holy Synod (the minister of the state church) and cabinet minister from 1880 to 1905. The emphasis on national identity and the mystical linkage of the Orthodox tsar and the Orthodox people created an environment for bypassing the written law, and undermined any intellectual inquiry into this topic within ecclesiastical circles. In the twentieth century, initiatives for change were few and short-lived. The mastery by bishops, priests, and the religious intelligentsia of a legal vocabulary that was adequate for responding to the social problems from the Predsobornoje Soveshchanije (1906) up to the Pomestnyj Sobor of 1917–1918 ended almost as soon as it began. During the Soviet era, there were no significant contributions—for obvious reasons. And in the émigré diaspora, the ROC Outside Russia turned a deaf ear to issues pertaining to the law, although some scholars did study the subject.

Developments in the Years 1990–2010

In the post-Soviet period, two stages in the activities of the ROC coincide with the changing political reality in Russia: 1990–2000 and 2000–2010. The Jubilee Pomestnyj Sobor in 2000, which promulgated the social policy of the ROC, was a milestone. While this social document is more of a declarative statement to the civil authorities, it is also interesting as an indicator of the intellectual state of the ROC. In the first place, the document is clearly not addressed to the average layperson; nor will every priest see a connection between it and everyday life. Second, the document's proposal, that theocracy is the highest form of governance and legal principles, effectively excludes any practical discussion of real legal issues.

The first period was focused on cultivating the identity of the ROC, of Russian Orthodoxy and Russia; and by a sharp distinction between Russian Orthodox civilization and the liberal, democratic West. The latter is presented as enmeshed in internal legal disputes emanating from various sources: the recognition of minority rights to the detriment of a supposedly conservative and traditionalist majority, the institutionalization of churches and their legal treatment as "minorities," the political and moral implications of secularization (including the notion of "political correctness"), and the complexities of implementing principles of national and international law.

As opposed to the actual law in post-Soviet Russia, which drew upon European principles, the ROC favored the principle of the symphony (*symphonia*) of ecclesiastical and civil powers. The ROC thereby demonstrated that it perceived itself in Russia as sharing in power, at least symbolically. And it was precisely from a perspective of power that representatives of the ROC leveled a critique at the secular civil authority.

The results of that first decade were assessed in a thematic, church-and-state issue of the magazine *Otechestvennyje zapiski*. The editor Tatyana Malkina found that there was considerable legal uncertainty about "church-state harmony" in the years 1990–2000. On the one hand, officials responsible for relations between the state and the ROC considered it impossible to infringe on the 1993 Constitution's provision on freedom of religious worship and practice. At that time, the Russian state did not yet see any prospects for restitution, whether for the ROC or for a wider range of potential claimants of the property confiscated by Soviet authorities. Many officials also believed that certain privileges the ROC had enjoyed during the 1990s, such as the duty-free import of alcohol and tobacco, only discredited it rather than advancing the cause of post-Soviet restoration. Nor were federal authorities prepared to introduce Orthodox religious instruction into the school system with ROC oversight, and the really multi-ethnic composition of the Russian armed forces hindered the introduction of Orthodox military chaplains. On the other hand, according to Malkina, "all these annoying reservations are negligible within the overall picture of the ROC's harmonious relations with the state." Malkina concludes that "the relationship between the ROC and the state is similar to a family relationship: it is based on categories and values that are in large measure irrational."[2] Thus, it is not considered appropriate to speak aloud of deep-rooted problems relating to Russian traditions.

Before proceeding to a characterization of the ROC's international relations, it is important to indicate another aspect of its perception of the West. In the ROC's constructions, Europe and the West appear as a kind of alter ego. When they refer to any current imperfections in Russian society, the church's speechwriters typically transfer them outside of the country. Since Russia and its people are thought to be undergoing a moral transformation under the leadership of the ROC, no such imperfections should exist. When ROC representatives speak of the West, quite often that discourse reflects what is happening in Russia. Because Russia has not legalized gay marriage, the ROC's position on that issue is expressed as an opposition to that in the "liberal, democratic and politically correct" West. But on other issues, the reference to "social vices" represents an effort to oust them from Russia and to send them back to their alleged "spiritual" and "historic" homeland—the West.

In the second period, 2000–2010, along with the ROC's establishment of direct relations with Russian civil authorities (very different from the West, whose secular states are separated from churches by law), the Moscow Patriarchate actively sought out traditionalist allies in the international arena, including churches, social movements, NGOs, and individual states.

In Russia, the ROC pursued ways to promote the formation of a "Russian national culture,"[3] and to play a decisive role in state-building.[4] This may appear to have been an affirmation of the ROC's leadership in the priority areas of spirituality and morality, over and against Western social orders that are based on legal norms. It is interesting to note the transfer of the symbols and attributes of power by the first Russian president Boris Yeltsin, who gave up his position prior to the end of his term in order to pave the way for his chosen successor Vladimir Putin, while respecting all the legal formalities that took place on December 31, 1999, in the presence of Patriarch Alexei II.

There are some significant differences between claims about the historic, state-building role of the ROC in Russian history and actual fact. First, according to Eastern Christian tradition, which came to ancient Rus' from Byzantium, the church was subordinated to the state. Second, Patriarch Nikon's seventeenth-century attempt to create a theocracy was suppressed by the emergence of Russian autocracy, which was similar but not identical to European absolutism. Third, the governance of the Russian empire in the eighteenth–nineteenth centuries did not serve the interests of a state church. In annexing the Caucasus and Central Asia, Tsarist Russia allied itself with the native nobility, which did not allow the state church to increase its flock.

Since 2000, a reorientation toward Europe has become a priority in the ROC's international diplomacy. It is not incidental that, after being elected primate in 2009, Patriarch Kirill appointed Bishop Hilarion (Alfeev) to his former position as head of the Department of External Church Relations.[5] The young bishop (born in 1966) had acquired leadership experience from his work in two European dioceses, including Vienna, a long-standing meeting place for representatives of the ROC and the Vatican. In a May 2007 address to a meeting of leaders of the European Union with religious leaders of Europe, Hilarion declared, "In speaking of the intolerance within anti-Semitism and Islamophobia, the political leaders of Europe often forget about various types of Christianophobia and anti-Christianity." He further affirmed, "It is impossible to erase two thousand years of Christianity...from the history of Europe...But the importance of Christianity is not limited to history. Christianity remains the most important moral and spiritual component of European identity." Human rights, in the bishop's interpretation, consist of both individual and collective rights. Collective rights, namely, the rights of religious communities, must be respected by the political leaders of European countries, and "this respect is necessary for the construction of a multi-polar society, in which religious communities can build a life in accordance with their traditional ethos."[6]

In its *Social Concept* (2000), the ROC rejects the "branch theory" of Christianity in order to justify again their membership in the World Council of Churches (WCC). In 1961 the ROC joined the organization, fulfilling the will of the Soviet state, which thereby acquired yet another influential diplomatic instrument. The ROC took that step under duress, fearing its own annihilation and an intensification of the religious persecution, which had already been unleashed by the head of state, Nikita Khrushchev.

The ROC considers its current participation in the WCC as a witness to the truth of Orthodoxy before the non-Orthodox world and a reminder to secularized Europe of its Christian roots and values. The first of these reasons had been used to explain and justify the ROC's involvement in the WCC in the past. That discourse on Christian roots also served the purpose of distinguishing sharply between the ROC and Western churches—the ROC positioned itself as a church that remained constant in the face of historical vicissitudes, while the secularized, Western "others" (in the WCC) were guided by the conventions of their own time.

Despite the ROC's apparent success in its relations with the EU and the UN, relations with other religious organizations and sectarian organizations in the same period were uneven. In the wake of the decision in 2002 to raise the status of Catholic Church structures in Russia to the level of full-fledged dioceses in 2002, the Russian church launched a campaign against Catholic proselytism in the "canonical territory" of the ROC. The term "canonical territory" had been applied to the ROC in the early 1990s. Despite the proclamation of religious equality in post-Soviet Russia, the ROC regarded Russia and other former Soviet republics as its own canonical territory. The ROC's relations with the Vatican began to change only after the election of Pope Benedict XVI. According to officials, the Vatican's revival of the Greek Catholic Church in Ukraine at the end of the 1980s had been a chief obstacle to dialogue with John Paul II—unofficial reasons included the pontiff's Polish roots and his commitment to humanist values. In addition to the establishment of Catholic dioceses in Russia, the visit of Pope John Paul II to Ukraine in the summer of 2001 had irritated the leadership of the ROC. Following the establishment of Catholic dioceses in Russia, the Russian Foreign Ministry blocked several Catholic priests and Bishop Jerzy Mazur from entry into the country.

And in 2008 the ROC withdrew from the Conference of European Churches, citing the admission into the organization of the Estonian Autonomous Orthodox Church

(Ecumenical Patriarchate) and no similar provision for the Estonian Autonomous Orthodox Church (Moscow Patriarchate).

In fact, the ROC today aims to create a kind of network of national and supranational organizations or alliances of a traditionalist religious orientation. In 2005, three years after the establishment of a representation at the EU, the World Russian National Sobor (WRNS) began to put in place a similar structure at the UN. The ROC had established the WRNS in 1993 to broadcast its positions on various issues. The WRNS, which conducts annual policy forums attended by government and public figures, is under the control of the ROC. In 2006, the WRNS promulgated a Declaration on Human Rights and Dignity—the first document that outlined the Orthodox understanding of human rights. Among other things, the declaration stated, "There are values that are not lower than human rights. These are values such as faith, morality, holiness, the Fatherland. When these values and the fulfillment of human rights conflict, society, state, and the law should reconcile them."[7]

In 2008, the ROC developed its own concept of human rights in a document titled *Fundamentals of the ROC's Teachings on Human Dignity, Freedom and Human Rights*, referred to unofficially as the *Orthodox Concept of Human Rights.* This document established the priority of the corporate rights of the church and the state over and above individual civil rights, which flies in the face of the fundamental legal principles in Russia today that affirm the priority of individual rights.

However, the ROC's search for allies to defend "traditional values" was limited to the international arena. Patriarch Kirill's successor as head of the Department for External Church Relations of Moscow Patriarchate, Metropolitan Hilarion (Alfeev), admitted that the ROC's relations with other denominations in Russia occur less frequently than contacts with churches from other states. Some attempts to revive the ROC's contacts with other denominations were undertaken by an international church structure—the Christian Interfaith Advisory Committee of the Commonwealth of Independent States and Baltic States.

Such a roundabout quest for potential allies, mainly from among Russian Protestant denominations, most of which hold very conservative views, does not appear to be incidental. A direct dialogue of the ROC with Protestants would inevitably demonstrate the formal, constitutional equality of Russian denominations, even as the ROC remains committed to the idea of its own privileged status, despite the absence of any such provisions in current Russian law.

Thus, we can speak about the conditions under which a positive perception of European secular law by the ROC is possible. The ROC typically holds the European legal system in very high regard, as long as it concerns the legal privileges of national churches in EC countries. As Archbishop Feofan (Ashurkov) of Chelyabinsk stated, "Ideally citizens should pay a church tax, as in developed countries, but we [in Russia] are not ready for this, and to this day no one has given parishes free electricity, or heat, or church buildings. Yet, in many countries the clergy receives a state salary."[8]

The Human Rights Doctrine of the ROC and the Transition from Theoretical Concepts to Practical Politics

As for the current social processes in Russia, particularly in the legal sphere, it would be easy to conclude that the Orthodox notion of human rights basically follows from the

Russian foreign policy doctrine of a multipolar world as expressed by Vladimir Putin, and which replaced the Cold War idea of two opposing superpowers. In addition, multipolarity requires a traditionalist foundation, which of course is different in each nation or society. Such an approach inevitably raises a number of questions—What precisely is meant by "tradition" and "traditional values?" By what mechanisms are they formed and developed? And how are the traditional values of one national culture transferred to other cultures?—but still it serves the formation of the Russian doctrine of a multipolar world. Second, in Russia the Orthodox concept of human rights serves to perpetuate stereotypes about the uniqueness of Russia and to sacralize the present civil power and the ROC. Third, a grassroots movement has emerged in Russia in opposition to law reform in the area of juvenile justice (proposing, among other things, the introduction of a separate system for young offenders) and inspired by ideas contained in the *Orthodox Concept of Human Rights*. At various stages, ROC eparchial structures have joined that movement.

The year 2011 was characterized by many important political events throughout the world. In Russia, the year concluded with mass demonstrations against the rigged parliamentary elections, which were in line with the developments of the foregoing 12 years. After the crisis in August 2008, Russian protests had diminished to a very low level because the population needed to attend to more basic concerns: subsistence and the maintenance of the standard of living. In addition, since Vladimir Putin was in office (from 2000 as president and later as prime minister) the government tried systematically to limit the right of citizens to participate in various forms of protest. At the same time, the mobilizing role of the Internet and of social networks, especially as applied to protest activities, has been significant. Prior to 2011, Internet communications had been seen almost exclusively through the prism of consumerism. Experts discussed information needs, services, and interpersonal contacts. The Internet was seen as a factor for the maximal individualization of humanity, although it was also recognized that it supported interpersonal communication. It was not yet seen as an instrument for mobilizing large numbers of people around common interests.

In the course of 2011, the ROC described the attacks in Arabian states on local Christian citizens as if radical Muslims were attacking universal civil rights. Two documents will serve as the basis for our survey of the ROC's position on the question. The first is the statement from the ROC's Holy Synod (May 30, 2011) concerning the global spread of Christianophobia and Patriarch Kirill's address to participants of the conference "Freedom of Conscience: The Problem of Discrimination and Persecution of Christians" on December 1, 2011.

The ROC attributed the anti-Christian violence to government incompetence in the Middle East, Africa, and Asia—in particular, their inability to guarantee equal human rights for their citizens, irrespective of their religious affiliations. The ROC Synod declared: "It is the duty of governments, which are responsible for their citizens, to respect the dignity and rights of every human being. Accordingly, they have to guarantee religious freedom and the safety of every religious community."[9] This synodal text employs the "dignity and rights" terminology of the *Orthodox Concept of Human Rights*; religious communities are described as subjects of religious activity; nevertheless, in that same statement, human rights are defined in their European understanding. Half a year later Patriarch Kirill emphasized: "According to our own understanding we do not portray ourselves as a victim in order to achieve exclusive rights or preferential treatment."[10] When the patriarch of the ROC talks about "us," it is clear that he is referring to the ROC and to Christians in general, including Christians living in the Arab world and in Africa.

This approach actually differs from the ROC's doctrine of human rights, which postulates the priority of collective rights—churches, nations, corporations—as opposed to individual or personal rights. Nevertheless, the Arabian case is very significant in another respect. In the early years of the post-Soviet period, when the ROC formulated its doctrine of human rights, beyond Russia this was addressed to European society, more precisely to an abstract "majority" within European society. The ROC considered the common Christian tradition of the European people as an indication of such a "majority." This "traditional majority" resembles the followers of "churches" in the ideal type construction of Max Weber.

The ROC's appeals were aimed at stirring the traditionalist sentiments of the European "majority" and in the national churches of Europe. The liberal values that had introduced a view of humanity during the Renaissance and which took their definitive shape under the influence of the Enlightenment now became an antipode of "traditional values," according to the ROC. In turn, that complex of ideas serves as the foundation for the priority of personal rights and cultural and moral pluralism, which are rooted in the value and autonomy of every individual person. Within this European model of rights, which is based on the separation of powers, on the acknowledgment of individual rights, and on the significant role of civil society in political decision-making, increased attention is paid to the rights and problems of various minorities.

In fact, both in Europe and in Russia practicing Christians (those who are religious to some degree in their daily lives) are in the minority. But the ROC never refers to European Christians or to Russian Christians as minorities.[11] Instead, secularism is always identified as the enemy of the Christian tradition of the ROC and is depicted as a departure from the proper, traditionalist direction of social life. It is precisely secularism, or "radical secularism," that is usually seen as a minority by the ROC.[12]

Until 2011, the term "minority" had very negative connotations for the ROC. At the same time, as demonstrated by recent events, the ROC's attitude toward the status of minorities was ambiguous, in that it was also informed by the Western European construction of justice and the positive treatment of minorities. So, on the one hand, "minorities" were seen by the ROC as a historical and social fact (e.g., the existence of Christian minorities in Islamic countries) and, on the other, as something akin to a discrepancy of norms within a regime (e.g., the public appearance of representatives of a "non-traditional sexual orientation" or of religious "sectarianism" in Russia). Such phenomena were not seen as having any relation to the ROC or to Orthodox Christians in Russia. It is noteworthy that the ROC's declarations still continue to perceive minorities in this way. At the same time, the ROC in present-day Russia strives to obtain privileges, which are proper to minorities and which are expressed through positive discrimination. Yet in those very efforts, the ROC still appeals to its status as the "church of the majority."

The ROC received such privileges on federal bases right before the Russian electoral campaign of 2011–2012. While no properties that were confiscated in Russia after 1917 were returned to their former possessors, a law that was favorable to the ROC was passed; this law was entitled the *Law on the return of properties with religious purpose, which are possessed by the state or local administrations, to religious communities.*[13] Although current juridical persons could make claims on such properties, such as the successors of denominations that were active in Russia before 1918, the principal beneficiary of this law was the ROC. Also, in April 2010, the recognition of religious communities as socially oriented, noncommercial organizations and thus partners of the state was taken by the ROC as an indication of support for its monopoly on such activities.[14]

The ROC reacts very sensitively whenever the government shows equal treatment toward other players on the religious scene, or when it considers the constitutional rights and interests of other religious communities and groups.[15] Even the extremely limited consideration of granting the status of corporate body (juridical person) to the other denominations—as demonstrated in the aforementioned statement of the vicar of the diocese of Voronezh—can be seen as an example of the corruption of Russian officials.

In their statements, the ROC and its representatives argue that the hypothetical preference of religious "minorities" (which, in accordance with Russian legal norms, means the legal recognition of the rights of all denominations) entails a derogation of the interests of the religious "majority." This argument of the ROC has the support of Russian civil authorities. This is clear in the prohibition of homosexual parades. Not even the decisions of the European Court of Human Rights, which must be acknowledged by the governments belonging to the Council of Europe, in particular its decision of October 21, 2010, which states that the prohibition of a gay parade in Moscow is illegal,[16] mattered in the decision of the administration of the Russian capital. In May 2011 the Moscow administration again denied permission for public activities of a homosexual association. In their rejection, the municipal authority systematically cites the incompatibility of homosexual behavior with the traditions of social morality and the consistently negative opinion of homosexuality among religious organizations and believers, and especially in the ROC.

For the first time, in the document of the synod the speech of Patriarch Kirill publicly referred to Christians in the Arabian world as "minorities." Following the synod, which affirmed that "in some countries, where Christians are a minority, their right to religious freedom is significantly restricted,"[17] Patriarch Kirill declared, "One of the most important tendencies of our time is the mass exodus of Christians out of the Middle East and North Africa, which is provoked by the unprecedented increase of violence against religious minorities in these regions."[18] The head of the ROC concludes that the religious majority of the world, constituted by Christians of all denominations, is today the most discriminated community: "Cases of persecution and discrimination of Christians in our times have assumed a systematic character. Numerous reports have demonstrated that this religious community—the largest in the world—finds itself in a vulnerable situation."[19]

In elaborating further on the relationship between "majority" and "minority," the patriarch addresses the verdict of the Great Chamber of the European Court of Human Rights of March 18, 2011, in the case of *Lautsi vs. Italy*. The applicant in this case had argued that the presence of a cross in Italian public schools has a compulsory character and thereby infringes on the European Convention on Human Rights. Russia entered this litigation in support of Italy only in its final stage, when the Italian state had launched an appeal against the judgment of the European Court of Human Rights in its Great Chamber. The Italian government attempted to challenge the decision of the European Court of Human Rights of November 3, 2009, No. 30814/06, *Lautsi vs. Italy*, which had recognized the cross as a religious symbol, by appealing to national traditions. In the end, the Great Chamber of the European Court of Human Rights rendered a contrary verdict by accepting the presence of the cross in Italian public schools as not contrary to the European Convention of Human Rights. The Great Chamber also added a qualifying comment, which expressed the necessity of considering fundamental civil rights, specifically drawing attention to the prohibition of religious education in public schools. The European Court of Human Rights justified its verdict "On Crosses" by pointing out that the European Council does not have a uniform standard for all member states concerning this question. Thus, the presence of the cross was treated as a "passive symbol," which does not have the same implication as religious education or the attendance of a religious rite.

However, in Patriarch Kirill's interpretation, with that decision of the Great Chamber of the European Court of Human Rights, the role of the symbol of Christianity was successfully defended—not through the efforts of civil society—but, remarkably, "through the joint efforts of several countries."[20] Indeed, numerous states—Armenia, Bulgaria, Greece, Lithuania, Malta, Monaco, and San Marino—had adopted positions analogous to that of Russia. The very fact that the cross issue had been investigated by the European Court of Human Rights led Patriarch Kirill to announce that even in Europe Christians have no guarantee of protection against discrimination.

In the context of real international relationships, the ROC's apparent attenuation of its initially rigid formulations of human rights is connected with the fact that the players of European politics expressed themselves on the rights of Christians from the point of view of international (basically European) law, rather than from abstract traditionalism. Prior to the promulgation on January 20, 2011, of the European Parliament's resolution on *The Situation of Christians in the Context of Freedom of Religion*, the ROC had considered this topic as its personal monopoly. The European Parliament's resolution condemns the persecution of Christians even outside European countries. In this way, an initiative previously advanced by the ROC and supported by its own ideas of rights and corresponding arguments finally changed hands. The ROC had to incorporate itself into the current process and to moderate its own doctrinal position on human rights.[21]

Notes

1. Пристенский В.Н. Правовой нигилизм: философско-антропологические корни // Credo new—2005—No. 1(41), C.175. A similar opinion has been formulated by the Russian researcher Eric Soloviev: Соловьев Э.Ю. Дефицит правопонимания в русской моральной философии // Прошлое толкует нас: Очерки по истории философии и культуры.—М.: Политиздат, 1991—С. 230–234.
2. Малкина Т. Титульная церковь РФ. Россиийская власть в поисках утраченного. // Отечественные Записки. No. 1, 2001, С. 10.
3. From the middle of the seventeenth century, with the direct participation of the authorities, the secularization of everyday life gained momentum and became firmly entrenched by the beginning of the eighteenth century.
4. The "culture-forming" and "state-forming" roles of the church are now formulas used in official texts and pronouncements by bishops, priests, and secular officials.
5. In 2002 Hilarion was appointed as the first head of the ROC to the European Institutions.
6. Представитель Московского Патриархата епископ Венский и Австрийский Иларион принял участие во встрече руководства Европейского Союза с религиозными лидерами Европы // http://www.patriarchia.ru/db/text/242445.html.

7. Декларация о правах и достоинстве человека X Всемирного Русского Народного Собора // http://www.patriarchia.ru/db/text/103235.html.
8. Онлайн-конференция. Феофан, архиерей Челябинской и Златоустовской епархии: «Я не считаю Челябинск ссылкой. Меня всегда посылали туда, где трудно»/Chelyabinsk.ru. Агентство новостей, 1 апреля 2011. //http://chelyabinsk.ru/conference/feofan74.html?p=1&qp=1#question.
9. Заявление Священного Синода Русской Православной Церкви в связи с ростом проявлений христианофобии в мире 30 мая 2011 г. http://www.patriarchia.ru/db/text/1498832.html.
10. Выступление Святейшего Патриарха Кирилла на встрече с участниками конференции «Свобода вероисповедания: проблема дискриминации и преследования христиан» // http://www.patriarchia.ru/db/text/1794559.html.
11. According to the nationwide survey conducted at the end of 2011 by one of the largest sociological institutes—the Public Opinion Foundation, in conjunction with the ROC's Sreda Research Centre—only 1 percent of respondents participate actively in parish life. http://www.interfax-religion.ru/?act=news&div=43709. Of those who call themselves Orthodox, 15 percent go to communion once or twice a year, 6 percent go several times a year, and only 2 percent—once a month. At the same time, 43 percent of respondents who call themselves Orthodox have never received communion, while 4 percent had difficulty answering the question. http://www.interfax-religion.ru/?act=news&div=43479. In addition, 56 percent of respondents opposed the idea of a church tax for the benefit of the ROC. http://www.interfax-religion.ru/?act=news&div=43269. The survey covered 1,500 people from 100 cities and villages in 44 regions of Russia, and the selection was random regarding sex, age, and education.
12. Заявление Священного Синода Русской Православной Церкви в связи с ростом проявлений христианофобии в мире 30 мая 2011 г. http://www.patriarchia.ru/db/text/1498832.html.Выступление Святейшего Патриарха Кирилла на встрече с участниками конференции «Свобода вероисповедания: проблема дискриминации и преследования христиан»// http://www.patriarchia.ru/db/text/1794559.html.
13. Федеральный закон Российской Федерации от 30 ноября 2010 г. N 327-ФЗ "О передаче религиозным организациям имущества религиозного назначения, находящегося в государственной или муниципальной собственности"// http://www.rg.ru/2010/12/03/tserkovnoedobro-dok.html.
14. Vicar Andrei (Tarasov) of the diocese of Voronezh explained that the possibility of a collaborative system of public, social, and religious organizations of various confessions could potentially lead to advantages for sects. http://www.portal-credo.ru/ сайт /? = акт новости и ID = 89362 & Type = зрения.

    The ROC's Siberian dioceses have begun to screen religious organizations working on the rehabilitation of drug addicts. This was reported at the antinarcotic conference in Tomsk, *Civil Society, Traditional Religions and State: Against Narcotic Aggression* (March 24–25, 2011). The organizers of this conference were the ROC dioceses of Tomsk and Novosibirsk, the Tomsk regional authority, a regional department fighting against illegal drug trade, and educational and medical institutions of the Tomsk region. http://www.portal-credo.ru/site/?act=news&id=83243&type=view.
15. Vsevolod Chaplin, an archpriest and ROC representative for state, society and church relations, argued that the state has the right to prefer some religious groups and to limit the rights of others. http://www.religare.ru/2_90329.html.
16. A selection of materials on this subject, including the positions of the civil authorities, the ROC, activists from Orthodox organizations, and the participants of gay parades are found on the Russian version of Wikipedia (http://ru.wikipedia.org/wiki), under "Гей-парады в России."

17. Заявление Священного Синода Русской Православной Церкви в связи с ростом проявлений христианофобии в мире 30 мая 2011 г. http://www.patriarchia.ru/db/text/1498832.html.
18. Выступление Святейшего Патриарха Кирилла на встрече с участниками конференции «Свобода вероисповедания: проблема дискриминации и преследования христиан» // http://www.patriarchia.ru/db/text/1794559.html.
19. Ibid.
20. Ibid.
21. Metropolitan Ilarion (Alfeyev) gave a positive assessment of the European Parliament's resolution: "The resolution has a revolutionary character. For the first time, European Parliamentarians addressed aloud a problem which they had previously preferred to ignore." He also described the persecution of Christians in Asia and Africa as a strategy of "some terrorist organizations and fundamentalist movements, whose goal is to annihilate or oust Christians who are living in Islamic countries as a 'fifth column' of the West." //Митрополит Волоколамский Иларион: «Резолюция Европарламента является революционной." РПЦ официальный сайт Отдела внешних церковных связей // http://www.mospat.ru/ru/2011/01/24/news34845/.

    The expression "fifth column of the West" was widely used under Putin's administration to characterize all irregular (*несистемной*) political opposition, which was not represented in parliament, regardless of their doctrinal orientation. It also referred to mainstream Western religious communities operating in Russia and to human rights organizations. For its part, the ROC describes the current religious situation in Russia by way of distinguishing between "traditional" (and, by implication, "legitimate") religions or confessions and "nontraditional" ones, whose moral and legal status is in doubt. The extremely arbitrary way in which religious communities are placed into either of the two categories is remarkable. According to widespread opinion within the ROC, not even the Catholic Church is included among the "traditional" religious communities of Russia.

14

The Russian Orthodox Church in a New Situation in Russia: Challenges and Responses

Olga Kazmina

The new religious situation that has emerged in post-Soviet Russia differs greatly from both Soviet and pre-Soviet religious realities, though both of those preceding periods also shaped the current situation. One of the specific features inherited from the pre-Soviet period is the close connection between religious and ethnic identities. This connection was historically typical for the country. The correlation of religion and ethnicity in Russia has deep historical roots, and the cultural dimension of religion was integral to ethnic identity. Religious affiliation was often ascribed according to birth within a particular ethnic group.[1] This created a situation in which religion was generally considered as not merely a private affair but also as a force of cultural tradition.

Before 1917, this link between religion and ethnicity was fixed by law. Most of Russia's ethnic groups were tightly connected with their "historical" religions, and the resulting interpenetration of church and state led to the involvement of the Russian Orthodox Church (ROC) in collective-identity construction, beyond its purely religious activity. The identity dimension of religion was so strong that even 70 years of state atheism and the suppression of religion could not eradicate religion. The specifics of Soviet-imposed secularization also produced a new religious situation. Soviet secularization differed greatly from Western secularization, which privatized religion and moved it from the social sphere to the private sphere, with an emphasis on personal religious choice.[2] In the Soviet Union, religion was not treated as a private matter, but rather as an alien or even hostile ideology. People had few opportunities to obtain a religious education or even elementary religious knowledge. In such a siutuation, religion remained for the most part restricted to rites and rituals as part of ethnic culture and tradition, though some latent religiosity was preserved indirectly through literature, art, proverbs, and so on.

In the post-Soviet period, the restoration of religion proceeded to a large extent by way of a "return to historical roots," and the identity dimension of religiosity was strengthened first of all. The absence of solid religious knowledge had a double effect—it contributed to the fusion of religious and ethnic identity, and it led some people to identify themselves as "simply Christians," with no particular denominational attachment. This facilitated the appearance and spread of many new denominations. However, throughout the whole post-Soviet period, despite increased religious diversity, the ROC has remained the religious organization with which most people in Russia affiliate themselves. In 2009, according to Patriarch Kirill, between 60 and 80 percent of Russia's population considered themselves Russian Orthodox.[3] In particular, the ROC's relations with other religious organizations and the state have largely shaped the main religious trends in the country.

In discussing religious developments in postcommunist Russia, we may distinguish three different periods: the early to mid-1990s, the late 1990s to the mid-2000s, and the mid-2000s to 2010. Each of these three periods may be characterized with reference to a number of factors: the official positions of the ROC and other religious organizations on various issues, the state's attitude toward religion, the balance between secular and postsecular tendencies, the conceptual dynamics underlying religious legislation, shifts in collective cultural identities and the place of religious identity in their hierarchy, and the understanding of human rights by religious organizations.

Legislative Liberalization, Proselytism, and a Defensive ROC

The first period is characterized by the firm neutrality of the state toward all religious organizations, by the intensive missionary activity of various religious organizations and a sharp increase in proselytism, the ROC's defensive posture and its vigorous competition with Protestant missionaries, and new religious movements. It was typical of this period that religion was perceived by the population as first and foremost a social and cultural phenomenon.

In the early 1990s religion began to restore its position in society. Religious thought, practice, and institutions acquired a new prominence in the social sphere. Most people welcomed the reopening of churches and monasteries, the revival of religious festivals and traditions, and the opportunity to profess their faith openly. It was also typical in those years for people to be disillusioned with state institutions, while religious organizations enjoyed a high level of public support. The prestige of the ROC was at a high point, and sociological surveys repeatedly confirmed higher popular ratings for the church than the president, the Parliament, and the government.[4]

Another feature of the early 1990s was the intense activization of all denominations. In that period, according to official estimates, 67 percent of the population considered themselves believers and only 33 percent nonbelievers.[5] All religious organizations experienced a significant growth in membership: whether those that had existed for a long time, or those that had been banned during the Soviet period, or even new arrivals on the scene. The population considered the activity of new denominations in a favorable light: people were open to everything new. For its part, the ROC viewed this proliferation of new religious organizations as a threat, and responded by adopting a defensive position. The years of Communist rule, during which the church had become, in effect, "locked" inside its own church buildings, had done their job. The ROC had lost its outreach experience in missionary and social work. In contrast, Christian denominations arriving from the West were very skilled in these types of activities.

The legal framework also favored religious pluralism. In the early 1990s the state faced an urgent need to adopt new religious laws. Russian society awaited full religious freedom as a decisive step in the break with the Soviet past. In 1990, the law "On Freedom of Beliefs"[6] granted virtually unlimited religious freedom, lifted all restrictions on the activity of religious organizations, guaranteed equal rights for all denominations, and permitted foreigners to become leaders of religious organizations. Though in Russia there was no tradition of considering religion as a private affair, the underlying philosophy of this law was grounded in ideas of individual religious choice, of the state's neutrality toward religious organizations, and of the privatization of religion. In addition, this law diminished the connection of religion and ethnicity, a connection that had been strong in Russia's history. According to the new law, the ROC no longer had privileges as compared to other denominations. Instead, the law placed all religious organizations on an equal footing.

However, within a few years a tension emerged between the 1990 law, with its ideal of individual religious rights, and a move to restore the old ties between religion and ethnicity. Whereas the 1990 law treated religion as a private affair, by the mid-1990s the idea of a special status for the ROC and other historical denominations and the recognition of their special role in supporting state interests began to gain ground. Thus, the 1990 law had a double effect: it introduced a new philosophy and conceptual framework for religious life and, a few years later, it brought to the fore a new concern in public policy debates—a concern for the legal protection of the historical church over and above sects and new denominations. Essentially, this created a sharper distinction between historical faiths and new religious organizations. From 1993, there were proposals for a new law on religion, and the debates around those proposals continued after the promulgation in December 1993 of a new constitution, which drew upon ideas of the 1990 law "On Freedom of Beliefs." The proposals for legislative reform on religion introduced a distinction between "traditional denominations," which were connected with the ethnic culture and history of the people, and "nontraditional denominations," which did not have such connections. The notion of "traditional denominations" took root and found its way into religious and sociopolitical discourses. There were even calls to apply it legislatively and officially with reference to the specific denominations.

The 1990 law had also opened the door to foreign missionaries. Thus, the ROC was not the only actor in the re-Christianization of the historically Orthodox population. Rather, it competed with many other Christian denominations, which engaged in proselytism. The ROC had not expected such competition. While its hierarchs had participated actively in the elaboration of the 1990 law, they had not indicated any desire to introduce restrictions. In its first encounters with proselytism, the ROC appealed to the ecumenical commitments of missionary organizations, arguing that proselytism was incompatible with ecumenism.[7] When those interventions proved fruitless, the ROC began to oppose the activities of Western Christian denominations more directly, and isolationist tendencies began to predominate in the ROC.

The debate around proselytism was complicated by the fact that the ROC and its competitors used different criteria to distinguish between acceptable missionary activity and unacceptable proselytism. According to Protestant evangelicals, any "nominal" Christian, baptized or not, can be a legitimate object of evangelism in any region of the world regardless whether another Christian Church exists there. Thus, a region like Russia would be viewed as a "legitimate missionary field."[8] Catholics add to this the idea of the universality of the Roman Catholic Church (RCC).

The ROC does not dispute that every individual should come into a personal relationship with God. But since most of the people of Russia are under its canonical jurisdiction and spiritual protection, insofar as they or their parents were baptized in this church, Russia cannot be viewed as an open field for the missionary work of other denominations. The ROC has thus considered missionary activity to be destructive when it is aimed at persons who were previously baptized as Russian Orthodox or who were linked with Orthodoxy historically.[9] In support of this position, the ROC cited the Apostle Paul: "It has always been my ambition to preach the gospel where Christ was not known, so that I would not be building on someone else's foundation" (Rom. 15:20). Thus, what evangelical denominations considered legitimate and useful missionary activity, the ROC perceived as impermissible proselytism.

Since the missionary impulse is inherent in the very nature of Christianity and there is no common definition of proselytism, the only way to draw a mutually agreed boundary between admissible and inadmissible activities would be to engage first of all in fruitful ecumenical dialogue. But, in the period under consideration, such dialogue was very limited. In the early and mid-1990s the ROC began to feel insecure because of the appearance of many new denominations and competition in the missionary field. In advancing its position on the inadmissibility of such competition, the ROC not only employed theological arguments but also appealed to feelings of ethnic identity and the historical and cultural traditions of the population. Unlike the early 1990s, by the mid- and late 1990s such concerns were received favorably by the general population. By the mid-1990s significant changes had taken place in the mentality of the majority Russian population: the initial, euphoric embrace of Western values gave way to more nationalistic tendencies and an increased interest in all things traditional, including religious traditions.

Special Status for Traditional Religions and the Ethnoreligious Connection

The main features of the second period were: the consolidation of the ROC's position in relation to the state and society, an increased correlation between religion and ethnicity, the politicization of religion, the emergence of major differences between the ROC and the RCC over proselytism, and the increased isolationism of the ROC in relation to Western Christianity. It is in such an atmosphere that a new law "On Freedom of Religion and on Religious Associations"[10] was adopted in 1997. Unlike the 1990 law, the new law reaffirmed a strong connection between religious life and the historical culture.

The 1997 law represented a new concept of religion-state-society relations and reflected changes in the mood of the population. Whereas the 1990 law had emphasized the inalienable right to religious freedom and a desire to follow the provisions of international legal charters, the 1997 law, while affirming the right of each person to freedom of conscience and freedom of creed, also linked religious life to the historical and cultural context. The preamble to the new law attached considerable importance to the "special contribution of Orthodoxy to the history of Russia and to the establishment and development of Russia's spirituality and culture."[11] The law limited the opportunities for new denominations to pursue missionary work and strengthened the primacy of the ROC.

Since mid-1990s, the church had also become more active. It issued a number of significant documents, including "The Concept of the Rebirth of the Missionary Activities of the ROC"[12] in 1995. This document pointed out that missionary activity is inherent in the very nature of the Christian Church and has always been a principal duty of Christians, according to Christ's command to his apostles "Go ye therefore, and teach all the nations, baptizing them in the name of the Farther, and of the Son, and of the Holy Ghost" (Matt. 28:19–20). In the same document, the ROC formulated the forms and methods of its missionary activity in response to the challenges faced by contemporary society. Informative, apologetic, educational, and "external" missions were also listed. The informative mission referred to Orthodox witness to large segments of the population through mass media, parish libraries, and special publications. The apologetic mission was aimed at providing a comparison of Orthodoxy with the doctrines of non-Orthodox denominations, which are viewed as inauthentic by the ROC. The intent of this distinction is to counter the proselytism of non-Orthodox organizations. The educational mission was focused on providing a basic knowledge of Orthodoxy to those who were preparing for Orthodox baptism and for those who were nominally Orthodox (i.e., baptized but unfamiliar with Orthodox teachings and practice), so that they could become "churched" persons. And finally, the external mission encompassed the Orthodox witness to non-Christian peoples, mostly migrants living within the canonical territory of the ROC.

In 2000, the ROC promulgated the *Bases of the Social Concept of the Russian Orthodox Church.*[13] This document exposed the church's position on the relations with the state and secular society and the church's views on a number of socially significant contemporary problems. For the first time in its history, the ROC formulated its position on a wide range of social problems and church-state issues. It also covered such issues as labor and its fruits; war and peace; crime, punishment, law reform; personal, family, and public morality; personal and national health; bioethics, ecological problems; secular science, culture, and education; mass media; international relations, problems of globalization and secularism. The adoption of *Bases of the Social Concept of the Russian Orthodox Church* also inspired other denominations in Russia to formulate their own perspectives on the role of religion in society. In the same year, the ROC also promulgated the *Basic Principles of the Russian Orthodox Church's Attitude toward the non-Orthodox.*[14] According to this document, the essential goal of the ROC in its relations with other Christian confessions is the pursuit of Christian unity, as required by the Gospel message (John 17–21). The document further states that the relationship of the ROC with the non-Orthodox Christian communities in the former Soviet republics should be maintained in a spirit of fraternal cooperation in order to coordinate social work, promote social harmony, and to put an end to proselytism on the canonical territory of the ROC. The social documents of the ROC thus outlined the church's activities in different spheres, reflected its views on theological and social problems, and reaffirmed its close ties to the national and cultural traditions of Russia.

As for the state, it modified its position from a demonstrative solidarity and favoritism toward the ROC in the latter part of the 1990s to a general neutrality and support for the ROC at critical moments in the 2000s.

The historical connection of Russian ethnic and religious identity, which had been weakened in early 1990s, was reinforced in this period. Consequently, other denominations were assessed through the prism of ethnicity as well. Thus, the ROC had better relations with other "traditional religions" of Russia, referring to them as "the religions of our neighboring peoples," than with non-Orthodox Christian denominations—referred to as "others," "aliens," or "competitors."

In its interfaith relations in the late 1990s the ROC preferred cooperation with the "traditional religions" of the country: along with Russian Orthodoxy, these were understood to be Islam, Buddhism, and Judaism. At the ROC's initiative in December 1998, representatives of these faith traditions established the Inter-religious Council of Russia. As to the relations of the ROC with Western Christian denominations, they were often complicated in the late 1990s and early 2000s. The ROC considered the main obstacle to improving these relations to be proselytism.

Whereas in the early 1990s the problem of proselytism had been associated primarily with the missionary activity of Protestant evangelical denominations, in the late 1990s and early 2000s, when mass gatherings and evangelical church services in stadiums and concert halls became less numerous, the RCC came to be seen as the main challenger to the ROC. As it happened, those denominations that were more theologically remote became more isolated in their spheres of activities, while those more proximate (like Orthodoxy and Catholicism) competed in the same field. It is easier for a nominal Orthodox person to convert to Catholicism than to a denomination whose theology is further removed.

In the debate over proselytism with the RCC and with other "contenders," the ROC held steadfastly to its claim of territorial-canonical jurisdiction. This claim is rooted in Orthodox theology and in the traditional connection between Russian religious and ethnic identity. As Patriarch Kirill indicated, "The canonical tradition of the early undivided Church formulated the very important principle: one city, one bishop, that is, in one city, or speaking more broadly, in one place there is one Church."[15]

The Catholic position on proselytism was centered in this period on the notions of the special status of the Apostle Peter, who is considered to be a founder of the Roman Church, and on the principle of universality, which justifies Catholic missionary work throughout the world.[16] The Catholic Church has emphasized that it is opposed to the enticement of believers from one Christian denomination to another. At the same time, it stressed the missionary nature of the Christian Church, which exhorted all Christians to missionary witness. An Orthodox believer should bring an Orthodox witness, whereas a Catholic believer should bring a Catholic witness.[17] The ROC saw this as an indication of the RCC's intent to substantiate its missionary activity in the canonical territory of the ROC.

On the matter of Catholic witness in Russia, the ROC stated:

> The Roman Catholic Church, as well as other Churches, should bring a Christian witness, however, its mission must be addressed to those who due to their national and cultural roots belong to a traditionally Catholic flock, but it must not be addressed to those people who have Orthodox roots, much less to those who were baptized into the Orthodox Church.[18]

During the late 1990s and early 2000s both churches repeatedly stated that they had aspired toward Christian unity and have condemned proselytism, understood as any pressure on conscience. At the same time, proselytism remained a principal concern of the ROC with the RCC. As before, the problem was grounded in different understandings of the scope of missionary work and of the meaning of proselytism. At the beginning of the twenty-first century, new tensions emerged between the two churches. Those tensions came to a head in 2002 in connection with the establishment of four Catholic dioceses as a separate church province. The ROC interpreted this as a form of proselytism. In the following years the problem of proselytism continued to be the main obstacle to improved ROC-RCC relations.

Diversification of Social Action: Missionary Work, the Youth, and Human Rights

The third period of religious developments in post-Communist Russia is marked by a further strengthening of the ROC's position, an expansion of its missionary activity, and its increased influence on the Russian state and society. In 2007, the Holy Synod of the ROC promulgated the *Concept of the Missionary Activity of the Russian Orthodox Church*,[19] and in 2008 the Bishops' Council approved this document and determined that the missionary activity of the ROC is mainly aimed at those who belong to Christian Orthodoxy by baptism or family and ethnic tradition, but who are not yet churched.[20] The *Concept* outlined the forms and methods of the ROC's missionary activity on a new stage, emphasizing the crucial importance of work with the youth. To the four previously elaborated forms of missionary activity, the new *Concept* added a fifth—the mission of reconciliation with people of different faiths, nationalities, ages, and social positions. The document also distinguished between mission and proselytism, defining proselytism as

> any direct or indirect attempt to influence the religious identification of a person belonging to another denomination in order to bring this person to apostasy through some "enticement," deception or concealment of truth, the exploitation of such a person's lack of experience or knowledge, his or her poverty, and so forth. Proselytism differs from missionary work in its violation of spiritual and moral laws and norms, including human free will.[21]

Thus, proselytism is understood as a change of religious affiliation, which occurs not by free choice but through deception.

Attention to the youth and its problems, and the encouragement of young people to become more involved in the life of the church was another key development in this third period. Many church documents of the first decade of the new century contained the elements of its emerging youth policy. ROC hierarchs began to address younger audiences more frequently. In the fall of 2009, Patriarch Kirill addressed youth gatherings on numerous occasions: in Moscow, Nizny Novgorod, and Kolomna. Prior to that, he had also met with the youth in Kaliningrad, Saint-Petersburg, and elsewhere. ROC youth conferences have become regularly scheduled events. Patriarch Kirill devoted a considerable part of his report to the 2010 Bishops' Meeting to youth ministry, stressing that it was a priority of the church at every level.[22] The church was also attentive to matters of peacekeeping, social service, charitable work, strengthening the family, and the morality of the population. The state in this period was generally neutral to religion but showed special respect to traditional religions, first of all to Orthodox Christianity and Islam.

In the third period, communion with the ROC Outside Russia was restored, thus ending the major twentieth-century split in Russian Orthodoxy. The ROC also expanded its dialogue with Western Christian denominations, intensifying its interfaith dialogue on missionary activity. In 2006, the RCC and the World Council of Churches (WCC) launched a joint study project aimed at developing a shared code of conduct on the controversial issue of religious conversion.[23] This project involved several interfaith consultations, which finalized the text of a Code of Conduct on Conversion.[24] In this period, the ROC pursued joint efforts with Roman Catholics and Protestants to uphold Christian values in the secular world. The ROC's relations with the RCC, which had been rather complicated in the early 2000s, began to improve from 2006 onward, as is evident from official documents and speeches of hierarchs of both churches. Another feature of the current situation is the emphasis, not on disagreements over proselytism, but on shared interdenominational perspectives on peacekeeping, solutions to social problems, and solidarity in defending traditional Christian values and preserving Christian morality and spirituality. Thus, the ROC set aside its previous isolationism and began to stress the need for common action with Roman Catholics and Protestants.

This new orientation was evident in 2009, when Metropolitan (then archbishop) Hilarion (Alfeev), chairman of the Department for the External Relations of Moscow Patriarchate, visited Rome and met with Pope Benedict XVI: proselytism was not mentioned. Instead, they discussed the importance of bearing a common Christian witness, defending traditional Christian values in a secular world, and joint actions in the field of culture and education. Among persisting problems Hilarion mentioned only the tension between Greek Catholics and Orthodox in Western Ukraine and the necessity for the ROC and RCC to settle this long-standing conflict.

In his Report to the 2010 Episcopal Synod Patriarch Kirill, while analyzing the current state of Orthodox-Catholic relations, did not mention proselytism either. Instead, he pointed out that in the ROC's dialogue with the RCC a number of positive tendencies had been established and that Russian Orthodox and Catholic perspectives on many issues are similar (e.g., on secularization, globalization, and moral norms). Patriarch Kirill also announced that the ROC and the RCC would cooperate with the UN, UNESCO, and other international organizations.[25]

In the third period the ROC further intensified its missionary activity abroad, and over the last several years it established parishes in many non-Orthodox countries.

At the same time, the ROC now takes a more moderate view of Western Christian missionary activity in Russia. Whereas in the 1990s Protestant denominations had been typically characterized as the main competitors, the current attitude is less confrontational: it appreciates that not all Protestants were aggressive proselytizers in the 1990s, but only some of the more fundamentalist, neo-charismatic, and pseudo-Protestant ones (referring to Protestant denominations, which had drifted away significantly from Protestant teaching). It also recognizes that even in 1990s the ROC had constructive relationships with Protestants in the WCC. As hegumen Philipp (Riabykh), vice chairman of the Department for the External Relations of Moscow Patriarchate, pointed out, the ROC had carried out joint social programs with them in the 1990s, and humanitarian assistance for Russia from these organizations had been transmitted through the ROC.[26] Thus, the ROC's initial opposition to increased religious diversity was largely a defensive reaction. Once the church had strengthened its position, the issue of proselytism receded into the background, even though the perceived problem had not been resolved.

In the area of human rights, in 2006 the ROC issued the *Declaration on Human Rights and Human Dignity*,[27] and in 2008 it adopted a more detailed document—- *Foundations of the Russian Orthodox Church's Teaching on Dignity, Freedom, and Human Rights*.[28] In the early 1990s non-Orthodox denominations had defended their right to engage in missionary activities by appealing to the idea of human rights. For its part, the ROC opposed such activities, which might have appeared to be a rejection of human rights principles. The 1997 law and its approach to traditional religions were often criticized by their opponents from a human rights perspective. This may also have created the impression that the ROC was opposed to the fundamental principles of human rights. In fact, prior to 2006 the church had made no official declaration on human rights.

In his report that introduced the adoption of the *Declaration on Human Rights and Dignity*, Metropolitan Kirill (Gundyaev) stressed that the ROC deeply appreciated that the Russian legislation since 1991 had affirmed human rights and liberties as a central norm for social and political relations. Since that legislation had guaranteed the free activity of the ROC and other religious organizations, the church could not oppose the idea of human rights.[29] However, he also noted that, under the banner of human rights, falsehoods and other affronts to religious and national values could be advanced. He also declared that the complex of human rights and liberties integrates ideas that are contrary to Christian and traditional moral views on the human person. Because of this, according to Patriarch Kirill, the theme of human rights exceeds the limits of the political arena and raises questions for the religious sphere as well. This also required that the church respond to questions relating to human rights.[30]

The main idea of the *Declaration on Human Rights and Dignity* is that "a human being as an image of God has special value, which cannot be taken away."[31] Furthermore, this value must be respected by society, the state, and every person. The notion of human value is connected to the idea of human dignity: "By doing good, a person gains dignity," the Declaration states.[32] Human value or worth is understood as a given, while human dignity is something that must be attained. The ROC's concept of human dignity thus differs fundamentally from the UN Universal Declaration of Human Rights (1948), which states: "All human beings are born free and equal in dignity and rights."[33]

Proceeding from its understanding of human dignity, the Declaration states that "human rights are grounded in human value, and they should be aimed toward the realization of human dignity."[34] Consequently, the content of human rights must be strictly bound with morality. Any separation of human rights from morality would entail a profanation of human rights, the declaration affirms, since immoral dignity cannot exist.[35] The church is also attentive to religious human rights: not only the right to freely practice religion but also the right to have a religious worldview and to look at the world from the perspective of one's religious and cultural tradition. The ROC holds that human liberty should be counterbalanced by the liberty of a cultural and/or religious community, and it assigns great importance to collective human rights (i.e., the human rights of religious communities).

The ROC's elaboration of human rights was not limited to the aforementioned declaration. Over the next two years, a special group of church hierarchs, Orthodox theologians, secular researchers, and lay activists worked on the document *Foundations of the Russian Orthodox Church's Teaching on Dignity, Freedom, and Human Rights*, which was adopted at the ROC Bishops' Council in June 2008. This document further developed the main ideas of the *Declaration on Human Rights and Dignity*, in particular, the church's view of human dignity. While human dignity is an inalienable feature of human nature, it can be corrupted by sin. Hence, it is connected with human responsibility. By virtue of free will, the image of God in a human person can either be diminished or manifested more fully.[36] The document draws a distinction between freedom of choice and freedom from evil (or from sin): "While recognizing the value of free choice, the Church asserts that such freedom fatally disappears when the choice is made in favor of evil. Evil and freedom are inconsistent."[37] According to the document, when a person uses freedom to choose evil, this necessarily leads to a degradation of their own dignity and another's dignity too. Hence, society should create mechanisms to restore the harmony of human dignity and freedom. Furthermore, it is unacceptable to bring into the sphere of human rights norms that would erode or undermine both Christian and natural morality. Individual human rights can never be in opposition to the values and interests of the motherland, community, and family, and no appeal to human rights can justify any compromise of religious sanctuaries, cultural values, and distinctive character of every people.[38] In keeping with this, the Orthodox Human Rights Center was founded in 2006 to develop human rights praxis.

Concluding Remarks

In the post-Soviet period, external challenges shaped the positions of the ROC and drove it to clarify or elaborate its attitudes on many urgent issues. One characteristic of the religious situation in post-Soviet Russia was common to all of the three periods considered here. The close connection of religion and ethnicity created an apparent paradox: throughout the whole post-Soviet period the number of adherents of traditional denominations was higher than the number of believers. In affiliating themselves with the ROC and with other traditional denominations, people usually expressed not only their religious worldview but also their ethnic or national self-consciousness. Some people did not consider themselves believers at all, but associated with a denomination because of a sense of connection to historical and cultural tradition—a sort of belonging without believing. The close connection between religious, ethnic, and cultural identities can also explain some apparently inconsistent behaviors of nonbelievers. According to sociological surveys in the 1990s, up to 50 percent of nonbelievers observed religious holidays; in addition, nonbelievers attended church services and even participated in religious sacraments and rituals.[39] The cultural component of religion is readily understandable to people who were raised in a secular society. However, religious practice has also been steadily increasing in the post-Soviet period. It therefore appears that this gap between the numbers of those who associate and those who practice, or between belonging and believing, is a clear indication that the "identity dimension," tightly bound to ethnicity, is of primary importance in the Russian context. This paradox, of belonging with variable degrees of believing, or not believing, also reveals potential paths for increasing the numbers of religious believers. For its part, the ROC recognizes the special importance of the cultural dimension of religiosity. In March 2010, Patriarch Kirill said that the ROC faced the enormous task of renewing the connection of the Russian people with the Orthodox spiritual and cultural traditions, from which they had been forcibly separated.[40] And it is precisely in the cultural dimension of religion that the church sees a tool by which people can be reoriented back to religious practice. Indeed, the gap between belonging and believing is seen by the church as a principal challenge for the future.

Notes

1. Eileen Barker, "The Opium Wars of the New Millennium: Religion in Eastern Europe and the Former Soviet Union," in *Religion on the International News Agenda*, ed. Mark Silk (Hartford, CT: The Leonard E. Greenberg Center for the Study of Religion in Public Life, 2000), p. 44.
2. See, e.g.: Bryan Wilson, *Religion in Secular Society* (London: Watts, 1966), p. 14.
3. *Doklad Sviateishego Patriarkha Kirilla na Arkhiereiskom Soveshchanii 2 Fevralia 2010 Goda* [Report of His Holiness Patriarch Kirill to the Bishops Meeting on February 2, 2010]. http://www.patriarchia.ru/db/text/106151.html (accessed May 20, 2010).
4. See: Stephen White and Ian McAllister, "The Politics of Religion in Postcommunist Russia," *Religion, State & Society* 25:3 (1997), 235–252; Mikhail Tulski. "Rol' Tserkvi v Zhizni Rossiiskogo obshchestva" [The role of the church in the life of Russian society], *Nezavisimaia Gazeta* (August 9, 2000).
5. Patrick Johnstone, *Operation World* (Grand Rapids, MI: Zondervan, 1993), p. 467.
6. "Zakon Rossiiskoi Sovetskoi Federativnoi Sotsialisticheskoi Respubliki 'O Svobode Veroispovedanii'" [Law of the Russian Soviet Federated Socialist Republic "On Freedom of Beliefs"]. *Vedomosti S'iezda Narodnykh Deputatov RSFSR i Verkhovnogo Soveta RSFSR* [Official Bulletin of the Congress of Peoples' Deputies of the RSFSR], no. 21 (October 25, 1990).
7. Kirill, Metropolitan of Smolensk and Kaliningrad, "Blagovestie i Kultura" [Good news and culture], in *Pravoslavnaya Missia Segodnia* [Orthodox mission today], ed. Vladimir Fedorov (Saint-Petersburg: Apostolski Gorod, 1999), p. 36.
8. John Witte, Jr., "Introduction," in *Proselytism and Orthodoxy in Russia. The New War for Souls*, ed. John Witte, Jr. and Michael Bourdeaux (Maryknoll, NY: Orbis Books, 1999), p. 21.
9. *Doklad Sviateishego Patriarkha Moskovskogo i Vseia Rusi Arkhiereiskomu Soboru v Moskve. 18–23 Fevralia 1997 g.* [Report of His Holiness Patriarch of Moscow and All Russia to the Bishops Council in Moscow on February 18–23, 1997]. http://sedmitza.ru/index.html?sid=50&did=40&p_comment=&call_action=print1 (accessed February 20, 2005).
10. Rossiiskaia Federatsia, "Federal'nyi Zakon o Svobode Sovesti i o Religioznykh Ob'edineniakh ot 26 sentiabria 1997 g." No. 125 F3. Priniat Gosudarstvennoy Dumoi 19 sentiabria 1997 goda. Odobren Sovetom Federatsii 24 sentiabria 1997 goda. Podpisan Prezidentom RF 26 sentiabria 1997 goda. Vstupil v silu 1 oktiabria 1997 goda [Russian Federation. Federal Law on Freedom of Conscience and on Religious Associations. September 26, 1997. No 125 F3. Adopted by the State Duma on September 19, 1997. Signed by the president of the RF on September 26, 1997. Came into force on October 1, 1997] *Rossiiskaya Gazeta*, October 1, 1997.
11. Ibid., preamble.
12. "Kontseptsia Vozrozhdenia Missionerskoi Deiatel'nosti Russkoi Pravoslavnoi Tserkvi" [Concept of the rebirth of the missionary activity of the Russian Orthodox Church], in *Pravoslavnaia Missia Segodnia*, pp. 11–16.
13. "Osnovy Sotsial'noi Kontseptsii Russkoi Pravoslavnoi Tserkvi" [Bases of the social concept of the Russian Orthodox Church], *Informatsionnyi Bulleten'. Otdel Vneshnikh Tserkovnykh Sviazei Moskovskogo Patriarkhata* [Information Bulletin. Department for the External Church Relations of Moscow Patriarchate] 8 (2000), pp. 5–105.

14. *Osnovnye Printsipy Otnoshenia Russkoi Pravoslavnoi Tserkvi k Inoslaviu* [Basic Principles of the Russian Orthodox Church's Attitude toward the non-Orthodox]. www.wco.ru/biblio/books/inoslavl/Main.htm?mes (accessed December 17, 2004).
15. *Pravoslavie i Inoslavie—Prodolzhaushchiisia Dialog. Otvety Predsedatelia Otdela Vneshnikh Tserkovnykh Sviazei Mitropolita Smolenskogo i Kaliningradskogo Kirilla na Voprosy Uchastnikov Internet-konferentsii portala "Luteranstvo v Rossii"* [Orthodoxy and non-orthodoxy—the ongoing dialogue. Answers of Metropolitan Kirill of Smolensk and Kaliningrad, Chairman of the Department for External Church Relations, to the Questions from Participants in the Internet-Conference held by the "Lutheranism in Russia" portal]. www.mospat.ru/text/e_publications/icl/7651.html (accessed August 1, 2005, now defunct).
16. *Katolichestvo v Rossii. Subkultura ili Kontrkultura? Kruglyi Stol v Redaktsii Internet-portala "Religuiia i SMI." 23 Dekabria 2003 g.* [Catholicism in Russia. Subculture or counterculture? Round-table in the Editors Office of the Internet Portal "Religion and Mass-Media" on December 23, 2003]. http://www.religare/ru/analitics7799.html (accessed October 19, 2008, now defunct).
17. Ibid.
18. "Doklad Sviateishego Patriarkha Moskovskogo i Vseia Rusi Aleksiia II na Arkhiereiskom Sobore Russkoi Pravoslavnoi Tserkvi," 18 Fevralia 1997 goda. Chast 11, Mezhkonfessionalnye i Mezhreliguioznye Otnosheniia. Uchastie v Deiatelnosti Mezhdunarodnykh Khristianskikh Organizatsiy [Report of His Holiness Patriarch of Moscow and All Russia to the Bishops Council of the Russian Orthodox Church. February 18, 1997. Part 11. Interdenominational and Interreligious Relations. Participation in the Activities of the International Christian Organizations], *Zhurnal Moskovskoy Patriarkhii* 3 (1997), 59.
19. *Kontseptsia Missionerskoi Deiatel'nosti Russkoi Pravoslavnoi Tserkvi* [Concept of the Missionary Activity of the Russian Orthodox Church]. http://www.patriarchia.ru/db/text/220902.html (accessed June 10, 2008).
20. *Opredelenie Osviashchennogo Arkhiereiskogo Sobora Russkoi Pravoslavnoi Tserkvi "O Voprosakh Vnutrennei Zhizni i Vneshnei Deiatel'nosti Russkoi Pravoslavnoi Tserkvi"* [Determination of the Holy Bishops Council of the Russian Orthodox Church "On the Issues of the Internal Life and External Activity of the Russian Orthodox Church"]. http://www.mospat.ru/center.php?page=41632&newwin=1&prn=1 (accessed July 10, 2008).
21. *Kontseptsia Missionerskoi Deiatel'nosti Russkoi Pravoslavnoi Tserkvi* [Concept of the missionary activity of the Russian Orthodox Church]. http://www.patriarchia.ru/db/text/220902.html (accessed June 10, 2008).
22. *Doklad Sviateishego Patriarkha Kirilla na Arkhiereiskom Soveshchanii 2 Fevralia 2010 Goda* [Report of His Holiness Patriarch Kirill to the Bishops Meeting on February 2, 2010].
23. *Vatican and WCC to Pursue Common Code of Conduct on Religious Conversion.* http://www2.wcc-coe.org/pressreleasen.nsf/index/pr-06-12.html (accessed October 24, 2007, now defunct).
24. *Dr. Coolins Geevarghese Attends the WCC-Vatican Consultation on a Code of Conduct on Conversion.* http://www.jacobiteonline.com/index.php?option=com_content+&view=article&id (accessed March 16, 2011).
25. *Doklad Sviateishego Patriarkha Kirilla na Arkhiereiskom Soveshchanii 2 Fevralia 2010 Goda* [Report of His Holiness Patriarch Kirill to the Bishops Meeting on February 2, 2010].
26. *Otvety Zamestitelia Predsedatelia Otdela Vneshnikh Tserkovnykh Sviazei Moskovskogo Patriarkhata Igumena Filippa (Riabykh) na Voprosy Korrespondenta Agentstva "Blagovest-info" 06.26.2010* [Answers of Hegumen Filipp (Riabykh), Vice-Chairman of the Department for the External Church Relations of Moscow Patriarchate to Questions

from the Correspondent of the Blagovest-info Agency on June 26, 2010]. http://www.patriarchia.ru/db/text/1187607.html (accessed July 2, 2010).
27. Deklaratsia o Pravakh i Dostoinstve Cheloveka [Declaration on Human Rights and Dignity]. *Zhurnal Moskovskoi Patriarkhii*, 2006, no. 6, pp. 77–78.
28. *Osnovy Uchenia Russkoi Pravoslavnoi Tserkvi o Dostoinstve, Svobode i Pravakh Cheloveka* [Foundations of the Russian Orthodox Church's Teaching on Dignity, Freedom, and Human Rights]. http://www.mospat.ru/center.php?page=41597&newwin=1&pm=1 (accessed July 10, 2008).
29. *Prava Cheloveka i Nravstvennaia Otvetstvennost'. Vystuplenie Mitropolita Smolenskogo i Kaliningaradskogo Kirilla, Predsedatelia Otdela Vneshnikh Tserkovnykh Sviazei Moskovskogo Patriarkhata, na X Vsemirnom Russkom Narodnom Sobore "Vera. Chelovek. Zemlia. Missia Rossii v XX Veke" (2006)* [Human rights and moral responsibility. Speech of Kirill, Metropolitan of Smolensk and Kaliningrad to the 10th World Russian Popular Sobor "Belief. Man. Earth. Russia's Mission in the 20th Century" (2006)]. http://www.mospat.ru/center.php?page=30688&newwin=1&prn=1 (accessed January 6, 2007).
30. Ibid.
31. *Deklaratsia o Pravakh i Dostoinstve Cheloveka* [Declaration on Human Rights and Dignity], p. 77.
32. Ibid.
33. *The Universal Declaration on Human Rights. Resolution 217 A (III) of the UN General Assembly. December 10, 1948.*
34. *Deklaratsia o Pravakh i Dostoinstve Cheloveka* [Declaration on Human Rights and Dignity], p. 77.
35. Ibid.
36. *Osnovy Uchenia Russkoi Pravoslavnoi Tserkvi o Dostoinstve, Svobode i Pravakh Cheloveka* [Foundations of the Russian Orthodox Church's teaching on dignity, freedom, and human rights].
37. Ibid.
38. Ibid.
39. Mikhail Mchedlov, "O Sostoianii Religioznosti v Sovremennoi Rossii" [On the state of religiosity in contemporary Russia], in *Natsionalnoie i Religioznoie* [National and religious], ed. Mikhail Mchedlov (Moscow: Rossiiskii Nezavisimyi Institut Sotsialnykh i Natsionalnykh Problem, 1996), pp. 26–27.
40. *Interview of Patriarch Kirill for the Greek newspaper "VIMA." 05.03.2010.* http://www.patriarchia.ru/db/text/1165090.html (accessed June 28, 2010).

Part V

Prospects for Religious Encounter, Consensus, and Cooperation

15

Neopatristic Synthesis and Ecumenism: Toward the "Reintegration" of Christian Tradition

Matthew Baker

The antithesis of "West" and "East" belongs more to the polemical and publicistic phraseology than to sober historical thinking. For at least a millennium, there was one world, despite all schisms and tensions, and at that time tension between "East" and "West" was by no means stronger than certain internal tensions in the East itself.[1]

An Orthodox seminary professor once quipped sarcastically: "Orthodox theology was invented in a 1930's Paris salon." With some adjustment, this cynical remark may be regarded as expressing a certain truth. The paradigm of Orthodox theology in the modern age—its "style," the envisioning of its contemporary task—was indeed refashioned in the West, sometime around the third decade of the twentieth century. This refashioning is generally associated with the idea of "neopatristic synthesis."

It is frequently remarked that the chief architect of the neopatristic program, Fr. Georges Florovsky, never left a clear blueprint.[2] This, however, has not stopped some from concluding that Florovsky's paradigm is anti-Western in orientation.[3] Closer study, however, reveals that his program for Orthodox theological renewal was, from the start, also an *ecumenical program*, aimed at the "reintegration" of Eastern and Western traditions. This essay uncovers the ecumenical background and shape of Florovsky's idea of neopatristic synthesis, and then draws lessons from its reception by later theologians (Lossky, Zizioulas), as regards Orthodox engagement with Western theology and culture.

Georges Florovsky (1893–1979)

Florovsky's ecumenical interests had their roots in his earliest thought. Having begun reading church history while yet a schoolboy, by 1909 or 1910 he had discovered the works of Vladimir Soloviev. In his first, adolescent publications, Florovsky defended Soloviev as a genuine voice of Orthodox catholicity, defining the task of thought in

Solovievian terms as "a genuine synthesis" of "faith and understanding."[4] While Florovsky would severely revise this judgment by the early 1920s, distinguishing his own conception of "synthesis" sharply from Soloviev's "synthesis of all-unity," something of Soloviev's ecumenical passion remained with him.[5] In particular, Soloviev's stress on *universal* Christian values as a source of culture, over against every religious nationalism,[6] may be heard echoing in Florovsky's engagement with the Eurasian movement.

The Eurasians were an eclectic group of Russian emigré intellectuals, formed in the early 1920s in Sofia under the leadership of Nikolai Trubetskoi, Peter Suvchinskiy, and Peter Savitsky. Eurasianianism was a theory of cultural autonomy and anti-Europeanization. For the Eurasians, Orthodox Russia and the non-Christian peoples of Central Asia stood together as a unique cultural type, over against the civilization of Germano-Latin West Europe. Borrowing a scheme from Nikolai Danilevsky's work *Rossiia i Evropa* (1869), Trubetskoi maintained a theory of cultural morphology according to which the multiethnic civilizations of Russian Eurasia and Western Europe were radically incommensurable. Under the impact of Oswald Spengler's *Der Untergang des Abendlandes* (1918–1923), some Eurasian thinkers, most notably Lev Karsavin, further developed the notion that each cultural type possesses the closed unity of a distinct organism, unfolding in history according to its own immanent developmental laws. Any cross-civilizational hybridization here could only be a kind of organic aberration: to use a Spenglerian term that Florovsky would also employ—yet in a very different sense, a *pseudomorphosis*. For the Eurasians, it was precisely such a pseudomorphosis of Russian culture under the impact of Western rationalism that had brought about the revolution.[7]

Florovsky's Eurasian association has occasionally been used to bolster the charge of "anti-Westernism."[8] In fact, from his earliest contributions, Florovsky can be seen critiquing the cultural morphology, geographical determinism, and identity politics that would soon become known as fundamental pillars of Eurasian ideology. This has led one recent Russian scholar to dub him "the most un-Eurasian Eurasian."[9] In his essays in the three Eurasian anthologies, *Iskhod k vostoku* (1921), *Na putyakh* (1922), and *Rossiia i latinstvo* (1923), Florovsky did excoriate the rationalism of modern Western *philosophes* as a cause of European cultural crisis,[10] and also reserved strong words against the Roman papacy.[11] In the same context, however, he rejected Danilevsky's concept of organic cultural types as a form of empiricist reductionism, a theory of culture based not on the revelation of the highest spiritual values, but on nationalism. Also censured was Trubetskoi's cultural relativism[12]: true, Florovsky argues, even Scripture speaks the language of its time and place; yet what makes its message transcendent is the expression of *universal* values. Cultural rebirth must begin, not with national tradition, but with the promise of Christ, who has conquered the world.[13] Already in this early phase, one finds the first distinct formulation of what would become his later concept of neopatristic synthesis: the principles of cultural rebirth, Florovsky insists to his fellow emigres, must be provided through a new philosophical synthesis of Orthodox patristics and Western learning.[14]

Florovsky broke with the Eurasians in August 1923—in his own words, "sickened" by their "spirit of intolerance" and "political intrigue."[15] In a 1928 essay, he attacked, as a form of fatalistic determinism, the Eurasian concept of the nation as an independent "cultural personality" (*kulturolichnost*) endowed from eternity with particular inclinations and systems, revealed organically in successive incarnations, each equally natural and necessary. To Florovsky, this was a departure from the Christian philosophy of history, for which culture should be understood as revealing a people's free inner spiritual life—a "morphology" for which people are creatively *responsible*. The Eurasians were consumed by problems of morphological "type." In contrast, a philosophy of history marked by genuine "Christocentricism," he argued, encourages a "sensitive responsiveness to authentic historical dynamics…not only of the organic gyre, but also creativity and sinful decay."[16]

These criticisms lead Florovsky right away to ecumenical conclusions.[17] The Eurasians did recognize valuable aspects of Christianity in the West. Yet in keeping with their conception of national culture as a closed organism, they regarded such aspects as "'alien to the Orthodox people and capable of being disclosed only to Roman-Germanic peoples,' and vital only for them." Florovsky charged:

> In their unbrotherly alienation, the Eurasians do not see, do not feel or hear the living, searching and suffering of Western people, who may be blind and even spiteful, but have nevertheless already touched the robe of Christ, and have already been anointed by His grace…There is in Eurasianism no sense of active and concrete religious and historical joint responsibility, no feeling of accountability for the truth of Orthodoxy that has been entrusted to Russia. Heresy and schism evoke in them disgust, anger and hatred, instead of compassion, pain, and the love which endures all things. They are content with a dry and self-satisfied demand for "repentance"…Russia is not Europe, says Danilevsky, and the Eurasians repeat it. Let us assume that this is so. Yes, Russia is not Europe, *but by what criterion* is it "not Europe"? In the Eurasian definition, geographic, ethnic, social, religious motifs are mixed, without a clear consciousness of their heterogeneity. Geographically and biologically, it is not so difficult to draw the western border of Russia, and perhaps even to build a wall on it. It is hardly so easy to separate Russia and Europe in terms of spiritual and historical dynamics; and it is hardly necessary. It is necessary to keep this firmly in mind: the name of Christ connects Russia and Europe, no matter how distorted and even profaned it may be in the West. There is a deep and enduring religious fissure between Russia and the West, but this does not negate their inner mystical and metaphysical bond and their mutual Christian responsibility. Russia, as the living successor to Byzantium, will remain the Orthodox East to the non-Orthodox but Christian West, *within a shared cultural and historical cycle*.[18]

The author who wrote these words had already had much experience of Western Christians. In 1926, Florovsky moved to Paris, taking up the chair of patrology at the Institut St.-Serge. Almost immediately, he joined Berdyaev's ecumenical colloquium, gathering weekly with such figures as Maritain, Gilson, and Gabriel Marcel; it was in this context that his earliest dogmatic papers (on creation and atonement) were first heard. Florovsky's work during this period shows an increasing engagement with Roman Catholic patristic scholarship: J. A. Möhler, Odo Casel, Maurice de la Taille, and, by the 1930s, Émile Mersch, all of whom were to exercise a decisive influence on his thought.[19]

Even more prominent was his involvement with Anglicans. From 1929 until World War II, Florovsky was highly active in the Anglo-Orthodox Fellowship of St. Alban and St. Sergius. Almost all his ecclesiological papers from this period were written for that context. An arrangement with St.-Serge allowed him to spend roughly five months a year in Britain throughout the 1930s, lecturing at theological colleges; during this time, he interacted closely with such important young Anglican theologians as Derwas Chitty, Eric Mascall, and Michael Ramsey.[20] It is important to recognize the ecumenical appeal that patristics enjoyed in this time and context, most especially with Anglicans. As Florovsky explained later, patristics provided him

> with access to non-Russian circles, because you can always intrigue the Westerners by presenting them with something peculiar, that is, *Russian*, but you can never join with Westerners unless you display an understanding of the Western tradition and are able to coordinate... I was interested when I was talking to Anglican students—I was interested to know what they are, and what is their background, and what they are searching. And this was emphasized—I got their heart because I offered them my own heart... not only as if coming from the True Church to preach to heretics—I never took this position, even if I had some doubts about the Church of England, canonical and others, but still—they were Christian and they were open,—they wanted to talk to me, etc.... Patristics was one of the links.[21]

These ecumenical connections extended also to Reformed Christians (in the "Scoto-Russian Fellowship of St. Andrew") and, beginning in 1937, to the Faith and Order Movement, at which time Florovsky was elected to the "Committee of Fourteen" charged with preparing the constitution of the World Council of Churches (WCC).[22]

It was in the midst of this ecumenical activity that Florovsky began to articulate his neopatristic paradigm. At the same time, however, he developed two other closely connected concepts: "Christian Hellenism" and the "pseudomorphosis" of post-Byzantine Orthodox theology. These ideas require some consideration here before passing on to neopatristic synthesis proper, if only because misunderstandings of them have contributed to misconceptions regarding the neopatristic synthesis.

Christian Hellenism

Florovsky's concept of Christian Hellenism was first developed within the distinct philosophical context of the "crisis" of German Idealism, a crisis he recognized as having worldwide import.[23] In Florovsky's view, to "philosophize about God" was no spiritual aberration or mere supererogatory work, but an essential moment in the Christian calling. No wonder, then, he argued, that the project of Idealist metaphysics arose in a Protestant milieu: in the vacuum created by the Reformation's rejection of medieval scholasticism—a rejection that had led to the repudiation of the project of Christian philosophy itself. In his view, however, German Idealism represented an atavism of pagan Hellenistic metaphysics, which failed to grasp the essential Christian doctrine of creation ex nihilo. His "Christian Hellenism" was coined in response to this diagnosis of Idealism, but also as a corrective to the fideism of anti-Idealist reaction he perceived in the philosophy of Lev Shestov and the "dialectical" theology of the early Barth and Emil Brunner. The "crisis" of Idealism had returned thought to the "crisis" of the Reformation. Though in conversation with Maritain and even sympathetic with Gilson, Florovsky tended to regard Thomism as an insufficient "baptism" of Aristotle. His appeal to the Christian Hellenism of the Fathers, then, was an affirmation of Christian *philosophy*, but one in which reason is converted and refounded upon the mysteries of revelation: an exercise in *fides quaerens intellectum*.[24]

This defense of Christian Hellenism was at the same time a defense of dogmatics,[25] understood not only in the sense of conciliar dogmas, but also that of the philosophical "systems" or doctrinal "synthesis" given in the fathers' explanation of these dogmas. Here Florovsky can be seen countering Harnack's critique of dogma as an "acute Hellenization" of the original Gospel,[26] as well as the attempt of Russian religious renaissance figures such as Bulgakov, Florensky, and Berdyaev to reinterpret the dogmas within the categories of modern Idealist philosophy. Although Florovsky stressed repeatedly the necessity of "creative" return to the fathers—*neo*-patristic synthesis—his work in the mid-1930s resounds with a note of sharp criticism for those who would search for a "new synthesis," while disregarding the already built-up philosophical synthesis inherent in the centuries of church tradition: in his view, patristic *dogma* could not be so easily disentangled from patristic *philosophy* or *doctrine*.[27] In his unique brand of Christian historicism, those fruits of intellectual creativity in theology accepted by the church throughout the centuries accumulate, solidify, and form a growing "body"—a synthesis—that any further creative synthesis must recapitulate and build upon, in an existential and hermeneutical way.

Florovsky's concept of Christian Hellenism has been criticized for equating patristic tradition with "Byzantinism," leaving no place for Latin or Oriental patristic thought.[28] The lack of attention to Latin fathers in his two patrological volumes is cited in evidence of this alleged cultural chauvinism. In fact, Florovsky's letters attest to his intention to complete this patrological work with a volume on the Latin fathers,[29] and his essays are peppered with references to Saints Cyprian, Vincent of Lérins, Hilary of Poitiers, and Augustine. Indeed, Augustine is the main patristic source for his ecclesiology,[30] a reliance especially attested by—though by no means limited to—his appeal to appropriate Augustine's views regarding the reality of sacraments in schismatic bodies outside the canonical boundaries of the church.[31] In Florovsky's words, "Augustine is a Father of the Church Universal, and we must take his testimony into account, if we are to attempt a true ecumenical synthesis."[32]

Florovsky's profound veneration for St. Augustine is unusual for a modern Orthodox theologian. In "The Vocation of the Orthodox in the Modern World," an unpublished lecture from the 1950s, he quoted St. Photius for the view that Augustine was "the greatest saint God ever gave his Church." In another unpublished lecture given at Fordham University in 1967, he called Augustine "the greatest Father of the Western church, and indeed of the Church Universal."[33] Far from being some kind of Eastern cultural chauvinism, then, Christian Hellenism in Florovsky's view "was never a peculiarly Eastern phenomenon." According to him, "The Fathers, both Greek and Latin, were interpreting the Apostolic message, the original Good News, in Greek categories."[34] In other places, he will include also Thomas Aquinas and Cardinal Newman as examples of this tradition of Christian Hellenism.

Ironically, while the Orthodox reception of Florovsky has typically failed to recognize this ecumenical character of Florovsky's idea of Hellenism,[35] Roman Catholic commentators have seen it clearly. As Dom Emmanuel Lanne observed in 1962, Christian Hellenism in Florovsky's understanding

> consists in the rediscovery of the "phronema" of the Fathers, and all the Fathers together in the widest possible sense. It explicitly includes Latin patristics and in particular St. Augustine whom the author frequently cites, and extends even up to the scholastics... This Christian Hellenism positively excludes an ethnic Hellenism and all manner of phyletism...If on this last point it has been too slowly and poorly understood, this is because of the ever-current tendencies of certain Orthodox theologians...We tend to think, however, that Florovsky has been misunderstood... To oppose Christian Hellenism to the religious culture of the West, as certain Orthodox appear to do today, seems to me artificial; it is to raise a false problem which disappears if one has grasped well what Father Florovsky understands by Christian Hellenism.[36]

Similarly, Jean Daniélou cites the "great orthodox theologian Florovsky" in support of his own view regarding the "persistent Hellenism of the Church." This Hellenism "belongs to the whole *catholica*": "The cultural divergence between the Eastern and Western Churches, which eventually led to doctrinal schism, need never have happened if the matter had been rightly understood." Like Florovsky, Daniélou asserts that the expression of true catholicity brings the requirement "to re-awaken the spirit of Hellenism in the heart of the Roman church."[37]

If this essentially catholic character of Florovsky's concept of Christian Hellenism can be seen to include Latin patristics, the same is true, granting the limitations of the scholarship of his time, for Syriac or other Oriental patristics—as witnessed in his inclusion of Ephrem the Syrian and Aphrahat in his patrologies. It must be recognized, too, that the existence of any purely Semitic patristic tradition, independent of Greek sources, is so doubtful as to be something of a scholarly pipe dream.[38] For Florovsky, the watershed in the formation of Christian Hellenism was the translation of the "Semitic" Gospel in the New Testament itself,[39] followed by its interpretation in the language of ecumenical councils common to classical Christendom—Greek, Latin, and Oriental. There is no reason why Florovsky's theological program cannot be expanded to encompass the fruits of the more recent explosion of Oriental patristic studies, provided these be appropriated in a catholic manner.

Pseudomorphosis

The interpretive problem surrounding Christian Hellenism is replicated with Florovsky's notion of the Westernizing "pseudomorphosis" of post-Byzantine Orthodox theology. F. J. Thomson glosses this idea as meaning that Florovsky allots "simply no role for the Western Latin part of the Church."[40] Similarly, Lutheran theologian Dorothea Wendebourg treats the theory of pseudomorphosis as essentially antiecumenical: in her view, it means that what was "wrong" with the post-Byzantine Orthodox theology was that "the East began to consider questions which were not its own—new, alien questions posed by the West, which did not develop naturally in the context of eastern Orthodox life." Correspondingly, Wendebourg suggests, Florovsky's neopatristic solution to this pseudomorphosis means that the East "must ask its own questions again and give its own answers. Or rather, it need not ask and answer questions at all." It is Wendebourg's conclusion that Florovsky's scheme makes "genuine dialogue . . . impossible": "it is hardly possible to take another's questions seriously when it has been previously established that these questions should never have been asked in the first place."[41]

"Pseudomorphosis" is a mineralogical term, describing a process by which a compound appears in an untypical form, in which its original dimensions remain constant while its form is replaced with the properties of another mineral. Oswald Spengler had used this term to refer to a process in which a nascent or half-developed culture is overtaken by the influence of an established foreign one, such that the undeveloped culture is not allowed to flourish creatively, but instead takes on the forms of the foreign culture and is crippled by them. Both Spengler and the Eurasians pointed to the Westernizing reforms of Czar Peter I (1672–1725) as the key moment in Russia's cultural pseudomorphosis.[42] Finally, in his *Ways of Russian Theology* (1937) and in several other essays, Florovsky famously applied this metaphor to the development of post-Byzantine Russian theology, the emblematic figure being the Latinizing Metropolitan of Kiev, Peter Moghila (1596–1646).

In keeping with his conviction that "'historical morphology' is a cheap substitute for theological analysis,"[43] however, the Spenglerian-Eurasian concept of pseudomorphosis is significantly changed in Florovsky's handling. As even Thomson admits, the "organism" that is the object of pseudomorphosis here is *not* Russian or Eastern *culture*, but precisely the *church.*[44] Unlike the Eurasians, Florovsky never doubted Russia's need to turn westward to overcome its own cultural isolation.[45] Moreover, in his view, the theological pseudomorphosis resulting from this westward turn was finally, in spite of all difficulties, "nevertheless a *sickness unto life and unto growth* and not a sickness unto death or degeneration"[46]: encounter with Western philosophy and historical methods ultimately helped Russian theologians in the nineteenth century to begin to recover from their isolation and imitation and to raise the question of Orthodoxy's unique inheritance and vocation in the ecumenical Christian world. "Pseudomorphosis" in Florovsky, then, signifies chiefly two things: (1) the alienation of "school" theology from the worshipping life of the church, with consequent loss of "existential" character; and (2) uncreative and "servile imitation" of foreign sources, making the constructive development of theology necessary for dialogue with the West on equal footing and on a truly Orthodox basis impossible.[47]

Ecumenically speaking, what was problematic about this pseudomorphosis of Russian theology was that it did not allow a genuine encounter between Orthodoxy and the West.[48] In Florovsky's view, the older anti-Western polemical theology was itself a pseudomorphic fruit.[49] Florovsky's response to this pseudomorphosis is not a walling-off, but rather, as he puts it, "a prayerful entry into the Church, an apocalyptical fidelity, a return to the fathers, a free encounter with the West."[50] As he poses the dilemma: "Is 'pseudomorphosis' and imitation the only possible form of meeting or the most natural one? The true meeting will only take place when the common ground is discovered."[51]

Too many readers have overlooked the way in which the sharp critical judgments regarding Western influence in *Ways of Russian Theology* issue out finally in the last chapter onto a rousing ecumenical imperative. *Pace* Wendebourg, it is *precisely* "Western questions" that Florovsky insists Orthodox theology today must grapple with, in faithful, sympathetic, and creative manner:

> It is not enough merely to repeat answers previously formulated in the West—the western questions must be discerned and relived. Russian theology must confidently penetrate the entire complex problematics of western religious thought and spirituality and trace and examine the difficult and bewildering path of the West from the time of the Great schism. Access to the inner creative life comes only through its problematics, and one must therefore sympathize with that life and experience it precisely in its full problematicality, searching, and anxiety... Only such compassionate co-experience provides a reliable path towards the reunification of the fractured Christian world and the embrace and recovery of departed brothers. It is not enough to refute or reject western errors or mistakes—they must be overcome and surpassed through a new creative act... Orthodox theology has been called upon to answer Western questions from the depths of its unbroken and catholic experience and to confront Western non-Orthodoxy not with accusations but with testimony: with the truth of Orthodoxy.[52]

Florovsky's critique of Russian theological "pseudomorphosis," then, is motivated in part by a concern for faithful and constructive ecumenical encounter with Western Christianity. And it must be noted also: while there is in *Ways* much criticism of Latin influence, it is aimed almost entirely, not at Latin patristics or even medieval scholasticism, but rather at Baroque-era, neoscholastic manual theology and its Russian imitations. Tellingly, the closest thing to the phrase "neo-patristic synthesis" occurring in *Ways of Russian Theology* comes in the last chapter, precisely in the context of stressing the need for the "newly sought Orthodox synthesis" to engage the thought of classical Latin scholasticism.[53] As Christoph Künkel interprets, Florovsky's program of "synthesis" suggests that "to encounter and appeal to the West, the Orthodox must either develop a theology corresponding to the complexity of western scholasticism, or else limit themselves in an archeological fashion to return to the patristic statements."[54] His answer to "pseudomorphosis" is therefore not monologic isolation, but a synthesis involving free dialogical engagement,[55] on the basis of the common patristic tradition of East and West, which Orthodoxy especially claims as her own.

Neopatristic Synthesis

The exact phrase, "neopatristic synthesis," does not occur in Florovsky's published writings until 1947. It first appeared in published form in an obscure Swedish-language essay,[56] the resumé of a planned book on the patristic doctrine of the atonement, drawn from his 1936 lectures on this theme at the University of London. The unpublished preface to this book, however, dated 1939, indicates that he was using the phrase already in the late 1930s, and in specifically ecumenical context.[57] Yet the terminology of neopatristic synthesis really belongs to Florovsky's later career, after he had moved to America and had become intensely involved in the WCC. The first really significant published use of the phrase appears in "The Legacy and Task of Orthodox Theology," his commencement address offered at St. Vladimir's Seminary in 1948, just a month after he had spoken at the First Assembly of the WCC in Amsterdam (August–September 1948).

In "The Legacy and Task of Orthodox Theology," the idea of neopatristic synthesis is introduced in a thoroughly ecumenical sense and context. The full passage must be quoted:

> The contemporary Orthodox theologian...cannot retire solely into a narrow shell of some local tradition—simply because his Orthodox, i.e. the Patristic, tradition is not a local one, but basically an ecumenical one. And he has to use all his skill to phrase this ecumenical message of the Fathers in such a way as to secure an ecumenical, universal appeal. This obviously cannot be achieved by any servile appeal to the Patristic letter, as it cannot be achieved by a Biblical fundamentalism. But servility is alien to the Bible and to the Fathers. They were themselves bold and courageous and adventurous seekers of the Divine truth. To walk truly in their steps means to break new ways, only in the same field as was theirs. No renewal is possible without a return to the sources. But it must be a return to the sources, and not simply a retirement into a library or museum of venerable and respectable, but outlived relics...The true theology can spring only out of a deep liturgical experience...Orthodox theology has, in recent decades, been speedily recovering from the unhappy "pseudomorphosis," by which it was paralyzed for rather too long. But to regain once more its own Eastern style and temper must mean for the Orthodox theology no detachment from the rest of the Christian world. What was to be rejected in the Westernizing school of Orthodox theology is its blind subservience to the foreign traditions of the school, and not its response to the challenge of other traditions, and not the fraternal appreciation of what has been achieved by the others. All reaches of

> the Orthodox tradition can be disclosed and consummated only in a standing intercourse with the whole of the Christian world. The East must meet and face the challenge of the West, and the West perhaps has to pay more attention to the legacy of the East, which after all was always meant to be an ecumenical and catholic message. We are perhaps on the eve of a new synthesis in theology—of a *neopatristic synthesis*, I would suggest. Theological tradition must be reintegrated, not simply summed up or accumulated. This seems to be one of the immediate objectives of the Church in our age. It seems to be the secure start for the healing of Christian desruption [*sic*]. An ecumenical cooperation in theology is already a fact; Roman Catholic and Protestant scholars are already working together in many directions. The Orthodox have to join in.[58]

Many themes come together here: return to the ecumenical theology of the fathers; creative freedom; the need to ground theology in liturgical experience; recovery from the "blind subservience" of pseudomophosis. What is most clear, however, is that neopatristic synthesis is, for Florovsky, *not only* an agenda for internal theological renewal within the Orthodox Church (though it is also, and equally, that), but *also* an ecumenical program: one that both grows out of concern for Christian unity and is ordered toward it. It is to be a work of cooperation, encounter, and mutual discernment between Orthodox, Roman Catholic, and Protestant scholars, aimed at the "reintegration" of Christian tradition, a work in which—Florovsky is convinced—Orthodox theology has a unique and critical role to play.

Florovsky uses the precise phrase "neopatristic synthesis" only very rarely in his published writings. It is thus highly significant that in two of his most prominent explicit discussions of this theme, both in "Legacy and Task" (1949) and in "Patristic Theology and the Ethos of the Orthodox Church" (1960), the idea appears together with a critique of the historiography of Arnold Toynbee. Florovsky regarded Toynbee as "an extremely dangerous man" and "a bad influence on historians" for his conception of Eastern and Western Christendom as two separate "intelligible fields of research."[59] Significantly, he connected Toynbee's idea of closed and "self-explanatory" worlds with Nikolai Danilevsky's *Rossiia i Evropa*—a key source for Eurasianism—and with the thought of Lev Karsavin, the chief Eurasian theorist after 1923.[60] The same critique of cultural morphology evident in Florovsky's work of the 1920s is heard again in his critique of Toynbee:

> The theory of independent "Christian societies" is a historical fiction, a sinful and dangerous fiction. Christendom is indeed divided. Yet the divided parts still belong together, since they are just "parts" and "fragments." Accordingly, they are intelligible only when taken together, in the context and against the background of the original Christian unity which had been broken. The recovery of the comprehensive Christian vision, of common Christian perspective, is by no means an easy task after so many centuries of estrangement and tension. But it is an impending task. The inveterate illusion of self-sufficiency must be broken down. It is the absolute prerequisite of any ecumenical encounter.[61]

Empirically speaking, then, "both East and West," Florovsky holds, "are incomplete." Their shared root and still-existing ties lead to the "*ecumenical idea*": "The task of Reunion is imposed on both by the inner logic of Christian history."[62] For Florovsky, this "logic" reflects the will of the Lord and Founder of the Church, and provides the basic imperative to work for the full concrete unity of Christians.

The basic ecumenical problem, in Florovsky's view, is that of *schism*. However, the reality of formal schism was prepared and then worsened by a long process of "progressive disintegration of the Christian mind."[63] This disintegration began with the loss of familiarity with the Greek fathers in the West, and the eventual equation of "Patristic" with "Augustinian." But conversely, "the rise of Latin-thinking Christianity in the West has been overlooked, or perhaps contemptuously ignored, in the East," which "took little notice of the rising 'Latin Christianity' and did not care for translations." There was "an inability, on both sides of the cultural schism, to ascertain even the existing agreements and the tendency to exaggerate all the distinctive marks."[64] Speaking of Lev Zander's idea that Eastern and Western Christianities represent different cultural-psychological "types" with differering blocs of insights into Christian faith—a kind of "liberal" variation on Eurasian morphology—Florovsky writes:

> We should not, however, overlook the fact that these different "blocs" of insights and convictions did actually grow out of a common ground and were, in fact, products of a *disintegration of mind.* Accordingly, the very problem of Christian reconciliation is not that of a *correlation* of parallel traditions, but precisely that of the *reintegration* of a distorted tradition. The two traditions may seem quite irreconcilable, when they are compared and confronted as they are at the present. Yet their differences are, to a great extent, simply the results of disintegration: they are, as it were, *distinctions* stiffened into *contradictions.* The East and the West can meet and find each other only if they remember their original kinship in the *common past.*[65]

"Reintegration of mind" is then what is required: not "just a toleration of the existing varieties or particular views." Rather, "the real reintegration of Christian tradition should be sought in a neo-patristic synthesis." But such "synthesis" can never be "achieved simply by arithmetical operation, either by subtraction of all distinction or by addition of all differences."[66] In some cases, it could be the "rediscovery of the consensus that was obscured by the use of discordant phraseologies,"[67] as in the reconciliation of "Old Nicenes" and "Homoiousians" at the Council of Alexandria in 362 under St. Athanasius. In other cases, however, as, for example, between "Nicenes" and "Arians," this would not be possible: some traditions are "purely negative and polemical," and "cannot be summed up as they are," but "must be reshaped and remolded to become fit for reintegration."

"The true synthesis," then, "presumes a discrimination."[68] Not every viewpoint can be reconciled. And Florovsky was adamant that the starting point of synthesis would have to be classical Orthodox Christology.[69] Theological reconciliation cannot be a kind of Hegelian *Aufhebung* in which, as for Soloviev's synthesis, "disruption and alienation, and all antagonisms and divergences, belong organically to the dialectics of integration."[70] Rather, we must "reintegrate our bits of the distorted Christian tradition into a new synthesis, which will at the same time be a recovery of the common mind of the Church of old," in which "there was no uniformity, but there was a common mind."[71]

Florovsky was clear that dogmatic divergences undoubtedly separate East and West. An opposition to easy doctrinal minimalism and ecumenical pragmatism characterizes all his work. He was firm in expressing that the Orthodox Church "*is* in very truth *the Church,* i.e. *the true* Church and the *only* true Church." However, he also stipulated, "the *true* church is not yet the *perfect* Church."[72] And there are also "many bonds still not broken, whereby the schisms are held together in a certain unity"—namely, "right belief, sincere devotion, the Word of God, and above all the Grace of God, 'which ever heals the weak and supplies what is lacking.'"[73] Separation from Orthodox faith and order constitutes a spiritual malady; yet there exists an imperfect, but still real and "objective"—not merely "subjective"—unity among Christians, in that the confession of faith in Christ as God and Savior establishes "a certain ontological circle which separates those inside it from the dark outside world, from all that is estranged from the Cross and that does not receive Christ the Lord and Savior at all."[74]

Further, Orthodoxy includes more than the present empirical "East": it is also the Church of Saints Augustine, Hilary, Ambrose, and so on. The body of Christ is one, and undivided. Yet, *culturally*, as regards the Christian *world*, the East too, as divided from the Christian West, is "incomplete" and a "fragment." Orthodox theologians also "had themselves to re-learn the dialects of the Fathers in recent times." And not only Westerners, but also Easterners "overemphasize and exaggerate" their peculiarity, acting as representatives of one local tradition alone.[75] Thus, the need "to create a true ecumenical and common language in theology and possibly to un-learn our party idioms."[76] It was Florovsky's belief that the basis for the creation of such a language was to be found in a joint constructive return to the fathers of both East and West—"not merely as historical documents... but as living masters from whom we may receive the message of life and truth."[77]

This program entails a unique method of dialogue, which Florovsky calls "ecumenism in time." Assessing his own contributions to theology in a 1973 letter to the Scots Reformed theologian T. F. Torrance, he wrote: "Personally I would underline two basic ideas: Ecumenism in time and the Neo-Patristic Synthesis, which are obviously correlated."[78] "Ecumenism in time" was formulated in critical counterpoint to "ecumenism in space." Whereas ecumenism in space aims at agreement between denominations as they exist at present, ecumenism in time searches the past for a common background in apostolic tradition, seeking "agreement with all ages" as "one of the normative prerequisites of unity." What is envisaged here is "no static restoration of old forms" or "rigid uniformity," "but rather a dynamic recovery of the perennial ethos," a catholicity in time, which allows for different manners of legitimate expression.[79] In Florovsky's view, this ecumenical method is especially fitted to the modern context, a major predicament of which is *provincialism in time*: an imprisonment in one's own epoch, a practical isolation from the wisdom and insight of ages past.

One final related point must be stressed here. It has now become fashionable among some Orthodox academics to charge Florovsky with encouraging "patristic fundamentalism"—a sterile and uncreative repetition of patristic texts. If this is so, it is only because his theology has not been read in tandem with his work in epistemology and historiography. Florovsky's sophisticated treatment of interpretation, sensitive to the contributions of such figures as Dilthey, Croce, Collingwood, and Marc Bloch, places him in many ways in relation to the modern continental tradition of philosophical hermeneutics. His affirmation of the dictum of F. A. Trendelenburg that "all understanding is interpretation" means for him that any living appropriation of tradition must be, by definition, creative and new.[80] In his usage, "reintegration" or "integration of mind" is not only an ecumenical method, but also a historical-hermeneutical task, in which the contributions of past thought must be continually "melted" together into a single interpreted whole of understanding, which is always present, and which will remain open-ended and provisional so long as history continues.[81] As he wrote in his later years:

> "The Neo-patristic synthesis"... should be more than just a collection of Patristic sayings or statements. It must be a *synthesis*, a creative reassessment of those insights which were

> granted to the Holy Men of old. It must be *Patristic,* faithful to the spirit and vision of the Fathers, *ad mentem Patrum*. Yet, it must also *Neo*-Patristic, since it is to be addressed to the new age, with its own problems and queries.[82]

Apart from a handful of dogmatic essays, Florovsky cannot be said to have produced such a synthesis himself—nor did he claim to have done so. He was a seminal thinker, writing programmatic essays, redirecting the course of Orthodox theology. Even the *aporiae* of his sentences are suggestive. A thorough study of his corpus discovers that many of his positive insights still have not been thoroughly mined and pursued by subsequent Orthodox theologians. It is certainly true that some have taken the formulas of "neopatristic synthesis," together with its related notions of "pseudomorphosis" and "Christian Hellenism," apart from their original sense, as slogans to be developed in distinctly antiecumenical directions. What is demonstrably false, however, is the claim that Florovsky's paradigm of neopatristic synthesis was a form of "anti-western polemicism towards the 'West' in an assertion of 'Eastern' Orthodox identity"—"an assertion of a particular ecclesial identity through a polemic against all that is different and alien to that identity."[83] The precise opposite would be even closer to the truth.

Neopatristic *Nachleben*: Developments and Challenges

Among the many theologians impacted by Florovsky, two figures stand out as most influential as regards the development of neopatristic synthesis and its ecumenical dimensions.

Although he never employed the phrase in his own work, Vladimir Lossky (1903–1958) was the first to produce, in Florovsky's own admiring estimation, "what can be described as a 'neo-patristic synthesis.'"[84] Lossky's *Essai sur la théologie mystique de l'Église d'Orient* (1944) had the advantage of having been written in French, providing a kind of one volume *dogmatica minora* at a time when very few books by modern Orthodox theologians were available in Western languages. It is partly for this reason that, as Rowan Williams observes, "Lossky remains probably the best known and most influential of all modern Orthodox writers."[85] It is Lossky's theology, more than any other, that has come to define received perceptions and developments of the theology of neopatristic synthesis.

Lossky's dogmatic synthesis depends heavily on work done by Florovsky in his essays on creation in the late 1920s.[86] At the same time, Lossky shows far greater Trinitarian speculation—ironically, given the youthful Lossky's fierce and public criticisms of Bulgakov's sophiology, some of it showing a significant influence from the thought of Pavel Florensky. The center of gravity in Lossky's reading of the tradition is also different: the focus is shifted away from classical Christology, and toward medieval debates regarding grace and the knowledge of God. Less historically minded and more rigidly apophatic than Florovsky, it was Lossky who made the essence/energies distinction the architectonic principle structuring his entire theology, thereby solidifying the later identification of neopatristic synthesis with so-called neo-Palamism.

Florovsky's perceptive comments on Lossky's theology in several essays as well as in his letters to Archimandrite Sophrony Sakharov form an extremely suggestive, and ecumenically significant, basis for a critique of "the ways of neo-patristic synthesis." While generally positive, Florovsky reserved strong criticisms for several aspects of Lossky's work: Lossky's insufficient Christocentrism and his division of ecclesiology into two "economies" of the Son and the Spirit; his one-sided apophaticism, low appraisal of the place of intellect and reason in theology and easy dismissal of Thomistic notions of analogy; and, finally, his treatment of Augustine's triadology and his separation of Christian East and West into two independent and irreconcilable blocs, even centuries before the schism.[87]

These problems are all connected at a deep level, and have to do in part with Lossky's particular Russian sources. Florovsky detected the influence of Florensky in Lossky's treatment of the Trinity as an "antinomy" for reason,[88] and saw Lossky's weak Christocentrism as a sign of his having succumbed in part to the "sea" of Russian religious renaissance thought.[89] The place once occupied by "Sophia" is now taken by the Holy Spirit or the divine energies; yet both remain still insufficiently integrated into a Christocentric framework. Florensky's oddly Joachimite-like pneumatology is palpable in Lossky's treatment of the Church and eschatology.[90] Yet these same motifs are equally tied to Lossky's fierce critique of the Latin *filioque*, and his concern to resist, in a strict and consistent way, any taint of "filioquism" throughout his theology. For Lossky, the *filioque* represents the height of Western rationalism: "the God of the philosophers and savants is introduced into the heart of the living God, taking the place of the *Deus absconditus.*" As such, it is "the sole dogmatic grounds for the separation of East and West," upon which all other issues depend.[91]

Lossky's treatment of the *filioque* brings us back to the problems of Eurasianism. In the early 1920s, Lossky studied in St. Petersburg under the guidance of the Russo-Polish medievalist and sometime Eurasian publicist Lev Karsavin. Karsavin's work *Lessons of the Repudiated Faith* (*Uroki otrechennoi very*, 1925) attempted to derive papal infallibility and "the entire system of Roman Catholicism, directly and one-sidedly, from one particular doctrine, the doctrine of the *filioque*." Florovsky criticizes the "excessive constructivism" of Karsavin's method: in the "implicit assumption of 'massive opposition' between East and West," there is "no desire for 'comprehension'"—only "distinctions, antitheses." He writes: "We get a brilliant construction of systems, and yet do we really grasp the 'existential' dimension of faith and life?"[92]

However, Florovsky noted, Karsavin's method is also continued in Lossky: "There is the same basic assumption that East and West are in permanent opposition to each other, the same skill in presenting the inner cohesion of ideas within each particular system, the same conviction that Filioque is at the root of the whole trouble."[93] Regarding his own views on this matter, Florovsky commented to Archimandrite Sophrony Sakharov:

> With respect to the Western (Roman) theology, I, too, for myself, anyway, prefer cautious judgments... I doubt very much the centrality of the *filioque* for the dogmatic development of the West, and I do not think that "papism" could derive from the *filoque*—that is, maybe you can "derive" it, but me as a historian, I'm not interested in logical deduction but in the actual filiation of ideas. "Papism" already existed when the *filioque* was not yet even in prospect. Leo the Great hardly knew Augustine's *De Trinitate*... this requires more careful and clear-cut analysis than we have so far known. The "fashion" regarding the *filioque* in modern Russian (diaspora) theology was started by Karsavin, and V.N. Lossky learned it from Karsavin, and then it was clumsily developed by Verkhovskoy, who does not know the history and adopted logical deductions from the course of existential developments. Finally, the belief of the Western church is not confined to Western

> "theology." I think that the faith of Catholicism is more Orthodox than in its school (or metaphysical) theology.[94]

There is a certain irony in the accusation of "rationalism" against the West in the ecumenical method of Karsavin and Lossky: if one "persistently assumes that there is absolute coherence and consistency in all systems, one always moves within the dimensions of systems." In the assumption of a single and unique "ethos" of Western Christianity, in tension with the East, cultural morphology is substituted for theological analysis, and the reality of the internal tensions that led to the Reformation is obscured.[95] As Florovsky stresses, "There were 'tensions' inside the 'Eastern tradition' itself, e.g., between Alexandria and Antioch"; and there is likewise no reason to assume that the tension between Cappadocian and Augustininan triadologies could not be overcome in some kind of "overarching synthesis." Florovsky's comments on Lossky contain finally an important lesson regarding neopatristic synthesis, which few Orthodox theologians since have yet to learn: "One should be 'ecumenical' rather than simply 'oriental' in the field of Patristic studies. One has to take into account the whole wealth of the Patristic tradition and wrestle impartially with its intrinsic variety and tensions."[96]

There is of course another side to Lossky: the Lossky who spent two decades writing his dissertation on Meister Eckhart under the tutelage of Gilson,[97] and who cultivated a deep intellectual friendship with Eric Mascall, being increasingly responsive to the new interpretations of Aquinas[98]; the Lossky revealed in the pages of his wartime journal, *Sept jours sur les routes de France,* in love with France and nourished by a deep devotion to St. Genevieve of Paris and to La Salette.[99] Lossky must be credited for having underscored, in a most profound way, the unity of theology and spiritual life. At the same time, his influence has left Orthodox thought with a host of problems—not least of which is the identification of historic Orthodox theology solely with "la théologie mystique de l'Église d'Orient." Some of this can be attributed more to a "vulgarised Losskianism" than to Lossky himself.[100] Yet these factors continue to impact in unnecessarily negative ways how Orthodox view Western Christianity—and how Western Christians view Orthodoxy.

If Lossky's thought is still generally treated as synonymous in content with neopatristic theology, it is John Zizioulas (1931–) who appears as the very first Orthodox theologian after Florovsky to categorize his own work explicitly as an attempt at "neopatristic synthesis." Zizioulas was Florovsky's student at Harvard and like his teacher has spent almost his whole theological career in ecumenical contexts. As Zizioulas describes his own project in the introduction to his hugely influential *Being as Communion*, after stressing his concern to communicate the Catholic faith of the Greek fathers and its existential relevance:

> As for the second concern of these texts, it is a result and a consequence of the first: it provokes and invites contemporary theology with a view to a synthesis between the two theologies, Eastern and Western. It is of course true that, in some respects, these two theologies seem incompatible. That is due, among other things, to the independent historical roads followed by East and West since the great schism or perhaps even earlier. However, this was not the case during the early patristic period. As the late Fr. Georges Florovsky liked to repeat, the authentic catholicity of the Church must include both East and West. It may be said in conclusion that these studies are intended to offer their contribution to a "neopatristic synthesis" capable of leading the West and the East nearer to their common roots, in the context of the existential quest of modern man.[101]

Almost uniquely among Orthodox theologians, Zizioulas understands the work of neopatristic synthesis in a manner explicitly akin to the original sense in which it was first conceived: as an ecumenical synthesis. In executing this task, Zizioulas is influenced by numerous aspects of Florovsky's own thinking: his sense of creative and existential return to the fathers; his Eucharistic ecclesiology; his interpretation of the Christian doctrine of creation clarified by Athanasius as initiating an "ontological revolution" in Greek thinking; and finally, the understanding of the person as the gift of Christianity to Hellenism, which itself could previously conceive of personhood only as a "mask."[102] Meanwhile, Zizioulas elaborates and develops these themes with far greater systematic presentation and synthetic force.

From an ecumenical standpoint, Zizioulas's greatest contributions are surely in the area of ecclesiology.[103] His work on apostolic succession especially constitutes a deeply constructive attempt to integrate Eastern and Western patristic understandings.[104] He has also made highly valuable offerings to the understanding of primacy and conciliarity, which are now proving to be crucial for the international Orthodox-Roman Catholic dialogue.[105] In contrast, his Trinitarian theology shows almost no attempt to engage positively the thought of Augustine or other Latin fathers, and even accentuates the Eastern-"personalism"-vs.-Western-"essentialism" paradigm common to many Orthodox theologians after Lossky.

It is in Zizioulas's personalism that one encounters lessons to be learned, not simply about "person" and "nature," but about theological "method" in the advancement of neopatristic synthesis. The organization of the masterful opening chapter in *Being as Communion*, "Personhood and Being," reveals Zizioulas's foundational theological method. This chapter begins with the contemporary ideal of "personal identity," and considers how that ideal might be secured. Zizioulas is firm that secular philosophy cannot give adequate access to the truth of the person: only theology can.[106] Only the person of Christ, as understood by the Greek fathers and experienced in the church's Eucharistic synaxis, can provide the answer to mortal man's tragic predicament. In framing the *question* to which this answer is to be given, however, Zizioulas articulates an existential phenomenology drawn from ancient Greek tragedians, Dostoyevsky, Heidegger, and Sartre. The problem of human existence is voiced by Dostoyevsky's tragic Kirilov: man's quest to affirm his existence in absolute freedom, not as a given reality, but by "free consent," "comes into conflict with his createdness," and with death. Only "at this point," says Zizioulas, does theology intervene, and he begins to construct his neopatristic synthesis.[107]

The framing of the question, however, shapes the form of the answer. In the first half of the chapter, Zizioulas established a concept of human "nature," identified as "necessity" and as Heidegger's *Sein-zum-Tode*. Now in the second half, this concept of nature is projected unrevised into Zizioulas's synthesis of Greek patristic theology—that is, unchallenged by the fathers' own understanding of "nature," or by the revelation of nature's *telos* in the resurrected Christ. This retention of the phenomenological conception of nature as necessity and being-toward-death established in the first half of the chapter results in a dualism between "nature" and "person," which is then replicated on every level of Zizioulas's theology. To be a "person" is to be free of one's nature. The "what" (*ti*) of human nature, including natural capacities of moral volition, biological functions and their use, contribute nothing to the "how" (*opos*) of human personhood in Christ. Action "according to nature" (*kata physin*)—for the Greek Fathers, necessary to the way of *theosis* "beyond nature" (*hyper physin*)—becomes, on the contrary, for Zizioulas, the way of individualism and death.[108]

Though lacking his Russian teacher's systematic treatment of hermeneutics and epistemology, Zizioulas appeals directly to Florovsky for his understanding of neopatristic synthesis as an "existential," always contemporaneous task of "*dogmatic hermeneutics*."[109] The hermeneutics shown in "Personhood and Being," however, join a confessedly Florovsky-inspired attempt at neopatristic synthesis to the correlational method of Zizioulas's other prominent teacher from his Harvard years, Paul Tillich.[110] In his attempt at "existential" synthesis, Zizioulas neglects to consider that knowledge of created "nature," as well as the apprehension of its tragic predicament under sin and death, are for patristic thought precisely *theological* understandings, grounded in the revelation of Christ—never purely phenomenologically derived. And where Florovsky's particular version of Christian personalism emphasized moral responsibility, Zizioulas's personalist ontology and its corresponding "ethical apophaticism," marked by a rejection of the "law of nature" (*nomos physeos*) as a realm of moral teleology, seem to lend themselves all too easily, like Tillich, to the antinomianism of a therapeutic age.

The question of acceptable cultural and philosophical "correlation" in theology should be an ecumenical concern. Probably no issue is more ecumenically divisive today—cutting not only *between* Christian confessions, but also *across* them—than that of Christian accommodation to secular thought and mores. As Pope Benedict XVI—himself an exponent of a kind of neopatristic ecumenism—reminds us, secularism is no friend to genuine ecumenical dialogue.[111] While Zizioulas himself continues to defend the basic project of neopatristic synthesis,[112] a number of other contemporary Orthodox thinkers, inspired in part by his existential correlational method, have now moved on to argue for a "post-patristic" and "contextual" theology.[113] Closely related to (but still distinct from) this tendency is also the recent scholarly attempt to revive—often against the achievements of neopatristic theology—the thought of Soloviev and Bulgakov as paradigms for Orthodox theology and a model of theological engagement with secular culture.[114]

These currents raise important questions, and may offer potential new insights. Yet they also carry potential hazards, not only for the integrity of Orthodox theology itself, but ecumenically—not least because they tend to represent more the liberal cultural values of the Western-trained academics to whose interest they are generally confined than the faith and piety of the Orthodox churches as a whole. Neither the political orientations of contemporary contextual theologies nor the idealist speculations of sophiology could be said to underscore clearly the ancient, perennial fundaments of apostolic faith able to unite Christians across diverse cultures and epochs. Noting the presence of aberrant gnostic tendencies in Russian sophiology, veteran ecumenist and Orthodox bishop Emilianos Timiadis has remarked on how "Orthodox teaching would have been misjudged by Western churches if such uncontrolled views had prevailed"; Florovsky, he says, offered a "corrective balance" and "an undefiled, authentic picture of Orthodoxy as it entered the arena of ecumenical debate."[115]

Such authenticity remains especially necessary if ecumenism is to be more than just a conversation between academics, but a truly representative meeting of churches in the apostolic tradition. Few questions divide the Orthodox more than ecumenism. Uniquely, Florovsky's neopatristic approach has commanded the respect both of career ecumenists and the most traditionalist elements of the Orthodox world, such as Mt. Athos.[116] Now, with the increasing influence of the patristic *ressourcement* upon the magisterial teaching of the Roman Catholic Church and the nascent interest in the fathers and the ancient councils among some Protestant evangelicals, new ecumenical opportunities arise for neopatristic theology. Without denying possible multilateral mediation, Orthodox theologians must consider which "West" they seek to draw near to most in dialogue. For Orthodox ecumenical witness to gain acceptance as truly representative within the broader Orthodox Church as well as to enter into constructive dialogue with the deepest traditions of the Christian West, it will, almost undoubtedly, have to continue to be a broadly neopatristic ecumenism, expanding further upon the basic program already established by Florovsky.

Conclusion

Florovsky noted of Origen that "his failures themselves were to become signposts on the road to a more satisfactory 'synthesis.'"[117] Something similar can be said of the shortcomings marking the incontestably great contributions of the neopatristic theologians. Here, in light of our reading of Lossky and Zizioulas, we can isolate two basic challenges.

First, there is the question of whether Orthodox theologians today can resist the temptation to "confine" themselves, as Florovsky noted of Lossky, "strictly to the Eastern tradition"—instead taking up the charge to "be 'ecumenical' rather than simply 'oriental' in the field of Patristic studies," assuming "the whole wealth of the Patristic tradition" as a source for theological teaching.[118] Undoubtedly, this means revising the caricatures of St. Augustine popularized in the twentieth century by figures such as Romanides and Yannaras, following Florovsky's call to weigh seriously the witness of Augustine as matter for Orthodox theological synthesis and teaching. Further, the more careful dialogue with the questions of Latin scholasticism in relation to Orthodox patristic theology, as called for in the conclusion to *Ways of Russian Theology*, should be seriously taken up.

Second, there is the question of hermeneutics, of "questioning in Christ," and the role of contemporary culture and philosophy within this questioning. An implicit consensus among Orthodox theologians prescribes that theology must be "existential" in character: addressed to living persons, with their problems and questions. Signs indicate, however, that with the arrival of Orthodox theology as a focus of academic interest in Western university contexts, Orthodox theologians may soon be facing a debate about theological method and hermeneutics not unlike that which divided "Barthians" and "correlationists" or, more recently, *ressourcement* theologians and transcendental Thomists. A vague appeal to "experience" served its relatively untroubled purpose for twentieth-century Orthodox theology. In a secularized academic context riveted by the political ideologies of "race, class, and gender," however, it will not suffice. The questions of "experience" and reason in theology[119]—its sources, first principles, and procedure—and of acceptable cultural "correlation," require a more rigorous dogmatic-philosophical treatment. Orthodox theologians must deal not only with Western theology, but also with the sources of Western secularism, with greater depth and care than has yet been shown. Undoubtedly, this will mean that political philosophy must be touched upon as well. In this work of discrimination, however, Florovsky's strictures that "'modern philosophy' must be examined from within the catholic self-consciousness of the Church,"[120] but equally, that "following the Holy Fathers" must be a "creative" and "existential" endeavor, will continue to guide those sensitive to the need to think with the church "of all ages" *and* zealous to advance her historic mission into the present.

Notes

1. Georges Florovsky, Review of Lev A. Zander, *Vision and Action*, in *St. Vladimir's Seminary Quarterly* 1:2 (Winter 1953), 28–34, at 32.
2. See, for instance, Alexander Schmemann, "In Memoriam Fr. Georges Florovsky," *St. Vladimir's Theological Quarterly* 23:3–4 (1979), 133–138, at 133; and Andrew Louth, "The Patristic Revival and Its Protagonists," in Mary B. Cunningham and Elizabeth Theokritoff (eds.), *The Cambridge Companion to Orthodox Christian Theology* (Cambridge University Press, 2008), pp. 188–203, at 193.
3. For the sharpest and most recent critique, see Brandon Gallaher, "'Waiting for the Barbarians': Identity and Polemicism in the Neo-Patristic Synthesis of Georges Florovsky," *Modern Theology* 27:4 (October 2011), 659–691.
4. G. V. Florovsky, "Iz proshlogo russkoi mysli" [1912], in his *Iz proshlogo russkoi mysli* (Moscow: Agraph, 1998), pp. 8, 12. From the same period was also his long review essay, "Novye knigi o Vladimire Solov'eve," *Izvestiya Odesskago bibliograficheskago Obshchestva pri Imperatorskom Novorossiiskom universitete* 1:7 (1912), 237–255.
5. "The true legacy of Soloviev is not his 'Romanism,' and of course not his utopian, theocratic dream, but his acute sense of Christian unity, of the common history and destiny of Christendom, his firm conviction that Christianity is the Church. It was a true ecumenical vision, as fantastic and dreamy, offensive and repelling, as his union plans had been. Soloviev's was the challenge. An earnest endeavor at an inclusive Catholic reintegration would be the answer. It would take us beyond all schemes of agreement." "Russian Orthodox Ecumenism in the 19th Century," in Florovsky, *Ecumenism II: A Historical Approach* (Vaduz: Büchervertriebsanstalt, 1989), p. 151 (translation of "L'Oecuménisme au XIXe siècle," part 2, *Irénikon* 27:4 (1954), 407–447, at 446–447). "Solovyov's true prophecy in the ecumenical search was that 'Catholic Unity' could be achieved not by way of 'conversion,' but only by the way of natural acknowledgement in the truth." Florovsky, "Solovyov Today," *Cross Currents* 12:1 (1962), 119.
6. See especially Vladimir Solovyov, *Russia and the Universal Church* (London: The Centenary Press, 1948).
7. Literature on Eurasianism is growing. For introduction, see Marlène Laruelle, *L'idéologie eurasiste russe ou comment penser l'empire* (Paris: L'Harmattan, 1999). For Russian scholarship on Florovsky's relation to Eurasianism as well as his published Eurasian-era correspondence, see Matthew Baker, "Bibliography of Literature on the Life and Work of Father Georges V. Florovsky," *Transactions of the Association of Russian-American Scholars in the U.S.A.* 37 (2011–2012) (forthcoming).
8. See Paul Gavrilyuk, "Florovsky's Neopatristic Synthesis and the Future Ways of Orthodox Theology," in George Demacopoulos and Aristotle Papanikolaou (eds.), *Orthodox Constructions of the West* (NY: Fordham University Press; forthcoming); also (following Gavrilyuk), Gallaher, "'Waiting for the Barbarians,'" 663–664.
9. G. V. Ivannikov, "G.V. Florovskii—Samyi neevraziiskii evraziets," *Aktual'nye problemy gumanitarnykh i estestvennykh nauk* 5 (2011), 274–276.
10. See Florovsky, "Breaks and Connections" and "The Cunning of Reason," in Ilya Vinkovetsky and Charles Schlacks (eds.), *Exodus to the East: Forebodings and Events—An Affirmation of the Eurasians* (Idyllwood, CA: Charles Schlacks, Jr., 1996), pp. 12–16, 30–40 (translation of the complete Eurasian volume *Iskhod k vostoku* [Sofia, 1921]).
11. See Florovsky, "Dva Zaveta," *Rossiia i latinstvo* (Berlin: Logos, 1923), pp. 152–176. In the same article, Florovsky stresses that what separates Christian confessions is a discrepancy

in the understanding of salvation, affecting religious life itself; while, on the other hand, Catholicism and Protestantism cannot be reduced to single doctrines, such as papal authority, or free inquiry. He also names charity (rather than persecution or religious compulsion) toward the heterodox as a mark of the apostolic Church.

12. As Florovsky noted later, speaking of Trubetskoi's *Evropa i chelovechestvo* (1920), Trubetskoi "published a wild theory denying the possibility of universal culture. I was never in agreement with this view because it was not acceptable from the Christian point of view. Of course it depends on the definition of culture... The other argument of Trubetskoi was that the origin was Romano-German, and therefore of course it does not influence the Slavs. But I could never accept this if only because the origin of an idea never determines its validity. Kant was a German, but it does not mean Kant's ideas are German or only for Germans." Andrew Blane, "Interview with Fr. Georges Florovsky on April 5, 1969" (unpublished typescript in my possession, pp. 40–41).
13. Florovsky, "Vechnoe i prekhodiashchee v uchenii russkikh slavianofilov" [1921], in his *Iz proshlogo russkoi mysli*, pp. 31–51, at 45–50.
14. Florovsky, "O patriotizme pravednom i grekhovnom," in his *Iz proshlogo russkoi mysli*, pp. 132–165, at 159–165; original publication in *Na putyakh: utverzhdenie evraziitsev*, Book 2 (Moscow-Berlin: Gelikon, 1922), pp. 230–293. This article, written in Sofia in 1921, is important for containing the earliest discussion of patristics in Florovsky's published oeuvre, as well as the earliest elaboration on the concept of "synthesis." Especially notable is the stress on the need for creative and constructive (*tvorcheskaia i sozidatel'naia*) response to modern problems, not a mere return to the past forms.
15. Andrew Blane, *Georges Florovsky: Russian Intellectual and Orthodox Churchman* (Crestwood, NY: St. Vladimir's Seminary Press, 1993), p. 39.
16. Florovsky, "Evraziskii soblazn," *Iz proshlogo russkoi mysli*, pp. 332–333.
17. It cannot be stressed enough how Florovsky's basic ecumenical outlook is tied to his personalist philosophy of freedom and the "creative deed" (*tvorcheskii podvig*) in history: being composed by free acting persons, the history of doctrine and spirituality in Christian schisms cannot be assumed to follow the pattern of quasi-organic laws of development or logical deductions; and being separated by a series of free acts, they may also be reconciled by a series of free acts. On this aspect of his philosophy of history, see Florovsky, "Evolution und Epigenesis. (Zur Problematik der Geschichte)," *Der Russische Gedanke* 1:3 (1930), 240–252.
18. Florovsky, "Evraziskii soblazn," pp, 332–333; emphasis in the original.
19. By the late 1940s, other names such as Karl Adam, Yves Congar, and Henri DeLubac would be added to this list: see Florovsky, "Le corps du Christ vivant: Une interprétation orthodoxe de l'Église," in F. J. Leenhardt et al., *La Sainte Église Universelle: Confrontation œcuménique* (Paris: Delachaux et Niestlé, 1948), pp. 9–57.
20. For recollections, see Eric Mascall, "Georges Florovsky (1893–1979)," *Sobornost* 2:1 (1980), 69–70; and *Saraband: The Memoirs of E.L. Mascall* (Herefordshire, England: Gracewing Publishing, 1992). Florovsky's influence on Ramsey's first book, *The Gospel and the Catholic Church* (1937), is palpable, particularly in its combination of a strong evangelical Christocentrism with a high sacramental doctrine of church order.
21. Andrew Blane and Thomas Bird, "Interview with G.V. Florovsky, Nov. 8, 1969," 76–77 (unpublished, in my possession); emphasis in the original.
22. Florovsky's participation in the ecumenical movement has yet to receive a close study. For a list of preliminary studies, see again my "Bibliography of Literature on the Life and Work of Father Georges V. Florovsky" (cited earlier).
23. For this paragraph, see Florovsky, Review of Lev Shestov, *Potestas clavium oder die Schlüsselgewalt*, in *Der Russische Gedanke* 2:2 (1931), 213–214; "The Crisis of German Idealism" [1931–1932], in Florovsky, *Philosophy: Philosophical Problems and Movements* (Vaduz: Büchervertriebsanstalt, 1989), pp. 23–41 [with dedication to Shestov];

"Revelation, Philosophy, and Theology" [1931], in Florovsky, *Creation and Redemption* (Belmont: Nordland, 1976); "Bogoslovskie otryvki," *Put'* 31 (December 1931), 3–21 (French translation: "Révélation, Expérience, Tradition [Fragments théologiques]," in Constantin Andronikof [ed.], *La Tradition: La Pensée Orthodoxe* (Paris: Institut St.-Serge, 1992), pp. 54–72); and "Hellenismus: Hellenisierung (des Christentums)," in *Weltkirchenlexikon: Handbuch der Ökumene* (Stuttgart: Kreuz-Verlag, 1960), pp. 540–541.

24. For references from Florovsky's work on this theme, see Matthew Baker, "'Theology reasons'—in History: Neo-patristic Synthesis and the Renewal of Theological Rationality," *Θεολογία* 81: 4 (2010), 81–118.
25. "Hellenism means philosophy... The Fathers... attempted a new philosophical synthesis on the basis of the Revelation... They vindicated the right of the human mind to ask questions. But it was the revealed truth they were interpreting and commending... The new and Christian mind emerges from this philosophical quest... the kernel, the very system of this new Philosophy... is Christian Dogmatics." (Florovsky, "Ad lectorem," unpublished preface to *In Ligno Crucis: The Patristic Doctrine of the Atonement*, typescript, 1939/1948, 5–6; Princeton University Rare Books and Archives, CO586, Box 2, f1/Box 3, f4).
26. See Florovsky, "Hellenismus," p. 541; and "Religion and Theological Tensions," *The Bostonian*, April 1950, 3–6, at 6.
27. Florovsky, "Patristics and Modern Theology," in Hamilcar Alivisatos (ed.), *Procès-verbaux du Premier Congrès de Théologie Orthodoxe à Athènes: 29 novembre-6 décembre 1936* (Athens, 1939), pp. 238–242; reprinted in *Diakonia* 4.3 (1969), 227–232.
28. See Hilarion Alfeyev, "The Patristic Heritage and Modernity," *The Ecumenical Review* 54 (2002), 91–111; and Konstantin Gavrilkin, *Church and Culture in the Thought of Father Georges Florovsky: The Role of Culture in the Making of Theology*, MTh. thesis, St. Vladimir's Seminary, 1998.
29. See Vladimir Janzen (ed.), "Materiali G.V. Florovskogo v Bazel'skom arkhiv F. Liba (1928–1954)," in M. Kolerov and N. S. Plotnikov (eds.), *Issledovaniia po istorii russkoi mysli: Ezhegodnik 2004 / 2005* [7] (Moscow, 2007), pp. 475–596, at 593. As George Williams has written, "Fr. Florovsky, to be sure, acknowledged proudly... his mastery of the Latin Fathers... There is no doubt but that St. Cyprian... and St. Augustine... were as important to Florovsky's vision of the world of the Church Fathers as were the Cappadocian Fathers." George H. Williams, "Fr. Florovsky's Vision of Ecumenism," *The Greek Orthodox Theological Review* 41:2–3 (1996), 136–158, at 154–155.
30. Very fittingly, Christoph Künkel, the author of the longest and most systematic study of Florovsky yet published, has encapsulated the subject of his work with an Augustinian phrase most beloved by Florovsky: Christoph Künkel, *Totus Christus: Die Theologie Georges V. Florovskys* (Göttingen: Vandenhoeck & Ruprecht, 1991).
31. See Florovsky, "The Limits of the Church," *Church Quarterly Review* 117:233 (October 1933), 117–133; "The Doctrine of the Church and the Ecumenical Problem," *The Ecumenical Review* 2:2 (1950), 152–161; and "A Holy Calling," *The Student World* 43:2 (1950), 169–171. Joseph Famerée emphasizes Florovsky's originality here: "In an Orthodoxy generally hostile to Augustine, culpable, in its eyes, of having created the doctrine of the *filioque* and a theory of original sin judged incompatible with the Eastern doctrine... not only does he defend personally the Augustinian ecclesiology, but with a bit of quiet provocation he also invites all Orthodox theologians to embrace it in order to explicate the traditional ecclesial attitude concerning the sacraments of schismatics and heretics": Joseph Famerée, SJ "Les limites de l'Eglise. L'apport de G. Florovsky au dialogue catholique-orthodoxe," *Revue théologique de Louvain* 3 (2003), 137–154, at 147–148.
32. Florovsky, "The Doctrine of the Church and the Ecumenical Problem," 156. Florovsky points to Augustine as a model of Christian Hellenism precisely because he did *not* attempt a "synthesis" of Christianity and Hellenism, but rather the latter's "conversion": see his comments in Edmund Fuller (ed.), *The Christian Idea of Education* (New Haven: Yale

University Press, 1957), pp. 166–167. What is to be "synthesized," then, is not the Gospel and Greek philosophy, but the fruits of the latter's conversion *by* the Gospel throughout history, in a creative, discriminating act of hermeneutic retrieval of Christian tradition.

33. Florovsky, "The Vocation of the Orthodox in the Modern World," Harvard University Library, audio archive; "Images of the Church in the Greek Fathers," Seminar IV, typescript, p. 1/17, Princeton University Rare Books and Archives, CO586.
34. Florovsky, "The Eastern Orthodox Church and the Ecumenical Movement," *Theology Today* 7:1 (April 1950), 68–79, at 74.
35. This applies not only to Florovsky's critics, but equally to his admirers. Regarding his student, the Greek American theologian John Romanides, Florovsky himself noted early on "a bias towards 'isolationism'": "He draws away from the West in everything and locks himself within the Byzantine tradition." Letter to S. Tyshkevich, SJ, December 17, 1960, in A. M. Pentkovskii (ed.), "Pis'ma G. Florovskogo S. Bulgakovu i S. Tyshkevichu," *Simvol* 29 (1993), 212.
36. Dom Emmanuel Lanne, OSB, "Le mystère de l'Église dans la perspective de la théologie Orthodoxe," *Irénikon* 35 (1962), 2, 171–212, at 203–204.
37. Jean Daniélou, SJ, *The Lord of History* (London: Longmans, 1958), pp. 41–43. Marko Marković, in his *La Philosophie de l'inégalité et les idées politiques de Nicolas Berdiaev* (Paris: Nouvelles Éditions Latines, 1978), p. 18, claims that Danielou's book took its inspiration from Florovsky. For a similar view of Christian Hellenism in the Roman Church, see Hugo Rahner, SJ, *Greek Mythos and Christian Mystery* (New York: Harper & Row, 1971), p. xv.
38. On this, see Ute Possekel, *Evidence of Greek Philosophical Concepts in the Writings of Ephrem the Syrian* (Louvain: Peeters, 1999).
39. See Florovsky, "Hellenismus," p. 541, and "The Christian Hellenism," *The Orthodox Observer* 442 (1957), 9; also, Florovsky, *Ways of Russian Theology*, vol. II (Vaduz: Büchervertriebsanstalt, 1987), p. 298: "The truth of 'Hebraism' is already incorporated in the Hellenic synthesis, for Hellenism became a part of the Church. Hellenism was integrated into the Church precisely through the Biblical engrafting."
40. F. J. Thomson, "Peter Mogila's Ecclesiastical Reforms and the Ukrainian Contribution to Russian Culture. A Critique of Georges Florovsky's Theory of the Pseudomorphosis of Orthodoxy," *Belgian Contributions to the 11th International Congress of Slavists, Bratislava, 30 Aug.-8 Sept. 1993.* In: *Slavica Gandensia* [Ghent, Belgium] 20 (1993), 67–119, at 103.
41. Dorothea Wendebourg, "'Pseudo-morphosis': A Theological Judgement as an Axiom in the History of Church and Theology," *The Greek Orthodox Theological Review* 42: 3/4 (1997), 321–342, at 323 and 340, n. 71.
42. For Florovsky's succinct summary of Spengler's idea, see "The Orthodox Churches and the Ecumenical Movement Prior to 1910," in Florovsky, *Christianity and Culture* (Belmont, MA: Nordland Publishing, 1974), p. 181.
43. Florovsky, Review of Lev A. Zander, *Vision and Action*, p. 33.
44. Thomson, "Peter Mogila's Ecclesiastical Reforms," 103.
45. On this, see Marc Raeff, "Florovsky and Eurasianism," in G. O. Mazur (ed.), *Twenty-Five Year Commemoration to the Life of Georges Florovsky* (1893–1979) (New York: Semenenko Foundation, 2005), pp. 87–100 (especially p. 91); and, in the same volume, Joseph Frank, "The Tragedy of Freedom," 202–212.
46. Florovsky, "Western Influences in Russian Theology," in his *Aspects of Church History* (Vaduz: Büchervertriebsanstalt, 1987), pp. 157–182, at 172, see 174–176 [original publication: "Westliche Einflüsse in der russischen Theologie," *Kyrios* 2:1 (1937), 212–231, at 225, see also 226–228]; emphasis in the original.
47. On the first, see especially Florovsky, "Patristic Theology and the Ethos of the Eastern Orthodox Church," in *Aspects of Church History*, pp. 11–31, at 20–22; "Western Influences in Russian Theology," p. 168; and *Ways of Russian Theology*, vol. II, p. 165. On the second, see note 48.

48. Florovsky, "The Problem of Ecumenical Encounter," in E. J. B. Fry and A. H. Armstrong, *Rediscovering Eastern Christendom. Essays in Memory of Dom Bede Winslow* (London: Dartman, Longman and Todd, 1963), pp. 63–76, at 68: "Not seldom Western manuals were directly used in Orthodox schools, in a rather promiscuous and eclectic manner, Roman and Protestant together. One may even speak of a certain 'pseudomorphosis' of Orthodox theology. And yet there was no real 'encounter' with the West. Influence and imitation are not yet 'encounter.' The study of the West in the East was limited to the needs of polemics and refutation. Western weapons were used to fight the West."
49. "The 'old polemical theology' has long ago lost its inner connection with any reality. Such theology was an academic discipline, and was always elaborated according to the same western 'textbooks.'" Florovsky, *Ways of Russian Theology*, vol. II, p. 302.
50. Ibid., p. 308.
51. Florovsky, "The Eastern Orthodox Church and the Ecumenical Movement," 78.
52. Florovsky, *Ways of Russian Theology*, vol. II, p. 301.
53. Ibid., p. 303: "In this newly-sought Orthodox synthesis, the centuries-old experience of the Catholic West must be studied and diagnosed by Orthodox theology with greater care and sympathy than has yet been the case up to now. What is meant here is not the adoption or acceptance of Roman doctrine, nor imitation 'Romanism.' In any case, the Orthodox thinker can find a more adequate source for creative awakening in the great systems of 'high scholasticism,' in the experience of the Catholic mystics, and in the theological experience of later Catholicism than in the philosophy of German idealism or in the Protestant critical scholarship of the nineteenth and twentieth centuries, or even in the 'dialectical theology' of our own day." Florovsky's published essays and letters from the mid-1920s up through the late 1950s attest to his special affinity for the thought of Duns Scotus, whom he cites on the themes of creation ex nihilo, contingent causality, and the "absolute decree" of the incarnation.
54. Künkel, *Totus Christus: Die Theologie Georges V. Florovskys*, pp. 264–265. Florovsky was less sanguine about Protestant theology, regarding the Reformation as a wholesale departure from historic church order. Yet a positive program is implied in his suggestion that Melanchthon's "attempt to interpret the message of the Reformation in the wider context of an ecumenical tradition embracing the East and the West... be repeated," with "all controversial points, dividing the East from the non-Roman West... analyzed again in the larger perspective of Patristic tradition": see "An Early Ecumenical Correspondance (Patriarch Jeremiah II and the Lutheran Divines)," in Florovsky, *Christianity and Culture*, pp. 143–155, at 155.
55. As Florovsky wrote, "Learning in general is not and must not be a dialectical, but rather a dialogical moment." Florovsky, *Ways of Russian Theology*, vol. II, pp. 306–307.
56. Florovsky, "In Ligno Crucis: Kyrkofädernas Lära om Försoningen, Tolkad från den Grekisk-ortodoxa Teologiens Synpunkt," *Svensk Teologisk Kvartalskrift* 23 (1947), 297–308, at 297.
57. Florovsky, "Ad lectorem," *In Ligno Crucis: The Patristic Doctrine of Atonement*, unpublished manuscript, Princeton University Rare Books and Archives, CO586 Box 2, folder 1. See Blane, *Georges Florovsky*, p. 154, where Florovsky indicates that he was led to the idea "quite early," even while the term came later.
58. Florovsky, "The Legacy and Task of Orthodox Theology," *Anglican Theological Review* XXXI:2 (1949), 69–70. It is notable that in this essay, Florovsky refers to *himself* also as a *Westerner* "by adoption."
59. Florovsky, "The Patterns of Historical Interpretation," *Anglican Theological Review* 50 (1968), 144–155, at 150.
60. See Florovsky, "The Problem of Ecumenical Encounter," pp. 63–76. Note, too, how Florovsky appeals to Soloviev's criticisms of this thesis of Danilevsky (p. 67).
61. Ibid., p. 67.
62. Florovsky, "The Legacy and Task of Orthodox Theology," 65–66.

63. Florovsky, "The Quest for Unity and the Orthodox Church," *Theology and Life* 4:3 (August 1961), 167–208, at 206.
64. Florovsky, "The Eastern Orthodox Church and the Ecumenical Movement," 70–71.
65. Florovsky, "Patristic Theology and the Ethos of the Eastern Orthodox Church," p. 29.
66. Florovsky, "The Eastern Orthodox Church and the Ecumenical Movement," 78–79.
67. Florovsky, "Terms of Communion in the Undivided Church," in Donald Baillie and John Marsh (eds.), *Intercommunion* (New York: Harper and Brothers, 1952), pp. 47–57, at 48.
68. Florovsky, "Determinations and Distinctions: Ecumenical Aims and Doubts," *Sobornost* 4:3 (Winter, 1948), 126–132, at 130.
69. See Florovsky, "Patristic Theology and the Ethos of the Eastern Orthodox Church."
70. Florovsky, "Reason and Faith in the Philosophy of Soloviëv," in E. J. Simmons, *Continuity and Change in Russian and Soviet Thought* (Cambridge, MA: Harvard University Press, 1955), pp. 283–297, at 284.
71. Florovsky, "Religion and Theological Tensions," 6.
72. He continues: "But in no way am I going to 'un-church' anybody. The judgment has been given to the Son. Nobody is entitled to anticipate His judgment. Yet the Church has her own authority in history. It is, first of all, an authority to teach and to keep faithfully the word of truth. There is a certain rule of faith and order that is to be regarded as normal. What is beyond that is just abnormal. But the abnormal should be cured, not just condemned." Florovsky, "Confessional Loyalty in the Ecumenical Movement," in Baillie and Marsh (eds.), *Intercommunion*, pp. 196–205, at 204; emphases in the original.
73. Florovsky, "The Doctrine of the Church and the Ecumenical Problem," 161.
74. Florovsky, "Une vue sur l'Assemblée d'Amsterdam," *Irénikon* 22:1 (1949), 4–25, at 13.
75. Florovsky, "The Eastern Orthodox Church and the Ecumenical Movement," 78.
76. Florovsky, "Confessional Loyalty in the Ecumenical Movement," p. 203. Speaking of Toynbee in "The Patterns of Historical Interpretation," 152: "Of course, you may say that you choose to study, let us say, the Latin Fathers. But don't pretend that Latin patristics is an intelligible field in itself, and therefore you may dispense with any knowledge of the Greek Fathers. Or vice versa."
77. Florovsky, "The Eastern Orthodox Church and the Ecumenical Movement," 78.
78. Letter of October 21, 1973, Princeton Theological Seminary Libraries, Thomas F. Torrance Manuscript Collection, Box 104.
79. Florovsky, "Primitive Tradition and the Traditions," in William S. Morris (ed.), *The Unity We Seek* (Toronto: Ryerson Press, 1962), pp. 28–38, at 29–30; see also, Florovsky, "Znamenie Prerekaemo," *Vestnik Russkago Studencheskago Khristianskago Dvizheniya* no. 72–73, I-II (1964), 1–7.
80. See especially Florovsky, "Types of Historical Interpretation" [1925] in Louis J. Shein (ed.), *Readings in Russian Philosophical Thought: Philosophy of History* (Waterloo: Wilfred Laurier University Press, 1977), pp. 89–108; and "The Predicament of the Christian Historian," in Florovsky, *Christianity and Culture* (Belmont, MA: Nordland Press, 1974), pp. 31–66. For the most insightful discussion of this deeply neglected but crucial dimension of Florovsky's thought, see Rowan Williams, "Eastern Orthodox Theology," in David F. Ford (ed.), *The Modern Theologians: An Introduction to Christian Theology in the Twentieth Century* (Cambridge, UK: Blackwell, 2005), pp. 499–510, at 508–509.
81. Florovsky, "The Predicament of the Christian Historian," pp. 50–51. Florovsky's thought here resembles H.-G. Gadamer's concept of *Horizontverschmelzung*, but with the critical correctives made to this concept by Emilio Betti, in that the identity of the original message remains stable and unchanged, even while the rational understanding and appropriation of it grows.
82. Blane, *Georges Florovsky*, p. 154.
83. Gallaher, "'Waiting for the Barbarians,'" 660, 677. The enormity of this claim is revealed especially when compared with Western theologians' reactions to Florovsky: see, for instance,

S. Tyszkiewicz, SJ Compte-rendu: "R.P. Georges Florovsky, Puti Russkago Bogosloviya," *Orientalia Christiana Periodica* 4 (1938), 288–291, at 290: "Concerning judgments regarding Catholicism, Fr. Florovsky is much more fair than the greater part of the other modern Orthodox theologians." See also, Dom Clement Lialine, Compte-rendu: "G. Florovskij.—Le problématisme de la réunion chrétienne," *Irénikon* 11 (1934), 601–602.

84. Florovsky, Review of *The Mystical Theology of the Eastern Church*, in *The Journal of Religion* 38:3 (July 1958), 207–208, at 207.
85. Williams, "Eastern Orthodox Theology," p. 507. Williams's unpublished doctoral dissertation still remains the most thorough study of Lossky's theology: Rowan Williams, *The Theology of Vladimir Nikolaievich Lossky*, DPhil thesis, University of Oxford, 1975.
86. As pointed out by Arkhimandrit Sofronii (Sakharov), *Perepiska s Protoiereem Georgiem Florovskim* (Essex/Moscow: Sviato-Ioanno-Predtechenskii Monastyr'/Sviato-Troitskaia Sergieva Lavra, 2008), pp. 65–69. In an unpublished lecture of 1956, Lossky went on record in expressing his view of Florovsky as the greatest Orthodox theologian of his age: cited in Williams, *The Theology of Vladimir Nikolaievich Lossky*, p. 281.
87. Florovsky, Review of *The Mystical Theology of the Eastern Church*, 207–208.
88. Sofronii, *Perepiska s Protoiereem Georgiem Florovskim*, pp. 78–79.
89. Ibid., p. 68.
90. Pavel Florensky, *The Pillar and Ground of Truth* (Princeton, NJ: Princeton University Press, 1997), pp. 82–83. In Lossky, this is also manifested in his view that "in the age to come" the Spirit, while "not having His image in another Hypostasis, will manifest Himself in deified persons: for the multitude of the saints will be His image": Vladimir Lossky, *The Mystical Theology of the Eastern Church* (Crestwood, NY: St. Vladimir's Seminary Press, 1998), p. 173.
91. "The Procession of the Holy Spirit in Orthodox Trinitarian Doctrine," in Vladimir Lossky, *In the Image and Likeness of God* (Crestwood, NY: St. Vladimir's Seminary Press, 1974), pp. 71–97, at 88 and 71.
92. Florovsky, "The Problem of Ecumenical Encounter," p. 73.
93. Ibid., p. 74. For a discussion of Florovsky's views on the *filioque*, see Matthew Baker, "The Eternal 'Spirit of the Son': Barth, Florovsky and Torrance on the *Filioque*," *International Journal of Systematic Theology* 12:4 (October 2010), 382–403.
94. Florovsky, letter of May 15, 1958, in Sofronii, *Perepiska s Protoiereem Georgiem Florovskim*, pp. 79–81. After expressing his admiration for Lossky's person, Florovsky stated later his belief that Lossky "was under the perverse influence of Karsavin." Andrew Blane and Thomas Bird, "Interview with GVF, Nov. 7, 1969" (unpublished typescript, in my possession).
95. Florovsky, "The Problem of Ecumenical Encounter," p. 73.
96. Florovsky, Review of *The Mystical Theology of the Eastern Church*, 207.
97. See Vladimir Lossky. *Théologie négative et connaissance de Dieu chez Maître Eckhart* (Paris: Vrin, 1973).
98. See, for instance, Vladimir Lossky, Review of E. L. Mascall, *Existence and Analogy*, in *Sobornost* 7 (Summer 1950), 295–297.
99. Vladimir Lossky, *Sept jours sur les routes de France: Juin 1940* (Paris: Cerf, 1998).
100. The phrase belongs to Aidan Nichols, *Light from the East* (London: Sheed and Ward, 1999), p. 32.
101. John D. Zizioulas, *Being as Communion: Studies in Personhood and the Church* (Crestwood, NY: St. Vladimir's Seminary Press, 1985). Henceforth cited as *BAC*.
102. See Florovsky, "The Idea of Creation in Christian Philosophy," *Eastern Churches Quarterly* 8:3 (1949), 53–77; and Zizioulas, *BAC*, pp. 83–86. The phrase "ontological revolution" originates from Florovsky (unpublished notes in my possession). On personhood and mask, compare Florovsky, "Revelation, Philosophy and Theology," 34, with *BAC*, pp. 31–35. Similar to Florovsky, Zizioulas also critiques Lossky for introducing an exaggerated "understanding of apophatic theology unknown to Greek patristic tradition": see Zizioulas, "The

Being of God and the Being of Anthropos," *Synaxis* (1991), 21–22. For a careful comparative study of Lossky and Zizioulas on this question, see Aristotle Papanikolaou, *Being with God: Trinity, Apophaticism, and Divine-Human Communion* (Notre Dame, IN: University of Notre Dame Press, 2006).

103. For two Roman Catholic appreciations, see Gaëtan Baillargeon, *Perspectives orthodoxes sur l'Eglise-communion: l'oeuvre de Jean Zizioulas* (Montréal: Éditions Paulines, 1989); and Paul McPartlan, *The Eucharist Makes the Church: Henri de Lubac and John Zizioulas in Dialogue* (Edinburgh: T&T Clark, 1993).
104. See *BAC*, Chapter 5, pp. 171–208; and "Apostolic Continuity of the Church and Apostolic Succession in the First Five Centuries," *Louvain Studies* 21:2 (1996), 153–168.
105. See Zizioulas, "Primacy in the Church: An Orthodox Approach," *Eastern Churches Journal* 5:2 (Summer 1998), 7–20; and "Recent Discussions on Primacy in Orthodox Theology," in Walter Kasper (ed.), *The Petrine Ministry* (Paulist Press, 2006), pp. 231–246. Zizioulas's influence is apparent in the "Ravenna Document" of October 13, 2007, "Ecclesiological and Canonical Consequences of the Sacramental Nature of the Church." In his insistence that the issue of primacy requires doctrinal development on the part of the Orthodox, Zizioulas echoes the view of Florovsky: see "On the Upcoming Council of the Roman Catholic Church," in Florovsky, *Ecumenism II*, 206 (original publication: "O predstoiashchem sobore Rimskoi Tserkvi," in *Vestnik Russkogo Studentchestogo Khristianskogo Dvizheniia* no. 52, I [1959], 5–10). Florovsky is reported to have said at Amsterdam in 1948, "qu'entre les deux Eglises, orthodoxe et catholique, il n'y avait au fond qu'une question, celle du Pape": Charles Boyer, SJ, *Le Movement Oecuménique: les Faits—le Dialogue* (Rome: Gregorianum, 1976), p. 109.
106. *BAC*, p. 43. See also *BAC*, pp. 45–46, f. 41; and Zizioulas, *Communion and Otherness* (London/New York: T&T Clark, 2006), p. 103 (henceforth cited as *CO*).
107. *BAC*, p. 43.
108. *CO*, p. 62.
109. Zizioulas, *Lectures in Christian Dogmatics*, ed. Douglas Knight (London/New York: T&T Clark, 2008), pp. ix–x.
110. "Philosophy formulates the questions implied in human existence, and theology formulates the answers implied in divine self-manifestation under the guidance of the questions implied in human existence." Paul Tillich, *Systematic Theology*, vol. 1 (Chicago: University of Chicago Press, 1973), p. 61; and see further, p. 64.
111. On secularism and ecumenism, see Daniel P. Payne and Jennifer M. Kent, "An Alliance of the Sacred: Prospects for a Catholic-Orthodox Partnership against Secularism in Europe," *Journal of Ecumenical Studies* 46:1 (Winter 2011), 41–66. For Benedict's neopatristic ecumenism, see Joseph Ratzinger, *Principles of Catholic Theology: Building Stones for a Fundamental Theology* (San Franscisco: Ignatius Press, 1987), pp. 140–141, 143: "Thomas Aquinas and the other great scholastics of the thirteenth century are 'Fathers' of a specifically Roman Catholic theology from which the Christian churches of the Reformation consider themselves completely separated and which, for the churches of the East, also expresses an alien mentality. But the teachers of the ancient Church represent a common past that, precisely as such, may well be a promise for the future. This thought must not be esteemed too lightly, for it is, in fact, to be regarded as the catalyst that can help to solve the problem of the relationship between patristic and modern theology... We are fairly certain today that, while the Fathers were not Roman Catholic as the thirteenth or nineteenth century would have understood the term, they were, nonetheless, 'Catholic,' and their Catholicism extended to the very canon of the New Testament itself... Who would deny that Thomas Aquinas and Luther are each Father of only one part of Christianity?... And so the question remains: If these Fathers can be Fathers for only a part of Christianity, must we not turn our attention to those who were once the Fathers of all?"

112. Zizioulas has also celebrated Florovsky's achievement in an article, John Zizioulas, "π. Γεώργιος Φλωρόφσκυ: ὁ οἰκουμενικός διδάσκαλος," *Θεολογία* 81: 4 (2010), 31–48.
113. The representative event here was the international conference held in Volos, Greece, June 3–6, 2010, "Neo-Patristic Synthesis or Post-Patristic Theology: Can Orthodox Theology Be 'Contextual'?" sponsored by the Volos Theological Academy and the Orthodox Studies Institute of Fordham University.
114. The representative work here is Paul Valliere, *Modern Russian Theology: Bukharev, Soloviev, Bulgakov: Orthodox Theology in a New Key* (Edinburgh: T&T Clark; Grand Rapids, Michigan: Wm. B. Eerdmans Publishing Co., 2000). Though not Orthodox himself, Valliere has recently exercised a strong influence on Orthodox academics in the English-speaking world with his championing of what he calls "liberal Orthodoxy."
115. Emilianos Timiadis, "Georges Florovsky 1893–1979," in Ioan Bria and Dagmar Heller (eds.), *Ecumenical Pilgrims: Profiles of Pioneers in Christian Reconciliation* (Geneva: WCC, 1995), pp. 94–95. Robert Bird registers a similar ecumenical caution regarding the attempt of such scholars as Valliere and Rowan Williams to promote the thought of Bulgakov: "The point would seem to be that Bulgakov's theological method represents a victory of modern, liberal values... a politically and culturally acceptable replacement for establishment Orthodoxy. But if any encounter is to occur between East and West, such replacement is inadmissible." Robert Bird, "The Tragedy of Russian Religious Philosophy: Sergei Bulgakov and the Future of Orthodox Theology," in J. Sutton and W. P. van den Bercken (eds.), *Orthodox Christianity and Contemporary Europe: Selected Papers of the International Conference Held at the University of Leeds, England, in June 2001* (Leuven: Peeters Publishers, 2003), pp. 223–224.
116. Indeed, there are some among the Athonites who would count Florovsky himself as a father of the church: see Alexander Golitzin, "'A Contemplative and a Liturgist': Father Georges Florovsky on the *Corpus Dionysiacum*," *St. Vladimir's Theological Quarterly* 43:2 (1999), 131–161, at 158. For an appreciation by an Orthodox ecumenist of latitudinarian strain with long experience in the WCC, see Thomas Fitzgerald, "'Florovsky at Amsterdam: his 'ecumenical aims and doubts,'" *Sobornost*, 21:1 (1999), 37–51.
117. "The Patristic Age and Eschatology," in Florovsky, *Aspects of Church History*, p. 72. In his later years, he made similar comments regarding the thinkers of the Russian religious renaissance—saying that his own work would not have been possible without them (unpublished papers in my possession).
118. Florovsky, Review of Vladimir Lossky, *The Mystical Theology of the Eastern Church*, p. 207.
119. On the question of rationality, as well as the issue of "nature" problematized by Zizioulas, no Orthodox theologian in modern times has made greater contributions than Dumitru Staniloae, who indeed may also have the greatest claim to having produced a neopatristic synthesis. The work of Nikolaos Loudovikos is also promising in this regard.
120. Florovsky, "Patristics and Modern Theology," p. 232. As he elaborates in "Western Influences in Russian Theology," p. 168: "The task of theology lies... in discovering in the ancient patristic tradition the perennial principles of Christian philosophy... not in controlling dogma by means of contemporary philosophy but rather in re-shaping philosophy on the experience of faith itself."

16

Justification in the Theological Conversations between Representatives of the Russian Orthodox Church and the Protestant Churches in Germany

Christoph Mühl

The doctrine of justification can be described as "the centre and boundary of Protestant theology" in so far as it delineated and brought into focus the new recognition of Christ (*Christuserkenntnis*) by the Reformers.[1] Given that this issue of justification triggered such a controversy between Protestants and the Roman Catholic Church that resulted in mutual condemnations, the theme of justification has thus come to occupy a central place in ecumenical dialogues in the last century. The *Joint Declaration on the Doctrine of Justification* signed in 1999 between the Lutheran World Federation and the Roman Catholic Church was certainly a significant milestone on the way toward ecumenical rapprochement. This declaration summarizes a consensus on justification determined in the dialogues that require us to see the divisive questions and condemnations of the sixteenth century in a new light.[2] But what about the Orthodox churches that were not involved in this doctrinal conflict? A forensic understanding of justification is an approach that is typical of Western theology, whereas in Orthodox theology salvation is seen rather as a process of *theosis*[3] (divinization/deification). This chapter assesses the extent to which the doctrine of justification was adequately understood and successfully communicated in the theological conversations between representatives of the Russian Orthodox Church (ROC) and the Protestant churches in Germany. On that account, the Protestant doctrine of justification and the Orthodox concept of *theosis* are summarized in terms of how they were formulated in the bilateral dialogue. After introducing the process of dialogue and the issue of justification, the chapter will then critically assess the agreement that has been reached thus far.

The Theological Conversations

The ROC and the Evangelical Church in Germany (Evangelische Kirche in Deutschland—EKD) have been conducting a bilateral ecumenical dialogue since 1959. Mutual visits of delegations to the Soviet Union and Germany throughout the 1950s as well as the exchange of professors paved the way for the first theological conference at the Evangelical Academy in Arnoldshain. All subsequent theological consultations were named "Arnoldshain conversations" after the site of this first meeting, though they actually took place in different locations. At the very beginning the dialogue thematically referred to a list of questions by the Russian theologian Lev Nikolaevič Parijskij; however, in the course of the dialogue the themes were defined from meeting to meeting. There was no master plan to discuss doctrinal differences, nor any long-term goal such as full communion, but rather the participants were concerned with breaking through obstacles and to cement ties. Theological issues arose from the confrontation with the realities of life of the respective churches. The dialogue was also shaped by the historical context: the Cold War era, church-state relations in the Soviet Union, and the emergence of two German states as competing political systems.

Thus, in 1969 the institutional unity of the Protestant[4] churches in East and West Germany within the EKD was rendered impossible by the new constitution of the German Democratic Republic, so that the Federation of the Evangelical Churches (Bund Evangelischer Kirchen in der DDR—BEK) was formed in the GDR. Hence, five years later the BEK and the Moscow Patriarchate established a separate dialogue in 1974 in Zagorsk[5] (the "Zagorsk conversations"). In order to avoid this dialogue becoming a mere duplication of the conversations with the EKD, the reflection on the existence of the church in socialist societies was intended to be the particular focus of these conversations.[6]

In view of the Cold War and the deeply damaged relations between Germany and the Soviet Union after World War II, the dialogues were also a vehicle for reconciliation and international understanding.[7]

After the reunification of Germany, the EKD and BEK were also reunited; in addition, after the dissolution of the Soviet Union the ROC found itself in an entirely new social and political situation. As a result, the churches renewed their dialogue under these changed conditions. This new phase of the dialogue, called the "Bad Urach conversations," was more about social ethics than about doctrinal issues.[8] After a critical evaluation of the results of the dialogue, the delegates analyzed the relationships between church, state, and society in Europe with a special focus on the churches' witness in today's world. In this context, the issue of religious education as well as the significance of Christian values in the face of secular and pluralistic societies were discussed at dialogue meetings in the years 2002 and 2005. The last theological conversation on "Freedom and Responsibility from a Christian Perspective"[9] held in 2008 in Wittenberg was also closely related to a Russian Orthodox statement on Human Rights.

If we look at these three strands of dialogues between the ROC and Protestant Churches in Germany as one process,[10] 24 dialogue meetings have been held thus far: 12 Arnoldshain conversations, 7 Zagorsk conversations, and 5 Bad Urach conversations. After 50 years of official theological conversations, the ROC declared that it was seeking new forms of dialogue. Ultimately unresolved obstacles all of a sudden made it harder for the ROC to continue the existing bilateral conversations. The call for reconsidering the dialogue in November 2009 had to do with the fact that the recently elected chair of the Council of the Evangelical Church in Germany, Margot Käßmann, was a woman. Since the chair of the EKD council had already been invited earlier to the planned anniversary celebrations of the dialogue to be held in Moscow and Berlin, some circles in the ROC were afraid that many Russian Orthodox believers would regard a meeting between the patriarch and a female bishop representing the EKD as an official acceptance of the ordination of women by the hierarchy of the Moscow Patriarchate. Unfortunately as a result the festivities were cancelled and the dialogue suspended until further notice.

As mentioned earlier, the dialogue concerned not just doctrinal issues, but also the endeavor of a true encounter of churches.[11] The ecclesiastical character of these talks was especially evident in that the mutual exchange of information about current developments in both churches played a significant role. A major aim of the dialogue was to promote a greater acquaintance with one another as well as an understanding of similarities and differences.

The Doctrine of Justification in the Dialogue

This was the reason for the initial focus by the participants on some basic questions concerning the life and teaching of Protestant churches, which the Russian theologian Lev Nikolaevič Parijskij had raised in a letter to the German theologian Hans Joachim Iwand in 1956.[12] Parijskij questioned the use of confessional stereotypes, observing in particular that the life of the Protestant churches did not correspond to the Protestant cliché employed in some (presumably Russian) textbooks of comparative theology. So, in addition to the discussion of the classic subject "Scripture and Tradition," the first conversations dealt with the Protestant doctrine of justification by faith alone. Considering that the Protestant churches have a strong tradition of diaconal work, the correlation of faith and good works was discussed in three papers. Nikolaj Dmitrievič Uspenskij presented the Russian perspective with a paper on "Salvation through Faith." Hans Joachim Iwand and Heinrich Vogel presented the doctrine of justification by faith alone from the Protestant perspective. In the course of the discussions, an unexpectedly high degree of convergence was discovered between the Protestant and the Orthodox positions. Consequently, the résumé formulated after the conference documented the common understanding of justification as follows:

> a) We receive justification through grace by faith in the salvation through the Lord Jesus Christ. b) There is no justification due to good works. c) Thereby the misunderstanding is eliminated that in Orthodox theology good works are a precondition for justification, and respectively that in Protestant theology the New Testament teaching on judgment according to deeds is rejected. d) The Reformation experience of justification by faith has much resonance in Orthodox liturgy and asceticism.[13]

As Harding Meyer observed, the common conviction outlined here comes close to the formulas of agreement of later dialogues.[14]

Thus, while the Protestant doctrine of justification was touched on in the course of the dialogue, no further common theses on justification were adopted after the first conference in Arnoldshain. In retrospect, Heinz Joachim Held explained that one wanted to treat "the question of justification by faith alone not as an isolated theological problem." Rather, the participants tried to "connect it to the general view of God's gracious deeds and to the sacraments of the church, through which people receive the salvific and sanctifying work of divine grace."[15] In other words, the Arnoldshain conversations focused on a common description of the work of God through the Holy Spirit, the sacraments, and the church. So the first meeting was followed by discussions "on the work of the Holy Spirit" in the liturgy, the sacraments, and synods in 1963. The third conversation (1967) dealt with the act of reconciliation between God and wo/men. Subsequently the sacrament of baptism, the new life that it confers, and its consequences for Christian ministry in the world were discussed at the fourth meeting. In addition, the question of the relation between word and sacrament, left open at the first Arnoldshain conversation, was also a subject of advanced discussions. Since the 1970s discussions have turned to the sacrament of the Eucharist and ecclesiology, in so far as they dealt with "the Risen Christ and the Salvation of the World," with the "Eucharist,"[16] and later with church ministry.[17]

Whereas in the Zagorsk conversations the proclamation of the Kingdom of God, "The Sanctifying Action of God's Grace in the Church and through the Church,"[18] and the discipleship of Christ in an atheistic environment were at the forefront from the beginning, here the doctrine of justification was contextualized by Günter Jacob, Christoph Wetzel, and Heino Falcke. At the first meeting in Zagorsk, Jacob addressed the pressing question of how justification could be preached in the context of the GDR. Raising the question of the social relevance of this doctrine today, he referred to Helmut Gollwitzer, who saw justification as a reinforcement of meaning—an account that did not mirror the "classic" Reformation formulas and their historical situation. However, other papers employed traditional Protestant perspectives. Discussing the church as a place of sanctification at the third Zagorsk conversation, Wetzel described the relation of justification and sanctification in accordance with the Augsburg Confession, and Falcke discussed the implications of divine justice of God for "the Church's ministry to promote justice in the world."

Justification and Theosis—Two Soteriological Concepts in Dialogue

The dialogue has revealed that the notion of justification is certainly also present in Orthodox theology, but salvation is rather seen as a process of sanctification, which aims at the deification (*theosis*[19]) of humanity. Thus, Orthodox theologians describe salvific events primarily in terms of illness and healing, rather than in juridical categories. And, whereas Protestant theology centers upon the Pauline writings, Orthodox theologians focus more on the Johannine literature.

These different ways of thinking about salvation in Eastern and Western theology are often viewed as opposites. However, some German participants were convinced from the outset that the differences are secondary and that the basic positions are in fact complementary.[20] But, as opposed to other Protestant-Orthodox dialogues, such as the theological conversations between the ROC and the Evangelical Lutheran Church of Finland or the international Lutheran-Orthodox dialogue, a comparative study of justification and *theosis* did not become a distinct theme in the German-Russian conversations.

Nevertheless, the papers and discussions allow some introductory remarks regarding these two systems of thought. Apart from the aforementioned papers, Ernst Wolf covered the doctrine of justification extensively in his presentation at the fourth Arnoldshain conversation,[21] though his deliberations were not incorporated into the theses.[22] Speaking about the new life in the faith after baptism, he developed the concept of justification within the terms of theological anthropology, an area in which Protestant and Orthodox theologies differ. In contrast to the Lutheran-Orthodox dialogue in the United States,[23] which focused on the anthropological principles underlying soteriological concepts, the German dialogue started from the connection between justification and good works. Nonetheless, it also dealt with issues such as grace, synergism, sin, the image of God, and the relation between justification and sanctification.

In Protestant teaching, the original relationship between God and human beings was fundamentally disrupted by the Fall. This ruptured relation can only be restored by divine grace (*sola gratia*). Wo/men remain sinners throughout their entire lives on account of their fallen nature. But at the same time they are justified by God if their faith accepts the salvific events in Jesus Christ (*simul iustus et peccator*). Then God no longer holds them accountable for sin, but declares them righteous, imputing Christ's righteousness to the faithful.[24] "In God's eyes—virtually from the outside—the person is made to something that one is not of his or her own accord."[25] In fact, through Christ and only through Him (*solus Christus*), wo/men become partakers of God's justice. Nevertheless this imputed justice continues to be an extrinsic gift.

At the first dialogue meeting, Iwand stated: "In Jesus Christ, in his death and his resurrection God proved to be just, that is (to say), here is a judgment judging the whole world and saving believers [...] God has judged all human justice."[26] In other words, the logic of distributive justice was abolished by the mediation of Christ's vicarious reparation.

God does not repay anyone according to their deeds, but declares a person righteous in accordance with his or her faith in Christ (*sola fide*). In this way, people are released from their "self-centeredness"; liberated from "the curse of selfishness,"[27] they become capable of turning toward Christ and attaining peace in themselves and with God. Hence, faith may be understood as a reconciled relationship with God that coincides with the call to discipleship of Christ.

Through faith, Christ becomes present in wo/man[28] and one is renewed from the inside, since "it is no longer I who live, but Christ who lives in me" (Gal. 2:20). Yet, "this transformation of man remains [...] an inner, private event,"[29] as stated in the common theses of the fifth Arnoldshain conversation.

In the life of faith, wo/man is called to abandon her-/himself and to look at Christ anew every day. This process involves an intensification of "self-perception"[30] (*Selbstwahrnehmung*) as a being before God. Realizing this enables the person to be free to act. So wo/man is not just deemed righteous but is actually made righteous by the Word of God, namely, Jesus Christ. Since justification is an event that seizes wo/man over and over again by God's grace, it always precedes sanctification, as Wolf stresses.[31]

In contrast to this, the Orthodox concept of *theosis* is focused on sanctification, though sanctification is not identical with *theosis*. As a Christian concept of the deification of humanity, *theosis* refers to the ongoing "transformation of believers into the likeness of God,"[32] which will be completed and fulfilled by God in the hereafter. It is a process of growing into union with God and in the eschatological holiness of the human person.[33]

In Orthodox thinking, wo/men still have spiritual power after the Fall and are thus called to pursue perfection.[34] "Human nature has preserved several features of the immortal image of God in the Fall and has kept the innate pursuit towards perfection,"[35] as Liverij Voronov pointed out at the third Arnoldshain meeting. These features are rationality and free will.[36] However, because of the Fall, true freedom was reduced to freedom of choice between good and evil, so that wo/men have to willingly and responsibly seek out and do the good, and thereby conform to the Divine will. In order to enable them to accomplish this, God informs wo/men with His grace, which turns back the natural powers to their original condition, making wo/men capable of further spiritual, primarily moral improvement in seeking the likeness of God.[37] The effect of God's grace is viewed as a healing of the "moral disease"[38] of humanity, which is sin.

Because in Jesus Christ the true image and likeness of God is revealed, the early Church Fathers taught that God's incarnation in Jesus Christ allows wo/men to partake in the divine nature. Consequently human beings are, on the one hand, called to imitate Christ, but, on the other hand, it is the Holy Spirit, through whom the divine energies are transmitted to people. Therefore it is wo/men's duty to open up to the Holy Spirit by asceticism and a virtuous life to become by grace what Christ is by nature—truly divine. In that sense Christ is the new Adam, the "archetype" for all people, as the true human.

Although baptism, as the incorporation into Christ, entails an ontological (physical) restoration of human nature, people remain involved in the fight against sin and cannot attain salvation by themselves, but only in cooperation with God.

Hence, the Russian theologian Nikolaj Uspenskij drew attention to the Orthodox theological distinction between an objective and a subjective side of salvation.[39] The objective side of salvation refers to the unique, historic event of salvation in Jesus Christ, while subjective salvation must be achieved through an active faith in Jesus Christ as the Savior.[40]

Consensus

We will now take a closer look at the agreements that have been reached thus far. As already quoted earlier, at the first consultation in Arnoldshain a consensus was expressed on the relation between faith and good works. For Orthodox Christians and Protestants alike, good works are "no precondition for justification."[41] In Protestant theology, good works are the fruits of faith.[42] "The deed that arises from faith [...] is a gift of the Holy Spirit,"[43] as Iwand pointed out, and Orthodox Christians generally agree with this. Nevertheless, from the Orthodox point of view it is indispensable for a person to cooperate with God, in order to accomplish the good works that are necessary for salvation. On this, the Protestant point of view differs—human deeds add nothing to justification and are not necessary for salvation. As for the distinction between objective and subjective salvation, for Iwand it simply reflects two perspectives on the same thing.[44] According to Protestant teaching wo/man is saved when s/he realizes and firmly believes that salvation is revealed in Jesus Christ for us, once and for all.

In addition to the agreement reached in Arnoldshain in 1959, a further statement of consensus on justification was expressed in a 1995 joint report to the governing bodies of the churches.[45] That document, which mainly refers to the first, third, and fourth Arnoldshain conversations, states:

> Both churches still attribute great importance to good works in the life of a Christian. For, by faith in Christ we stand in a vital, reconciled communion with the Triune God, who endows us with the strength of his Spirit and who calls and empowers us to be his co-workers in the conduct of the good.

> Salvation or justification by faith is a unique divine act of grace upon us through which we become Christians as well as an ongoing gracious process occurring to us by which we are taught a life in Christ within the communion of the church and through which we stay and prosper in Christian life.[46]

This consensus, apparently colored by the Protestant view, certainly requires further elaboration. Various terms, such as "co-worker" and "grace,"[47] are understood differently by Orthodox and Protestants. Similarly, the anthropological categories of sin and free will need further clarification.

Differences—The Problem of Sin and Free Will

For both Orthodox and Protestants, God's promise of salvation is related to His call into the discipleship of Christ. Because in this world wo/man remains involved in sinful structures, staying and prospering in Christian life means always to struggle against sin. This is called "daily repentance" by Protestants and "internal renewal" by the Orthodox.[48] However, a significant difference can be observed in the understanding of sin. As summarized in the Zagorsk conversations, in Orthodox theology sin means to fall along the path of discipleship, whereas in Protestant theology sin means to completely abandon this path.[49]

While agreeing in their understanding of the discipleship of Christ, as letting Christ become present in oneself, Orthodox and Protestants have different views of the range of human capabilities. For the Orthodox, discipleship means that the person is called to cooperate with the divine will through a virtuous life and asceticism. Protestants stress that "a life in discipleship always arises anew from the justifying grace of God,"[50] since wo/man can only go astray by her or his own will. Since discipleship arises from faith, the substance of faith also needs to be clarified. In Protestant theology, faith can also be described as the reconciled relationship between God and wo/man.[51] The connection between justifying faith and God's reconciling work needs to be considered attentively. Inasmuch as the term "justification" is synonymous with the term "reconciliation" in the Pauline writings, as is noted in the third Arnoldshain conversation,[52] a closer look at the reconciled communion with God mentioned in the report seems necessary.

According to the Russian theologian Dmitrij Petrovič Ogickij, the reconciliation of wo/man and God requires a radical refusal of sin.[53] This appears to contrast with the Protestant view that wo/man is radically sinful. However, from an Orthodox point of view wo/man cannot overcome sin by her- or himself, but only with God's help and in cooperation with God.[54] According to Vasilij Dmitrievič Saryčev, reconciliation is a moral change, a God-human "struggle" that "is absolutely necessary for the education of the will, for the development of the moral personality, for the attainment of true holiness, which is necessary for a true reconciliation and communion with God."[55]

Throughout Orthodox theology, a strong emphasis is placed on human free will. In fact, Ogickij speaks not only of the human answer to God's call, but also of "human participation in the work of reconciliation,"[56] which sounds very much like synergism to Protestants. On the other hand, there was consensus in the dialogue that cooperation also comes from God, since it is an effect of God's presence in us.[57]

Following this, the Zagorsk conversations also considered that the synergistic formulations of Orthodox theologians were formed apart from the development of the doctrine of grace in Western theology, and that Orthodox theology cannot therefore be compared with the controversial formulations of Protestantism.[58]

Some Conclusions

While in Orthodoxy justification is seen as the starting point of sanctification, Protestantism, in particular Lutheranism, strictly distinguishes between justification and sanctification, although the two aspects are indissolubly connected. For Protestant theology, sanctification is "no result or proof of justification" in human action, it is no "self-justification," nor is it a perfection of the new existence before God, which is established in baptism. In a Protestant perspective, wo/man is not a "co-worker" of his or her own salvation.[59] Thus, justification cannot be displayed ethically, because "faith cannot be imaged as an action that intends what or how God wants,"[60] as Gerhard Sauter emphasizes.[61] In contrast, Russian theologians emphasize the moral consequences and link them to the process of salvation.

So, despite similarities in many areas (such as the absolute priority of God's grace,[62] the relation of faith and good works as well as the new life under the guidance of the Holy Spirit), an important question remains: What is the "nature of faith that leads to salvation"?[63] According to Heinz Joachim Held, there is "still no comprehensive and adequate theological agreement (*Verständnis*) on the doctrine of justification," but some progress cannot be denied.[64] Admittedly, the delegations agreed that "faith in Christ turns out to be a life in Christ" and that "faith is always a faith which is active through love."[65] But, as Saarinen has noted, "by avoiding some central notions [such as justification and *synergeia* in the common theses] and replacing them by such confessionally neutral expressions, such as 'reconciliation' and 'new life,' the dialogue partners leave many issues undefined."[66] Of course, this does not resolve the terminological problems[67] that come along with the confessional vocabulary (of the past) but it might be seen as a step toward developing a common theological language in the future. At the same time, such an approach can also be a hindrance to understanding insofar as differences are blurred or neglected.

Numerous issues will require further study, and they include: the understanding of grace, free will, human cooperation, being created in the image of God, the assurance of salvation and the relation between imputative and effective notions of justification.

Remaining Lack of Understanding— The Debate on Human Rights as an Indicator

There remains a significant lack of understanding in the ecumenical debate on human rights. In 2008, the Bishop's Council of the ROC adopted the document "The Russian Orthodox Church's Basic Teaching on Human Dignity, Freedom and Rights,"[68] which was accompanied by an invitation to study and discuss this "follow-up to her [the ROC's] Basic Social Concept."[69] The Community of Protestant Churches in Europe (CPCE) was the first to respond to this document.

In their statements on human dignity, the ROC and the CPCE appealed to theological anthropology and to their confessional notions of salvation.[70] Consequently, they came to a different evaluation of human rights. The most significant obstacle to understanding appears to be underlying anthropological presuppositions.

Protestant and Orthodox alike consider the creation in God's image (*imago Dei*) as the basis of inalienable human dignity. In the ROC document, this dignity is also referred to as "ultimate worth."[71] But Russian theologians define the concept of dignity from the morality and virtue of a person. They equally underscore the importance of pursuing moral perfection and of taking moral responsibility in the process of becoming God-like. A morally unworthy life "darkens the dignity"[72] given by God, according to the ROC. Thus, they criticize modern freedom rights for their possible use of the freedom of choice for an immoral and therefore God-contrary life. In that way, freedom rights could potentially turn wo/men away from salvation. The Protestant Churches in Europe are critical of this position, pointing out that human dignity is derived from the gospel of justification.

Clearly, the dialogue still has a long way to go, but the remaining questions and challenges in no way mean that the doctrinal consensus achieved so far should be questioned at its core.[73] Thus far, the dialogue has revealed itself as a meeting place of two language systems that originated in distinct philosophical traditions. Many of the doctrinal differences between Eastern and Western theology are embedded and reflected in language. Differences in perspective may also arise from different selections and interpretations of biblical texts, or from difficulties in translating certain terms adequately from one language into the other. The specific connotations of concepts are especially important because they release different sets of perceptions in dissimilar contexts: like numerous other terms, "salvation" is expressed and understood within diverse semantic and lexical fields. Not the least significant achievement of the dialogue has been that it has clarified two central tasks for the future—to seek a deeper mutual understanding of soteriology and anthropology, and to work toward a common theological language.[74]

Notes

1. See Ernst Wolf, "Die Rechtfertigungslehre als Mitte und Grenze reformatorischer Theologie," in Ernst Wolf (ed.), *Peregrinatio. Bd. II: Studien zur reformatorischen Theologie, zum Kirchenrecht und zur Sozialethik* (München: Kaiser, 1965), pp. 11–21, 11.
2. See *Joint Declaration on the Doctrine of Justification*, Article 7, <http://www.lutheranworld.org/LWF_Documents/EN/JDDJ_99-jd97e.pdf> and <http://www.vatican.va/roman_curia/pontifical_councils/chrstuni/documents/rc_pc_chrstuni_doc_31101999_cath-luth-joint-declaration_en.html> (accessed March 7, 2012).
3. For an introduction to the concept of deification, see Stephen Finlan and Vladimir Kharlamov, *Theōsis. Deification in Christian Theology* (James Clarke, Cambridge, 2006). See also Michael J. Christensen and Jeffrey A. Wittung (eds.), *Partakers of the Divine Nature. The History and Development of Deification in the Christian Traditions* (Madison, NJ: Fairleigh Dickinson University Press, 2007).
4. The term "Protestant" refers here to the EKD/BEK as a community of Lutheran, Reformed, and United churches of Germany. However, it should be noted that the Lutheran position was predominant in the dialogue as a whole, and in the discussions of justification in particular.
5. Today's Sergiyev Posad.
6. See, e.g., Christoph Demke (ed.), *Sagorsk I-III. Die theologischen Gespräche zwischen der Russischen Orthodoxen Kirche und dem Bund der Evangelischen Kirchen in der DDR* (Berlin: Evangelische Verlagsanstalt, 1982), pp. 4–5, 11, 18.

7. See Heinz Joachim Held, "Neubeginn in der Kraft des Evangeliums. Zu den Anfängen der Beziehungen zwischen der Evangelischen Kirche in Deutschland und der Russischen Orthodoxen Kirche nach dem Zweiten Weltkrieg," in Rüdiger Schloz (ed.), *Partner der Ökumene. Zeugnisse der Lebensarbeit von Heinz Joachim Held* (Bielefeld: Luther Verlag, 1993), pp. 153–156.
8. See Dagmar Heller, "Divergenzen und Perspektiven im Dialog zwischen Orthodoxie und Protestantismus," *G2W* 38:9 (2010), 16.
9. The papers and theses of this meeting have not been published yet. A download of the communiqué is accessible here: http://www.ekd.de/download/Kommunique_Wittenberg_Schlussvers_Ende.pdf (accessed July 23, 2010).
10. The EKD considers the three dialogues as part of one process; thus, e.g., the second Bad Urach conversation is also referred to as the twenty-first meeting between the ROC and the EKD.
11. Reinhard Slenczka, "25 Jahre theologische Gespräche zwischen Evangelischer Kirche in Deutschland und Moskauer Patriarchat," *Ökumenische Rundschau* 34 (1985), 452–453.
12. The letter is published in *Tradition und Glaubensgerechtigkeit. Das Arnoldshainer Gespräch zwischen Vertretern der Evangelischen Kirche Deutschlands und der Russischen Orthodoxen Kirche vom Oktober 1959*, Außenamt der Evangelischen Kirche in Deutschland, ed., Studienheft 3 (Witten: Luther-Verlag, 1961), pp. 76–79.
13. Tradition und Glaubensgerechtigkeit, p. 11.
14. *Rechtfertigung im ökumenischen Dialog. Dokumente und Einführung*, Harding Meyer and Günther Gaßmann, eds., Ökumenische Perspektiven 12 (Frankfurt am Main: Otto Lembeck, 1987), p. 36.
15. Heinz Joachim Held, "Schritte und Markierungen auf dem Weg der zwölf Arnoldshain-Gespräche. Eine Zwischenbilanz," in Rüdiger Schloz (ed.), *Partner der Ökumene. Zeugnisse der Lebensarbeit von Heinz Joachim Held* (Bielefeld: Luther-Verlag, 1993), p. 205. Translations from the original German texts are by the author.
16. The quotation marks indicate that these are the official titles of the dialogue meetings.
17. Risto Saarinen delivers a fine and critical review, *Faith and Holiness. Lutheran-Orthodox Dialogue 1959–1994*, Kirche und Konfession 40 (Göttingen: Vandenhoeck und Ruprecht, 1997), pp. 84–127. In chapter 7.2 he examines the "Achievements and Remaining Tasks" in the field of soteriology.
18. This was the title of the third Zagorsk conversation.
19. For an introduction to the concept of deification, see Finlan and Kharlamov, *Theōsis*. See also Michael J. Christensen and Jeffrey A. Wittung (eds.), *Partakers of the Divine Nature. The History and Development of Deification in the Christian Traditions* (Madison, NJ: Fairleigh Dickinson University Press, 2007).
20. This may be observed in the discussions and in papers dealing with the concept of *theosis*. See, e.g., the contribution of Georg Kretschmar, "Die Heiligen als Zeichen der Erfüllung von Gottes Verheißung für den Menschen," in Kirchliches Außenamt der Evangelischen Kirche in Deutschland, ed., *Die Hoffnung auf die Zukunft der Menschheit unter der Verheißung Gottes. Eine Dokumentation über das Achte Theologische Gespräch mit der Russischen Orthodoxen Kirche in Odessa 1979*, Studienheft 12; BÖR 41 (Frankfurt am Main: Lembeck, 1979), p. 133. See also Hans Joachim Iwand's comments at the first Arnoldshain meeting in *Tradition und Glaubensgerechtigkeit*, pp. 71–72.
21. Ernst Wolf, "Der getaufte Mensch als Mitarbeiter im Versöhnungshandeln Gottes an der Welt," in Außenamt der Evangelischen Kirche in Deutschland, ed., *Taufe—Neues Leben—Dienst. Das Leningrader Gespräch über die Verantwortung der Christen für die Welt zwischen Vertretern der Evangelischen Kirche in Deutschland und der Russischen Orthodoxen Kirche*, Studienheft 6 (Witten: Luther-Verlag, 1970), pp. 33–45.
22. See Saarinen, *Faith and Holiness. Lutheran-Orthodox Dialogue 1959–1994*, Kirche und Konfession 40 (Göttingen: Vandenhoeck und Ruprecht, 1997), p. 101.

23. This dialogue is documented in *Salvation in Christ. A Lutheran-Orthodox Dialogue*, John Meyendorff and Robert Tobias (eds.) (Minneapolis, MN: Augsburg Fortress, 1992).
24. See Gerhard Sauter, "Art. Rechtfertigung, IV. Reformatorische Theologie," *TRE* 28 (1997), 318.
25. Hans Joachim Iwand, "Rechtfertigungslehre; Glaube und Werke," in *Tradition und Glaubensgerechtigkeit*, p. 46.
26. Ibid.
27. Wolf, "Der getaufte Mensch," p. 38.
28. Ibid., pp. 38–39.
29. "Theological talks 'Arnoldshain-V' between Representatives of the Evangelical Church in the Federal Republic of Germany and the Russian Orthodox Church," *The Journal of the Moscow Patriarchate* 2:1 (1972), 50. The literal translation from the German text would be: "this change of the person remains [...] a hidden event." For the German version, see thesis I.3 in Kirchliches Außenamt der Evangelischen Kirche in Deutschland, ed., *Der auferstandene Christus und das Heil der Welt. Das Kirchberger Gespräch über die Bedeutung der Auferstehung für das Heil der Welt zwischen Vertretern der Evangelischen Kirche in Deutschland und der Russischen Orthodoxen Kirche*, Studienheft 7 (Witten: Luther-Verlag, 1972), p. 20.
30. Gerhard Sauter, "Art. Rechtfertigung, VII. Dogmatisch," *TRE* 28 (1997), 359.
31. Wolf, "Der getaufte Mensch," p. 39.
32. Finlan and Kharlamov, *Theōsis. Deification in Christian Theology*, p. 1.
33. Ibid., p. 5
34. See W. Ssarytschew, "Das Wesen der Versöhnung und deren biblische Grundlage," in Außenamt der Evangelischen Kirche in Deutschland (ed.), *Versöhnung. Das deutsch-russische Gespräch über das christliche Verständnis der Versöhnung zwischen Vertretern der Evangelischen Kirche in Deutschland und der Russischen Orthodoxen Kirche 1967*, Studienheft 5 (Witten: Luther-Verlag, 1967), p. 81.
35. L. Woronow, "Die Verwirklichung der Versöhnung im Leben und in der Tätigkeit der Kirche," in *Versöhnung*, p. 108.
36. See *Salvation in Christ*, pp. 26–27.
37. Ssarytschew, "Das Wesen der Versöhnung," p. 91.
38. Ibid., p. 85.
39. Nikolaj D. Uspenskij, "Die Rettung durch den Glauben," in *Tradition und Glaubensgerechtigkeit*, p. 41. See Aleksej Osipov, "Die Heiligen als Zeichen der Erfüllung von Gottes Verheißung für den Menschen," in *Die Hoffnung auf die Zukunft*, pp. 96–113.
40. Uspenskij, "Die Rettung durch den Glauben," p. 37f.
41. See thesis 2 c) in *Tradition und Glaubensgerechtigkeit*, p. 11.
42. See thesis I.3 in *Taufe—Neues Leben—Dienst*, p. 26.
43. Iwand, "Rechtfertigungslehre," p. 45.
44. See discussion in *Tradition und Glaubensgerechtigkeit*, p. 71.
45. "Gemeinsamer Bericht an die Leitungen der Russischen Orthodoxen Kirche und der Evangelischen Kirche in Deutschland über den Stand des bilateralen theologischen Dialogs," in *Bilaterale theologische Dialoge mit der Russischen Orthodoxen Kirche*, Klaus Schwarz (ed.), Studienheft 22 (Hermannsburg: Missionshandlung, 1996), pp. 387–396.
46. Ibid., p. 392.
47. The terminological problem that the Russian word *blagodat* is not entirely identical with the term "grace" is mentioned in the summary of Zagorsk III. See Sagorsk I–III, p. 149.
48. Thesis V.5 in *Taufe—Neues Leben—Dienst*, p. 31.
49. See "Kommuniqué des IV. Theologischen Gesprächs zwischen Vertretern des Bundes der Evangelischen Kirchen in der DDR und der Russischen Orthodoxen Kirche," in *Sagorsk. Theologische Gespräche mit der Russischen Orthodoxen Kirche*, Rolf Koppe (ed.), Studienheft 25 (Hermannsburg: Missionshandlung, 1998), p. 137.
50. Ibid.

51. Cf. Heinz Joachim Held, "Kirchen im Gespräch," in Kirchenamt der EKD in Hannover / Kirchliches Außenamt des Moskauer Patriarchats, ed., *Hinhören und Hinsehen. Beziehungen zwischen der Russischen Orthodoxen Kirche und der Evangelischen Kirche in Deutschland* (Leipzig: Evangelische Verlagsanstalt, 2003), p. 138. The phrasing Held uses here is almost identical with the stated consensus. This is not surprising since Held was a leading figure in the drafting of the common report.
52. Thesis II.4 in *Versöhnung*, p. 23.
53. P. Ogickij, "Der getaufte Mensch als Mitarbeiter im Versöhnungswerk Gottes in der Welt," in *Taufe—Neues Leben—Dienst*, p. 51.
54. Ssarytschew, "Das Wesen der Versöhnung," p. 91.
55. Ibid.
56. Ogickij, "Der getaufte Mensch," p. 53.
57. Ibid., p. 50. Cf. also Ssarytschew, "Das Wesen der Versöhnung," p. 90.
58. See Werner Krusche's foreword in *Sagorsk I-III*, p. 6. See also the minutes in *Tradition und Glaubensgerechtigkeit*, p. 70f.
59. See Wolf, "Der getaufte Mensch," p. 40.
60. Sauter, "Rechtfertigung, VII. Dogmatisch," p. 359.
61. Ibid., p. 358.
62. See Iwand's contribution to the discussion at Arnoldshain I in *Tradition und Glaubensgerechtigkeit*, p. 71.
63. "Gemeinsamer Bericht," p. 392.
64. Held, "Schritte und Markierungen," p. 206.
65. Held, "Kirchen im Gespräch," 139.
66. Saarinen, *Faith and Holiness*, p. 103.
67. Ibid.
68. "The Russian Orthodox Church's Basic Teaching on Human Dignity, Freedom and Rights," *Russian Orthodox Church*, 2008: http://www.mospat.ru/en/documents/dignity-freedom-rights/, (accessed July 23, 2010).
69. Ibid.
70. "Human Rights and Morality. A Response of the Community of Protestant Churches in Europe (CPCE)—Leuenberg Church Fellowship—to the Principles of the Russian Orthodox Church on "Human Dignity, Freedom and Rights," *Community of Protestant Churches in Europe*, 2009: http://www.leuenberg.net/daten/File/Upload/doc-9806-2.pdf (accessed July 23, 2010).
71. See "Basic Teaching," I.2.
72. Ibid., I.4.
73. See *Rechtfertigung im ökumenischen Dialog*, Meyer and Günther, p. 82. Considering the example of marriage, Meyer shows that there might still be differences in the criteriological application of the doctrine of justification on other theological subjects, though a formula of consensus has been elaborated by the two dialogue partners.
74. See Held, "Schritte und Markierungen," p. 199.

17

Constructing Interreligious Consensus in the Post-Soviet Space: The Ukrainian Council of Churches and Religious Organizations

Andrii Krawchuk

Interreligious conversation is a recent development within the post-Soviet space. While encounters across religious boundaries did occur even during the Soviet period, they were for the most part limited to contacts among dissidents of different faiths or to the officially sanctioned, and closely monitored, representations at international venues such as the World Council of Churches. Since the collapse of the USSR, the legislative and constitutional reforms in various states have produced a new climate of religious liberty, permitting traditional religious communities to reemerge and to embark upon a laborious path of resuming their place in society. In the process, they have found themselves in a wholly new environment—a religious marketplace of unprecedented diversity, connected globally through the Internet, and one in which newly arrived, nontraditional religious movements and organizations aspire to the same right of religious freedom as the historically rooted, "native" religious communities. Within this environment, the traditional religions have felt a need to join together and form interreligious coalitions that could articulate their shared concerns. In 1998, the Interreligious Council of Russia was established, comprising representatives of Russian Orthodoxy, Islam, Buddhism, and Judaism. Two years earlier in Ukraine, a similar consortium was created—the Ukrainian Council of Churches and Religious Organizations (UCCRO).

This chapter analyzes official statements of the UCCRO and assesses the nature of its interreligious consensus.[1] Focusing on the social and political problems and challenges that the council has identified as priorities, its responses to those challenges and the religious considerations that informed and shaped the consensus, the study concludes with reflections on the UCCRO's work as a case study in interreligious encounter.

Background: Origin and Purpose of the UCCRO

The UCCRO was formed in 1996 as a "representative, inter-confessional consultative body with the aim of bringing together the efforts of churches and religious organizations for the spiritual renewal of Ukraine, for interchurch dialogue in Ukraine and abroad, for participation in the drafting of legislation relating to the state's relations with churches and religious organizations, and to carry out comprehensive charitable initiatives."[2] Its founding members included the leaders of the three Orthodox jurisdictions in Ukraine (Moscow and Kyiv Patriarchates, and the Ukrainian Autocephalous Orthodox Church), two Catholic jurisdictions (Greek Catholic and Roman), evangelical denominations (Baptists, German Lutherans, and Pentecostals), three Muslim leaders of Ukraine and Crimea, and the chief rabbi of Kyiv and Ukraine. Among those representatives were Metropolitan Volodymyr (Sabodan—Moscow Patriarchate), Patriarch Filaret (Denysenko—Kyiv Patriarchate), Metropolitan Mefodii (Kudriakov—Ukrainian Autocephalous Orthodox Church), Cardinal Lubomyr (Husar—Ukrainian Catholic Church), and Rabbi Yaakov Dov Bleich. Today the council comprises 18 churches and religious organizations, representing over 95 percent of the religious network in Ukraine. In its beginnings, the UCCRO had direct links with the state—the State Committee on Religious Affairs convoked the founding meeting in 1996, and its representatives participated in subsequent council meetings and cosigned some of its early statements.[3] However, in 1998 the council's statute limited membership status exclusively to religious organizations, by the end of 2005 UCCRO documents no longer included state signatories and a 2007 membership list was without state representatives.

In a 2006 address to the citizens of Ukraine, the UCCRO described itself and its work in terms of interreligious collaboration in the midst of diversity:

> We are the leaders of various churches and religious organizations. Our faith traditions [*konfesii*] glorify God and exercise their ministry in diverse languages and in diverse ways. We engage in discussions, and we have different approaches to many questions. But, for the sake of the common good, for the unity of Ukrainian society, and in order to protect the rights and freedoms of everyone who lives in Ukraine, we find common ground and work together for the good of our native land, and we call all of our fellow citizens to join us in this work. (2006–3: 501)

Understanding the common good in Ukraine in terms of social unity, civil rights, and freedoms, the UCCRO constituted a basic consensus on the need to work together across religious boundaries to safeguard and promote those social values.

The principal activities of the UCCRO are its meetings and its joint statements addressed to the government or to the Ukrainian public. In keeping with its primary focus on matters of public policy, the council's communications to the state have addressed law reform, with particular attention to religious freedom, the promotion and protection of religious values in social life, and the relationship between the state and religious organizations. In addition, the council's statements to the Ukrainian public have addressed, among other things, patriotic consciousness, social unity, and the promotion of democracy and civil society—all under the heading of overriding religious, spiritual values and respect for the diverse religious traditions in Ukraine.

Both religious and secular considerations inform the UCCRO's position statements. While the council is not a forum for interreligious exchange on theological matters, its members and signatories of documents are the leaders of the principal religious groups in Ukraine, and religious considerations inevitably inform their participation in discussions. In turn, their consensus statements usually contain at least a subtext of broadly framed religious agreement, and occasionally they do make explicit reference to divinity. In addition to the underlying religious perspectives, the UCCRO repeatedly enunciates its commitment to the touchstones of Ukraine's identity and civil society values today: its independent statehood, the Constitution and legal framework, the principles of religious freedom, and the equal, nondiscriminatory treatment of citizens of diverse traditions before the law.

In a 2007 address to newly elected members of Parliament, the council elaborated further on its mandate of addressing matters of public policy on behalf of religious believers in Ukraine. Informed by the religious values and diverse traditions of its members, the UCCRO committed itself to addressing a wide range of social issues in ethical terms and to cooperate with the state in promoting a just social order.

> The Churches and religious organizations are an important and essential component of society. Like all citizens, we are not indifferent to the future of Ukraine. In particular, we are concerned about matters of spirituality and morality, which are directly tied to matters of faith. That is why the Ukrainian Council of Churches and Religious Organizations will continue to monitor the extent to which our social, political and state life adheres to high spiritual and moral ideals. We will strive to respond in a timely way to the challenges of our time, promoting what is true and good and exposing what is false and evil, regardless of its source. (2007–4: 519)

The UCCRO thus represents a unique and unprecedented forum for working toward interreligious consensus in Ukraine. The council includes some members who meet only in this venue and of some Christian churches, which are not in communion with one another. Meetings are convened primarily to discuss public policy and legislative matters on issues of mutual concern, common ground is identified and positions are formulated collectively in joint statements. In those official pronouncements, the UCCRO understands itself as a unified body: when it has formulated a mutually agreed position, it speaks with one voice. The often-employed self-designation "We, the leaders of Churches and religious organizations of Ukraine" expresses its collaborative, corporate consciousness, which is further reinforced by the council's core commitment to religious values in society, interreligious respect, and the welfare of Ukraine and its people.

The council's working principle of consensus is generally understood to mean that no joint statement will be issued without the *unanimous* agreement of members present at a meeting—any member can veto any draft. In fact, some documents contain more signatures than others, which suggests that there is some flexibility in the formulation of official positions. Another implication of consensus as unanimous agreement is that it can potentially disincline the current members of "traditional" religious organizations to admit more recently registered religious groups, or to grant them full membership with veto power.

Individual UCCRO members, of course, freely exercise their own public and pastoral activity with independent statements and responses to a variety of issues. Occasionally, they also issue joint declarations as part of smaller, interdenominational groups—Catholic Churches and Christian Churches are two examples of such occasional collaborations. But the council, now well into its second decade of work, has become a unique meeting place for the leaders of the major religious communities of Ukraine. While the scope of its joint statements is limited to those areas in which common ground exists, an interreligious agenda has definitely assumed its place in the public policy debates of Ukraine.

Historical Memory and Ethical Interpretations of the Past

In pursuing interreligious consensus and formulating constructive proposals for the future, the UCCRO has recognized that historical self-awareness is essential: "Only by understanding our past and by assessing it properly will we be able to understand our path into the future" (2007–5: 521). On numerous occasions, the council has referred to specific moments in Ukraine's past, which in its view help to identify ethical principles and values that remain relevant today.

The UCCRO took account of its own emergence in the wake of Ukraine's independence in 1991. Within the post-Soviet environment, the challenges of social harmony and political unity were at the forefront and the council connected them with historical precedents: from Kyivan Rus' to the twentieth century, discord, enmity, misunderstanding, and distrust had been the main reasons for the repeated failures of Ukrainian statehood. In the council's view, the present reality is no different and, for the sake of Ukraine and its future, social reconciliation and unity are needed above all (2005–3: 489).

Concern for historical truth was likewise at the center of the council's statement on the seventy-fifth anniversary of the Great Famine of 1932–1933 (or "Holodomor") in Ukraine, in which millions of Ukrainians died—even more than in World War II—as a result of a deliberate, planned policy of the Soviet leadership. Describing the Famine as a "crime," a "collective tragedy," and a "terrible genocide of the Ukrainian people," the council declared that the truth about this event, silenced in the Communist period, must be now heard. It was not a matter of vengeance, which was neither necessary nor possible, since the perpetrators would be judged in the next world. Rather, the memory and respect for the victims should unify all citizens, regardless of their national, religious, or political convictions, "for only unity in the truth can enable a people to survive the most terrible stages on its historical path" (2007–5: 520–521). Four years earlier, the UCCRO had written to UN secretary general Kofi Annan with a request that the "deliberate and viciously executed" famine, which had claimed almost ten million lives, be recognized by the United Nations as an act of genocide against the Ukrainian people (2003–1: 25).

The Volyn' tragedy of 1943–1944, the wartime Polish-Ukrainian conflict that claimed tens of thousands of lives, was remembered on its sixtieth anniversary in 2003. In an open letter, the UCCRO framed its reflection within the common historical experiences of Ukrainians and Poles: "Over many centuries, history has repeatedly interwoven the fate of Ukrainians and Poles, whether uniting them in a single empire or separating them by borders in peace and in conflict" (2003–2:

26). By virtue of their shared Christian heritage, both peoples upheld the sanctity of human life, which was challenged to the core in times of armed conflict. Their common Christian identity was also a source of shared responsibility in duly remembering the past and moving together into the future. As declassified archival materials were brought to light, the moral imperative would be to avoid using them to stir up distrust or prejudice and to ensure "that *the truth of Christ's love* may not be darkened by feelings of injury, that the *irremediable mistakes* of the past may not be repeated in the future, that reciprocal forgiveness, mutual respect, peace and understanding may prevail in the relations between *our Christian—Ukrainian and Polish—peoples*" (ibid.; emphasis mine). A separate letter on this same subject to Pope John Paul II explained that, as Poland and Ukraine embarked on a path of forgiveness and reconciliation with a view to ensuring "that the past shall not determine their future," the religious leaders of Ukraine pledged their commitment to introduce a spiritual dimension into the process of reconciliation (2003-3: 27).

In its reading of Ukraine's history, the UCCRO thus affirmed the vital importance of memory for understanding present-day moral responsibilities: to honor the innocent victims of the Soviet régime, to uphold the ideals of those who gave their lives for a better future, to be mindful of shared religious beliefs and values that cut across ethnic borders, to summon the courage to acknowledge the truth, and to learn from the mistakes of the past. In facing the current challenges of state-building, social harmony, and international relations, the council aligned itself with the political pursuit of unity and peace, and in that work it committed itself to draw upon the spiritual resources of its diverse religious traditions. Connected to such broader political considerations is the immediate concern for social peace and political stability in independent Ukraine. Here as well, historical consciousness could be of great service:

> The history of the world demonstrates that those states in which the secular and spiritual authorities attend equally to [ensuring] a high level of morality have seen a consistent growth of vibrant prosperity, military strength and international recognition. But whenever licentiousness, disrespect and the setting aside of ethical norms gain the upper hand, social ruin is inevitable. As a result of such decline, most civilizations were destroyed forever—not only physically, but also from the memory of subsequent generations. (2008-1)

The UCCRO's interpretation of the past is thus primarily ethical. While leaving the actual reconstruction of facts and details to historians, the council's statements seek to identify the overarching moral lessons of history and the priorities for Ukrainian society today from a multireligious perspective. Its principal guidelines are that the truth of the past must be remembered, studied, and known—not forgotten; that it is not discord, enmity, and prejudice but good relations, understanding, and respect that provide a solid foundation for the state and for the community of states; and that the past *can* inform a positive transformation of humanity. Rather than a mere recitation of commonplaces, there is a practical aim: to establish, in the current socio-political discourse and in the public consciousness, a sense of the organic, ethical linkage between the historical past and the present reality. In the UCCRO's elaboration, the memory that mediates between the past and the present can have a profound ethical significance when it is informed by shared religious values (truth, love, respect), values that in turn establish the primacy of forgiveness over vengeance, and of reconciliation over conflict. Nor is the duty of historical memory understood as a mere accumulation of facts that may be interpreted freely. Rather, it is a call to a new social consciousness, comprising self-critical courage and empathy for the other. By attending to the experiential lessons of the past and situating them within the framework of its traditional religious values, the council trusts that Ukraine's social and political structures will develop a clear sense of direction for the future. In order to truly learn from the past, the UCCRO insists that the religious, spiritual element is essential; without it, there can be no meaningful transformation of society and no exit from the cyclical patterns of violence and enmity of the past.

In addition to deriving moral lessons from the past, the council alluded to another, practical rationale for historical memory. In addressing the types of political agitation that had become all too familiar in recent electoral campaigns, the council stated:

> Before every election in our country some politicians try to exploit issues that are harmful to the unity of the Ukrainian people and introduce division and confusion into the social and political organism. Unfortunately, the object of such political manipulation are such things as language, history and religion, which are sacred for the sovereignty and stability of the state. (2012–2)

Through its ethical reflection on the historical past, the UCCRO has tried to articulate a vision for the country that is grounded in the notion of continuity with the traditional, historical values of the people.[4] The council is convinced that continuity with the past is crucial to the identity of the "socio-political organism," that it must therefore be maintained and protected, and that any threat to that continuity is a direct threat to Ukrainian statehood.

Relations with the State and the Idea of a Partnership

An early formulation of the idea of a religion-state partnership in Ukraine was the *Draft Conception of Religion-State Relations in Ukraine*, elaborated in 2004 by parliamentarians in collaboration with the Razumkov Center for Economic and Political Research and the UCCRO.[5] This study laid out a number of fundamental principles for religion-state relations in Ukraine: freedom of conscience, understood as the freedom to believe or not to believe; the equality of all citizens before the law, irrespective of their attitude toward religion; the absence of a state religion, or a required system of religious beliefs; the separation of religious organizations and the state, and the noninterference by each social institution in the specific spheres of activity of the other (the exclusive competence or jurisdiction of each in its own internal affairs); the secular, religiously neutral character of education in state schools and the prohibition of the propagation of religion or atheism in the education system of the state; the right of religious organizations to participate in social life and to cooperate with the state; the right of religious organizations to establish their own schools (2004–1: 1.1, 1.2).

The proposed partnership model for religion-state relations would recognize that, notwithstanding the distinctiveness and separation of the two institutions, both work in the interests of Ukrainian society with a common goal: to protect freedom of conscience, to consolidate Ukrainian society, to maintain and develop its "traditional religious culture," to provide an orientation for its values and to resolve social problems (ibid., 1.3). The principal goals of such a partnership would be to promote social harmony, tolerance, interreligious peace, and good religion-state relations. In turn, those goals would be pursued through a range of jointly funded religion-state social programs with more specific objectives: promoting a healthy lifestyle; strengthening the family and protecting children; socially integrating the physically challenged; disaster relief; social rehabilitation; public education connected with the preservation of "the traditional religious culture of Ukrainian society" and the protection of social values against the incursion of a culture of violence, cruelty, and pornography; and the creation of educational opportunities for the poor (ibid.).

Taking its cue from this proposal, on April 13, 2005, the UCCRO declared in its letter to President Viktor Yushchenko that "a stable social order and its harmonious development are impossible without the creation of a partnership between the state and the religious communities" (2005–1: 478). The UCCRO was convinced that a deeper relationship or partnership with the state was realistic in light of key provisions of the Constitution of Ukraine: freedom of conscience and religious belief, and the equality of religions before the law. Furthermore, the new administration's declared commitment to the priority of spiritual values over material ones was taken as a promising sign, and a partnership would ensure that such declarations were implemented in practice. Any contraventions of the law by religious groups—such as those that had been noted in the previous presidential elections, when some religious groups took part in political "agitation"—could also be addressed more effectively through a partnership between the council and the state. The council therefore proposed that it be elevated to the status of a presidential Advisory Group "as a mechanism of interreligious and religion-state relations" (2005–1: 479).[6]. At a meeting with the council on June 14, 2005, President Yushchenko apparently expressed support for the creation of such an advisory group. However, seeing no progress on this in the course of the following year, the UCCRO wrote again to the president, emphasizing that it considered such a relationship as an *essential precondition* to effective law reform relating to religion: "Before passing any legislation relating to freedom of religion and the activities of religious communities, it is essential first of all to work out the conceptual principles of religion-state relations in Ukraine, which would establish the basis for a partnership between the state, the churches and religious organizations" (2006–2: 498).

It is not clear why the council continued to press for a special relationship with the state, or what, beyond the already existing constitutional common ground, it expected such a partnership to establish. Perhaps some of the euphoria of the Orange Revolution still persisted, along with a desire to align the religious communities of Ukraine with what was perceived as a benevolent and democratizing Yushchenko administration. There may have been a sense that this was a unique opportunity to put in place a stable structure, one that would endure and keep religion-state relations and related law reform on the civil society track, even as administrations changed. Or, as the full extent of unresolved religious questions revealed itself, the UCCRO may have concluded that, without an expanded commitment of personnel and resources by the government, the council on its own would be unable to meet new challenges in a systematic, comprehensive way. Whatever the motivation, the UCCRO continued to push for a formal partnership with the state as a priority and a precondition for progress in law reform and socioreligious harmony. But whereas the state had participated in the creation of the UCCRO and continued to recognize it as an authoritative, interreligious voice in Ukraine, it appeared reluctant to take any further steps. By November 2006 the only response was a letter from the State Department for Religious Affairs, stating that the issues were "either already resolved or impossible to resolve" (2006–6: 506). To the council's disappointment, government officials were satisfied with the existing structure of dialogue and saw no need to forge any stronger connections—to do so might have blurred the separation of religious organizations and the state. Just as the UCCRO had, in its early years, opted for an arm's length relationship by removing government officials from its membership roster, it was now the state that set aside the idea of integrating the UCCRO into its own structures. The state would certainly continue to consult with the religious groups, but the responsibility for legislation and law reform would be left to elected officials. In 2011 and 2012, the UCCRO was still returning to the partnership idea in letters to the president (2011–1, 2012–1).

Regardless whether or not a more formalized partnership is ever established, the UCCRO views the state as its principal dialogue partner. The council endorses and promotes the Constitution of Ukraine, with its principles of religious freedom and the equality of all religions before the law; the unity and stability of the Ukrainian state; and the progress toward a just civil society. It sees common cause with the state in advancing social and political values that it considers socially constructive insofar as they can inform the transition from Soviet ways of being and doing to democratic ones.

Occasionally, the UCCRO has also expressed what it expects from the state. In 2007, in three separate documents, it focused on the fundamental responsibility of individual politicians as the elected representatives of their constituencies. In the aftermath of the parliamentary election of March 2006, the council voiced concern about an apparent lack of accountability by elected officials to the voting public. In its view, the ensuing political crisis had been caused by "individual representatives of political parties, who set aside their campaign promises and programs" and instead "began to act as though they represented only themselves, and not the voters" (2007–1: 513). In opposing such behavior, the council emphasized that "the only [legitimate] bearers of the fullness of the state are the Ukrainian people" (ibid.). Members of Parliament were therefore exhorted to set aside their personal ambitions and to focus on national unity, the common good, and the future of the state—only by doing so would they remove suspicions that they were disregarding the will of the electorate. As the UCCRO elaborated further:

> The only bearer of authority in the state is the Ukrainian people, that is, all of us together. It is neither the secret arrangements of politicians, nor bribery or other forms of corruption, but exclusively the trust of the people that confers authority to political parties and their leaders. Our members of Parliament are referred to as "of the people," and every one of them must remember that they are elected for selfless service not to their own needs, but to the people. If they forget this, we can always elect others, who are more worthy and who will serve not their own interests, but the good of those who elected them. (2007–3: 517)

After the elections, the council addressed the newly elected members of Parliament with a message on accountability to the electorate. Parliamentarians were reminded that they had been called to office "by the will of the people" in order to serve the people responsibly and to enact just and wise laws (2007–4: 518). Even according to secular principles, if politicians would recognize that "the highest secular value is the social good," rather than personal, family, social, or even party interests, then their conscience would be their guide in distinguishing between authentic public service and the false path of corruption and the pursuit of personal gain. For the UCCRO, this is an essential requirement for establishing a new consciousness of the true meaning of political service.

As for religion, its place in the public sphere is an objective fact that should inform political decisions, according to the council. Since the majority of Ukrainian citizens are religious believers, any neglect or disregard of this significant sector of society would indicate "political immaturity" and would be assessed accordingly by voters (2007–4: 519). The UCCRO saw its primary role in civil society as monitoring social and political life, speaking out in the name of spiritual and moral ideals and putting forward legislative proposals on behalf of its multireligious constituency. On the presumption that these fundamentals of accountability and due respect for the religious values of the majority were in place, the UCCRO was prepared to cooperate with the state in constructing the legal framework of a just, civil society.

One further element of this religion-state discussion deserves to be mentioned: the matter of including minority, nontraditional religious groups as equal partners. While the UCCRO claims to represent over 95 percent of the religious network in Ukraine, the absence of minority religious movements in the council (which represent 37 of the 55 religious organizations in Ukraine—67 percent; 2010–2012) suggests that there may be a conceptual and practical divide between two classes of religious organizations—those that are established and traditional, and those that are not. In fact, we have an indication of just such a conceptual divide in the *Draft Conception of Religion-State Relations in Ukraine* (2004–1). Endorsed by the UCCRO and posted on its website, this proposal defined the crucial notion of the "traditional religious culture" of Ukrainian society as

> the aggregate of historically original religions of the Ukrainian people ("sukupnist' relihii, istorychno prytamannykh narodu Ukrainy"), which shaped their culture and mentality, and which society recognizes de facto as a common value and a common cultural possession. Also indicative is the de facto recognition by the state and by society of the significant role of the Kyivan Church tradition of Christianity in Ukraine (Orthodox and Greek Catholic) in shaping the culture of Ukraine and the mentality of the Ukrainian people, which has been manifested by the establishment of major Christian feasts as federal holidays in Ukraine, and by broadcasts of Christian liturgical services on state radio and television. Also undeniable has been the contribution to the culture and mentality of the Ukrainian people as an ethnic and political society by the religions of national minorities—Roman Catholicism, Protestantism, Islam, Judaism—which have lived in Ukraine for centuries, which enrich Ukraine's spiritual-cultural wealth, which enhance its independence ("spryiaiut' ii samobutnosti") and openness to the world community, and which prevent the homogenization of the population and the depersonalization of Ukraine in a world that is becoming globalized." (2004–1: "Dodatok—Holovni terminy ta poniattia: 'Tradytsiina relihiina kul'tura ukrains'koho suspil'stva'")

Thus, we have an ethnoreligiously and historically based distinction between two classes of "traditional religions": the Orthodox and Greek Catholic forms of

Ukrainian Christianity, recognized by the state and by Ukrainian society as *the historically original religions of the Ukrainian people*, as rooted in the millennial history of Kyivan Rus', and as having shaped the culture and mentality of the Ukrainian people; and the non-Christian "religions of national minorities," which appeared in Ukraine after Kyivan Rus', which are not connected to the country's origins, but which *contributed to* the culture and mentality of the Ukrainian people. The implicit primacy reserved for the heirs of Kyivan Christianity has been captured elsewhere in the expression "the Churches of Volodymyr's Baptism."

New religious movements, a class apart, are understood by the authors of the *Draft Conception* as faiths that appeared on the scene since the middle of the twentieth century:

> Because of their recent appearance, the religious practices of these faiths are not sufficiently known, which creates problems with their social acceptance and legal recognition by the state. A particular problem, which is recognized internationally, is the existence of some new religious movements, whose practices can be *harmful* to the life and health of citizens, to social morality, to civil order and to the *preservation of the traditional religious culture* of a society. (2004–1: "Dodatok—Holovni terminy ta poniattia: 'Novitni relihiini rukhy (neorelihii)'"; emphasis mine)

If the UCCRO were to fully embrace such reasoning, its very understanding of religious freedom and equality could potentially set up a hierarchy of "preferred religions" and "second-class religions"—in effect, ensuring freedom and equality for some, but not for all. Taken to its logical conclusion, such a position could be challenged on constitutional grounds. It would also run counter to the principle enunciated by the president that "for the Ukrainian state all Churches and religious organizations are equal and native" ("rivni i vodnochas ridni," May 13, 2010, statement by Viktor Yanukovych, cited in 2010–1). Sooner or later, the council will have to face this potential inconsistency directly and decide whether its tradition-centered discourse on religious freedom and equality can retain its credibility if some religious minorities are excluded.

Responding to Processes in Society: The Social Role of Religious Institutions

Beyond its juridical-political representations to the state, the UCCRO's social activity has been guided by an idea of solidarity across religious boundaries. As Bishop Yevstratii (Ukrainian Orthodox Church-Kyiv Patriarchate) explained, it is the idea "that we, as a community of religious organizations—while adhering to different religions, belonging to different denominations, without altering our identities, or faith traditions, or beliefs—aspire to give a practical example to society of how to speak with one voice."[7]

Individually, the council's member institutions have been committed to service in their communities and beyond, providing social assistance on the ground, wherever it was needed. Lest such vital contributions to society be ignored, or religious communities be considered as peripheral or indifferent to pressing social concerns, the UCCRO explained: "In addition to their work in the spheres of spirituality and ethics, religious institutions consider it their responsibility to care for the more vulnerable members of society—orphans, the sick, the homeless, alcoholics and drug addicts—thus to a large extent carrying out the social work which should be done by the state" (2006–5: 505).

Embedded within the raison d'être of political and religious institutions, social philanthropy constituted an additional area of common ground between the two. Just as religious communities were living up to their responsibility in these matters, the UCCRO felt that the state should also do its part by allocating sufficient funds for social assistance and by allowing religious groups to expand the scope of their social philanthropy. Inevitably, this raised the issue of budgets, finances, and the allocation of scarce resources:

> Churches and religious organizations have a broad range of opportunities to undertake activities that raise the level of spirituality and ethics in society. At the same time, some unresolved, problematic issues prevent churches and religious organizations from delivering social services of the highest quality. These issues relate to legal provisions for churches and religious organizations to carry out social services, and to enhanced material support for such activities. (2005–1: 479 #3)

Thus, both the state and the religious communities of Ukraine were duty-bound to respond to urgent needs in society, and the most effective approach to nationwide social assistance would be one in which they joined their efforts.

Beyond its commitment to provide social assistance, the UCCRO also identified other areas of social life in which the core beliefs of diverse traditions could inform joint initiatives. An early instance of this was the *Memorandum of Agreement on the Coverage of Religious Issues by the Mass Media* (1998: 19–21), jointly signed by Metropolitan Volodymyr Sabodan (Ukrainian Orthodox Church—Moscow Patriarchate) on behalf of the UCCRO, Information Minister Z. Kulyk, and the Chair of the State Committee on Religious Affairs V. Bondarenko. Having reviewed the state of the question in Ukraine, the signatories noted three areas of concern: "the denominational patiality of certain publications, which creates conflicts in the religious milieu; the increasing dissemination of literature, videos and periodical publications that promote licentious and violent behavior and undermine social morality; and televised broadcasts of foreign missions, which do not contribute to the development of Ukrainian spirituality and culture" (ibid., 19). Recognizing the "important roles of the mass media in shaping the religious culture and the interfaith climate in our country, and of religious organizations, whose faith-based principles strengthen the humanitarian principles of society," the signatories agreed that corrective measures were needed, in particular, the development of high-quality educational programming with a balanced, unbiased presentation of the role of religion in society; ending the distribution of publications that promote violence and sexual immorality; public information about the teachings and practices of new religious movements, particularly those of "totalitarian cults" and groups with tarnished international reputations; and restricting access to the mass media by foreign missions in favor of the "historical churches" (ibid., 19–20).

Related issues were addressed in the UCCRO's *Letter to the Ukrainian People on the Ethical Content of Advertising* (2005–2). Affirming the priority of spiritual over material values, the document inveighed against hedonism and consumerism in social life. Specifically targeting the abuse of alcohol and tobacco and pointing to their profound social costs, the council called for legal restrictions (and in some cases, a full prohibition) on their advertising, on their sponsorship of recreational and sports events, and regulations on their use in public spaces (2005–2: 485). Yet another type of "morally inadmissible" advertising was one that abused the ideas and symbols, which were sacred to believers. The UCCRO deplored the increase in the "inappropriate use of religious symbols" and distortions of religious traditions that offended the religious feelings of believers. In some cases, this had led to physical violence associated with religious or ethnic intolerance. In raising these concerns, the council acknowledged that its pronouncements went against the grain of popular culture: "The Churches and religious organizations realize that their spiritual and moral values stand in sharp contrast to current, so-called 'liberal values,' behind which we find egoism, hedonism, amorality and a consumer attitude towards life and the natural environment" (2006–1: 495).

As for the rights of free speech and free expression in artistic and literary works, they were not to be misinterpreted as a license to disregard or disrespect other religious or ethnic identities:

> "The dissemination of false, offensive and humiliating ideas, the fueling of suspicion and hatred by one group in society towards another, the desire to assert one's own ego at any cost—these are signs not of free speech and self-expression, but a distortion of that freedom. Everyone has the right to free speech and self-expression, but the use of that right must be firmly tied to respect for others, their opinions and traditions—including religious ones." (Ibid.)

Observing that the mass media, publishers, and people in the creative arts were at the center of the problem, the council exhorted the professionals working in those fields to be mindful of their social responsibility, to draw religious knowledge from primary sources, rather than from "distorted theories," and to present disputed questions in a balanced way. Churches and religious organizations were likewise entitled to teach their own perspectives and traditions, while maintaining the same spirit of respect for others.

Education policy was also a priority on the UCCRO's social agenda. As with the concerns around the mass media, this religion-state conversation began with a memorandum of agreement signed on April 18, 2000, by Patriarch Filaret (Ukrainian Orthodox Church-Kyiv Patriarchate) as chair of the UCCRO, Education Minister V. Kremen', and the Chair of the State Committee on Religious Affairs V. Bondarenko. The preamble recognized that

> the historical and cultural development of the Ukrainian people over the past millennium is connected with the ideas of Christianity; the establishment of higher education in Ukraine has its origin in theological studies; the social, political and cultural particularities of Ukrainian society have been shaped to a significant degree by the Christian worldview of the majority of the Ukrainian people; and it is therefore necessary to renew, maintain and develop Ukraine's educational traditions within the discipline of theology. (2000: 22)

In light of those considerations, the signatories resolved, first of all, to take measures to introduce the study of Christian ethics in state-run primary and secondary schools, with a view toward teaching students the foundations of the Christian worldview, the ethical principles, and the core elements of "the Christian tradition of Ukraine." They further agreed that the introduction of theology as an academic discipline in universities would advance social harmony:

> Insofar as there is a significant number of faith traditions in Ukraine, each of which has its own dogmatic particularities, the signatories feel that the establishment of a university-level program of theological education should be based on fundamental principles and dogmatic positions which are common to all, and which do not evoke irreconcilable disputes among the theologians of different faith traditions. (2000: 22–23)

But while this desire to promote social harmony was germane to the argument for the social relevance of theology, the notion of theological studies as a unified, comprehensive body of material reflected an understanding of "Christian tradition" in its official, institutional formulations, rather than a diversity of expressions elaborated through free theological exploration. Second, the implicit primacy of the Christian tradition accords a special, preferential status to Christian communities with a historical track record in Ukraine over that of non-Christian religious organizations.[8] Further studies of this document may shed light on the UCCRO's internal discussions—in particular, on the views of its non-Christian members on this question. Some of these unresolved issues may explain why the memorandum of agreement of 2000 had still not been implemented by 2005.

Although Patriarch Filaret had formally signed the memorandum of 2000 on behalf of the UCCRO, in light of the statement's sharp focus on the Christian tradition, follow-ups were taken over by the leaders of the Christian churches of Ukraine on their own. Thus, in 2005 this subgroup of the UCCRO, speaking only for themselves, wrote a letter to the president, the prime minister, the education minister, and the speaker of parliament and called for a program of moral education in the primary and secondary schools that would be based on "the principles of the Christian cultural heritage," and would include the teaching of the foundations of Christian ethics in Ukrainian culture. However, this time the proposal was framed more broadly and inclusively:

> The study of this subject [i.e., the foundations of Christian ethics] as a non-denominational subject, unaccompanied by any religious rituals, will promote social consolidation centered on common cultural symbols, ethical values and pedagogical principles. In the interests of advancing tolerance and neighborly relations, we propose that an exposure to other religious cultures and traditions of Ukraine also be included in the curriculum.[9]

This revised proposal, which replaced ritual and denominational particularity with an attentiveness to other faith traditions suggested that informal consultations may have taken place with government officials, and that their feedback was incorporated into the document. In the end, while still coming only from the heads of Christian churches, the revised proposal was more attuned to secular and pluralist dimensions of current Ukrainian social life. The earlier affirmation of the central importance of (Christian) theology was reduced here to a call for "an appropriate specialization" at the university level.

By the end of 2005, there was some progress on the introduction of an ethics program for public schools. Through the joint efforts of church representatives, of education administrators, and of teachers of ethics, the *Concept for the Teaching of Courses with Spiritual-Moral Content* was drafted.[10] Rather than having an exclusively Christian thrust, the program would provide an option between two parallel streams: Christian ethics and philosophical ethics. Here as well, the teaching of Christian ethics would involve no rituals or prayers and would include information about the non-Christian traditions and cultures of Ukraine. However, both the Christian and the philosophical streams would emphasize *specifically Ukrainian* moral and cultural values.

If the education issue initially appeared to have divided the UCCRO into Christian and non-Christian camps and to have required some compromise in order to move forward, there was no such division on homosexuality. "Deeply disturbed by efforts in our country to legally establish so-called same-sex marriages or the registration of same-sex partnerships," the council issued two statements that expressed its categorical opposition to the legal recognition of such unions and of the right of gay couples to adopt children (2006–4, 2007–2). Signed by all the members of the UCCRO, an open letter to the Parliament of Ukraine and a separate public declaration spelled out a particular instance of interreligious consensus. Emphasizing that their collective position was that of representatives of Christian, Muslim, and Jewish faith traditions, the council declared:

> The sacred writings of our religions state unequivocally that sexual relations between members of the same sex are a *grave sin*. Divine punishment comes not only to those who personally engage in such relations, but also to those who endorse it publicly or silently. Consequently, religious organizations cannot stand by with indifference when, under the guise of a struggle for human rights and democracy, a tolerant and even positive attitude towards same-sex sexual relations is advanced in Ukrainian society. (2006–4: 503–504; emphasis mine. Cf. 2007–2: 515 #4: "*contrary to nature and evil*" and #6)

But while these public statements sent a crystal-clear message to both the state and Ukrainian society at large about the council's vehement opposition to gay marriage, the human rights dimension of that position remained vague and problematic. Beyond the UCCRO's rejection of human rights arguments by the advocates of gay marriage, both documents had also made two significant affirmations: (1) "Religious believers do not hate or hold prejudices against people with homosexual inclinations" (2006–4: 503; 2007–2: 515 #5); and (2) "We do not advocate discrimination against people who consider themselves to be homosexuals" (2006–4: 504; 2007–2: 516 #9). The implication was that the homosexual community is entitled, from the standpoint of the various religions, to basic human protections—against hatred, prejudice, and discrimination. Yet the use of religious argument to marginalize the community in Ukraine on moral grounds undermines the human rights premise of these two affirmations, even though it is unlikely that they were made gratuitously. The various religious traditions also have scriptural teachings that, beyond the passing of moral judgments, enable believers to embrace the other in his/her humanity. The crucial question is whether the UCCRO's official position on homosexuality will overshadow more conciliatory, pastoral approaches, and whether it will aggravate an already troubling social marginalization. In the face of alarming levels of homophobia, of violence perpetrated against homosexuals, and of the high incidence of suicide among socially marginalized groups in Ukraine, the majority religions will have to consider whether, in light of their core beliefs, it suffices merely to declare that they do not hate or discriminate against homosexuals.

In April 2010, as the Parliamentary Assembly of the Council of Europe prepared to discuss a draft resolution on discrimination on the basis of sexual orientation and gender identity, the UCCRO expressed its reservations to President Yanukovych about any such move that would require "all CE member countries to guarantee legal recognition of same-sex partnerships and to extend the rights of representatives of the homosexual community" (2010–1). Disappointed that the Ukrainian delegation had supported the proposal at the draft stage, the UCCRO restated its categorical opposition to "the introduction, internationally or in Ukraine, of any initiatives oriented towards the propaganda of homosexuality and efforts to legalize same-sex relations." Relying on its earlier position statements on this subject, the UCCRO did not reiterate its arguments, but pointed out that the core idea of its *Declaration of Opposition to the Phenomenon of Homosexuality* (2007–2)—that people of faith "cannot be reconciled with homosexuality, other amoral acts and their propaganda, as phenomena in spiritual and social life"—represented "the convictions and the worldview of the absolute majority of Ukrainian society" (2010–1).[11] Subsequent UCCRO statements have affirmed marriage as an exclusively heterosexual alliance (2011–1b; 2012–3), the latter explicitly linking this notion to traditional, theological values—and to the ultimate, legislative goal of these religion-state initiatives: "These and other Eternal Truths, which were given to us by the Almighty through the Books of Sacred Scripture and which were reflected naturally in the particularities ('samobutnostiakh') of our peoples, should be the foundations of national legal systems, since only they can guarantee constant and secure social development if they are duly recognized and respected" (2012–3).

On abortion, in 2008 the UCCRO adopted a set of proposed amendments to the Constitution of Ukraine, which were submitted to President Yanukovych in April 2011. The proposals included recognizing "every person's inviolable right to life *from conception*" (2011–1b; emphasis mine). The UCCRO's public policy voice on the issue was given special prominence in 2009, when the Ukrainian Ministry of Health established a Community Council on Cooperation with the UCCRO. The goals of this consultative Community Council, no less than two-thirds of which would be comprised of representatives of churches and religious organizations (i.e., the UCCRO or its delegates), include "elaborating *and representing* the positions of the Churches and religious organizations when making health and bioethics policy recommendations to the Ministry of Health."[12] In addition, two UCCRO chairs have addressed the issue on separate occasions. In a word of greeting to the IV National Congress of Bioethics in Kyiv (September 2010), the Roman Catholic Bishop Markian Trofimiak declared that human life begins "from the moment of conception we are dealing with a human person," and that the artificial termination of pregnancy is both a form of homicide and a violation of the dignity of women. He then urged the congress to consider "the protection of the rights and dignity of every person from the moment of conception to the moment of natural death."[13] And in his letter to Hungarian president János Áder, the Greek Catholic Major Archbishop Sviatoslav Shevchuk reiterated that human life from conception should be constitutionally protected (2012–3). While legislative reform in this area remains a future prospect, the UCCRO has certainly positioned itself very strategically through its guaranteed majority on the Community Council. But in a country where, according to official statistics, there were 180,000 abortions in 2009 and an estimated 8 million since independence, the council faces a greater challenge at the level of social attitudes.[14]

The UCCRO's primary focus for achieving social change is on law reform. Observing that "the average citizen is without any authentic moral authorities," the council cited an array of "pseudo-values" ("free love," legalized licentiousness, sexual perversions, narcotics, the cultivation of greed, intolerance, ignorance, anti-Semitism, xenophobia, and disrespect toward national and religious values) and a causal link between the decline of social morality and the incidence of alcoholism, drug abuse, venereal diseases, the AIDS epidemic, and the collapse of family values. The council therefore called for adherence to Ukraine's social morality laws (2008–1) and for law reform to improve the protection of social morality (2011–1a: 1.2). Furthermore, new legislation on marriage and the family, on the protection of motherhood and childhood, and on the mutual responsibilities of parents and children should, in its view, provide "clear, legislative criteria of morality in society" and return to traditional values by drawing upon "the experience and wisdom of our ancestors" (2011–2). Such new laws were to be clear and effective, not merely declarative, and accompanied by "an effective mechanism for its implementation" (ibid.).

Concluding Reflections

In the ongoing post-Soviet transition, the legalized religions of Ukraine have formed a coalition, the interreligious UCCRO, which has undertaken a formidable task: to secure religious freedom provisions in the law and to transform the social and national consciousness of the population. The following reflections are an attempt to link this experience with some ideas from the broader, international discussion of interreligious dialogue, to situate the UCCRO's work within that wider discussion, and to raise some questions.

Is this a type of interreligious dialogue? The UCCRO's terms of reference do not foresee a dialogue that would focus on core theological beliefs with the goal of religious rapprochement, and no such dialogue is planned.[15] It is important to note that the prospect of faith-based consensus is especially problematic in Ukraine, given the absence of canonical recognition and communion among some of the Christian denominations. In fact, precisely in light of this, the very existence of the UCCRO is a remarkable achievement. The council has produced a substantial body of material that identifies common ground on social ethics and the place of religious values in the social and political arenas. In its joint statements, the council has explicitly referred to fundamental values that are shared by its members. Individual participants have even suggested that the council may be considered a unique type of ecumenical or interfaith encounter. Certainly, the numerous deliberations, regular meetings, joint statements, and various activities over the years have produced a sense of solidarity, mutual trust, and common cause within this group of religious leaders. The groundwork is definitely there, yet a full-fledged, interreligious dialogue would need to encompass more—the unrestricted exploration of a wider range of issues, such as: differences at the level of core beliefs, particular religious identities, historical experiences and grievances, a respectful study of past conflicts and enmity, all with an explicit goal of relationship-building. Such a reorientation can only be decided by the council itself, and only when its members are ready. But it would mark a significant turning point in the council's evolution, a coming of age of its vision for the future of Ukraine. Thus far, the UCCRO has looked outward at the state and at society, and pronounced largely on matters in which agreement already exists. By choosing to look also self-critically inward, the major religions of Ukraine could bear powerful testimony to the way in which religion can be a constructive, peace-building factor for the state and society alike.

Martin Marty has proposed several criteria for determining whether interreligious understanding is present among the monotheistic religions.[16] One of these involves coming to an awareness of boundaries: who is included or excluded, and who decides the boundaries. For the UCCRO, this raises a question about its current modes of operation and future orientation. While the council is a unified body, and enjoys state recognition as the representative voice of the majority of religious believers in the country, religious minorities and new religious movements are not members and there appears to be little prospect of their admission in the foreseeable future. The council may reserve the right to maintain its membership standards, but if that exclusion were to be extended to pronouncements in the public sphere it could undermine the UCCRO's declared commitments to religious freedom and equality.

Another criterion asks more pointedly about attitudes toward the outsider, the excluded other, and reminds us that interreligious dialogue involves both a readiness to listen to the other and an intention to learn from the other. We have noted that the council has aligned itself with a notion of "traditional religions," whose leaders feel that their values are threatened by minority religions. A similar theme of threat to traditional values is employed in its denunciations of homosexuality, and informs its critical stance toward globalization and secular trends in society. If left unchecked, this discourse of a threat to core values and the corresponding retreat to traditions of the past, a characteristic pattern of conservative or fundamentalist tendencies in religion, could become a cornerstone of the council's identity and sense of mission. In the worst case, the UCCRO could lose sight of the capacity of nontraditional, minority constituencies to make significant contributions to civil society and to participate meaningfully in articulating what Eboo Patel has referred to as "a vision of society where no one is victimized."[17] The emergence of a subgroup comprised of Christian members of the council suggests that the border-making impulse may be at work even within the UCCRO, charting out a hierarchy of denominationally based priorities. Thus, it appears that the organization faces a fundamental option. One path is through a process of isolation, exclusion, and retreat into the past, to refuse encounter with the marginalized other and to withdraw, gradually and deliberately, from participation in the construction of an inclusive, new order. The other path is to apply its valuable experience in partnership-building toward addressing all forms of injustice, discrimination, and prejudice, and to embrace all of society, including minority religions, marginalized groups, and nonbelievers. In this fundamental option, much will depend on effective religious leadership that can build on the experiential knowledge that some of the most prosperous and successful local communities are those that welcome the marginalized through outreach, inclusion and embrace.

It may well be that the missing link is what Raimundo Panikkar called the "intra-religious dialogue," and which he introduced as a vital prerequisite for interreligious dialogue: "No *inter*-religious dialogue can yield any fruit unless it is... preceded by an *intra*-religious dialogue within the partners themselves."[18] By intrareligious dialogue, he meant (1) a critical awareness that one's own belief, even regarded as ultimate and exhaustive, does not preclude a capacity to step back intellectually and to adopt a perspective from which one's own tradition may be seen, judged, and even criticized; and (2) a recognition of the possibility that one's own expression of faith allows room for enrichment by the other. In this view, only those who were able to "critically undergo an internal dialogue within themselves" were ready for the religious dialogue.

It is likely that many of the UCCRO's collective statements were only possible precisely because some form of "internal dialogue" had indeed informed the individual representatives over the years. However, authentic dialogue goes deeper still—Panikkar distinguished between the "ecclesiastical meetings" of official representatives of religious groups and a more profound level of interreligious encounter. He noted a built-in limitation of the official encounters of religious leaders, where the rules of the game are premised on the stability and integrity of established perspectives. While such encounters may identify common ground, shared interests, and concerns, they would not necessarily require any self-critical scrutiny or revision of established positions:

> Ecclesiastical dignitaries are bound to preserve tradition; they must consider the multitude of believers who follow that religion, for and to whom they are responsible. They are faced with practical and immediate problems; they must discover ways to tolerate, to collaborate, to understand. But in general they cannot risk new solutions. They have to approve and put into practice already proven and fruitful ways. But where are those proofs to come from? The religious encounter we have in mind will certainly pave the way for ecclesiastical meetings and vice versa but must be differentiated and separated from them.[19]

What, then, might be some steps toward the further consolidation and expansion of the interreligious effort in Ukraine?

Bridging National and Local Initiatives

The UCCRO's achievements in interreligious consensus may be numerous and significant, however they have yet to unlock the full potential of an interreligious dialogue. If Panikkar is correct in pointing out the practical limitations of religious leaders and their "top-down" approach in the interreligious dialogue, then the missing *intra*religious link will be found in a complementary "bottom-up," or grassroots, engagement in the dialogical process. The intellectual and spiritual potential of regional and local, community-based initiatives for advancing the interreligious dialogue cannot be overstated—nor should it be underestimated. In addition to the existing high-level talks and nationwide declarations, the UCCRO's goals of promoting tolerance and social harmony can be effectively advanced through local, grassroots interfaith projects. The council's experience of collaborative, practical reflection and solidarity needs to inform and be informed by local and regional initiatives. Just as the UCCRO itself drew upon the valuable experience of spontaneous, local initiatives, its consensus on the national scene does not mean that it should ignore the equally important work on the ground, in the villages, cities and oblasts (provinces). In order for local initiatives to flourish and to bear fruit, they will require the encouragement and active support of those leaders who participate in the national council. Jews, Christians, Muslims, and other religious believers in Ukraine are meeting and working out new modes of encounter and coexistence in the secular, public sphere. On their own initiative, local religious communities are establishing new levels of understanding and mutual learning with their neighbors across religious boundaries. There is a great potential for interreligious progress, both at the top and on the ground. Perhaps the most crucial first step would be to bridge the gap between the UCCRO and local initiatives for interreligious understanding. How can this be done? The stories of local initiatives, both successes and challenges, should inform and shape the council's agenda, while the council's experience and insights should be effectively communicated to local communities.

Education

The structure, content, and goals of religious education in Ukraine also hold great potential for significant interreligious advances. Diana Eck and others have pointed out the importance and the challenge of promoting higher levels of religious literacy: "The idea that someone would deliberately study someone else's religion is really almost unheard of in many parts of the world."[20] As interreligious encounters and dialogues proceed throughout the world, religious literacy, a more profound understanding of the religious and cultural other, can further substantiate the progress that has been made. Of special importance are the curricula of denominational seminaries and theological schools, which form the future leaders of religious communities. In Ukraine, the experience of concerted efforts at religious encounter, consensus, and trust can serve as a foundation for curriculum reforms and new courses that would broaden the intercultural knowledge and sensitivity of future ministers, priests, rabbis, and imams—and through them, understanding and respect across religious boundaries in local communities. Eck has emphasized the transformative role that can be played by programs of theological education attuned to the realities of global and local diversity:

> How must theological education be reconceptualized to prepare candidates for ministry in a world in which one's neighbors are not only other Christians, but Muslims, Sikhs, Hindus, Jews, Buddhists, and people of native traditions? *The study of the world's religious traditions can no longer be a peripheral concern in preparing Christian ministers for professional work. Both the global situation and the local situation require an understanding of people of other faiths —their scriptures, rituals, loyalties and aspirations.* Yet still most theological schools, with only a few exceptions, have made no move to integrate the study of other religious traditions into the preparation for an educated Christian ministry.[21]

This argument for the urgency of educational reforms that would prepare a different kind of Christian minister may be beneficial to all the faith traditions and religious organizations of Ukraine. Each in its own right would stand to gain from a new generation of leaders, who would be educated in the religious ways of their neighbors, equipped to face the social challenges of prejudice, mistrust, and enmity, proactive in local interreligious initiatives and growing together with others through understanding, mutual respect, and cooperation in a vibrant socioreligious milieu.

Such a reorientation would require a measure of theological courage proceeding from an awareness that interreligious dialogue does not pose a threat to the integrity of religions. What it does represent is a shift from monologue to dialogue, from the unilateral language of "proclaiming," "announcing," and "professing" to one that is balanced with a language of listening and mutuality.[22] In order for interreligious dialogue to occur, the fear of "syncretism," the misconception that dialogue is aimed at religious assimilation, or structural fusion should be set aside. The goal of interreligious dialogue is to discover both common ground *and differences*, and to move toward deeper understandings, both of the religious other and of oneself. To those who would maintain that a discussion of one's core beliefs with people of other traditions is risky or fraught with danger, Eck points out: "It is the parochialism and ethnocentrism, not the particularity, of the denominations and churches that are challenged and overcome in ecumenical encounter. Similarly, in encounter with people of other faiths, it is Christian parochialism, not Christian particularity, that is challenged and overcome."[23] The promotion of a robust, intercultural dimension in religious and theological education will be a litmus test for the presence of a genuine desire in Ukraine to pursue interreligious dialogue. Conversely, resistance to it would suggest that there is not yet a readiness to part ways with the patterns of monologue and isolation.

New Readings of the Historical Past

Much like theological language, historical language can be used to draw borders, bolster ethnoreligious identity, and exclude the religious and cultural other. The reorientation toward interreligious dialogue involves a shift away from the paths of monologue and isolation. A number of the UCCRO's historical reflections have demonstrated such a shift, and a willingness to reread one's own past in light of the neighbor's reading, perceptions, memories, and sensitivities. This is a vitally important project, and its further development holds much promise for the future of interreligious understanding and cooperation in Ukraine. As a collective project of the traditional religions (Christians representing some 96 percent of Ukraine's population), it can enrich the (78 percent Ukrainian) national historical narrative by including other ethnic voices: Russian, Polish, Jewish, Tatar. The work of critically and self-critically reviewing the historical past—together with one's neighbor—is a noble undertaking, which could lay the groundwork for well-informed and respectful intercultural dialogue, understanding, and cooperation. The challenges are huge (the Russian-Ukrainian dialogue being a case in point) and much remains to be done, but it must be recognized that the UCCRO, with its Russian and Ukrainian members, has in fact set a historical precedent. As with other areas of the interreligious dialogue, a new and more inclusive reading of history is not about renouncing one's identity, but rather about situating it within its dynamic, relational context—within a common history that is shared with other cultural communities.

The rereading and rethinking of religious history can also involve a recuperation of forgotten values and practices. Ever since the publication of John Boswell's

Same-Sex Unions in Pre-modern Europe (1994), the premodern Greco-Slavic practice of brother-making (Greek: *adelphopoiesis*, Slavonic: *bratotvorenie*) has been a subject of controversy. Yet, regardless whether it was a marriage-like union or a form of adoption, it was indisputably a type of spiritual fraternity or partnership and was confirmed and blessed in Eastern Christian rituals, including those of the Kyivan tradition. The return to the historical traditions of Ukraine can become a source of enrichment if it is not carried out selectively and if it takes account of the diversity of human partnerships, which elicited no controversy in the past.[24] The issue for the UCCRO is not about whether to change its declared position and adopt the contrary view—that is as unlikely as a sudden climate change in social attitudes on this subject. For now, the issue is about how religious objections to gay marriage will be articulated—through a language of exclusion and condemnation toward an entire community—or whether an alternative language can be found, even in disagreement, which will go a step beyond the dismissive, minimalist terminology of "non-hatred and non-discrimination" and demonstrate that official religious pronouncements can still maintain an authentic respect toward others as human beings and as citizens. Mindfulness of the diverse, traditional forms of spiritual relationship could also temper the impulse to a reactionary language of exclusion and condemnation.

The ongoing quest for democratic values, civil society, and religious understanding in post-Soviet Ukraine is occurring with fits and starts. There is the benefit of historical hindsight—the recent memory of totalitarianism, and a firm resolve to chart out a course that is noncoercive and respectful. In the religious sphere, this is most evident in the UCCRO's core commitment to religious freedom and equality. At the same time, there are also enduring habits and impulses—notably, to seek out and prefer that which is certain, clear, and unequivocal. Some patterns of religiously motivated exclusion or marginalization are visible in the UCCRO's attitudes toward minority religious and social communities; patterns of isolation and protectionism are likewise evident in its suspicion toward globalization and secularization. But all in all, the council's track record remains quite impressive—both in its representations of religious concerns to the state and in its social initiatives, it has achieved interreligious consensus and formulated significant pronouncements.

The question of building on this to create a climate for interreligious dialogue in Ukraine will be bound up with a number of important requirements. Perhaps chief among them is a clear understanding of what interreligious dialogue is, and what it is not: the old antiecumenical theses, borrowed from external sources, which presumed that the goal is to produce a "superchurch," or that it involves some sort of coercion, simply do not correspond to the reality of contemporary dialogues and must be put to rest. A new understanding will only emerge from a thorough, analytical study of the ecumenical movement and the global interreligious dialogues—their origins, evolving ideas and goals. Until they are studied and understood, these processes of recognizing and acting on the ethical imperative to build the common good in a global community will remain vulnerable to distortion and unfounded fears.

In 2008, Archbishop Rowan Williams of Canterbury responded to *A Common Word between Us and You* (2007), the open letter of Islamic leaders to Christian leaders, which called for common ground and understanding between the two religious traditions. A profound reflection on the Muslim document and on the nature of dialogue, Williams' seminal statement contained the following passage: "We interpret your invitation as saying 'let us find a way of recognizing that on some matters we are speaking enough of a common language for us to be able to pursue both exploratory dialogue and peaceful co-operation with integrity and without compromising fundamental beliefs.'"[25]

The UCCRO has demonstrated that it possesses some core elements of dialogue: a sufficient common language and common ground that have permitted the pursuit of peaceful cooperation, without compromising fundamental beliefs. Even exploratory, theological dialogue must already exist at some tacit level, whether in the selection of issues to be jointly addressed or in the working out of common positions and religious rationales. The interreligious conversation in Ukraine has certainly made great strides over the years, building new relationships of understanding and trust through encounter across religious borders. The next phase, full-fledged interreligious dialogue, will require a shift of focus from social policy and religion-state relations to core beliefs and values.

Documentary Sources Cited

Collections

SZD — "Spil'ni zvernennia predstoiateliv Ukrains'koi Hreko-Katolyts'koi Tserkvy ta inshykh Tserkov i relihiinykh spil'not Ukrainy." [Joint Addresses of the Primates of the Ukrainian Greek Catholic Church with the heads of other churches and religious communities in Ukraine] in *Sotsial'no Zoriientovani Dokumenty Ukrains'koi Hreko-Katolyts'koi Tserkvy 1989–2008*. L'viv: Vydavnytstvo Ukrains'koho Katolyts'koho Universytetu, 2008, pp. 455–524.

VRTs — *Vseukrains'ka Rada Tserkov i Relihiinykh Orhanizatsii, 1996–2007. Zbirnyk ofitsiinykh Dokumentiv.* [The Ukrainian Council of Churches and Religious Organizations, 1996–2007. Collected Official Documents]. Kyiv: Sekretariat Vseukrains'koi Rady Tserkov i Relihiinykh Orhanizatsii, 2007.

Website—UCCRO — Selected Documents posted on the UCCRO's official website: http://vrciro.org.ua (accessed on September 14, 2012).

Selected Documents of the Ukrainian Council of Churches and Religious Organizations

1998 — February 17—"Memorandum Vseukrains'koi Rady Tserkov i relihiinykh orhanizatsii, Mininformu ta Derzhkomrelihii shchodo vysvitlennia zasobamy informatsii problem relihiino-tserkovnoho zhyttia" [Memorandum of Agreement of the UCCRO, the Ministry of Information and the State Committee for Religious Affairs on the Coverage of Religious Issues by the Mass Media], in *VRTs*, pp. 19–21.

2000 — April 18—"Memorandum pro Spivpratsiu Ministerstva osvity i nauky Ukrainy, Derzhavnoho Komitetu Ukrainy u spravakh relihii ta Vseukrains'koi Rady Tserkov i relihiinykh orhanizatsii" [Memorandum of Agreement of the Ministry of Education, the State Committee for Religious Affairs and the UCCRO], in *VRTs*, pp. 22–23.

2003–1 April 2—"Heneral'nomu Sekretarevi Orhanizatsii Ob'iednanykh Natsii Panovi Kofi Annanu." [To UN Secretary General Kofi Annan], in *VRTs*, p. 25.

2003–2 "Zvernennia do viruiuchykh i vsikh liudei dobroi voli z pryvodu 60-oi richnytsi Volyns'koi Trahedii periodu Druhoi svitovoi viiny" [Letter to the faithful and to all people of good will on the 60-th anniversary of the Volyn' tragedy of World War II], in *VRTs*, p. 26.

2003–3 "Papi Ryms'komu Yoho Sviatosti Ioannu Pavlu II" [Letter to His Holiness Pope John Paul II], in *VRTs*, p. 27.

2004–1 "Proekt Kontseptsii derzhavno-konfesiinykh vidnosyn v Ukraini" [Draft Conception of Religion-State Relations in Ukraine]. Elaborated by members of the UCCRO, parliamentarians, and the Razumkov Center for Economic and Political Research. Reissued July 18, 2008, *Website—UCCRO.*

2005–1 April 13—"Zvernennia do Prezydenta Ukrainy Viktora Yushchenka shchodo derzhavno-konfesiinykh vidnosyn v Ukraini" [Letter to President Yushchenko on Religion-State Relations in Ukraine], in *SZD*, doc. no. 288, pp. 478–480.

2005–2 June 24—"Zvernennia do ukrains'koho narodu shchodo Moral'no-etychnoho zmistu reklamnoi produktsii" [Letter to the Ukrainian People on the Ethical Content of Advertising], in SZD, doc. no. 291, pp. 485–487.

2005–3 October 25—"Zvernennia do Ukrains'koho Narodu iz zaklykom do molytvy za Ukrains'ku Derzhavu" [Letter to the Ukrainian People with a Call for Prayers for the Ukrainian State], in *SZD*, doc. no. 293, pp. 488–489.

2006–1 June 2—"Zaiava shchodo neobkhidnosty povazhaty relihiini pochuttia, symvoly i tradytsii" [Declaration on the Need to Respect Religious Sentiments, Symbols and Traditions], in *SZD*, doc. no. 298, pp. 495–496.

2006–2 June 6—"Zvernennia do Prezydenta Ukrainy Viktora Yushchenka shchodo derzhavno-kofesiinykh vidnosyn v Ukraini" [Letter to President Yushchenko on Religion-State Relations in Ukraine], in *SZD*, doc. no. 300, pp. 497–498; Addendum, pp. 498–500.

2006–3 July 24—"Zvernennia do Ukrains'koho Narodu shchodo funktsionuvannia mov v Ukraini ta zahrozy separatyzmu" [Letter to the Ukrainian People on the Functioning of Languages in Ukraine and the Threat of Separatism], in *SZD*, doc. no. 302, pp. 500–502.

2006–4 November 24—"Vidkrytyi Lyst do Verkhovnoi Rady Ukrainy z pryvodu initsiatyv lehalizatsii tak zvanykh Odnostatevykh Shliubiv (reiestratsii odnostatevykh partnerstv)" [Open Letter to the Parliament of Ukraine regarding Efforts to Legalize So-called Same-Sex Marriages (the Registration of Same-Sex Partnerships)], in *SZD*, doc. no. 304, pp. 503–505.

2006-5 November 24—"Zvernennia do Premier-Ministra Ukrainy Viktora Yanukovycha shchodo taryfiv na spozhytyi haz dlia relihiinykh orhanizatsii" [Letter to Prime Minister Viktor Yanukovych on Gas Tariffs for Religious Organizations], in *SZD*, doc. no. 305, pp. 505–506.

2006-6 November 24—"Zvernennia do Prezydenta Ukrainy Viktora Yushchenka shchodo neobkhidnosty podal'shoho rozvytku derzhavno-konfesiinoho dialohu v Ukraini" [Letter to President Yushchenko on the Need for Further Development of Religion-State Dialogue in Ukraine], in *SZD*, doc. no. 306, pp. 506–507.

2007-1 April 4—"Zvernennia do Ukrains'koho Narodu z pryvodu suchasnoi politychnoi sytuatsii" [Letter to the Ukrainian People on the Current Political Situation], in *SZD*, doc. no. 315, pp. 513–514.

2007-2 May 15—"Deklaratsiia pro nehatyvne stavlennia do yavyshcha homoseksualizmu ta sprob lehalizatsii tak zvanykh Odnostatevykh Shliubiv (reiestratsii odnostatevykh partnerstv)" [Declaration of Opposition to the Phenomenon of Homosexuality and Efforts to Legalize So-called Same-Sex Marriages (the Registration of Same-Sex Partnerships)], in *SZD*, doc. no. 316, pp. 514–516.

2007-3 September 30—"Zvernennia do Ukrains'koho Narodu z nahody pozacherhovykh vyboriv do Verkhovnoi Rady Ukrainy 30 veresnia 2007 roku" [Letter to the Ukrainian people on the Early Parliamentary Elections of 30 September 2007 to the Parliament of Ukraine], in *SZD*, doc. no. 317, pp. 517–518.

2007-4 November 23—"Zvernennia do novoobranykh narodnykh deputativ Ukrainy" [Letter to the Newly Elected People's Deputies of Ukraine], in *SZD*, doc. no. 318, pp. 518–520.

2007-5 November 23—"Zvernennia z pryvodu 75-richchia pochatku Holodomoru v Ukraini" [Letter on the 75-th Anniversary of the Beginning of the Great Famine in Ukraine], in *SZD*, doc. no. 319, pp. 520–522.

2008-1 December 16—"Spil'ne zvernennia VRTsRO ta Natsional'noi ekspertnoi komisii Ukrainy z pytan' zakhystu suspil'noi morali do derzhavnykh ta hromads'kykh orhanizatsii, ZMI ta vsikh hromadian Ukrainy" [Joint Statement of the UCCRO and the National Commission of Experts of Ukraine for the Protection of Social Morality to State and Community Organizations, the Mass Media and to all Citizens of Ukraine]. *Website—UCCRO*.

2010-1 April 19—"Zvernennia do Prezydenta Ukrainy proty amoral'nykh initsiatyv u Parlaments'kii Asamblei Rady Yevropy" [Letter to President Viktor Yanykovych against Amoral Initiatives at the Parliamentary Assembly of the Council of Europe]. *Website—UCCRO*.

2010-2 December 20—"Rezoliutsiia Kruhloho stolu 'Dialoh mizh vladoiu i konfesiamy v konteksti ievropeis'koi systemy tsinnostei'" [Resolution of the Round Table on "Religion-State Dialogue in the Context of the European System of Values"], cosigned by members of the UCCRO, of the Institute of Religious Freedom, and other participants of the round table. *Website—UCCRO.*

2011–1 April 21—"Zvernennia do Prezydenta Ukrainy Viktora Yanukovycha." [Memorandum to President Viktor Yanukovych]. *Website—UCCRO.*

2011–1a Appendix #1—"Perelik aktual'nykh pytan' derzhavno-konfesiinykh vidnosyn v Ukraini." [List of Current Issues relating to Religion-State Relations in Ukraine]. *Website—UCCRO.*

2011–1b Appendix #2—"Propozytsii shchodo zmin Konstytutsii Ukrainy." [UCCRO Proposals for Amendments to the Constitution of Ukraine]. Adopted at a meeting of the UCCRO on December 16, 2008. *Website—UCCRO.*

2011–2 November 9—"Zvernennia do uchasnykiv parlaments'kykh slukhan' 'Stan suspil'noi morali v Ukraini'" [Address to Participants of the Parliamentary Hearings on the State of Social Morality in Ukraine]. *Website—UCCRO.*

2012–1 March 21—"Zvernennia do Prezydenta Ukrainy Viktora Yanukovycha" [Memorandum to President Viktor Yanukovych]. *Website—UCCRO.*

2012–2 May 27—"Vseukrains'ka Rada Tserkov sturbovana sprobamy rozkoloty suspil'stvo za movnoiu oznakoiu" [The UCCRO is Troubled by Attempts to Divide the Population along Linguistic Lines]. *Website—UCCRO.*

2012–3 July 13—"Zvernennia do Prezydenta Uhors'koi Respubliky" [Letter to President János Áder of Hungary]. Adopted at a meeting of the UCCRO on May 30, 2012. *Website—UCCRO.*

Notes

1. UCCRO documents have been published in two collections: *The Ukrainian Council of Churches and Religious Organizations, 1996–2007. Collected Official Documents* (2007) and *Joint Addresses of the Primates of the Ukrainian Greek Catholic Church with the heads of other Churches and religious communities in Ukraine* (2008). More recent documents appear on the council's website, http://vrciro.org.ua (accessed September 14, 2012), and additional information is drawn from the author's interviews with UCCRO representatives in the summer of 2011.
2. "Informatsiia pro Vseukrains'ku Radu Tserkov i Relihiinykh Orhanizatsii," in *Vseukrains'ka Rada Tserkov i Relihiinykh Orhanizatsii, 1996–2007. Zbirnyk ofitsiinykh Dokumentiv* [The Ukrainian Council of Churches and Religious Organizations, 1996–2007. Collected Official Documents] (Kyiv: Sekretariat Vseukrains'koi Rady Tserkov i Relihiinykh Orhanizatsii, 2007), p. 9.
3. The UCCRO's 1996 membership list included the head of the State Committee on Religious Affairs, Anatolii D. Koval'. "Spysok Chleniv Vseukrains'koi Rady Tserkov i relihiinykh orhanizatsii," in *VRTs*, p. 10. Among the council's published documents, the last one cosigned by a head of the State Committee was the Memorandum to the President of Ukraine on April 13, 2005. See 2005–1.
4. This sentiment was tellingly echoed in the council's letter to President János Áder of Hungary, greeting him "on the occasion of your country's ratification of its Constitution,

which protects your traditional, moral, religious-spiritual and national values" (2012–3). In fact, Áder assumed office in May 2012—over a year after the ratification under his predecessor, Pal Schmitt. The document—protective of families and foetuses, and exclusionary toward gays—has been cited as an affirmation of the country's Christian traditions.

5. Though it was not drafted exclusively by the UCCRO, the *Draft Conception* defined many of the operative concepts and presuppositions of the current religion-state discourse in Ukraine. Endorsed by the council, it has been posted on the UCCRO's website. In 2011, the council included the approval of the *Draft Conception* in its list of religion-state priorities (2011–1: Appendix #1, II.3.2).
6. "mekhanizm konfesiinoi i derzhavno-konfesiinoi spivpratsi." Beyond the limits of Christian denominations only, the statement referred to all the UCCRO's member religious communities.
7. The author's interview with Bishop Yevstratii, at the Patriarchal Residence in Kyiv, June 15, 2011.
8. In line with this setting apart of the "traditional" institutions in Ukraine, recent statements of Christian churches introduced a further, historical demarcation with the expression "Churches of Volodymyr's Baptism" (*Tserkvy Volodymyrs'koho Khreshchennia*).
9. "Spil'ne zvernennia hlav Tradytsiinykh Khrystyians'kykh Konfesii Ukrainy do Prezydenta Ukrainy, Holovy Verkhovnoi Rady Ukrainy, Prem'ier-Ministra Ukrainy pro Khrystyians'ki Tsinnosti v Osviti" [Collective Letter of the Leaders of the Traditional Christian Denominations to the President, the Speaker of Parliament, the Prime Minister and the Minister of Education On Christian Values in Education], June 29, 2005, in *SZD*, doc. no. 292, p. 487. The signatories were: Metropolitan Volodymyr Sabodan (Ukrainian Orthodox Church-Moscow Patriarchate), Patriarch Filaret Denysenko (Ukrainian Orthodox Church-Kyiv Patriarchate), Metropolitan Mefodii Kudriakov (Ukrainian Autocephalous Orthodox Church), and Major Archbishop Lubomyr Husar (Ukrainian Greek-Catholic Church).
10. It is mentioned in: "Vidkrytyi lyst Kerivnykiv khrystyians'kykh Tserkov Ukrainy Prezydentovi Ukrainy V. A. Yushchenkovi pro zaprovadzhennia do shkil'noho kursu navchal'noho predmeta *Khrystyians'ka Etyka*" [Open Letter of the Leaders of the Christian Churches of Ukraine to President Yushchenko on the Introduction of the Subject of Christian Ethics into Schools], in *SZD*, doc. no. 294, December 9, 2005, pp. 489–490. The list of signatories is not provided in this publication.
11. In fact, Council of Europe Resolution 1728 (April 29, 2010) does not mandate or impose, but only recommends the legal recognition of same-sex partnerships by CE member states. In Art 16.9, the Assembly "calls on member states... to ensure legal recognition of same-sex partnerships *when national legislation envisages such recognition*, as already recommended by the Assembly in 2000." http://assembly.coe.int/Mainf.asp?link=/Documents/AdoptedText/ta10/ERES1728.htm (accessed October 10, 2012; emphasis mine).

    In 2010, Ukraine was—along with neighboring Poland and Russia—one of 26 European Council member states that had no legal recognition of same-sex partnerships. However, the situation is evolving: in 2009, Norway and Sweden became the fourth and fifth CE countries to pass legislation on civil marriage for same-sex partners, and Hungary became the third to recognize the formal registration of same-sex partnerships, though with a status inferior to that of married couples. A detailed description of the situation is given in: http://assembly.coe.int/Main.asp?link=/Documents/WorkingDocs/Doc10/EDOC12185.htm (accessed October 10, 2012).
12. "Nakaz Ministerstva Okhorony Zdorovia pro stvorennia Hromads'koi rady pry MOZ Ukrainy z pytan' spivpratsi z VRTsiRO" [Order of the Ministry of Health on the Estblishment of a Community Council of the Ministry for Cooperation with the UCCRO], June 1, 2009. *Website—UCCRO* (emphasis mine).

13. Markian Trofimiak, "Vitannia uchasnykam IV Natsional'noho konhresu z bioetyky, 20.09.2010" [Greeting to the Participants of the IV National Congress of Bioethics in Kyiv, 20.09.2010], *Website—UCCRO*. The Congress adopted a resolution comprising a series of recommendations, including the establishment of educational and consultative services for the cultivation of "moral and family values," and to propose amendments to Ukraine's Constitution and Civil Code that would recognize the right to life from the moment of conception. See "Rezoliutsiia Sympoziumu 'Moral'no-etychni aspekty shtuchnoho pereryvannia vahitnosti'" [Resolution of the Symposium on Ethical and Moral Aspects of the Artificial Termination of Pregnancy], IV Natsional'nyi Konhres z bioetyky, Kyiv, September 22, 2010. *Website—UCCRO*.
14. "Rezoliutsiia Sympoziumu 'Moral'no-etychni aspekty shtuchnoho pereryvannia vahitnosti'" (ibid.).
15. Bishop Yevstratii feels that there are various ways of defining ecumenism, and that the UCCRO's modus operandi is unique. He attributes the UCCRO's success to its avoidance of direct dialogues on doctrine, practice, liturgy, and denominational particularities, and instead a focus on areas in which there is common ground ("spil'nist' dumok") among the religions. These areas are the main sectors of the UCCRO's work: religion-state relations, social relations and social morality, and the defense of the freedom of conscience and religious belief. According to Bishop Yevstratii, "This *new form of ecumenism*, which we try to maintain as a matter of principle, has demonstrated its effectiveness," and he believes that the UCCRO will remain effective in the future as long as it does not touch on questions of faith and doctrine. The author's interview with Bishop Yevstratii, at the Patriarchal Residence (Ukrainian Orthodox Church-Kyiv Patriarchate) in Kyiv, June 15, 2011 (emphasis mine).
16. Martin Marty's observations were given at the book discussion: Jacob Neusner et al., *Do Jews, Christians, & Muslims Worship the Same God?* (Nashville, TN: Abingdon Press, 2012). Annual meeting of the American Academy of Religion, Chicago, November 12, 2012.
17. Patel recalls *la Convivencia* in Muslim-ruled, medieval Cordoba and Andalusia, which was characterized by an active cooperation of Jews, Christians, and Muslims. Eboo Patel, *Sacred Ground: Pluralism, Prejudice and the Promise of America* (Boston: Beacon Press, 2012), xii–f.
18. Raimundo Panikkar, "Inter-Religious Dialogue: Some Principles," *Journal of Ecumenical Studies* 12:3 (Summer 1975), 408.
19. Raimon Panikkar, *The Intra-Religious Dialogue* (New York: Paulist Press, 1999), 69. The idea of a preliminary, internal dialogue has been elaborated in various contexts. In his encyclical on ecumenism *Ut Unum Sint* (*UUS*—1995), Pope John Paul II referred to internalization as an essential component at the other end of dialogue—at its completion. While the ecumenical quest for truth necessarily entails an examination of conscience (*UUS*, 33–35), no less important is the "reception of the results already achieved." The effectiveness of dialogue requires that agreements on religious matters be communicated to, and implemented within, religious communities. Such agreements "cannot remain the statements of bilateral commissions but *must become a common heritage*" (*UUS*, 80. Emphasis mine). As a follow-up phase of dialogue, reception should engage the practical reflection of theologians and faculties of theology (*UUS*, 81). The full text of *UUS* is available at: w.vatican.va/holy_father/john_paul_ii/encyclicals/documents/hf_jp-ii_enc_25051995_ut-unum-sint_en.html (accessed July 15, 2013).

    Likewise, the Faith and Order Commission of the World Council of Churches noted that religious dialogue without reception ran the risk of retrenchment, reconfessionalization, and an antiecumenical spirit. Instead, it pointed out, the goal of mutual recognition requires a movement beyond preconceived boundaries and beyond declarative expressions of convergence to "a reconciled common life." See *The Nature and Mission of the Church*, Faith and Order Paper 198 (Geneva: World Council of Churches, 2005), par. 120–122. http://archived.oikoumene.org/fileadmin/files/wcc-main/documents/p2/FO2005_198_en.pdf (accessed July 15, 2013).

The shared insights are that, without reception of the introspective and self-critical insights of dialogue, faith-based particularities remain enshrined but not subjected to closer scutiny; and without reception, there is no transformative movement beyond declarative expressions of common understanding.

20. Diana Eck, "Globalization and Religious Pluralism—Discussion," 2009 Gifford Lecture #1, St. Cecilia's Hall, University of Edinburgh. At 1:03–1:04. www.youtube.com/watch?v=M0wDxV4vOqU&list=PLEA9467E8E8D991AE (accessed December 16, 2012).
21. Diana L. Eck, "Inter-religious Dialogue as a Christian Ecumenical Concern," *Ecumenical Review* 37:4 (October 1985), 418 (emphasis mine).
22. Ibid., 414.
23. Ibid., 416.
24. Nor would a return to such past practice be unheard of in the Christian East. In her critical review of Boswell's book, *Same-Sex Unions in Premodern Europe* (New York: Villard Books, 1994), Robin Darling Young recounts her own experience at St. Mark's Monastery in Jerusalem in 1985. There, Syrian Orthodox archbishop Dionysius Behnam Jajaweh united Young and her travel companion in a spiritual sisterhood that "would last beyond the grave." The ritual was performed and understood strictly as a spiritual union, with no nuptial connotations. Robin Darling Young, "Review Essay—Gay Marriage: Reimagining Church History," *First Things* 47 (1994), 43.

    A 1904 *Euchologion* of the Edinovertsi, Old Believers who reunited with the Russian Orthodox Church while retaining some ritual practices, contains the following prayer from the rite of brother-making: "O Lord God, Almighty, You made mankind after Your image and likeness and have granted us eternal life. You thought it right that Your holy and glorious apostles Peter and Paul, as well as Philip and Bartholomew, be joined as brothers: not by birth, but by faith, love, and the Holy Spirit. Likewise, Your holy martyrs Sergius and Bacchus were made brothers. Now bless Your servants (N. and N.) to be joined in brotherhood: not by birth, but by faith and love. Grant them mutual love without envy or temptation all the days of their lives, through the prayers of Your saints who have pleased You throughout the ages." Excerpt from: *Velikii Potrebnik* (Moscow: Edinovertsi, 1904), trans. Basil Isaacks, at: www.qrd.org/qrd/religion/judeochristian/eastern_orthodox/bratotvorenie.edinovertsii.1904 (accessed December 16, 2012).
25. Rowan Williams, Archbishop of Canterbury, "A Common Word for the Common Good," July 14, 2008, p. 2. www.acommonword.com/category/site/christian-responses/.

Part VI

Emerging Encounters and New Challenges in Post-Soviet Central Asia

18

Muslim-Orthodox Relations in Russia: Contextual Readings of *A Common Word*

Andrii Krawchuk

The publication in 2007 of *A Common Word between Us and You* (*ACW*) was an unprecedented instance of outreach by Muslim leaders to Christianity on a global scale. The website dedicated to it contains hundreds of related materials, including over 70 responses from Christian leaders and scholars. The response by Russian Orthodox Patriarch Alexy II was a significant contribution to the discussion, which set a precedent in the Muslim-Orthodox relationship by introducing a theological reflection on biblical texts that was applied to the Russian context. While neither *ACW* nor Alexy claimed that their assessments were exhaustive, their substantive insights and observations may well encourage future collaborative studies and dialogue on the founding texts and core values of both traditions. This chapter first examines Muslim-Orthodox relations in Russia today, then studies the use of biblical texts in the two documents. After an overview of other Orthodox responses to *ACW*, it concludes with a reflection on the significance of this exchange for future Muslim-Orthodox dialogue.

The Russian Context of Muslim-Orthodox Relations

The coexistence of the two largest religious communities in Russia, Orthodoxy and Islam, is rooted in the history of Mongol and Tartar rule in the thirteenth and fourteenth centuries and in the subsequent Russian expansion into the Muslim territories of Asia. The Russian Orthodox Church (ROC) represents the majority of Orthodox believers in the land, an estimated 58.8 million self-declared adherents, or 41 percent of the population. The Muslim community in the former Soviet sphere has established five major institutions since the 1990s, and its self-declared adherents in Russia are estimated at 9.4 million, or 6.5 percent of the population.[1] This demographic imbalance is less marked, and even reversed, in a number of republics and regions of Russia that have significant or absolute majority Muslim populations,[2] and areas that receive a steady flow of illegal immigrants from the North Caucasus, Azerbaijan, and Central Asia.

In its post-Soviet policies and positions, the ROC strives to combine its declared openness to diversity, pluralism, and religious equality in the public space with active engagement in the social and political spheres.[3] This general approach receives various interpretations and applications, depending upon which subgroup of the ROC one chooses to focus: the liberals, who favor church reforms and ecumenical engagement; the fundamentalists, who prefer isolation to involvement in global processes and ecumenical dialogues; or the conservatives, the predominant group, whose pragmatic cooperation with the state and other religions, and promotion of Orthodox tradition and a specifically Russian religious identity has shaped the Orthodox agenda over the past few decades. This latter group is also behind a newly articulated social vision for the church, which set forth the terms of its involvement with society and the state.

These priorities indicate the principal challenges that the ROC has identified and the responses that it has enacted. In the domestic transition toward democratic reform, the church has supported new laws on religious freedom and equality, which lends credibility to its advancement of Russian Orthodox minorities in other countries. And, because it considers itself as a (or the) "traditional religion" of Russia, the ROC is committed to democratic pluralism to the extent that this does not compromise the primacy of the Orthodox component of Russian national identity.

The Muslim institutions of Russia recognize the vital importance of state support in their efforts to protect and advance the rights of Muslims. In the pursuit of that goal, the key difference in strategic orientation is between the proponents of accommodation and harmonization with the status quo (Talgat Tadzhuddin and Ismail Berdiev) and the advocates of continued reform in favor of greater Muslim visibility and equality in society (Ravil Gainutdin and Nafigulla Ashirov).[4] The former pursue a line of "political correctness" in their relations with the ROC and the state, and are critical of Islamic fundamentalism, while the latter are more tolerant of fundamentalism and critical of perceived instances of Orthodox "clericalism." The accommodationists also favor the idea of "neo-Eurasianism"—that Orthodoxy and Islam are equal and integral to Russian civilization, and that the two should work together in responding to challenges from the West. The reformists see full equality as a goal yet to be achieved, mainly through legislative and institutional initiatives.

The core value of religious identity has emerged as a major preoccupation of both the ROC and the Muslim communities in the post-Soviet environment. In extensive reflection and debates, each community is seeking to define its place within the ongoing social and political transformation, as well as the nature of its relations with the religious neighbor. For both, it is an opportunity to reassess their goals for the future and the nature of their contributions toward shaping the new Russia.

Russian Orthodox reflection on identity over the past decade has been informed by perceptions of a decline of Russia as a political and cultural force and of the simultaneous emergence of Islam as a potential ally in addressing the challenges of modernity, particularly those that are associated with "the West."[5] On the Muslim side, various forms of cultural synthesis have been proposed. They endorse basic loyalty to the Russian state, but differ on the desirable degree of cultural assimilation of Muslims.

The Central Muslim Spiritual Board of Russia under Mufti Tadzhuddin endorses the harmony of Orthodoxy and Islam by virtue of their shared Abrahamic roots and as the two major religions in Russia. Many of its members are associated with the cluster of ideas referred to as "neo-Eurasianism," which presents Orthodoxy and Islam as the two pillars of Russia; the true nature of Russia as both Orthodox and oriental, or Asian; Islam as an essential component of Russia's rebirth; and both communities as sharing the common enemies of Western liberalism and secularism.[6] Russian Orthodox circles debated and ultimately rejected the neo-Eurasian ideology in the 1990s, favoring instead the view of Russia as an "ethnic Russian and Orthodox civilization," with Russian Islam as a junior partner.[7] The Council of Muftis of Russia (CMR), a heterogeneous group, also rejects neo-Eurasianism and sees the two religious traditions as distinct and even mutually opposed. In sharp contrast to the ROC, the CMR advocates an equal status for Islam in a "bi-religious" Russia and it challenges the ROC's pursuit of special privileges.

Considering some of the key divergences in Russian Islam, Alexey Malashenko of the Carnegie Moscow Center refers to two Islams in Russia—traditional Islam and nontraditional Islam. Traditional Islam fuses religion with ethnic identity and adherence to "one's own" theological and legal school of thought (*mazhab*). Generally loyal to the Russian state and enjoying the support of the state, the adherents of Hanafism (Bashkirs and Tatars), Shafiism (Muslims in the North Caucasus), and Tariqatism and other strains of Sufism (North Caucasus) are considered part of traditional Islam. Nontraditional Islam includes branches of Islam that appeared in Russia only after the Soviet period: Salafism, fundamentalism, and Wahhabism. Russian authorities consider nontraditional Islam as hostile and a source of extremism and terrorism.[8]

A significant development for the consolidation of Muslim ideas in Russia was the publication of the *Elementary Guidelines of the Social Program of Russian Muslims* (2001) by the CMR. The document advanced the separation of religion and state, loyalty to the Russian state as a religious obligation of Muslim citizens, and the creation of a "social partnership" with the state—for cooperation on a range of social programs and to protect Muslim civil rights and equality.[9]

From the perspective of the Muslim communities, the main cause of religious tensions has been Orthodox clericalization, which they see in the ROC's cultivation of privileged relations with the state and affirmations of its predominance as the main religious voice in Russian society. Orthodox initiatives that elicited criticism from Muslim circles have included the proposal of obligatory school courses on Orthodox culture, anniversary celebrations of the fourteenth-century Russian victory over the Tatars at Kulikovo, and the translation of the Bible into the languages of traditional Muslim Kumyk and Avar communities. Summing up the concerns of Muslims, Djannat Sergei Markus characterized this pattern as "antidemocratic clericalism," echoing the CMR, which in 2007 had declared its categorical opposition to "replacing the spiritual revival of a multiethnic and multireligious Russia with the restoration of a feudal state monopoly on the faith," and viewed such a process as a threat to Russia's national security. The CMR formulated its alternative vision in relation to the principles of social pluralism and religious equality: "We Muslims want to see peace and harmony in our multinational and multireligious country; we want diversity to become a genuine source of prosperity and the welfare for all the peoples of Russia. To that end, it is essential that clericalism in all its forms be decisively ended."[10]

The overriding concern among Muslims is that the advancement of Orthodox tradition as the primary element of national identity in Russia demonstrates a lack of commitment to a multiethinic and secular model of the Russian state. This in turn reveals a growing distance between two competing models of Russian religious, cultural, and political identity: one views Russian ethnicity and Orthodox tradition as tightly interwoven components of a coherent, monolithic culture, while the other draws upon principles of democracy, pluralism, and religious equality to propose a new path for the state and society. Thus, rather than a clash of religious traditions, Russian Muslims frame this as a debate on the respective merits of confessional and secular models of the state.

Interreligious dialogue is a major priority of Russian domestic and foreign policy. The state actively promotes and supports it in the interests of social harmony, national security, and the construction of a "Eurasian" image of Russia, as a cultural bridge between Europe and Asia, Orthodoxy and Islam. In the words of Dmitry Medvedev, "Islam is an inseparable part of Russian history and culture...Our country is an organic part of the [Muslim] world."[11] The post-Soviet search for a new model of the Russian state involves making space for religious communities in the public forum, tapping into their capacity for integration and containing their potential for conflict. The peaceful coexistence of the two major religions is recognized as a necessary precondition for the social and political reinvention of Russia, and the state pursues those related goals by promoting religious dialogue and cooperation—and by balancing the competing, Orthodox and secular-multicultural, visions for the future.

For the two major religions of Russia, the interreligious dialogue can become a forum for constructive Orthodox-Muslim exchange on the contested issues of religious equality and the desired paths toward democracy. Both religious communities recognize that mutual understanding and consensus-building hold the best promise for improving their bilateral relations and their relations with the state. But whereas the state views the cultivation of Orthodox-Muslim relations as a means toward "spiritual security" and the prevention of domestic conflicts, the religious communities are no less committed to ensuring their own stability and growth, attending to the needs of their members and contributing meaningfully and proactively to civil society—above and beyond merely passive compliance with the law.

Interreligious relations in Russia take place under the auspices of the Interreligious Council of Russia (IRC), a federal forum of the four "traditional religions" (Russian Orthodoxy, Islam, Judaism, and Buddhism), which was established in 1998. Criticized for becoming an "exclusive club of privileged religious communities" that monopolizes communication with the state,[12] and for having exhausted its usefulness,[13] the IRC nevertheless meets regularly and is regarded as an influential collective voice for common ground and advocacy on a range of issues, among other things denouncing proselytism and religious extremism. Significant interreligious encounters have included two conferences in Moscow: *Christianity and Islam: On the Way to Dialogue* (2005) and *Russia and the Muslim World* (2009). The CMR was actively involved in these initiatives, and created its own Muslim-Christian Dialogue Commission.[14] Still, the cooperation of IRC members and their corresponding sense of equality has not always been matched by the ROC, whose Metropolitan Kirill (Gundyaev) referred to the institution as "the church of the majority" in "a predominantly Orthodox country with some national and religious minorities."[15]

In moments of tension between Orthodox and Muslims in Russia, public debates are often colored by a "clash of civilizations" discourse, which inevitably pits Orthodoxy against Islam, aggravates Islamophobia, and escalates conflict between the two communities.[16] However, when this discourse is reoriented in the global setting toward the "liberal and secular" West, the common enemy becomes a rallying cry for interreligious cooperation.

Biblical Texts in *A Common Word*

In seeking to identify significant common ground between Christianity and Islam, *ACW* explored the Christian understanding of the commandment to love God and neighbor through reflections on various biblical texts. In this connection, four basic points were made:

1. *Love of God—ACW* focuses on the text of the Shema, "You shall love the LORD your God with all your heart, and with all your soul, and with all your strength" (Deut. 6:4–5) and its reaffirmation in the teaching of Jesus (Mark 12:28–31 and Matt. 22:34–40). It notes that the basic formula of the commandment is reiterated in many other biblical texts, and that despite some variation from the original formula of "heart-soul-strength"—such as "heart-soul" (Josh. 22:5); "heart-soul-mind-strength" (Mark 12:30, Luke 10:27); "heart-mind-strength" (Mark 12:32); and "heart-soul-mind" (Matt. 22:37)—they all express the same command: "to love God fully with one heart and soul and to be fully devoted to Him." Further, an "effective similarity in meaning" is found between this commandment and the Muslim formula "You shall love the Lord your God with all your heart, and with all your soul, and with all your strength." Despite their different expressions in different contexts, both the Muslim and the Christian formulas are understood by *ACW* to express the same religious idea—that of "the primacy of total love and devotion to God."
2. *Love of neighbour*—on this, *ACW* points to the second Christian commandment, "You shall love your neighbour as yourself," and to its Hebrew precursor in Leviticus 19:17–18, "You shall not take vengeance, nor bear any grudge against the children of your people, but you shall love your neighbour as yourself." This too is connected to the teachings of the Prophet Muhammad, in particular: "None of you has faith until you love for your brother what you love for yourself" (Sahih Al-Bukhari, Kitab al-Iman, Hadith no. 13), and: "None of you has faith until you love for your neighbour what you love for yourself" (Sahih Muslim, Kitab al-Iman, 67–1, Hadith no. 45). *ACW* concludes that these two commandments constitute "an area of common ground and a link between the Qur'an, the Torah and the New Testament."
3. *The unity of God—ACW* next observes that the principle of only one God immediately precedes the two great commandments in both the Torah and the New Testament—the Shema invocation "Hear, O Israel: The Lord our God, the Lord is one!" (Deut. 6:4) is faithfully restated in Mark (12:29). *ACW* takes this as an indication that the principle of divine unity is integrally linked to the two commandments, and that it is also included in Jesus's affirmation "On these two commandments hang all the Law and the Prophets" (Matt. 22:40). Declaring that the very same truths are confirmed by the Qur'an, *ACW* concludes that "the Unity of God, love of Him, and love of the neighbour form a common ground upon which Islam and Christianity (and Judaism) are founded."

4. *A foundation and an imperative for interfaith dialogue*—*ACW*'s final biblical reflection reinforces the connection of the Muslim-Christian common ground with biblical teaching and the Christian imperative to make peace. The common ground identified in the first three points, the two great commandments and the oneness of God, are core values of Christianity and "that on which hangs all the Law and the Prophets" (Matt. 22:40). While recognizing that Islam and Christianity are different religions, whose formal differences should not be minimized, *ACW* argues that this scripturally based common ground should become the basis for Muslim-Christian dialogue.

For the authors of *ACW*, the urgency of Muslim-Christian interfaith dialogue arises from the global reality that their common future and world peace are at stake. In a more theological vein, "our very eternal souls are all also at stake if we fail to sincerely make every effort to make peace and come together in harmony." The pursuit of interfaith harmony and global peace, and ultimately salvation are seen as Christian imperatives that find support in the seventh Beatitude ("Blessed are the peacemakers," Matt. 5:9) and in the warning about losing sight of the priority of salvation ("For what profit is it to a man if he gains the whole world and loses his soul?" Matt. 16:26). *ACW* thus reads Christian scripture with a primary reflection on the commandment of love of God and neighbor,[17] but it also uses biblical texts to illustrate another area of common ground—monotheism—and to propose a shared Muslim-Christian ethical imperative to collaborate in the pursuit of world peace.

Biblical Texts in the Russian Orthodox Response

The official Russian Orthodox response to *ACW* by Patriarch Alexy II is of interest to the discussion of Muslim-Orthodox relations in the Russian context because biblical texts and theological considerations are brought into the picture as never before.[18] While acknowledging that the commandment of love of God and neighbor brings Christians and Muslims together, Alexy cautions at the very outset against a selective focus on any individual doctrine apart from its larger context:

> Any doctrinal affirmation in Christianity or Islam cannot be viewed in isolation from its unique place in the integral theological system. Otherwise, one's religious identity will be obliterated and there is a danger of moving along the path of blending the faiths. It seems to be more fruitful, therefore, to study the integral faith of each side and to compare them. (Alexy II 2008: par. 4)

The argument for a contextual reading of one religious tradition by another is hardly controversial, nor is the suggestion that a faith tradition should be studied in its entirety—as long as this does not set up insurmountable prerequisites for interreligious encounter. As for the concern about the potential threat to religious identity, a recurring refrain in Russian Orthodox writings on ecumenism and religious dialogue, it may be understood here as a precaution against reductionism and simplification, which can only impede authentic dialogue and understanding.

What, then, is the larger context, the "integral theological system" in which the commandment of love must be situated in order to avoid an obliteration of Orthodox

Christian identity? Patriarch Alexy develops his critique of *ACW* through five biblically grounded observations. He begins by setting forth the Christian understanding of the divine nature in order to address what he considers the first major oversight of *ACW*'s reading of the Christian tradition: namely, that "in Christianity, a discourse about love of God and love of one's neighbor is impossible without a discourse about God." In other words, the Christian discourse on the divine-human relationship is grounded in a number of biblical descriptions of the nature of divine and human love.

1. *"God is love"*—Alexy's first point about the Christian understanding of divinity has to do with God's self-revelation, as illustrated by two texts from the first letter of John: "Whoever does not love does not know God, because God is love" (1 John 4:8); and "And so we know and rely on the love God has for us. God is love, and whoever lives in love lives in God, and God in him" (1 John 4:16). For Alexy, this establishes that divine nature has love as its "most essential, characteristic and important property."[19] However, Alexy does not examine the Muslim understanding of the divine nature, nor does he indicate whether he considers this Christian perspective to be a point of convergence or of divergence with Islam.

2. *"Just as you are in me"*—Alexy next connects the notion of the divine nature as love with the Christian understanding of the Trinity. Love, says the patriarch, "presupposes the existence of the other," and the only way for God to be a personal being is "through love of another personal being."[20] In other words, the relational and personal nature of God means that the one God is not an "isolated essence of love," but Being in three persons.

Alexy affirms a biblical foundation for this belief ("the New Testament speaks of God as one Being in three persons—the Father, the Son and the Holy Spirit")[21] and refers to two passages in the Gospel of John, which presumably should be read by analogy with tradition, harmonizing with later formulations of the doctrine. He proposes that the words "just as you are in me and I am in you" (John 17:21) reflect the self-aware relationship of the Son with the Father, and that Jesus's pronouncement about the Spirit of truth, "He will bring glory to me by taking from what is mine and making it known to you" (John 16:14) completes the union of three divine persons. However, he does not enter into the historical context of Christian controversies that preceded the definitive formulation of the doctrine, or indeed of the period before those controversies.

3. *"Not that we loved God"*—The third specificity of Christian theology, according to Alexy, is that God as love is "the main driving force of Divine Providence for humanity," which makes human knowledge of God and salvation possible. In particular, God's self-revelation through Jesus is a "natural manifestation of God's love of human beings."[22] The cited biblical sources are the classic Johannine formula "For God so loved the world" (John 3:16) and its echo in "This is how God showed his love among us: He sent his one and only Son into the world that we might live through him. This is love: *not that we loved God, but that he loved us* and sent his Son as an atoning sacrifice for our sins" (1 John 4:9–10; emphasis mine).

The second passage is especially significant: in addition to God's self-manifestation in Jesus, John emphatically insists that in the divine and human relationship it is God's love that takes precedence; it is God's initiative that breathes life, so to speak, into the relationship and makes it possible. By using this text, Alexy lays out the uniquely Christian theological understanding of love in the divine-human relationship.

4. *"That we should be called children of God"*—Patriarch Alexy next addresses the nature of humanity and its place in the relationship with divinity. By virtue of its creation "in the image and after the likeness of God" (Gen. 1:26), humanity has the inherent capacity to receive and experience the divine message of love. This knowledge becomes "their inner property, their living force that determines, penetrates and forms their whole lives."[23] As explained in the first letter of John, this acquired knowledge consists of an awareness of the relationship as that between the Father and his children: "How great is the love the Father has lavished on us, that we should be called children of God!" (1 John 3:1). The same understanding of humanity's relationship with the Heavenly Father is reflected in the Lord's Prayer (Luke 11:2). Furthermore, humanity has the capacity to respond to God's love, and it is precisely through such response that love arises in humanity. Here, Alexy makes his point with a sharp distinction: "God expects from man not so much a slave's devotion as a filial feeling of love."[24]

5. *"Through the love of our own heart"*—The patriarch's final point is that the human response to God's love includes a selfless desire to fulfil God's commandments, and that this is only possible if man is free. On this, he cites the words of the seventh-century Eastern Christian mystic Isaac the Syrian: "Because of His great love, God was not pleased to restrict our freedom but was pleased to draw us near to Him through the love of our own heart." For Alexy, human freedom is also connected to the evangelical call to perfection (Matt. 5:48): a key element of Christian love and morality is the pursuit of perfection through the emulation of the Creator, and the human progress along that path is marked by growth in the love of God—and in freedom. Again, Alexy underscores this observation with a contrast: "the exercise of human freedom involves fulfilling the will of God by choice, not only out of fear or for the sake of reward."[25]

Patriarch Alexy explains that his aim was not to set forth the whole of Christian theology, but to offer a reflection on the divine-human relationship of love, "which underlies the whole theological system of Christianity and which cannot be reduced to a few laconic formulations."[26] The core of his response to and critique of *ACW* is that while the commandment of love is indeed central to Christianity, its proper understanding requires that it be situated in a broader reflection on the divine and human natures and the relationship between them. Thus, the Muslim-Christian dialogue cannot be limited only to an acknowledgment of common ground, as *ACW* would appear to suggest. It must also recognize the distinctiveness of Christian and Islamic theologies. Concerned with maintaining a sense of secure identities in the face of a perceived, real potential for religious assimilation, Alexy believes that it is essential to establish clear and inviolable religious boundaries from the very outset of dialogue. In his view, authentic and legitimate dialogue can only take place when the lines of demarcation are in place.

The second requirement is that interfaith dialogue be, first and foremost, a work of theology that adheres to the official, traditional elaboration of the faith. An underlying institutional ecclesiology is clearly at work here, affirming the central authority in the role of custodian and teacher of the "integral theological system." And it is likely that the most "appropriate" participants of interfaith dialogue would be sought first of all among trained theologians and members of the clergy, duly authorized to speak on behalf of the official ROC and held accountable for doctrinal correctness through the course of the dialogue.

For the ROC, the essential theological framework for properly situating the commandment of love is a discourse on the nature of God the Creator and created humanity. The Christian affirmation that God is love is understood as part of God's relational (Trinitarian) essence and God's self-revelation in Jesus. The Creator initiates the relationship of love, and humanity possesses the capacity to receive that love and to respond to it. Humanity's response to God's love is a love that proceeds from the knowledge of God as Father and from a desire to imitate God's perfection, and it is expressed through a free choice to obey God's commandments.

Patriarch Alexy thus approached *ACW*'s discourse on the commandment of love as an opportunity to reflect on what the Muslim-Orthodox dialogue could and should be. Although the main thrust of his scriptural reflection appears to be more polarizing than harmonizing, Alexy insisted that further dialogue must also attend to the larger contexts of scripture, tradition and the challenges of the contemporary world. Looking to the future of Muslim-Orthodox dialogue and relations in Russia as a particular case of Muslim-Christian relations in the global setting, he gave support to the transition to the next phase of dialogue—from consensus on social and political issues to a more thoroughgoing theological exploration of common ground, and distinctiveness, on core values.

Reflections on Text and Context in Other Orthodox Responses

A number of other Orthodox leaders also employed scriptural references in their responses to *ACW*. These contributions are relevant to the international setting of Muslim-Orthodox relations and their insights resonate with Alexy's thoughts—in fact, some of them may well have informed the patriarch's intervention. In essence, they welcome the invitation to dialogue and provide constructive methodological proposals for making a transition to a deeper, more comprehensive interreligious exchange. Reflecting a variety of Orthodox contexts, these responses echo the Russian Orthodox patriarch's desire for a comprehensive and meaningful dialogue with Muslims.

Beyond Superficial Similarities to an Appreciation of Conceptual Differences

Mor Eustathius Matta Roham, archbishop of Jezira and the Euphrates (Syrian Orthodox Church of Antioch), points out that fruitful dialogue requires an accurate representation of religious concepts across religious traditions.[27] He is concerned that *ACW* discussed the two notions of love as if they carried the same meaning in both religious traditions, whereas in his view they do not:

> When we talk about the love of God in Christianity, we mean God's love for humanity and human's [*sic*] love of God. In the letter, the love of God in Islam is actually closer to the fear of God in Christianity. The concept of God's love for humanity in Christianity has no similarity in Islam as this concept in Christianity refers to the Doctrine of Salvation, which is the core of Christian faith... Similarly, the love of neighbour in Islam reflects the geographical sense of the word "neighbour" (in Arabic, Jar جار). In Christianity, love

of neighbour (in Arabic, Qarib قريب) surpasses all geographical and religious boundaries and takes on a whole new dimension encompassing all of humanity.[28]

Aram I, Catholicos of Cilicia (Armenian Orthodox Church), also feels that there is a distinctively Christian understanding of the love of neighbor.[29] It must be understood in the context of God's other commands, in particular the instruction to "be fruitful and multiply, and fill the earth, and subdue it" (Gen, 1:28), which Aram I considers to be integral to God's call and the proper human response, "harmonious and meaningful" coexistence. He too distinguishes between two connotations of the "neighbor," noting that the parable of the Good Samaritan (Luke 10:24ff) demonstrates that the Christian understanding is not about proximity or kinship, but about "the 'other' who is in need of our love, help and fellowship."[30] At the same time, he also sees common ground in that both sacred books understand love of neighbor as "the beginning of just relation with the 'other.'"[31]

These responses preceded Alexy's by over two months, and it is possible that the patriarch had access to them while that final draft of his intervention was being edited. Certainly his argument reiterates these earlier observations, but his critical elaboration is more comprehensive.

Beyond Literal Readings to Critical Interpretation and Contextual Application

According to Mor Eustathius, *ACW* relied exclusively on sacred texts as the basis of dialogue and thus neglected the need for other bases, such as the human ability to reason. He cites the historical example of the Al-Mu'tazela group in Baghdad, which at the height of the Abbasid civilization had recognized the priority of reasoning over religious texts, apparently favoring a critical approach to the interpretation of sacred texts in the dialogue, rather than merely a literal one.[32]

A similar concern is raised by Catholicos Aram, for whom the construction of a new Muslim-Christian relationship requires more than a reflection on sacred texts alone—the interpretation of texts across religious boundaries must also be tied to their practical application: "Christians and Muslims can shape a life together based on the love of God and neighbor, provided we apply the basic thrusts of our Scriptures in our particular contexts."[33] This addresses the primary Orthodox concern with respecting religious boundaries. Such concern does not preclude more thorough studies of the respective scriptural texts, nor does it exclude the possibility that the critical interpretations and contextual applications of those scriptural teachings by the respective faith communities may become an additional area of interreligious convergence and consensus on practical questions.

Beyond Texts to Human Contexts

In the same vein, all of the Orthodox commentators stress the importance of moving from a discussion of sacred texts to a frank exchange on specific contextual issues as a sign of progress in the dialogue. Some of these issues relate to the shared historical experiences of Muslims and Orthodox Christians, while others are current matters that require attention.

For Alexy, the history of Muslim-Christian relations in Russia is a long-standing record of peaceful coexistence, based on respect for religious identities and loyalty to the "common Motherland."[34] This model of distinct religious identities, a shared history and common cause in defending the Russian state, also informs his understanding of the goals of the interreligious dialogue. Alexy alluded to a pressing issue in Muslim-Christian relations—that of legislative restrictions on Christian minorities "in some Islamic countries"—but left its further elaboration to another bishop.[35]

Syrian Orthodox Archbishop Mor Eustathius notes "an obscure accusation" in *ACW*, which is made without any reference to time or place: "As Muslims, we say to Christians that we are not against them and that Islam is not against them—so long as they do not wage war against Muslims on an account of their religion, oppress them and drive them out of their homes."[36]

Mor Eustathius feels that such a statement should be more specific, and considers some of the possible contexts. If the reference is to the Crusades, then those "wars of the Franks" brought equal suffering to Muslims and Christians of the East. If the reference is to the more recent interventions of Western powers in Iraq, Afghanistan, and other countries, Eustathius points out that those same powers stood by the Muslims of Bosnia-Herzegovina and liberated Kuwaitis together with several Muslim countries. In the present context, he too notes serious human rights concerns among Christians living in Muslim countries and suggests that the war in south Sudan was precipitated by laws that discriminated against the Christian minority.

Archbishop Chrisostomos of Cyprus contrasts 450 years of "absolutely harmonious" Muslim-Christian coexistence in his native Cyprus with the situation after the 1974 invasion by Turkey, and considers the deprivation of the Christian community's fundamental religious rights and freedoms unacceptable.[37]

Perhaps the most conciliatory contextualization among the Orthodox responses is that of Archbishop Yeznik Petrosyan of the Armenian Apostolic Church.[38] He cites specific historical examples of encounter and cooperation between Armenian Christians and Muslims: an agreement in 652 that provided for religious freedom, a respectful exchange of thoughts on faith in 720 between the Armenian Catholicos St. John of Odzun and Omar, the Arabian Chief Emir, and the reception, shelter, and support of millions of refugees of the Armenian Genocide of 1915–1923 by predominantly Muslim countries of the Middle East. He acknowledges that problems exist in the region, but expresses hope that the quadrilateral dialogue established in 1994 will continue to work toward peaceful solutions in the Caucasus and the Middle East.

Beyond Mere Coexistence toward a New Global Community

For Patriarch Alexy II, the global context presents challenges whose magnitude surpasses the response capacities of the traditional religions of Russia on their own. These challenges include an antireligious worldview that seeks to impose itself on all spheres of social life, a "new morality" that undermines the core values of traditional religions, and common enemies who want to see Christians and Muslims either clash or enter into a false, secular unity based on religious indifference.[39] An effective response to these challenges demands a recognition of the urgency of the situation and a sense of common cause between Christians and Muslims both inside Russia and beyond its borders.

Armenian Catholicos Aram I sees Muslim-Christian common ground in the shared historical experiences and geographical contexts, as well as in the global setting. In his view, the urgency of global awareness arises not so much from external challenges as from an internal ethical motivation that is equally applicable in both traditions: "We belong to one humanity and one world under one sovereign God."[40] This common belonging is connected to the God-given responsibility to work together to build a new human community governed by love, justice, dignity, and peace. Aram I sees the project of human transformation as a moral obligation for which Muslims and Christians are already equipped:

> In addition to their theological teachings our two religions have the rich experience and inner potential *to transform mere coexistence into a broader community of shared values*, interactive diversity, common participation and mutual trust. We must acknowledge, however, that we have differences which may not be easy to overcome. We must accept and respect the way we are, by suspending our desire to emphasize differences and committing ourselves to living together with the fear of God and not with the fear of one another.[41]

Despite numerous historical instances of Muslim-Christian cooperation and recent advances in dialogue, it would be premature to claim that all differences and challenges have been resolved. Much remains to be done in order to create a climate of understanding and trust. There appears to be basic agreement that cooperation on global issues is needed, as is the mutual respect for distinctive religious identities, but not at the expense of sustained efforts to expand and deepen the relationship between the two religious traditions.

Conclusion

Within the post-Soviet processes of normalization of religious life and the quest for a new Russian social and political identity, Russian Orthodoxy and Islam are pursuing similar strategic goals. Both see their own institutional consolidation and stabilization as reliable bulwarks against internal diversification and dissent, and against the external pressures of secularism and democratic pluralism. Both rely on legislative support from the state, and both reciprocate with declarations of loyalty, a spirit of partnership with the state, and the endorsement of its principles of religious freedom and equality. Beyond the legal framework, the religious identity debate also has a cultural dimension, and here the two religious communities differ in their approaches—the ROC standing for the primacy of Russian language and culture, and the Muslim community supporting, with varying degrees of assertiveness, a culturally diverse model of Russia.

Interreligious relations are also subsumed under the pragmatic agenda of the state, which sees religious harmony as an essential component of "spiritual security," social consolidation, and the articulation of a new vision for Russia. The two major religious communities are thus invited to demonstrate solidarity with the state's principal strategic objectives. At the same time, each community has its own self-awareness, priorities, and internal dynamics, and the Muslim-Orthodox dialogue in Russia will probably not be shaped by state interest alone. Beyond the pragmatic goal of peaceful religious coexistence, which is quite sufficient for the state, the religious communities are also free to choose a more thoroughgoing and comprehensive dialogue with the goal of transforming self-identity through a new relationship with the other. The reflections outlined in this chapter suggest that there is openness to such a transformative approach and the creation of a new type of interreligious solidarity, "a broader community of shared values." That kind of openness has the potential to take the relationship beyond the limits of the secular, pragmatic agenda.

The shared exploration of founding scriptural texts initiated by *ACW* and the Orthodox responses has opened up new motivations and possibilities for interreligious understanding in Russia. Despite conceptual and doctrinal differences that remain unresolved, the initial exchange has identified areas of profound concern to both communities, and the global context appears to be a very promising area for common cause and cooperation as Orthodoxy and Islam respond to challenges that surpass their individual capacities. In turn, advocacy on international issues such as the minority rights of Christians in Islamic countries could encourage broader support on the home front for Russia's largest religious minority—the Islamic community.

Notes

1. For the results of the 2012 sociological survey and mapping of religious adherents in Russia based on self-identification, see: "Арена. Атлас религий и национальностей России." Проект службы *Среда*—http://sreda.org/arena (accessed April 21, 2013). The 2010 Census had estimated the ethnic Muslim population of Russia at 16 million. See Alexey Malashenko, "The Dynamics of Russian Islam" (Muslim Migrants in Russia), February 1, 2013—www.carnegie.ru/2013/02/01/dynamics-of-russian-islam/f890# (April 21, 2013). On the main Muslim institutions: the Central Spiritual Board of Muslims in Russia led by Sheikh ul-Islam Talgat Tadzhuddin; the Council of Muftis of Russia under Sheikh Ravil Gainutdin; the Spiritual Board of Muslims of the Asian Part of Russia led by Sheikh Nafigulla Ashirov; the Coordination Center for Muslims in the Northern Caucasus under Mufti Ismail Berdiev; and the Muslim Spiritual Board of the Republic of Tatarstan led by Mufti Gusman Iskhakov, see Alicja Cecylia Curanović, "Relations between the Orthodox Church and Islam in the Russian Federation," *Journal of Church and State* 52:3 (2010), 507.
2. Chechnia, Ingushetia, Dagestan (82.6 percent), and Kabardino-Balkaria (55.4 percent); Karachay-Cherkessia (48 percent), Bashkortonstan (38.6 percent), and Tatarstan (33.7 percent)—en.wikipedia.org/wiki/Religion_in_Russia (April 21, 2013).
3. James W. Warhola, "Religion and Politics under the Putin Administration: Accommodation and Confrontation within 'Managed Pluralism,'" *Journal of Church and State* 49 (Winter 2007), 79.
4. Curanović, "Relations between the Orthodox Church and Islam," 512.
5. Malashenko, "The Dynamics of Russian Islam" (Conversions to Islam).
6. Alexander Verkhovsky, "Public Interactions between Orthodox Christian and Muslim Organisations at the Federal Level in Russia Today," *Religion, State & Society* 36:4 (December 2008), 385.
7. Ibid., 386.
8. Malashenko, "The Dynamics of Russian Islam" (Islam's Complexities). Malashenko elaborates further on this: "In the latter case [of nontraditional Islam], the regime convinces everyone and itself that it is dealing with bandits, against whom armored vehicles and helicopters have to be used from time to time. Both 'bad' and 'good' Islams have long been factors of Russian politics. It seems that in the foreseeable future, these two Islams will remain separate, given that dialogue between the adherents of different Islams has

not been working thus far." See Alexey Malashenko, "Religion in Russia: Politicization and Disengagement" (September 3, 2012), Carnegie Moscow Center, carnegieendowment.org/2012/09/03/religion-in-russia-politicization-and-disengagement/drje (April 21, 2013).

9. Curanović, "Relations between the Orthodox Church and Islam," 516.
10. Shavkat Avviasov et al., "Clericalism—A Threat to the National Security of Russia," August 15, 2007, Institute of Religion and Policy: i-r-p.ru/page/stream-document/index-15042.html (April 20, 2013). Nor were Muslim communities the only source of such criticism: in a letter to the president that same year, ten members of the Russian Academy of Sciences voiced their rejection of "the growing clericalization of Russian society" and the interference of the ROC "in all spheres of social life." See "Российские академики—против вмешательства церкви во все сферы общественной жизни," *Институт религии и политики*, 23.07.2007. i-r-p.ru/page/stream-event/index-14477.html (April 20, 2013).
11. "Ислам является неотъемлемой частью российской истории и культуры. Уважение к вере, обычаям и традициям наших народов—это основа гражданского мира в нашей стране. Скажу прямо, у России нет необходимости добиваться дружбы с мусульманским миром. Наша страна сама по себе является органичной частью этого мира." Dimitry Medvedev, Speech to the League of Arab States (Cairo, June 23, 2009), "Выступление на встрече с постоянными представителями стран—членов Лиги арабских государств,"—www.kremlin.ru/transcripts/4804 (April 21, 2013).
12. Curanović, "Relations between the Orthodox Church and Islam," 525.
13. Djanat Sergei Markus, "Mezhreligiozny sovet Rossii ischerpal svoi vozmozhnosti," http://www.islam.ru/pressclub/gost/markus_ric—cited in Curanović, "Relations between the Orthodox Church and Islam," 529. No longer accessible on the site.
14. Curanović, "Relations between the Orthodox Church and Islam," 523.
15. Verkhovsky, "Public Interactions between Orthodox Christian and Muslim Organisations," 384–385. Since this statement in 2002, Verkhovsky also noted a parallel motif of Russia as a multiethnic and multireligious country in the discourses of the future patriarch of Moscow.
16. Ibid., 388.
17. See *A Common Word: Muslims and Christians on Loving God and Neighbor*, Miroslav Volf, Muhammad bin Ghazi and Melissa Yarrington (eds.) (Grand Rapids, MI: Eerdmans, 2010).
18. Alexy II, Patriarch of Moscow and All Russia, "Response to the open letter of 138 Muslim Theologians" (# 55—April 14, 2008), *Christian Responses to A Common Word*. www.acommonword.com/response-from-his-holiness-patriarchy-alexy-ii-of-moscow-and-all-russia/ (accessed April 20, 2013).
19. Alexy II, par. 5.
20. Alexy II, par. 6.
21. Alexy II, par. 6.
22. Alexy II, par. 7–8.
23. Alexy II, par. 9.
24. Alexy II, par. 9.
25. Alexy II, par. 10.
26. Alexy II, par. 11.
27. Mor Eustathius Matta Roham, archbishop of Jezira and the Euphrates, Syrian Orthodox Church of Antioch, "Christian Responses to A Common Word: Response #44," January 31, 2008, www.acommonword.com/response-from-mor-eustathius-matta-roham-archbishop-of-jezira-and-the-euphrates-syrian-orthodox-church-of-antioch/ (accessed April 21, 2013).
28. Mor Eustathius Matta Roham, par. 3.

29. Aram I, Catholicos of Cilicia, Armenian Orthodox Church, "Christian Responses to A Common Word: Response #46," February 6, 2008, www.acommonword.com/category/site/christian-responses/ (accessed April 21, 2013).
30. Aram I, par. 2.
31. Aram I, par. 2.
32. Mor Eustathius Matta Roham, par. 2.
33. Aram I, par. 1.
34. "The traditional religions in our country have never come into conflict while preserving their identity for a thousand years...Various religious communities lived side-by-side, working together and defending together their common Motherland." Alexy II, par. 15–16.
35. See Bishop Hilarion (Alfeyev), "Setting Objectives for Christian-Muslim Dialogue and Cooperation," June 2, 2008, www.orthodoxytoday.org/articles8/Bp-Hilarion-Setting-Objectives-For-Christian-Muslim-Dialogue-And-Cooperation.php (accessed January 30, 2013). Hilarion reiterates the main points of Alexy's original response and expands on a number of them. On the matter of Christian minority rights, he singles out places where the situation of Christians is desperate (Iraq, Afghanistan, Saudi Arabia), where Christians have been persecuted and killed (Pakistan, Indonesia, the Philippines), where Christians have suffered religious persecution (the Kosovo region, the Turkish-occupied part of Cyprus), and where the needs of Christians are neglected (Turkey). Hilarion echoes Alexy's hope that Muslim-Christian dialogue will improve conditions in all of these trouble spots.
36. Mor Eustathius Matta Roham,, par. 5.
37. Chrisostomos, archbishop of Cyprus, "Christian Responses to A Common Word: Response #64," November 10, 2008, www.acommonword.com/response-from-his-beatitude-chrisostomos-archbishop-of-cyprus/ (accessed February 25, 2013).
38. Archbishop Yeznik Petrosyan, Armenian Apostolic Church, "Christian Responses to A Common Word: Response #52," April 2, 2008, www.acommonword.com/response-from-archbishop-yeznik-petrosyan-general-secretary-for-inter-church-relations-on-behalf-of-his-holiness-karekin-ii-supreme-patriarch-and-catholicos-of-all-armenians-the-mother-see-of-holy/ (accessed February 25, 2013).
39. Alexy II, par. 12–14.
40. Aram I, par. 5.
41. Aram I, par. 4. Emphasis mine.

19

Radical Islam in the Ferghana Valley

Galina M. Yemelianova

The Ethnocultural and Historical Background

The Ferghana Valley is situated in the heart of Central Asia, which includes present-day Kazakhstan, Uzbekistan, Tajikistan, Kyrgyzstan, and Turkmenistan. Historically, Central Asia has been an important part of the Islamic world. It also represents one of the largest Muslim regions of the former Soviet Union (45 million) along with the Caucasus (11 million) and the Volga-Urals (7 million). For historical, demographic, and socioeconomic reasons the Ferghana Valley has been the center of Islam and Islamic activism in the region. At present, the Ferghana Valley is shared by Uzbekistan, Tajikistan, and Kyrgyzstan. The total territory of the valley is 120,000 square kilometers and the total population exceeds 11 million. The numerically dominant ethnic groups of the Ferghana Valley are Uzbeks (Turkic people), Tajiks (Iranian people), and Kyrgyz (Turkic people). Smaller ethnic groups include Russians, Ukrainians, Dungans, Uighurs, Germans, and others.

The Islamization of the Ferghana Valley began in the seventh century AD when Arabs from Mesopotamia invaded the region which they called *Mawarannahr* (i.e., "that which lies beyond the river" [Amu-Darya]). By the beginning of the eighth century AD *Mawarannahr* was incorporated into the Islamic Caliphate. The proliferation of Islam was a relatively peaceful process. Its main agents were Arab merchants and farmers. Islam first found strongholds among urban peoples in Bukhara and Samarkand, situated on the territory of present-day Uzbekistan, and later it gradually spread among various rural peoples and nomadic tribes of the Central Asian steppes. From the end of the ninth century Islam had been the official religion of numerous states that emerged and declined in the region. The dominant form of Islam has been the Hanafi *madhhab* (juridical school of Sunni Islam). This is the most flexible juridical school of the four schools. It is characterized by tolerance toward representatives of other juridical schools, toward *'adats* (customary norms), and toward non-Muslims. The inhabitants of the Pamir mountains of Tajikistan have adhered to Shiism, Ismailism in particular. In the Middle Ages the cities of

Bukhara and Samarkand were renowned centers of Islamic culture and scholarship in the Islamic world. In the medieval period the region was part of the empires of Genghizids, Timurids, and other great Islamic empires. From the late nineteenth century until 1991 it was under Russian/Soviet control.

Central Asia's geographic alienation from the Islamic mainland and its lengthy existence under Russian and Soviet control, which was characterized by a physical, political, and ideological assault on Islam, accounted for the prevalence of nonofficial, so-called folk, or traditional Islam, which represents an amalgamation of Islamic beliefs, *'urf* (tribal law), *'adat* (customary law), Zoroastrianism, Buddhism, Nestorian Christianity, Shamanism, and other pre-Islamic beliefs and ethnic customs. In some parts of the Ferghana Valley Sufi Islam (Islamic mysticism) constitutes an important element of "traditional Islam."

Following the Bolshevik takeover of Central Asia and especially since the late 1920s Central Asian Muslims were subjected, like all peoples of the former Russian empire, to Sovietization, central elements of which were Communist indoctrination and atheization. Under the Soviet regime thousands of Muslim clerics and Sufi shaykhs perished; almost all mosques, Islamic schools, and other Islam-related institutions were either destroyed, closed, or converted into various mundane premises. The dual script change (first from Arabic to Latin in 1927 and later from Latin to Cyrillic in 1937) cut off the Muslims of Central Asia and other Muslim-populated regions of the USSR (since 1922) from their Islamic heritage and their coreligionists abroad. As a result, the traditions of "high," intellectual Islam were severely undermined. The dominant form of Islam became "folk," ritualistic Islam, which functioned unofficially and in disguised forms. From the 1920s it coexisted with "official Islam," represented by Islamic clerics[1] who complied with the Soviet regime. From 1943 the focus of "official Islam" was the Islamic Spiritual Board of Muslims of Central Asia (SADUM), centered in Tashkent. In 1948 it became the leading Islamic board on the territory of the USSR. (Other Islamic Boards were in Ufa, Bashkortostan; Buynaksk, Dagestan and Baku, Azerbaijan.)

On the positive side, however, Soviet rule enhanced the significant economic and societal modernization of Central Asian Muslims. The region was integrated into the nationwide modern transport and energy systems. Among the obvious gains were the eradication of widespread illiteracy, the elimination of numerous deadly diseases and the emancipation of Muslim women, who at least legally acquired economic and social equality with men. The corollary was a significant increase in living standards of local people and demographic growth. It is worth noting that due to comprehensive free secondary education and the accessibility of free higher education, Central Asian Muslims greatly surpassed their coreligionists abroad in their levels of education and professional training (Yemelianova 2002: 135).

The Soviet invasion of Afghanistan following the Marxist coup of 1978 had an "awakening" effect on Central Asian Muslims, who from the very beginning of the conflict had ambivalent feelings about it. Of special significance was their exposure in Afghanistan to different and more puritanical forms of Islam. So, upon their return home many Central Asian soldiers began to question the validity of their "folk" Islamic practices and beliefs. It is worth noting that those ex-soldiers became particularly receptive to the principles of fundamentalist Islam, which began to proliferate in the region during the 1980s.

Vectors of Islamic Activism

The Gorbachevian political liberalization and the adoption of a more liberal religious approach facilitated the emergence of a so-called Islamic revival in the region. Its pioneers were the so-called young imams, graduates of Central Asian madrasahs (Islamic schools) and foreign Islamic colleges and universities, who challenged the official "old imams" for their alleged passivity, theological incompetence, low moral standards, and their conformity with the Soviet establishment and the KGB. They began a campaign for the restoration of an Islamic infrastructure on a prerevolutionary scale, for the promotion of knowledge of Islam and Arabic language and for the wider involvement of Central Asian Muslims in the social and political life of their respective republics. The leading figures among the "young imams" were Muhammad Sadiq Yusuf,[2] Akbar Turajonzade,[3] Ratbek Nysanbai-uly,[4] and Nasrullah ibn Ibadullah.[5] In the summer of 1990 Kazakh and Kyrgyz "young imams" split from the Uzbek-dominated SADUM and established separate Kazakh and Kyrgyz muftiates. The movement for Islamic enlightenment was enhanced by moral, educational, and material assistance from foreign Islamic foundations and organizations, which acquired the rights to operate in Central Asian republics. Foreign Islamic assistance was pivotal in the Islamic construction and publishing boom, which began in the region in the late 1980s. During the late Soviet and the early post-Soviet period hundreds of new mosques, dozens of madrasahs, Islamic colleges, and universities were built and many Arabic-language courses were established. A number of new Islamic periodicals, TV and radio programs were launched.

Parallel to the advance of official "young imams" there appeared nonofficial Islamic modernizers of *Salafi*[6] orientation, some of who allegedly enjoyed considerable financial support from various nongovernment Islamic funds and organizations, based in Saudi Arabia, Kuwait, the UAE, Afghanistan, Pakistan, and other Muslim countries. In the Ferghana Valley these Islamic preachers organized informal underground circles, which offered local young people basic Islamic education and Arabic-language training. Many of them criticized some aspects of "folk" Islam, although they emphasized their adherence to Hanafism. The most prominent among them were Muhammadjan Hindustani Rustamov, known as *Hajjee* Domla[7] (1892–1989), and his disciples Abduwali Qari Mirzaev, Hakimjan Qari of Margelan, and 'Allama Rahmatulla Qari. Their disciples began to operate in local mosques and madrasahs and to distribute audio and videotapes of a *Salafi* nature. The authorities and media dubbed them "Wahhabis" by alleging their foreign connections and treated them with suspicion. However, some credible sources revealed that the Uzbekistan Communist leadership had secretly forged links with proto-*Salafi*s in order to use them against influential representatives of traditional Islam (Akiner 2002:74; Naumkin 2005: 52).

The Islamic Renaissance Party of Tajikistan

An important consequence of the late Soviet political thaw was the formation of Islamic, Islamo-national, and Islamist parties and organizations. The most influential among them was the Islamic Renaissance Party of Tajikistan (IRPT), initially represented by regional branches of the all-union Islamic Renaissance Party (IRP), which was founded in June 1990 in Astrakhan. The party's ideologists included some former disciples of Hindustani. In the early 1990s the Tajik branch of the pan-Soviet IRP emerged as the major Islamic political party. During the 1990s the IRPT claimed over 10,000 active and over 20,000 passive members. Initially, its proclaimed aim was the re-Islamicization of Tajikistan through parliamentary means. During the political crisis in 1991–1992 the position of the IRP radicalized toward acceptance of a violent jihad. Its members became the driving force of the United Tajik Opposition (UTO) during the Tajik civil war (1992–1997) under the leadership of Sayid Abdulloh Nuri.[8] As a result of the compromise Peace Agreement of 1997, which ended the war, the IRPT was legalized and some of its members joined the coalition government of Tajikistan. This led to a change in the IRPT's position regarding jihad, the new position involving a denunciation of armed conflict and the interpretation of jihad as mainly a Muslim's internal, spiritual struggle for self-perfection.

Parties of Adolat, Baraka, Tawba, and Islam Lashkarlari

In the late 1990s the epicenter of Islamism shifted to the Uzbekistan part of the Ferghana Valley. The first Islamist groups and organizations were formed in the valley in the early 1990s. They were the Baraka (Blessing), the Tawba (Repentance), the Islam Lashkarlari (Islamic Warriors), and its splinter group—the Adolat (Justice).[9] These organizations established contacts with Saudi[10] and other foreign Islamic foundations and organizations. By the mid-1990s the Adolat turned into a noticeable factor of the social landscape in the valley. It is interesting that initially the Adolat was particularly concerned with the provision of welfare and safety to the local population. The motto of its activists was the establishment of social equality, justice, and public order. They organized the *mahalla* militia, which patrolled roads and monitored prices at local markets (Rashid 2002: 139; Naumkin 2005: 58, 69, 97). Later on, however, they began to emphasize their Islamic identity and to refer to the sharia as the exclusive legal basis of their activities. They distributed leaflets and audiotapes, which promoted *Salafi* Islam, and imposed a strict Islamic dress code, including the veiling of women, in the areas under their control. In political terms most local Islamists subscribed to the concept of *Musulman-abad* (The land of Islam), that is, the Islamic unification of the whole of Central Asia. However, in practice they were mainly concerned with the Islamic unification of the Ferghana Valley. In the early 1990s Islamists de facto controlled most of Namangan, Andijan, and Margelan *oblasts* of the Ferghana Valley.

The Islamic Movement of Uzbekistan

President Karimov's ruthless political and administrative suppression of Islamists had a radicalizing effect on them and led to the formation of the Islamic Movement of Uzbekistan (IMU) in 1996 by Tahir Yuldashev ("Faruq")[11] and Juma Hojiev (Namangani).[12] Both leaders unambiguously embraced political Islam and advocated the violent removal of President Karimov from office and the creation of an Islamic state in the Ferghana Valley. Unlike the Islam Lashkarlari, the Adolat, and Tawba, the IMU prioritized political and military engagement rather than religious education and indoctrination. Its members were predominantly ethnic Uzbeks who portrayed themselves as *mujahedeen* (Islamic warriors) waging a jihad against the rule of *kafir* President Karimov of Uzbekistan. Many of them underwent combat training in jihadist camps in Afghanistan, Pakistan, and Chechnia (Rashid 2002: 137–140; Naumkin 2005: 88, 97). The IMU militants used largely guerrilla tactics against the Uzbek state and police employees and other official targets. They strongly relied on foreign support, especially from the Pakistani-based *Jamiat Ulema-e- Islam* (Assembly of Islamic clergy)[13] and later the Taliban in Afghanistan. Other means of cash flow to the IMU involved its drug trafficking activities from Afghanistan to Tajikistan and Kyrgyzstan, hostage-taking, robberies, and other forms of criminal activity (Fredholm 2002: 27).

It is alleged that the IMU played a pivotal role in the bombings in Tashkent in February 1999, which killed sixteen and wounded more than a hundred people. These terrorist incidents triggered a new wave of official political and administrative repression against the IMU activists, their sympathizers, and ordinary Muslims who behaved, or only dressed, "suspiciously." As a result, the IMU was significantly weakened and fragmented. Those IMU members who escaped arrest moved to neighboring Tajikistan (Tavildara district), Afghanistan, and Pakistan. In August 1999 and in August–September 2000 the IMU militants invaded the Batken *oblast'* of Kyrgyzstan. After September 11, 2001, some of the IMU members fought on the side of the Taliban and its allies against the US-led coalition forces in Afghanistan. Following the Taliban's defeat the IMU's remnants either went deep underground in some areas of the Ferghana Valley, Kazakhstan (Taraz and Shymkent), and Xinjiang province in China, or fled to Pakistan. Between 2001 and 2003 their actual activities in Central Asia were minimal. Since 2003, however, they have resurfaced under different names (*Islamic Jihad Union* [IJU] and others) as part of the global multiethnic, although still mainly Turkic, jihadist network. Thus, according to some sources, in April and July 2004 natives of southern Kazakhstan, who allegedly received military training in Pakistan's Waziristan region, carried out bombings against the Israeli and US embassies in Tashkent.[14] Jihadist attacks also took place in Tajikistan in January and July 2005 and then in July 2006. The IJU and other small jihadist groupings represent a localized threat to Uzbekistan and its neighbors, whilst also having the ability to undertake operations in Europe, and maintaining a residual or nominal support base in some parts of the Ferghana Valley, Turkey, the Caspian region, and the Greater Middle East including tribal regions in Afghanistan, Pakistan, and Iran.[15]

Hizb at-Tahrir al-Islamii

Since 1999 the major agency of Islamism in the region has been the *Hizb at-Tahrir al-Islamii* (Party of Islamic Liberation, hereafter referred to as *HT*).[16] Compared to the aforementioned Islamist organizations, the *HT* represents an international Islamist organization, which combines characteristics of religious and political movement. The correlation between religious and political engagement of *HT* members is congruent to the level of their Islamic awareness and "preparedness" for a political action in the name of Islam. *HT* ideology is *Salafi* Islam and its declared goal "to resume the Islamic way of life and to convey the Islamic call to the world" through the construction of the worldwide Caliphate under the rule of a caliph who combines functions of political and religious leader. Members of *HT* denounce the West and its major attributes such as democracy, pluralism, free markets, and human rights.

It is significant that *HT* has been successful in recruiting new members in various parts of the Muslim world due to its doctrinal and political flexibility and its ability to adjust to local conditions and to modify its *da'awa* (summon to Islam) message and tactics accordingly. Importantly, it has been consistent in advocating nonviolent means to promote its salvation message. The leaders of the Central Asian outlet of *HT* have subscribed to the *HT* main religious and political principles. However, their emphasis has been the re-education of local people in Islamic religion and sharia due to their lengthy existence under the Soviet atheistic rule. *Tahriris*' educational message has been supported by their provision of welfare and other assistance to the most needy members of local communities.

The first evidence of *HT*'s activity in Uzbekistan's Andijan, Surkhan Darya, and Namangan *oblast'* of the Ferghana Valley was reported in the early 1990s.[17] Throughout the 1990s and the early 2000s *HT*'s popularity steadily grew despite tough state control and suppression. In 1996 a group under the leadership of Akram Yuldashev split from *HT* and formed a separate Uzbekified Islamist organization, known as *Al-Akramiyya*. Its cells were formed in Andijan, Margelan, Namangan, and Kokand *oblast'* of the valley. In 1999, yet another group *Hizb an-Nusra* (Party of victory) split from *HT*. However, the scope of activities and popularity of both splinter groups have been very limited. From the late 1990s *HT* has been also active in northwestern Tajikistan and Jalal-Abad and Osh *oblast'* of Kyrgyzstan. Since the early 2000s the *Tahriris*' presence has been reported in the Shimkent *oblast'* of southern Kazakhstan. Although it has been impossible, given the dearth of verified data, to establish the actual membership of *HT* in the region, it is plausible to assume that it has united between thirty and fifty thousand active members. However, *Tahriris*' relatives have constituted a much larger group of sympathizers.

Organization, Ideology, and Tactics of Islamic Radicals

The continuing advance of the *HT* in the Ferghana Valley has been largely due to its pyramidal organization, its high level of secrecy, its strict discipline, the simplicity of its salvation message, its social projects, its tolerance of traditional "folk" Islam, in particular, and its skillful propaganda. The primary cell of HT has been a *halaqa*, or a *da'ira* (circle), which has been headed by a *mushrif* (local leader), and which has included up to five party members. Rank-and-file members knew only those who belonged to their immediate circle. Therefore, the arrest, or elimination, of one, or several *Tahriris* did not seriously affect the whole network. The identities of the party's district and regional leaders have been kept secret (Naumkin 2005: 145). *HT* members had to pay a monthly membership, which amounted to 5–20 percent of their individual monthly income.

My research has revealed that *HT* activists have been intelligent and articulate men in their mid-and late-twenties. Among them were former journalists, students, and businessmen. As for the ethnonational profile of *Tahriris* the vast majority of them were Uzbeks, followed by Tajiks and then Uighurs, Kyrgyz, and representatives of other Muslim ethnic minorities. An average age of a *Tahriri* was 25 years.

Tahriris have recruited new members predominantly from two major social groups. The first group consisted of young dwellers of the valley's small towns who were unhappy with their existing social and professional status. Although many of them were involved in casual business activities, they did not have stable employment and income and did not see any prospects of a positive change in the future. The second group included members of the extended family of a *Tahriri* who had been jailed or persecuted by the authorities. In that case feelings of family solidarity, rather than ideological imperatives, played a central role in their decision to join. This group also generated most female recruits of the *HT*. A sign of the growing female involvement in the *Tahriris*' movement was a noticeable increase in the number of women wearing the hijab. It is worth noting that the rise in the female membership of the *HT* has had particular significance given the central role of women in the upbringing of children and in supporting their families.

Factors of Islamic Radicalization

Economic and Social Factors

Research has shown that economic hardships have been among the main causes of Islamic radicalization in the Ferghana Valley. Following the collapse of the USSR the life of the vast majority of the valley's dwellers has been reduced to basic survival. They have suffered from the diminishing size of arable land resulting from the disruption of the previously unified water system and the lack of state loans for agriculture. As a result, a significant part of the economically active population found themselves without work. High unemployment forced many men to leave their families in search of work in Kazakhstan and Russia, while women were left to look after elderly relatives and children. Desperation drew some residents of the valley into involvement in drug-trafficking, kidnapping, prostitution, hostage-taking, and other illegal activities. The valley's dwellers have been badly affected by the post-Soviet border controls and customs, which severely restricted their previously free movement across the three republics. Numerous border controls jeopardized the support networks, which had played a central role in the well-being of many families. Local people also suffered from the arbitrary actions of border guards and customs officers who supplemented their meager incomes through extortionate customs fines on local traders.

The rise of interest in Islam and political Islam, in particular, among young residents of the valley was also linked to the continuing deterioration in the standards of primary and secondary education in comparison with the Soviet period. Religious education in state schools has remained inadequate and has not provided pupils with a basic knowledge of Islam and sharia, which would have assisted them in negotiating their position toward various Islamic and Islamist organizations. On the other hand, the introduction of university fees and a partial privatization of higher education, which was free in the Soviet times, made higher education inaccessible for the vast majority of impoverished families. As a result, a growing number of young people began to seek alternative sources of knowledge within informal Islamic study groups. An aggravating factor was the absence of governmental youth policies and relevant funding analogous to the pioneer and *komsomol* organizations of the Soviet period. It appears that among the implications of the de-Sovietization of Central Asia, and the Ferghana Valley, in particular, has been the retraditionalization of local rural societies and the social marginalization of its young people. Of special concern was the reversal of the relative gender equality, which had existed in the Soviet period, and its replacement by relations based on male supremacy and domination. There has been a growing trend of girls' early withdrawal from formal schooling, their early marriages, and their subsequent confinement to Islamicized household routine.

Political Factors

The advance of Islamism has also been linked to the lack of democracy and the widespread disillusionment and frustration with corrupt and inefficient state institutions and officials. Some dwellers of the valley became receptive to the Islamist salvation message because they lost hope of any positive change in their lives through legitimate political channels. They felt defenseless against the arbitrariness and the heavy-handedness of law-enforcement officers and border-guards. The repression against Islamists and their sympathizers has intensified even further in the aftermath of the Andijan uprising in May 2005. Consequently, many previously law-abiding and loyal people have been antagonized and have turned into militant Islamists. It is also worth noting that the official portrayal and treatment of *Tahriri*s as criminals has created an aura of martyrdom around them. Often the arrest of one *Tahriri* served as a catalyst of Islamic radicalization among the members of his immediate family, as well as a wider kinship community. Furthermore, jailed *Tahriri*s promoted their Islamist propaganda among prison inmates. As a result, there has been a growing merger between Islamism and terrorism.

The *Tahriris*' promise of fair government in a border-free Central Asian Caliphate has appealed to those people who have been frustrated by the reluctance of regional governments to address the acute ecological and socioeconomic problems of the valley. In particular, the authorities' refusal, or inability, to demarcate clearly the borders of the three republics has been causing conflict over arable land and water resources. It appears that the governments' preoccupation with the military, administrative, and political assault on real and imagined Islamists has further aggravated the alienation of ordinary people from the authorities. This alienation has occurred in parallel to increased government control and interference in the life of local Muslim communities.

Yet another noticeable factor has been the official foreign policies of Uzbekistan, Tajikistan, and Kyrgyzstan, especially their initial siding with the United States and their Western allies in "the war on terror," which was not popular among the ordinary people. However, this factor has been less significant than among Muslim communities in the West.

The Inadequacy of Traditional Islamic "Clergy"

An important factor behind the proliferation of *Tahriris*' message has been continuing domination of poorly educated "traditional" Islamic clergy (over 90 percent in the Ferghana Valley). Their theological incompetence, corruption, and progovernment position, as well as their avoidance of a debate with Islamists on vital socioeconomic political and ideological issues, have undermined public trust in them and led to their religious and political marginalization. As a result, young people have been turning to *Tahriri*s and other unofficial Islamic preachers and activists, who have provided them with ideological guidance and practical assistance.

Of particular appeal has been *Tahriris*' idea of the establishment of a Caliphate, which would dissolve the existing state borders. *Tahriris* believed that a Caliphate would ensure justice for everyone and eliminate corruption and social inequality. Unlike other Islamic fundamentalists, and especially *Wahhabis* in the North Caucasus, who have denounced local Islamic traditions, *Tahriris* have attuned their propaganda to local "folk" Islamic traditions and customs. Compared to the IMU, which advocated an armed jihad in order to remove *kafir* (nonbeliever) President Karimov from power, *HT* has stressed its rejection of any violent actions and its reliance on peaceful methods of *da'awa*. *Tahriris* have propagated their ideas through preaching and disseminating printed, audio-, video-, and online materials, produced both abroad and locally. For this reason the definition of *HT* as a jihadist organization is questionable (Williams 2003: 13).

Islamist Propaganda, Tactical and Financial Advantages

The continuing proliferation of Islamism in the region has been also due to the Islamists' advantages in terms of their propaganda, organization, tactics, and financial resources.

It is significant that, although *Tahriris* acknowledged their belonging to the international organization of *HT*, most of them were natives of the Ferghana Valley who studied at Islamic universities in Egypt, Saudi Arabia, and Pakistan. The *Tahriris*' good knowledge of the region and its inhabitants enabled them to adjust the party's priorities and tactics to particular local conditions. Thus, they emphasized the peaceful nature of jihad, which they described as an internal struggle of an individual toward becoming a better Muslim. Because of this, many ordinary residents of the valley treated *Tahriris* as their representatives, rather than as outsiders.

In comparison to representatives of official Islam, who refrained from any critique of the authorities, *Tahriris* have exposed corruption, bribery, arbitrariness, extortion, and other improper practices of government officials, police, and Muslim clerics at all levels. *Tahriris* have also gained sympathy by directing their critique against those members of law-enforcement agencies who literally terrorized local populations in the name of fighting Islamic extremism.

Yet another selling point of the *Tahriris*' propaganda has been their bold denunciation of Western democracy, which was widely associated with moral and spiritual degradation and with the allegedly anti-Islamic policies of the leading Western powers. Compared to government officials and the IRPT activists, who claimed their adherence to democracy and human rights as guiding principles, *Tahriris* openly rejected Western democracy and human rights as incompatible with Islam. Instead, they have advocated sharia law as the main social and political regulator in the Ferghana Valley. It is worth noting that the introduction of some elements of the sharia law into the existing juridical system has been viewed favorably by those who were frustrated by the rising crime rates, corruption, prostitution, and alcohol and drug abuse.

The *Tahriris*' advance has been ensured by their clandestine pyramidal organization and their proselytizing methods. They have been able to operate under conditions of tough official control. Their preferred tactics have included the night-time distribution of leaflets, posters, CDs, audio and videotapes at mosques and public buildings. They have skillfully attuned their verbal propaganda, as well as their audio, video, and printed materials, to the specific problems of local communities. Compared to registered Muslim clerics, who in their sermons avoided politics, the *Tahriris* have actively engaged in the ongoing political debate and offered their interpretation of the conflicts in Afghanistan and Iraq along the lines of a Western assault on Muslim brothers and sisters worldwide.

Finally, the vital condition of the *Tahriris*' relative proselytizing success has been their substantial material and financial resources, which has enabled them to design and produce locally and in local languages their propaganda video and audio materials, leaflets and other Islamic publications, as well as to provide material help to impoverished locals. The *Tahriris* insist that they are fully self-funded and rely on membership dues, proceeds from publishing activities, and their involvement in small business for funds. However, their opponents allege that the *HT* has been funded from abroad.

Conclusion

Following the disintegration of the USSR in 1991, the Ferghana Valley, which is administratively divided among Uzbekistan, Tajikistan, and Kyrgyzstan, has been one of epicenters of Islamic radicalization in Muslim Eurasia and a wider Muslim world. The rise of radical Islam there has occurred against the background of dramatic political and socioeconomic changes associated with the post-Communist transition. The region, which in the Soviet era had been highly subsidized by Moscow, has experienced a sharp deterioration in its social and economic situation and a proliferation of crime and violence. At the same time, the end of institutionalized atheism and the relaxation of border controls have prompted the gradual cultural and religious reintegration of the valley's Muslims within the wider Islamic world. A corollary of this process has been the proliferation among them of "foreign" Islam, including that of a *Salafi* and radical nature. Among the contributing factors to the advance of *Salafi* Islam there have been the endemic corruption and inefficiency of ruling regimes, the repressive policies of Uzbekistan president Karimov and his likes, as well as the theological incompetence and complacency of the official Muslim "clergy" who have been unable to provide the much-sought-after spiritual guidance and practical support to poverty-stricken and ideologically confused people.

Islamic radicalization has occurred in both jihadist (proviolent) and nonjihadist (nonviolent) forms. The main agencies of jihadism in the region have been Islamic Movement of Uzbekistan (IMU), Islamic Jihad Union (IJU), and some other IMU splinter groups, which have been integrated within a global jihadist movement. The region's main nonjihadist Islamist organization has been *Hizb al-Tahrir al-Islamii*. In the past two decades there has been a rise in the number of Islamists in the region. At the same time, Islamists' presence has remained limited and restricted to a few enclaves in the Ferghana Valley (Namangan, Kokand, Margelan, and Andijan). The estimated number of Islamists and their sympathizers in the Ferghana Valley ranges from 8 to 20 percent of the valley's population.

The main deterrents to a wider proliferation of Islamism were the Soviet-era legacy of secularism, the resilience and conservatism of local societies, based on a *mahalla*,[18] and strong positions of "folk" Islam, rooted in *Al-Maturidiyya*,[19] a local form of Sunni Islam of Hanafi *maddhab* (juridical school), which emphasizes patience and tolerance, as well as Muslims' noninvolvement in politics. However, the prolongation of the current dire socioeconomic conditions, the ineffectiveness, pervasive corruption, and repressive nature of the regional and local authorities, as well as the official treatment of devout Muslims with suspicion as potential extremists may further enhance the proliferation of Islamism in the region.[20]

Notes

1. Strictly speaking, the use of the Christian terms "clerics" and "clergy" in relation to mullahs, imams, muftis, shaykhs, and other representatives of Islamic authority is incorrect, because Islam does not accept the concept of mediation between God and believers and therefore does not require an institutionalized hierarchy. A Muslim who leads a prayer or presents a sermon is trusted by the community to perform these functions simply because of his superior knowledge of Islam compared to his coreligionists. In this chapter the term is used for the sake of utility and simplicity alone.
2. Muhammad Sadiq Yusuf, an ethnic Uzbek, was born in 1952 in Andijan province of Uzbekistan. He received training in Islamic studies from the *Mir-i Arab madrasah* in Bukhara, the Islamic Institute in Tashkent, and the Islamic University in Libya. He is one of the most prominent theologians in Central Asia and the wider Islamic world.
3. Akbar Turajonzade, an ethnic Tajik, was born in 1954 in the Kofarnihon province of Tajikistan. He received a structured Islamic education and in 1988–1991 served as the *Qazi Qalon* (supreme Islamic authority) of Tajikistan. In 1993–1999 he was the second in command of the IRPT and the UTO. After the end of the Tajik Civil War he served as the deputy prime minister of Tajikistan.
4. In 1990–2000 Ratbek Nysanbai-uly served as the first mufti of independent Kazakhstan. In 2000 he was succeeded by Shaykh Absattar *hajjee* Derbisali, a professional diplomat and scholar of Arabic.
5. In 1990–2003 Nasrullah ibn Ibadullah served as the first mufti of independent Turkmenistan. In 2003 he was removed from his office and charged with alleged assassination attempt on the late President Saparmurad Niyazov. He was sentenced to 22 years in prison.
6. The term *Salafi* Islam (lit. "Islam of ancestors") refers to an "unadulterated Islam" of Prophet Muhammad and four righteous caliphs.
7. Muhammadjan Hindustani Rustamov (*Hajjee* Domla), a renowned Islamic scholar, was born in 1892 in Kokand and was educated in madrasahs of Kokand and Bukhara. He subsequently traveled to Afghanistan, India, and Mecca. In 1947 he returned to the Ferghana Valley, but was charged with espionage and sent to a labor camp in Kazakhstan. He was rehabilitated at the end of the 1950s and settled in Dushanbe, where he died in 1989.
8. Sayid Abdulloh Nuri (1974–2006), an ethnic Tajik, born in Sangvor, Qarateghin Valley, Tajikistan. In 1974 he founded an Islamic educational organization *Nahzat-i Islomi*. During the Tajik Civil War (1992–1997) he was the leader of the UTO. In 1997 Sayid Nuri and Tajik president Emomali Rakhmonov signed the Tajik National Peace Accord, which ended the Civil War.
9. For a detailed discussion of those parties, see chapter 20 in this volume.
10. The special role of Saudi Arabia as a benefactor of the Islamic revival in the region could be attributed to the existence in the country of a 300,000-strong Central Asian diaspora, which is comprised of descendants of *basmachis* (Naumkin 2005: 38).
11. Tahir Yuldashev (1967–2009) an ethnic Uzbek, born in Namangan, was an underground imam who underwent combat training in an Islamist camp in Afghanistan. Prior to

organizing the IMU he was one of central leading figures in the IRP and the Adolat. He fought in the Tajik Civil War, in the "Namangani battalion," and had close links with jihadists in Pakistan and Afghanistan. See more on this in chapter 20 of this volume.

12. Juma Namangani (1969–2002), an ethnic Uzbek, was a former Soviet paratrooper who fought in Afghanistan. Like Tahir Yoldashev, he was one of the leaders of Adolat. He fought in the Tajik Civil war, in the "Namangani battalion," and had close links with jihadists in Pakistan and Afghanistan. See more in chapter 20 of this volume.
13. The *Jamiat Ulema-e-Islam* is a Deobandi Islamic political party, which was formed in Pakistan in 1945. The party established thousands of madrasahs in Pakistan and was involved in the creation of Taliban movement in Afghanistan.
14. www.rferl.org/content/article/1078560.html (accessed March 13, 2012).
15. On the IMU's activities outside the Ferghana Valley, see chapter 20 of this volume.
16. *HT* was founded in 1953 in Jordan by a Palestinian judge, Taqi ad-Din Nabhani (1909–1977), a member of the Muslim Brotherhood. From 1977 to 2003 the *HT* was headed by 'Abd al-Qadim Zallum, a Jordanian national of Palestinian descent. Since 2003, the *HT* leader has been 'Ata Abu ar-Rushta, a Palestinian. *HT* operates in many countries of the Middle East, Europe, and the former USSR. It is banned in most Middle Eastern and former Soviet countries. Since 2001, *HT* has been banned in all Central Asian states.
17. Allegedly, the first *HT* regional leaders were 'Isam Abu Mahmud Qiyadati and Abd al-Qadim Zallum, both Jordanians.
18. *Mahalla* is a neighborhood community, which unites dwellers of towns and large villages. Each *mahalla* represents a semi-self-governed unit, which has a mosque and a *maktab* (an Islamic primary school). The imam plays a central role in the life of a *mahalla*.
19. The term "Al-Maturidiyya" derives from the name of Abu Mansur al-Maturidi al-Samarqandi (d. 944), one of the most prominent local followers of Abu Hanifa. Al-Maturidi created his school of scholastic theology (*kalam*), which together with that of al-Ash'ari, formed the essence of Sunni Islamic theology. *Al-Maturidiyya* legitimized the interwovenness of Hanafi Islam with traditional clan and tribal networks, which endured for centuries almost without change.
20. For a fuller elaboration of the arguments set out in this chapter, see Yemelianova (2010).

References

Akiner, Sh. (2002) "Islam in Post-Soviet Central Asia: Contested Territory." In A. Strasser, S. Haas, G. Mangott, and V. Heuberger (eds.), *Zentralasien und Islam*. Hamburg: Deutsches Orient-Institut. 73–101.

Baran, Z., S. F. Starr, and S. E. Cornell. (2006) *Islamic Radicalism in Central Asia and the Caucasus: Implications for the EU*. Silk Road Paper, July, Uppsala.

Fredholm, M. (2002) *Islamic Extremism as a Political Force in Central Asia*. Research Report no. 6, Forum for Central Asia Studies, Stockholm University.

Naumkin, V. (2005) *Radical Islam in Central Asia*. Lanham: Rowman & Littlefield Publishers.

Rashid, J. (2002) *Jihad. The Rise of Militant Islam in Central Asia*. New Haven: Yale University Press.

Williams, B. (2003) "Jihad and Ethnicity in Post-Communist Eurasia. On the Trail of Transnational Islamic Holy Warriors in Kashmir, Afghanistan, Central Asia, Chechnya and Kosovo." *The Global Review of Ethnopolitics* 2:3–4. 3–24.

Yemelianova, G. (2002) *Russia and Islam: A Historical Survey*. New York: Palgrave Macmillan.

———. (2010) *Radical Islam in the Former Soviet Union*. London & New York: Routledge.

Map 19.1 Central Asian States—Setting.

Map 19.2 Central Asian States—Detail.

20

Uzbek Islamic Extremists in the Civil Wars of Tajikistan, Afghanistan, and Pakistan: From Radical Islamic Awakening in the Ferghana Valley to Terrorism with Islamic Vocabulary in Waziristan

Michael Fredholm

The Islamic Movement of Uzbekistan—Origins of the Movement

The Islamic Movement of Uzbekistan (IMU), or *O'zbekiston Islomiy Harakati* as it is known locally (*Harakat ul-Islamiyyah* in Arabic),[1] had its origin in the Islamic movement called *Adolat* ("Justice"), a faction of a larger group known as *Islom lashkarlari* ("Islamic Warriors"). This group arose in the city of Namangan in the Uzbekistani part of the Ferghana Valley in about 1990 as a response to what was perceived as widespread corruption and social injustice exposed by the liberal perestroika era as well as the resurgence in religious activities no longer prohibited by the Soviet government. The movement was reportedly founded, or at least inspired, by Abdulhakim Qori, the well-known preacher of radical Islam. Supported by imams and preachers such as Obidkhon Qori Nazarov from Tashkent, and Umarkhon Domla and Davudkhon Qori from Namangan, who also contributed funds from their mosques, the movement grew rapidly.

However, funded by sources in Saudi Arabia, the movement became increasingly radicalized by the variety of Salafism known as Wahhabism, thus producing a form of Islamic extremism by then rare in the Central Asian region. Yet, few of the movement's members had the theological skills to recognize the differences in various types of Islam, so these names are of little value in analyzing their religious beliefs. For practical purposes, perhaps the best definition of Islamic extremism is that proposed by the Council of the Muftis (Islamic religious leaders) of Russia on

June 30, 2000. The council then singled out as extremist those movements that (1) rejected the basic Islamic traditions, (2) claimed the right to brand as "non-Muslims" traditional believers who happened to disagree with their interpretation of Islamic law, and (3) claimed the right to kill "infidels" including traditional Muslims who had failed to side with them.[2] This will be the definition of Islamic extremism adopted here, since it subsumes all varieties of Sunni extremism, whether referred to as Salafi or Wahhabi.

The basic traditions referred to by the Council of Muftis as rejected by extremists were those of Sufism and popular traditions of Islam in Central Asia. Interestingly, one could make a case for the extremists here since they reject such aspects of Islam as did not form part of the religion at the time of the Prophet Muhammad. On the other hand, in particular the Sufi-inspired traditions and practices of "folk Islam" do play a central role in the religious life of many Central Asian Muslims, who thus were alienated by the extremists.[3]

The movement came to be led by two young men: the college drop-out and local mullah Tohir Yo'ldosh and the former conscript soldier Jumaboy Hojiyev (later known as Juma Namangani or, at times, Tojiboy). Both were young, and neither is likely to have had a history of involvement in Central Asian Sufism or folk Islam. Indeed, Yo'ldosh had been inspired by the radical preaching of those imams who in turn had found their inspiration in Salafism and/or Wahhabism.

Tohir (or Tohirjon) Abduhalilovich Yo'ldosh (also known in Russian as Tahir Yuldashev and in Arabic as Muhammad Tahir Farooq (Farukh in Russian), was born in 1967 in Namangan.[4] His father died when he was five, and he was brought up by his mother, Karomat Asqarova.[5] An early member of the Uzbekistani branch of the All-Union Islamic Renaissance Party (IRP), founded in Astrakhan in June 1990, he had grown disillusioned with this party's refusal to demand an Islamic state. Together with other likeminded young Uzbeks, Yo'ldosh formed *Adolat* as a platform for his demand for an Islamic revolution.[6]

Jumaboy Ahmadjonovich Hojiyev, an ethnic Uzbek born in 1967 in Namangan, graduated from agricultural vocational school before he was drafted into the Soviet army in 1987. He reportedly served as an airborne soldier in Afghanistan during the last phase of the Soviet war there, eventually becoming promoted to sergeant, unless the elite airborne episode too is part of the myth that soon grew around his person. He is said to have become interested in Islam during his term in Afghanistan.[7]

In January 1990, Yo'ldosh renamed the movement, which he now controlled, *Islom adolati* (Islamic justice) and introduced the taking of an oath of allegiance (*bayah*) by its members, promising to introduce Islamic law first in Namangan, then the rest of Uzbekistan. In the same year, the movement built the first of several mosques and madrasahs. Of the various centers, Yo'ldosh operated out of the Otavalikhon mosque in Namangan. From November 1991 to the spring of 1992, the movement, which primarily consisted of unemployed young men, perhaps as many as five thousand altogether although other reports indicate numbers ranging from three to five hundred active members only, went on to organize protest meetings and occupy government buildings. The movement formed its own vigilante religious police force, the most militant of which became known as *yurishlar* (conquerors), which administered summary justice in the streets. Each member was paid a salary from mosque funds as well as taxes imposed on local traders. In April 1991, President Karimov, arriving to talk to the militants, was shouted down. Tohir Yo'ldosh even grabbed the microphone from the president's hands, shouting "No! Now and here, I'm the ruler! You can talk only when I allow you! Now, shut up and listen!" In December 1991, militants occupied the headquarters of the Communist Party of Uzbekistan (CPU) in Namangan. Among other things, they demanded that the government immediately proclaim the establishment of an Islamic state, use Islamic law as the only legal system, cease to orient the country toward Turkey, and introduce separate schools for boys and girls. They also began to refer to themselves as *mujohidlar* (mujahidin). Yo'ldosh assumed the title *bosh amir* (commander-in-chief). Branches of Adolat rose across the Ferghana Valley, in Andijan, Margelan, Kuva, Farghona, and Osh (in Kyrgyzstan).[8]

Little reliable information is available today on what the preachers who inspired these demands for an Islamic state actually said to their followers. As far as can be ascertained, the religious content was primarily inspired by Saudi Wahhabism but were not identical to the forms taken by Wahhabism in Saudi Arabia. As for the young leaders of Adolat at the time, their demands were no doubt motivated by personal religious convictions but they simultaneously used the religion as a political tool to achieve personal power. Many of them rejected their own teachers in Islamic theology and wished to take their places in mosques and elsewhere.[9]

Adolat was banned in March 1992, and the Uzbekistani government restored order, dissolving the movement. Several Adolat leaders, including Yo'ldosh and Hojiyev, who now took the name Juma Namangani after his hometown, fled to Tajikistan in 1992, where they joined the Tajikistani branch of the IRP, which by then was preparing to launch a violent civil war in Tajikistan.[10]

There the two young men embarked upon very different careers, although aiming for the same broad goals. Yo'ldosh began what can only be called a political career, while Namangani became a guerrilla leader. Their militant activities took them first to Tajikistan, then Afghanistan, where they formed the Islamic Movement of Uzbekistan (IMU) in 1998 and on August 25, 1999, issued their only substantially argued declaration of jihad. This was a document written in Arabic and signed by Zubayr ibn Abdur Raheem, a somewhat mysterious individual who appears to have been a Saudi Wahhabi of Uzbek origin. The group subsequently claimed that he was a descendant of the Mangit family, which once ruled Bukhara in today's Uzbekistan. Zubayr ibn Abdur Raheem had been appointed head of the IMU religious leadership and also appeared to be the chairman of the group's supreme council, while Namangani was military commander and Yo'ldosh, despite his previous claims to have been a mullah, fulfilled no religious role but that of *amir* (general commander) and chief political leader. Yet, while the declaration of jihad was signed by Zubayr ibn Abdur Raheem, it stated that the jihad was declared by Yo'ldosh, in his capacity as *amir* of the movement, and the decision had been taken following agreement by the religious leadership of the IMU. The declaration concluded that there was "clear evidence" on the obligation of jihad against the infidels as well as on the obligation to liberate the lands and the people of the Muslim community. Even so, the declaration of jihad never properly explained why this was so, or what the "clear evidence" was. The declaration included a total of four citations from the Quran, but of these, only three were referenced. In the final analysis, only one Quran quote, the first of the four and the one that headed the entire declaration, sheds some light upon the motivation for the jihad: "And fight them until there is no more *fitnah* (strife; diversity of belief) and the religion is all for Allah" (Al Anfaal 39).[11] While the word "jihad" had been used already in Namangan in 1991, when the militants began to refer to themselves as mujahidin, the 1999 declaration of jihad by Yo'ldosh and his associates does not support a conclusion that they had substantially added to their previous beliefs.

Indeed, unlike certain other groups such as the Hizb ut-Tahrir, there was apparently little Islamic theological reflection on jihad among the IMU and its successor, the Islamic Jihad Union (IJU—see later). In fact, what strikes the reader of the documents available from these groups is the lack of theological reflection in them. The reader finds references to the Quran among the political statements and manuals on how to build bombs but despite these isolated sentences, the documents contain only little theological content. Perhaps this is not surprising. Many of the followers of the IMU indeed have but little formal theological training and would themselves be hard pressed to explain their position from a theological point of view. They simply know that they are right because this is what they have been told by their religious leaders. Yet, these are personal religious beliefs held strongly enough to fight and die for, so the simplicity of these beliefs does not warrant a conclusion that they are unimportant.

The history of the IMU in Afghanistan, the death of Namangani in battle against the American-led invasion in late 2001, and the flight of the IMU survivors into Pakistan have been dealt with elsewhere and will not be repeated here.[12]

The Surviving IMU Networks in Central Asia

To the surprise of many, it soon turned out that the IMU had survived in Central Asia as well as in Pakistan. Details are sketchy, but a few facts can be ascertained. In Uzbekistan, militants believed to have been members of the IMU by mid-2003 still remained in the south, in the Surkhondaryo (Surkhandarya) province, where the IMU had been known to have sleeper cells as late as in 2001.[13]

The IMU had also survived in Kyrgyzstan. Several alleged IMU bombings took place in Kyrgyzstan during 2002 and 2003. In the United States, the State Department issued several warnings, possibly based on American intelligence information, that the IMU might attack American citizens in Uzbekistan and Kyrgyzstan.[14]

Other alleged IMU incidents took place in Tajikistan. In January and June 2005, explosions occurred near the Ministry of Emergency Situations in Dushanbe, and Tajikistan accused the IMU of involvement. On January 25, 2006, a small group of militants managed to free a prison inmate, who was accused of links with the IMU, from Ghayroghum district of Soghd province in northern Tajikistan, killing the prison director in the process. The group then disappeared by car toward the nearby border with Kyrgyzstan, where they presumably went into hiding. However, there remains some doubt whether the militants in fact belonged to the IMU. Suspicions have also been directed toward another organization, Bayat (oath of allegiance), which had been accused of the murder of a Baptist missionary on January 12, 2004, and of several subsequent arson attacks on the homes and shops of sellers of alcohol as well as local mosques in Chorkuh, Isfara district. A number of Bayat members were reported once to have been members of the Islamic Renaissance Party of Tajikistan.[15]

There may also have been a connection between the IMU and the Andijan affair on May 13, 2005.[16] Although there is no evidence that the IMU was directly involved in the events on that day, the Uzbekistani prosecutor-general's office on September 16 of the same year noted that a certain Ilhom Hojiyev in April 2005 had smuggled up to $200,000 into Uzbekistan in support of the group involved in the affair.[17] Whether this Ilhom Hojiyev was the relative of the late Namangani who previously had joined Yo'ldosh in Pakistan is unknown, but the Uzbekistani investigators may have thought so, since they also requested Kyrgyzstan to return a certain Dilshod Hojiyev, who had sought asylum there after the Andijan affair. A criminal case was opened against him in Uzbekistan, while several human rights organizations expressed their rage that the Kyrgyzstanis considered handing him and three other named Uzbekistani citizens over to Uzbekistan for criminal charges. Again, it is unknown whether this Dilshod Hojiyev was the same man who was the son-in-law and second-in-command of Yo'ldosh, and also the one in charge of IMU finances, or merely an unfortunate bystander who happened to have the same name.[18] Yet, the fact that his name was on the list of four named suspects requested by Uzbekistan certainly indicates that the Uzbekistani investigators thought he belonged to the IMU.

On May 12, 2006, militants from Tajikistan reputedly associated with the IMU attacked a Tajikistani border post and a Kyrgyzstani customs office, presumably to acquire weapons. Four militants were killed and one captured. Tajikistani law enforcement noted that their captive was a member of the IMU and was on the wanted list. In early 2008, one of the remaining wanted gunmen, alleged IMU activist Abdulhai Yuldashev, was arrested in southern Kyrgyzstan. Three other gunmen remained wanted, two of them Tajikistani citizens and one a Kyrgyzstani.[19] It is difficult to assess whether these and several other acts of violence attributed to the IMU in the Central Asian republics were planned acts of terrorism or merely the side effects of continued drug smuggling activities.

In 2006, Yo'ldosh issued statements to the Muslims of Central Asia on three occasions, speaking in Uzbek. Interestingly, he devoted considerable time toward a refutation of the ideology of the Hizb ut-Tahrir. Yet, while the statements were couched in religious terms, they contained no real religious content. Yo'ldosh seemed content to conclude that he was right and those others were wrong. He also denounced the perpetrators of the March and April 2004 suicide bombings in Tashkent and Bukhara, that is, the IJU, severely. He may have felt that he was losing support in his Central Asian core territories due to his long absence and the comparable success of other Islamic groups there. Indeed, in August 2005, dozens of people who claimed to be former IMU members rallied at the Dutch embassy in Tehran to demand refugee status.[20] Yet more Uzbek Muslims contacted other European countries for the same purpose.[21] However, Yo'ldosh also denounced the presidents of Uzbekistan, Kyrgyzstan, and Tajikistan, and vowed vengeance for the Muslims killed in Andijan in 2005,[22] a statement that may support the supposition that the IMU had provided funding there in anticipation of the affair.

The IMU in Waziristan

The IMU also suffered an uneasy existence in Waziristan. Already in June 2002, Pakistani security forces killed six alleged IMU members in South Waziristan and Kohat after they had killed a policeman and an intelligence officer.[23] Further conflicts soon followed. The fighting with Pakistani security forces around Wana in

South Waziristan became particularly severe in March 2004, and a general Pakistani offensive followed from late 2003 onward.[24]

In Afghanistan, the IMU had been protected by the Taliban. In Pakistan, the IMU henceforth fell under the protection of the Mehsuds, a powerful local tribe that dominated South Waziristan. In particular, the IMU became associated with the important Taliban-supporter Baitullah Mehsud, who led large numbers of Pakistani Taliban and soon came into conflict with the Pakistan Army. The IMU henceforth became as closely allied to the Pakistani Taliban as it had been to the Afghan Taliban. Yo'ldosh was reportedly present as a witness to the 2006 peace agreement between the Pakistan Army and the Taliban in South Waziristan. In December 2007, Baitullah Mehsud formed the Tehrik-e-Taliban Pakistan (TTP), which he then led from its formation until his death in a CIA drone attack in September 2009. The IMU supported the TTP in its various activities, for instance, by sending fighters to Swat when the Mehsud ally Maulana Fazlullah began his militant activities there. The IMU also retained its international networks. So did, for instance, several Uighurs train with the IMU in South Waziristan, before they reportedly returned to China to attack targets in Xinjiang.[25]

However, problems soon arose in the relationship between the IMU and local Pashtuns in Waziristan. The exact cause for this largely remains unknown, although it seems likely that the IMU was caught up in internecine rivalry within the local Ahmadzai Wazirs, many of whom were hostile to the Mehsuds.[26] In March 2007, Uzbek extremists and local Pashtun militants clashed in the town of Azam Varsak in South Waziristan, close to the Afghan border. At least 15 people died as a result of the fight, and the IMU was forced to leave its bases in and around Wana, at least for the time being.[27]

In January 2008, Yo'ldosh confirmed his support for Baitullah Mehsud, calling for intensified jihad against the Pakistani security forces.[28] Following Baitullah Mehsud's death in September 2009, Yo'ldosh reiterated his support for the new TTP leader, Hakimullah Mehsud.[29] However, on September 26, 2009, Yo'ldosh was himself mortally wounded in a CIA drone attack in South Waziristan.[30] He reportedly died on October 1 and was replaced as head of the IMU by Usman Jan, the group's deputy leader till that time.[31] Usman Jan was in his turn targeted by a CIA drone in January 2010, but he may have survived the attack.[32] On August 17, 2010, the IMU finally confirmed the death of Yo'ldosh, and announced that he had been replaced as amir by one Usmon Odil (Usman Adil), presumably the Usman Jan already mentioned.[33]

The IMU Networks in Europe

Despite the IMU's operations in Waziristan and apparent activities in the Central Asian republics, the organization had not neglected the war in Afghanistan, which it continued to fight, either in rivalry or in cooperation with another Uzbek group, the IJU (see later, including the section on the continued activities of the IMU and IJU in Afghanistan). The IMU also did not neglect its supporters elsewhere.

It soon became clear that the IMU had at its disposal networks of supporters and activists in Turkey and Europe as well as in Central Asia. In May 2008, French, German, and Dutch security agencies reported that they had detained ten individuals, most of them of Turkish background, on suspicion of running a network to send money to the IMU. The network had been led by Irfan Demirtaş, of Turkish and Dutch origin.[34] Although this particular network was broken up, it seems likely that the IMU still enjoys the assistance of support networks in Turkey and Western Europe.

In September 2008, for instance, the IMU posted a German-language propaganda video on the Internet in support of the Afghan Taliban. The IMU asked Muslim men and women to come to join the jihad.[35] This may have been a deliberate attempt to copy the success of the IJU in attracting German-speaking recruits. It may also have been a sign of increased cooperation between the two groups.

The Islamic Jihad Union—The Younger Generation of Uzbek Extremists Comes of Age

Following the Taliban defeat in Afghanistan and their 2001/2002 rout into Pakistan, the surviving Uzbek extremist leaders within the IMU could not agree on how best to continue the holy war. Some IMU leaders stayed with Yo'ldosh, who hid in South Waziristan and henceforth appeared to concentrate on the war in Afghanistan and local rivalries in Pakistan. Others, led by Najmiddin Jalolov and Suhail Buranov, presumably in early 2002, withdrew to North Waziristan. There, most likely in March 2002, they founded a new group, which somewhat later came to be called the Islamic Jihad Union (IJU; *Islomiy Jihod Ittihodi*, or *Itihaad al-Jihad al-Islami*, perhaps more correctly translated as the Alliance of Islamic Jihad; its original name was *Jamaat al-Jihad al-Islami*, Society of Islamic Jihad, or simply *Jamoat* in Uzbek). Unlike Yo'ldosh, Jalolov and Buranov seem to have been more interested in a global jihad of the type waged by Al-Qaida.[36]

Najmiddin Kamolitdinovich Jalolov (born in 1972 in Andijan; alias Abu Yahya Muhammad Fatih, Muhammad Foteh Bukhoriy, and Abdurakhmon; Fatih or Foteh signifies "conqueror") appears to have been a member of the IMU since at least the late 1990s and perhaps from the outset. He was known to have been trained at Al-Qaida camps, presumably in Afghanistan. Jalolov was sentenced to death by an Uzbekistani court in 2000 for his role in the 1999 Tashkent bombings but was never apprehended. Jalolov now appointed another Uzbek named Suhail Fatilloyevich Buranov (born in 1983 in Tashkent; alias Sohail Mansur, alias Abu Huzaifa) his deputy. Buranov was known to have been trained at an Al-Qaida camp in Khost province, Afghanistan. Criminal charges had been filed against him in 2000, which would seem to confirm that he too then belonged to the IMU.[37] However, considering his young age at the time, he is unlikely to have been a founding member.

The core of the IJU accordingly consisted of former IMU members who had broken away from Yo'ldosh to work more closely with Al-Qaida against its global rather than regional enemies.[38] For them, unlike the first generation of Uzbek extremists in Afghanistan and the Afghan Taliban movement, the territory of Afghanistan was only one front, and not the most important one, in the global jihad as envisaged by Al-Qaida and its supporters. Besides, the loss of bases in Afghanistan, which had followed the Taliban defeat, made them yet more interested in following a global agenda, in particular as a new base could then be found among Al-Qaida sympathizers in Pakistan. The IJU had its headquarters and ran training camps in North Waziristan (in Mir Ali), unlike those of the IMU, which were located in South Waziristan (around Wana). While the IMU turned toward the Mehsuds for protection, the IJU instead became the junior partner in an alliance with the Haqqani network (a fundamentally autonomous wing of the Afghan Taliban movement based in Miram Shah, the administrative center of North Waziristan, and named after its leader, Jalaluddin Haqqani) and Al-Qaida.[39] In time, the relationship with Al-Qaida became increasingly public. In late January 2008, Abu Laith al-Libi, the Libyan liaison officer between the Al-Qaida leadership and the IJU, was killed in a CIA drone attack in Pakistan. The IJU confirmed his death, referring to him as "our Shaikh."[40] The IJU again acknowledged its relationship with Al-Qaida in a video communiqué on June 5, 2009, showing several IJU commanders with another Libyan Al-Qaida member, Abu Yahya al-Libi.[41]

Even so, it was soon shown that the IJU, first known to outsiders simply as the Islamic Jihad Group, was even more involved in the Central Asian republics than the IMU. Indeed, the IJU, as it became known in 2005 in the American and British lists of banned terrorist organizations, first rose to fame only for a series of plots to use suicide bombers in Uzbekistan.[42] The IJU is generally believed to have been behind the suicide bombings in Tashkent and Bukhara in March and April 2004, in which both male and female suicide bombers were used, and almost certainly conducted the coordinated suicide bombing attacks in Tashkent on July 30, 2004, against the American and Israeli embassies and the office of the Uzbekistani prosecutor-general, all of which the IJU claimed responsibility for in a statement. The beginning of this statement mirrored the 1999 declaration of jihad by the IMU in that it repeated the quote from the Quran, "And fight them until there is no more *fitnah* (strife; diversity of belief) and the religion is all for Allah" (Al Anfaal 39).[43]

In the trials that followed the events and arrests of 2004, the evidence presented indicated that a radical Jamoat group led by one Farkhad Kazabkhayev had been operating in Tashkent, Bukhara, and Samarkand since 2000. The trial proceedings also indicated that others, including overall leader Jalolov based in Waziristan, may have played a role linking this Jamoat with a network that facilitated the movement of small amounts of weapons and men to training camps in Pakistan.[44] There was also an IJU cell in Kazakhstan, headed by Akhmed Biymurzayev (Ahmad Bekmirzayev) and Zhakshybek Biymurzayev. The former had died in one of the attacks in Uzbekistan. The latter had apparently received training in Afghanistan, and had played a significant role in the IMU incursions into the Batken region in 1999 and 2000, which if correct would have made him yet another early IMU member who had changed his allegiance to the IJU, presumably along with Jalolov and Buranov.[45] Several Kazakh members of the cell had been trained in Shymkent in southern Kazakhstan.[46]

On the eve of the Andijan affair on May 13, 2005, the IJU rapidly posted a communiqué on the Internet, in which it expressed its support for any uprising against the Uzbekistani government, declared war on the Karimov government, and called on all Muslims to join in the attack. The statement, which was written in vague terms and signified no particular knowledge of the events in Andijan, was signed by the amir of the IJU, Muhammad Foteh Bukhoriy, that is, Jalolov. As with previous statements, the text was couched in religious terms but contained no real religious content.[47]

The US and Israeli embassies in Tashkent took the threat from the IJU very seriously. In response to a "specific terrorist threat" the two embassies in early June 2005 withdrew nonessential staff from the country.[48]

The IJU Networks in Europe

The IJU then turned its attention toward Europe. On September 4, 2007, a plot to attack possibly Frankfurt airport and an American air base in Germany was foiled with the arrest of three men, two of them German converts to Islam (Fritz Gelowicz and Daniel Schneider) and the third a Turk (Adem Yılmaz). The group, which became known in the media as the "Sauerland cell," had trained in Pakistan and had links with the IJU. Later on, a German Turk, Atilla Selek, was arrested as well.[49]

On September 11, 2007, the IJU posted a communiqué on a Turkish website, which stated that the three men arrested in Germany had planned attacks on the Ramstein air base and the US and Uzbekistani consulates in Germany.[50] The IJU had by then come to rely on several Turkish-language websites.[51] In them, the IJU used a Turkish name, İslami Cihad İttehadi (ICI, translated by the group into English as Ittihad Islamic Jihad).

It soon became clear that the "Sauerland cell" formed part of a larger group, consisting of about 30 extremists, mostly ethnic Turks living in Germany but also several converts. Between 10 and 20 of them had participated in terrorist training in IJU camps in Pakistan. This was unprecedented, since ethnic Turks in Europe had not earlier been seen to turn to extremism. Now several had been to IJU camps in North Waziristan.[52] Previously, IJU recruits had been sent to commit terrorist acts in Central Asia or to participate in guerrilla warfare in Afghanistan; now the IJU had trained European recruits and dispatched them back to Europe to engage in terrorism there.

The IJU networks in Europe were not confined to Germany. In April 2009, Turkish security forces arrested over 30 militant extremists, most of them allegedly IJU members, including the IJU leader in Turkey, Mahmut Kaplan (alias Abu Muhammad).[53] IJU networks may have existed in other countries too, since in May 2008, as noted, French, German, and Dutch security agencies detained several people, most of them of Turkish origin, for suspicion of supporting the IMU.[54] It does not seem too far-fetched to argue that in communities where one Uzbek group would have supporters, another one would most likely find a few of its own.

The IJU Media Wings

The IJU maintained a rather professional media wing, known as Badr at-Tawhid (Full moon of monotheism). The group also published in German and Turkish with another media outfit named Elif Medya.[55] Both seem to have understood what kind of media strategy goes down well in the West. The media campaign focused on fighting crusaders, which appealed to an extremist Muslim audience, and to fight dictatorships such as those of Central Asia, which appealed to the Western media. The IJU in October 2009 even claimed not to be connected to Al-Qaida, in order to present itself in better light to a Western audience.[56]

Badr at-Tawhid by early 2010 seemed to have some relationship to yet another jihadist web site, tawba.info, allegedly produced by the Jamaat Bulgar group of Russian-speaking Islamic extremists.[57] This was not surprising, since already in 2007 Andrey Batalov, a Russian convert to Islam, had been arrested in Afghanistan, disguised in a burqa, in a truck loaded with explosives. He admitted to having received some kind of training presumably in an IJU camp in North Waziristan, although he denied that he had ever intended to take part in fighting.[58] Indeed, the IJU made considerable efforts to maintain contacts and recruits in many different countries and among many different ethnic backgrounds. In May 2007, Jalolov in an interview confirmed that the IJU had been in contact and worked on common targets with jihadists from the Caucasus.[59]

The IJU and Pakistan

Despite its apparent focus on Europe and Turkey, the IJU, true to its allegiance to Waziristani militants, remained engaged in hostilities with Pakistani security forces. In October 2006, three Pakistanis trained and supported by the IJU and its leader Jalolov went so far as to attempt improvised explosive devices (IED) attacks on government targets in the Pakistani capital of Islamabad.[60]

In October 2007, the Pakistan Army launched an offensive against Uzbek fighters in Mir Ali in North Waziristan. The IJU was also active elsewhere in Pakistan. The group claimed to have attacked Pakistani military targets in Swat in late 2007.[61]

Jalolov was killed on September 14, 2009, in North Waziristan in a CIA drone attack. He was replaced as amir by Abdullah Fatih.[62]

The IJU (and IMU?) in the Central Asian Republics

From 2009, Uzbek terrorism appeared to have returned to its place of origin. On May 25–26, 2009, several attacks took place in Uzbekistan. A police checkpoint was attacked in Khonobod on the border with Kyrgyzstan and bombings occurred in nearby Andijan. The IJU claimed responsibility for the attacks a few days later.[63] In July, the IJU again voiced its support for jihad against Uzbekistan.[64]

On June 23, 2009, Kyrgyzstan claimed to have killed five IMU terrorists in a special operation.[65] On August 29, 2009, a series of shootings took place in Tashkent, in which one alleged IMU member was killed.[66] In early June 2010, Tajikistan too claimed to have killed two IMU members in a special operation.[67]

It is hard to assess the level of involvement, if any, of the IJU or IMU in these events. Both organizations have expressed their participation in and support for jihad against the governments of Uzbekistan, Kyrgyzstan, and Tajikistan. Both organizations certainly appear to have networks in place in these countries. Since the IJU split from the IMU, there exists the possibility that individuals cooperate with each other, even if they have given their allegiance to separate groups. There is also the possibility that security organs may mistake members of one organization for that of the other. On the other hand, there is some doubt whether all these incidents were properly attributed by the law enforcement organs of the countries involved. The temptation to label regular violent crime as terrorism may be strong. It may even be that individual IMU and IJU members have turned to regular crime to fund their activities, or even to support themselves. As described elsewhere,[68] the IMU once played a substantial role in narcotics trafficking out of Central Asia. The two groups may still be involved in such activities.[69]

The IJU's Recruitment in Turkey and Europe and the Concept of Jihad Tourism

Arguably, the main impact of the IJU has been as a promoter of international jihad and facilitator for extremist recruits from Turkey and Europe who wish to fight in Afghanistan.

The memoirs of the German convert and IJU recruit Eric Breininger (who died in action on April 28, 2010[70]) give a vivid description of how new recruits from Turkey and Europe from the mid-2000s onward reached the IJU training camps in Waziristan. Recruits to Waziristan first traveled by air to Iran (for which they needed a visa, something that caused difficulties for Breininger and his friend, the German Lebanese Hussayn al-Mallah, although they eventually got seven-day transit visas upon landing in Tehran). Then they would board a domestic flight or bus from Tehran to Bam, from where they continued to Zahedan. There the recruits typically changed their names or adopted *noms de guerre*, apparently due to the fact that from there on the clandestine part of their journey began. Having arrived in Zahedan, they would take a taxi to a certain mosque (possibly the large Makki Mosque, reportedly an important center for IJU logistics[71]), where a contact would be waiting. This contact brought them to a safe house inhabited by facilitators (*ansar*), where they would wait a few days until a small group of recruits had shown up. The group would travel together along the apparently usual route, by bus across the Iranian-Pakistani border. Foreign-looking recruits such as Germans would instead travel in a private car to the Iranian-Pakistani border, disguised in burqas while crossing, since women were usually not searched. From the border, they would then take one of the waiting Pakistani taxis to a certain hotel, while a native facilitator bought bus tickets and then put them on a bus, presumably to Quetta. Foreign-looking recruits would remain in burqas during the ride. Upon arrival, other facilitators would meet them and take them to a safe house, where they finally could get out of their burqas. From there on, the final leg of the journey was by car along a mountain road to a house belonging to yet other facilitators, this time of the IJU. Judging from Breininger's memoirs, it is quite possible that all other facilitators met during the journey were freelancers rather than IJU members, presumably as part of regular smuggling networks that moved recruits for money (although the IJU may well have been the ultimate broker and financier of the journey). At the IJU safe house, the new recruits would await other recruits, from countries as far apart as Turkey and Tajikistan, after which they went as a group to the training camp.[72]

To hide foreign jihadists in burqas was by then standard operating procedure for both the IJU and IMU. In addition to the already mentioned Breininger and the Russian Batalov, who both hid in burqas, the IMU in a 2008 interview pointed out that a dark-skinned Sudanese too had been successfully smuggled into Pakistan by the same means.[73] The same method was again used in June 2010, when another suspected IJU recruit from Germany was detained in Bannu district, northwestern Pakistan, traveling from Mir Ali to Peshawar with a fake Pakistani passport and a burqa to hide his foreign appearance.[74]

In fact, so many German and German-speaking recruits reached the IJU that Breininger and friends founded the "Deutsche Taliban Mujahideen" (German Taliban Mujahidin), comprising six men, with a certain Abu Ishaaq al-Muhajir elected as amir.[75] This was not all, however. Breininger wanted unmarried Muslim girls to travel to their camp, so they all could get married. The girls would also learn to use weapons, "just like the mujahidin." Then the newlyweds, he argued, would raise a new generation of mujahidin who would know Arabic, Turkish, English, Pashto, Urdu, and the mother tongue of the parents, in his case German. The children would learn Islam and temper their bodies through sports and martial arts, and early on learn the use of weapons and military tactics. This would, he planned, produce a new "generation of terrorists" whose names did not exist in any security service database.[76]

Indeed, from the mid- to late 2000s a growing number of Islamic extremists from Germany, including converts but many of Turkish or North African descent, traveled to Waziristan. Swedish extremists too joined them, as did several of apparently Kurdish extraction, although their choice of names alone does not reveal whether they were Kurds from Europe, Turkey, Iraq, or Iran. Some commentators even referred to the establishment of a jihadist village of European fighters.[77] The white-faced European recruits had a reputation as dedicated fighters, since for them, unless they had less obviously foreign faces, it took some perseverance to reach Waziristan. Indeed, in July 2008 complaints were voiced in an IJU communiqué that too many new recruits, in particular among Turks, were useless as jihadist fighters, since "they grew up in a democratic society" and therefore were prone to discuss commands rather than accepting and obeying them without questions. Furthermore, many had come to the IJU only to prove to their friends back home that they were more religious than them, or had come to escape social or other secular problems. Many were indeed no more than jihad tourists, who had come to Afghanistan only so that they could tell stirring tales of their exploits when they returned home to friends and family.[78]

The issue of how individuals in Europe and Turkey are being radicalized and recruited, in many cases by voluntarily searching out groups such as the IJU, would warrant an essay of its own. Still, in particular the phenomenon of "jihad tourists" from Europe and Turkey is a fascinating one. While these individuals typically express very strong personal religious beliefs, they often lack the theological skills needed to define which tradition of Islam they support. In this, interestingly, they are quite similar to most Central Asian recruits to the IMU and IJU. They are certainly not religious scholars, and usually have had no real contact with such theologians.[79]

The IMU and IJU in Afghanistan

The fact that both the IMU and IJU continued to maintain networks for recruitment and presumably smuggling in the Central Asian republics and in Europe did not mean that they neglected the war in Afghanistan. Both groups continued to support jihadist activities against Afghan security forces and foreign troops there.

On January 3, 2008, the IJU claimed to have attacked British troops in Paktika province, Afghanistan. On March 3, the IJU announced on a Turkish website that a second-generation Turk living in Germany had carried out a suicide attack on American and Afghan troops in the same province. In April, this was followed by a video call for jihad by Eric Breininger, the German convert then in an IJU camp in Waziristan.[80] Then the IJU claimed responsibility for two other suicide attacks (on May 31 and June 4) in Jalalabad city and Khost province, respectively, the first on an American convoy and the second on a military post.[81] In the same year, the IJU also claimed responsibility for several additional attacks in Paktika and Paktia provinces.[82] There was then no longer any question of whether the IJU had begun to participate in the war in Afghanistan, at least in the named provinces, which formed part of the region traditionally dominated by the group's protector in Waziristan, the Haqqani network.[83] However, from 2009, if not before, the IJU was also active in Kunduz province, further to the north. On May 12, 2009, two IJU operatives were arrested there.[84]

This was a new development, since the IJU had not previously been known to fight in northern Afghanistan. However, later in the year, it seems that the IMU too had moved combat teams there. By October and November 2009, several reports mentioned that IMU fighters (usually only referred to as "Uzbeks and Chechens") had been killed in Kunduz, fighting German and Afghan troops.[85] Whether or not the attribution by the security forces of these "Uzbeks and Chechens" to the IMU was correct remains unknown and should not be taken for granted, even though the IMU had a long history of fighting in Afghanistan.[86] Be that as it may, in December 2009 further details from the north followed. The Afghan National Security Directorate's press service stated that four IMU fighters led by Hafiz Nurillah, a resident of Faryab province, had been arrested.[87] If correct, this would indicate that the IMU by then had acquired local roots in northern Afghanistan. In January 2010, reports suggested that armed groups comprising Chechens, Uzbeks, and Tajiks had moved into positions in Ghowr-Teppa, Kunduz province. Whether they belonged to the IMU or IJU was unknown; yet, the participation of Tajiks, and their identification as such by Afghan security forces, again suggested that networks that included local militants as well and not only foreign fighters may have been formed.[88] By February 2010, IMU fighers were reported in Jowzjan province too.[89] By April 2010, IMU fighters were noted in Baghlan province as well as in Kunduz province.[90] In Baghlan province, the government forces had in May 2010 not yet gained control over the Ahmadzai area of Dahan-e Ghowri District, where Pakistani, Chechen, Uzbek, and other foreign fighters were reported as being part of the resistance.[91] By June 2010, IMU fighters were reported even in the hitherto fairly calm Balkh province.[92]

Concluding Remarks

This brief history of the IMU and IJU shows that the two groups changed considerably in character on several occasions during the two decades in which their members have engaged in violence. Yet, many of their goals, tactics, and means of finance remained the same. The IMU and IJU accordingly remain a source of violence and instability in their many and varied areas of operations. Although the eyes of the world are focused on Afghanistan and Pakistan, it will not be enough to ensure stability there (in itself a difficult task). Tajikistan, Kyrgyzstan, and to some extent Uzbekistan remain fragile states with militant networks closely connected to those south of their borders.

Uzbek extremists have played major roles in civil conflicts, such as in Tajikistan, Afghanistan, and Pakistan, and in transnational narcotics smuggling. In civil conflicts, they have indeed played the role of a foreign legion.

Uzbek extremists have also encouraged further radicalization as far away as in Turkey, Russia, and Europe. The existence of IJU and IMU bases in Waziristan has encouraged jihad tourism from Europe and Turkey to Pakistan and Afghanistan.

The IMU and IJU have been rivals for funds and recruits; however, now all original leaders are dead. It is likely that the causes of rivalry between the IMU and IJU will have died with them. The survivors will probably cooperate or even merge, since their networks already seem to overlap in many places and some of their members very possibly already collaborate on an individual basis. Any increased level of cooperation will probably be seen first in Afghanistan.

The IMU and IJU have been a catalyst for terror and instability. Their propensity for violence should not be ignored, nor their effect in pushing state structures into excessive repression in the name of combating terrorism. Indeed, the activities of Uzbek extremists have been central to the retention, and even strengthening, of authoritarianism within the Central Asian state structures, thereby directly preventing these states from acquiring any increased level of democracy and popular legitimacy. This was attained by the extremists through the role of catalyst rather than through direct participation in government. As in many other countries, including outside the region, the state confronted with terrorism responded with the tools at its disposal, including increased powers to the security services and harsher legislation. Although neither the IMU nor IJU ever stood a chance of assuming power in Central Asia, their negative impact on state development there, and elsewhere, has been considerable.

Yet, there is but little religious content in the statements issued by these groups. They employ Islamic vocabulary but display little or no theological reflection. Despite this lack of religious reflection, these groups have not encountered any difficulties in attracting new recruits to their cause. Mere faith in the righteousness of their cause and statements sprinkled with Islamic vocabulary but with little religious content have proven sufficient to inspire willing recruits from several, widely different cultural backgrounds. Group dynamics have enabled potential recruits first to radicalize, then to prepare themselves psychologically for battle and death for each other and the cause. The armed struggle has seemingly become a goal in itself and may no longer be regarded as a means to build an Islamic society. Religious reflection and motivation has been exchanged for faith in the righteousness of one's comrades, the group, and its cause. Participation in armed jihad has become not one among several religious activities, but the one religious act that is believed to lead to salvation.

Notes

1. The movement's website, www.furqon.com; International Crisis Group (ICG), *Central Asia: Islamist Mobilisation and Regional Security* (Osh/Brussels: ICG Asia Report 14, March 1, 2001), p. 4. The present report is an updated and expanded version of the chapters on the IMU and IJU in Michael Fredholm, *Islamic Extremism as a Political Force in Central Asia: A Comparative Study of Central Asian Extremist Movements* (Stockholm: Stockholm University, Asian Cultures and Modernity 12, October 2006).
2. Alexander Ignatenko, "Islamic Radicalism: A Cold War By-Product," *Central Asia and the Caucasus* 1 (2001), 101–112. See also Fredholm, *Islamic Extremism as a Political Force.*
3. Michael Fredholm, *Islam and Modernity in Contemporary Central Asia: Religious Faith versus Way of Life—A Story of Four Radical Disruptions* (Stockholm: Stockholm University, Asian Cultures and Modernity 14, January 2007).

4. Yo'ldosh was born on October 2, 1967. Official records, Uzbekistan; Interpol website, www.interpol.int.
5. Ahmed Rashid, *Jihad: The Rise of Militant Islam in Central Asia* (New Haven: Yale University Press, 2002), p. 146. She publicly disowned her son in 1999.
6. Ibid., pp. 138–139; Ahmed Rashid, "Heart of Darkness," *Far Eastern Economic Review*, August 5, 1999, pp. 8–12; "The Taliban: Exporting Extremism," *Foreign Affairs*, November/December 1999, pp. 22–35; "From Deobandism to Batken: Adventures of an Islamic Heritage," CACI Forum Transcription, April 13, 2000.
7. Orozbek Moldaliev, "An Incongruous War in the Valley of Poison: The Religious Conflict in Southern Kyrgyzstan," *Central Asia and the Caucasus* 1 (2000), 11–20; Rashid, "From Deobandism to Batken"; *Washington Post*, November 10, 2001; Rashid, *Jihad*, pp. 137–138. Some report his year of birth as 1968. Other reports indicate that Hojiyev was born in 1967 (Vitaly V. Naumkin, *Militant Islam in Central Asia: The Case of the Islamic Movement of Uzbekistan* [Berkeley: University of California, Berkeley Program in Soviet and Post-Soviet Studies, Working Paper, 2003], p. 22) or 1969 (Vitaly V. Naumkin, *Radical Islam in Central Asia: Between Pen and Rifle* [Lanham, MD: Rowman & Littlefield, 2005], p. 68). He reportedly returned from Afghanistan in 1988, which would seem to suggest the earlier year as his year of birth. Hojiyev was later publicly disowned by his sister Makhbuba Ahmedova and his brother Nasyr Hojiyev (both arrested in 2000). Soon after, so did his mother. Rashid, *Jihad*, p. 147.
8. On the origin of the movement, see Mehrdad Haghayeghi, *Islam and Politics in Central Asia* (New York: St. Martin's Press, 1995), pp. 93–94; William Fierman, "Political Development in Uzbekistan: Democratization?" in Karen Dawisha and Bruce Parrott (eds.), *Conflict, Cleavage, and Change in Central Asia and the Caucasus* (Cambridge: Cambridge University Press, 1997), pp. 360–408, on p. 382; Bakhtiar Babadzhanov [Babajanov], "Islam in Uzbekistan: From the Struggle for 'Religious Purity' to Political Activism," in Boris Rumer (ed.), *Central Asia: A Gathering Storm?* (London: M. E. Sharpe, 2002), pp. 299–330, on pp. 315–316, 328 n.55; Rashid, *Jihad*, pp. 137–140; Naumkin, *Radical Islam*, pp. 66–67; Bahtijar Babadžanov [Babajanov], "Le jihad comme idéologie de l''Autre' et de 'l'Exilé' à travers l'étude de documents du Mouvement islamique d'Ouzbekistan," *Cahiers d'Asie centrale* 15/16 (2007), 141–166. The words of Yo'ldosh are translated from Babadžanov, p. 150.
9. Fredholm, *Islamic Extremism as a Political Force*, pp. 11–13.
10. Rashid, *Jihad*, p. 140.
11. Fredholm, *Islamic Extremism as a Political Force*, pp. 21–23, which also reprints the declaration of jihad in the original Arabic and in translation.
12. Fredholm, *Islamic Extremism as a Political Force*.
13. Esmer Islamov, "Sightings of IMU Militants Reported in Remote Area of Uzbekistan," *Eurasia Insight*, July 9, 2003 (www.eurasianet.org).
14. Richard Weitz, "Storm Clouds over Central Asia: Revival of the Islamic Movement of Uzbekistan (IMU)?" *Studies in Conflict & Terrorism* 27: 6 (2004), 505–530, on 512–513.
15. Zafar Abdullaev, "Tajikistan: Concern at New Islamic Group," *IWPR's Reporting Central Asia* 280, April 27, 2004; Zoya Pylenko, "Suspected IMU Member Escapes from Tajik Prison," *Central Asia-Caucasus Analyst*, February 22, 2006.
16. On the events in Andijan, see Shirin Akiner, *Violence in Andijan, 13 May 2005* (London, June 7, 2005). Her report was subsequently published as Shirin Akiner, *Violence in Andijan, 13 May 2005: An Independent Assessment* (Washington, DC, & Uppsala: Central Asia-Caucasus Institute & Silk Road Studies Program, July 2005). The media's somewhat one-sided focus on repression in the Central Asian states, in particular in Uzbekistan, has influenced the international community in several ways. First, any information received from Central Asian law enforcement organs will routinely be treated as unsubstantiated, regardless of content. While it has to be said that such information at times is biased and

incorrect, it would appear unwise to disregard all information derived from these sources simply because they have received a bad press. Second, the way the situation in Uzbekistan in particular has been framed in the Western media means that Western governments can refuse asylum to Uzbekistani citizens only with great difficulty, or not at all, even if they are known or suspected terrorists, since there are difficulties in separating bona fide refugees escaping from persecution by authoritarian government from terrorists and extremists fleeing from bona fide Central Asian counterterrorism efforts.

17. Interfax, September 20, 2005.
18. RFE/RL *Newsline*, June 13, 2005; IWPR's *Reporting Central Asia* 387, June 15, 2005.
19. *Kommersant*, May 13, 2006; IWPR's *Reporting Central Asia* 448, June 19, 2006; Sanobar Shermatova, "IMU May Return into Politics Only If and When the Existing Geopolitical Parity in Central Asia Is Ruined," Ferghana.ru, February 8, 2008. The captive was identified as 30-year-old Abdurahim Khojayev from the Syrdarya region of Uzbekistan. His name is a common one, but it is possible that the Kyrgyzstanis, perhaps wrongly, connected him with the already mentioned IMU leader Ilhom Hojiyev, alias Commander Abdurahmon, the relative of the late Namangani.
20. Ikbaldjon Mirsayitov, "The Islamic Movement of Uzbekistan: Development Stages and Its Present State," *Central Asia and the Caucasus* 6 (42) (2006), 110–114. The video statements were issued on January 10, in August, and on September 11, 2006. The IMU maintains a website in Uzbek (www.furqon.com).
21. In Sweden, e.g., no less than 530 people born in Uzbekistan received asylum in 2005. In comparison, in the period 1994–2001 this number varied between 16 and 32 per year, rising to between 57 and 120 annually in the period 2002–2004. SCB national statistics.
22. Ferghana.ru, September 13, 2006.
23. Weitz, "Storm Clouds," 510.
24. Mike Redman, "Central Asian Militant Group Remains Active in Pakistan," *Eurasia Insight*, March 24, 2004 (www.eurasianet.org); Daan van der Schriek, "War in Waziristan," *Central Asia-Caucasus Analyst*, November 3, 2004.
25. See, e.g., *Daily Times* (Pakistan), October 3, 2009.
26. See, e.g., Guido Steinberg, *A Turkish al-Qaeda: The Islamic Jihad Union and the Internationalization of Uzbek Jihadism* (Center for Contemporary Conflict, n.d. (July 2008)).
27. See, e.g., RIA Novosti, March 8, 2007.
28. See, e.g., Steinberg, *A Turkish al-Qaeda*.
29. Yo'ldosh was, for instance, shown with Hakimullah Mehsud in a video released by the IMU's media wing, Studio Jundullah. NEFA Foundation website, www.nefafoundation.org.
30. See, e.g., *Daily Times* (Pakistan), October 3, 2009; Jim Nichols, *Central Asia's Security: Issues and Implications for U.S. Interests* (Congressional Research Service Report RL30294, March 11, 2010), p. 9.
31. *Hindustan Times*, October 3, 2009. There have been conflicting reports on both the date of the drone attack and on whether Yo'ldosh survived or not. However, the appointment of a new head would seem to confirm his death before this date.
32. *USA Today*, January 17, 2010; *Dawn*, January 18, 2010.
33. IMU website, http://furqon.com.
34. Europe1 (www.europe1.fr), July 19, 2008; AFP, July 20, 2008.
35. NEFA Foundation website, www.nefafoundation.org; NEFA release date January 29, 2009, original date September 2008.
36. Europol, *TE-SAT 2008: EU Terrorism Situation and Trend Report* (The Hague: European Police Office, 2008), p. 18. The IJU eventually confirmed that the group had been established in 2002. Michail Logvinov, "Islamische Dschihad-Union," *Die Kriminalpolizei*, March 2010; citing an IJU communiqué dated May 31, 2007 (www.sehadetzamani.com).

37. Jalolov was born on April 1, 1972, Buranov on October 11, 1983. Details on the various names, aliases, and addresses of the IJU leaders, and criminal charges against them, were published in, among others, United Nations Security Council Al-Qaida and Taliban Sanctions Committee, SC/9396, April 23, 2008; United States Department of the Treasury, press release hp-1035, June 18, 2008; Office of Foreign Assets Control, Specially Designated Nationals and Blocked Persons: Financial Institution Letter FIL-60–2008 (Washington, DC: Federal Deposit Insurance Corporation [FDIC], June 26, 2008).
38. In June 2008, an IJU video claimed that one Uzbek IJU member had taken part already in IMU's 1999 attack in Kyrgyzstan, and later had fought in Afghanistan against the Northern Alliance and then against Coalition forces. Nichols, *Central Asia's Security*, p. 9.
39. See, e.g., Steinberg, *A Turkish al-Qaeda*.
40. He was probably killed on January 29, 2008, in North Waziristan, according to the Pakistani military. See, e.g., CNN, January 31, 2008; Steinberg, *A Turkish al-Qaeda*.
41. *Der Spiegel* (www.spiegel.de), June 5, 2009.
42. See, e.g., the presentation to the British Parliament by Home Office Minister Hazel Blears, October 13, 2005.
43. Press statement by Richard Boucher, spokesman for the Department of State, Washington, DC, May 26, 2005, upon the inclusion of the group in the list of specially designated global terrorist organizations under Executive Order 13224. For a brief summary of the suicide bombings in March and April 2004, see RFE/RL *Central Asia Report* 4:14, April 7, 2004; 4:15, April 14, 2004; 4:33, September 1, 2004; Artie McConnell, "Tashkent Bombings Signal Rise in Islamist Activities," *Jane's Intelligence Review*, May 2004, 14–17. The group claimed responsibility for the March and April 2004 attacks in a communiqué conveyed by an opponent of the Karimov government in exile, Hazratqul Khudoyberdi, through the website www.centrasia.ru, April 3, 2004. The group claimed responsibility for the July 30, 2004, attacks in a second communiqué, signed by Deputy Amir Sayfurrahmon and again conveyed by Hazratqul Khudoyberdi through the website www.centrasia.ru, July 31, 2004.
44. AP, July 27, 2004; Cerwyn Moore, "Uzbek Terror Networks: Germany, Jamoat and the IJU," *Terrorism Monitor* 5:21 (November 2007). Yet another member was mentioned as being called Abu Muhammad.
45. Naumkin, *Radical Islam*, p. 117; IWPR's *Reporting Central Asia* 380, May 20, 2005; Marat Yermukanov, "Kazakh Security Services Trumpet Victory over 'Al-Qaida Members.'" *Central Asia-Caucasus Analyst*, November 3, 2004.
46. See, e.g., Steinberg, *A Turkish al-Qaeda*.
47. The communiqué was as before conveyed by Hazratqul Khudoyberdi through the website www.centrasia.ru, May 13, 2005.
48. Reuters, June 6, 2005. On June 2, 2005, the US Department of State issued a travel warning due to the sudden terrorist threat.
49. See, e.g., *Economist*, September 8, 2007; *Der Spiegel*, September 12, 2007, October 9, 2007 (www.spiegel.de). The group was reportedly first identified by the NSA. The operation was later handled by a joint CIA and German task force set up in Berlin. See also Moore, "Uzbek Terror Networks"; Logvinov, "Islamische Dschihad-Union."
50. *Der Spiegel*, September 12, 2007 (www.spiegel.de); IJU communiqué, September 11, 2007 (www.sehadetvakti.com).
51. The September 11, 2007, communiqué was posted on www.sehadetvakti.com ("Time for Martyrdom"), now defunct. The IJU has also posted information on www.sehadetzamani.com (in Turkish) and the more general jihadist websites www.sodiqlar.com (in Uzbek) and www.cihaderi.net (in Turkish). The first communiqué posted on Turkish websites seems to be dated April 2007. Logvinov, "Islamische Dschihad-Union."
52. See, e.g., Steinberg, *A Turkish al-Qaeda*.

53. *Turkish Weekly*, April 21, 2009 (www.turkishweekly.net).
54. Europel (www.europel.fr), July 19, 2008; AFP, July 20, 2008.
55. See, e.g., the movement's various websites.
56. Thomas M. Sanderson, Daniel Kimmage, and David A. Gordon, *From the Ferghana Valley to South Waziristan: The Evolving Threat of Central Asian Jihadists* (Washington, DC: Center for Strategic and International Studies, March 2010), p. 12, citing www.sehadet-zamani.com, October 22, 2009.
57. The group's website, http://tawba.info/ru.
58. *New York Times*, October 30, 2007. Batalov's case can be found among the secret US military reports covering the war in Afghanistan that in July 2010 were exposed by the Wikileaks website (http://wikileaks.org/wiki/Afghan_War_Diary,_2004–2010). See Report Key 759114F2-5F50-4303-B45F-790FEE8B7526, document AFG20070826n804. According to this initial report, Batalov was unknowingly going to be used as a suicide bomber.
59. NEFA Foundation website, www.nefafoundation.org; NEFA release date, September 23, 2009, original date May 31, 2007.
60. *Dawn*, November 4, 2006.
61. IJU communiqué, December 19, 2007 (www.sehadetvakti.com). See, e.g., Steinberg, *A Turkish al-Qaeda*; Ronald Sandee, *The Islamic Jihad Union (IJU)* (NEFA Foundation, October 14, 2008), p. 15.
62. GEO TV Pakistan (www.geo.tv), September 17, 2009; Bill Roggio, "Two al Qaeda Leaders Reported Killed in North Waziristan Strike," *Long War Journal* (www.longwarjournal.org), September 16, 2009; Badr at-Tawheed communiqué, September 27, 2009 (www.sehadetzamani.com).
63. RIA Novosti, May 26, 2009; Deirdre Tynan, "Uzbekistan: Kyrgyz Officials Deny Islamic Militant Raids Originated in Kyrgyzstan," *Eurasia Insight*, May 27, 2009 (www.eurasianet.org); *Der Spiegel* (www.spiegel.de), June 5, 2009. See also Nichols, *Central Asia's Security*, p. 6.
64. In a communiqué dated July 3, 2009. Logvinov, "Islamische Dschihad-Union."
65. Roman Muzalevsky, "Kyrgyz Operation Against IMU Reveals Growing Terrorist Threat," *Central Asia-Caucasus Analyst*, July 1, 2009.
66. Deirdre Tynan, "Uzbekistan: Authorities Link Tashkent Shootout in August to Islamic Movement of Uzbekistan," *Eurasia Insight*, September 9, 2009 (www.eurasianet.org).
67. Interfax, June 4, 2010. The same news report indicated that some 15 suspected members of the IMU were convicted in Tajikistan each year.
68. Fredholm, *Islamic Extremism as a Political Force*.
69. For a list of terrorist attacks in Tajikistan, Kyrgyzstan, and Uzbekistan in the period 2004–2009, not all of which can be attributed to the IMU or IJU, see Sanderson, Kimmage, and Gordon, *From the Ferghana Valley to South Waziristan*, 27–29.
70. Abdul Ghaffar El Almani [Eric Breininger], *Mein Weg nach Jannah* (ElifMedya, posted online on May 5, 2010), p. 106.
71. Sandee, *Islamic Jihad Union*, p. 11. Sandee does not provide a source for this statement, and Breininger never identifies the mosque in his memoirs.
72. Abdul Ghaffar El Almani [Eric Breininger], *Mein Weg*, pp. 82–85.
73. NEFA Foundation website, www.nefafoundation.org; NEFA release date January 29, 2009, original date September 2008.
74. BBC News, June 22, 2010.
75. Abdul Ghaffar El Almani [Eric Breininger], *Mein Weg*, p. 102.
76. Ibid., pp. 103–104. The implication of this, and his choice of languages, is that he also foresaw attacks in Germany itself.
77. *Daily Telegraph* (www.telegraph.co.uk), September 25, 2009.

78. Logvinov, "Islamische Dschihad-Union"; citing an IJU communiqué dated July 23, 2008 (www.sehadetzamani.com).
79. See, e.g., Marc Sageman, *Leaderless Jihad: Terror Networks in the Twenty-First Century* (Philadelphia: University of Pennsylvania Press, 2008).
80. IJU communiqué, March 3, 2008. The suicide bomber, Cüneyt Çiftçi, had lived in Germany until April 2007. *Der Spiegel* (www.spiegel.de), March 15, 2009; Logvinov, "Islamische Dschihad-Union." See also, e.g., Steinberg, *A Turkish al-Qaeda*; Sandee, *Islamic Jihad Union*, p. 15.
81. IJU communiqués, June 1, 2008, June 5, 2008 (http://sodiqlar.narod.ru). Judging from the chosen names of the suicide bombers, Said Kurdi and Abu Muslim Kurdi, they were presumably of Kurdish origin. The Jalalabad attack killed a US Marine. NPR (www.npr.org), May 31, 2008.
82. Sandee, *Islamic Jihad Union*, pp. 16–17; based on IJU communiqués.
83. Thomas Ruttig, "Loya Paktia's Insurgency: The Haqqani Network as an Autonomous Entity," in Antonio Giustozzi, *Decoding the New Taliban: Insights from the Afghan Field* (London: Hurst & Company, 2009), pp. 57–88.
84. Kunduz Executive Summary, September 15, 2009 (Program for Culture & Conflict Studies).
85. See, e.g., Afghan Islamic Press news agency (Peshawar), October 11, 2009; Reuters, October 20, 2009; Pajhwok Afghan News (Kabul), November 5, 2009.
86. Doubts on whether the Afghan security forces in fact could correctly identify what they customarily referred to as "Uzbeks and Chechens" were also expressed by foreign intelligence officers in Afghanistan, for instance, among the secret US military reports exposed by the Wikileaks website. See Report Key EDD3627E-B5D4-417E-B0B6-CBEDA3B8F08F, document AFG20071009n1041. According to this report, "PRT CO spoke with ANP 6 today regarding his comments in an open source report on the 5 OCT air strike in Sarobi. In the source, ANP 6 stated that 16 Uzbek fighters were killed and one was captured; however, this conflicted with TF Eagles own assessment of the fighters and the BDA. ANP 6 received his intelligence from the Sarobi Chief of Police, and it seems likely that the COP and the locals assumed the fighters were Uzbeks only because they did not speak Pashto. TF Eagle identified the fighters as Turkish based off of SIGINT and the 1 captured EWIA."
87. Arzu TV (Mazar-e Sharif), December 3, 2009.
88. Avesta (Dushanbe), January 22, 2010, citing the governor of Kunduz province. The Tajiks may of course have come from Tajikistan.
89. Shamshad TV (Kabul), February 10, 2010, citing the governor of Jowzjan province.
90. Arzu TV (Mazar-e Sharif), April 15, 2010, citing General Gholam Sakhi, deputy commander of Shahin Military Corps No. 209 in northern Afghanistan.
91. Afghan Islamic Press news agency (Peshawar), May 17, 2010, citing Morad Ali Morad, commander of Shahin Military Corps No. 209.
92. Arzu TV (Mazar-e Sharif), June 22, 2010, citing General Abdol Rauf Taj, commander of the Balkh provincial police.

Contributors

Matthew Baker is a PhD student in systematic theology at Fordham University, whose current research focuses on modern Orthodox theology and philosophical hermeneutics. His articles have been published in several scholarly journals, including *International Journal of Systematic Theology, Participatio, Theologia*, and *Crkvene Studije*. He serves on the advisory board of the Fr. Georges Florovsky Orthodox Christian Theological Society of Princeton University, as well as the Society for Orthodox Christian History in America, and is editorial assistant for *Participatio: The Journal of the TF Torrance Theological Fellowship.*

Thomas Bremer is professor of ecumenical theology and Eastern Christian studies at the University of Münster, Germany. He is a board member of the German Association for East European Studies, of the Executive Committee of the International Council for Central and East European Studies, and coeditor of the present volume. He is author and editor of several books, among them *Kreuz und Kreml*, a short history of the Russian Orthodox Church, published in English as *Cross and Kremlin* in 2013. His research focuses on ecumenical relations between Eastern and Western Churches, on Orthodoxy in Russia, Ukraine, and in the Balkans, and on churches and politics in Eastern Europe.

Anna Briskina-Müller completed studies in Orthodox theology in St. Petersburg (1990–1996), and studied Protestant theology and church history at Heidelberg University, obtaining her doctorate in 2005. The dissertation examined the dispute over the doctrine of justification between Philip Melanchthon and Andreas Osiander from an Orthodox perspective. Her publications include *LOGOS im DIALOGOS. Auf der Suche nach der Orthodoxie. Gedenkschrift für Hermann Goltz (1946–2010)*, A. Briskina-Müller, A. Drost-Abgarjan, A. Meißner, eds. (Berlin: LIT, 2011). Since 2004, she has taught courses on the Orthodox Church in the Faculty for Protestant Theology of Halle-Wittenberg University, Germany.

Alfons Brüning is a lecturer at the Institute for Eastern Christian Studies, St. Radboud University Nijmegen, the Netherlands, and professor of Orthodoxy and Peacebuilding in Europe at the Department of Philosophy of Religion and Comparative Study of Religions, University of Amsterdam. His research interests and teaching relate to the early modern and modern history of Christianity in Eastern and Central Europe, mainly along the border zone between Eastern and Western Christianity. His research has focused on Orthodoxy and human rights in historical and theological perspective. His publications include a monograph on the religious history of early modern Poland-Lithuania (*"Unio non est unitas"—Polen-Litauens Weg im Konfessionellen Zeitalter (1569–1648)* [Wiesbaden, 2008]) and numerous scholarly articles on aspects of church history in Poland, Ukraine, and Russia from the seventeenth to the twentieth centuries. He also edited, with Evert van der Zweerde, *Orthodox Christianity and Human Rights* (Leuven, 2012).

Dorothée de Nève is visiting professor at the Institute for Political Science at FernUniversität in Hagen, Germany. Her research centers on governance, democracy and democratization, political participation, research on politics and religion. Her publications include "Das Evangelium ist (k)ein Programmersatz—Religiöse Parteien in der Schweiz," in Georg Pfleiderer and Alexander Heit, *Sphärendynamik II* (Zürich/Baden Baden, 2012); and "Grenzen der Religionsfreiheit," *Religionsrechtliche Studien* 2 (2011).

Regina Elsner studied Jewish studies and Catholic theology in Berlin and Münster, Germany. From 2005 to 2010, she worked for *Caritas Russia* in the Russian Federation. Since 2010, she is a researcher for the "Institutions and Institutional Change in Postsocialism" network at the Ecumenical Institute in Muenster, analyzing the role of Russian Orthodoxy in present-day Russia and the theological debate about modern values. Her publications on the social engagement of the churches in Russia and the current position of Russian Orthodoxy in Russia include: "Die Russische Orthodoxe Kirche—Stütze des neuen Autoritarismus?" In *Rückkehr zum Autoritarismus? Vormoderne, Moderne und Postmoderne im postsozialistischen Europa,* Beate Apelt and Irene Hahn, eds. (Bremen, 2011); "Zwischen Staatskirche und Privatangelegenheit—die Russische Orthodoxe Kirche und die moderne russische Gesellschaft," In *Staat oder privat? Akteure und Prozesse zwischen Staaten und Gesellschaften in Osteuropa* (Bremen, 2010); and "Sozialarbeit der katholischen Kirche in Russland" *G2W* 38:4 (2010).

Michael Fredholm is a historian and defense analyst who has written extensively on the history, defense strategies, security policies, and energy sector developments of Eurasia. Educated at Uppsala, Stockholm, and Lund Universities, he has taught at Stockholm University (South and Central Asia Programme), Uppsala University (Orientalist Programme), the Swedish Royal Military Academy and Defence Academy (various courses), and a special educational and advisory program on East Asia for the commander-in-chief. He is currently affiliated with the Division of South and Central Asian Studies at Stockholm University, where he has made a special study of Central Asian geopolitics, Afghanistan, and Islamic extremism.

Ciprian Ghişa is a lecturer in church history at the Faculty of Greek Catholic Theology—Babes-Bolyai University in Cluj-Napoca, Romania. His research interests include the interconfessional relations in the Romanian and Eastern European areas in the eighteenth–twentieth centuries; the evolution and elaboration of the identitary discourses of the Romanian Orthodox and Greek Catholic Churches; and the evolution of the ecclesiastical institutions in the eighteenth and nineteenth centuries. He has published a book on the Greek Catholic identity discourse in Transylvania between 1700 and 1850, and another on the Greek Catholic Church in the mid-nineteenth century.

Dagmar Heller is a specialist in church history and ecumenical theology and an ordained minister in the Protestant Church in Germany (EKD). Since 2007, she has served as study secretary for Faith and Order at the World Council of Churches (Geneva) and professor of ecumenical theology at the Ecumenical Institute in Bossey, Switzerland. In the years 2001–2007, she was executive secretary for ecumenism and for the relations between the EKD and Orthodox Churches at the EKD office for external relations in Hannover, Germany. Her recent publications include: "Der

Dialog zwischen der Orthodoxie und den Kirchen der Reformation—Probleme und Perspektiven," *Una Sancta* 66 (2011); "Menschenrechte, Menschenwürde und sittliche Verantwortung im kirchlichen Dialog zwischen Ost und West," *ÖR* 59 (2010); "A Spirituality of Time in Times of Globalization," *Studia Liturgica* 40 (2010); "Сакраментология в герменевтической перспективе," *Церковь и время* 1 (2009); and numerous books, including the forthcoming *Baptized into Christ. A Guide to the Ecumenical Discussion on Baptism*.

Daniela Kalkandjieva is a researcher at the Scientific Research Department of Sofia University "St. Kliment Ohridski," whose academic interests focus on Bulgarian religious history and the comparative study of Orthodox churches and societies. She is author of the dissertation *Ecclesio-Political Aspects of the International Activities of the Moscow Patriarchate (1917–1948)* and the monograph *The Bulgarian Orthodox Church and the State, 1944–1953* (Sofia, 1997). Her recent articles include: "A Comparative Analysis on Church-State Relations in Eastern Orthodoxy: Concepts, Models and Principles," *Journal of Church and State* 53:4 (Autumn 2011); "The Bulgarian Orthodox Church and the 'Ethics of Capitalism,'" *Social Compass* 57:1 (2010); and "Pre-Modern Orthodoxy: Church Features and Transformations" *Études Balkaniques* 4 (2010). She has also worked on numerous national and international research projects, including *Religious Pluralism and Interfaith Dialogue in Bulgaria*, *Religion and the Public Sphere: Interdisciplinary Approaches*, and *Religions and Values: Central and Eastern European Research Network*.

Olga Kazmina is a professor in the Department of Ethnology and deputy dean for international affairs at the Faculty of History in Moscow State University. She is coauthor of two monographs (in Russian): *Religious Organizations of the Contemporary World* (Moscow, 2010) and *The Russian Orthodox Church in a New Religious Situation in Russia* (Moscow, 2009).

Natalia Kochan PhD, is a senior researcher of the Ivan F. Kuras Institute of Political and Ethnic Studies, National Academy of Sciences of Ukraine. Specializing in the areas of religion and politics, ethnicity and nationalism, she has published numerous scholarly articles in Ukraine and abroad.

Andrii Krawchuk is professor of religious studies and former president of the University of Sudbury (Canada). He is a member of the Religion in Europe Group (American Academy of Religion), of the Executive Committee of the International Council for Central and East European Studies. Author of *Christian Social Ethics in Ukraine: The Legacy of Andrei Sheptytsky* and editor of several documentary collections, his publications focus on religion, society, and ethics in Eastern Europe. His current research is on interreligious dialogue and intercultural ethics.

Julia Anna Lis obtained her PhD from the Theological Faculty in Münster, Germany. Her dissertation studies anti-Westernism in Serbia, Bulgaria, and Greece. In 2008–2011, she took part in the international project "New Borders and Old Frontiers. Orthodox Churches and European Integration," which was supported by the Volkswagen Foundation.

Vasilios N. Makrides is professor of religious studies (specializing in Orthodox Christianity) at the Faculty of Philosophy, University of Erfurt, Germany. He has many scholarly publications in comparative religious and cultural history, and the sociology of Orthodox Christianity to his credit. He is author of *Hellenic Temples and Christian Churches: A Concise History of the Religious Cultures of Greece from Antiquity to the Present* (New York/London, 2009), and coeditor, with Victor Roudometof, of *Orthodox Christianity in Twenty-First Century Greece: The Role of Religion in Culture, Ethnicity and Politics* (Farnham, 2010).

Christoph Mühl a doctoral candidate, is preparing a dissertation on *Justification and God's Justice in Ecumenical Dialogues Involving the Participation of the Russian Orthodox Church*. He is also a research assistant at the Ecumenical Institute at the Faculty of Catholic Theology at the University of Münster/Germany, and participated in the joint research project "Cultures of Justice. Normative Discourses in the Cultural Transfers between Western Europe and Russia" (2009–2012).

Tina Olteanu is a researcher and lecturer at the Fern Universität in Hagen, Germany, specializing in democratic theory, empirical and comparative research on democracy, transformation and corruption. Her publications include *Korrupte Demokratie?* (Wiesbaden, 2012).

Jennifer Wasmuth is an assistant professor at the Faculty of Theology of the Humboldt University of Berlin. She studied Protestant theology and Slavic literatures in Münster and Heidelberg and Orthodox theology in St. Petersburg. She is author of a dissertation on the nineteenth-century influence of Protestantism on Russian Orthodoxy, focusing on "Liberal Orthodox Theology," which was published as *Der Protestantismus und die russische Theologie. Zur Rezeption und Kritik des Protestantismus in den Zeitschriften der Geistlichen Akademien an der Wende vom 19. zum 20. Jahrhundert* (Göttingen, 2007), and numerous articles, including: "Georges V. Florovsky," in the forthcoming *Encyclopedia of the Bible and its Reception*; "Die Russische Orthodoxe Kirche und die Menschenrechte," *G2W* 38:5 (2010); "Politisches und soziales Engagement der orthodoxen Kirche in Russland" *Ost-West* 11:1 (2010); (with Thomas Bremer) "Gott und die Welt. Kirche und Religion in Osteuropa," *Osteuropa* 59:6 (2009); and "Sozialethik in der russisch-orthodoxen Kirche der Gegenwart. 'Die Grundlagen der Sozialkonzeption' in kritischer Betrachtung," *Evangelische Theologie* 64:1 (2004).

Galina M. Yemelianova is senior lecturer in Eurasian studies at the Centre for Russian and East European Studies, The University of Birmingham, United Kingdom. She has been researching and teaching history and contemporary politics in the Middle East and Muslim Eurasia for more than two decades. Her publications include *Yemen During the First Ottoman Rule (1538)* (1988), *Russia and Islam: A Historical Survey* (2002), *Islam in Post-Soviet Russia: Public and Private Faces* (2003), and *Radical Islam in the Former Soviet Union* (2010). Since 2008, she has headed the University of Birmingham Research Group on the Caucasus and Central Asia.

Mikhail Zherebyatyev is associate professor at Voronezh State University in the Russian Federation. His primary fields of research are political science and religious studies. He has provided numerous consultations to the religious news website Портал-Credo.Ru and contributed the study "Понимание принципа светскости властью и обществом в регионах Центральной России" to the collection *Светскость государства: мировой опыт и его применение к России* / под ред. А. Агаджаняна и Кати Русселе (Moscow, 2008).

Index

Note: Italicized references are to charts, endnotes and bibliographic notes.

CPSIA information can be obtained
at www.ICGtesting.com
Printed in the USA
LVOW13s0509100817
544485LV00021B/462/P

9 781349 480180